SIXTH EDITION

PROGRAMMING LOGIC AND DESIGN

COMPREHENSIVE

JOYCE FARRELL

COURSE TECHNOLOGY
CENGAGE Learning

Australia • Brazil • Japan • Korea • Mexico • Singapore • Spain • United Kingdom • United States

COURSE TECHNOLOGY
CENGAGE Learning

Programming Logic and Design, Comprehensive, Sixth Edition
Joyce Farrell

Executive Editor: Marie Lee

Acquisitions Editor: Amy Jollymore

Managing Editor: Tricia Coia

Developmental Editor: Dan Seiter

Content Project Manager: Jennifer Feltri

Editorial Assistant: Zina Kresin

Marketing Manager: Bryant Chrzan

Art Director: Marissa Falco

Text Designer: Shawn Girsberger

Cover Designer: Cabbage Design Company

Cover Image: iStockphoto

Print Buyer: Julio Esperas

Copy Editor: Michael Beckett

Proofreader: Vicki Zimmer

Indexer: Alexandra Nickerson

Compositor: Integra

For product information and technology assistance, contact us at
Cengage Learning Customer & Sales Support, 1-800-354-9706

For permission to use material from this text or product, submit all requests online at **cengage.com/permissions**
Further permissions questions can be emailed to
permissionrequest@cengage.com

Library of Congress Control Number: 2009938501

ISBN-13: 978-0-5387-4476-8

ISBN-10: 0-538-74476-6

Course Technology
20 Channel Center Street
Boston, MA 02210
USA

Some of the product names and company names used in this book have been used for identification purposes only and may be trademarks or registered trademarks of their respective manufacturers and sellers.

Course Technology, a part of Cengage Learning, reserves the right to revise this publication and make changes from time to time in its content without notice.

Cengage Learning is a leading provider of customized learning solutions with office locations around the globe, including Singapore, the United Kingdom, Australia, Mexico, Brazil, and Japan. Locate your local office at:
www.cengage.com/global

Cengage Learning products are represented in Canada by Nelson Education, Ltd.

To learn more about Course Technology, visit
www.cengage.com/coursetechnology

Purchase any of our products at your local college store or at our preferred online store **www.ichapters.com**

Printed in Canada
1 2 3 4 5 6 7 14 13 12 11 10

Brief Contents

vi

Contents

ix

x

CHAPTER 10   Object-Oriented Programming **426**

CHAPTER 11   More Object-Oriented Programming
Concepts **469**

CHAPTER 12   Event-Driven GUI Programming, Multithreading, and Animation. **515**

CHAPTER 13   System Modeling with the UML **550**

CHAPTER 14   Using Relational Databases **585**

Preface

Programming Logic and Design, Comprehensive, Sixth Edition provides the beginning programmer with a guide to developing structured program logic. This textbook assumes no programming language experience. The writing is nontechnical and emphasizes good programming practices. The examples are business examples; they do not assume mathematical background beyond high school business math. Additionally, the examples illustrate one or two major points; they do not contain so many features that students become lost following irrelevant and extraneous details.

The examples in *Programming Logic and Design* have been created to provide students with a sound background in logic, no matter what programming languages they eventually use to write programs. This book can be used in a stand-alone logic course that students take as a prerequisite to a programming course, or as a companion book to an introductory programming text using any programming language.

Organization and Coverage

Programming Logic and Design, Comprehensive, Sixth Edition introduces students to programming concepts and enforces good style and logical thinking. General programming concepts are introduced in Chapter 1. Chapter 2 discusses using data and introduces two important concepts: modularization and creating high-quality programs. It is important to emphasize these topics early so that students start thinking in a modular way and concentrate on making their programs efficient, robust, easy to read, and easy to maintain.

Chapter 3 covers the key concepts of structure, including what structure is, how to recognize it, and most importantly, the advantages to writing structured programs. This early overview gives students a solid foundation for thinking in a structured way before they have to manage the details of the structures.

Chapters 4, 5, and 6 explore the intricacies of decision making, looping, and array manipulation. Chapter 7 provides details of file handling so students can create programs that handle a significant amount of data.

In Chapters 8 and 9, students learn more advanced techniques in array manipulation and modularization. Chapters 10 and 11 provide a thorough, yet accessible, introduction to concepts and terminology used in object-oriented programming. Students learn about classes, objects, instance and static class members, constructors, destructors, inheritance, and the advantages provided by object-oriented thinking.

Chapter 12 explores additional object-oriented programming issues: event-driven GUI programming, multithreading, and animation. Chapter 13 discusses system design issues and details the features of the Unified Modeling Language. Chapter 14 is a thorough introduction to the most important database concepts business programmers should understand.

The first three appendices give students summaries of numbering systems, flowchart symbols, and structures. Additional appendices allow students to gain extra experience with structuring large unstructured programs, creating print charts, and understanding posttest loops and case structures.

Programming Logic and Design combines text explanation with flowcharts and pseudocode examples to provide students with alternative means of expressing structured logic. Numerous detailed, full-program exercises at the end of each chapter illustrate the concepts explained within the chapter, and reinforce understanding and retention of the material presented.

Programming Logic and Design distinguishes itself from other programming logic books in the following ways:

- It is written and designed to be non-language specific. The logic used in this book can be applied to any programming language.

- The examples are everyday business examples; no special knowledge of mathematics, accounting, or other disciplines is assumed.

- The concept of structure is covered earlier than in many other texts. Students are exposed to structure naturally, so they will automatically create properly designed programs.

- Text explanation is interspersed with flowcharts and pseudocode so students can become comfortable with both logic development tools and understand their interrelationship. Screen shots of running programs also are included, providing students with a clear and concrete image of the programs' execution.

- Complex programs are built through the use of complete business examples. Students see how an application is constructed from start to finish instead of studying only segments of programs.

Features

This edition of the text includes many features to help students become better programmers and understand the big picture in program development. Many new features have been added, and the popular features from the first five editions are still included.

Features maintained from previous editions include:

OBJECTIVES Each chapter begins with a list of objectives so the student knows the topics that will be presented in the chapter. In addition to providing a quick reference to topics covered, this feature provides a useful study aid.

FLOWCHARTS This book has plenty of figures and illustrations, including flowcharts, which provide the reader with a visual learning experience, rather than one that involves simply studying text. You can see examples of flowcharts beginning in Chapter 1.

PSEUDOCODE This book also includes numerous examples of pseudocode, which illustrate correct usage of the programming logic and design concepts being taught.

 NOTES These tips provide additional information—for example, another location in the book that expands on a topic, or a common error to watch out for.

THE DON'T DO IT ICON It is sometimes illustrative to show an example of how NOT to do something—for example, having a dead code path in a program. However, students do not always read carefully and sometimes use logic similar to that shown in what is intended to be a "bad" example. When the instructor is critical, the frustrated student says, "But that's how they did it in the book!" Therefore, although the text will continue to describe bad examples, and the captions for the related figures will mention that they are bad examples, the book also includes a "Don't Do It" icon near the offending section of logic. This icon provides a visual jolt to the student, emphasizing that particular figures are NOT to be emulated.

THE TWO TRUTHS AND A LIE QUIZ This quiz appears after each chapter section, with answers provided. The quiz contains three statements based on the preceding section of text—two true and one false. Over the years, students have requested answers to problems, but we have hesitated to distribute them in case instructors want to use problems as assignments or test questions. These true-false mini-quizzes provide students with immediate feedback as they read, without "giving away" answers to the multiple-choice questions and programming problems later in the chapter.

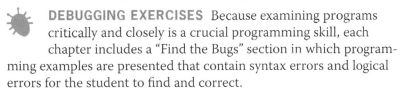

GAME ZONE EXERCISES These exercises are included at the end of each chapter. Students can create games as an additional entertaining way to understand key concepts presented in the chapter.

CHAPTER SUMMARIES Following each chapter is a summary that recaps the programming concepts and techniques covered in the chapter. This feature provides a concise means for students to review and check their understanding of the main points in each chapter.

KEY TERMS Each chapter lists key terms and their definitions; the list appears in the order the terms are encountered in the chapter. Along with the chapter summary, the list of key terms provides a snapshot overview of a chapter's main ideas. A glossary at the end of the book lists all the key terms in alphabetical order, along with working definitions.

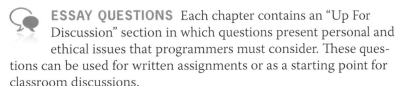

DEBUGGING EXERCISES Because examining programs critically and closely is a crucial programming skill, each chapter includes a "Find the Bugs" section in which programming examples are presented that contain syntax errors and logical errors for the student to find and correct.

REVIEW QUESTIONS Twenty multiple-choice review questions appear at the end of every chapter to allow students to test their comprehension of the major ideas and techniques presented.

EXERCISES Multiple end-of-chapter flowcharting and pseudocoding exercises are included so students have more opportunities to practice concepts as they learn them. These exercises increase in difficulty and are designed to allow students to explore logical programming concepts. Each exercise can be completed using flowcharts, pseudocode, or both. In addition, instructors can assign the exercises as programming problems to be coded and executed in a particular programming language.

ESSAY QUESTIONS Each chapter contains an "Up For Discussion" section in which questions present personal and ethical issues that programmers must consider. These questions can be used for written assignments or as a starting point for classroom discussions.

New to this Edition!

VIDEO LESSONS Each chapter is accompanied by two or more video lessons that help explain an important chapter concept. A listing of the videos provided can be found on the inside back cover of this text. These videos are designed and narrated by the author and are available for free with a new book. (They can also be purchased separately at iChapters.com.)

If you have a new book, it will contain a URL and PIN code. Once you go to this URL and enter your PIN code, follow the prompts to locate the videos for this text. If you are a user of an online course cartridge, such as BlackBoard, WebCT, or Angel, you will also have access to these videos through that platform.

INCREASED EMPHASIS ON MODULARITY From the second chapter, students are encouraged to write code in concise, easily manageable, and reusable modules. Instructors have found that modularization is a technique that should be encouraged early to instill good habits and a clearer understanding of structure. This edition explains modularization early, using global variables instead of local passed and returned values, and saves parameter passing for later when the student has become more adept.

CLEARER EXPLANATIONS This edition has been rewritten to provide clearer, simpler explanations that are appropriate for the beginning programming student. As a result of the new, cleaner approach, the length of the book has been reduced.

NEW APPENDICES FOR EASY REFERENCE New appendices have been added that cover numbering systems, flowchart symbols, and structures.

DECREASED EMPHASIS ON CONTROL BREAKS Professional programmers should understand control break logic, but creating such logic is not as common a task as it was years ago. Therefore, the topic is still covered briefly as part of the file-handling chapter, but with reduced emphasis from previous editions of the book.

Instructor Resources

The following supplemental materials are available when this book is used in a classroom setting. All of the instructor resources available with this book are provided to the instructor on a single CD-ROM.

ELECTRONIC INSTRUCTOR'S MANUAL The Instructor's Manual that accompanies this textbook provides additional instructional material to assist in class preparation, including items such as Sample Syllabi, Chapter Outlines, Technical Notes, Lecture Notes, Quick Quizzes, Teaching Tips, Discussion Topics, and Key Terms.

EXAMVIEW® This textbook is accompanied by ExamView, a powerful testing software package that allows instructors to create and administer printed, computer (LAN-based), and Internet exams. ExamView includes hundreds of questions that correspond to the topics covered in this text, enabling students to generate detailed study guides that include page references for further review. The computer-based and Internet testing components allow students to take exams at their computers, and save the instructor time by grading each exam automatically.

POWERPOINT PRESENTATIONS This book comes with Microsoft PowerPoint© slides for each chapter. These are included as a teaching aid for classroom presentation, to make available to students on your network for chapter review, or to be printed for classroom distribution. Instructors can add their own slides for additional topics they introduce to the class.

SOLUTIONS Suggested solutions to Review Questions and Exercises are provided on the Instructor Resources CD and may also be found on the Course Technology Web site at *www.cengage.com/coursetechnology*. The solutions are password protected.

DISTANCE LEARNING Course Technology offers WebCT© and Blackboard© courses for this text to provide the most complete and dynamic learning experience possible. When you add online content to one of your courses, you're adding a lot: automated tests, topic reviews, quick quizzes, and additional case projects with solutions. For more information on how to bring distance learning to your course, contact your Course Technology sales representative.

Software Options

You have the option to bundle software with your text! Please contact your Course Technology sales representative for more information.

MICROSOFT® OFFICE VISIO® PROFESSIONAL Visio is a diagramming program that helps users create flowcharts and diagrams easily while working through the text, enabling them to visualize concepts and learn more effectively.

VISUAL LOGIC™ This simple but powerful tool teaches programming logic and design without traditional high-level programming language syntax. Visual Logic uses flowcharts to explain essential programming concepts, including variables, input, assignment, output, conditions, loops, procedures, graphics, arrays, and files. It also has the ability to interpret and execute flowcharts, providing students with immediate and accurate feedback about their solutions. By executing student solutions, Visual Logic combines the power of a high-level language with the ease and simplicity of flowcharts.

Acknowledgments

I would like to thank all of the people who helped to make this book a reality, especially Dan Seiter, Development Editor, whose hard work and attention to detail have made this a high-quality textbook. I have worked with Dan for many years now, and he is indispensable in producing accurate and approachable technical instruction. Thanks also to Tricia Coia, Managing Editor; Amy Jollymore, Acquisitions Editor; Jennifer Feltri, Content Project Manager; and Green Pen QA, Technical Editors. I am grateful to be able to work with so many fine people who are dedicated to producing high-quality instructional materials.

I am grateful to the many reviewers who provided helpful and insightful comments during the development of this book, including Gilbert Armour, Virginia Western Community College; John Buerck, Saint Louis University; Karen Cummings, McLennan Community College; Clara Groeper, Illinois Central College; and Jeff Hedrington, Colorado Technical University.

Thanks, too, to my husband, Geoff, and our daughters, Andrea and Audrey, for their support. This book, as were all its previous editions, is dedicated to them.

–Joyce Farrell

About the Inside Front Cover

Check out our interviews with recent graduates who are now working in the IT field. One is featured on the inside front cover of this book. If you know people who recently landed a job in IT, we'd like to interview them too! Send your suggestions via e-mail to Amy Jollymore, Acquisitions Editor, at Amy.Jollymore@Cengage.com.

CHAPTER 1

An Overview of Computers and Programming

In this chapter, you will learn about:

- ◎ Computer systems
- ◎ Simple program logic
- ◎ The steps involved in the program development cycle
- ◎ Pseudocode statements and flowchart symbols
- ◎ Using a sentinel value to end a program
- ◎ Programming and user environments
- ◎ The evolution of programming models

2

Understanding Computer Systems

A **computer system** is a combination of all the components required to process and store data using a computer. Every computer system is composed of multiple pieces of hardware and software.

- **Hardware** is the equipment, or the physical devices, associated with a computer. For example, keyboards, mice, speakers, and printers are all hardware. The devices are manufactured differently for large mainframe computers, laptops, and even smaller computers that are embedded into products such as cars and thermostats, but the types of operations performed by different-sized computers are very similar. When you think of a computer, you often think of its physical components first, but for a computer to be useful it needs more than devices; a computer needs to be given instructions. Just as your stereo equipment does not do much until you provide music, computer hardware needs instructions that control how and when data items are input, how they are processed, and the form in which they are output or stored.

- **Software** is computer instructions that tell the hardware what to do. Software is **programs**: instructions written by programmers. You can buy prewritten programs that are stored on a disk or that you download from the Web. For example, businesses use word-processing and accounting programs, and casual computer users enjoy programs that play music and games. Alternatively, you can write your own programs. When you write software instructions, you are **programming**. This book focuses on the programming process.

Software can be classified as application software or system software. **Application software** comprises all the programs you apply to a task— word-processing programs, spreadsheets, payroll and inventory programs, and even games. **System software** comprises the programs that you use to manage your computer, including operating systems such as Windows, Linux, or UNIX. This book focuses on the logic used to write application software programs, although many of the concepts apply to both types of software.

Together, computer hardware and software accomplish three major operations in most programs:

- **Input**—Data items enter the computer system and are put into memory, where they can be processed. Hardware devices that perform input operations include keyboards and mice. **Data items** include all the text, numbers, and other information that are processed by a computer.

In business, much of the data used is facts and figures about such entities as products, customers, and personnel. However, data can also be items such as the choices a player makes in a game or the notes required by a music-playing program.

Many computer professionals distinguish between the terms *data*, which describes items that are input, and *information*, which describes data items that have been processed and sent to a device where people can read and interpret them. For example, your name, Social Security number, and hourly pay rate are data items when they are input to a program, but the same items are information after they have been processed and output on your paycheck.

- **Processing**—Processing data items may involve organizing or sorting them, checking them for accuracy, or performing calculations with them. The hardware component that performs these types of tasks is the **central processing unit**, or **CPU**.

- **Output**—After data items have been processed, the resulting information usually is sent to a printer, monitor, or some other output device so people can view, interpret, and use the results.

Some people consider storage as a fourth major computer operation. Instead of sending output to a device such as a printer, monitor, or speaker where a person can interpret it, you sometimes store output on **storage devices**, such as a disk or flash media. People cannot read data directly from these storage devices, but the devices hold information for later retrieval. When you send output to a storage device, sometimes it is used later as input for another program.

You write computer instructions in a computer **programming language**, such as Visual Basic, C#, C++, or Java. Just as some people speak English and others speak Japanese, programmers also write programs in different languages. Some programmers work exclusively in one language, whereas others know several programming languages and use the one that is best suited to the task at hand.

The instructions you write using a programming language are called **program code**; when you write instructions, you are **coding the program**.

Every programming language has rules governing its word usage and punctuation. These rules are called the language's **syntax**. If you ask, "How the geet too store do I?" in English, most people can figure out what you probably mean, even though you have not used proper English syntax—you have mixed up the word order, misspelled a word, and used an incorrect word. However, computers are not nearly as smart as most people; in this case, you might as well have asked the computer, "Xpu mxv ort dod nmcad bf B?" Unless the syntax is perfect, the computer cannot interpret the programming language instruction at all.

When you write a program, you usually type its instructions using a keyboard. When you type program instructions, they are stored in **computer memory**, which is a computer's temporary, internal

4

Random access memory, or **RAM**, is a form of internal, volatile memory. It is hardware on which the programs that are currently running and the data items that are currently being used are stored for quick access.

The program statements you write in a programming language are known as **source code**. The translated machine language statements are known as **object code**.

storage. Internal storage is **volatile**—its contents are lost when the computer is turned off or loses power. Usually, you want to be able to retrieve and perhaps modify the stored instructions later, so you also store them on a permanent storage device, such as a disk. Permanent storage devices are **nonvolatile**—that is, their contents are persistent and are retained even when power is lost.

After a computer program is stored in memory, it must be translated from your programming language statements to **machine language** that represents the millions of on/off circuits within the computer. Each programming language uses a piece of software, called a **compiler** or an **interpreter**, to translate your program code into machine language. Machine language is also called **binary language**, and is represented as a series of 0s and 1s. The compiler or interpreter that translates your code tells you if any programming language component has been used incorrectly. Syntax errors are relatively easy to locate and correct because the compiler or interpreter you use highlights every syntax error. If you write a computer program using a language such as C++ but spell one of its words incorrectly or reverse the proper order of two words, the software lets you know that it found a mistake by displaying an error message as soon as you try to translate the program.

Although there are differences in how compilers and interpreters work, their basic function is the same—to translate your programming statements into code the computer can use. When you use a compiler, an entire program is translated before it can execute; when you use an interpreter, each instruction is translated just prior to execution. Usually, you do not choose which type of translation to use—it depends on the programming language. However, there are some languages for which both compilers and interpreters are available.

Only after program instructions are successfully translated to machine code can the computer carry out the program instructions. When instructions are carried out, a program **runs**, or **executes**. In a typical program, some input will be accepted, some processing will occur, and results will be output.

Besides the popular full-blown programming languages such as Java and C++, many programmers use **scripting languages** (also called **scripting programming languages** or **script languages**) such as Python, Lua, Perl, and PHP. Scripts written in these languages usually can be typed directly from a keyboard and are stored as text rather than as binary executable files. Scripting language programs are interpreted line by line each time the program executes, instead of being stored in a compiled (binary) form.

Understanding Simple Program Logic

A program with syntax errors cannot execute. A program with no syntax errors can execute, but might contain **logical errors**, and produce incorrect output as a result. For a program to work properly, you must give the instructions to the computer in a specific sequence, you must not leave any instructions out, and you must not add extraneous instructions. By doing this, you are developing the **logic** of the computer program.

Suppose you instruct someone to make a cake as follows:

```
Get a bowl
Stir
Add two eggs
Add a gallon of gasoline
Bake at 350 degrees for 45 minutes
Add three cups of flour
```

Don't Do It
Don't bake a cake like this!

Even though you have used the English language syntax correctly, the cake-baking instructions are out of sequence, some instructions are missing, and some instructions belong to procedures other than baking a cake. If you follow these instructions, you are not going to make an edible cake, and you most likely will end up with a disaster. Logical errors are much more difficult to locate than syntax errors—it is easier for you to determine whether "eggs" is spelled incorrectly in a recipe than it is for you to tell if there are too many eggs or if they are added too soon.

The dangerous cake-baking instructions are shown with a Don't Do It icon. You will see this icon when the book contains an unrecommended programming practice that is used as an example of what *not* to do.

If you misspell a programming language word, you commit a syntax error, but if you use an otherwise correct word that does not make sense in the current context, programmers say you have committed a **semantic error**. Either way, the program will not execute.

After you learn French, you automatically know, or can easily figure out, many Spanish words. Similarly, after you learn one programming language, it is much easier to understand several other languages.

You will learn about the odd elimination of the space between words like my and Number in Chapter 2.

Programmers use an asterisk to indicate multiplication. You will learn more about arithmetic statements in Chapter 2.

Just as baking directions can be given correctly in Mandarin, Urdu, or Spanish, the same program logic can be expressed in any number of programming languages. Because this book is not concerned with any specific language, the programming examples could have been written in Visual Basic, C++, or Java. For convenience, this book uses instructions written in English!

Most simple computer programs include steps that perform input, processing, and output. Suppose you want to write a computer program to double any number you provide. You can write such a program in a programming language such as Visual Basic or Java, but if you were to write it using English-like statements, it would look like this:

```
input myNumber
set myAnswer = myNumber * 2
output myAnswer
```

The number-doubling process includes three instructions:

- The instruction to input myNumber is an example of an input operation. When the computer interprets this instruction, it knows to look to an input device to obtain a number. When you work in a specific programming language, you write instructions that tell the computer which device to access for input. For example, when a user enters a number as data for a program, the user might click on the number with a mouse, type it from a keyboard, or speak it into a microphone. Logically, however, it doesn't really matter which hardware device is used, as long as the computer knows to look for a number. When the number is retrieved from an input device, it is placed in the computer's memory at the location named myNumber. The location myNumber is a variable. A **variable** is a named memory location whose value can vary—for example, the value of myNumber might be 3 when the program is used for the first time and 45 when it is used the next time.

From a logical perspective, when you input a value, the hardware device is irrelevant. The same is true in your daily life. If you follow the instruction "Get eggs for the cake," it does not really matter if you purchase them from a store or harvest them from your own chickens—you get the eggs either way. There might be different practical considerations to getting the eggs, just as there are for getting data from a large database as opposed to an inexperienced user. For now, this book is only concerned with the logic of the operation, not the minor details.

- The instruction set myAnswer = myNumber * 2 is an example of a processing operation. Mathematical operations are not the only kind of processing operations, but they are very typical. As with input operations, the type of hardware used for processing is irrelevant—after you write a program, it can be used on computers of different brand names, sizes, and speeds. The instruction takes the value stored in memory at the myNumber location, multiplies it by 2, and stores the result in another memory location named myAnswer.

- In the number-doubling program, the output myAnswer instruction is an example of an output operation. Within a particular program, this statement could cause the output to appear on the monitor (which might be a flat-panel plasma screen or a cathode-ray tube), or the output could go to a printer (which could be laser or ink-jet), or the output could be written to a disk or DVD. The logic of the output process is the same no matter what hardware device you use. When this instruction executes, the value stored in memory at the location named myAnswer is sent to an output device.

Watch the video *A Simple Program*.

Computer memory consists of millions of numbered locations where data can be stored. The memory location of **myNumber** has a specific numeric address—for example, 48604. Your program associates **myNumber** with that address. Every time you refer to **myNumber** within a program, the computer retrieves the value at the associated memory location. When you write programs, you seldom need to be concerned with the value of the memory address; instead, you simply use the easy-to-remember name you created.

Computer programmers often refer to memory addresses using hexadecimal notation, or base 16. Using this system, they might use a value like 42FF01A to refer to a memory address. Despite the use of letters, such an address is still a hexadecimal number. Appendix A contains information on this numbering system.

TWO TRUTHS & A LIE

Understanding Simple Program Logic

1. A program with syntax errors can execute but might produce incorrect results.

2. Although the syntax of programming languages differs, the same program logic can be expressed in different languages.

3. Most simple computer programs include steps that perform input, processing, and output.

The false statement is #1. A program with syntax errors cannot execute; a program with no syntax errors can execute, but might produce incorrect results.

Understanding the Program Development Cycle

A programmer's job involves writing instructions (such as those in the doubling program in the preceding section), but a professional programmer usually does not just sit down at a computer keyboard and start typing. Figure 1-1 illustrates the **program development cycle**, which can be broken down into at least seven steps:

1. Understand the problem.

2. Plan the logic.

3. Code the program.

4. Use software (a compiler or interpreter) to translate the program into machine language.

5. Test the program.

6. Put the program into production.

7. Maintain the program.

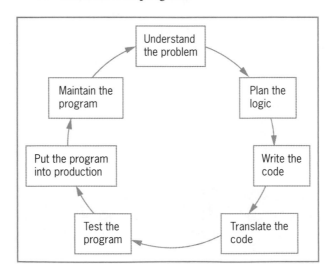

Figure 1-1   The program development cycle

Understanding the Problem

Professional computer programmers write programs to satisfy the needs of others, called **users** or **end users**. Examples could include a Human Resources department that needs a printed list of all employees, a Billing department that wants a list of clients who are 30 or more days overdue on their payments, and an Order department that needs a Web site to provide buyers with an online shopping cart in which to gather their orders. Because programmers are providing a service to these users, programmers must first understand what the users want. Although when a program runs, you usually think of the logic as a cycle of input-processing-output operations; when you plan a program, you think of the output first. After you understand what the desired result is, you can plan what to input and process to achieve it.

 The term *end user* distinguishes those who actually use and benefit from a software product from others in an organization who might purchase, install, or have other contact with the software.

Suppose the director of Human Resources says to a programmer, "Our department needs a list of all employees who have been here over five years, because we want to invite them to a special thank-you dinner." On the surface, this seems like a simple request. An experienced programmer, however, will know that the request is incomplete. For example, you might not know the answers to the following questions about which employees to include:

- Does the director want a list of full-time employees only, or a list of full- and part-time employees together?

- Does she want people who have worked for the company on a month-to-month contractual basis over the past five years, or only regular, permanent employees?

- Do the listed employees need to have worked for the organization for five years as of today, as of the date of the dinner, or as of some other cutoff date?

- What about an employee who, for example, worked three years, took a two-year leave of absence, and has been back for three years?

The programmer cannot make any of these decisions; the user (in this case, the Human Resources director) must address these questions.

More decisions still might be required. For example:

- What data should be included for each listed employee? Should the list contain both first and last names? Social Security numbers? Phone numbers? Addresses?

- Should the list be in alphabetical order? Employee ID number order? Length-of-service order? Some other order?

- Should the employees be grouped by any criteria, such as department number or years of service?

Several pieces of documentation are often provided to help the programmer understand the problem. **Documentation** consists of all the supporting paperwork for a program; it might include items such as original requests for the program from users, sample output, and descriptions of the data items available for input.

10

Watch the video *The Program Development Cycle, Part 1.*

You may hear programmers refer to planning a program as "developing an algorithm." An **algorithm** is the sequence of steps necessary to solve any problem.

You will learn more about flowcharts and pseudocode later in this chapter.

In addition to flowcharts and pseudocode, programmers use a variety of other tools to help in program development. One such tool is an **IPO chart**, which delineates input, processing, and output tasks. Some object-oriented programmers also use **TOE charts**, which list tasks, objects, and events.

Really understanding the problem may be one of the most difficult aspects of programming. On any job, the description of what the user needs may be vague—worse yet, users may not really know what they want, and users who think they know frequently change their minds after seeing sample output. A good programmer is often part counselor, part detective!

Planning the Logic

The heart of the programming process lies in planning the program's logic. During this phase of the process, the programmer plans the steps of the program, deciding what steps to include and how to order them. You can plan the solution to a problem in many ways. The two most common planning tools are flowcharts and pseudocode. Both tools involve writing the steps of the program in English, much as you would plan a trip on paper before getting into the car or plan a party theme before shopping for food and favors.

The programmer shouldn't worry about the syntax of any particular language at this point, but should focus on figuring out what sequence of events will lead from the available input to the desired output. Planning the logic includes thinking carefully about all the possible data values a program might encounter and how you want the program to handle each scenario. The process of walking through a program's logic on paper before you actually write the program is called **desk-checking**. You will learn more about planning the logic throughout this book; in fact, the book focuses on this crucial step almost exclusively.

Coding the Program

After the logic is developed, only then can the programmer write the program. Hundreds of programming languages are available. Programmers choose particular languages because some have built-in capabilities that make them more efficient than others at handling certain types of operations. Despite their differences, programming languages are quite alike in their basic capabilities—each can handle input operations, arithmetic processing, output operations, and other standard functions. The logic developed to solve a programming problem can be executed using any number of languages. Only after choosing a language must the programmer be concerned with proper punctuation and the correct spelling of commands—in other words, using the correct *syntax*.

Some very experienced programmers can successfully combine logic planning and program coding in one step. This may work for planning and writing a very simple program, just as you can plan and write a postcard to a friend using one step. A good term paper or a Hollywood screenplay, however, needs planning before writing—and so do most programs.

Which step is harder: planning the logic or coding the program? Right now, it may seem to you that writing in a programming language is a very difficult task, considering all the spelling and syntax rules you must learn. However, the planning step is actually more difficult. Which is more difficult: thinking up the twists and turns to the plot of a best-selling mystery novel, or writing a translation of an existing novel from English to Spanish? And who do you think gets paid more, the writer who creates the plot or the translator? (Try asking friends to name any famous translator!)

Using Software to Translate the Program into Machine Language

Even though there are many programming languages, each computer knows only one language: its machine language, which consists of 1s and 0s. Computers understand machine language because they are made up of thousands of tiny electrical switches, each of which can be set in either the on or off state, which is represented by a 1 or 0, respectively.

Languages like Java or Visual Basic are available for programmers because someone has written a translator program (a compiler or interpreter) that changes the programmer's English-like **high-level programming language** into the **low-level machine language** that the computer understands. If you write a programming language statement incorrectly (for example, by misspelling a word, using a word that doesn't exist in the language, or using "illegal" grammar), the translator program doesn't know how to proceed and issues an error message identifying a **syntax error**, which is a misuse of a language's grammar rules. Although making errors is never desirable, syntax errors are not a major concern to programmers, because the compiler or interpreter catches every syntax error and displays a message that notifies you of the problem. The computer will not execute a program that contains even one syntax error.

Typically, a programmer develops a program's logic, writes the code, and compiles the program, receiving a list of syntax errors. The programmer then corrects the syntax errors and compiles the program again. Correcting the first set of errors frequently reveals new errors that originally were not apparent to the compiler. For example, if you could use an English compiler and submit the sentence "The dg chase

When you learn the syntax of a programming language, the commands you learn will work on any machine on which the language software has been installed. However, your commands are translated to machine language, which differs depending on your computer make and model.

Watch the video *The Program Development Cycle, Part 2.*

After a program has been translated into machine language, the machine language program is saved and can be run any number of times without repeating the translation step. You only need to retranslate your code if you make changes to your source code statements.

the cat," the compiler at first might point out only one syntax error. The second word, "dg," is illegal because it is not part of the English language. Only after you corrected the word to "dog" would the compiler find another syntax error on the third word, "chase," because it is the wrong verb form for the subject "dog." This doesn't mean "chase" is necessarily the wrong word. Maybe "dog" is wrong; perhaps the subject should be "dogs," in which case "chase" is right. Compilers don't always know exactly what you mean, nor do they know what the proper correction should be, but they do know when something is wrong with your syntax.

When writing a program, a programmer might need to recompile the code several times. An executable program is created only when the code is free of syntax errors. When you run an executable program, it typically also might require input data. Figure 1-2 shows a diagram of this entire process.

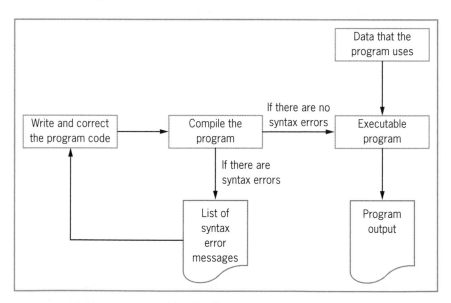

Figure 1-2   Creating an executable program

Testing the Program

A program that is free of syntax errors is not necessarily free of logical errors. A logical error results when you use a syntactically correct statement but use the wrong one for the current context. For example, the English sentence "The dog chases the cat," although syntactically perfect, is not logically correct if the dog chases a ball or the cat is the aggressor.

Once a program is free of syntax errors, the programmer can test it—that is, execute it with some sample data to see whether the results are logically correct. Recall the number-doubling program:

```
input myNumber
set myAnswer = myNumber * 2
output myAnswer
```

If you execute the program, provide the value 2 as input to the program, and the answer 4 is displayed, you have executed one successful test run of the program.

However, if the answer 40 is displayed, maybe the program contains a logical error. Maybe the second line of code was mistyped with an extra zero, so that the program reads:

```
input myNumber
set myAnswer = myNumber * 20
output myAnswer
```

Don't Do It
The programmer typed "20" instead of "2".

Placing 20 instead of 2 in the multiplication statement caused a logical error. Notice that nothing is syntactically wrong with this second program—it is just as reasonable to multiply a number by 20 as by 2—but if the programmer intends only to double myNumber, then a logical error has occurred.

The process of finding and correcting program errors is called **debugging**.

Programs should be tested with many sets of data. For example, if you write the program to double a number, then enter 2 and get an output value of 4, that doesn't necessarily mean you have a correct program. Perhaps you have typed this program by mistake:

Don't Do It
The programmer typed "+" instead of "*".

```
input myNumber
set myAnswer = myNumber + 2
output myAnswer
```

An input of 2 results in an answer of 4, but that doesn't mean your program doubles numbers—it actually only adds 2 to them. If you test your program with additional data and get the wrong answer—for example, if you enter 7 and get an answer of 9—you know there is a problem with your code.

Selecting test data is somewhat of an art in itself, and it should be done carefully. If the Human Resources department wants a list of the names of five-year employees, it would be a mistake to test the program with a small sample file of only long-term employees. If no newer employees are part of the data being used for testing, you do not really know if the program would have eliminated them

Chapter 4 contains more information on testing programs.

14

from the five-year list. Many companies do not know that their software has a problem until an unusual circumstance occurs—for example, the first time an employee has more than nine dependents, the first time a customer orders more than 999 items at a time, or when (as well-documented in the popular press) a new century begins.

Putting the Program into Production

Once the program is tested adequately, it is ready for the organization to use. Putting the program into production might mean simply running the program once, if it was written to satisfy a user's request for a special list. However, the process might take months if the program will be run on a regular basis, or if it is one of a large system of programs being developed. Perhaps data-entry people must be trained to prepare the input for the new program; users must be trained to understand the output; or existing data in the company must be changed to an entirely new format to accommodate this program. **Conversion**, the entire set of actions an organization must take to switch over to using a new program or set of programs, can sometimes take months or years to accomplish.

Maintaining the Program

After programs are put into production, making necessary changes is called **maintenance**. Maintenance can be required for many reasons: new tax rates are legislated, the format of an input file is altered, or the end user requires additional information not included in the original output specifications, to name a few. Frequently, your first programming job will require maintaining previously written programs. When you maintain the programs others have written, you will appreciate the effort the original programmer put into writing clear code, using reasonable variable names, and documenting his or her work. When you make changes to existing programs, you repeat the development cycle. That is, you must understand the changes, then plan, code, translate, and test them before putting them into production. If a substantial number of program changes are required, the original program might be retired, and the program development cycle might be started for a new program.

Watch the video *The Program Development Cycle, Part 3.*

TWO TRUTHS & A LIE

Understanding the Program Development Cycle

1. Understanding the problem that must be solved can be one of the most difficult aspects of programming.

2. The two most commonly used logic-planning tools are flowcharts and pseudocode.

3. Flowcharting a program is a very different process if you use an older programming language instead of a newer one.

The false statement is #3. Despite their differences, programming languages are quite alike in their basic capabilities—each can handle input operations, arithmetic processing, output operations, and other standard functions. The logic developed to solve a programming problem can be executed using any number of languages.

Using Pseudocode Statements and Flowchart Symbols

When programmers plan the logic for a solution to a programming problem, they often use one of two tools: pseudocode (pronounced "sue-doe-code") or flowcharts. **Pseudocode** is an English-like representation of the logical steps it takes to solve a problem. A **flowchart** is a pictorial representation of the same thing. *Pseudo* is a prefix that means "false," and to *code* a program means to put it in a programming language; therefore, *pseudocode* simply means "false code," or sentences that appear to have been written in a computer programming language but do not necessarily follow all the syntax rules of any specific language.

Writing Pseudocode

You have already seen examples of statements that represent pseudocode earlier in this chapter, and there is nothing mysterious about them. The following five statements constitute a pseudocode representation of a number-doubling problem:

```
start
   input myNumber
   set myAnswer = myNumber * 2
   output myAnswer
stop
```

Using pseudocode involves writing down all the steps you will use in a program. Usually, programmers preface their pseudocode with a beginning statement like start and end it with a terminating statement like stop. The statements between start and stop look like English and are indented slightly so that start and stop stand out. Most programmers do not bother with punctuation such as periods at the end of pseudocode statements, although it would not be wrong to use them if you prefer that style. Similarly, there is no need to capitalize the first word in a sentence, although you might choose to do so. This book follows the conventions of using lowercase letters for verbs that begin pseudocode statements and omitting periods at the end of statements.

Pseudocode is fairly flexible because it is a planning tool, and not the final product. Therefore, for example, you might prefer any of the following:

- Instead of start and stop, some pseudocode developers would use the terms begin and end.

- Instead of writing input myNumber, some developers would write get myNumber or read myNumber.

- Instead of writing set myAnswer = myNumber * 2, some developers would write calculate myAnswer = myNumber times 2 or compute myAnswer as myNumber doubled.

- Instead of writing output myAnswer, many pseudocode developers would write display myAnswer, print myAnswer, or write myAnswer.

The point is, the pseudocode statements are instructions to retrieve an original number from an input device and store it in memory where it can be used in a calculation, and then to get the calculated answer from memory and send it to an output device so a person can see it. When you eventually convert your pseudocode to a specific programming language, you do not have such flexibility because specific syntax will be required. For example, if you use the C# programming language and write the statement to output the answer, you will code the following:

```
Console.Write (myAnswer);
```

The exact use of words, capitalization, and punctuation are important in the C# statement, but not in the pseudocode statement.

Drawing Flowcharts

Some professional programmers prefer writing pseudocode to drawing flowcharts, because using pseudocode is more similar to writing the final statements in the programming language. Others prefer drawing flowcharts to represent the logical flow, because flowcharts allow programmers to visualize more easily how the program statements will connect. Especially for beginning programmers, flowcharts are an excellent tool to help them visualize how the statements in a program are interrelated.

When you create a flowchart, you draw geometric shapes that contain the individual statements and that are connected with arrows. You use a parallelogram to represent an **input symbol**, which indicates an input operation. You write an input statement in English inside the parallelogram, as shown in Figure 1-3.

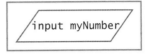

Figure 1-3 Input symbol

Arithmetic operation statements are examples of processing. In a flowchart, you use a rectangle as the **processing symbol** that contains a processing statement, as shown in Figure 1-4.

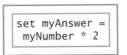

Figure 1-4 Processing symbol

To represent an output statement, you use the same symbol as for input statements—the **output symbol** is a parallelogram, as shown in Figure 1-5.

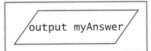

Figure 1-5 Output symbol

You can draw a flowchart by hand or use software, such as Microsoft Word and Microsoft PowerPoint, that contains flowcharting tools. You can use several other software programs, such as Visio and Visual Logic, specifically to create flowcharts.

Because the parallelogram is used for both input and output, it is often called the **input/output symbol** or **I/O symbol**.

Some software programs that use flowcharts (such as Visual Logic) use a left-slanting parallelogram to represent output. As long as the flowchart creator and the flowchart reader are communicating, the actual shape used is irrelevant. This book will follow the most standard convention of always using the right-slanting parallelogram for both input and output.

To show the correct sequence of these statements, you use arrows, or **flowlines**, to connect the steps. Whenever possible, most of a flowchart should read from top to bottom or from left to right on a page. That's the way we read English, so when flowcharts follow this convention, they are easier for us to understand.

Appendix B contains a summary of all the flowchart symbols you will see in this book.

Programmers seldom create both pseudocode and a flowchart for the same problem. You usually use one or the other. In a large program, you might even prefer to use pseudocode for some parts and draw a flowchart for others.

To be complete, a flowchart should include two more elements: **terminal symbols**, or start/stop symbols, at each end. Often, you place a word like start or begin in the first terminal symbol and a word like end or stop in the other. The standard terminal symbol is shaped like a racetrack; many programmers refer to this shape as a lozenge, because it resembles the shape of the medication you might use to soothe a sore throat. Figure 1-6 shows a complete flowchart for the program that doubles a number, and the pseudocode for the same problem. You can see from the figure that the flowchart and pseudocode statements are the same—only the presentation format differs.

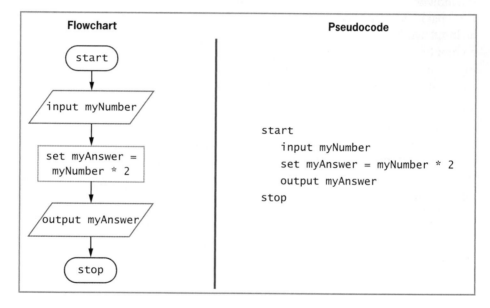

Figure 1-6　Flowchart and pseudocode of program that doubles a number

Repeating Instructions

After the flowchart or pseudocode has been developed, the programmer only needs to: (1) buy a computer, (2) buy a language compiler, (3) learn a programming language, (4) code the program, (5) attempt to compile it, (6) fix the syntax errors, (7) compile it again, (8) test it with several sets of data, and (9) put it into production.

"Whoa!" you are probably saying to yourself. "This is simply not worth it! All that work to create a flowchart or pseudocode, and *then* all those other steps? For five dollars, I can buy a pocket calculator that will double any number for me instantly!" You are absolutely right. If this were a real computer program, and all it did was double the value of a number, it would not be worth the effort. Writing a computer program would be worthwhile only if you had many—let's say 10,000—numbers to double in a limited amount of time—let's say the next two minutes.

Unfortunately, the number-doubling program represented in Figure 1-6 does not double 10,000 numbers; it doubles only one. You could execute the program 10,000 times, of course, but that would require you to sit at the computer and tell it to run the program over and over again. You would be better off with a program that could process 10,000 numbers, one after the other.

One solution is to write the program shown in Figure 1-7 and execute the same steps 10,000 times. Of course, writing this program would be very time consuming; you might as well buy the calculator.

 When you tell a friend how to get to your house, you might write a series of instructions or you might draw a map. Pseudocode is similar to written, step-by-step instructions; a flowchart, like a map, is a visual representation of the same thing.

19

```
start
    input myNumber
    set myAnswer = myNumber * 2
    output myAnswer
    input myNumber
    set myAnswer = myNumber * 2
    output myAnswer
    input myNumber
    set myAnswer = myNumber * 2
    output myAnswer
    ...and so on for 9,997 more times
```

Don't Do It
You would never want to write such a repetitious list of instructions.

Figure 1-7   Inefficient pseudocode for program that doubles 10,000 numbers

A better solution is to have the computer execute the same set of three instructions over and over again, as shown in Figure 1-8. The repetition of a series of steps is called a **loop**. With this approach, the computer gets a number, doubles it, displays the answer, and then starts over again with the first instruction. The same spot in memory, called myNumber, is reused for the second number and for any subsequent numbers. The spot in memory named myAnswer is reused each time to store the result of the multiplication operation. The logic illustrated in the flowchart in Figure 1-8 contains a major problem—the sequence of instructions never ends. This programming situation is known as an **infinite loop**—a repeating flow of logic with no end. You will learn one way to handle this problem later in this chapter; you will learn a superior way in Chapter 3.

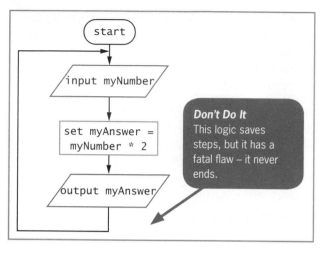

Figure 1-8 Flowchart of infinite number-doubling program

TWO TRUTHS & A LIE

Using Pseudocode Statements and Flowchart Symbols

1. When you draw a flowchart, you use a parallelogram to represent an input operation.

2. When you draw a flowchart, you use a parallelogram to represent a processing operation.

3. When you draw a flowchart, you use a parallelogram to represent an output operation.

The false statement is #2. When you draw a flowchart, you use a rectangle to represent a processing operation.

Using a Sentinel Value to End a Program

The logic in the flowchart for doubling numbers, shown in Figure 1-8, has a major flaw—the program contains an infinite loop. If, for example, the input numbers are being entered at the keyboard, the program will keep accepting numbers and outputting doubles forever. Of course, the user could refuse to type any more numbers. But the computer is very patient, and if you refuse to give it any more numbers, it will sit and wait forever. When you finally type a number, the program will double it, output the result, and wait for another. The program cannot progress any further while it is waiting for input; meanwhile, the program is occupying computer memory and tying up operating system resources. Refusing to enter any more numbers is not a practical solution. Another way to end the program is simply to turn off the computer. But again, that's neither the best way nor an elegant solution.

A superior way to end the program is to set a predetermined value for myNumber that means "Stop the program!" For example, the programmer and the user could agree that the user will never need to know the double of 0, so the user could enter a 0 to stop. The program could then test any incoming value contained in myNumber and, if it is a 0, stop the program. Testing a value is also called **making a decision**.

You represent a decision in a flowchart by drawing a **decision symbol**, which is shaped like a diamond. The diamond usually contains a question, the answer to which is one of two mutually exclusive options—often yes or no. All good computer questions have only two mutually exclusive answers, such as yes and no or true and false. For example, "What day of the year is your birthday?" is not a good computer question because there are 366 possible answers. However, "Is your birthday June 24?" is a good computer question because, for everyone in the world, the answer is either yes or no.

 A yes-or-no decision is called a **binary decision**, because there are two possible outcomes.

The question to stop the doubling program should be "Is the value of myNumber just entered equal to 0?" or "myNumber = 0?" for short. The complete flowchart will now look like the one shown in Figure 1-9.

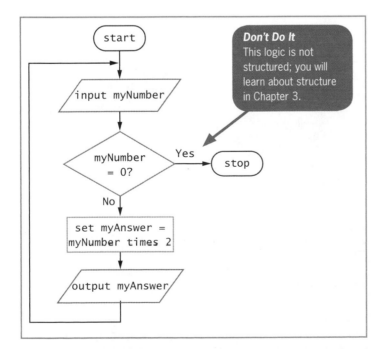

Figure 1-9 Flowchart of number-doubling program with sentinel value of 0

One drawback to using 0 to stop a program, of course, is that it won't work if the user does need to find the double of 0. In that case, some other data-entry value that the user will never need, such as 999 or −1, could be selected to signal that the program should end. A preselected value that stops the execution of a program is often called a **dummy value** because it does not represent real data, but just a signal to stop. Sometimes, such a value is called a **sentinel value** because it represents an entry or exit point, like a sentinel who guards a fortress.

Not all programs rely on user data entry from a keyboard; many read data from an input device, such as a disk. When organizations store data on a disk or other storage device, they do not commonly use a dummy value to signal the end of the file. For one thing, an input record might have hundreds of fields, and if you store a dummy record in every file, you are wasting a large quantity of storage on "nondata." Additionally, it is often difficult to choose sentinel values for fields in a company's data files. Any `balanceDue`, even a zero or a negative number, can be a legitimate value, and any `customerName`, even "ZZ", could be someone's name. Fortunately, programming languages can recognize the end of data in a file automatically, through a code that is stored at the end of the data. Many programming languages use the term **eof** (for "end of file") to refer to this marker that automatically acts as a sentinel. This book, therefore, uses eof to indicate the end of data whenever using a dummy value is impractical or inconvenient. In the flowchart shown in Figure 1-10, the eof question is shaded.

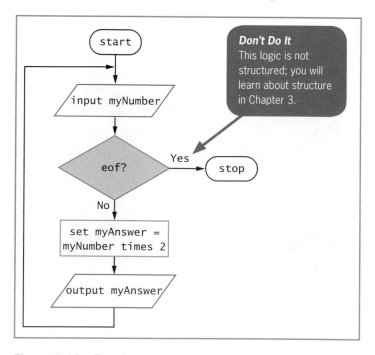

Figure 1-10   Flowchart using eof

TWO TRUTHS & A LIE

Using a Sentinel Value to End a Program

1. A program that contains an infinite loop is one that never ends.

2. A preselected value that stops the execution of a program is often called a dummy value or a sentinel value.

3. Many programming languages use the term fe (for "file end") to refer to a marker that automatically acts as a sentinel.

The false statement is #3. The term eof (for "end of file") is the common term for a file sentinel.

Understanding Programming and User Environments

Many approaches can be used to write and execute a computer program. When you plan a program's logic, you can use a flowchart or pseudocode, or a combination of the two. When you code the program, you can type statements into a variety of text editors. When your program executes, it might accept input from a keyboard, mouse, microphone, or any other input device, and when you provide a program's output, you might use text, images, or sound. This section describes the most common environments you will encounter as a new programmer.

Understanding Programming Environments

When you plan the logic for a computer program, you can use paper and pencil to create a flowchart, or you might use software that allows you to manipulate flowchart shapes. If you choose to write pseudocode, you can do so by hand or by using a word-processing program. To enter the program into a computer so you can translate and execute it, you usually use a keyboard to type program statements into an editor. You can type a program into one of the following:

- A plain text editor

- A text editor that is part of an integrated development environment

A **text editor** is a program that you use to create simple text files. It is similar to a word processor, but without as many features. You can use a text editor such as Notepad that is included with Microsoft Windows. Figure 1-11 shows a C# program in Notepad that accepts a number and doubles it. An advantage to using a simple text editor to type and save a program is that the completed program does not require much disk space for storage. For example, the file shown in Figure 1-11 occupies only 314 bytes of storage.

This line contains a prompt that tells the user what to enter. You will learn more about prompts in Chapter 2.

```
NumberDoublingProgram.cs - Notepad

File  Edit  Format  View  Help
using System;
public class NumberDoublingProgram
{
    public static void Main()
    {
        int myNumber;
        int myAnswer;
        Console.Write("Please enter a number >> ");
        myNumber = Convert.ToInt32(Console.ReadLine());
        myAnswer = myNumber * 2;
        Console.WriteLine(myAnswer);
    }
}
```

Figure 1-11   A C# number-doubling program in Notepad

You can use the editor of an **integrated development environment (IDE)** to enter your program. An IDE is a software package that provides an editor, compiler, and other programming tools. For example, Figure 1-12 shows a C# program in the **Microsoft Visual Studio IDE**, an environment that contains tools useful for creating programs in Visual Basic, C++, and C#.

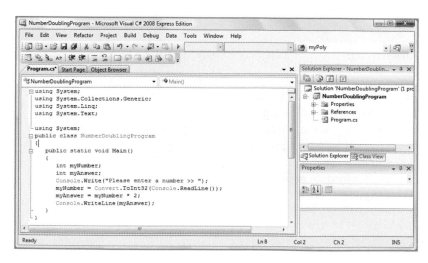

Figure 1-12   A C# number-doubling program in Visual Studio

Using an IDE is helpful to programmers because IDEs usually provide features similar to those you find in many word processors. In particular, an IDE's editor commonly includes such features as the following:

- It uses different colors to display various language components, making elements like data types easier to identify.

- It highlights syntax errors visually for you.

- It employs automatic statement completion; when you start to type a statement, the IDE suggests a likely completion, which you can accept with a keystroke.

- It provides tools that allow you to step through a program's execution one statement at a time so you can more easily follow the program's logic and determine the source of any errors.

When you use the IDE to create and save a program, you occupy much more disk space than when using a plain text editor. For example, the program in Figure 1-12 occupies more than 49,000 bytes of disk space.

Although various programming environments might look different and offer different features, the process of using them is very similar. When you plan the logic for a program using pseudocode or a flowchart, it does not matter which programming environment you will use to write your code, and when you write the code in a programming language, it does not matter which environment you use to write it.

Understanding User Environments

A user might execute a program you have written in any number of environments. For example, a user might execute the number-doubling program from a command line like the one shown in Figure 1-13. A **command line** is a location on your computer screen at which you type text entries to communicate with the computer's operating system. In the program in Figure 1-13, the user is asked for a number, and the results are displayed.

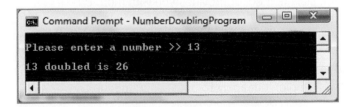

Figure 1-13 Executing a number-doubling program in a command-line environment

Many programs are not run at the command line in a text environment, but are run using a **graphical user interface**, or **GUI** (pronounced "gooey"), which allows users to interact with a program in a graphical environment. When running a GUI program, the user might type input into a text box or use a mouse or other pointing device to select options on the screen. Figure 1-14 shows a number-doubling program that performs exactly the same task as the one in Figure 1-13, but this program uses a GUI.

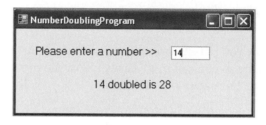

Figure 1-14 Executing a number-doubling program in a GUI environment

A command-line program and a GUI program might be written in the same programming language. (For example, the programs shown in Figures 1-13 and 1-14 were both written using C#.) However, no matter which environment is used to write or execute a program, the logical process is the same. The two programs in Figures 1-13 and 1-14 both accept input, perform multiplication, and perform output. In this book, you will not concentrate on which environment is used to type a program's statements, nor will you care about the type of environment the user will see. Instead, you will be concerned with the logic that applies to all programming situations.

TWO TRUTHS & A LIE

Understanding Programming and User Environments

1. You can type a program into an editor that is part of an integrated development environment, but using a plain text editor provides you with more programming help.

2. When a program runs from the command line, a user types text to provide input.

3. Although GUI and command-line environments look different, the logic processes of input, processing, and output apply to both program types.

The false statement is #1. An integrated development environment provides more programming help than a plain text editor.

Understanding the Evolution of Programming Models

People have been writing modern computer programs since the 1940s. The oldest programming languages required programmers to work with memory addresses and to memorize awkward codes associated with machine languages. Newer programming languages look much more like natural language and are easier to use, partly because they allow programmers to name variables instead of using awkward memory addresses. Also, newer programming languages allow programmers to create self-contained modules or program segments that can be pieced together in a variety of ways. The oldest computer programs were written in one piece, from start to finish, but modern programs are rarely written that way—they are created by teams of programmers, each developing reusable and connectable program procedures. Writing several small modules is easier than writing one large program, and most large tasks are easier when you break the work into units and get other workers to help with some of the units.

Currently, two major models or paradigms are used by programmers to develop programs and their procedures. One technique, **procedural programming**, focuses on the procedures that programmers create. That is, procedural programmers focus on the actions that are carried out—for example, getting input data for an employee and writing the calculations needed to produce a paycheck from the data. Procedural programmers would approach the job of producing a paycheck by breaking down the process into manageable subtasks.

The other popular programming model, **object-oriented programming**, focuses on objects, or "things," and describes their features (or attributes) and their behaviors. For example, object-oriented programmers might design a payroll application by thinking about employees and paychecks, and describing their attributes (e.g. employees have names and Social Security numbers, and paychecks have names and check amounts). Then the programmers would think about the behaviors of employees and paychecks, such as employees getting raises and adding dependents and paychecks being calculated and output. Object-oriented programmers would then build applications from these entities.

With either approach, procedural or object oriented, you can produce a correct paycheck, and both models employ reusable program modules. The major difference lies in the focus the programmer takes during the earliest planning stages of a project. For now, this book focuses on procedural programming techniques. The skills you gain in programming procedurally—declaring variables, accepting input, making decisions, producing output, and so on—will serve you well whether you eventually write programs in a procedural or object-oriented fashion, or in both.

Ada Byron Lovelace predicted the development of software in 1843; she is often regarded as the first programmer. The basis for most modern software was proposed by Alan Turing in 1935.

You will learn to create program modules in Chapter 2.

You can write a procedural program in any language that supports object orientation. The opposite is not always true.

Object-oriented programming employs a large vocabulary; you can learn this terminology in Chapter 10 of the comprehensive version of this book.

TWO TRUTHS & A LIE

Understanding the Evolution of Programming Models

1. The oldest computer programs were written in many separate modules.

2. Procedural programmers focus on actions that are carried out by a program.

3. Object-oriented programmers focus on a program's objects and their attributes and behaviors.

The false statement is #1. The oldest programs were written in a single piece; newer programs are divided into modules.

Chapter Summary

- Together, computer hardware (physical devices) and software (instructions) accomplish three major operations: input, processing, and output. You write computer instructions in a computer programming language that requires specific syntax; the instructions are translated into machine language by a compiler or interpreter. When both the syntax and logic of a program are correct, you can run, or execute, the program to produce the desired results.

- For a program to work properly, you must develop correct logic. Logical errors are much more difficult to locate than syntax errors.

- A programmer's job involves understanding the problem, planning the logic, coding the program, translating the program into machine language, testing the program, putting the program into production, and maintaining it.

- When programmers plan the logic for a solution to a programming problem, they often use flowcharts or pseudocode. When you draw a flowchart, you use parallelograms to represent input and output operations, and rectangles to represent processing. Programmers also use decisions to control repetition of instruction sets.

- To avoid creating an infinite loop when you repeat instructions, you can test for a sentinel value. You represent a decision in a flowchart by drawing a diamond-shaped symbol that contains a question, the answer to which is either yes or no.

- You can type a program into a plain text editor or one that is part of an integrated development environment. When a program's data values are entered from a keyboard, they can be entered at the command line in a text environment or in a GUI. Either way, the logic is similar.

- Procedural and object-oriented programmers approach problems differently. Procedural programmers concentrate on the actions performed with data. Object-oriented programmers focus on objects and their behaviors and attributes.

Key Terms

A **computer system** is a combination of all the components required to process and store data using a computer.

Hardware is the collection of physical devices that comprise a computer system.

Software consists of the programs that tell the computer what to do.

Programs are sets of instructions for a computer.

Programming is the act of developing and writing programs.

Application software comprises all the programs you apply to a task.

System software comprises the programs that you use to manage your computer.

Input describes the entry of data items into computer memory using hardware devices such as keyboards and mice.

Data items include all the text, numbers, and other information processed by a computer.

Processing data items may involve organizing them, checking them for accuracy, or performing mathematical operations on them.

The **central processing unit**, or **CPU**, is the hardware component that processes data.

Output describes the operation of retrieving information from memory and sending it to a device, such as a monitor or printer, so people can view, interpret, and work with the results.

Storage devices are types of hardware equipment, such as disks, that hold information for later retrieval.

Programming languages, such as Visual Basic, C#, C++, Java, or COBOL, are used to write programs.

Program code is the set of instructions a programmer writes in a programming language.

Coding the program is the act of writing programming language instructions.

The **syntax** of a language is its grammar rules.

Computer memory is the temporary, internal storage within a computer.

Volatile describes storage whose contents are lost when power is lost.

Nonvolatile describes storage whose contents are retained when power is lost.

Random access memory (RAM) is temporary, internal computer storage.

Machine language is a computer's on/off circuitry language.

A **compiler** or **interpreter** translates a high-level language into machine language and tells you if you have used a programming language incorrectly.

Binary language is represented using a series of 0s and 1s.

Source code is the statements a programmer writes in a programming language.

Object code is translated machine language.

To **run** or **execute** a program is to carry out its instructions.

Scripting languages (also called **scripting programming languages** or **script languages**) such as Python, Lua, Perl, and PHP are used to write programs that are typed directly from a keyboard. Scripting languages are stored as text rather than as binary executable files.

A **logical error** occurs when incorrect instructions are performed, or when instructions are performed in the wrong order.

You develop the **logic** of the computer program when you give instructions to the computer in a specific sequence, without omitting any instructions or adding extraneous instructions.

A **semantic error** occurs when a correct word is used in an incorrect context.

A **variable** is a named memory location whose value can vary.

The **program development cycle** consists of the steps that occur during a program's lifetime.

Users (or **end users**) are people who employ and benefit from computer programs.

Documentation consists of all the supporting paperwork for a program.

An **algorithm** is the sequence of steps necessary to solve any problem.

An **IPO chart** is a program development tool that delineates input, processing, and output tasks.

A **TOE chart** is a program development tool that lists tasks, objects, and events.

Desk-checking is the process of walking through a program solution on paper.

A **high-level programming language** supports English-like syntax.

Machine language is the **low-level language** made up of 1s and 0s that the computer understands.

A **syntax error** is an error in language or grammar.

Debugging is the process of finding and correcting program errors.

Conversion is the entire set of actions an organization must take to switch over to using a new program or set of programs.

Maintenance consists of all the improvements and corrections made to a program after it is in production.

Pseudocode is an English-like representation of the logical steps it takes to solve a problem.

A **flowchart** is a pictorial representation of the logical steps it takes to solve a problem.

An **input symbol** indicates an input operation and is represented by a parallelogram in flowcharts.

A **processing symbol** indicates a processing operation and is represented by a rectangle in flowcharts.

An **output symbol** indicates an output operation and is represented by a parallelogram in flowcharts.

An **input/output symbol** or **I/O symbol** is represented by a parallelogram in flowcharts.

Flowlines, or arrows, connect the steps in a flowchart.

A **terminal symbol**, or start/stop symbol, is used at each end of a flowchart. Its shape is a lozenge.

A **loop** is a repetition of a series of steps.

An **infinite loop** occurs when repeating logic cannot end.

Making a decision is the act of testing a value.

A **decision symbol** is shaped like a diamond and used to represent decisions in flowcharts.

A **binary decision** is a yes-or-no decision with two possible outcomes.

A **dummy value** is a preselected value that stops the execution of a program.

A **sentinel value** is a preselected value that stops the execution of a program.

The term **eof** means "end of file."

A **text editor** is a program that you use to create simple text files; it is similar to a word processor, but without as many features.

An **integrated development environment (IDE)** is a software package that provides an editor, compiler, and other programming tools.

Microsoft Visual Studio IDE is a software package that contains useful tools for creating programs in Visual Basic, C++, and C#.

A **command line** is a location on your computer screen at which you type text entries to communicate with the computer's operating system.

A **graphical user interface**, or **GUI** (pronounced "gooey"), allows users to interact with a program in a graphical environment.

Procedural programming is a programming model that focuses on the procedures that programmers create.

Object-oriented programming is a programming model that focuses on objects, or "things," and describes their features (or attributes) and their behaviors.

Review Questions

1. Computer programs are also known as _____.

    a. hardware

    b. software

    c. data

    d. information

2. The major computer operations include _____.

   a. hardware and software

   b. input, processing, and output

   c. sequence and looping

   d. spreadsheets, word processing, and data
   communications

3. Visual Basic, C++, and Java are all examples of computer
   _____.

   a. operating systems

   b. hardware

   c. machine languages

   d. programming languages

4. A programming language's rules are its _____.

   a. syntax

   b. logic

   c. format

   d. options

5. The most important task of a compiler or interpreter
   is to _____.

   a. create the rules for a programming language

   b. translate English statements into a language the computer
   can understand, such as Java

   c. translate programming language statements into machine
   language

   d. execute machine language programs to perform useful
   tasks

6. Which of the following is temporary, internal storage?

   a. CPU

   b. hard disk

   c. keyboard

   d. memory

7. Which of the following pairs of steps in the programming process is in the correct order?

    a. code the program, plan the logic

    b. test the program, translate it into machine language

    c. put the program into production, understand the problem

    d. code the program, translate it into machine language

8. The programmer's most important task before planning the logic of a program is to _____.

    a. decide which programming language to use

    b. code the problem

    c. train the users of the program

    d. understand the problem

9. The two most commonly used tools for planning a program's logic are _____.

    a. flowcharts and pseudocode

    b. ASCII and EBCDIC

    c. Java and Visual Basic

    d. word processors and spreadsheets

10. Writing a program in a language such as C++ or Java is known as _____ the program.

    a. translating

    b. coding

    c. interpreting

    d. compiling

11. An English-like programming language such as Java or Visual Basic is a _____ programming language.

    a. machine-level

    b. low-level

    c. high-level

    d. binary-level

12. Which of the following is an example of a syntax error?

    a. producing output before accepting input

    b. subtracting when you meant to add

    c. misspelling a programming language word

    d. all of the above

13. Which of the following is an example of a logical error?

    a. performing arithmetic with a value before inputting it

    b. accepting two input values when a program requires only one

    c. dividing by 3 when you meant to divide by 30

    d. all of the above

14. The parallelogram is the flowchart symbol representing _____.

    a. input

    b. output

    c. both a and b

    d. none of the above

15. In a flowchart, a rectangle represents _____.

    a. input

    b. a sentinel

    c. a question

    d. processing

16. In flowcharts, the decision symbol is a _____.

    a. parallelogram

    b. rectangle

    c. lozenge

    d. diamond

17. The term "eof" represents _____.

    a. a standard input device

    b. a generic sentinel value

    c. a condition in which no more memory is available for storage

    d. the logical flow in a program

18. When you use an IDE instead of a simple text editor to develop a program, _____.

    a. the logic is more complicated

    b. the logic is simpler

    c. the syntax is different

    d. some help is provided

19. When you write a program that will run in a GUI environment as opposed to a command-line environment, _____.

    a. the logic is very different

    b. some syntax is different

    c. you do not need to plan the logic

    d. users are more confused

20. As compared to procedural programming, with object-oriented programming _____.

    a. the programmer's focus differs

    b. you cannot use some languages, such as Java

    c. you do not accept input

    d. you do not code calculations; they are created automatically

Exercises

1. Match the definition with the appropriate term.

   1. Computer system devices   a. compiler
   2. Another word for programs   b. syntax
   3. Language rules   c. logic
   4. Order of instructions   d. hardware
   5. Language translator   e. software

2. In your own words, describe the steps to writing a computer program.

3. Match the term with the appropriate shape.

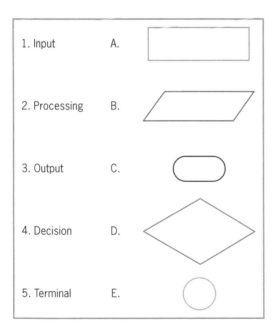

   1. Input   A.

   2. Processing   B.

   3. Output   C.

   4. Decision   D.

   5. Terminal   E.

4. Draw a flowchart or write pseudocode to represent the logic of a program that allows the user to enter a value. The program multiplies the value by 10 and outputs the result.

5. Draw a flowchart or write pseudocode to represent the logic of a program that allows the user to enter a value for the radius of a circle. The program calculates the diameter by multiplying the radius by 2, and then calculates the circumference by multiplying the diameter by 3.14. The program outputs both the diameter and the circumference.

6. Draw a flowchart or write pseudocode to represent the logic of a program that allows the user to enter two values. The program outputs the sum of the two values.

7. Draw a flowchart or write pseudocode to represent the logic of a program that allows the user to enter three values. The values represent hourly pay rate, the number of hours worked this pay period, and percentage of gross salary that is withheld. The program multiplies the hourly pay rate by the number of hours worked, giving the gross pay. Then, it multiplies the gross pay by the withholding percentage, giving the withholding amount. Finally, it subtracts the withholding amount from the gross pay, giving the net pay after taxes. The program outputs the net pay.

 ## Find the Bugs

8. Since the early days of computer programming, program errors have been called "bugs." The term is often said to have originated from an actual moth that was discovered trapped in the circuitry of a computer at Harvard University in 1945. Actually, the term "bug" was in use prior to 1945 to mean trouble with any electrical apparatus; even during Thomas Edison's life, it meant an "industrial defect." However, the term "debugging" is more closely associated with correcting program syntax and logic errors than with any other type of trouble.

Your student disk contains files named DEBUG01-01.txt, DEBUG01-02.txt, and DEBUG01-03.txt. Each file starts with some comments that describe the problem. Comments are lines that begin with two slashes (//). Following the comments, each file contains pseudocode that has one or more bugs you must find and correct.

Game Zone

9. In 1952, A. S. Douglas wrote his University of Cambridge Ph.D. dissertation on human-computer interaction, and created the first graphical computer game—a version of Tic-Tac-Toe. The game was programmed on an EDSAC vacuum-tube mainframe computer. The first computer game is generally assumed to be "Spacewar!", developed in 1962 at MIT; the first commercially available video game was "Pong," introduced by Atari in 1972. In 1980, Atari's "Asteroids" and "Lunar Lander" became the first video games to be registered with the U. S. Copyright Office. Throughout the 1980s, players spent hours with games that now seem very simple and unglamorous; do you recall playing "Adventure," "Oregon Trail," "Where in the World Is Carmen Sandiego?," or "Myst"?

Today, commercial computer games are much more complex; they require many programmers, graphic artists, and testers to develop them, and large management and marketing staffs are needed to promote them. A game might cost many millions of dollars to develop and market, but a successful game might earn hundreds of millions of dollars. Obviously, with the brief introduction to programming you have had in this chapter, you cannot create a very sophisticated game. However, you can get started.

Mad Libs© is a children's game in which players provide a few words that are then incorporated into a silly story. The game helps children understand different parts of speech because they are asked to provide specific types of words. For example, you might ask a child for a noun, another noun, an adjective, and a past-tense verb. The child might reply with such answers as "table," "book," "silly," and "studied." The newly created Mad Lib might be:

> Mary had a little *table*
>
> Its *book* was *silly* as snow
>
> And everywhere that Mary *studied*
>
> The *table* was sure to go.

Create the logic for a Mad Lib program that accepts five words from input, then creates and displays a short story or nursery rhyme that uses those words.

Up for Discussion

10. Which is the better tool for learning programming—flowcharts or pseudocode? Cite any educational research you can find.

11. What is the image of the computer programmer in popular culture? Is the image different in books than in TV shows and movies? Would you like that image for yourself?

CHAPTER 2

Working with Data, Creating Modules, and Designing High-Quality Programs

In this chapter, you will learn about:

- ◎ Declaring and using variables and constants
- ◎ Assigning values to variables
- ◎ The advantages of modularization
- ◎ Modularizing a program
- ◎ The most common configuration for mainline logic
- ◎ Hierarchy charts
- ◎ Some features of good program design

42

Declaring and Using Variables and Constants

As you learned in Chapter 1, data items include all the text, numbers, and other information that are processed by a computer. When you input data items into a computer, they are stored in variables in memory where they can be processed and converted to information that is output.

When you write programs, you work with data in three different forms: variables; literals, or unnamed constants; and named constants.

Watch the video *Declaring Variables and Constants.*

Working with Variables

Variables are named memory locations whose contents can vary or differ over time. For example, in the number-doubling program in Figure 2-1, myNumber and myAnswer are variables. At any moment in time, a variable holds just one value. Sometimes, myNumber holds 2 and myAnswer holds 4; at other times, myNumber holds 6 and myAnswer holds 12. The ability of variables to change in value is what makes computers and programming worthwhile. Because one memory location can be used repeatedly with different values, you can write program instructions once and then use them for thousands of separate calculations. *One* set of payroll instructions at your company produces each individual's paycheck, and *one* set of instructions at your electric company produces each household's bill.

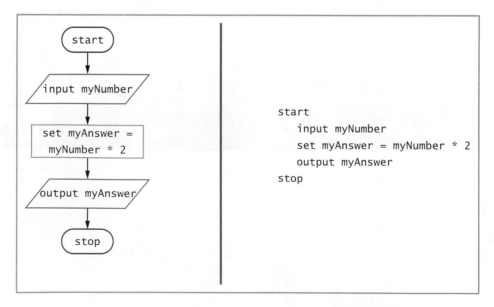

Figure 2-1   Flowchart and pseudocode for the number-doubling program

In most programming languages, before you can use any variable, you must include a declaration for it. A **declaration** is a statement that provides a data type and an identifier for a variable. An **identifier** is a variable's name. A data item's **data type** is a classification that describes the following:

The process of naming program variables and assigning a type to them is called **making declarations**, or **declaring variables**.

43

• What values can be held by the item

• How the item is stored in computer memory

• What operations can be performed on the data item

In this book, two data types will be used: num and string. When you declare a variable, you provide both a data type and an identifier. Optionally, you can declare a starting value for any variable. Declaring a starting value is known as **initializing the variable**. For example, each of the following statements is a valid declaration. Two of the statements include initializations, and two do not:

Later in this chapter, you will learn that you select identifiers for program modules as well as for variables.

```
num mySalary
num yourSalary = 14.55
string myName
string yourName = "Juanita"
```

Figure 2-2 shows the number-doubling program from Figure 2-1 with the added declarations shaded. Variables must be declared before they are used in a program for the first time.

```
start
    Declarations
        num myNumber
        num myAnswer
    input myNumber
    set myAnswer = myNumber * 2
    output myAnswer
stop
```

Figure 2-2 Flowchart and pseudocode of number-doubling program with variable declarations

Some languages require all variables to be declared at the beginning of the program; others allow variables to be declared anywhere as long as they are declared before their first use. This book will follow the convention of declaring all variables together.

44

In many programming languages, if you declare a variable and do not initialize it, the variable contains an unknown value until it is assigned a value. A variable's unknown value is commonly called **garbage**. In many languages it is illegal to use a garbage-holding variable in an arithmetic statement or to display it as output. Even if you work with a language that allows you to display garbage, it serves no purpose to do so and constitutes a logical error. When you create a variable without assigning it an initial value (as with myNumber and myAnswer in Figure 2-2), your intention is to assign a value later—for example, by receiving one as input or placing the result of a calculation there.

Naming Variables

The number-doubling example in Figure 2-2 requires two variables: myNumber and myAnswer. Alternatively, these variables could be named userEntry and programSolution, or inputValue and twiceTheValue. As a programmer, you choose reasonable and descriptive names for your variables. The language interpreter then associates the names you choose with specific memory addresses.

Although some languages use a default value for some variables (such as assigning 0 to any unassigned numeric variable), this book will assume that an unassigned variable holds garbage.

Every computer programming language has its own set of rules for creating identifiers. Most languages allow letters and digits within variable names. Some languages allow hyphens in variable names, such as hourly-wage, and some allow underscores, as in hourly_wage. Other languages allow neither. Some languages allow dollar signs or other special characters in variable names (for example, hourly$); others allow foreign-alphabet characters, such as π or Ω.

You can also refer to a variable name as a **mnemonic**. In everyday language, a mnemonic is a memory device, like the musical reference "Every good boy does fine," which makes it easier to remember the notes that occupy the lines on the staff in sheet music. In programming, a variable name is a device that makes it easier to reference a memory address.

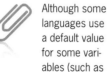

Each programming language has a few (perhaps 80) reserved **keywords** that are not allowed as variable names because they are part of the language's syntax. When you learn a programming language, you will learn its list of keywords.

Different languages put different limits on the length of variable names, although in general, the length of identifiers in newer languages is virtually unlimited. In many languages, identifiers are case sensitive, so HoUrLyWaGe, hourlywage, and hourlyWage are three separate variable names. The format used in the last example, in which the variable starts with a lowercase letter and any subsequent word begins with an uppercase letter, is called **camel casing**—variable names such as hourlyWage have a "hump" in the middle. The variable names in this book are shown using camel casing.

When the first letter of a variable name is uppercase, as in `HourlyWage`, the format is known as **Pascal casing**. Adopting a naming convention for variables and using it consistently will help make your programs easier to read and understand.

Even though every language has its own rules for naming variables, you should not concern yourself with the specific syntax of any particular computer language when designing the logic of a program. The logic, after all, works with any language. The variable names used throughout this book follow only two rules:

 Almost all programming languages prohibit variable names that start with a digit. This book follows the most common convention of starting variable names with a letter.

1. *Variable names must be one word*. The name can contain letters, digits, hyphens, underscores, or any other characters you choose, with the exception of *spaces*. Therefore, r is a legal variable name, as are `rate` and `interestRate`. The variable name `interest rate` is not allowed because of the space.

2. *Variable names should have some appropriate meaning*. This is not a formal rule of any programming language. When computing an interest rate in a program, the computer does not care if you call the variable g, u84, or `fred`. As long as the correct numeric result is placed in the variable, its actual name doesn't really matter. However, it's much easier to follow the logic of a statement like `set finalBalance = initialInvestment * interestRate`, than a statement like `set f = i * r`, or `set someBanana = j89 * myFriendLinda`. When a program requires changes, which could be months or years after you write the original version, you and your fellow programmers will appreciate clear, descriptive variable names in place of cryptic identifiers.

 When you write a program using an editor that is packaged with a compiler in an IDE, the compiler may display variable names in a different color from the rest of the program. This visual aid helps your variable names stand out from words that are part of the programming language.

Notice that the flowchart in Figure 2-2 follows the preceding two rules for variables: both variable names, `myNumber` and `myAnswer`, are one word without embedded spaces, and they have appropriate meanings. Some programmers name variables after friends or create puns with them, but computer professionals consider such behavior unprofessional and amateurish.

 Another general rule in all programming languages is that variable names may not begin with a digit, although usually they may contain digits. Thus, in most languages `budget2013` is a legal variable name, but `2013Budget` is not.

Understanding Unnamed, Literal Constants and their Data Types

Computers deal with two basic types of data—text and numeric. When you use a specific numeric value, such as 43, within a program, you write it using the digits and no quotation marks. A specific numeric value is often called a **numeric constant**

When you store a numeric value in computer memory, additional characters such as dollar signs and commas are not input or stored. Those characters can be added to output for readability, but then the output is a string and not a number.

String values are also called **alphanumeric values** because they can contain alphabetic characters, numbers, and punctuation. Numeric values, however, cannot contain alphabetic characters.

Some languages allow for several types of numeric data. Languages such as C++, C#, Visual Basic, and Java distinguish between **integer** (whole number) numeric variables and **floating-point** (fractional) numeric variables that contain a decimal point. (Floating-point numbers are also called **real numbers**.) Thus, in some languages, the values 4 and 4.3 would be stored in different types of numeric variables.

(or **literal numeric constant**) because it does not change—a 43 always has the value 43. When you use a specific text value, or string of characters, such as "Amanda", you enclose the **string constant** (or **literal string constant**) within quotation marks. The constants 43 and "Amanda" are examples of **unnamed constants**—they do not have identifiers like variables do.

Understanding the Data Types of Variables

Like literals, variables can also be different data types.

- A **numeric variable** is one that can hold digits and have mathematical operations performed on it. Also, you usually have the option of having a numeric variable hold a decimal point and a sign indicating positive or negative. In the statement `set myAnswer = myNumber * 2`, both `myAnswer` and `myNumber` are numeric variables; that is, their intended contents are numeric values, such as 6 and 3, 14.8 and 7.4, or −18 and −9.

- A **string variable** can hold text, such as letters of the alphabet, and other special characters, such as punctuation marks. If a working program contains the statement `set lastName = "Lincoln"`, then `lastName` is a string variable. A string variable can also hold digits either with or without other characters. For example, "235 Main Street" and "86" are both strings. A string like "86" is stored differently than the numeric value 86, and you cannot perform arithmetic with the string.

Computers handle string data differently from the way they handle numeric data. You may have experienced these differences if you have used application software such as spreadsheets or database programs. For example, in a spreadsheet, you cannot sum a column of words. Similarly, every programming language requires that you distinguish variables as to their correct type, and that you use each type of variable appropriately.

Object-oriented programming languages allow you to create new data types called classes. Classes are covered in all object-oriented programming language textbooks, as well as in Chapter 10 of the comprehensive version of this book.

You can assign data to a variable only if it is the correct type. If you declare `taxRate` as a numeric variable and `inventoryItem` as a string, then the following statements are valid:

```
set taxRate = 2.5
set inventoryItem = "monitor"
```

The following are invalid because the type of data being assigned does ot match the variable type:

```
set taxRate = "2.5"
set inventoryItem = 2.5
```

Don't Do It
If taxRate is numeric and inventoryItem is a string, then these assignments are invalid.

Watch the video *Understanding Data Types*.

In addition to setting a variable to a constant value, you can set it to the value of another variable of the same data type. If taxRate and oldRate are both numeric, and inventoryItem and orderedItem are both strings, then the following are valid:

```
set taxRate = oldRate
set orderedItem = inventoryItem
```

Declaring Named Constants

Besides variables, most programming languages allow you to create named constants. A **named constant** is similar to a variable, except it can be assigned a value only once. You use a named constant when you want to assign a useful name to a value that will never be changed during a program's execution. Using named constants makes your programs easier to understand by eliminating magic numbers. A **magic number** is an unnamed constant, like 0.06, whose purpose is not immediately apparent.

For example, if a program uses a sales tax rate of 6%, you might want to declare a named constant as follows:

```
num SALES_TAX = 0.06
```

You then might use SALES_TAX in a program statement similar to the following:

```
set taxAmount = price * SALES_TAX
```

The way in which named constants are declared differs among programming languages. This book follows the convention of using all uppercase letters in constant identifiers, and using underscores to separate words for readability. Using these conventions makes named constants easier to recognize.

When you declare a named constant, program maintenance becomes easier. For example, if the value of the sales tax changes from 0.06 to 0.07 in the future, and you have declared a named constant SALES_TAX, then you only need to change the value assigned to the named constant at the beginning of the program, and all references to SALES_TAX are automatically updated. If you have used the unnamed literal 0.06 instead, you would have to search for every instance of the value and replace it with the new one.

In many languages a constant must be assigned its value when it is declared, but in some languages, a constant can be assigned its value later. In both cases, however, a constant's value can never be changed after the first assignment. This book follows the convention of initializing all constants when they are declared.

Sometimes, using unnamed literal constants is appropriate in a program, especially if their meaning is clear to most readers. For example, in a program that calculates half of a value by dividing by two, you might choose to use the literal 2 instead of incurring the extra time and memory costs of creating a named constant HALF and assigning 2 to it. Extra costs that result from adding variables or instructions to a program are known as **overhead**.

48

TWO TRUTHS & A LIE

Declaring and Using Variables and Constants

1. A variable's data type describes the kind of values the variable can hold and the types of operations that can be performed with it.

2. If name is a string variable, then the statement set name = "Ed" is valid.

3. If salary is a numeric variable, then the statement set salary = "12.50" is valid.

The false statement is #3. If salary is a numeric variable, then the statement set salary = 12.50 (with no quotation marks) is valid. If salary is a string variable, then the statement set salary = "12.50" is valid.

Assigning Values to Variables

The assignment operator is an example of a **binary operator**, meaning it requires two operands—one on each side.

When you create a flowchart or pseudocode for a program that doubles numbers, you can include a statement such as the following:

```
set myAnswer = myNumber * 2
```

Such a statement is an **assignment statement**. This statement incorporates two actions. First, the computer calculates the arithmetic value of myNumber * 2. Second, the computed value is stored in the myAnswer memory location.

An operator that works from right to left, like the assignment operator, has **right-associativity** or **right-to-left associativity**.

The equal sign is the **assignment operator**. The assignment operator always operates from right to left; the value of the expression to the right of the operator is evaluated before the assignment to the operand on the left occurs. The operand to the right of an assignment statement can be a value, a formula, a named constant, or a variable. The operand to the left of an assignment operator must be a name that represents a memory address—the name of the location where the result will be stored.

For example, if you have declared a numeric variable named someNumber, then each of the following is a valid assignment statement:

```
set someNumber = 2
set someNumber = 3 + 7
```

Additionally, if you have declared another numeric variable named someOtherNumber and assigned a value to it, then each of the following is a valid assignment statement:

```
set someNumber = someOtherNumber
set someNumber = someOtherNumber * 5
```

In each case, the expression to the right of the assignment operator is evaluated and stored at the location referenced on the left side.

The result to the left of an assignment operator is called an **lvalue**. The *l* is for left. Lvalues are always memory address identifiers.

The following statements, however, are *not* valid:

Don't Do It
The operand to the left of an assignment operator must represent a memory address.

```
set 2 + 4 = someNumber
set someOtherNumber * 10 = someNumber
```

In each of these cases, the value to the left of the assignment operator is not a memory address, so the statements are invalid.

When you write pseudocode or draw a flowchart, it might help you to use the word "set" in assignment statements, as shown here, to emphasize that the left-side value is being set. However, in most programming languages, the word "set" is not used, and assignment statements take the following form:

```
someNumber = 2
someNumber = someOtherNumber
```

Because the abbreviated form is how assignments appear in most languages, it is used for the rest of this book.

Performing Arithmetic Operations

Most programming languages use the following standard arithmetic operators:

+ (plus sign)—addition

– (minus sign)—subtraction

* (asterisk)—multiplication

/ (slash)—division

Many languages also support operators that calculate the remainder after division (often the percent sign, %) and that raise a number to a higher power (often the carat, ^).

For example, the following statement adds two test scores and assigns the sum to a variable named totalScore:

```
totalScore = test1 + test2
```

The following adds 10 to totalScore and stores the result in totalScore:

```
totalScore = totalScore + 10
```

In other words, this example increases the value of totalScore. This last example looks odd in algebra because it might appear to say that the value of totalScore and totalScore plus 10 are equivalent. You must remember that the equal sign is the assignment operator, and that the statement is actually taking the original value of totalScore,

The assignment operator has a very low precedence. Therefore, in a statement such as d = e * f + g, the operations on the right of the assignment operator are always performed before the final assignment to the variable on the left.

When you learn a specific programming language, you will learn about all the operators that are used in that language. Many programming language books contain a table that specifies the relative precedence of every operator used in the language.

adding 10 to it, and assigning the result to the memory address on the left of the operator, which is totalScore.

In programming languages, you can combine arithmetic statements. When you do, every operator follows **rules of precedence** (also called the **order of operations**) that dictate the order in which operations in the same statement are carried out. The rules of precedence for the basic arithmetic statements are as follows:

- Expressions within parentheses are evaluated first. If there are multiple sets of parentheses, the expression within the innermost parentheses is evaluated first.

- Multiplication and division are evaluated next, from left to right.

- Addition and subtraction are evaluated next, from left to right.

For example, consider the following two arithmetic statements:

```
firstAnswer = 2 + 3 * 4
secondAnswer = (2 + 3) * 4
```

After these statements execute, the value of firstAnswer is 14. According to the rules of precedence, multiplication is carried out before addition, so 3 is multiplied by 4, giving 12, and then 2 and 12 are added, and 14 is assigned to firstAnswer. The value of secondAnswer, however, is 20, because the parentheses force the contained addition operation to be performed first. The 2 and 3 are added, producing 5, and then 5 is multiplied by 4, producing 20.

Forgetting about the rules of arithmetic precedence, or forgetting to add parentheses when you need them, can cause logical errors that are difficult to find in programs. For example, the following statement might appear to average two test scores:

```
average = score1 + score2 / 2
```

However, it does not. Because division has a higher precedence than addition, the preceding statement takes half of score2, adds it to score1, and stores the result in average. The correct statement is:

```
average = (score1 + score2) / 2
```

You are free to add parentheses even when you don't need them to force a different order of operations; sometimes you use them just to make your intentions clearer. For example, the following statements operate identically:

```
totalPriceWithTax = price + price * TAX_RATE
totalPriceWithTax = price + (price * TAX_RATE)
```

In both cases, `price` is multiplied by TAX_RATE first, then it is added to `price`, and finally the result is stored in `totalPriceWithTax`. Because multiplication occurs before addition on the right side of the assignment operator, both statements are the same. However, if you feel the statement with the parentheses makes your intentions clearer to someone reading your program, then you should use them.

All the arithmetic operators have **left-to-right associativity**. This means that operations with the same precedence take place from left to right. Consider the following statement:

```
answer = a + b + c * d / e - f
```

Multiplication and division have higher precedence than addition or subtraction, so the multiplication and division are carried out from left to right as follows:

Watch the video
Arithmetic Operator Precedence.

`c` is multiplied by `d`, and the result is divided by `e`, giving a new result.

Therefore, the statement becomes:

```
answer = a + b + (temporary result just calculated) - f
```

Then, addition and subtraction are carried out from left to right as follows:

`a` and `b` are added, the temporary result is added, and then `f` is subtracted. The final result is then assigned to `answer`.

Another way to say this is that the following two statements are equivalent:

```
answer = a + b + c * d / e - f
answer = a + b + ((c * d) / e) - f
```

Table 2-1 summarizes the precedence and associativity of the five most frequently used operators.

Operator symbol	Operator name	Precedence (compared to other operators in this table)	Associativity
=	Assignment	Lowest	Right-to-left
+	Addition	Medium	Left-to-right
−	Subtraction	Medium	Left-to-right
*	Multiplication	Highest	Left-to-right
/	Division	Highest	Left-to-right

Each operator in Table 2-1 is a binary operator.

Table 2-1   Precedence and associativity of five common operators

52

TWO TRUTHS & A LIE

Assigning Values to Variables

1. The assignment operator always operates from right to left; programmers say it has right-associativity or right-to-left associativity.

2. The operand to the right of an assignment operator must be a name that represents a memory address.

3. The following adds 5 to a variable named `points`:

    ```
    points = points + 5
    ```

The false statement is #2. The operand to the left of an assignment operator must be a name that represents a memory address—the name of the location where the result will be stored. Any operand on the right of an assignment operator can be a memory address (a variable) or a constant.

Understanding the Advantages of Modularization

You can learn about modules that receive and return data in Chapter 9 of the comprehensive version of this book.

Programmers seldom write programs as one long series of steps. Instead, they break down the programming problem into reasonable units, and tackle one small task at a time. These reasonable units are called **modules**. Programmers also refer to them as **subroutines**, **procedures**, **functions**, or **methods**.

The name that programmers use for their modules usually reflects the programming language they use. For example, Visual Basic programmers use "procedure" (or "subprocedure"). C and C++ programmers call their modules "functions," whereas C#, Java, and other object-oriented language programmers are more likely to use "method." Programmers in COBOL, RPG, and BASIC (all older languages) are most likely to use "subroutine."

The process of breaking down a large program into modules is called **modularization**. You are never required to modularize a large program in order to make it run on a computer, but there are at least three reasons for doing so:

Reducing a large program into more manageable modules is sometimes called **functional decomposition**.

- Modularization provides abstraction.

- Modularization allows multiple programmers to work on a problem.

- Modularization allows you to reuse your work more easily.

Modularization Provides Abstraction

One reason modularized programs are easier to understand is that they enable a programmer to see the big picture. **Abstraction** is the process of paying attention to important properties while ignoring nonessential details. Abstraction is selective ignorance. Life would be tedious without abstraction. For example, you can create a list of things to accomplish today:

```
Do laundry
Call Aunt Nan
Start term paper
```

Without abstraction, the list of chores would begin:

```
Pick up laundry basket
Put laundry basket in car
Drive to Laundromat
Get out of car with basket
Walk into Laundromat
Set basket down
Find quarters for washing machine
. . . and so on.
```

You might list a dozen more steps before you finish the laundry and move on to the second chore on your original list. If you had to consider every small, low-level detail of every task in your day, you would probably never make it out of bed in the morning. Using a higher-level, more abstract list makes your day manageable. Abstraction makes complex tasks look simple.

Likewise, some level of abstraction occurs in every computer program. Fifty years ago, a programmer had to understand the low-level circuitry instructions the computer used. But now, newer high-level programming languages allow you to use English-like vocabulary in which one broad statement corresponds to dozens of machine instructions. No matter which high-level programming language you use, if you display a message on the monitor, you are never required to understand how a monitor works to create each pixel on the screen. You write an instruction like `output message` and the details of the hardware operations are handled for you.

Modules provide another way to achieve abstraction. For example, a payroll program can call a module named `computeFederalWithholdingTax()`. When you call this module from your program, you use one statement; the module itself might contain dozens of statements. You can write the mathematical details of the module later, someone else can write them, or you can purchase them from an outside source. When you plan your main payroll program,

Abstract artists create paintings in which they see only the "big picture"—color and form—and ignore the details. Abstraction has a similar meaning among programmers.

your only concern is that a federal withholding tax will have to be calculated; you save the details for later.

Modularization Allows Multiple Programmers to Work on a Problem

When you dissect any large task into modules, you gain the ability to more easily divide the task among various people. Rarely does a single programmer write a commercial program that you buy. Consider any word-processing, spreadsheet, or database program you have used. Each program has so many options, and responds to user selections in so many possible ways, that it would take years for a single programmer to write all the instructions. Professional software developers can write new programs in weeks or months, instead of years, by dividing large programs into modules and assigning each module to an individual programmer or team.

Modularization Allows You to Reuse Your Work

If a module is useful and well written, you may want to use it more than once within a program or in other programs. For example, a routine that verifies the validity of dates is useful in many programs written for a business (e.g., a month value is valid if it is not lower than 1 or higher than 12, a day value is valid if it is not lower than 1 or higher than 31 if the month is 1, and so on). If a computerized personnel file contains each employee's birth date, hire date, last promotion date, and termination date, the date-validation module can be used four times with each employee record. Other programs in an organization can also use the module, including programs that ship customer orders, plan employees' birthday parties, and calculate when loan payments should be made. If you write the date-checking instructions so they are entangled with other statements in a program, they are difficult to extract and reuse. On the other hand, if you place the instructions in their own module, the unit is easy to use and portable to other applications. The feature of modular programs that allows individual modules to be used in a variety of applications is known as **reusability**.

You can find many real-world examples of reusability. When you build a house, you don't invent plumbing and heating systems; you incorporate systems with proven designs. This certainly reduces the time and effort it takes to build a house. The plumbing and electrical systems you choose are in service in other houses, so they also improve the reliability of your house's systems—they have been tested under a variety of circumstances and have been proven to function correctly. **Reliability** is the feature of programs that assures you a module has been tested and proven to function correctly. Reliable software saves time and money. If you create the functional components of your programs as stand-alone modules and test them in your current programs, much of the work will already be done when you use the modules in future applications.

TWO TRUTHS & A LIE

Understanding the Advantages of Modularization

1. Modularization eliminates abstraction, a feature that makes programs more confusing.

2. Modularization makes it easier for multiple programmers to work on a problem.

3. Modularization allows you to reuse your work more easily.

The false statement is #1. Modularization enables abstraction, which allows you to see the big picture.

Modularizing a Program

Most programs consist of a **main program**, which contains the basic steps, or the **mainline logic**, of the program. The main program then accesses modules that provide more refined details.

When you create a module, you include the following:

- A header—A **module's header** includes the module identifier and possibly other necessary identifying information.

- A body—A **module's body** contains all the statements in the module.

- A return statement—A **module's return statement** marks the end of the module and identifies the point at which control returns to the program or module that called the module.

Naming a module is similar to naming a variable. The rules for naming modules are slightly different in every programming language, but in this text, module names follow the same two rules used for variable identifiers:

- Module names must be one word.

- Module names should have some meaning.

In most programming languages, if you do not include a return statement at the end of a module, the logic will still return. This book follows the convention of explicitly including a return statement with every module.

As you learn more about modules in specific programming languages, you will find that you sometimes place variable names within the parentheses of module names. Any variables enclosed in the parentheses contain information you want to send to the module. For now, the parentheses we use at the end of module names will be empty.

A module can call another module, and the called module can call another. The number of chained calls is limited only by the amount of memory available on your computer.

When you call a module, the action is similar to putting a DVD player on pause. You abandon your primary action (watching a video), take care of some other task (for example, making a sandwich), and then return to the main task exactly where you left off.

Although it is not a requirement of any programming language, it frequently makes sense to use a verb as all or part of a module's name, because modules perform some action. Typical module names begin with action words such as `get`, `calculate`, and `display`. When you program in visual languages that use screen components such as buttons and text boxes, the module names frequently contain verbs representing user actions, such as `click` or `drag`.

Additionally, in this text, module names are followed by a set of parentheses. This will help you distinguish module names from variable names. This style corresponds to the way modules are named in many programming languages, such as Java, C++, and C#.

When a main program wants to use a module, it "calls" the module's name. The flowchart symbol used to call a module is a rectangle with a bar across the top. You place the name of the module you are calling inside the rectangle.

Some programmers use a rectangle with stripes down each side to represent a module in a flowchart, and this book uses that convention if a module is external to a program. For example, prewritten, built-in modules that generate random numbers, compute standard trigonometric functions, and sort values are often external to your programs. However, if the module is one being created as part of the program, the book uses a rectangle with a single stripe across the top.

In a flowchart, you draw each module separately with its own sentinel symbols. The symbol that is the equivalent of the `start` symbol in a program contains the name of the module. This name must be identical to the name used in the calling program. The symbol that is the equivalent of the `stop` symbol in a program does not contain `stop`; after all, the program is not ending. Instead, the module ends with a "gentler," less final term, such as `exit` or `return`. These words correctly indicate that when the module ends, the logical progression of statements will exit the module and return to the calling program. Similarly, in pseudocode, you start each module with its name, and end with a `return` or `exit` statement; the module name and return statements are vertically aligned and all the module statements are indented between them.

For example, consider the program in Figure 2-3, which does not contain any modules. It accepts a customer's name and balance due as input and produces a bill. At the top of the bill, the company's name and address are displayed on three lines, which are followed by the customer's name and balance due. To display the company name and address, you can simply include three `output` statements in the mainline logic of a program, as shown in Figure 2-3, or you can modularize the program by creating both the mainline logic and a `displayAddressInfo()` module, as shown in Figure 2-4.

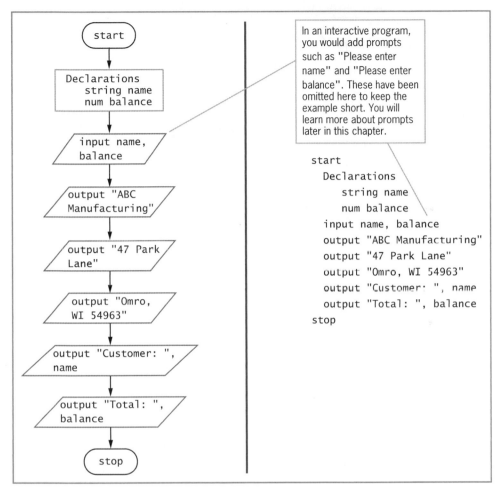

Figure 2-3   Program that produces a bill using only main program

In Figure 2-4, when the `displayAddressInfo()` module is called, logic transfers from the main program to the `displayAddressInfo()` module, as shown by the large red arrow in both the flowchart and the pseudocode. There, each module statement executes in turn before logical control is transferred back to the main program, where it continues with the statement that follows the module call, as shown by the large blue arrow.

Neither of the programs in Figures 2-3 and 2-4 is superior to the other in terms of functionality; both perform exactly the same tasks in the same order. However, you may prefer the modularized version of the program for at least two reasons:

- First, the main program remains short and easy to follow because it contains just one statement to call the module, rather than three separate `output` statements to perform the work of the module.

Programmers say the statements that are contained in a module have been **encapsulated**.

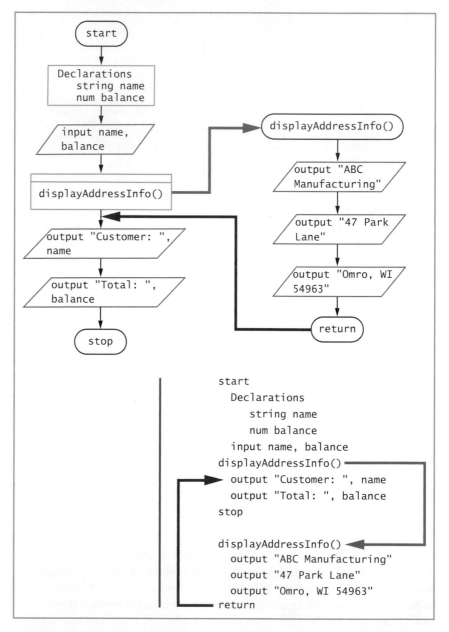

Figure 2-4   Program that produces a bill using main program that calls `displayAddressInfo()` module

- Second, a module is easily reusable. After you create the address information module, you can use it in any application that needs the company's name and address. In other words, you do the work once, and then you can use the module many times.

A potential drawback to creating modules and moving between them is the overhead incurred. The computer keeps track of the correct memory address to which it should return after executing a module by recording the memory address in a location known as the **stack**. This process requires a small amount of computer time and resources. In most cases, the advantage to creating modules far outweighs the small amount of overhead required.

Determining when to break down any particular program into modules does not depend on a fixed set of rules; it requires experience and insight. Programmers do follow some guidelines when deciding how far to break down modules, or how much to put in each of them. Some companies may have arbitrary rules, such as "a module's instructions should never take more than a page," or "a module should never have more than 30 statements," or "never have a module with only one statement." Rather than use such arbitrary rules, a better policy is to place together statements that contribute to one specific task. The more the statements contribute to the same job, the greater the **functional cohesion** of the module. A routine that checks the validity of a date variable's value, or one that asks a user for a value and accepts it as input, is considered cohesive. A routine that checks date validity, deducts insurance premiums, and computes federal withholding tax for an employee would be less cohesive.

Watch the video
*Modularizing
a Program.*

Declaring Variables and Constants within Modules

You can place any statements within modules, including input, processing, and output statements. You can also include variable and constant declarations within modules. For example, you might decide to modify the billing program shown in Figure 2-4 so it looks like the one in Figure 2-5. In this version of the program, three named constants that hold the three lines of company data are declared within the displayAddressInfo() module. (See shading.)

The variables and constants declared in a module are usable only within the module. Programmers say the data items are **visible** only within the module in which they are declared. That means the program only recognizes them there. Programmers say that variables and constants declared within a module are **in scope** only within that module. Programmers also say that variables and constants are **local** to the module in which they are declared. In other words, when the strings LINE1, LINE2, and LINE3 are declared in the displayAddressInfo() module in Figure 2-5, they are not recognized and cannot be used by the main program.

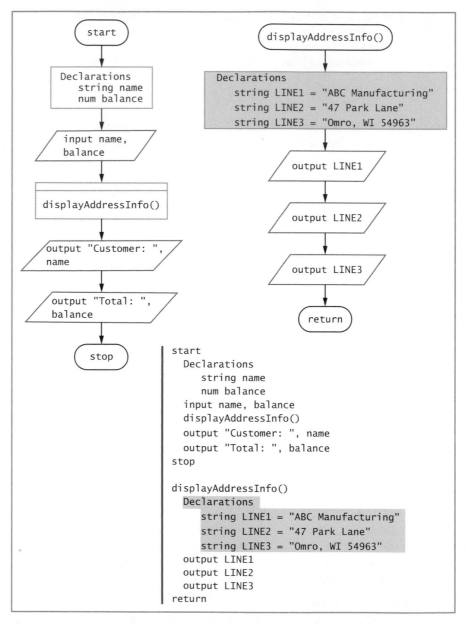

Figure 2-5   The billing program with constants declared within the module

One of the motivations for creating modules is that separate modules are easily reusable in multiple programs. If the displayAddressInfo() module will be used by several programs within the organization, it makes sense that the definitions for its variables and constants must come with it. This makes the modules more **portable**; that is, they are self-contained units that are easily transported.

Besides local variables and constants, you can create global variables and constants. **Global** variables and constants are known to the entire program; they are said to be declared at the **program level**. That means they are visible to and usable in all the modules called by the program. The opposite is not true—variables and constants declared within a module are not usable elsewhere; they are visible only to that module. In this book, variables and constants declared in the main program will be global. (For example, in Figure 2-5, the main program variables `name` and `balance` are global variables, although in this case they are not used in any modules.) For the most part, this book will use only global variables and constants so that the examples are easier to follow and you can concentrate on the main logic.

Many programmers do not approve of using global variables and constants. They are used here so you can more easily understand modularization without yet learning the techniques of sending local variables from one module to another. Chapter 9 of the comprehensive version of this book will describe how you can make every variable local.

61

TWO TRUTHS & A LIE

Modularizing a Program

1. Most programs contain a main program, which contains the mainline logic; this program then accesses other modules or subroutines.

2. A calling program calls a module's name when it wants to use the module.

3. Whenever a main program calls a module, the logic transfers to the module; when the module ends, the program ends.

The false statement is #3. When a module ends, the logical flow transfers back to the main calling program and resumes where it left off.

Understanding the Most Common Configuration for Mainline Logic

In Chapter 1, you learned that a procedural program contains procedures that follow one another in sequence. The mainline logic of almost every procedural computer program can follow a general structure that consists of four distinct parts:

1. Declarations include data types, identifiers, and (sometimes) initial values for global variables and constants.

2. **Housekeeping tasks** include any steps you must perform at the beginning of a program to get ready for the rest of the program. They can include tasks such as displaying instructions

Inputting the first data item is always part of the housekeeping module. You will learn the theory behind this practice in Chapter 3.

Chapter 7 covers file handling, including what it means to open and close a file.

You learned that repetitions are called loops in Chapter 1.

In Chapter 1, you learned that when input data comes from a file, the end-of-file sentinel value is commonly called eof.

to users, displaying report headings, opening any files the program requires, and inputting the first piece of data.

3. **Detail loop tasks** do the core work of the program. When a program processes many records, detail loop tasks execute repeatedly for each set of input data until there are no more. For example, in a payroll program, the same set of calculations is executed repeatedly until a check has been produced for each employee.

4. **End-of-job tasks** are the steps you take at the end of the program to finish the application. You can call these finish-up or clean-up tasks. They might include displaying totals or other final messages and closing any open files.

Figure 2-6 shows the relationship of these three typical program parts. Notice how the housekeeping() and endOfJob() tasks are executed just once, but the detailLoop() tasks repeat as long as the eof condition has not been met. The flowchart uses an arrow to show how the detailLoop() module repeats; the pseudocode uses the words while and endwhile to contain statements that execute in a loop. You will learn more about the while and endwhile terms in subsequent chapters; for now, understand that they are a way of expressing repeated actions.

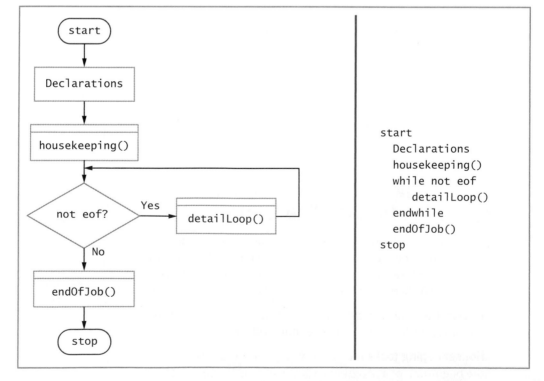

Figure 2-6 Flowchart and pseudocode of mainline logic for a typical procedural program

Many everyday tasks follow the three-module format just described. For example, a candy factory opens in the morning, and the machines are started and filled with ingredients. These housekeeping tasks occur just once at the start of the day. Then, repeatedly during the day, candy is manufactured. This process might take many steps, each of which occurs many times. These are the steps in the detail loop. Then, at the end of the day, the machines are cleaned and shut down. These are the end-of-job tasks.

The module names used in Figure 2-6 can be any legal identifiers you choose. The point is that almost all programs have start-up and finishing tasks that surround the major repetitive program work.

Not all programs take the format of the logic shown in Figure 2-6, but many do. Keep this general "shape" in mind as you think about how you might organize many programs. For example, Figure 2-7 shows a sample payroll report for a small company. A user enters employee names until there are no more to enter, at which point the user enters "XXX". As long as the entered name is not "XXX", the user enters the employee's weekly gross pay. Deductions are computed as a flat 25 percent of the gross pay, and the statistics for each employee are output. The user enters another name, and as long as it is not "XXX", the process continues. Examine the logic in Figure 2-8 to identify the components in the housekeeping, detail loop, and end-of-job tasks. You will learn more about the payroll report program in the next few chapters. For now, concentrate on the big picture of how a typical application works.

Payroll Report

Name	Gross	Deductions	Net
Andrews	1000.00	250.00	750.00
Brown	1400.00	350.00	1050.00
Carter	1275.00	318.75	956.25
Young	1100.00	275.00	825.00
***End of report			

Figure 2-7   Sample payroll report

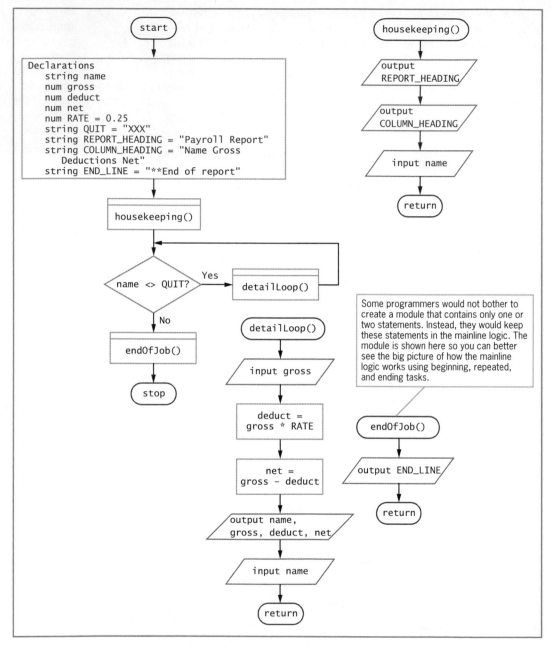

Some programmers would not bother to create a module that contains only one or two statements. Instead, they would keep these statements in the mainline logic. The module is shown here so you can better see the big picture of how the mainline logic works using beginning, repeated, and ending tasks.

Figure 2-8   Logic for payroll report

```
start
   Declarations
      string name
      num gross
      num deduct
      num net
      num RATE = 0.25
      string QUIT = "XXX"
      string REPORT_HEADING = "Payroll Report"
      string COLUMN_HEADING = "Name   Gross   Deductions   Net"
      string END_LINE = "**End of report"
   housekeeping()
   while not name = QUIT
      detailLoop()
   endwhile
   endOfJob()
stop

housekeeping()
   output REPORT_HEADING
   output COLUMN_HEADING
   input name
return

detailLoop()
   input gross
   deduct = gross * RATE
   net = gross - deduct
   output name, gross, deduct, net
   input name
return

endOfJob()
   output END_LINE
return
```

Figure 2-8   Logic for payroll report (continued)

TWO TRUTHS & A LIE

Understanding the Most Common Configuration for Mainline Logic

1. Housekeeping tasks include any steps you must perform at the beginning of a program to get ready for the rest of the program.

2. The detail loop of a program contains the housekeeping and finishing tasks.

3. The end-of-job tasks are the steps you take at the end of the program to finish the application.

The false statement is #2. The detail loop executes repeatedly, once for every record. The loop executes after housekeeping tasks are completed and before end-of-job tasks are executed.

Creating Hierarchy Charts

You may have seen hierarchy charts for organizations, such as the one in Figure 2-9. The chart shows who reports to whom, not when or how often they report.

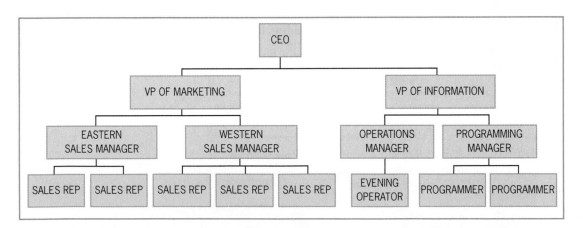

Figure 2-9   An organizational hierarchy chart

When a program has several modules calling other modules, programmers often use a program **hierarchy chart** that operates in a similar manner to show the overall picture of how modules are related to one another. A hierarchy chart does not tell you what tasks are to be performed *within* a module, *when* the modules are called, *how* a module executes, or *why* they are called—that information is in the flowchart or pseudocode. A hierarchy chart tells you only *which* modules exist within a program and *which* modules call others. The hierarchy chart for the program in Figure 2-8 looks like Figure 2-10. It shows that the main module calls three others—housekeeping(), detailLoop(), and endOfJob().

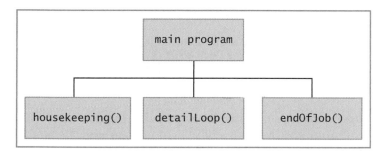

Figure 2-10 Hierarchy chart of payroll report program in Figure 2-8

Figure 2-11 shows an example of a hierarchy chart for the billing program of a mail-order company. The hierarchy chart is for a more complicated program, but like the payroll report chart in Figure 2-10, it supplies module names and a general overview of the tasks to be performed, without specifying any details.

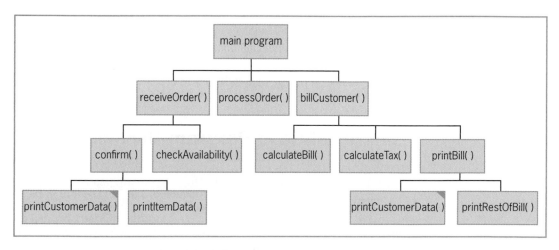

Figure 2-11 Billing program hierarchy chart

Because program modules are reusable, a specific module may be called from several locations within a program. For example, in the billing program hierarchy chart in Figure 2-11, you can see that the printCustomerData() module is used twice. By convention, you

Hierarchy charts are used in procedural programming, but other types of diagrams frequently are used in object-oriented environments. Chapter 13 of the comprehensive edition of this book describes the Unified Modeling Language, which is a set of diagrams you use to describe a system.

blacken a corner of each box that represents a module used more than once. This action alerts readers that any change to this module will affect more than one location.

A hierarchy chart can be both a planning tool for developing the overall relationship of program modules before you write them and a documentation tool to help others see how modules are related after a program is written. For example, if a tax law changes, a programmer might be asked to rewrite the calculateTax() module in the billing program diagrammed in Figure 2-11. As the programmer changes the calculateTax() module, the hierarchy chart shows other dependent routines that might be affected. If a change is made to printCustomerData(), the programmer is alerted that changes will occur in multiple locations. A hierarchy chart is useful for "getting the big picture" in a complex program.

TWO TRUTHS & A LIE

Creating Hierarchy Charts

1. You can use a hierarchy chart to illustrate modules' relationships.

2. A hierarchy chart tells you what tasks are to be performed within a module.

3. A hierarchy chart tells you only which modules call other modules.

The false statement is #2. A hierarchy chart tells you nothing about tasks performed within a module; it only depicts how modules are related to each other.

Features of Good Program Design

As your programs become larger and more complicated, the need for good planning and design increases. Think of an application you use, such as a word processor or a spreadsheet. The number and variety of user options are staggering. Not only would it be impossible for a single programmer to write such an application, but without thorough planning and design, the components would never work together properly. Ideally, each program module you design needs to work well as a stand-alone module and as an element of larger systems. Just as a house with poor plumbing or a car with bad brakes is fatally flawed, a computer-based application can be highly functional only if each component is designed well. Walking through your program's logic on paper (called desk-checking, as you learned in Chapter 1) is an important step to achieving superior programs. Additionally, you can implement several design features while creating programs that can make the programs easier to write and maintain:

- You should use program comments where appropriate.

- Your identifiers should be well-chosen.

- You should strive to design clear statements within your programs and modules.

- You should write clear prompts and echo input.

- You should continue to maintain good programming habits as you develop your programming skills.

Using Program Comments

When you write programs, you might often want to insert program comments. **Program comments** are written explanations that are not part of the program logic but that serve as documentation for readers of the program. In other words, they are nonexecuting statements that help readers understand programming statements. The syntax used to create program comments differs among programming languages. This book starts comments in pseudocode with two front slashes. For example, Figure 2-12 contains comments that explain the origins and purposes of some variables in a real estate program.

 Program comments are a type of **internal documentation.** This term distinguishes them from supporting documents outside the program, which are called **external documentation.** Appendix D discusses other types of documentation.

```
Declarations
    num sqFeet
        // sqFeet is an estimate provided by the seller of the property
    num pricePerFoot
        // pricePerFoot is determined by current market conditions
    num lotPremium
        // lotPremium depends on amenities such as whether lot is waterfront
```

Figure 2-12 Pseudocode that declares some variables and includes comments

In a flowchart, you can use an annotation symbol to hold information that expands on what is stored within another flowchart symbol. An **annotation symbol** is most often represented by a three-sided box that is connected to the step it references by a dashed line. Annotation symbols are used to hold comments, or sometimes statements that are too long to fit neatly into a flowchart symbol. For example, Figure 2-13 shows how a programmer might use some annotation symbols in a flowchart for a payroll program.

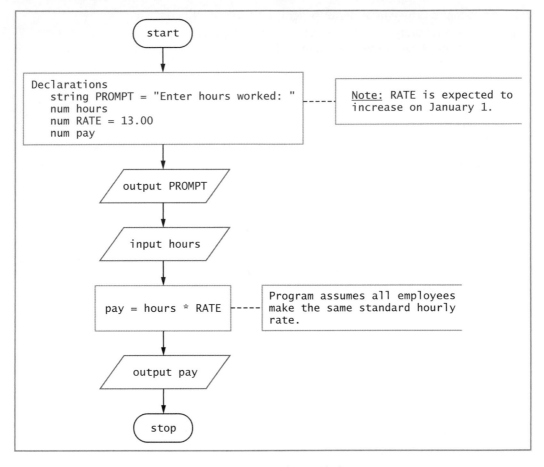

Figure 2-13   Flowchart that includes some annotation symbols

You probably will use program comments in your coded programs more frequently than you use them in pseudocode or flowcharts. For one thing, flowcharts and pseudocode are more English-like than the code in some languages, so your statements might be less cryptic. Also, your comments will remain in the program as part of the program documentation, but your planning tools are likely to be discarded once the program goes into production.

A drawback to comments is that they must be kept current as a program is modified. Outdated comments can provide misleading information about a program's status.

Including program comments is not necessary to create a working program, but comments can help you to remember the purpose of variables or to explain complicated calculations. Some students do not like to include comments in their programs because it takes time to type them and they aren't part of the "real" program, but the programs you write in the future probably will require some comments. When you acquire your first programming job and modify a program written by another programmer, you will appreciate well-placed comments that explain complicated sections of the code.

Choosing Identifiers

The selection of good identifiers is an often-overlooked element in program design. When you write programs, you choose identifiers for variables, constants, and modules. Choosing good names for these components makes your programming job easier and makes it easier for others to understand your work.

Some general guidelines include the following:

- Although it is not required in any programming language, it usually makes sense to give a variable or a constant a name that is a noun (or a combination of an adjective and a noun) because it represents a thing. Similarly, it makes sense to give a module an identifier that is a verb, or a combined verb and noun, because a module takes action.

- Use meaningful names. Creating a data item named `someData` or a module named `firstModule()` makes a program cryptic. Not only will others find it hard to read your programs, but you will forget the purpose of these identifiers even within your own programs. All programmers occasionally use short, nondescriptive names such as `x` or `temp` in a quick program; however, in most cases, data and module names should be meaningful. Programmers refer to programs that contain meaningful names as **self-documenting**. This means that even without further documentation, the program code explains itself to readers.

Don't forget that not all programmers share your culture. An abbreviation whose meaning seems obvious to you might be cryptic to someone in a different part of the world.

- Usually, you should use pronounceable names. A variable name like `pzf` is neither pronounceable nor meaningful. A name that looks meaningful when you write it might not be as meaningful when someone else reads it; for instance, `preparead()` might mean "Prepare ad" to you, but "Prep a read" to others. Look at your names critically to make sure they are pronounceable. Very standard abbreviations do not have to be pronounceable. For example, most businesspeople would interpret `ssn` as Social Security number.

- Be judicious in your use of abbreviations. You can save a few keystrokes when creating a module called `getStat()`, but is its purpose to find the state in which a city is located, input some statistics, or determine the status of some variables? Similarly, is a variable named `fn` meant to hold a first name, file number, or something else?

To save typing time when you develop a program, you can use a short name like `efn`. After the program operates correctly, you can use a text editor's Search and Replace feature to replace your coded name with a more meaningful name such as `employeeFirstName`.

Many IDEs support an automatic statement-completion feature that saves typing time. After the first time you use a name like `employeeFirstName`, you need to type only the first few letters before the compiler editor offers a list of available names from which to choose. The list is constructed from all the names you have used that begin with the same characters.

72

- Usually, avoid digits in a name. Zeroes get confused with the letter "O", and lowercase "l"s are misread as the numeral 1. Of course, use your judgment: budgetFor2012 probably will not be misinterpreted.

- Use the system your language allows to separate words in long, multiword variable names. For example, if the programming language you use allows dashes or underscores, then use a module name like initialize-data() or initialize_data(), which is easier to read than initializedata(). Another option is to use camel casing to create an identifier such as initializeData(). If you use a language that is case sensitive, it is legal but confusing to use variable names that differ only in case. For example, if a single program contains empName, EmpName, and Empname, confusion is sure to follow.

Many languages support a Boolean data type, which you assign to variables meant to hold only true or false. Using a form of "to be" in identifiers for Boolean variables is appropriate.

- Consider including a form of the verb *to be*, such as *is* or *are*, in names for variables that are intended to hold a status. For example, use isFinished as a variable that holds a "Y" or "N" to indicate whether a file is exhausted. The shorter name finished is more likely to be confused with a module that executes when a program is done.

- Many programmers follow the convention of naming constants using all uppercase letters, inserting underscores between words for readability. In this chapter you saw examples such as LINE1.

Programmers sometimes create a **data dictionary**, which is a list of every variable name used in a program, along with its type, size, and description. When a data dictionary is created, it becomes part of the program documentation.

- Organizations sometimes enforce different rules for programmers to follow when naming variables. It is your responsibility to find out the conventions used in your organization and to adhere to them. As an example, some organizations use a variable-naming convention called **Hungarian notation**, in which a variable's data type or other information is stored as part of the name. For example, a numeric field might always start with the prefix num, as in numAge or numSalary.

When you begin to write programs, the process of determining what data variables, constants, and modules you need and what to name them all might seem overwhelming. The design process is crucial, however. When you acquire your first professional programming assignment, the design process might very well be completed already. Most likely, your first assignment will be to write or modify one small member module of a much larger application. The more the original programmers stuck to these guidelines, the better the original design was, and the easier your job of modification will be.

Designing Clear Statements

In addition to adding program comments and selecting good identifiers, you can use the following tactics to contribute to the clarity of the statements within your programs:

- Avoid confusing line breaks.

- Use temporary variables to clarify long statements.

Avoiding Confusing Line Breaks

Some older programming languages require that program statements be placed in specific columns. Most modern programming languages are free-form; you can arrange your lines of code any way you see fit. As in real life, with freedom comes responsibility; when you have flexibility in arranging your lines of code, you must take care to make sure your meaning is clear. With free-form code, programmers are allowed to place two or three statements on a line, or, conversely, to spread a single statement across multiple lines. Both make programs harder to read. All the pseudocode examples in this book use appropriate, clear spacing and line breaks.

Using Temporary Variables to Clarify Long Statements

When you need several mathematical operations to determine a result, consider using a series of temporary variables to hold intermediate results. A **temporary variable** (or a **work variable**) is not used for input or output, but instead is just a working variable that you use during a program's execution. For example, Figure 2-14 shows two ways to calculate a value for a real estate `salespersonCommission` variable. Each module achieves the same result—the salesperson's commission is based on the square feet multiplied by the price per square foot, plus any premium for a lot with special features, such as a wooded or waterfront lot. However, the second example uses two temporary variables: `basePropertyPrice` and `totalSalePrice`. When the computation is broken down into less complicated, individual steps, it is easier to see how the total price is calculated. In calculations with even more computation steps, performing the arithmetic in stages would become increasingly helpful.

 Programmers might say using temporary variables, like the second example in Figure 2-14, is *cheap*. When executing a lengthy arithmetic statement, even if you don't explicitly name temporary variables, the programming language compiler creates them behind the scenes (although without descriptive names), so declaring them yourself does not cost much in terms of program execution time.

```
// Using a single statement to compute commission
salespersonCommission = (sqFeet * pricePerFoot + lotPremium) * commissionRate

// Using multiple statements to compute commission
basePropertyPrice = sqFeet * pricePerFoot
totalSalePrice = basePropertyPrice + lotPremium
salespersonCommission = totalSalePrice * commissionRate
```

Figure 2-14 Two ways of achieving the same `salespersonCommission` result

Writing Clear Prompts and Echoing Input

When program input should be retrieved from a user, you almost always want to provide a prompt for the user. A **prompt** is a message that is displayed on a monitor to ask the user for a response and perhaps explain how that response should be formatted. Prompts are used both in command-line and GUI interactive programs.

For example, suppose a program asks a user to enter a catalog number for an item the user is ordering. The following prompt is not very helpful:

```
Please enter a number.
```

The following prompt is more helpful:

```
Please enter a five-digit catalog order number.
```

The following prompt is even more helpful:

```
The five-digit catalog order number appears to the right of
the item's picture in the catalog. Please enter it now.
```

When program input comes from a stored file instead of a user, prompts are not needed. However, when a program expects a user response, prompts are valuable. For example, Figure 2-15 shows the flowchart and pseudocode for the beginning of the bill-producing program shown earlier in this chapter. If the input was coming from a data file, no prompt would be required, and the logic might look like the logic in Figure 2-15.

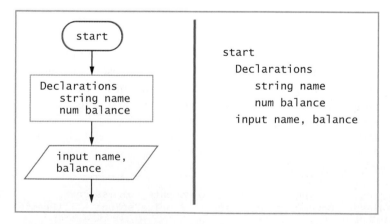

Figure 2-15 Beginning of a program that accepts a name and balance as input

However, if the input was coming from a user, including prompts would be helpful. You could supply a single prompt such as "Please enter a customer's name and balance due", but inserting more requests into a prompt generally makes it less likely that the user can remember to enter all the parts or enter them in the correct order. It is almost always best to include a separate prompt for each item to be entered. Figure 2-16 shows an example.

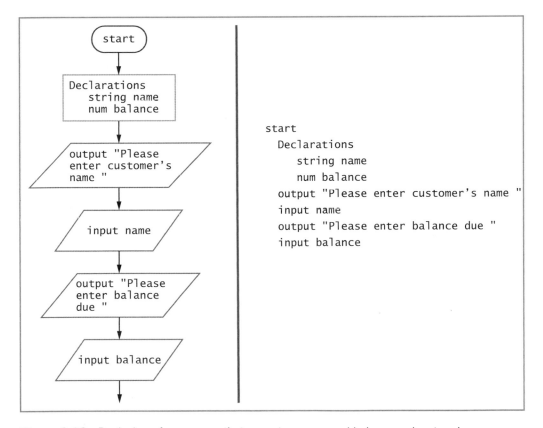

Figure 2-16 Beginning of a program that accepts a name and balance as input and uses a separate prompt for each item

Users also find it helpful when you echo their input. **Echoing input** is the act of repeating input back to a user either in a subsequent prompt or in output. For example, Figure 2-17 shows how the second prompt in Figure 2-16 can be improved by echoing the user's first piece of input data in the second prompt. When a user runs the program that is started in Figure 2-17 and enters "Green" for the customer name, the second prompt will not be "Please enter balance due". Instead, it will be "Please enter balance due for Green". For example, if a clerk was about to enter the balance for the wrong customer, the mention of "Green" might be enough to alert the clerk to the potential error.

 Notice the space before the ending quote in the prompt "Please enter balance due for ". The space will appear between "for" and the last name.

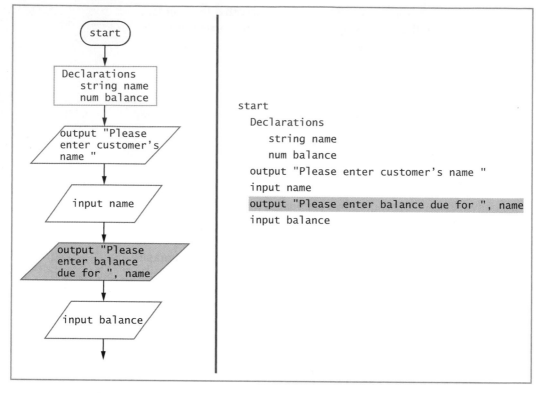

Figure 2-17   Beginning of a program that accepts a customer's name and uses it in the second prompt

Maintaining Good Programming Habits

When you learn a programming language and begin to write lines of program code, it is easy to forget the principles you have learned in this text. Having some programming knowledge and a keyboard at your fingertips can lure you into typing lines of code before you think things through. But every program you write will be better if you plan before you code. If you maintain the habit of first drawing flowcharts or writing pseudocode, as you have learned here, your future programming projects will go more smoothly. If you desk-check your program logic on paper before starting to type statements in a programming language, your programs will run correctly sooner. If you think carefully about the variable and module names you use, and design your program statements to be easy to read and use, your programs will be easier to develop and maintain.

TWO TRUTHS & A LIE

Features of Good Program Design

1. A program comment is a message that is displayed on a monitor to ask the user for a response and perhaps explain how that response should be formatted.

2. It usually makes sense to give each variable a name that contains a noun and to give each module a name that contains a verb.

3. Echoing input can help a user to confirm that a data item was entered correctly.

The false statement is #1. A program comment is a written explanation that is not part of the program logic but that serves as documentation for those reading the program. A prompt is a message that is displayed on a monitor to ask the user for a response and perhaps explain how that response should be formatted.

Chapter Summary

- Variables are named memory locations, the contents of which can vary. Before you can use a variable in any program, you must include a declaration for it. A declaration includes a data type and an identifier. Every computer programming language has its own set of rules for naming variables; however, all variable names must be written as one word without embedded spaces, and should have appropriate meaning. Data types include numeric and string. A named constant is similar to a variable, except it can be assigned a value only once.

- The equal sign is the assignment operator; it is used in an assignment statement. The assignment operator has right-associativity or right-to-left associativity. Most programming languages use +, −, *, and / as the four standard arithmetic operators. Every operator follows rules of precedence that dictate the order in which operations in the same statement are carried out; multiplication and division always take precedence over addition and subtraction. The rules of precedence can be overridden using parentheses.

- Programmers break down programming problems into reasonable units called modules, subroutines, procedures, functions, or methods. To execute a module, you call it from another program or module. Any program can contain an unlimited number of modules, and each module can be called an unlimited number of times. Modularization provides abstraction, allows multiple programmers to work on a problem, and makes it easier for you to reuse your work.

- When you create a module, you include a header, a body, and a return statement. When a main program wants to use a module, it "calls" the module's name. The flowchart symbol used to call a module is a rectangle with a bar across the top. In a flowchart, you draw each module separately with its own sentinel symbols. You can place any statements within modules, including input, processing, and output statements, and variable and constant declarations. The variables and constants declared in a module are usable only within the module; they are local to the module. Global variables and constants are those that are known to the entire program.

- The mainline logic of almost every procedural computer program can follow a general structure that consists of four distinct parts: declarations, housekeeping tasks, detail loop tasks, and end-of-job tasks.

- You can use a hierarchy chart to illustrate modules' relationships. A hierarchy chart tells you which modules exist within a program and which modules call others.

- As your programs become larger and more complicated, the need for good planning and design increases. You should use program comments where appropriate. Choose identifiers wisely, strive to design clear statements within your programs and modules, write clear prompts and echo input, and continue to maintain good programming habits as you develop your programming skills.

Key Terms

A **declaration** is a statement that provides a data type and an identifier for a variable.

An **identifier** is a variable's name.

A data item's **data type** is a classification that describes what values can be assigned, how the variable is stored, and what types of operations can be performed with the variable.

Making declarations or **declaring variables** describes the process of naming variables and assigning a data type to them.

Initializing a variable is the act of assigning its first value, often at the same time the variable is created.

Garbage describes the unknown value stored in an unassigned variable.

Keywords comprise the limited word set that is reserved in a language.

A **mnemonic** is a memory device; variable identifiers act as mnemonics for hard-to-remember memory addresses.

Camel casing is the format for naming variables in which the initial letter is lowercase, multiple-word variable names are run together, and each new word within the variable name begins with an uppercase letter.

Pascal casing is the format for naming variables in which the initial letter is uppercase, multiple-word variable names are run together, and each new word within the variable name begins with an uppercase letter.

A **numeric constant** (or **literal numeric constant**) is a specific numeric value.

A **string constant** (or **literal string constant**) is a specific group of characters enclosed within quotation marks.

An **unnamed constant** is a literal numeric or string value.

Alphanumeric values can contain alphabetic characters, numbers, and punctuation.

A **numeric variable** is one that can hold digits, have mathematical operations performed on it, and usually can hold a decimal point and a sign indicating positive or negative.

An **integer** is a whole number.

A **floating-point** number is a number with decimal places.

Real numbers are floating-point numbers.

A **string variable** can hold text that includes letters, digits, and special characters such as punctuation marks.

A **named constant** is similar to a variable, except that its value cannot change after the first assignment.

A **magic number** is an unnamed constant whose purpose is not immediately apparent.

Overhead describes the extra resources a task requires.

An **assignment statement** assigns a value from the right of an assignment operator to the variable or constant on the left of the assignment operator.

The **assignment operator** is the equal sign; it is used to assign a value to the variable or constant on its left.

A **binary operator** is an operator that requires two operands—one on each side.

Right-associativity and **right-to-left associativity** describe operators that evaluate the expression to the right first.

An **lvalue** is the memory address identifier to the left of an assignment operator.

Rules of precedence dictate the order in which operations in the same statement are carried out.

The **order of operations** describes the rules of precedence.

Left-to-right associativity describes operators that evaluate the expression to the left first.

Modules are small program units that you can use together to make a program. Programmers also refer to modules as **subroutines**, **procedures**, **functions**, or **methods**.

Modularization is the process of breaking down a program into modules.

Functional decomposition is the act of reducing a large program into more manageable modules.

Abstraction is the process of paying attention to important properties while ignoring nonessential details.

Reusability is the feature of modular programs that allows individual modules to be used in a variety of applications.

Reliability is the feature of modular programs that assures you a module has been tested and proven to function correctly.

A **main program** runs from start to stop and calls other modules.

The **mainline logic** is the logic that appears in a program's main module; it calls other modules.

A **module's header** includes the module identifier and possibly other necessary identifying information.

A **module's body** contains all the statements in the module.

A **module's return statement** marks the end of the module and identifies the point at which control returns to the program or module that called the module.

Encapsulation is the act of containing a task's instructions in a module.

A **stack** is a memory location in which the computer keeps track of the correct memory address to which it should return after executing a module.

The **functional cohesion** of a module is a measure of the degree to which all the module statements contribute to the same task.

Visible describes the state of data items when a module can recognize them.

In scope describes the state of data that is visible.

Local describes variables that are declared within the module that uses them.

A **portable** module is one that can more easily be reused in multiple programs.

Global describes variables that are known to an entire program.

Global variables are declared at the **program level**.

Housekeeping tasks include steps you must perform at the beginning of a program to get ready for the rest of the program.

Detail loop tasks of a program include the steps that are repeated for each set of input data.

End-of-job tasks hold the steps you take at the end of the program to finish the application.

A **hierarchy chart** is a diagram that illustrates modules' relationships to each other.

Program comments are written explanations that are not part of the program logic but that serve as documentation for those reading the program.

Internal documentation is documentation within a coded program.

External documentation is documentation that is outside a coded program.

An **annotation symbol** contains information that expands on what appears in another flowchart symbol; it is most often represented by a three-sided box that is connected to the step it references by a dashed line.

Self-documenting programs are those that contain meaningful data and module names that describe the programs' purpose.

Hungarian notation is a variable-naming convention in which a variable's data type or other information is stored as part of its name.

A **data dictionary** is a list of every variable name used in a program, along with its type, size, and description.

A **temporary variable** (or a **work variable**) is a working variable that you use to hold intermediate results during a program's execution.

A **prompt** is a message that is displayed on a monitor to ask the user for a response and perhaps explain how that response should be formatted.

Echoing input is the act of repeating input back to a user either in a subsequent prompt or in output.

Review Questions

1. What does a declaration provide for a variable?

   a. a name

   b. a data type

   c. both of the above

   d. none of the above

2. A variable's data type describes all of the following *except* _____.

   a. what values the variable can hold

   b. how the variable is stored in memory

   c. what operations can be performed with the variable

   d. the scope of the variable

3. The value stored in an uninitialized variable is
   _____.

   a. garbage

   b. null

   c. compost

   d. its identifier

4. The value 3 is a _____.

   a. numeric variable

   b. numeric constant

   c. string variable

   d. string constant

5. The assignment operator _____.

   a. is a binary operator

   b. has left-to-right associativity

   c. is most often represented by a colon

   d. two of the above

6. Which of the following is true about arithmetic precedence?

   a. Multiplication has a higher precedence than division.

   b. Operators with the lowest precedence always have left-to-right associativity.

   c. Division has higher precedence than subtraction.

   d. all of the above

7. Which of the following is a term used as a synonym for "module" in any programming language?

   a. method

   b. procedure

   c. both of these

   d. none of these

8. Which of the following is a reason to use modularization?

   a. Modularization avoids abstraction.

   b. Modularization reduces overhead.

   c. Modularization allows you to more easily reuse your work.

   d. Modularization eliminates the need for syntax.

9. What is the name for the process of paying attention to important properties while ignoring nonessential details?

   a. abstraction

   b. extraction

   c. extinction

   d. modularization

10. Every module has all of the following except _____.

    a. a header

    b. local variables

    c. a body

    d. a return statement

11. Programmers say that one module can _____ another, meaning that the first module causes the second module to execute.

    a. declare

    b. define

    c. enact

    d. call

12. The more that a module's statements contribute to the same job, the greater the _____ of the module.

    a. structure

    b. modularity

    c. functional cohesion

    d. size

13. In most modern programming languages, when a variable or constant is declared in a module, the variable or constant is _____ in that module.

   a. global

   b. invisible

   c. in scope

   d. undefined

14. Which of the following is *not* a typical housekeeping task?

   a. displaying instructions

   b. printing summaries

   c. opening files

   d. displaying report headings

15. Which module in a typical program will execute the most times?

   a. the housekeeping module

   b. the detail loop

   c. the end-of-job module

   d. It is different in every program.

16. A hierarchy chart tells you _____.

   a. what tasks are to be performed within each program module

   b. when a module executes

   c. which routines call which other routines

   d. all of the above

17. What are nonexecuting statements that programmers place within their code to explain program statements in English?

   a. comments

   b. pseudocode

   c. trivia

   d. user documentation

18. Program comments are _____.

    a. required to create a runnable program

    b. a form of external documentation

    c. both of the above

    d. none of the above

19. Which of the following is valid advice for naming variables?

    a. To save typing, make most variable names one or two letters.

    b. To avoid conflict with names that others are using, use unusual or unpronounceable names.

    c. To make names easier to read, separate long words by using underscores or capitalization for each new word.

    d. To maintain your independence, shun the conventions of your organization.

20. A message that asks a user for input is a _____.

    a. comment

    b. prompt

    c. echo

    d. declaration

Exercises

1. Explain why each of the following names does or does not seem like a good variable name to you.

    a. c

    b. cost

    c. costAmount

    d. cost amount

    e. cstofdngbsns

    f. costOfDoingBusinessThisFiscalYear

    g. costYear2012

    h. 2012YearCost

2. If myAge and yourRate are numeric variables, and
   departmentName is a string variable, which of the following
   statements are valid assignments? If a statement is not valid,
   explain why not.

   a. myAge = 23

   b. myAge = yourRate

   c. myAge = departmentName

   d. myAge = "departmentName"

   e. 42 = myAge

   f. yourRate = 3.5

   g. yourRate = myAge

   h. yourRate = departmentName

   i. 6.91 = yourRate

   j. departmentName = Personnel

   k. departmentName = "Personnel"

   l. departmentName = 413

   m. departmentName = "413"

   n. departmentName = myAge

   o. departmentName = yourRate

   p. 413 = departmentName

   q. "413" = departmentName

3. Assume that cost = 10 and price = 12. What is the value of
   each of the following expressions?

   a. price − cost * 2

   b. 15 + price − 3 * 2

   c. (price + cost) * 3

   d. 4 − 3 * 2 + cost

   e. cost * ((price − 8) + 5) + 100

4. Draw a typical hierarchy chart for a paycheck-producing
   program. Try to think of at least 10 separate modules that
   might be included. For example, one module might calculate
   an employee's dental insurance premium.

5. a. Draw the hierarchy chart and then plan the logic for a program for the sales manager of The Couch Potato Furniture Company. The manager needs a program to determine the profit on any item sold. Input includes the wholesale price and retail price for an item. The output is the item's profit, which is the retail price minus the wholesale price. Use three modules. The main program declares global variables and calls housekeeping, detail, and end-of-job modules. The housekeeping module prompts for and accepts a wholesale price. The detail module prompts for and accepts the retail price, computes the profit, and displays the result. The end-of-job module displays the message "Thanks for using this program".

    b. Revise the profit-determining program so that it runs continuously for any number of items. The detail loop executes continuously while the wholesale price is not 0; in addition to calculating the profit, it prompts the user for and gets the next wholesale price. The end-of-job module executes after 0 is entered for the wholesale price.

6. a. Draw the hierarchy chart and then plan the logic for a program that calculates the gown size a student needs for a graduation ceremony. The program uses three modules. The first prompts a user for and accepts the student's height in inches. The second module accepts the student's weight in pounds and converts the student's height to centimeters and weight to grams. Then, it calculates the graduation gown size needed by adding 1/3 of the weight in grams to the value of the height in centimeters. The program's output is the gown size the student should order. There are 2.54 centimeters in an inch and 453.59 grams in a pound. Use named constants wherever you think they are appropriate. The last module displays the message "End of job".

    b. Revise the size-determining program to execute continuously until the user enters 0 for the height in inches.

7. Draw the hierarchy chart and design the logic for a program that contains housekeeping, detail loop, and end-of-job modules, and that calculates the service charge customers owe for writing a bad check. The main program declares any needed global variables and constants and calls the other modules. The housekeeping module displays a prompt for and accepts a customer's last name. While the user does not enter "ZZZZ" for the name, the detail loop accepts the amount of the check in dollars and cents. The service charge is computed as $20 plus 2 percent of the check amount. The detail loop also displays the service charge and then prompts the user for the next customer's name. The end-of-job module, which executes after the user enters the sentinel value for the name, displays a message that indicates the program is complete.

8. Draw the hierarchy chart and design the logic for a program for the owner of Bits and Pieces Manufacturing Company, who needs to calculate an employee's projected salary following a raise. The input is the name of the employee, the employee's current weekly salary, and the percentage increase expressed as a decimal (for example, 0.04 for a 4 percent raise). Design the program so that it runs continuously for any number of employees using three modules. The housekeeping module prompts the user for the percent raise that will be applied to every employee, and prompts for the first employee's name. The detail loop executes continuously until the user enters "XXX" for the employee's name. The detail loop gets the employee's weekly salary, applies the raise, produces the result, and prompts for the next employee name. The end-of-job module, which executes after the user enters the sentinel value for the name, displays a message that indicates the program is complete.

9. Draw the hierarchy chart and design the logic for a program for the manager of the Jeter County softball team who wants to compute batting averages for his players. A batting average is computed as hits divided by at-bats, and is usually expressed to three decimal positions (for example, .235). Design a program that prompts the user for a player jersey number, the number of hits, and the number of at-bats, and then displays all the data, including the calculated batting average. The program accepts players continuously until 0 is entered for the jersey number. Use appropriate modules, including one that displays "End of job" after the sentinel is entered for the jersey number.

Find the Bugs

10. Your student disk contains files named DEBUG02-01.txt, DEBUG02-02.txt, and DEBUG02-03.txt. Each file starts with some comments that describe the problem. Comments are lines that begin with two slashes (//). Following the comments, each file contains pseudocode that has one or more bugs you must find and correct.

 Game Zone

11. For games to hold your interest, they almost always include some random, unpredictable behavior. For example, a game in which you shoot asteroids loses some of its fun if the asteroids follow the same, predictable path each time you play. Therefore, generating random values is a key component in creating most interesting computer games. Many programming languages come with a built-in module you can use to generate random numbers. The syntax varies in each language, but it is usually something like the following:

```
myRandomNumber = random(10)
```

In this statement, myRandomNumber is a numeric variable you have declared and the expression random(10) means "call a method that generates and returns a random number between 1 and 10." By convention, in a flowchart, you would place a statement like this in a processing symbol with two vertical stripes at the edges, as shown below.

```
myRandomNumber =
random(10)
```

Create a flowchart or pseudocode that shows the logic for a program that generates a random number, then asks the user to think of a number between 1 and 10. Then display the randomly generated number so the user can see whether his or her guess was accurate. (In future chapters you will improve this game so that the user can enter a guess and the program can determine whether the user was correct.)

Up for Discussion

12. Many programming style guides are published on the Web. These guides suggest good identifiers, explain standard indentation rules, and identify style issues in specific programming languages. Find style guides for at least two languages (for example, C++, Java, Visual Basic, or C#) and list any differences you notice.

13. In this chapter, you learned the term *mnemonic*, which is a memory device like the sentence "Every good boy does fine." Another popular mnemonic is "May I have a large container of coffee?" What is its meaning? Have you learned other mnemonics as you have studied various subjects? Describe at least five other mnemonics that people use for remembering lists of items.

14. What advantages are there to requiring variables to have a data type?

15. Would you prefer to write a large program by yourself, or work on a team in which each programmer produces one or more modules? Why?

16. Extreme programming is a system for rapidly developing software. One of its tenets is that all production code is written by two programmers sitting at one machine. Is this a good idea? Does working this way as a programmer appeal to you? Why or why not?

CHAPTER 3

Understanding Structure

In this chapter, you will learn about:

◎ The features of unstructured spaghetti code

◎ The three basic structures—sequence, selection, and loop

◎ Using a priming input to structure a program

◎ The need for structure

◎ Recognizing structure

◎ Structuring and modularizing unstructured logic

Understanding Unstructured Spaghetti Code

Professional computer programs usually get far more complicated than the examples you have seen so far in Chapters 1 and 2. Imagine the number of instructions in the computer program that NASA uses to calculate the launch angle of a space shuttle, or in the program the IRS uses to audit your income tax return. Even the program that produces your paycheck at your job contains many, many instructions. Designing the logic for such a program can be a time-consuming task. When you add several thousand instructions to a program, including several hundred decisions, it is easy to create a complicated mess. The popular name for logically snarled program statements is **spaghetti code**, because the logic is as hard to follow as one noodle through a plate of spaghetti. Programs that use spaghetti code logic are **unstructured programs**; that is, they do not follow the rules of structured logic that you will learn in this chapter. **Structured programs** *do* follow those rules.

For example, suppose you start a job as a dog washer, and you receive instructions for how to wash a dog, as shown in Figure 3-1. This kind of flowchart is an example of unstructured spaghetti code. A computer program that is structured similarly might "work"—that is, it might produce correct results—but would be difficult to read and maintain, and its logic would be difficult to follow.

You might be able to follow the logic of the dog-washing procedure in Figure 3-1 for two reasons:

- You probably already know how to wash a dog.

- The flowchart contains a very limited number of steps.

However, imagine that the described process was far more complicated or that you were not familiar with the process. (For example, imagine you must wash 100 dogs concurrently while applying flea and tick medication, giving them haircuts, and researching their genealogy.) Depicting more complicated logic in an unstructured way would be cumbersome. By the end of this chapter, you will understand how to make the unstructured process in Figure 3-1 clearer and less error-prone.

 Software developers say that spaghetti code has a shorter life than structured code. This means that programs developed using spaghetti code exist as production programs in an organization for less time. Such programs are so difficult to alter that when improvements are required, developers often find it easier to abandon the existing program and start from scratch. Obviously, this costs more money.

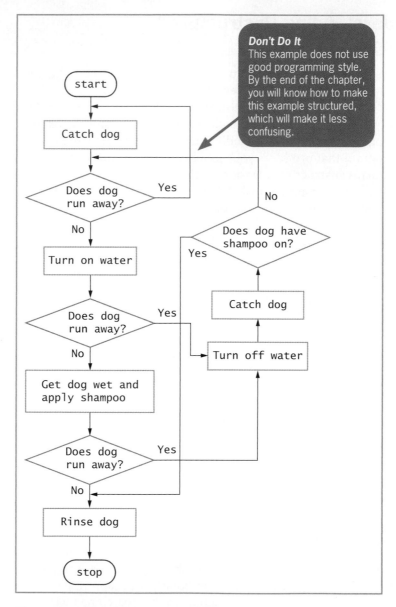

Figure 3-1   Spaghetti code logic for washing a dog

Understanding the Three Basic Structures

In the mid-1960s, mathematicians proved that any program, no matter how complicated, can be constructed using one or more of only three structures. A **structure** is a basic unit of programming logic; each structure is one of the following:

- sequence

- selection

- loop

With these three structures alone, you can diagram any task, from doubling a number to performing brain surgery. You can diagram each structure with a specific configuration of flowchart symbols.

The first of these three basic structures is a sequence, as shown in Figure 3-2. With a **sequence structure**, you perform an action or task, and then you perform the next action, in order. A sequence can contain any number of tasks, but there is no option to branch off and skip any of the tasks. (In other words, a flowchart that describes a sequence structure never contains a decision symbol, and pseudocode that describes a sequence structure never contains an if or a while.) Once you start a series of actions in a sequence, you must continue step by step until the sequence ends.

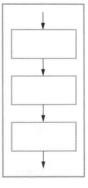

Figure 3-2
Sequence structure

As an example, driving directions often are listed as a sequence. For example, to tell a friend how to get to your house from school, you might provide the following sequence, in which one step follows the other and no steps can be skipped:

```
go north on First Avenue for 3 miles
turn left on Washington Boulevard
go west on Washington for 2 miles
stop at 634 Washington
```

The second of the three structures is a **selection structure** or **decision structure**, as shown in Figure 3-3. With this structure, you ask a question and, depending on the answer, you take one of two courses of action. Then, no matter which path you follow, you continue with the next task. (In other words, a flowchart that describes a selection structure must begin with a decision symbol, and the branches of the

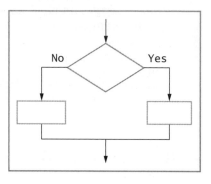

Figure 3-3   Selection structure

decision must join at the bottom of the structure. Pseudocode that describes a selection structure must start with if and end with endif.)

Some people call the selection structure an **if-then-else** because it fits the following statement:

```
if someCondition is true then
    do oneProcess
else
    do theOtherProcess
```

For example, you might provide part of the directions to your house as follows:

```
if traffic is backed up on Washington Boulevard then
    continue for 1 block on First Avenue and turn left on
    Adams Lane
else
    turn left on Washington Boulevard
```

Similarly, a payroll program might include a statement such as:

```
if hoursWorked is more than 40 then
    calculate regularPay and overtimePay
else
    calculate regularPay
```

The previous examples can also be called **dual-alternative ifs** (or **dual-alternative selections**), because they contain two alternatives—the action taken when the tested condition is true and the action taken when it is false. Note that it is perfectly correct for one branch of the selection to be a "do nothing" branch. In each of the following examples, an action is taken only when the tested condition is true:

```
if it is raining then
    take an umbrella
```

```
if employee participates in
the dental plan then
    deduct $40 from employee
    gross pay
```

The previous examples are **single-alternative ifs** (or **single-alternative selections**); a diagram of their structure is shown in Figure 3-4. In these cases, you do not take any special action if it is not raining or if the employee does not belong to the dental plan. The case in which nothing is done is often called the **null case**.

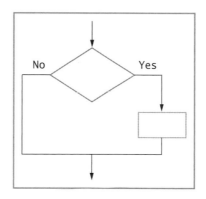

Figure 3-4 Single-alternative selection structure

The third of the three basic structures, shown in Figure 3-5, is a loop. In a **loop structure**, you continue to repeat actions while a condition remains true. The action or actions that occur within the loop are known as the **loop body**. In the most common type of loop, a condition is evaluated; if the answer is true, you

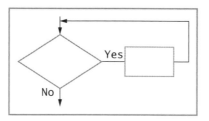

Figure 3-5 Loop structure

execute the loop body and evaluate the condition again. If the condition is still true, you execute the loop body again and then reevaluate the original condition. This continues until the condition becomes false, and then you exit the structure. (In other words, a flowchart that describes a loop structure always begins with a decision symbol that has a branch that returns to a spot prior to the decision. Pseudocode that describes a loop starts with `while` and ends with `endwhile`.) You may hear programmers refer to looping as **repetition** or **iteration**.

 Sometimes you must ask a negative question to execute a loop body. The most common example is to repeat a loop while a sentinel condition has *not* been met.

Some programmers call this structure a **while...do**, or more simply, a **while loop**, because it fits the following statement:

```
while testCondition continues to be true
    do someProcess
```

When you provide directions to your house, part of the directions might be:

```
while the address of the house you are passing remains
below 634
    travel forward to the next house and look at the address
```

You encounter examples of looping every day, as in each of the following:

```
while you continue to be hungry
    take another bite of food and see if you still feel
    hungry
```

```
while unread pages remain in the reading assignment
    read another unread page and see if there are more pages
```

Whether you are drawing a flowchart or writing pseudocode, you can use either of the following pairs to represent decision outcomes: Yes and No or true and false. This book follows the convention of using Yes and No in flowchart diagrams and true and false in pseudocode.

All logic problems can be solved using only these three structures—sequence, selection, and loop. The three structures can be combined in an infinite number of ways. For example, you can have a sequence of tasks followed by a selection, or a loop followed by a sequence. Attaching structures end to end is called **stacking structures**. For example, Figure 3-6 shows a structured flowchart achieved by stacking structures, and shows pseudocode that might follow that flowchart logic.

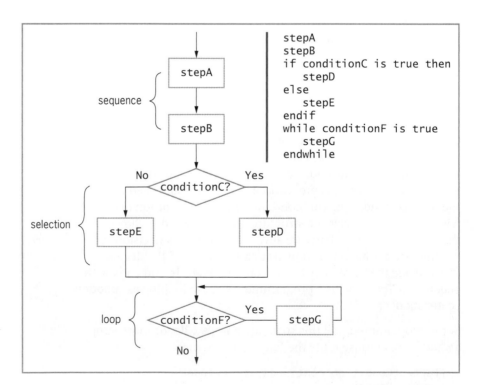

Figure 3-6   Structured flowchart and pseudocode with three stacked structures

The pseudocode in Figure 3-6 shows two **end-structure statements**—endif and endwhile. You can use an endif statement to clearly show where the actions that depend on a decision end. The instruction that follows if occurs when its tested condition is true, the instruction that follows else occurs when the tested condition is false, and any instructions that follow endif occur in either case—instructions after the endif are not dependent on the if statement at all. In other words, statements beyond the endif statement are "outside" the decision structure. Similarly, you use an endwhile statement to show where a loop structure ends. In Figure 3-6, while conditionF continues to be true, stepG continues to execute. If any statements followed the endwhile statement, they would be outside of, and not a part of, the loop. (You first saw the endwhile statement in Chapter 2.)

Besides stacking structures, you can replace any individual tasks or steps in a structured flowchart diagram or pseudocode segment with additional structures. In other words, any sequence, selection, or loop can contain other sequences, selections, or loops. For example, you can have a sequence of three tasks on one side of a selection, as shown in Figure 3-7. Placing a structure within another structure is called **nesting structures**.

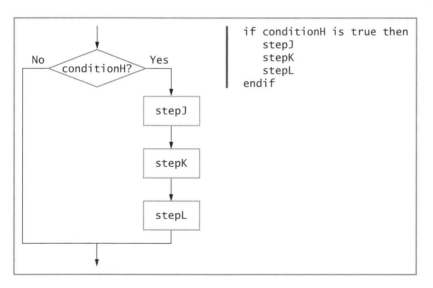

Figure 3-7 Flowchart and pseudocode showing nested structures—a sequence nested within a selection

In the pseudocode for the logic shown in Figure 3-7, the indentation shows that all three statements (stepJ, stepK, and stepL) must execute if conditionH is true. The three statements constitute a **block**, or a group of statements that executes as a single unit.

In place of one of the steps in the sequence in Figure 3-7, you can insert a selection. In Figure 3-8, the process named stepK has been replaced with a loop structure that begins with a test of the condition named conditionM.

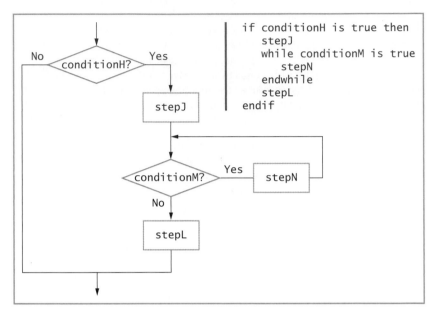

```
if conditionH is true then
    stepJ
    while conditionM is true
        stepN
    endwhile
    stepL
endif
```

Figure 3-8 Flowchart and pseudocode showing nested structures—a loop nested within a sequence, nested within a selection

When you nest structures, the statements that start and end a structure are always on the same level and always in pairs. Structures cannot overlap. For example, if you have an if that contains a while, then the endwhile statement will come before the endif. On the other hand, if you have a while that contains an if, then the endif statement will come before the endwhile.

In the pseudocode shown in Figure 3-8, notice that if and endif are vertically aligned. This shows that they are all "on the same level." Similarly, stepJ, while, endwhile, and stepL are aligned, and they are evenly indented. In the flowchart in Figure 3-8, you could draw a vertical line through the symbols containing stepJ, the entry and exit points of the while loop, and stepL. The flowchart and the pseudocode represent exactly the same logic.

There is no limit to the number of levels you can create when you nest and stack structures. For example, Figure 3-9 shows logic that has been made more complicated by replacing stepN with a selection. The structure that performs stepP or stepQ based on the outcome of conditionO is nested within the loop that is controlled by conditionO. In the pseudocode in Figure 3-9, notice how the if, else, and endif that describe the condition selection are aligned with each other and within the while structure that is controlled by conditionM. As before, the indentation used in the pseudocode reflects the logic laid out graphically in the flowchart.

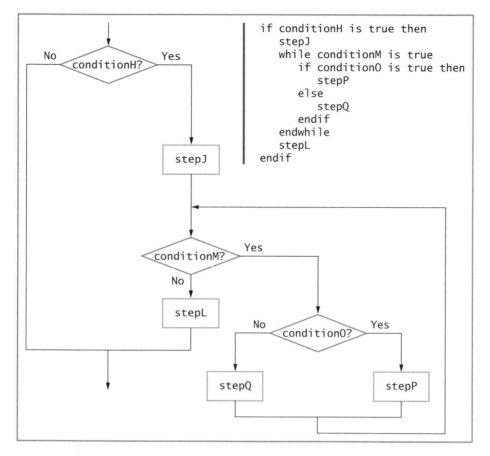

```
if conditionH is true then
    stepJ
    while conditionM is true
        if conditionO is true then
            stepP
        else
            stepQ
        endif
    endwhile
    stepL
endif
```

Figure 3-9 Flowchart and pseudocode for loop within selection within sequence within selection

Many of the preceding examples are generic so that you can focus on the relationships of the shapes without worrying what they do. Keep in mind that generic instructions like stepA and generic conditions like conditionC can stand for anything. For example, Figure 3-10 shows the process of buying and planting flowers outdoors in the spring after the danger of frost is over. The flowchart and pseudocode structures are identical to the ones in Figure 3-9. In the exercises at the end of this chapter, you will be asked to develop more scenarios that fit the same pattern.

The possible combinations of logical structures are endless, but each segment of a structured program is a sequence, a selection, or a loop. The three structures are shown together in Figure 3-11. Notice that each structure has one entry and one exit point. One structure can attach to another only at one of these points.

 Try to imagine physically picking up any of the three structures using the entry and exit "handles." These are the spots at which you could connect a structure to any of the others. Similarly, any complete structure, from its entry point to its exit point, can be inserted within the process symbol of any other structure.

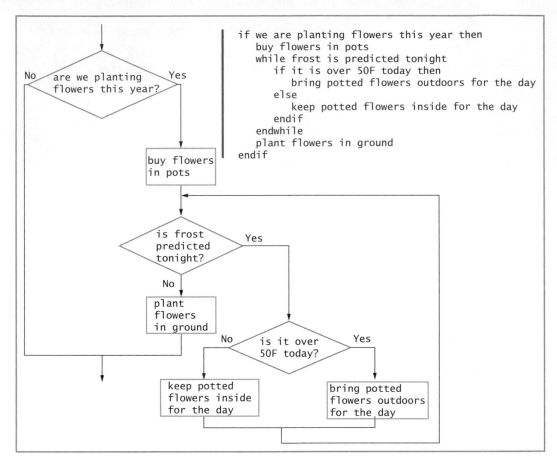

```
if we are planting flowers this year then
      buy flowers in pots
      while frost is predicted tonight
         if it is over 50F today then
            bring potted flowers outdoors for the day
         else
            keep potted flowers inside for the day
         endif
      endwhile
      plant flowers in ground
endif
```

Figure 3-10   The process of buying and planting flowers in the spring

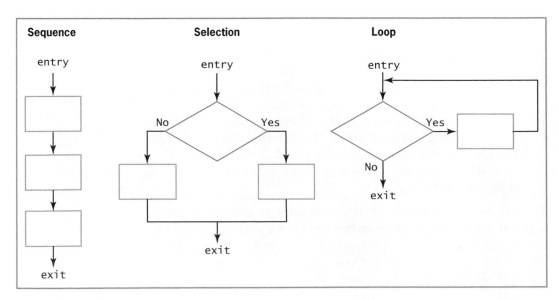

Figure 3-11   The three structures

In summary, a structured program has the following characteristics:

- A structured program includes only combinations of the three basic structures—sequence, selection, and loop. Any structured program might contain one, two, or all three types of structures.

- Each of the structures has a single entry point and a single exit point.

- Structures can be stacked or connected to one another only at their entry or exit points.

- Any structure can be nested within another structure.

Watch the video
Understanding Structure.

103

A structured program is never *required* to contain examples of all three structures. For example, many simple programs contain only a sequence of several tasks that execute from start to finish without any needed selections or loops. As another example, a program might display a series of numbers, looping to do so, but never making any decisions about the numbers.

TWO TRUTHS & A LIE

Understanding the Three Basic Structures

1. Each structure in structured programming is a sequence, selection, or loop.

2. All logic problems can be solved using only these three structures—sequence, selection, and loop.

3. The three structures cannot be combined in a single program.

The false statement is #3. The three structures can be stacked or nested in an infinite number of ways.

Using a Priming Input to Structure a Program

Recall the number-doubling program discussed in Chapter 2; Figure 3-12 shows a similar program. The program inputs a number and checks for the end-of-file condition. If it is not the end of file, then the number is doubled, the answer is displayed, and the next number is input.

Is the program represented by Figure 3-12 structured? At first, it might be hard to tell. The three allowed structures were illustrated in Figure 3-11, and the flowchart in Figure 3-12 does not look exactly like any of those three shapes.

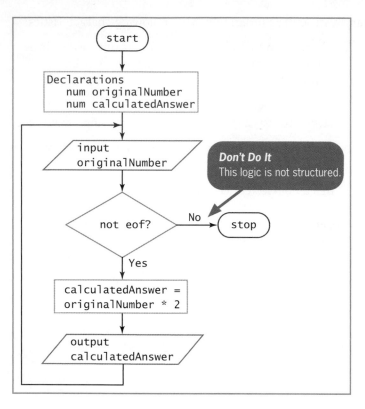

Figure 3-12   Unstructured flowchart of a number-doubling program

Recall from Chapter 1 that this book uses **eof** to represent a generic end-of-data condition when the exact tested parameters are not important to the discussion. In this example, the test is for **not eof**, because processing will continue while it is true that the end of the data has not been reached.

However, because you may stack and nest structures while retaining overall structure, it might be difficult to determine whether a flowchart as a whole is structured. It is easiest to analyze the flowchart in Figure 3-12 one step at a time. The beginning of the flowchart looks like Figure 3-13. Is this portion of the flowchart structured? Yes, it is a sequence of two events.

Adding the next piece of the flowchart looks like Figure 3-14. The sequence is finished; either a selection or a loop is starting. You might not know which one, but you do know the sequence is not continuing, because sequences cannot contain questions. With a

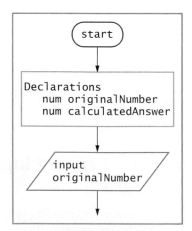

Figure 3-13   Beginning of a number-doubling flowchart

sequence, each task or step must follow without any opportunity to branch off. So, which type of structure starts with the question in Figure 3-14? Is it a selection or a loop?

Selection and loop structures differ as follows:

- In a selection structure, the logic goes in one of two directions after the question, and then the flow comes back together; the question is not asked a second time within the structure.

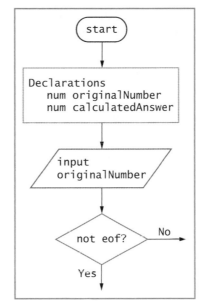

Figure 3-14   Number-doubling flowchart continued

- In a loop, if the answer to the question results in the loop being entered and the loop statements executing, then the logic returns to the question that started the loop. When the body of a loop executes, the question that controls the loop is always asked again.

If the number-doubling problem in the original Figure 3-12 is not eof (that is, if the end-of-file condition is not met), then some math is performed, an answer is output, a new number is obtained, and the logic returns to the eof question. In other words, while the answer to the eof question continues to be *No*, a body of statements continues to execute. Therefore, the eof question starts a structure that is more like a loop than a selection.

The number-doubling problem *does* contain a loop, but it is not a structured loop. In a structured loop, the rules are:

1. You ask a question.

2. If the answer indicates you should execute the loop body, then you do so.

3. If you execute the loop body, then you must go right back to repeat the question.

The flowchart in Figure 3-12 asks a question. If the answer is *No* (that is, while it is true that the eof condition has not been met), then the program performs two tasks in the loop body: it does the arithmetic and it displays the results. Doing two things is acceptable because two tasks with no possible branching constitute a sequence, and it is fine to nest a structure within another structure. However, when the sequence ends, the logic does not flow right back to the loop-controlling question. Instead, it goes *above* the question to get another number. For the loop in Figure 3-12 to be a structured loop, the logic must return to the eof question when the embedded sequence ends.

The flowchart in Figure 3-15 shows the flow of logic returning to the eof question immediately after the sequence. Figure 3-15 shows a structured flowchart, but the flowchart has one major flaw—it does not do the job of continuously doubling different numbers.

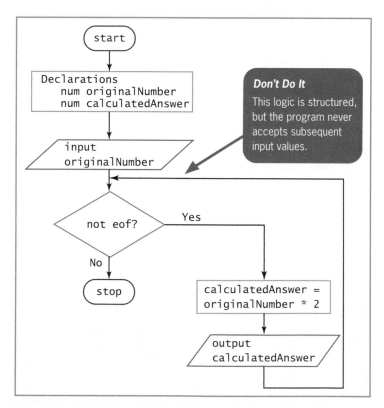

Figure 3-15   Structured, but nonfunctional, flowchart of number-doubling problem

Follow the flowchart in Figure 3-15 through a typical program run, assuming the eof condition is an input value of 0. Suppose when the program starts, the user enters a 9 for the value of originalNumber. That is not eof, so the number is multiplied by 2, and 18 is displayed as the value of calculatedAnswer. Then the question eof? is asked again. It cannot be eof because a new value representing the sentinel (ending) value cannot be entered. The logic never returns to the `input originalNumber` task, so the value of `originalNumber` never changes. Therefore, 9 doubles again and the answer 18 is displayed again. It is still not `eof`, so the same steps are repeated. This goes on *forever*, with the answer 18 being output repeatedly. The program logic shown in Figure 3-15 is structured, but it does not work as intended. Conversely, the program in Figure 3-16 works, but it is not structured!

The loop in Figure 3-16 is not structured because after the tasks execute within a structured loop, the flow of logic must return directly to the loop-controlling question. In Figure 3-16, the logic does not return to this question; instead, it goes "too high" outside the loop to repeat the `input originalNumber` task.

107

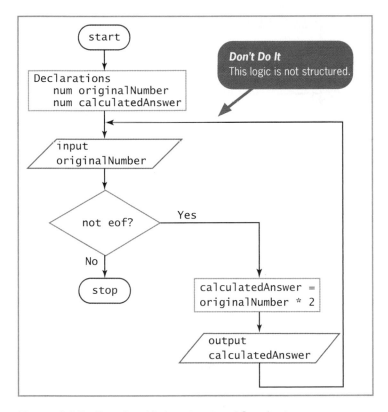

Figure 3-16 Functional but unstructured flowchart

How can the number-doubling problem be both structured and work as intended? Often, for a program to be structured, you must add something extra. In this case, it is a priming input step. A **priming input** or **priming read** is an added statement that gets the first input value in a program. For example, if a program will receive 100 data values as input, you input the first value in a statement that is separate from the other 99. You must do this to keep the program structured.

Consider the solution in Figure 3-17; it is structured *and* it does what it is supposed to do. It contains a shaded, additional input originalNumber statement. The program logic illustrated in Figure 3-17 contains a sequence and a loop. The loop contains another sequence.

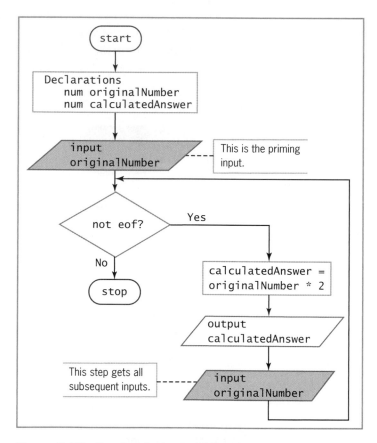

Figure 3-17   Functional, structured flowchart and pseudocode for the number-doubling problem

In Chapter 2, you learned that the group of preliminary tasks that sets the stage for the main work of a program is called the housekeeping section. The priming read is an example of a housekeeping task.

The additional input originalNumber step shown in Figure 3-17 is typical in structured programs. The first of the two input steps is the priming input. The term *priming* comes from the fact that the read is first, or *primary* (it gets the process going, as in "priming the pump"). The purpose of the priming input step is to control the upcoming loop that begins with the eof question. The last element within the structured loop gets the next, and all subsequent, input values. This is also typical in structured loops—the last step executed within the loop alters the condition tested in the question that begins the loop, which in this case is the eof question.

Figure 3-18 shows another way you might attempt to draw the logic for the number-doubling program. At first glance, the figure might seem to show an acceptable solution to the problem—it is structured, contains a single loop with a sequence of three steps within it, and appears to eliminate the need for the priming input statement. When the program starts, the **eof** question is asked. The answer is *No*, so the program gets an input number, doubles it, and displays it. Then, if it is still not **eof**, the program gets another number, doubles it, and displays it. The program continues until **eof** is encountered when getting input. The last time the `input originalNumber` statement executes, it encounters **eof**, but the program does not stop—instead, it calculates and displays a result one last time. Depending on the language you are using and on the type of input being used, you might receive an error message or you might output garbage. In either case, this last output is extraneous—no value should be doubled and output after the **eof** condition is encountered. As a general rule, an **eof** question should always come immediately after an input statement because the end-of-file condition will be detected at input. Therefore, the best solution to the number-doubling problem remains the one shown in Figure 3-17—the solution containing the priming input statement.

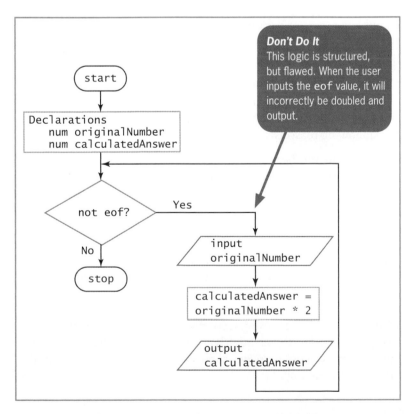

Figure 3-18 Structured but incorrect solution to the number-doubling problem

110

TWO TRUTHS & A LIE

Using a Priming Input to Structure a Program

1. A priming input is the statement that repeatedly gets all the data that is input in a program.

2. A structured program is sometimes longer than an unstructured one.

3. A program can be structured yet still be incorrect.

The false statement is #1. A priming input gets the first input.

Understanding the Reasons for Structure

At this point, you may very well be saying, "I liked the original number-doubling program back in Figure 3-12 just fine. I could follow it. Also, the first program had one less step in it, so it was less work. Who cares if a program is structured?"

Until you have some programming experience, it is difficult to appreciate the reasons for using only the three structures—sequence, selection, and loop. However, staying with these three structures is better for the following reasons:

- *Clarity*—The number-doubling program is small. As programs get bigger, they get more confusing if they are not structured.

- *Professionalism*—All other programmers (and programming teachers you might encounter) expect your programs to be structured. It is the way things are done professionally.

- *Efficiency*—Most newer computer languages are structured languages with syntax that lets you deal efficiently with sequence, selection, and looping. Older languages, such as assembly languages, COBOL, and RPG, were developed before the principles of structured programming were discovered. However, even programs that use those older languages can be written in a structured form. Newer languages such as C#, C++, and Java enforce structure by their syntax.

In older languages, you could leave a selection or loop before it was complete by using a "go to" statement. The statement allowed the logic to "go to" any other part of the program whether it was within the same structure or not. Structured programming is sometimes called **goto-less programming.**

- *Maintenance*—You and other programmers will find it easier to modify and maintain structured programs as changes are required in the future.

- *Modularity*—Structured programs can be easily broken down into routines or modules that can be assigned to any number of programmers. The routines are then pieced back together like modular furniture at each routine's single entry or exit point. Additionally, a module often can be used in multiple programs, saving development time in the new project.

TWO TRUTHS & A LIE

Understanding the Reasons for Structure

1. Structured programs are clearer than unstructured programs.

2. You and other programmers will find it easier to modify and maintain structured programs as changes are required in the future.

3. Structured programs are not easily divided into parts, making them less prone to error.

The false statement is #3. Structured programs can be easily broken down into modules that can be assigned to any number of programmers.

Recognizing Structure

When you are beginning to learn about structured program design, it is difficult to detect whether a flowchart of a program's logic is structured. For example, is the flowchart segment in Figure 3-19 structured?

Yes, it is. It has a sequence and a selection structure.

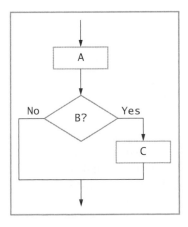

Figure 3-19   Example 1

Is the flowchart segment in Figure 3-20 structured?

Yes, it is. It has a loop, and within the loop is a selection.

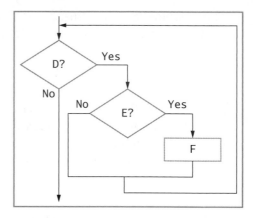

Figure 3-20   Example 2

Is the flowchart segment in Figure 3-21 structured?

No, it is not constructed from the three basic structures. One way to straighten out an unstructured flowchart segment is to use the "spaghetti bowl" method; that is, picture the flowchart as a bowl of spaghetti that you must untangle. Imagine you can grab one piece of pasta at the top of the bowl and start pulling. As you "pull" each symbol out of the tangled mess, you can untangle the separate paths until the entire segment is structured.

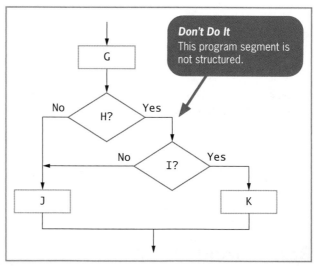

Figure 3-21   Example 3

For example, look at the diagram in Figure 3-21. If you could start pulling at the top, you would encounter a procedure box labeled G. (See Figure 3-22.) A single process like G is part of an acceptable structure—it constitutes at least the beginning of a sequence structure.

Figure 3-22   Untangling Example 3, first step

Imagine that you continue pulling symbols from the tangled segment. The next item in the flowchart is a question that tests a condition labeled H, as you can see in Figure 3-23. At this point, you know the sequence that started with G has ended. Sequences never have decisions in them, so the sequence is finished; either a selection or a loop is beginning with question H. A loop must return to the loop-controlling question at some later point. You can see from the original logic in Figure 3-21 that whether the answer to H is *Yes* or *No*, the logic never returns to H. Therefore, H begins a selection structure, not a loop structure.

To continue detangling the logic, you would pull up on the flowline that emerges from the left side (the *No* side) of Question H. You encounter J, as shown in Figure 3-24. When you continue beyond J, you reach the end of the flowchart.

Now you can turn your attention to the *Yes* side (the right side) of the condition tested in H. When you pull up on the right side, you encounter Question I. (See Figure 3-25.)

In the original version of the flowchart in Figure 3-21, follow the line on the left side of Question I. The line emerging from the left side of selection I is attached to J, which is outside the selection structure. You might say the I-controlled selection is becoming entangled with the H-controlled selection, so you

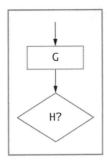

Figure 3-23 Untangling Example 3, second step

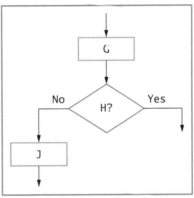

Figure 3-24 Untangling Example 3, third step

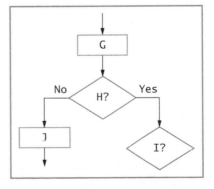

Figure 3-25 Untangling Example 3, fourth step

114

must untangle the structures by repeating the step that is causing the tangle. (In this example, you repeat Step J to untangle it from the other usage of J.) Continue pulling on the flowline that emerges from J until you reach the end of the program segment, as shown in Figure 3-26.

Now pull on the right side of Question I. Process K pops up, as shown in Figure 3-27; then you reach the end.

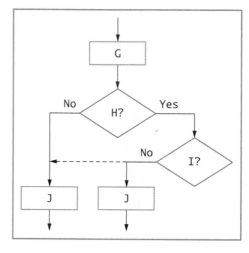

Figure 3-26   Untangling Example 3, fifth step

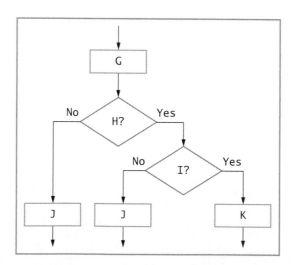

Figure 3-27   Untangling Example 3, sixth step

If you want to try structuring a very difficult example of an unstructured program, see Appendix E.

At this point, the untangled flowchart has three loose ends. The loose ends of Question I can be brought together to form a selection structure; then the loose ends of Question H can be brought together to form another selection structure. The result is the flowchart shown in Figure 3-28. The entire flowchart segment is structured—it has a sequence followed by a selection inside a selection.

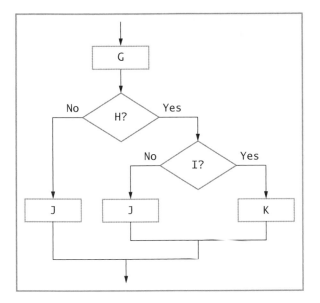

Figure 3-28   Finished flowchart and pseudocode for untangling Example 3

TWO TRUTHS & A LIE

Recognizing Structure

1. Most, but not all, sets of instructions can be expressed in a structured format.

2. When you are first learning about structured program design, it can be difficult to detect whether a flowchart of a program's logic is structured.

3. Any unstructured flowchart can be "detangled" to become structured.

The false statement is #1. Any set of instructions can be expressed in a structured format.

Structuring and Modularizing Unstructured Logic

Recall the dog-washing process illustrated in Figure 3-1 at the beginning of this chapter. When you look at it now, you should recognize it as an unstructured process. Can this process be reconfigured to perform precisely the same tasks in a structured way? Of course!

Figure 3-29 shows the beginning of the process. The first step, *Catch dog*, is a simple sequence.

Figure 3-30 contains the next part of the process. When a question is encountered, the sequence is over, and either a loop or a selection starts. In this case, after the dog runs away, you must catch the dog and determine whether he runs away again, so a loop begins. To create a structured loop like the ones you have seen earlier in this chapter, you can repeat the *Catch dog* process and return immediately to the *Does dog run away?* question.

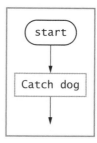

Figure 3-29 Washing the dog, part 1

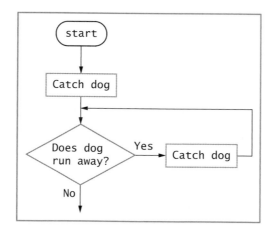

Figure 3-30 Washing the dog, part 2

In the original flowchart in Figure 3-1, you turn on the water when the dog does not run away. This step is a simple sequence, so it can correctly be added after the loop. When the water is turned on, the original logic checks to see whether the dog runs away after this new development. This starts a loop. In the original flowchart, the lines cross, creating a tangle, so you repeat as many steps as necessary to detangle the lines. After you turn off the water and catch the dog, you encounter the question *Does dog have shampoo on?* Because the logic has not yet reached the shampooing step, there is no need to ask this question; the answer at this point always will be *No*. When one of the logical paths emerging from a question can never be traveled, you can eliminate the question. Figure 3-31 shows that if the dog runs away after you turn on the water, but before you've gotten the dog wet and shampooed it, you must turn the water off, catch the dog, and return to the step that asks whether the dog runs away.

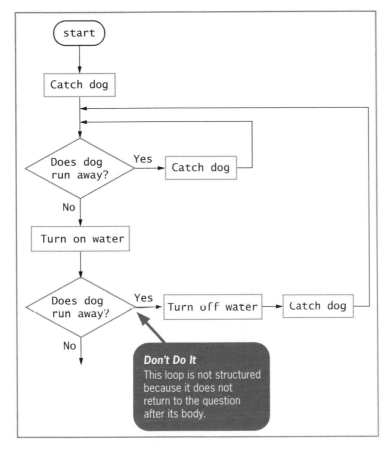

Figure 3-31   Washing the dog, part 3

The logic in Figure 3-31 is not structured because the second loop that begins with the question *Does dog run away?* does not immediately return to the loop-controlling question after its body executes. So, to make the loop structured, you can repeat the actions that occur before returning to the loop-controlling question. (See Figure 3-32.)

The flowchart segment in Figure 3-32 is structured; it contains a sequence, a loop, a sequence, and a final, larger loop. This last loop contains its own sequence, loop, and sequence.

After the dog is caught and the water is on, you wet and shampoo the dog, as shown in Figure 3-33. Then, according to the original flowchart in Figure 3-1, you once again check to see whether the dog has run away. If he has, you turn off the water and catch the dog. From this location in the logic, the answer to the *Does dog have shampoo on?* question will always be Yes; so, as before, there is no need to ask a question when there is only one possible answer. So, if the dog runs away, the last loop executes. You turn off the water, continue to catch the dog as it repeatedly escapes, and turn the water on.

When the dog is caught at last, you rinse the dog and end the program. Figure 3-33 shows both the complete flowchart and pseudocode.

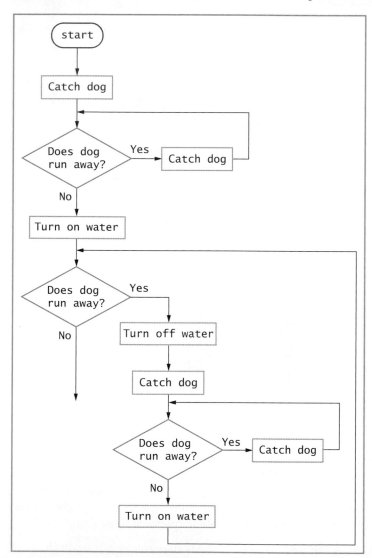

Figure 3-32 Washing the dog, part 4

The flowchart in Figure 3-33 is complete and is structured. It contains alternating sequence and loop structures.

Figure 3-33 shows three places where the sequence-loop-sequence of catching the dog and turning the water on are repeated. So, if you wanted to, you could modularize the duplicate sections so that their instruction sets are written once and contained in their own module. Figure 3-34 shows a modularized version of the program; the three module calls are shaded.

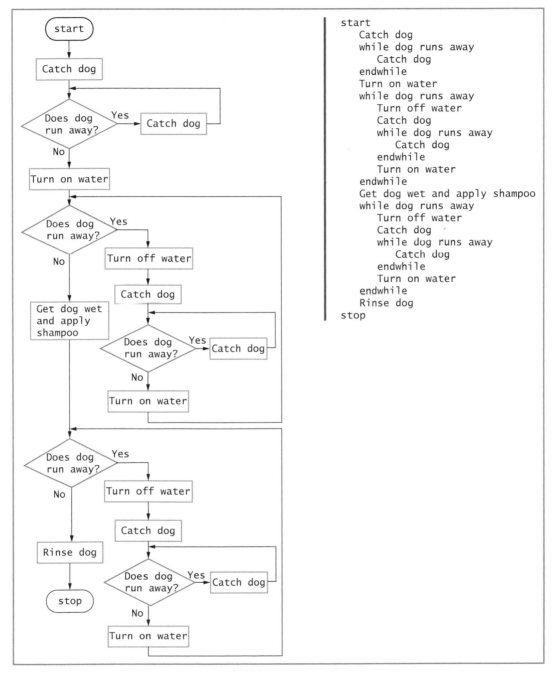

Figure 3-33 Structured dog-washing flowchart and pseudocode

120

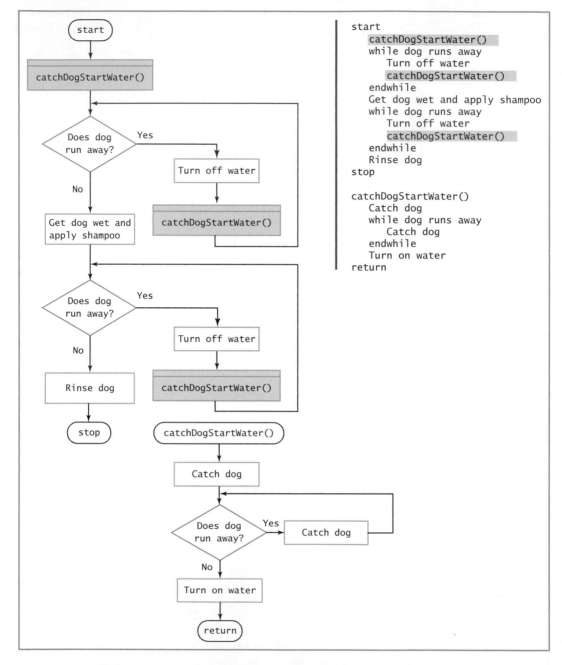

Figure 3-34   Modularized version of the dog-washing program

No matter how complicated it is, any set of steps can always be reduced to combinations of the three basic structures of sequence, selection, and loop. These structures can be nested and stacked in an infinite number of ways to describe the logic of any process and to create the logic for every computer program written in the past, present, or future.

Watch the video *Structuring Unstructured Logic*.

121

For convenience, many programming languages allow two variations of the three basic structures. The `case` structure is a variation of the selection structure and the `do` loop is a variation of the `while` loop. You can learn about these two structures in Appendix F. Even though these extra structures can be used in most programming languages, all logical problems can be solved without them.

TWO TRUTHS & A LIE

Structuring and Modularizing Unstructured Logic

1. When you encounter a question in a logical diagram, a sequence should be ending.

2. In a structured loop, the logic returns to the loop-controlling question after the loop body executes.

3. If a flowchart or pseudocode contains a question to which the answer never varies, you can eliminate the question.

The false statement is #1. When you encounter a question in a logical diagram, either a selection or a loop should start. Any structure might end before the question is encountered.

Chapter Summary

- Spaghetti code is the popular name for unstructured program statements that do not follow the rules of structured logic.

- Clearer programs can be constructed using only three basic structures: sequence, selection, and loop. These three structures can be combined in an infinite number of ways by stacking and nesting them. Each structure has one entry and one exit point; one structure can attach to another only at one of these points.

- A priming input is the statement that gets the first input value prior to starting a structured loop. The last step within the loop gets the next, and all subsequent, input values.

- Programmers use structured techniques to promote clarity, professionalism, efficiency, and modularity.

- One way to order an unstructured flowchart segment is to imagine it as a bowl of spaghetti that you must untangle.

- Any set of logical steps can be rewritten to conform to the three structures.

Key Terms

Spaghetti code is snarled, unstructured program logic.

Unstructured programs are programs that do *not* follow the rules of structured logic.

Structured programs are programs that do follow the rules of structured logic.

A **structure** is a basic unit of programming logic; each structure is a sequence, selection, or loop.

With a **sequence structure**, you perform an action or task, and then you perform the next action, in order. A sequence can contain any number of tasks, but there is no option to branch off and skip any of the tasks.

With a **selection structure** or **decision structure**, you ask a question, and, depending on the answer, you take one of two courses of action. Then, no matter which path you follow, you continue with the next task.

An **if-then-else** is another name for a selection structure.

Dual-alternative ifs (or **dual-alternative selections**) define one action to be taken when the tested condition is true and another action to be taken when it is false.

Single-alternative ifs (or **single-alternative selections**) take action on just one branch of the decision.

The **null case** is the branch of a decision in which no action is taken.

With a **loop structure**, you continue to repeat actions based on the answer to a question.

A **loop body** is the set of actions that occur within a loop.

Repetition and **iteration** are alternate names for a loop structure.

In a **while...do**, or more simply, a **while loop**, a process continues while some condition continues to be true.

Stacking structures is the act of attaching structures end to end.

End-structure statements designate the ends of pseudocode structures.

Nesting structures is the act of placing a structure within another structure.

A **block** is a group of statements that executes as a single unit.

A **priming input** or **priming read** is the statement that reads the first input data record prior to starting a structured loop.

Goto-less programming is a name to describe structured programming, because structured programmers do not use a "go to" statement.

Review Questions

1. Snarled program logic is called _____ code.

   a. snake

   b. spaghetti

   c. string

   d. gnarly

2. The three structures of structured programming are _____.

   a. sequence, order, and process

   b. selection, loop, and iteration

   c. sequence, selection, and loop

   d. if, else, and then

3. A sequence structure can contain _____.

   a. any number of tasks

   b. exactly three tasks

   c. no more than three tasks

   d. only one task

4. Which of the following is *not* another term for a selection structure?

   a. decision structure

   b. if-then-else structure

   c. dual-alternative if structure

   d. loop structure

5. The structure in which you ask a question, and, depending on the answer, take some action and then ask the question again, can be called all of the following except a(n) _____.

   a. iteration

   b. loop

   c. repetition

   d. if-then-else

6. Placing a structure within another structure is called _____ the structures.

   a. stacking

   b. untangling

   c. building

   d. nesting

7. Attaching structures end to end is called _____.

   a. stacking

   b. untangling

   c. building

   d. nesting

8. The statement `if age >= 65 then seniorDiscount="yes"` is an example of a _____.

   a. sequence

   b. loop

   c. dual-alternative selection

   d. single-alternative selection

9. The statement `while temperature remains below 60, leave the furnace on` is an example of a _____.

   a. sequence

   b. loop

   c. dual-alternative selection

   d. single-alternative selection

10. The statement `if age<13 then movieTicket=4.00 else movieTicket=8.50` is an example of a _____.

    a. sequence

    b. loop

    c. dual-alternative selection

    d. single-alternative selection

11. Which of the following attributes do all three basic structures share?

    a. Their flowcharts all contain exactly three processing symbols.

    b. They all have one entry and one exit point.

    c. They all contain a decision.

    d. They all begin with a process.

12. Which is true of stacking structures?

    a. Two incidences of the same structure cannot be stacked adjacently.

    b. When you stack structures, you cannot nest them in the same program.

    c. Each structure has only one point where it can be stacked on top of another.

    d. When you stack structures, the top structure must be a sequence.

13. When you input data in a loop within a program, the input statement that precedes the loop _____.

    a. is the only part of the program allowed to be unstructured

    b. cannot result in `eof`

    c. is called a priming input

    d. executes hundreds or even thousands of times in most business programs

14. A group of statements that executes as a unit is a
_____.

   a. block

   b. family

   c. chunk

   d. cohort

15. Which of the following is acceptable in a structured program?

   a. placing a sequence within the true half of a dual-alternative decision

   b. placing a decision within a loop

   c. placing a loop within one of the steps in a sequence

   d. All of these are acceptable.

16. In a selection structure, the structure-controlling question is _____.

   a. asked once at the beginning of the structure

   b. asked once at the end of the structure

   c. asked repeatedly until it is false

   d. asked repeatedly until it is true

17. In a loop, the structure-controlling question is
_____.

   a. asked exactly once

   b. never asked more than once

   c. asked before and after the loop body executes

   d. asked only if it is true, and not asked if it is false

18. Which of the following is *not* a reason for enforcing structure rules in computer programs?

   a. Structured programs are clearer to understand than unstructured ones.

   b. Other professional programmers will expect programs to be structured.

    c. Structured programs usually are shorter than unstructured ones.

    d. Structured programs can be broken down into modules easily.

19. Which of the following is *not* a benefit of modularizing programs?

    a. Modular programs are easier to read and understand than nonmodular ones.

    b. If you use modules, you can ignore the rules of structure.

    c. Modular components are reusable in other programs.

    d. Multiple programmers can work on different modules at the same time.

20. Which of the following is true of structured logic?

    a. You can use structured logic with newer programming languages, such as Java and C#, but not with older ones.

    b. Any task can be described using some combination of the three structures.

    c. Structured programs require that you break the code into easy-to-handle modules that each contain no more than five actions.

    d. All of these are true.

Exercises

1. In Figure 3-10, the process of buying and planting flowers in the spring was shown using the same structures as the generic example in Figure 3-9. Using exactly the same structure for the logic, create a flowchart or pseudocode that describes some other process with which you are familiar.

2. Each of the flowchart segments in Figure 3-35 is unstructured. Redraw each flowchart segment so that it does the same thing but is structured.

128

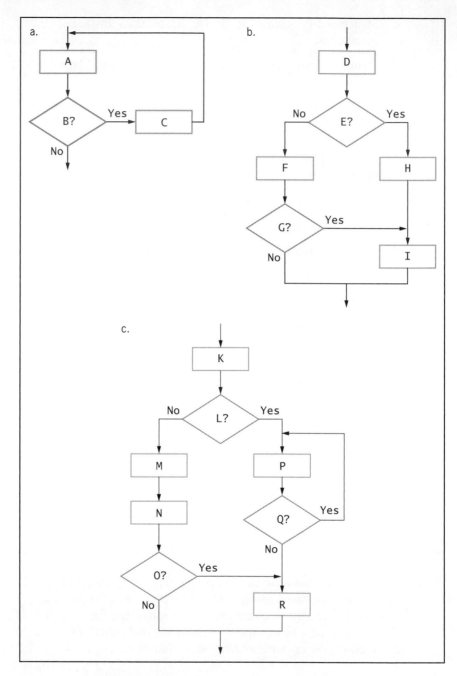

Figure 3-35 Flowcharts for Exercise 2

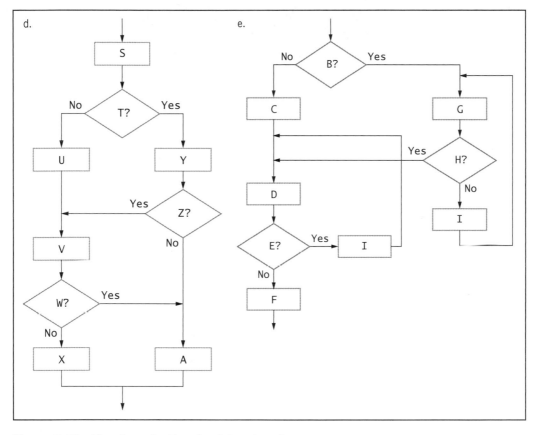

Figure 3-35 Flowcharts for Exercise 2 (continued)

3. Write pseudocode for each example (a through e) in Exercise 2, making sure your pseudocode is structured but accomplishes the same tasks as the flowchart segment.

4. Assume you have created a mechanical arm that can hold a pen. The arm can perform the following tasks:

    • Lower the pen to a piece of paper.

    • Raise the pen from the paper.

    • Move the pen 1 inch along a straight line. (If the pen is lowered, this action draws a 1-inch line from left to right; if the pen is raised, this action just repositions the pen 1 inch to the right.)

    • Turn 90 degrees to the right.

    • Draw a circle that is 1 inch in diameter.

Draw a structured flowchart or write structured pseudocode describing the logic that would cause the arm to draw or write the following. Have a fellow student act as the mechanical arm and carry out your instructions.

   a.   a 1-inch square

   b.   a 2-inch by 1-inch rectangle

   c.   a string of three beads

   d.   a short word (for example, "cat"). Do not reveal the word to your partner until the exercise is over.

5.   Assume you have created a mechanical robot that can perform the following tasks:

   • Stand up.

   • Sit down.

   • Turn left 90 degrees.

   • Turn right 90 degrees.

   • Take a step.

   Additionally, the robot can determine the answer to one test condition:

   • Am I touching something?

   Place two chairs 20 feet apart, directly facing each other. Draw a structured flowchart or write pseudocode describing the logic that would allow the robot to start from a sitting position in one chair, cross the room, and end up sitting in the other chair. Have a fellow student act as the robot and carry out your instructions.

6.   Looking up a word in a dictionary can be a complicated process. For example, assume you want to look up "logic." You might open the dictionary to a random page and see "juice." You know this word comes alphabetically before "logic," so you flip forward and see "lamb." That is still not far enough, so you flip forward and see "monkey." You have gone too far, so you flip back, and so on. Draw a structured flowchart or write pseudocode that describes the process of looking up a word in a dictionary. Pick a word at random and have a fellow student attempt to carry out your instructions.

7. Draw a structured flowchart or write structured pseudocode describing your preparation to go to work or school in the morning. Include at least two decisions and two loops.

8. Draw a structured flowchart or write structured pseudocode describing your preparation to go to bed at night. Include at least two decisions and two loops.

9. Draw a structured flowchart or write structured pseudocode describing how your paycheck is calculated. Include at least two decisions.

10. Draw a structured flowchart or write structured pseudocode describing the steps a retail store employee should follow to process a customer purchase. Include at least two decisions.

 ## Find the Bugs

11. Your student disk contains files named DEBUG03-01.txt, DEBUG03-02.txt, and DEBUG03-03.txt. Each file starts with some comments that describe the problem. Comments are lines that begin with two slashes (//). Following the comments, each file contains pseudocode that has one or more bugs you must find and correct.

 ## Game Zone

12. Choose a very simple children's game and describe its logic, using a structured flowchart or pseudocode. For example, you might try to explain Rock, Paper, Scissors; Musical Chairs; Duck, Duck, Goose; the card game War; or the elimination game Eenie, Meenie, Minie, Moe.

13. Choose a television game show such as *Deal or No Deal* or *Jeopardy!* and describe its rules using a structured flowchart or pseudocode.

14. Choose a sport such as baseball or football and describe the actions in one limited play period (such as an at-bat in baseball or a possession in football) using a structured flowchart or pseudocode.

Up for Discussion

15. Find more information about one of the following people and explain why he or she is important to structured programming: Edsger Dijkstra, Corrado Bohm, Giuseppe Jacopini, and Grace Hopper.

16. Computer programs can contain structures within structures and stacked structures, creating very large programs. Computers can also perform millions of arithmetic calculations in an hour. How can we possibly know the results are correct?

17. Develop a checklist of rules you can use to help you determine whether a flowchart or pseudocode segment is structured.

CHAPTER 4

Making Decisions

In this chapter, you will learn about:

- ◎ Evaluating Boolean expressions to make comparisons
- ◎ The relational comparison operators
- ◎ AND logic
- ◎ OR logic
- ◎ Making selections within ranges
- ◎ Precedence when combining AND and OR operators

Evaluating Boolean Expressions to Make Comparisons

Mathematician George Boole (1815–1864) approached logic more simply than his predecessors did, by expressing logical selections with common algebraic symbols. He is considered the founder of mathematical logic, and Boolean (true/false) expressions are named for him.

The reason people frequently think computers are smart lies in the computer program's ability to make decisions. A medical diagnosis program that can decide if your symptoms fit various disease profiles seems quite intelligent, as does a program that can offer different potential vacation routes based on your destination.

Every decision you make in a computer program involves evaluating a **Boolean expression**—an expression whose value can be only true or false. True/false evaluation is "natural" from a computer's standpoint because computer circuitry consists of two-state on-off switches, often represented by 1 or 0. Every computer decision yields a true-or-false, yes-or-no, 1-or-0 result. A Boolean expression is used in every selection structure. The selection structure is not new to you—it's one of the basic structures you learned about in Chapter 3. See Figures 4-1 and 4-2.

This book follows the convention that the two logical paths emerging from a decision are drawn to the right and left of a diamond in a flowchart. Some programmers draw one of the flowlines emerging from the bottom of the diamond. The exact format of the diagram is not as important as the idea that one logical path flows into a selection, and two possible outcomes emerge.

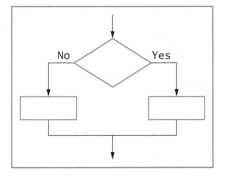

Figure 4-1   The dual-alternative selection structure

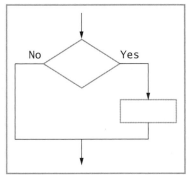

Figure 4-2   The single-alternative selection structure

In Chapter 3 you learned that you can refer to the structure in Figure 4-1 as a dual-alternative, or binary, selection because an action is associated with each of two possible outcomes: depending on the answer to the question represented by the diamond, the logical flow proceeds either to the left branch of the structure or to the right. The choices are mutually exclusive; that is, the logic can flow only to one of the two alternatives, never to both.

You can call a single-alternative decision (or selection) a *single-sided decision*. Similarly, a dual-alternative decision is a *double-sided decision* (or selection).

The flowchart segment in Figure 4-2 represents a single-alternative selection in which action is required for only one outcome of the question. You call this form of the selection structure an **if-then**, because no alternative or "else" action is necessary.

Figure 4-3 shows the flowchart and pseudocode for an interactive program that computes pay for employees. The program displays the weekly pay for each employee at the same hourly rate ($10.00) and assumes there are no payroll deductions. The mainline logic calls `housekeeping()`, `detailLoop()`, and `finish()` modules. The `detailLoop()` module contains a typical `if-then-else` decision that determines whether an employee has worked more than a standard workweek (40 hours), and pays one and one-half times the employee's usual hourly rate for hours worked in excess of 40 per week.

Throughout this book, many examples are presented in both flowchart and pseudocode form. When you analyze a solution, you might find it easier to concentrate on just one of the two design tools at first. When you understand how the program works using one tool (for example, the flowchart), you can confirm that the solution is identical using the other tool.

135

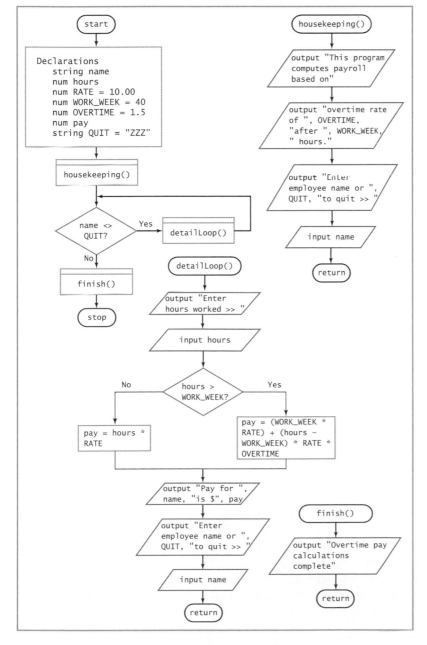

Figure 4-3 Flowchart and pseudocode for overtime payroll program

```
start
   Declarations
      string name
      num hours
      num RATE = 10.00
      num WORK_WEEK = 40
      num OVERTIME = 1.5
      num pay
      string QUIT = "ZZZ"
   housekeeping()
   while name <> QUIT
      detailLoop()
   endwhile
   finish()
stop

housekeeping()
   output "This program computes payroll based on"
   output "overtime rate of ", OVERTIME, "after ", WORK_WEEK, " hours."
   output "Enter employee name or ", QUIT, "to quit >> "
   input name
return

detailLoop()
   output "Enter hours worked >> "
   input hours
   if hours > WORK_WEEK then
      pay = (WORK_WEEK * RATE) + (hours - WORK_WEEK) * RATE * OVERTIME
   else
      pay = hours * RATE
   endif
   output "Pay for ", name, "is $", pay
   output "Enter employee name or ", QUIT, "to quit >> "
   input name
return

finish()
   output "Overtime pay calculations complete"
return
```

Figure 4-3   Flowchart and pseudocode for overtime payroll program (continued)

In the detailLoop() module of the program in Figure 4-3, the longer overtime calculation is the **then clause** of the decision—the part of the decision that holds the action or actions that execute when the tested condition in the decision is true. The shorter calculation, which calculates pay by multiplying hours by RATE, constitutes the **else clause** of the decision—the part that executes only when the tested condition in the decision is false.

Figure 4-4 shows a typical execution of the program in a command-line environment. Data values are entered for three employees. The first two employees do not work more than 40 hours, so their pay is displayed simply as hours times $10.00. The third employee, however, has worked one hour of overtime, and so makes $15 for the last hour instead of just $10.

Watch the video *Boolean Expressions and Decisions.*

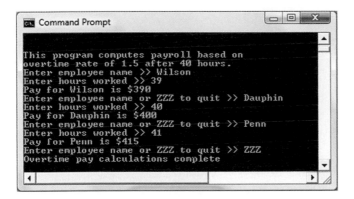

Figure 4-4 Typical execution of the overtime payroll program in Figure 4-3

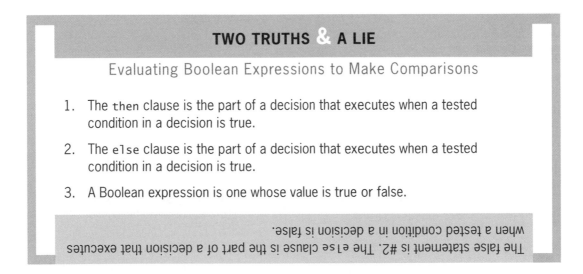

TWO TRUTHS & A LIE

Evaluating Boolean Expressions to Make Comparisons

1. The then clause is the part of a decision that executes when a tested condition in a decision is true.

2. The else clause is the part of a decision that executes when a tested condition in a decision is true.

3. A Boolean expression is one whose value is true or false.

The false statement is #2. The else clause is the part of a decision that executes when a tested condition in a decision is false.

Using Relational Comparison Operators

Table 4-1 describes the six **relational comparison operators** supported by all modern programming languages. Each of these operators is binary—that is, each requires two operands. When you construct an expression using two operands and one of the operators

In Chapter 2 you learned that the assignment operator is also a binary operator.

138

When an operator is formed using two keystrokes, you never insert a space between them.

Some programming languages allow you to compare a character to a number. If you do, then a single character's numeric code value is used in the comparison. Appendix A contains more information on coding systems.

described in Table 4-1, the expression evaluates to true or false based on the operands' values. Usually, both operands in a comparison must be the same data type; that is, you can compare numeric values to other numeric values, and text strings to other strings.

The term "relational comparison operators" is somewhat redundant. You can also call these operators **relational operators** or **comparison operators**.

Operator	Name	Discussion
=	Equivalency operator	Evaluates as true when its operands are equivalent. Many languages use a double equal sign (==) to avoid confusion with the assignment operator.
>	Greater-than operator	Evaluates as true when the left operand is greater than the right operand.
<	Less-than operator	Evaluates as true when the left operand is less than the right operand.
>=	Greater-than or equal-to operator	Evaluates as true when the left operand is greater than or equivalent to the right operand.
<=	Less-than or equal-to operator	Evaluates as true when the left operand is less than or equivalent to the right operand.
<>	Not-equal-to operator	Evaluates as true when its operands are not equivalent. Some languages use an exclamation point followed by an equal sign to indicate not equal to (!=). Because the not-equal-to operator differs in the common programming languages, this book will most often spell out "is not equal to" in flowcharts and pseudocode.

Table 4-1   Relational comparison operators

In any Boolean expression, the two values compared can be either variables or constants. For example, the expression currentTotal = 100? compares a variable, currentTotal, to a numeric constant, 100. Depending on the `currentTotal` value, the expression is true or false. In the expression `currentTotal = previousTotal?`, both values are variables, and the result is also true or false depending on the values stored in each of the two variables. Although it's legal, you would never use expressions in which you compare two constants—for example, 20 = 20? or 30 = 40?. Such expressions are **trivial expressions** because each will always evaluate to the same result: true for 20 = 20? and false for 30 = 40?.

Any decision can be made using combinations of just three types of comparisons: equal, greater than, and less than. You never need the three additional comparisons (greater than or equal, less than or equal, or not equal), but using them often makes decisions more convenient. For example, assume you need to issue a 10 percent discount to any customer whose age is 65 or greater, and charge full price to other customers. You can use the greater-than-or-equal-to symbol to write the logic as follows:

```
if customerAge >= 65 then
    discount = 0.10
else
    discount = 0
endif
```

As an alternative, if the >= operator did not exist, you could express the same logic by writing:

```
if customerAge < 65 then
    discount = 0
else
    discount = 0.10
endif
```

In any decision for which a >= b is true, then a < b is false. Conversely, if a >= b is false, then a < b is true. By rephrasing the question and swapping the actions taken based on the outcome, you can make the same decision in multiple ways. The clearest route is often to ask a question so the positive or true outcome results in the action that was your motivation for making the test. When your company policy is to "provide a discount for those who are 65 and older," the phrase "greater than or equal to" comes to mind, so it is the most natural to use. Conversely, if your policy is to "provide no discount for those under 65," then it is more natural to use the "less than" syntax. Either way, the same people receive a discount.

Comparing two amounts to decide if they are *not* equal to each other is the most confusing of all the comparisons. Using "not equal to" in decisions involves thinking in double negatives, which can make

When you write pseudocode or draw a flowchart for your own use, you can indicate relationships in any way you prefer. For example, to indicate equivalency, you can use "=", "==", or spell out "is equal to". When you take a class or work in an organization, you might be required to use a specific format for consistency.

Usually, string variables are not considered to be equal unless they are identical, including the spacing and whether they appear in uppercase or lowercase. For example, "black pen" is *not* equal to "blackpen", "BLACK PEN", or "Black Pen".

you prone to include logical errors in your programs. For example, consider the flowchart segment in Figure 4-5.

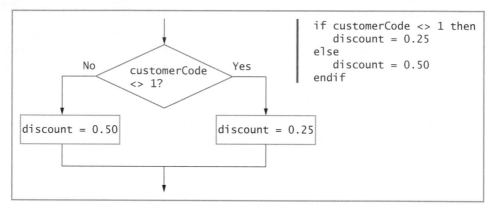

```
if customerCode <> 1 then
    discount = 0.25
else
    discount = 0.50
endif
```

Figure 4-5   Using a negative comparison

In Figure 4-5, if the value of customerCode *is* equal to 1, the logical flow follows the false branch of the selection. If customerCode <> 1 is true, discount is 0.25; if customerCode <> 1 is not true, it means customerCode *is* 1, and discount is 0.50. Even saying the phrase "if the customer code is not equal to one is not true" is awkward.

Figure 4-6 shows the same decision, this time asked in a positive way. Making the decision if customerCode *is* 1 then discount = 0.50 is clearer than trying to determine what customerCode is *not*.

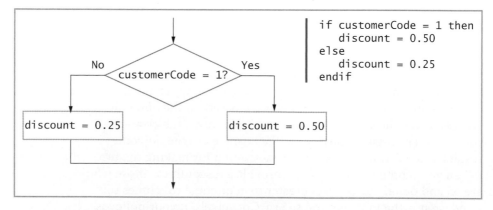

```
if customerCode = 1 then
    discount = 0.50
else
    discount = 0.25
endif
```

Figure 4-6   Using the positive equivalent of the negative comparison in Figure 4-5

Although negative comparisons can be awkward to use, your meaning is sometimes clearest when using them. Frequently, this occurs when you use an if without an else, taking action only when some comparison is false. An example would be: if customerZipCode is not equal to LOCAL_ZIP_CODE then add deliveryCharge to total.

Avoiding a Common Error with Relational Operators

A common error that occurs when you use relational operators is using the wrong one and missing the boundary or limit required for a selection. If you use > to make a selection when you should have used >=, all the cases that are = will go unselected. Unfortunately, those who request programs do not always speak as precisely as a computer. If, for example, your boss says, "Write a program that selects all employees over 65," does she mean to include employees who are 65 or not? In other words, is the comparison age > 65 or age >= 65? Although the phrase "over 65" indicates "greater than 65," people do not always say what they mean, and the best course of action is to double-check the intended meaning with the person who requested the program—for example, the end user, your supervisor, or your instructor. Similar phrases that can cause misunderstandings are "no more than," "at least," and "not under."

TWO TRUTHS & A LIE

Using Relational Comparison Operators

1. Usually, you can compare only values that are of the same data type.

2. A Boolean expression is defined as one that decides whether two values are equal.

3. In any Boolean expression, the two values compared can be either variables or constants.

The false statement is #2. Although deciding whether two values are equal is a Boolean expression, so is deciding whether one is greater than or less than another. A Boolean expression is one that results in a true or false value.

Understanding AND Logic

Often, you need more than one selection structure to determine whether an action should take place. When you ask multiple questions before an outcome is determined, you create a **compound condition**. For example, suppose you work for a cell phone company that charges customers as follows:

- The basic monthly service bill is $30.

- An additional $20 is billed to customers who make more than 100 calls that last for a total of more than 500 minutes.

You first learned about nesting structures in Chapter 3. You can always stack and nest any of the basic structures.

142

The logic needed for this billing program includes an **AND decision**—a decision in which two conditions must be true for an action to take place. In this case, both a minimum number of calls must be made *and* a minimum number of minutes must be used before the customer is charged the additional amount. An AND decision can be constructed using a **nested decision**, or a **nested if**—that is, a decision "inside of" another decision. The flowchart and pseudocode for the program that determines the charges for customers is shown in Figure 4-7.

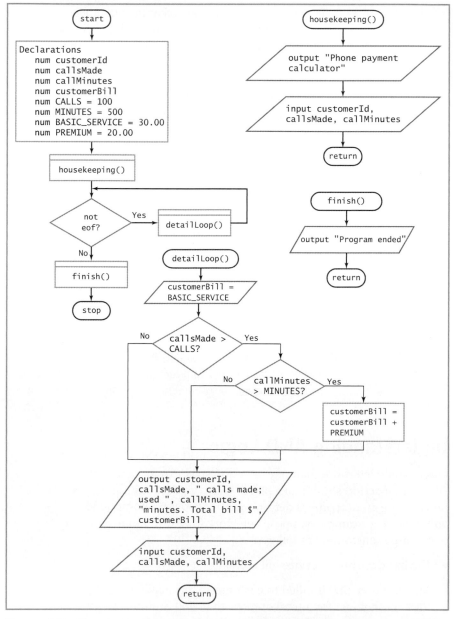

Figure 4-7 Flowchart and pseudocode for cell phone billing program

```
start
   Declarations
      num customerId
      num callsMade
      num callMinutes
      num customerBill
      num CALLS = 100
      num MINUTES = 500
      num BASIC_SERVICE = 30.00
      num PREMIUM = 20.00
   housekeeping()
   while not eof
      detailLoop()
   endwhile
   finish()
stop

housekeeping()
   output "Phone payment calculator"
   input customerId, callsMade, callMinutes
return

detailLoop()
   customerBill = BASIC_SERVICE
   if callsMade > CALLS then
      if callMinutes > MINUTES then
         customerBill = customerBill + PREMIUM
      endif
   endif
   output customerId, callsMade, " calls made; used ",
      callMinutes, " minutes. Total bill $", customerBill
   input customerId, callsMade, callMinutes
return

finish()
   output "Program ended"
return
```

Figure 4-7 Flowchart and pseudocode for cell phone billing program (continued)

In the cell phone billing program, the customer data is retrieved from a file. This eliminates the need for prompts and keeps the program shorter so you can concentrate on the decision-making process. If this was an interactive program, you would use a prompt before each input statement. Chapter 7 covers file processing and explains a few additional steps you can take when working with files.

A series of nested if statements is also called a **cascading if statement**.

Most languages allow you to use a variation of the decision structure called the *case structure* when you must nest a series of decisions about a single variable. Appendix F contains information about the case structure.

In Figure 4-7, the appropriate variables and constants are declared, and then the housekeeping() module displays an introductory heading and gets the first set of input data. After control returns to the mainline logic, the eof condition is tested, and if it is not eof, the detailLoop() module executes. In the detailLoop() module, the customer's bill is set to the standard fee, and then the nested decision executes. In the nested if structure in Figure 4-7, the expression callsMade > CALLS is evaluated first. If this expression is true, only then is the second Boolean expression (callMinutes > MINUTES) evaluated. If that expression is also true, then the $20 premium is added to the customer's bill. If neither of the tested conditions is true, the customer's bill value is never altered, retaining the initially assigned value of $30.

Nesting AND Decisions for Efficiency

When you nest decisions because the resulting action requires that two conditions be true, you must decide which of the two decisions to make first. Logically, either selection in an AND decision can come first. However, when there are two selections, you often can improve your program's performance by correctly choosing which selection to make first.

For example, Figure 4-8 shows two ways to design the nested decision structure that assigns a premium to customer bills if they make more than 100 cell phone calls and use more than 500 minutes in a billing period. The program can ask about calls made first, eliminate customers who have not made more than the minimum, and ask about the minutes used only for customers who "pass" the minimum calls test. Or, you could ask about the minutes first, eliminate those who do not qualify, and ask about the number of calls only for customers who "pass" the minutes test. Either way, only customers who exceed both limits must pay the premium. Does it make a difference which question is asked first? As far as the result goes, no. Either way, the same customers pay the premium—those who qualify on the basis of both criteria. As far as program efficiency goes, however, it *might* make a difference which question is asked first.

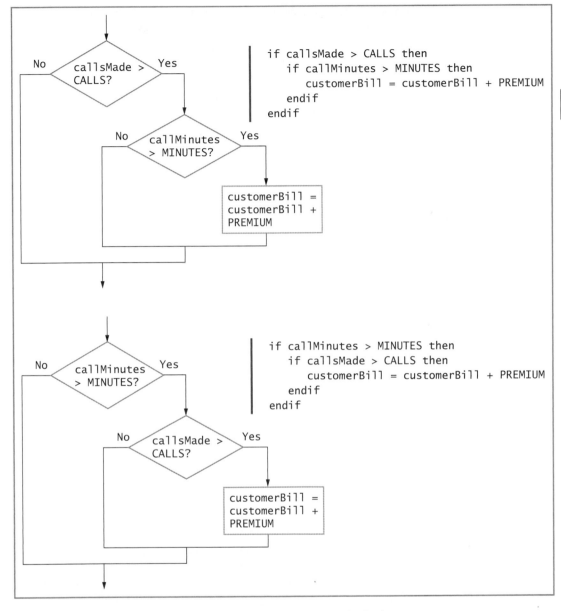

Figure 4-8 Two ways to produce cell phone bills using identical criteria

Assume you know that out of 1000 cell phone customers, about 90 percent, or 900, make more than 100 calls in a billing period. Assume you also know that only about half the 1000 customers, or 500, use more than 500 minutes of call time.

If you use the logic shown first in Figure 4-8, and you need to produce 1000 phone bills, the first question, `callsMade > CALLS?`, will execute 1000 times. For approximately 90 percent of the customers, or 900 of them, the answer is `true`, so 100 customers are eliminated from the premium assignment, and 900 proceed to the next question about the minutes used. Only about half the customers use more than 500 minutes, so 450 of the 900 pay the premium, and it takes 1900 questions to identify them.

Using the alternate logic shown second in Figure 4-8, the first question, `callMinutes > MINUTES?`, will also be asked 1000 times—once for each customer. Because only about half the customers use the high number of minutes, only 500 will "pass" this test and proceed to the question for number of calls made. Then, about 90 percent of the 500, or 450 customers, will pass the second test and be billed the premium amount. It takes 1500 questions to identify the 450 premium-paying customers.

Whether you use the first or second decision order in Figure 4-8, the same 450 employees who satisfy both criteria pay the premium. The difference is that when you ask about the number of calls first, the program must ask 400 more questions than when you ask about the minutes used first.

The 400-question difference between the first and second set of decisions doesn't take much time on most computers. But it does take *some* time, and if a corporation has hundreds of thousands of customers instead of only 1000, or if many such decisions have to be made within a program, performance time can be significantly improved by asking questions in the more efficient order.

Watch the video *Writing Efficient Nested Selections.*

Often, when you must make nested decisions, you have no idea which event is more likely to occur; in that case, you can legitimately ask either question first. However, if you do know the probabilities of the conditions, or can make a reasonable guess, the general rule is: *In an AND decision, first ask the question that is less likely to be true.* This eliminates as many instances of the second decision as possible, which speeds up processing time.

Using the AND Operator

Most programming languages allow you to ask two or more questions in a single comparison by using a **conditional AND operator**, or more simply, an **AND operator** that joins decisions in a single statement. For example, if you want to bill an extra amount to cell phone customers who make more than 100 calls that total more than 500 minutes in a billing period, you can use nested decisions, as shown in the previous section, or you can include both decisions in a single statement by writing the following question:

```
callsMade > CALLS AND callMinutes > MINUTES?
```

When you use one or more AND operators to combine two or more Boolean expressions, each Boolean expression must be true for the entire expression to be evaluated as true. For example, if you ask, "Are you a native-born U.S. citizen and are you at least 35 years old?", the answer to both parts of the question must be "yes" before the response can be a single, summarizing "yes." If either part of the expression is false, then the entire expression is false.

One tool that can help you understand the AND operator is a truth table. **Truth tables** are diagrams used in mathematics and logic to help describe the truth of an entire expression based on the truth of its parts. Table 4-2 shows a truth table that lists all the possibilities with an AND decision. As the table shows, for any two expressions x and y, the expression x AND y is true only if both x and y are individually true. If either x or y alone is false, or if both are false, then the expression x AND y is false.

The conditional AND operator in Java, C++, and C# consists of two ampersands, with no spaces between them (&&). In Visual Basic, you use the word And.

147

x	y	x AND y
True	True	True
True	False	False
False	True	False
False	False	False

Table 4-2   Truth table for the AND operator

If the programming language you use allows an AND operator, you must realize that the question you place first (to the left of the operator) is the one that will be asked first, and cases that are eliminated based on the first question will not proceed to the second question. In other words, each part of an expression that uses an AND operator is evaluated only as far as necessary to determine whether the entire expression is true or false. This feature is called **short-circuit evaluation**. The computer can ask only one question at a time; even when your pseudocode looks like the first example in Figure 4-9, the computer will execute the logic shown in the second example.

You are never required to use the AND operator because using nested if statements can always achieve the same result, but using the AND operator often makes your code more concise, less error-prone, and easier to understand.

Using an AND operator does not eliminate your responsibility for determining which condition to test first. Even when you use an AND operator, the computer makes decisions one at a time, and makes them in the order you ask them. If the first question in an AND expression evaluates to false, then the entire expression is false, and the second question is not even tested.

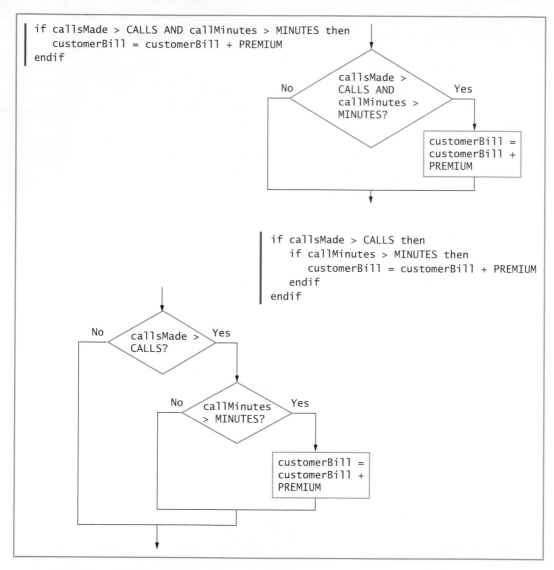

```
if callsMade > CALLS AND callMinutes > MINUTES then
    customerBill = customerBill + PREMIUM
endif
```

```
if callsMade > CALLS then
    if callMinutes > MINUTES then
        customerBill = customerBill + PREMIUM
    endif
endif
```

Figure 4-9   Using an AND operator and the logic behind it

Avoiding Common Errors in an AND Selection

When you need to satisfy two or more criteria to initiate an event in a program, you must make sure that the second decision is made entirely within the first decision. For example, if a program's objective is to add a $20 premium to the bill of cell phone customers who exceed 100 calls and 500 minutes in a billing period, then the program segment shown in Figure 4-10 contains three different types of logic errors.

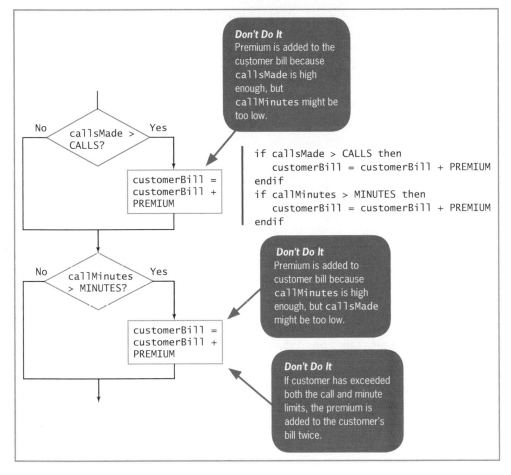

Figure 4-10   Incorrect logic to add a $20 premium to the bills of cell phone customers who meet two criteria

The logic in Figure 4-10 shows that $20 is added to the bill of a customer who makes too many calls. This customer should not necessarily be billed extra—the customer's minutes might be below the cutoff for the $20 premium. In addition, a customer who has made few calls is not eliminated from the second question. Instead, all customers are subjected to the minutes question, and some are assigned the premium even though they might not have passed the criterion for number of calls made. Additionally, any customer who passes both tests has the premium added to his bill twice. For many reasons, the logic shown in Figure 4-10 is *not* correct for this problem.

When you use the AND operator in most languages, you must provide a complete Boolean expression on each side of the operator. In other words, `callMinutes > 100 AND callMinutes < 200` would be a valid expression to find `callMinutes` between 100 and 200. However, `callMinutes > 100 AND < 200` would not be valid because what follows the AND operator (`< 200`) is not a complete Boolean expression.

To override the default precedence of the AND operator over the OR operator, or simply for clarity, you can surround each Boolean expression in a compound expression with its own set of parentheses. Use this format if it is clearer to you. For example, you might write the following:

```
if (callMinutes > MINUTES) AND (callsMade > CALLS)
   customerBill = customerBill + PREMIUM
endif
```

TWO TRUTHS & A LIE

Understanding AND Logic

1. When you nest decisions because the resulting action requires that two conditions be true, either decision logically can be made first and the same selections will occur.

2. When two selections are required for an action to take place, you often can improve your program's performance by appropriately choosing which selection to make first.

3. To improve efficiency in a nested selection in which two conditions must be true for some action to occur, you should first ask the question that is more likely to be true.

The false statement is # 3. For efficiency in a nested selection, you should first ask the question that is less likely to be true.

Understanding OR Logic

Sometimes you want to take action when one *or* the other of two conditions is true. This is called an **OR decision** because either one condition *or* some other condition must be met in order for an event to take place. If someone asks, "Are you free for dinner Friday or Saturday?", only one of the two conditions has to be true for the answer to the whole question to be "yes"; only if the answers to both halves of the question are false is the value of the entire expression false.

For example, suppose you want to add $20 to the bills of cell phone customers who either make more than 100 calls or use more than 500 minutes. Figure 4-11 shows the altered detailLoop() module of the billing program that accomplishes this objective.

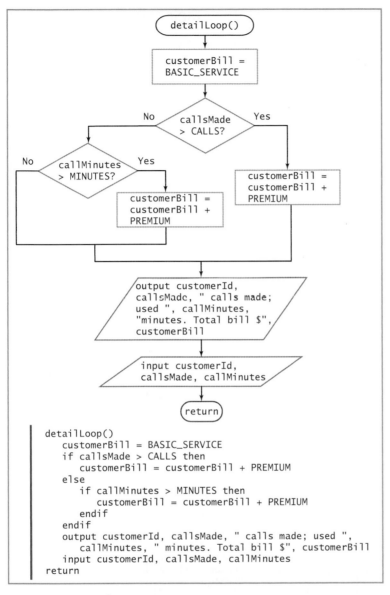

```
detailLoop()
    customerBill = BASIC_SERVICE
    if callsMade > CALLS then
        customerBill = customerBill + PREMIUM
    else
        if callMinutes > MINUTES then
            customerBill = customerBill + PREMIUM
        endif
    endif
    output customerId, callsMade, " calls made; used ",
        callMinutes, " minutes. Total bill $", customerBill
    input customerId, callsMade, callMinutes
return
```

Figure 4-11 Flowchart and pseudocode for cell phone billing program in which a customer must meet one or both of two criteria to be billed a premium

The `detailLoop()` in the program in Figure 4-11 asks the question `callsMade > CALLS?`, and if the result is true, the extra amount is added to the customer's bill. Because just making too many calls (more than 100) is enough for the customer to incur the premium, there is no need for further questioning. If the customer has not made more than 100 calls, only then does the program need to ask whether `callMinutes > MINUTES` is true. If the customer did not make over 100 calls, but used more than 500 minutes nevertheless, then the premium amount is added to the customer's bill.

Writing OR Decisions for Efficiency

As with an AND selection, when you use an OR selection, you can choose to ask either question first. For example, you can add an extra $20 to the bills of customers who meet one or the other of two criteria using the logic in either part of Figure 4-12.

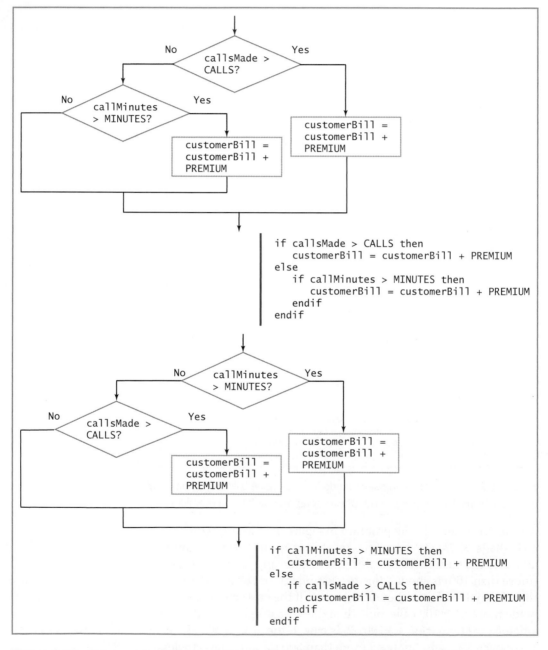

```
if callsMade > CALLS then
    customerBill = customerBill + PREMIUM
else
    if callMinutes > MINUTES then
        customerBill = customerBill + PREMIUM
    endif
endif
```

```
if callMinutes > MINUTES then
    customerBill = customerBill + PREMIUM
else
    if callsMade > CALLS then
        customerBill = customerBill + PREMIUM
    endif
endif
```

Figure 4-12 Two ways to assign a premium to bills of customers who meet one of two criteria

You might have guessed that one of these selections is superior to the other when you have some background information about the relative likelihood of each condition you are testing. For example, assume you know that out of 1000 cell phone customers, about 90 percent, or 900, make more than 100 calls in a billing period. Assume you also know that only about half the 1000 customers, or 500, use more than 500 minutes of call time.

When you use the logic shown in the first half of Figure 4-12, you first ask about the calls made. For 900 customers the answer is true, and you add the premium to their bills. Only about 100 sets of customer data continue to the next question regarding the call minutes, where about 50 percent of the 100, or 50, are billed the extra amount. In the end, you have made 1100 decisions to correctly add premium amounts for 950 customers.

If you use the OR logic in the second half of Figure 4-12, you ask about minutes used first—1000 times, once each for 1000 customers. The result is true for 50 percent, or 500 customers, whose bill is increased. For the other 500 customers, you ask about the number of calls made. For 90 percent of the 500, the result is true, so premiums are added for 450 additional people. In the end, the same 950 customers are billed an extra $20—but after executing 1500 decisions, 400 more decisions than when using the first decision logic.

The general rule is: *In an OR decision, first ask the question that is more likely to be true.* This approach eliminates as many executions of the second decision as possible, and the time it takes to process all the data is decreased. As with the AND situation, in an OR situation, it is more efficient to eliminate as many extra decisions as possible.

Using the OR Operator

If you need to take action when either one or the other of two conditions is met, you can use two separate, nested selection structures, as in the previous examples. However, most programming languages allow you to ask two or more questions in a single comparison by using a **conditional OR operator** (or simply the **OR operator**). For example, you can ask the following question:

```
callsMade > CALLS OR callMinutes > MINUTES
```

When you use the logical OR operator, only one of the listed conditions must be met for the resulting action to take place. Table 4-3 shows the truth table for the OR operator. As you can see in the table, the entire expression x OR y is false only when x and y each are false individually.

C#, C++, C, and Java use the symbol || as the logical OR operator. In Visual Basic, the operator is Or.

As with the AND operator, most programming languages require a complete Boolean expression on each side of the OR operator.

x	y	x OR y
True	True	True
True	False	True
False	True	True
False	False	False

Table 4-3   Truth table for the OR operator

If the programming language you use supports the OR operator, you still must realize that the question you place first is the question that will be asked first, and cases that pass the test of the first question will not proceed to the second question. As with the AND operator, this feature is called short-circuiting. The computer can ask only one question at a time; even when you write code, as shown at the top of Figure 4-13, the computer will execute the logic shown at the bottom.

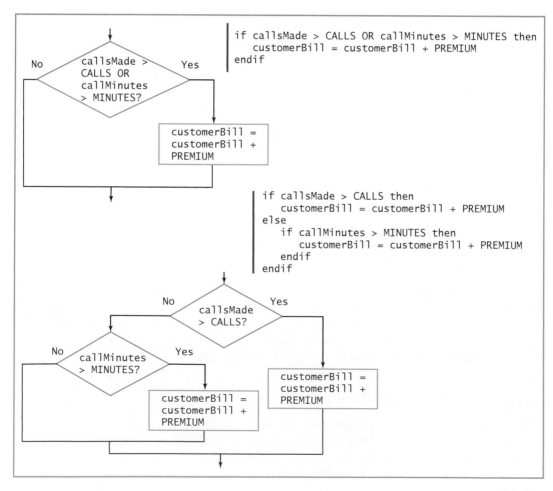

Figure 4-13   Using an OR operator and the logic behind it

Avoiding Common Errors in an OR Selection

You might have noticed that the assignment statement `customerBill = customerBill + PREMIUM` appears twice in the decision-making processes in Figures 4-12 and 4-13. When you create a flowchart, the temptation is to draw the logic to look like Figure 4-14. Logically, you might argue that the flowchart in Figure 4-14 is correct because the correct customers are billed the extra $20. However, this flowchart is not structured. The second question is not a self-contained structure with one entry and exit point; instead, the flowline "breaks out" of the inner selection structure to join the true side of the outer selection structure.

If you do not understand why the flowchart segment in Figure 4-14 is unstructured, review Chapter 3.

155

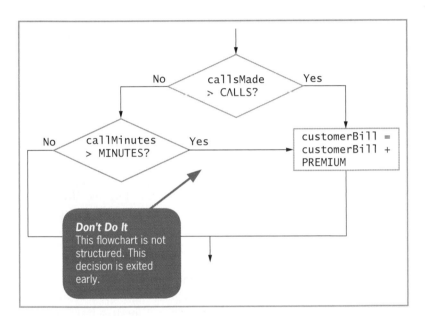

Figure 4-14 Unstructured flowchart for determining customer cell phone bill

An additional source of error that is specific to the OR selection stems from a problem with language and the way people use it more casually than computers do. When your boss wants to add an extra amount to bills of cell phone customers who have made more than 100 calls or used more than 500 minutes, she is likely to say, "Add $20 to the bill of anyone who makes more than 100 calls and to anyone who has used more than 500 minutes." Her request contains the word "and" between two types of people—those who made many calls and those who used many minutes—placing the emphasis on the people. However, each decision you make is about the added $20 for a single customer who has met one criterion *or* the other *or* both. In other words, the OR condition is between each customer's attributes, and not between different customers. Instead of the manager's previous statement, it would be clearer if she said, "Add $20 to the bill of anyone who has made more than 100 calls or has used more than 500 minutes," but you can't count on people to speak like computers. As a programmer, you have the job of clarifying what really is being requested. Often, a casual request for A *and* B logically means a request for A *or* B.

The way we casually use English can cause another type of error when you are required to find whether a value falls between two other values. For example, a movie theater manager might say, "Provide a discount to patrons who are under 13 years old and to those who are over 64 years old; otherwise, charge the full price." Because the manager has used the word "and" in the request, you might be tempted to create the decision shown in Figure 4-15; however, this logic will not provide a discounted price for any movie patron. You must remember that every time the decision is made in Figure 4-15, it is made for a single movie patron. If `patronAge` contains a value lower than 13, then it cannot possibly contain a value over 64. Similarly, if it contains a value over 64, there is no way it can contain a lesser value. Therefore, no value could be stored in `patronAge` for which both parts of the AND question could be true—and the price will never be set to the discounted price for any patron. Figure 4-16 shows the correct logic.

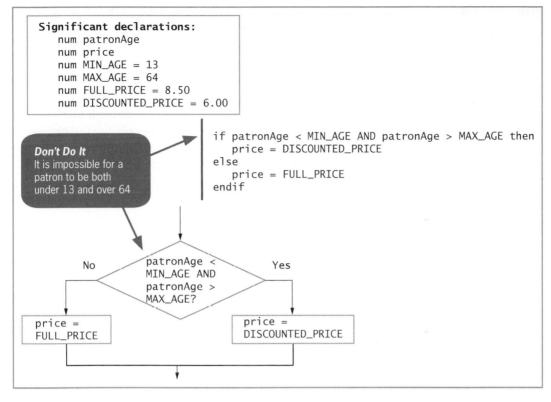

Figure 4-15 Incorrect logic that attempts to provide a discount for young and old movie patrons

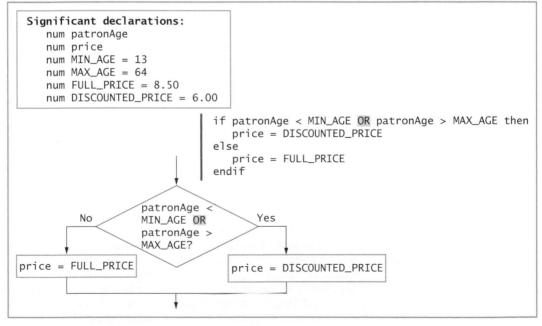

Figure 4-16 Correct logic that provides a discount for young and old movie patrons

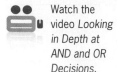 Watch the video *Looking in Depth at AND and OR Decisions.*

A similar error can occur in your logic if the theater manager says something like, "Don't give a discount—that is, charge full price—if a patron is over 12 or under 65." Because the word "or" appears in the request, you might plan your logic to resemble Figure 4-17. No patron ever receives a discount, because every patron is either over 12 or under 65. Remember, in an OR decision, only one of the conditions needs to be true for the entire expression to be evaluated as true. So, for example, because a patron who is 10 is under 65, the full price is charged, and because a patron who is 70 is over 12, the full price also is charged. Figure 4-18 shows the correct logic for this decision.

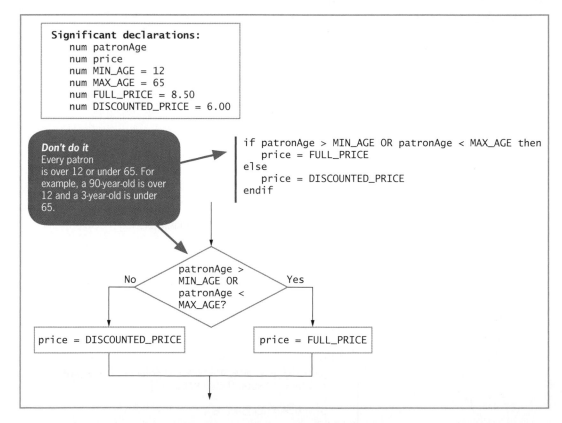

Significant declarations:
```
num patronAge
num price
num MIN_AGE = 12
num MAX_AGE = 65
num FULL_PRICE = 8.50
num DISCOUNTED_PRICE = 6.00
```

Don't do it
Every patron is over 12 or under 65. For example, a 90-year-old is over 12 and a 3-year-old is under 65.

```
if patronAge > MIN_AGE OR patronAge < MAX_AGE then
    price = FULL_PRICE
else
    price = DISCOUNTED_PRICE
endif
```

patronAge > MIN_AGE OR patronAge < MAX_AGE?

No → price = DISCOUNTED_PRICE

Yes → price = FULL_PRICE

Figure 4-17 Incorrect logic that attempts to charge full price for patrons whose age is over 12 and under 65

 Besides AND and OR operators, most languages support a NOT operator. You use the **logical NOT operator** to reverse the meaning of a Boolean expression. For example, the statement `if NOT (age < 21) output "OK"` outputs "OK" when `age` is greater than or equal to 21. The NOT operator is unary instead of binary—that is, you do not use it between two expressions, but you use it in front of a single expression. In C++, Java, and C#, the exclamation point is the symbol used for the NOT operator. In Visual Basic, the operator is `Not`.

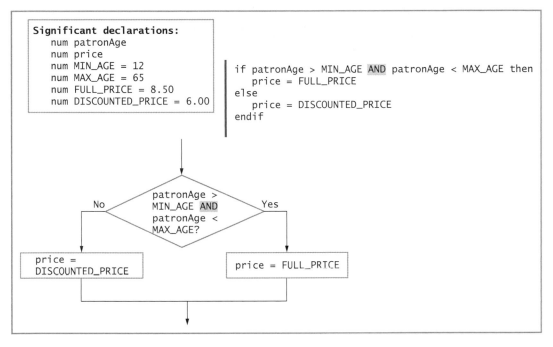

```
Significant declarations:
   num patronAge
   num price
   num MIN_AGE = 12
   num MAX_AGE = 65
   num FULL_PRICE = 8.50
   num DISCOUNTED_PRICE = 6.00
```

```
if patronAge > MIN_AGE AND patronAge < MAX_AGE then
   price = FULL_PRICE
else
   price = DISCOUNTED_PRICE
endif
```

Figure 4-18   Correct logic that charges full price for patrons whose age is over 12 and under 65

TWO TRUTHS & A LIE

Understanding OR Logic

1. In an OR selection, two or more conditions must be met in order for an event to take place.

2. When you use an OR selection, you can choose to ask either question first and still achieve a usable program.

3. The general rule is: In an OR decision, first ask the question that is more likely to be true.

The false statement is #1. In an OR selection, only one of two conditions must be met in order for an event to take place.

Making Selections within Ranges

You often need to make selections based on a variable falling within a range of values. For example, suppose your company provides various customer discounts based on the number of items ordered, as shown in Figure 4-19.

Items Ordered	Discount Rate (%)
0 to 10	0
11 to 24	10
25 to 50	15
51 or more	20

Figure 4-19 Discount rates based on items ordered

When you write the program that determines a discount rate based on the number of items, you could make hundreds of decisions, such as itemQuantity = 1?, itemQuantity = 2?, and so on. However, it is more convenient to find the correct discount rate by using a range check.

When you use a **range check**, you compare a variable to a series of values that mark the limiting ends of ranges. To perform a range check, make comparisons using either the lowest or highest value in each range of values. For example, to find each discount rate listed in Figure 4-19, you can use one of the following techniques:

- Make comparisons using the low ends of the ranges.

  - You can ask: Is itemQuantity less than 11? If not, is it less than 25? If not, is it less than 51? (If the value could be negative, you would also check for values less than 0 and take action if necessary.)

  - You can ask: Is itemQuantity greater than or equal to 51? If not, is it greater than or equal to 25? If not, is it greater than or equal to 11? (If the value could be negative, you would also check for values greater than or equal to 0 and take action if necessary.)

- Make comparisons using the high ends of the ranges.

  - You can ask: Is itemQuantity greater than 50? If not, is it greater than 24? If not, is it greater than 10? (If there is a maximum allowed value for itemQuantity, you would also check for values greater than that limit and take action if necessary.

  - You can ask: Is itemQuantity less than or equal to 10? If not, is it less than or equal to 24? If not, is it less than or equal to 50? (If there is a maximum allowed value for itemQuantity, you would also check for values less than or equal to that limit and take action if necessary.

Figure 4-20 shows the flowchart and pseudocode that represent the logic for a program that determines the correct discount for each order quantity. In the decision-making process, itemsOrdered is compared to the high end of the lowest-range group (RANGE1). If itemsOrdered is less than or equal to that value, then you know the correct discount, DISCOUNT1; if not, you continue checking. If itemsOrdered is less than or equal to the high end of the next range (RANGE2), then the customer's discount is DISCOUNT2; if not, you continue checking, and the customer's discount eventually is set to DISCOUNT3 or DISCOUNT4.

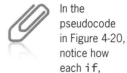 In the pseudocode in Figure 4-20, notice how each if, else, and endif group aligns vertically.

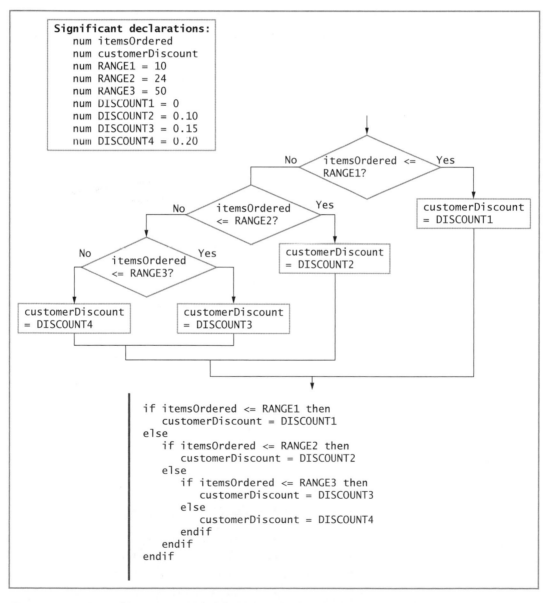

Figure 4-20   Flowchart and pseudocode of logic that selects correct discount based on items

In computer memory, a percent sign (%) is not stored with a value that represents a percentage. Instead, the mathematical equivalent is stored. For example, 15% is stored as 0.15.

For example, consider an order for 30 items. The expression `itemsOrdered <= RANGE1` evaluates as `false`, so the `else` clause of the decision executes. There, `itemsOrdered <= RANGE2` also evaluates to `false`, so its `else` clause executes. The expression `itemsOrdered <= RANGE3` is `true`, so `customerDiscount` becomes `DISCOUNT3`, which is 0.15. Walk through the logic with other values for `itemsOrdered` and verify for yourself that the correct discount is applied each time.

Avoiding Common Errors When Using Range Checks

When new programmers perform range checks, they are prone to including logic that has too many decisions, entailing more work than is necessary.

Figure 4-21 shows a program segment that contains a range check in which the programmer has asked one question too many—the shaded question in the figure. If you know that `itemsOrdered` is not less than or equal to `RANGE1`, not less than or equal to `RANGE2`, and not less than or equal to `RANGE3`, then `itemsOrdered` must be greater than `RANGE3`. Asking whether `itemsOrdered` is greater than `RANGE3` is a waste of time; no customer order can ever travel the logical path on the far left of the flowchart. You might say such a path is a **dead** or **unreachable path,** and that the statements written there constitute dead or unreachable code. Although a program that contains such logic will execute and assign the correct discount to customers who order more than 50 items, providing such a path is inefficient.

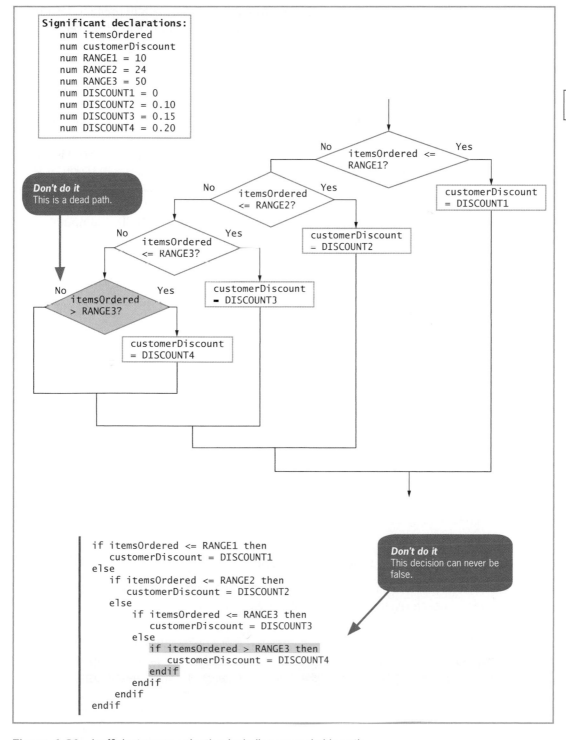

Significant declarations:
```
num itemsOrdered
num customerDiscount
num RANGE1 = 10
num RANGE2 = 24
num RANGE3 = 50
num DISCOUNT1 = 0
num DISCOUNT2 = 0.10
num DISCOUNT3 = 0.15
num DISCOUNT4 = 0.20
```

Don't do it
This is a dead path.

itemsOrdered <= RANGE1?   No   Yes

customerDiscount = DISCOUNT1

itemsOrdered <= RANGE2?   No   Yes

customerDiscount = DISCOUNT2

itemsOrdered <= RANGE3?   No   Yes

customerDiscount = DISCOUNT3

itemsOrdered > RANGE3?   No   Yes

customerDiscount = DISCOUNT4

```
if itemsOrdered <= RANGE1 then
   customerDiscount = DISCOUNT1
else
   if itemsOrdered <= RANGE2 then
      customerDiscount = DISCOUNT2
   else
      if itemsOrdered <= RANGE3 then
         customerDiscount = DISCOUNT3
      else
         if itemsOrdered > RANGE3 then
            customerDiscount = DISCOUNT4
         endif
      endif
   endif
endif
```

Don't do it
This decision can never be false.

Figure 4-21   Inefficient range selection including unreachable path

When you ask questions of human beings, you sometimes ask a question to which you already know the answer. For example, a good trial lawyer seldom asks a question in court if the answer will be a surprise. With computer logic, however, such questions are an inefficient waste of time.

Beginning programmers sometimes justify their use of unnecessary questions as "just making really sure." Such caution is unnecessary when writing computer logic.

In Figure 4-21, it is easier to see the useless path in the flowchart than in the pseudocode representation of the same logic. However, anytime you use an `if` without an `else`, you are doing nothing when the question's answer is false.

Another error that programmers make when writing the logic to perform a range check also involves asking unnecessary questions. You should never ask a question if there is only one possible answer or outcome. Figure 4-22 shows an inefficient range selection that asks two unneeded questions. In the figure, if `itemsOrdered` is less than or equal to RANGE1, `customerDiscount` is set to DISCOUNT1. If `itemsOrdered` is not less than or equal to RANGE1, then it must be greater than RANGE1, so the next decision (shaded in the figure) does not have to check for values greater than RANGE1. The computer logic will never execute the shaded decision unless `itemsOrdered` is already greater than RANGE1—that is, unless it follows the `false` branch of the first selection. If you use the logic in Figure 4-22, you are wasting computer time asking a question that has previously been answered. The same logic applies to the second shaded decision in Figure 4-22.

TWO TRUTHS & A LIE

Making Selections within Ranges

1. When you perform a range check, you compare a variable to every value in a series of ranges.

2. You can perform a range check by making comparisons using the lowest value in each range of values you are using.

3. You can perform a range check by making comparisons using the highest value in each range of values you are using.

The false statement is #1. When you use a range check, you compare a variable to a series of values that represents the ends of ranges. Depending on your logic, you can use either the high or low end of each range.

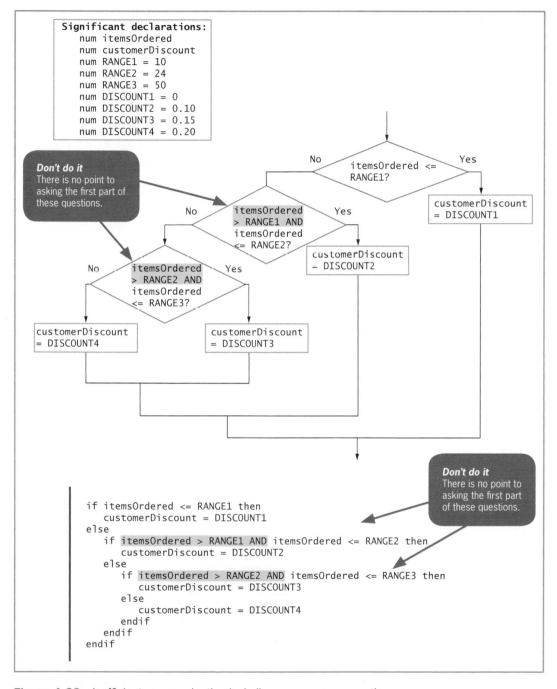

Significant declarations:
```
num itemsOrdered
num customerDiscount
num RANGE1 = 10
num RANGE2 = 24
num RANGE3 = 50
num DISCOUNT1 = 0
num DISCOUNT2 = 0.10
num DISCOUNT3 = 0.15
num DISCOUNT4 = 0.20
```

Don't do it
There is no point to asking the first part of these questions.

Don't do it
There is no point to asking the first part of these questions.

```
if itemsOrdered <= RANGE1 then
   customerDiscount = DISCOUNT1
else
   if itemsOrdered > RANGE1 AND itemsOrdered <= RANGE2 then
      customerDiscount = DISCOUNT2
   else
      if itemsOrdered > RANGE2 AND itemsOrdered <= RANGE3 then
         customerDiscount = DISCOUNT3
      else
         customerDiscount = DISCOUNT4
      endif
   endif
endif
```

Figure 4-22 Inefficient range selection including unnecessary questions

Understanding Precedence When Combining AND and OR Operators

Most programming languages allow you to combine as many AND and OR operators in an expression as you need. For example, assume you need to achieve a score of at least 75 on each of three tests to pass a course. You can declare a constant MIN_SCORE equal to 75 and test the multiple conditions with a statement like the following:

```
if score1 >= MIN_SCORE AND score2 >= MIN_SCORE AND
score3 >= MIN_SCORE then
    classGrade = "Pass"
else
    classGrade = "Fail"
endif
```

On the other hand, if you are enrolled in a course in which you need to pass only one of three tests to pass the course, then the logic is as follows:

```
if score1 >= MIN_SCORE OR score2 >= MIN_SCORE OR score3 >=
MIN_SCORE then
    classGrade = "Pass"
else
    classGrade = "Fail"
endif
```

The logic becomes more complicated when you combine AND and OR operators within the same statement. When you do, the AND operators take **precedence**, meaning their Boolean values are evaluated first.

 In Chapter 2 you learned that in every programming language, multiplication has precedence over addition in an arithmetic statement. That is, the value of 2 + 3 * 4 is 14 because the multiplication occurs before the addition. Similarly, in every programming language, AND has precedence over OR because computer circuitry treats the AND operator as multiplication and the OR operator as addition.

For example, consider a program that determines whether a movie theater patron can purchase a discounted ticket. Assume discounts are allowed for children and senior citizens who attend "G"-rated movies. The following code looks reasonable, but it produces incorrect results because the expression that contains the AND operator (see shading) evaluates before the one that contains the OR operator.

Don't Do It
The AND evaluates first, which is not the intention.

```
if age <= 12 OR age >= 65 AND rating = "G" then
    output "Discount applies"
endif
```

For example, assume a movie patron is 10 years old and the movie rating is "R". The patron should not receive a discount (or be allowed to see the movie!). However, within the `if` statement, the part of the expression that contains the `AND`, `age >= 65 AND rating = "G"`, is evaluated first. For a 10-year-old and an "R"-rated movie, the question is false (on both counts), so the entire `if` statement becomes the equivalent of the following:

```
if age <= 12 OR aFalseExpression then
    output "Discount applies"
endif
```

Because the patron is 10, `age <= 12` is `true`, so the original `if` statement becomes the equivalent of:

```
if aTrueExpression OR aFalseExpression then
    output "Discount applies"
endif
```

The combination `true OR false` evaluates as `true`. Therefore, the string `"Discount applies"` prints when it should not.

Many programming languages allow you to use parentheses to correct the logic and force the `OR` expression to be evaluated first, as shown in the following pseudocode.

```
if (age <= 12 OR age >= 65) AND rating = "G" then
    output "Discount applies"
endif
```

With the added parentheses, if the patron's `age` is 12 or under `OR` the `age` is 65 or over, the expression is evaluated as:

```
if aTrueExpression AND rating = "G" then
    output "Discount applies"
endif
```

When the age value qualifies a patron for a discount, then the rating value must also be acceptable before the discount applies. This was the original intention.

You can use the following techniques to avoid confusion when mixing `AND` and `OR` operators:

- You can use parentheses to override the default order of operations, as in the movie discount example.

- You can use parentheses for clarity even though they do not change what the order of operations would be without them. For example, if a customer should be between 12 and 19 or have a school ID to receive a high school discount, you can use the expression `(age > 12 AND age < 19) OR validId = "Yes"`, even though the evaluation would be the same without the parentheses.

- You can use nesting if statements instead of using AND and OR operators. With the flowchart and pseudocode shown in Figure 4-23, it is clear which movie patrons receive the discount. In the flowchart, you can see that the OR is nested entirely within the Yes branch of the rating = "G"? selection. Similarly, in the pseudocode in Figure 4-23, you can see by the alignment that if the rating is not "G", the logic proceeds directly to the last endif statement, bypassing any checking of age at all.

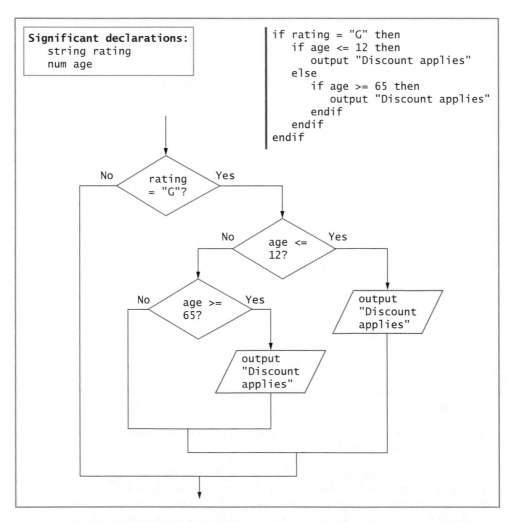

Significant declarations:
```
   string rating
   num age
```

```
if rating = "G" then
    if age <= 12 then
        output "Discount applies"
    else
        if age >= 65 then
            output "Discount applies"
        endif
    endif
endif
```

Figure 4-23 Nested decisions that determine movie patron discount

---

TWO TRUTHS & A LIE

Understanding Precedence When Combining AND and OR Operators

1. Most programming languages allow you to combine as many AND and OR operators in an expression as you need.

2. When you combine AND and OR operators, the OR operators take precedence, meaning their Boolean values are evaluated first.

3. You can always avoid the confusion of mixing AND and OR decisions by nesting if statements instead of using AND and OR operators.

The false statement is #2. When you combine AND and OR operators, the AND operators take precedence, meaning the Boolean values of their expressions are evaluated first.

Chapter Summary

- Every decision you make in a computer program involves evaluating a Boolean expression. You can use if-then-else or if-then structures to choose between two possible outcomes. You use if-then-else structures when action is required whether the selection is true or false. Use if-then structures when there is only one outcome for the question for which action is required.

- You can use relational comparison operators to compare two operands of the same type. The standard comparison operators are =, >, <, >=, <=, and <>.

- In an AND decision, two conditions must be true for a resulting action to take place. An AND decision requires a nested decision, or a nested if. In an AND decision, it is most efficient to first ask the question that is less likely to be true. Most programming languages allow you to ask two or more questions in a single comparison by using a conditional AND operator.

- In an OR decision, at least one of two conditions must be true for a resulting action to take place. In an OR decision, first ask the question that is more likely to be true. Most programming languages allow you to ask two or more questions in a single comparison by using a conditional OR operator.

- To perform a range check, make comparisons with either the lowest or highest value in each range of values you are using. Common errors that occur when programmers perform range checks include asking unnecessary and previously answered questions.

- When you combine AND and OR operators in an expression, the AND operators take precedence, meaning their Boolean values are evaluated first.

Key Terms

A **Boolean expression** is one that represents only one of two states, usually expressed as true or false.

In an **if-then** decision structure, action is taken only when the Boolean expression in the decision is true.

A **then clause** of a decision holds the action that results when the Boolean expression in the decision is true.

The **else clause** of a decision holds the action or actions that execute only when the Boolean expression in the decision is false.

Relational comparison operators are the symbols that express Boolean comparisons. Examples include =, >, <, >=, <=, and <>. These operators are also called **relational operators** or **comparison operators**.

A **trivial expression** is one that always evaluates to the same value.

A **compound condition** is constructed when you need to ask multiple questions before determining an outcome.

With an **AND decision**, two conditions must both be true for an action to take place.

A **nested decision**, or a **nested if**, is a decision "inside of" another decision.

A series of nested if statements can also be called a **cascading if statement**.

A **conditional AND operator** (or, more simply, an **AND operator**) is a symbol that you use to combine decisions so that two (or more) conditions must be true for an action to occur.

Truth tables are diagrams used in mathematics and logic to help describe the truth of an entire expression based on the truth of its parts.

Short-circuit evaluation is a logical feature in which expressions in each part of a larger expression are evaluated only as far as necessary to determine the final outcome.

An **OR decision** contains two (or more) decisions; if at least one condition is met, the resulting action takes place.

A **conditional OR operator** (or, more simply, an **OR operator**) is a symbol that you use to combine decisions when any one condition can be true for an action to occur.

The **logical NOT operator** is a symbol that reverses the meaning of a Boolean expression.

When you use a **range check**, you compare a variable to a series of values that marks the limiting ends of ranges.

A **dead** or **unreachable path** is a logical path that can never be traveled.

When an operator has **precedence**, it is evaluated before others.

Review Questions

1. The selection statement `if quantity > 100 then discountRate = RATE` is an example of a _____.

   a. dual-alternative selection

   b. single-alternative selection

   c. structured loop

   d. all of these

2. The selection statement `if dayOfWeek = "Sunday" then price = LOWER_PRICE else price = HIGHER_PRICE` is an example of a _____.

   a. dual-alternative selection

   b. single-alternative selection

   c. unary selection

   d. all of the above

3. All selection statements must have _____.

    a. a **then** clause

    b. an **else** clause

    c. both of these

    d. none of these

4. An expression like **amount** < 10 is a(n) _____ expression.

    a. Gregorian

    b. Edwardian

    c. Machiavellian

    d. Boolean

5. Usually, you compare only variables that have the same _____.

    a. type

    b. size

    c. name

    d. value

6. Symbols such as > and < are known as _____ operators.

    a. arithmetic

    b. sequential

    c. relational comparison

    d. scripting accuracy

7. If you could use only three relational comparison operators, you could get by with _____.

    a. greater than, less than, and greater than or equal to

    b. equal to, less than, and greater than

    c. less than, less than or equal to, and not equal to

    d. equal to, not equal to, and less than

8. If a > b is false, then which of the following is always true?

   a. a <= b

   b. a < b

   c. a = b

   d. a >= b

9. Usually, the most difficult comparison operator to work with is _____.

   a. equal to

   b. greater than

   c. less than

   d. not equal to

10. Which of the lettered choices is equivalent to the following decision?

```
if x > 10 then
    if y > 10 then
        output "X"
    endif
endif
```

   a. if x > 10 OR y > 10 then output "X"

   b. if x > 10 AND x > y then output "X"

   c. if y > x then output "X"

   d. if x > 10 AND y > 10 then output "X"

11. The Midwest Sales region of Acme Computer Company consists of five states—Illinois, Indiana, Iowa, Missouri, and Wisconsin. About 50 percent of the regional customers reside in Illinois, 20 percent in Indiana, and 10 percent in each of the other three states. Suppose you have input records containing Acme customer data, including state of residence. To most efficiently select and display all customers who live in the Midwest Sales region, you would ask first about residency in _____.

   a. Illinois

   b. Indiana

   c. either Iowa, Missouri, or Wisconsin—it does not matter which one of these three is first

   d. any of the five states—it does not matter which one is first

12. The Boffo Balloon Company makes helium balloons. Large balloons cost $13.00 a dozen, medium-sized balloons cost $11.00 a dozen, and small balloons cost $8.60 a dozen. About 60 percent of the company's sales are of the smallest balloons, 30 percent are medium, and large balloons constitute only 10 percent of sales. Customer order records include customer information, quantity ordered, and size. To write a program that makes the most efficient determination of an order's price based on size ordered, you should ask first whether the size is _____ .

    a. large

    b. medium

    c. small

    d. It does not matter.

13. The Boffo Balloon Company makes helium balloons in three sizes, 12 colors, and with a choice of 40 imprinted sayings. As a promotion, the company is offering a 25 percent discount on orders of large, red "Happy Valentine's Day" balloons. To most efficiently select the orders to which a discount applies, you would use _____ .

    a. nested if statements using OR logic

    b. nested if statements using AND logic

    c. three completely separate unnested if statements

    d. Not enough information is given.

14. In the following pseudocode, what percentage raise will an employee in Department 5 receive?

```
if department < 3 then
   raise = SMALL_RAISE
else
   if department < 5 then
      raise = MEDIUM_RAISE
   else
      raise = BIG_RAISE
   endif
endif
```

    a. SMALL_RAISE

    b. MEDIUM_RAISE

    c. BIG_RAISE

    d. impossible to tell

15. In the following pseudocode, what percentage raise will an employee in Department 8 receive?

```
if department < 5 then
   raise = SMALL_RAISE
else
   if department < 14 then
      raise = MEDIUM_RAISE
   else
      if department < 9
         raise = BIG_RAISE
      endif
   endif
endif
```

 a. SMALL_RAISE

 b. MEDIUM_RAISE

 c. BIG_RAISE

 d. impossible to tell

16. In the following pseudocode, what percentage raise will an employee in Department 10 receive?

```
if department < 2 then
   raise = SMALL_RAISE
else
   if department < 6 then
      raise = MEDIUM_RAISE
   else
      if department < 10
         raise = BIG_RAISE
      endif
   endif
endif
```

 a. SMALL_RAISE

 b. MEDIUM_RAISE

 c. BIG_RAISE

 d. impossible to tell

17. When you use a range check, you compare a variable to the _____ value in the range.

 a. lowest

 b. middle

 c. highest

 d. lowest or highest

18. If sales = 100, rate = 0.10, and expenses = 50, which of the following expressions is true?

    a. sales >= expenses AND rate < 1

    b. sales < 200 OR expenses < 100

    c. expenses = rate OR sales = rate

    d. two of the above

19. If a is true, b is true, and c is false, which of the following expressions is true?

    a. a OR b AND c

    b. a AND b AND c

    c. a AND b OR c

    d. two of the above

20. If d is true, e is false, and f is false, which of the following expressions is true?

    a. e OR f AND d

    b. f AND d OR e

    c. d OR e AND f

    d. two of the above

Exercises

1. Assume the following variables contain the values shown:

   ```
   numberRed = 100    numberBlue = 200   numberGreen = 300
   wordRed = "Wagon" wordBlue = "Sky"   wordGreen = "Grass"
   ```

   For each of the following Boolean expressions, decide whether the statement is true, false, or illegal.

   a. numberRed = numberBlue?

   b. numberBlue > numberGreen?

   c. numberGreen < numberRed?

   d. numberBlue = wordBlue?

   e. numberGreen = "Green"?

   f. wordRed = "Red"?

   g. wordBlue - "Blue"?

   h. numberRed <= numberGreen?

   i. numberBlue >= 200?

   j. numberGreen >= numberRed + numberBlue?

   k. numberRed > numberBlue AND numberBlue < numberGreen?

   l. numberRed = 100 OR numberRed > numberBlue?

   m. numberGreen < 10 OR numberBlue > 10?

   n. numberBlue = 30 AND numberGreen = 300 OR numberRed = 200?

2. Chocolate Delights Candy Company manufactures several types of candy. Design a flowchart or pseudocode for the following:

   a. A program that accepts a candy name (for example, "chocolate-covered blueberries"), price per pound, and number of pounds sold in the average month, and displays the item's data only if it is a best-selling item. Best-selling items are those that sell more than 2000 pounds per month.

   b. A program that accepts candy data continuously until a sentinel value is entered and displays a list of high-priced, best-selling items. Best-selling items are defined in Exercise 2a. High-priced items are those that sell for $10 per pound or more.

3. Pastoral College is a small college in the Midwest. Design a flowchart or pseudocode for the following:

   a. A program that accepts a student's data as follows: ID number, first and last name, major field of study, and grade point average. Display a student's data if the student's grade point average is below 2.0.

   b. A program that continuously accepts students' data until a sentinel value is entered and displays a list of all students whose grade point averages are below 2.0.

   c. A program for the Literary Honor Society that continuously reads student data and displays every student who is an English major with a grade point average of 3.5 or higher.

4. The Summerville Telephone Company charges 10 cents per minute for all calls outside the customer's area code that last over 20 minutes. All other calls are 13 cents per minute. Design a flowchart or pseudocode for the following:

   a. A program that accepts the following data about one phone call: customer area code (three digits), customer phone number (seven digits), called area code (three digits), called number (seven digits), and call time in minutes (four digits). Display the calling number, called number, and price for the call.

   b. A program that continuously accepts data about phone calls until a sentinel value is entered, and displays all the details only about calls that cost over $10.

   c. A program that continuously accepts data about phone calls until a sentinel value is entered, and displays details only about calls placed from the 212 area code to the 704 area code that last over 20 minutes.

   d. A program that prompts the user for a three-digit area code from which to select phone calls. Then the program continuously accepts phone call data until a sentinel value is entered, and displays data only for phone calls placed to or from the specified area code.

5. The Drive-Rite Insurance Company provides automobile insurance policies for drivers. Design a flowchart or pseudo-code for the following:

   a. A program that accepts insurance policy data, including a policy number; customer last name; customer first name; age; premium due month, day, and year; and number of driver accidents in the last three years. If an entered policy number is not between 1000 and 9999 inclusive, set the policy number to 0. If the month is not between 1 and 12 inclusive, or the day is not correct for the month (for example, not between 1 and 31 for January or 1 and 29 for February), set the month, day, and year to 0. Display the policy data after any revisions have been made.

   b. A program that continuously accepts policy holders' data until a sentinel value has been entered, and displays the data for any policy holder over 35 years old.

   c. A program that accepts policy holders' data and displays the data for any policy holder who is at least 21 years old.

   d. A program that accepts policy holders' data and displays the data for any policy holder no more than 30 years old.

   e. A program that accepts policy holders' data and displays the data for any policy holder whose premium is due no later than March 15 any year.

   f. A program that accepts policy holders' data and displays the data for any policy holder whose premium is due up to and including January 1, 2012.

   g. A program that accepts policy holders' data and displays the data for any policy holder whose premium is due by April 27, 2011.

   h. A program that accepts policy holders' data and displays the data for any policy holder who has a policy number between 1000 and 4000 inclusive, whose policy comes due in April or May of any year, and who has had fewer than three accidents.

6. The Barking Lot is a dog day care center. Design a flowchart or pseudocode for the following:

   a. A program that accepts data for an ID number of a dog's owner, and the name, breed, age, and weight of the dog. Display a bill containing all the input data as well as the weekly day care fee, which is $55 for dogs under 15 pounds, $75 for dogs from 15 to 30 pounds inclusive, $105 for dogs from 31 to 80 pounds inclusive, and $125 for dogs over 80 pounds.

   b. A program that continuously accepts dogs' data until a sentinel value is entered, and displays billing data for each dog.

   c. A program that continuously accepts dogs' data until a sentinel value is entered, and displays billing data for dog owners who owe more than $100.

7. Rick Hammer is a carpenter who wants an application to compute the price of any desk a customer orders, based on the following: desk length and width in inches, type of wood, and number of drawers. The price is computed as follows:

   - The minimum charge for all desks is $200.

   - If the surface (length * width) is over 750 square inches, add $50.

   - If the wood is mahogany, add $150; for oak, add $125. No charge is added for pine.

   - For every drawer in the desk, there is an additional $30 charge.

   Design a flowchart or pseudocode for the following:

   a. A program that accepts data for an order number, customer name, length and width of the desk ordered, type of wood, and number of drawers. Display all the entered data and the final price for the desk.

   b. A program that continuously accepts desk order data and displays all the relevant information for oak desks that are over 36 inches long and have at least one drawer.

8. Black Dot Printing is attempting to organize carpools to save energy. Each input record contains an employee's name and town of residence. Ten percent of the company's employees live in Wonder Lake; 30 percent live in the adjacent town of Woodstock. Black Dot wants to encourage employees who live in either town to drive to work together. Design a flowchart or pseudocode for the following:

    a. A program that accepts an employee's data and displays it with a message that indicates whether the employee is a candidate for the carpool.

    b. A program that continuously accepts employee data until a sentinel value is entered, and displays a list of all employees who are carpool candidates.

9. Diana Lee, a supervisor in a manufacturing company, wants to know which employees have increased their production this year over last year. These employees will receive certificates of commendation and bonuses. Design a flowchart or pseudocode for the following:

    a. A program that continuously accepts each worker's first and last names, this year's number of units produced, and last year's number of units produced. Display each employee with a message indicating whether the employee's production has increased over last year's production.

    b. A program that accepts each worker's data and displays the name and a bonus amount. The bonuses will be distributed as follows:

    If this year's production is greater than last year's production and this year's production is:

- 1000 units or fewer, the bonus is $25.

- 1001 to 3000 units, the bonus is $50.

- 3001 to 6000 units, the bonus is $100.

- 6001 units and up, the bonus is $200.

    c. Modify Exercise 9b to reflect the following new facts, and have the program execute as efficiently as possible:

- Thirty percent of employees have greater production rates this year than last year.

- Sixty percent of employees produce over 6000 units per year; 20 percent produce 3001 to 6000; 15 percent produce 1001 to 3000 units; and only 5 percent produce fewer than 1001.

Find the Bugs

10. Your student disk contains files named DEBUG04-01.txt, DEBUG04-02.txt, and DEBUG04-03.txt. Each file starts with some comments that describe the problem. Comments are lines that begin with two slashes (//). Following the comments, each file contains pseudocode that has one or more bugs you must find and correct.

Game Zone

11. In Chapter 2, you learned that many programming languages allow you to generate a random number between 1 and a limiting value named LIMIT by using a statement similar to randomNumber = random(LIMIT). Create the logic for a guessing game in which the application generates a random number and the player tries to guess it. Display a message indicating whether the player's guess was correct, too high, or too low. (After you finish Chapter 5, you will be able to modify the application so that the user can continue to guess until the correct answer is entered.)

12. Create a lottery game application. Generate three random numbers, each between 0 and 9. Allow the user to guess three numbers. Compare each of the user's guesses to the three random numbers and display a message that includes the user's guess, the randomly determined three digits, and the amount of money the user has won, as follows:

Matching Numbers	Award ($)
Any one matching	10
Two matching	100
Three matching, not in order	1000
Three matching in exact order	1,000,000
No matches	0

Make certain that your application accommodates repeating digits. For example, if a user guesses 1, 2, and 3, and the randomly generated digits are 1, 1, and 1, do not give the user credit for three correct guesses—just one.

Up for Discussion

13. Computer programs can be used to make decisions about your insurability as well as the rates you will be charged for health and life insurance policies. For example, certain pre-existing conditions may raise your insurance premiums considerably. Is it ethical for insurance companies to access your health records and then make insurance decisions about you? Explain your answer.

14. Job applications are sometimes screened by software that makes decisions about a candidate's suitability based on keywords in the applications. Is such screening fair to applicants? Explain your answer.

15. Medical facilities often have more patients waiting for organ transplants than there are available organs. Suppose you have been asked to write a computer program that selects which of several candidates should receive an available organ. What data would you want on file to be able to use in your program, and what decisions would you make based on the data? What data do you think others might use that you would choose not to use?

Looping

In this chapter, you will learn about:

- ◎ The advantages of looping
- ◎ Using a loop control variable
- ◎ Nested loops
- ◎ Avoiding common loop mistakes
- ◎ Using a `for` loop
- ◎ Common loop applications

Understanding the Advantages of Looping

Although making decisions is what makes computers seem intelligent, it's looping that makes computer programming both efficient and worthwhile. When you use a loop, you can write one set of instructions that operates on multiple, separate sets of data.

Recall the loop structure that you learned about in Chapter 3; it looks like Figure 5-1. As long as a Boolean expression remains true, a `while` loop's body executes.

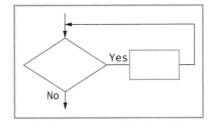

Figure 5-1   The loop structure

Using fewer instructions not only results in less time required for design and coding, but in less compile time and reduced errors.

You have already learned that many programs use a loop to control repetitive tasks. For example, Figure 5-2 shows the basic structure of many business programs. After some housekeeping tasks are taken care of, the detail loop repeats once for every data record that must be processed.

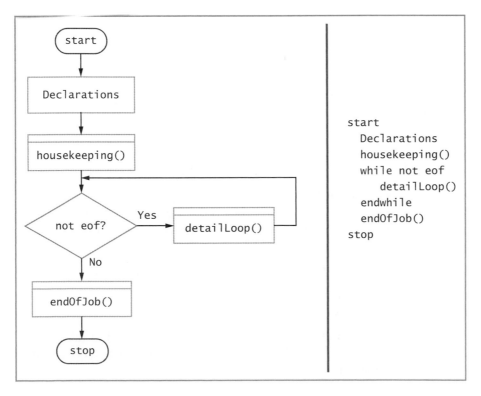

Figure 5-2   The mainline logic common to many business programs

Watch the video *A Quick Introduction to Loops.*

186

For example, Figure 5-2 might represent the mainline logic of a typical payroll program. The first employee's data would be entered in the housekeeping() module, and while the eof condition is not met, the detailLoop() module would perform such tasks as determining regular and overtime pay, and deducting taxes, insurance premiums, charitable contributions, union dues, and other items. Then, after the employee's paycheck is output, the next employee's data would be entered, and the detailLoop() module would repeat. The advantage to having a computer produce payroll checks is that all of the calculation instructions need to be written only once and can be repeated indefinitely.

TWO TRUTHS & A LIE

Understanding the Advantages of Looping

1. When you use a loop, you can write one set of instructions that operates on multiple, separate sets of data.

2. A major advantage of having a computer perform complicated tasks is the ability to repeat them.

3. A loop is a structure that branches in two logical paths before continuing.

The false statement is #3. A loop is a structure that repeats actions while some condition continues.

Using a Loop Control Variable

You can use a while loop to execute a body of statements continuously as long as some condition continues to be true. To make a while loop end correctly, you should declare a variable to control the loop's execution, and three separate actions should occur:

- The **loop control variable** is initialized before entering the loop.

- The loop control variable is tested, and if the result is true, the loop body is entered.

- The body of the loop must take some action that alters the value of the loop control variable (so that the while expression eventually evaluates as false).

When you write a loop, you must control the number of repetitions it performs; if you do not, you run the risk of creating an infinite loop. Commonly, you can control a loop's repetitions in one of two ways:

You first learned about infinite loops in Chapter 1; they are loops that do not end.

- Use a counter to create a definite, counter-controlled loop.

- Use a sentinel value to create an indefinite loop.

The body of a loop might contain any number of statements, including method calls, decisions, and other loops. Once your logic enters the body of a structured loop, the entire loop body must execute. Your program can leave a structured loop only at the comparison that tests the loop control variable.

Using a Definite Loop with a Counter

Figure 5-3 shows a loop that displays "Hello" four times. The variable count is the loop control variable. This loop is a **definite loop** because it executes a definite, predetermined number of times—in this case, four. The loop is a **counted loop** or **counter-controlled loop** because the program keeps track of the number of loop repetitions by counting them.

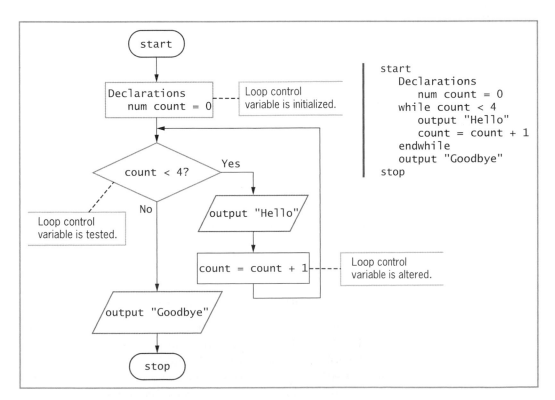

Figure 5-3 A counted while loop that outputs "Hello" four times

Watch the video *Looping*.

188

The loop in Figure 5-3 executes as follows:

- The loop control variable is initialized to 0.

- The `while` expression compares `count` to 4.

- The value of `count` is less than 4, and so the loop body executes. The loop body shown in Figure 5-3 consists of two statements. The first statement displays "Hello" and the second statement adds 1 to `count`.

- The next time `count` is evaluated, its value is 1, which is still less than 4, so the loop body executes again. "Hello" is displayed a second time and `count` becomes 2, "Hello" displays a third time and `count` becomes 3, then "Hello" displays a fourth time and `count` becomes 4. Now when the expression `count<4` evaluates, it is `false`, so the loop ends.

Because you so frequently need to increment a variable, many programming languages contain a shortcut operator for incrementing. You will learn about these shortcut operators when you study a programming language that uses them.

Within a correctly functioning loop's body, you can change the value of the loop control variable in a number of ways. Many loop control variable values are altered by **incrementing**, or adding to them, as in Figure 5-3. Other loops are controlled by reducing, or **decrementing**, a variable and testing whether the value remains greater than some benchmark value. For example, the loop in Figure 5-3 could be rewritten so that `count` is initialized to 4, and reduced by 1 on each pass through the loop. The loop should then continue while `count` remains greater than 0. Loops are also controlled by adding or subtracting values other than 1. For example, to display company profits at five-year intervals for the next 50 years, you would want to add 5 to a loop control variable during each iteration.

The looping logic shown in Figure 5-3 uses a counter. A **counter** is any numeric variable you use to count the number of times an event has occurred. In everyday life, people usually count things starting with 1. Many programmers prefer starting their counted loops with a variable containing a 0 value for two reasons:

- In many computer applications, numbering starts with 0 because of the 0-and-1 nature of computer circuitry.

- When you learn about arrays in Chapter 6, you will discover that array manipulation naturally lends itself to 0-based loops.

Using an Indefinite Loop with a Sentinel Value

Often, the value of a loop control variable is not altered by arithmetic, but instead is altered by user input. For example, perhaps you want to continue performing some task while the user indicates a desire to continue. In that case, you do not know when you write the program whether the loop will be executed two times, 200 times, or not at all. This type of loop is an **indefinite loop**.

Consider an interactive program that displays "Hello" repeatedly as long as the user wants to continue. The loop is indefinite because each time the program executes, the loop might be performed a different number of times. The program appears in Figure 5-4.

 The first **input** statement in the application in Figure 5-4 is a priming input statement. You learned about the priming input statement in Chapter 3.

 The program shown in Figure 5-4 continues to display "Hello" while the user's response is Y. If the user enters anything other than Y, the program ends. The loop could also be written to display while the response is not N. In that case, a user entry of anything other than N would cause the program to continue. In Chapter 1, you learned that a value such as Y or N that stops a loop is called a sentinel value.

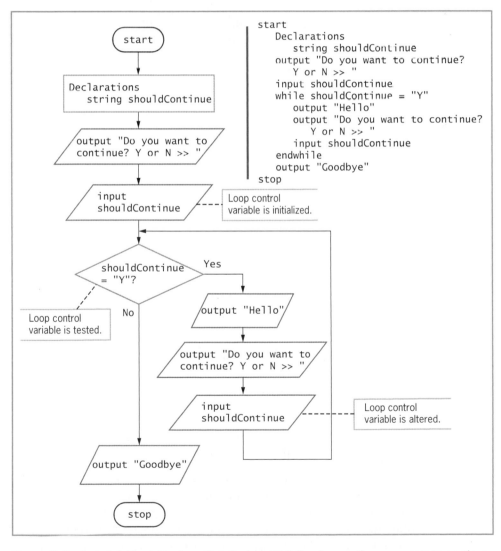

```
start
    Declarations
        string shouldContinue
    output "Do you want to continue?
        Y or N >> "
    input shouldContinue
    while shouldContinue = "Y"
        output "Hello"
        output "Do you want to continue?
            Y or N >> "
        input shouldContinue
    endwhile
    output "Goodbye"
stop
```

Figure 5-4 An indefinite `while` loop that displays "Hello" as long as the user wants to continue

In most programming languages, comparisons are case sensitive. If a program tests shouldContinue="Y", a user response of y will result in a false evaluation.

190

In the program in Figure 5-4, the loop control variable is shouldContinue. The program executes as follows:

● The loop control variable is initialized by the user's first response.

● The while expression compares the loop control variable to Y.

● If the user has entered Y, then "Hello" is output and the user is asked whether the program should continue.

● At any point, if the user enters N, the loop ends.

Figure 5-5 shows how the program might look when it is executed at the command line and in a GUI environment. The screens in Figure 5-5 show programs that perform exactly the same tasks using different environments. In each environment, the user can continue to choose to see "Hello" messages, or can choose to quit the program and display "Goodbye".

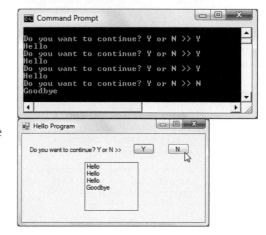

Figure 5-5 Typical executions of the program in Figure 5-4 in two environments

Understanding the Loop in a Program's Mainline Logic

The flowchart and pseudocode segments in Figure 5-4 contain three steps that should occur in every properly functioning loop:

1. You must provide a starting value for the variable that will control the loop.

2. You must test the loop control variable to determine whether the loop body executes.

3. Within the loop, you must alter the loop control variable.

In Chapter 2 you learned that the mainline logic of many business programs follows a standard outline that consists of housekeeping tasks, a loop that repeats, and finishing tasks. The three crucial steps that occur in any loop also occur in standard mainline logic. Figure 5-6 shows the flowchart for the mainline logic of the payroll program that you saw in Figure 2-8. In Figure 5-6, the three loop-controlling steps are highlighted. In this case, the three steps—initializing, testing, and altering the loop control variable—are in different modules. However, the steps all occur in the correct places, showing that the mainline logic uses a standard and correct loop.

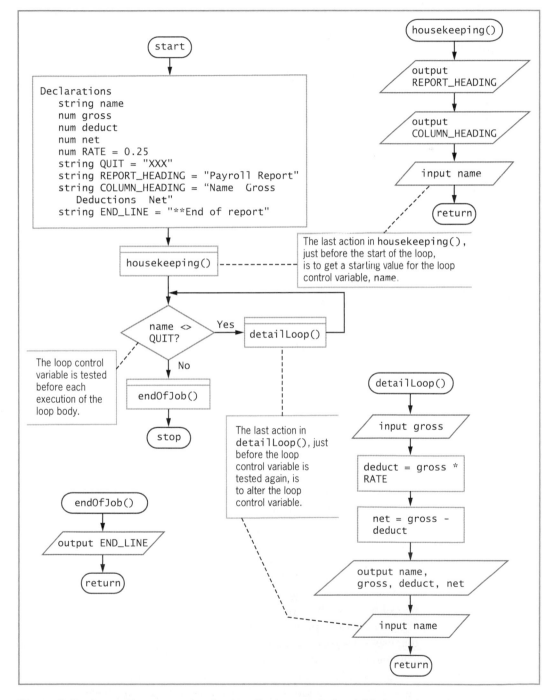

Figure 5-6 A payroll program showing how the loop control variable is used

---

TWO TRUTHS & A LIE

Using a Loop Control Variable

1. To make a `while` loop execute correctly, a loop control variable must be set to 0 before entering the loop.

2. To make a `while` loop execute correctly, a loop control variable should be tested before entering the loop body.

3. To make a `while` loop execute correctly, the body of the loop must take some action that alters the value of the loop control variable.

The false statement is #1. A loop control variable must be initialized, but not necessarily to 0.

Nested Loops

Program logic gets more complicated when you must use loops within loops, or **nested loops**. When one loop appears inside another, the loop that contains the other loop is called the **outer loop**, and the loop that is contained is called the **inner loop**. You need to create nested loops when the values of two (or more) variables repeat to produce every combination of values. Usually, when you create nested loops, each loop has its own loop control variable.

For example, suppose you want to write a program that produces quiz answer sheets like the ones shown in Figure 5-7. Each answer sheet has a unique heading followed by five parts with three questions in each part, and you want a fill-in-the-blank line for each question. You could write a program that uses 63 separate output statements to produce three sheets, but it is more efficient to use nested loops.

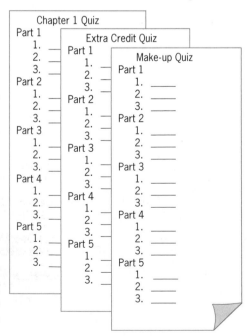

Figure 5-7   Quiz answer sheets

Figure 5-8 shows the logic for the program that produces answer sheets. Three loop control variables are declared for the program:

- `quizName` controls the `detailLoop()` module that is called from the mainline logic.

- `partCounter` controls the outer loop within the `detailLoop()` module; it keeps track of the answer sheet parts.

- `questionCounter` controls the inner loop in the `detailLoop()` module; it keeps track of the questions and answer lines within each part section on each answer sheet.

Five named constants are also declared. Three of these constants (QUIT, PARTS, and QUESTIONS) hold the sentinel values for each of the three loops in the program. The other two hold the text that will be output (the word "Part" that precedes each part number, and the period-space-underscore combination that forms a fill-in line for each question).

When the program starts, the `housekeeping()` module executes and the user enters the name to be output at the top of the first quiz.

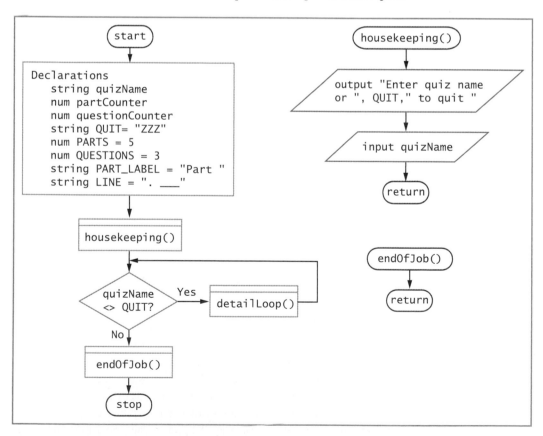

Figure 5-8 Flowchart and pseudocode for `AnswerSheet` program

194

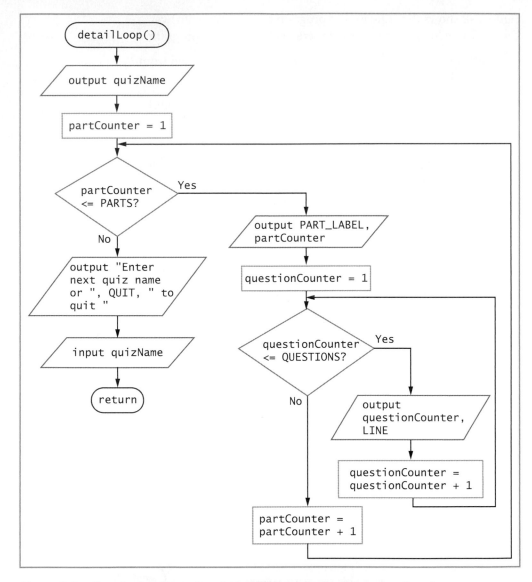

Figure 5-8   Flowchart and pseudocode for `AnswerSheet` program (continued)

If the user enters the `QUIT` value, the program ends immediately, but if the user enters anything else, such as "Make-up Quiz", then the `detailLoop()` module executes.

In the `detailLoop()` the quiz name is output at the top of the answer sheet. Then `partCounter` is initialized to 1. The `partCounter` variable is the loop control variable for the outer loop in this module. The outer loop continues while `partCounter` is less than or equal to `PARTS`. The last statement in the outer loop adds 1 to `partCounter`. In other words, the outer loop will execute when `partCounter` is 1, 2, 3, 4, and 5.

```
start
   Declarations
      string quizName
      num partCounter
      num questionCounter
      string QUIT = "ZZZ"
      num PARTS = 5
      num QUESTIONS = 3
      string PART_LABEL = "Part "
      string LINE = ". _____"
   housekeeping()
   while quizName <> QUIT
      detailLoop()
   endwhile
   endOfJob()
stop

housekeeping()
   output "Enter quiz name or ", QUIT, "to quit "
   input quizName
return

detailLoop()
   output quizName
   partCounter = 1
   while partCounter <= PARTS
      output PART_LABEL, partCounter
      questionCounter = 1
      while questionCounter <= QUESTIONS
         output questionCounter, LINE
         questionCounter = questionCounter + 1
      endwhile
      partCounter = partCounter + 1
   endwhile
   output "Enter next quiz name or ", QUIT, " to quit "
   input quizName
return

endOfJob()
return
```

Figure 5-8   Flowchart and pseudocode for `AnswerSheet` program (continued)

In Figure 5-8, some output would be sent to one output device, such as a monitor. Other output would be sent to another output device, such as a printer. The statements needed to send output to separate devices differs among languages. Chapter 7 provides more details.

The `endOfJob()` module is included in the program in Figure 5-8, even though it contains no statements, so that the mainline logic contains all the parts you have learned. An empty module that acts as a placeholder is called a **stub**.

In the program in Figure 5-8, it is important that `questionCounter` is reset to 1 within the outer loop, just before entering the inner loop. If this step was omitted, Part 1 would contain questions 1, 2, and 3, but subsequent parts would be empty.

In the outer loop in the `detailLoop()` module in Figure 5-8, the word "Part" and the current `partCounter` value are output. Then the following steps execute:

- The loop control variable for the inner loop is initialized by setting `questionCounter` to 1.

- The loop control variable `questionCounter` is evaluated by comparing it to QUESTIONS, and while `questionCounter` does not exceed QUESTIONS, the loop body executes: the value of `questionCounter` is output, followed by a period and a fill-in-the-blank line.

Watch the video
Nested Loops.

- At the end of the loop body, the loop control variable is altered by adding 1 to `questionCounter` and the `questionCounter` comparison is made again.

In other words, when `partCounter` is 1, the part heading is output and underscore lines are output for questions 1, 2, and 3. Then `partCounter` becomes 2, the part heading is output, and underscore lines are created for another set of questions 1, 2, and 3. Then `partCounter` in turn becomes 3, 4, and 5, and three underscore lines are created for each part.

TWO TRUTHS & A LIE

Nested Loops

1. When one loop is nested inside another, the loop that contains the other loop is called the outer loop.

2. You need to create nested loops when the values of two (or more) variables repeat to produce every combination of values.

3. The number of times a loop executes always depends on a constant.

The false statement is #3. The number of times a loop executes can depend on a constant or a value that varies.

Avoiding Common Loop Mistakes

The mistakes programmers most often make with loops are:

- Neglecting to initialize the loop control variable
- Neglecting to alter the loop control variable
- Using the wrong comparison with the loop control variable
- Including statements inside the loop that belong outside the loop

The following sections explain these common mistakes in more detail.

Mistake: Neglecting to Initialize the Loop Control Variable

It is always a mistake to fail to initialize a loop's control variable. For example, consider the program in Figure 5-9. It prompts the user for a name, and while the name continues not to be the sentinel value "ZZZ", it outputs a greeting that uses the name and asks for the next name. This program works correctly.

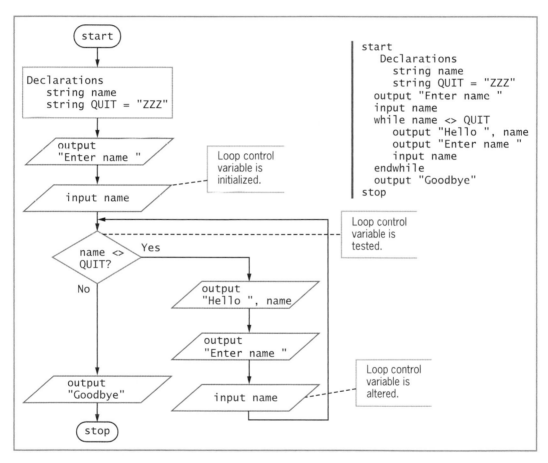

Figure 5-9 Correct logic for greeting program

Figure 5-10 shows an incorrect program in which the loop control variable is not assigned a starting value. If the **name** variable is not set to a starting value, then when the **eof** condition is tested, there is no way to predict whether or not it will be true. That's because if the user does not enter a value for name, the garbage value originally held by that variable might or might not be "ZZZ". So, one of two scenarios follows:

- Most likely, the uninitialized value of name is not "ZZZ", so the first greeting output will include garbage—for example, "Hello 12BGr5".

- By a remote chance, the uninitialized value of name *is* "ZZZ", so the program ends immediately before the user can enter any names.

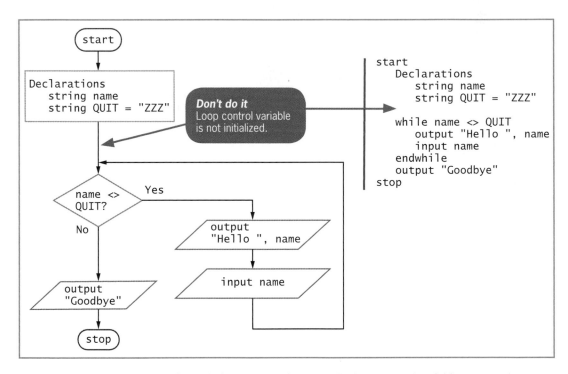

Figure 5-10 Incorrect logic for greeting program because the loop control variable initialization is missing

Mistake: Neglecting to Alter the Loop Control Variable

Different sorts of errors will occur if you fail to alter a loop control variable within the loop. For example, in the program in Figure 5-9 that accepts and displays names, you create such an error if you don't accept names within the loop. Figure 5-11 shows the resulting incorrect logic.

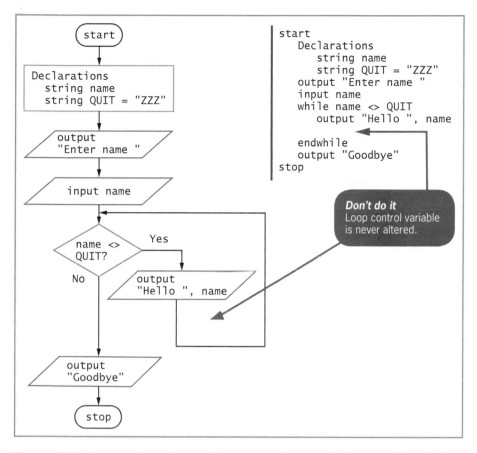

```
start
   Declarations
      string name
      string QUIT = "ZZZ"
   output "Enter name "
   input name
   while name <> QUIT
      output "Hello ", name

   endwhile
   output "Goodbye"
stop
```

Don't do it
Loop control variable
is never altered.

Figure 5-11 Incorrect logic for greeting program because the loop control variable is not altered

If you remove the `input name` instruction from the end of the loop in the program, no name is ever entered after the first one. For example, assume that when the program starts, the user enters "Fred". The name will be compared to the sentinel value, and the loop will be entered. After a greeting is output for Fred, no new name is entered, so when the logic returns to the loop-controlling question, the `name` will still not be "ZZZ", and greetings for Fred will continue to be output infinitely. It is always incorrect to create a loop that cannot terminate.

Mistake: Using the Wrong Comparison with the Loop Control Variable

Programmers must be careful to use the correct comparison in the statement that controls a loop. A comparison is correct only when the correct operands and operator are used. For example, although only one keystroke differs between the original greeting program in Figure 5-9 and the one in Figure 5-12, the original program correctly produces named greetings and the second one does not.

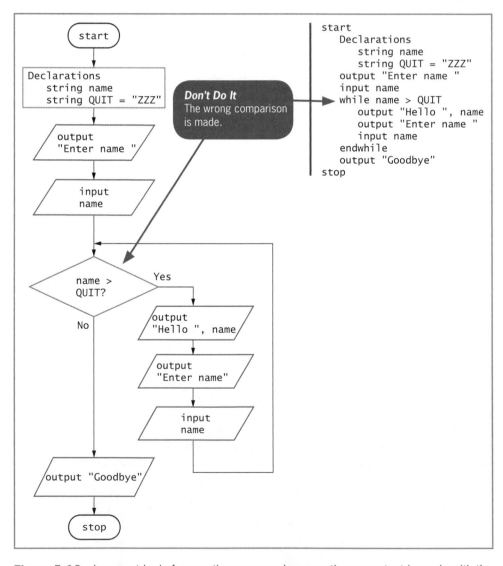

Figure 5-12 Incorrect logic for greeting program because the wrong test is made with the loop control variable

In the example in Figure 5-12, a greater-than comparison (>) is made instead of a not-equal-to (<>) comparison. Suppose that when the program executes, the user enters "Fred" as the first name. In most programming languages, when the comparison between "Fred" and "ZZZ" is made, the values are compared alphabetically. "Fred" is not greater than "ZZZ", so the loop is never entered, and the program ends.

Using the wrong comparison can have serious effects. For example, in a counted loop, if you use <= instead of < to compare a counter to a sentinel value, the program will perform one loop execution too many. If the loop displays greetings, the error might not be critical, but if such an error occurred in a loan company application, each customer might be charged a month's additional interest. If the error occurred in an airline's application, it might overbook a flight. If it occurred in a pharmacy's drug-dispensing application, each patient might receive one extra (and possibly harmful) unit of medication.

Mistake: Including Statements Inside the Loop that Belong Outside the Loop

Suppose that you want to write a program for a store manager who wants to discount every item he sells by 30 percent. The manager wants 100 new price label stickers for each item. The user enters a price, the new price is calculated, 100 stickers are printed, and the next price is entered. Figure 5-13 shows a program that performs the job, albeit somewhat inefficiently. The program is inefficient because the same value, newPrice, is calculated 100 separate times for each price that is entered.

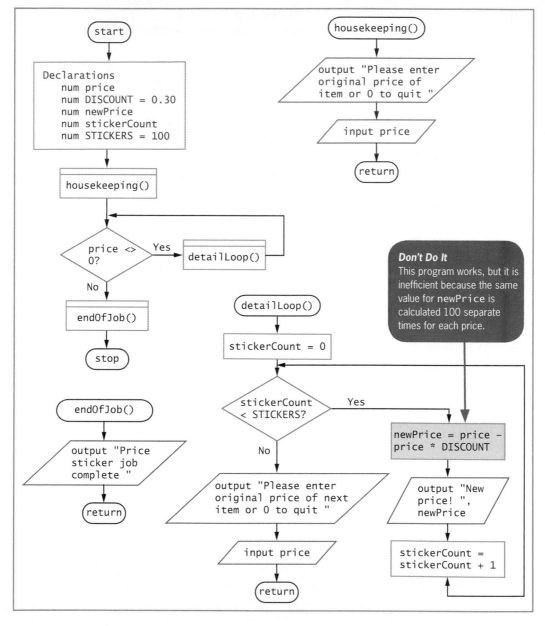

Figure 5-13 Inefficient way to produce 100 discount price stickers for differently priced items

```
start
    Declarations
        num price
        num DISCOUNT = 0.30
        num newPrice
        num stickerCount
        num STICKERS = 100
    housekeeping()
    while price <> 0
        detailLoop()
    endwhile
    endOfJob()
stop

housekeeping()
    output "Please enter original price of item or 0 to quit "
    input price
return

detailLoop()
    stickerCount = 0
    while stickerCount < STICKERS
        newPrice = price - price * DISCOUNT
        output "New price! ", newPrice
        stickerCount = stickerCount + 1
    endwhile
    output "Please enter original price of
        next item or 0 to quit "
    input price
return

endOfJob()
    output "Price sticker job complete"
return
```

Don't Do It
This program works, but it is inefficient because the same value for newPrice is calculated 100 separate times for each price.

Figure 5-13 Inefficient way to produce 100 discount price stickers for differently priced items (continued)

Figure 5-14 shows the same program, in which the newPrice value that is output on the sticker is calculated only once per new price; the calculation has been moved to a better location. The programs in Figures 5-13 and 5-14 do the same thing. However, the one in Figure 5-14 does it more efficiently. As you become more proficient at programming, you will recognize many opportunities to perform the same tasks in alternate, more elegant, and more efficient ways.

When you describe people or events as "elegant," you mean they possess a refined gracefulness. Similarly, programmers use the term "elegant" to describe programs that are well designed and easy to understand and maintain.

204

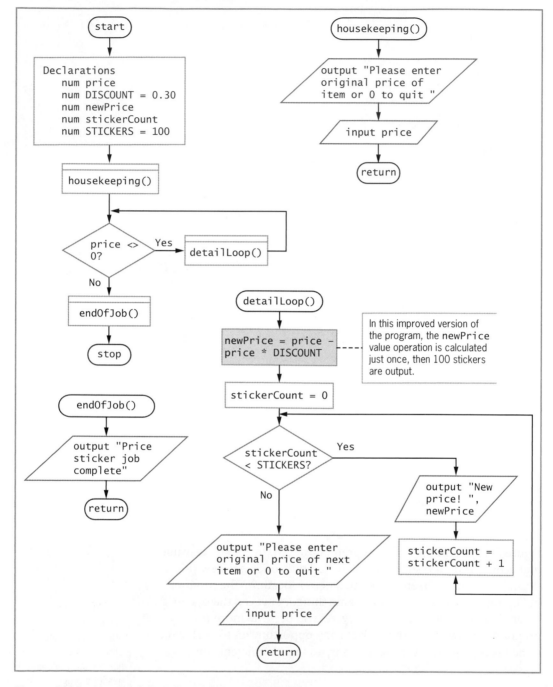

Figure 5-14 Improved discount sticker-making program

```
start
    Declarations
        num price
        num DISCOUNT = 0.30
        num newPrice
        num stickerCount
        num STICKERS = 100
    housekeeping()
    while price <> 0
        detailLoop()
    endwhile
    endOfJob()
stop

housekeeping()
    output "Please enter original price of item or 0 to quit "
    input price
return

detailLoop()
    newPrice = price - price * DISCOUNT
    stickerCount = 0
    while stickerCount < STICKERS
        output "New price! ", newPrice
        stickerCount = stickerCount + 1
    endwhile
output "Please enter original price of next item or 0 to quit "
input price
return

endOfJob()
    output "Price sticker job complete"
return
```

In this improved version of the program, the newPrice value operation is calculated just once, then 100 stickers are output.

Figure 5-14 Improved discount sticker-making program (continued)

TWO TRUTHS & A LIE

Avoiding Common Loop Mistakes

1. In a loop, neglecting to initialize the loop control variable is a mistake.

2. In a loop, neglecting to alter the loop control variable is a mistake.

3. In a loop, it is a mistake to compare the loop control variable using >= or <=.

The false statement is #3. Many loops are created correctly using <= or >=.

Using a for Loop

Every high-level computer programming language contains a while statement that you can use to code any loop, including both indefinite and definite loops. In addition to the while statement, most computer languages support a for statement. You usually use the **for statement**, or **for loop**, with definite loops—those that will loop a specific number of times—when you know exactly how many times the loop will repeat. The for statement provides you with three actions in one compact statement. In a for statement, a loop control variable is:

- Initialized

- Evaluated

- Incremented

The for statement sometimes takes the form:

```
for loopControlVariable = initialValue to
   finalValue step stepValue
      do something
endfor
```

For example, to display "Hello" four times, you can write either of the sets of statements in Figure 5-15.

```
   count = 0                      for count = 0 to 3 step 1
   while count <= 3                  output "Hello"
      output "Hello"              endfor
      count = count + 1
   endwhile
```

Figure 5-15   Comparable while and for statements that each output "Hello" four times

The code segments in Figure 5-15 each accomplish the same tasks:

- The variable count is initialized to 0.

- The count variable is compared to the limit value 3; while count is less than or equal to 3, the loop body executes.

- As the last statement in the loop execution, the value of count increases by 1. After the increase, the comparison to the limit value is made again.

The for loop simply expresses the same logic in a more compact form. The amount by which a for loop control variable changes is often called a **step value**. The step value can be positive or negative; that is, it can increment or decrement. You never are required to use a for statement for any loop; a while statement can always be used instead. However, when a loop's execution is based on a loop control variable progressing from a known starting value to a known ending value in equal steps, the for loop provides you with a convenient shorthand. It is easy for others to read, and because the loop control variable's initialization, testing, and alteration are all performed in one location, you are less likely to leave out one of these crucial elements.

 The programmer doesn't need to know the starting value, ending value, or step value for the loop control variable when the program is written; only the application must know those values while the program is running. For example, any of the values might be entered by the user, or might be the result of a calculation.

207

 In Java, C++, and C#, a for loop that displays 20 values might look similar to the following:

```
for(count = 0; count < 20; count++)
{
    output count
}
```

The three actions (initialization, comparison, and altering of the loop control variable) all take place within a set of parentheses that follows the keyword for and are separated by semicolons. The expression count++ adds 1 to count. The block of statements that depends on the loop sits between a pair of curly braces.

 The for loop is particularly useful when processing arrays. You will learn about arrays in Chapter 6.

 Both the while loop and the for loop are examples of *pretest loops*. That means the loop control variable is tested before each iteration. Most languages allow you to use a variation of the looping structure known as a *posttest loop*, which tests the loop control variable after each iteration. Appendix F contains information about posttest loops.

TWO TRUTHS & A LIE

Using a for Loop

1. The for statement provides you with three actions in one compact statement: initializing, evaluating, and incrementing.

2. A for statement body always executes at least one time.

3. In most programming languages, you can provide a for loop with any step value.

The false statement is #2. A for statement body might not execute depending on the initial value of the loop control variable.

Common Loop Applications

Although every computer program is different, many techniques are common to a variety of applications. Loops, for example, are frequently used to accumulate totals and to validate data.

Using a Loop to Accumulate Totals

Some business reports list only totals, with no individual item details. Such reports are called **summary reports**.

Business reports often include totals. The supervisor requesting a list of employees who participate in the company dental plan is often as interested in the number of participating employees as in who they are. When you receive your telephone bill at the end of the month, you are usually more interested in the total than in the charges for the individual calls.

For example, a real estate broker might want to see a list of all properties sold in the last month as well as the total value for all the properties. A program might read sales data that includes the street address of the property sold and its selling price. The data records might be entered by a clerk as each sale is made, and stored in a file until the end of the month; then they can be used in the month-end report. Figure 5-16 shows an example of such a report.

```
MONTH-END SALES REPORT

Address          Price

287 Acorn St     150,000
12 Maple Ave     310,000
8723 Marie Ln     65,500
222 Acorn St     127,000
29 Bahama Way    450,000

Total          1,102,500
```

Figure 5-16 Month-end real estate sales report

To create the sales report, you must output the address and price for each property sold and add its value to an accumulator. An **accumulator** is a variable that you use to gather or accumulate values. An accumulator is very similar to a counter that you use to count loop iterations. However, usually you add just one to a counter, whereas you add some other value to an accumulator. If the real estate broker wants to know how many listings the company holds, you count them. When she wants to know total real estate value, you accumulate it.

To accumulate total real estate prices, you declare a numeric variable such as `accumPrice` and initialize it to 0. As you get each real estate transaction's data, you output it and add its value to the accumulator `accumPrice`, as shown shaded in Figure 5-17.

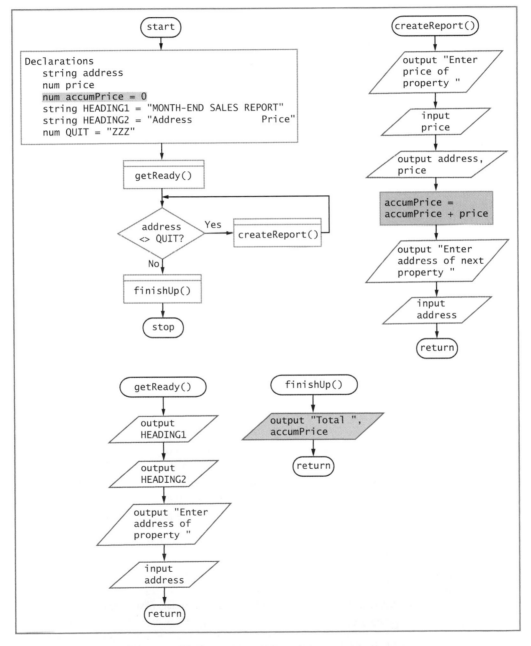

Figure 5-17 Flowchart and pseudocode for real estate sales report program

210

```
start
   Declarations
      string address
      num price
      num accumPrice = 0
      string HEADING1 = "MONTH-END SALES REPORT"
      string HEADING2 = "Address            Price"
      num QUIT = "ZZZ"
   getReady()
   while address <> QUIT
      createReport()
   endwhile
   finishUp()
stop

getReady()
   output HEADING1
   output HEADING2
   output "Enter address of property "
   input address
return

createReport()
   output "Enter price of property "
   input price
   output address, price
   accumPrice = accumPrice + price
   output "Enter address of next property "
   input address
return

finishUp()
   output "Total ", accumPrice
return
```

Figure 5-17 Flowchart and pseudocode for real estate sales report program (continued)

Some programming languages assign 0 to a numeric variable you fail to initialize explicitly, but many do not—when you try to add a value to an uninitialized variable, they either issue an error message or let you incorrectly start with an accumulator that holds garbage. The safest and clearest course of action is to assign the value 0 to accumulators before using them.

After the program in Figure 5-17 gets and displays the last real estate transaction, the user enters the sentinel value, and loop execution ends. At that point, the accumulator will hold the grand total of all the real estate values. The program displays the word "Total" and the accumulated value, accumPrice. Then the program ends.

Figure 5-17 highlights the three actions you usually must take with an accumulator:

- Accumulators are initialized to 0.

- Accumulators are altered, usually once for every data set processed.

- At the end of processing, accumulators are output.

After outputting the value of `accumPrice`, new programmers often want to reset it to 0. Their argument is that they are "cleaning up after themselves." Although you can take this step without harming the execution of the program, it does not serve any useful purpose. You cannot set `accumPrice` to 0 in anticipation of having it ready for the next program, or even for the next time you execute this program. Variables exist only during an execution of the program, and even if a future application happens to contain a variable named `accumPrice`, the variable will not necessarily occupy the same memory location as this one. Even if you run the same application a second time, the variables might occupy physical memory locations different from those they occupied during the first run. It is the programmer's responsibility to initialize all variables that must start with a specific value. There is no benefit to changing a variable's value when it will never be used again during the current execution.

Using a Loop to Validate Data

When you ask a user to enter data into a computer program, you have no assurance that the data will be accurate. Loops are frequently used to **validate data**; that is, to make sure it is meaningful and useful. For example, validation might ensure that a value is the correct type, or that it falls within an acceptable range.

For example, suppose part of a program you are writing asks a user to enter a number that represents his or her birth month. If the user types a number lower than 1 or greater than 12, you must take some sort of action. For example:

- You could display an error message and stop the program.

- You could choose to assign a default value for the month (for example, 1) before proceeding.

- You could reprompt the user for valid input.

If you choose this last course of action, at least two approaches could be used. You could use a selection, and if the month is invalid, you could ask the user to reenter a number, as shown in Figure 5-18.

Incorrect user entries are by far the most common source of computer errors. The programs you write will be improved if you employ **defensive programming**, which means trying to prepare for all possible errors before they occur.

Programmers employ the acronym **GIGO** for "garbage in, garbage out." It means that if your input is incorrect, your output is worthless.

211

212

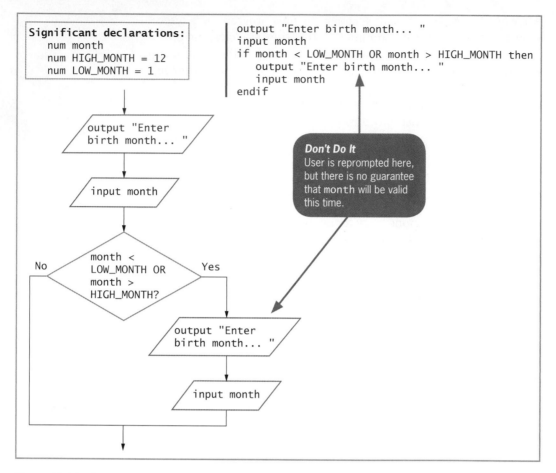

Figure 5-18 Reprompting a user once after an invalid month is entered

The problem with the logic in Figure 5-18 is that the user still might not enter valid data on the second attempt to enter a month. Of course, you could add a third decision, but you still couldn't control what the user enters.

The superior solution is to use a loop to continuously prompt a user for a month until the user enters it correctly. Figure 5-19 shows this approach.

Just because a data item is valid does not mean that it is correct. For example, a program can determine that 5 is a valid birth month, but not that your birthday actually falls in month 5.

Most languages provide a built-in way to check whether an entered value is numeric or not. When you rely on user input, you frequently accept each piece of input data as a string and then attempt to convert it to a number. The procedure for accomplishing numeric checks is slightly different in different programming languages.

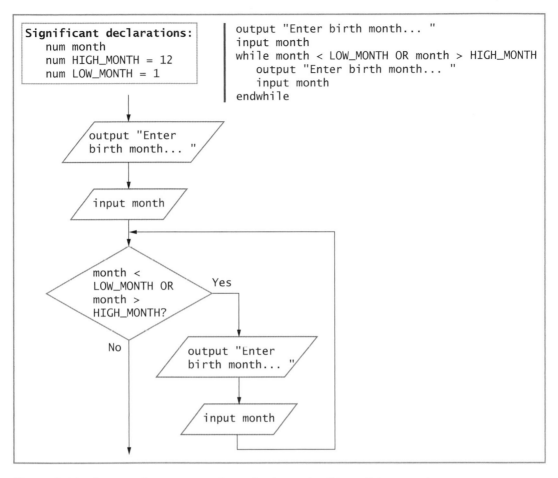

Significant declarations:
```
num month
num HIGH_MONTH = 12
num LOW_MONTH = 1
```

```
output "Enter birth month... "
input month
while month < LOW_MONTH OR month > HIGH_MONTH
    output "Enter birth month... "
    input month
endwhile
```

Figure 5-19   Reprompting a user continuously after an invalid month is entered

Limiting a Reprompting Loop

Reprompting a user is a good way to ensure valid data, but it can be frustrating to a user if it continues indefinitely. For example, suppose the user must enter a valid birth month, but has used another application in which January was month 0, and keeps entering 0 no matter how many times you repeat the prompt. One helpful addition to the program would be to use the limiting values as part of the prompt. In other words, instead of the statement output "Enter birth month ... ", the following statement might be more useful:

```
output "Enter birth month between ", LOW_MONTH, ", and ",
    HIGH_MONTH, " ... "
```

Still, the user might not understand the prompt or not read it carefully, so you might want to employ the tactic used in Figure 5-20, in which a count of the number of reprompts is maintained. In this example, a constant named ATTEMPTS is set to 3. While a count of the user's attempts at correct data entry remains below this limit, and the user enters invalid data, the user continues to be reprompted. If the user exceeds the limited number of allowed attempts, the loop ends. The next action depends on the application. If count equals ATTEMPTS after the data-entry loop ends, you might want to force the invalid data to a default value. **Forcing** a data item means you override incorrect data by setting the variable to a specific value. For example, you might decide that if a month value does not fall between 1 and 12, you will force the month to 0 or 99, which indicates to users that no valid value exists. In a different application, you might just choose to end the program. In an interactive, Web-based program, you might choose to have a customer service representative start a chat session with the user to offer help.

Programs that frustrate users can result in lost revenue for a company. For example, if a company's Web site is difficult to navigate, users might just give up and not do business with the organization.

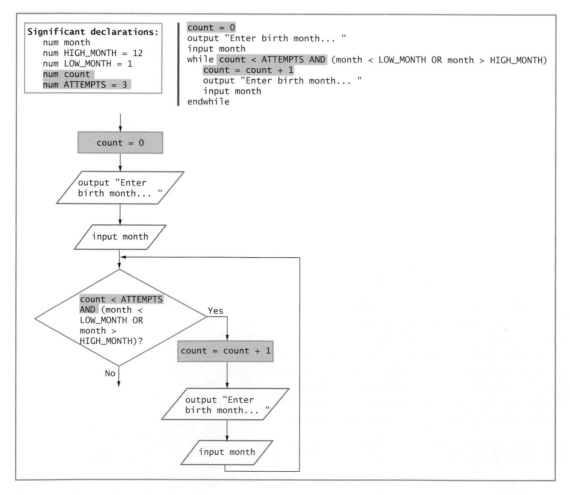

Figure 5-20   Limiting user reprompts

Validating a Data Type

The data you use within computer programs is varied. It stands to reason that validating data requires a variety of methods. For example, some programming languages allow you to check data items to make sure they are the correct data type. Although this technique varies from language to language, you can often make a statement like the one shown in Figure 5-21. In this program segment, isNumeric() represents a method call; it is used to check whether the entered employee salary falls within the category of numeric data. You check to ensure that a value is numeric for many reasons—an important one is that only numeric values can be used correctly in arithmetic statements. A method such as isNumeric() is most often provided with the language translator you use to write your programs. Such a method operates as a black box; in other words, you can use the method's results without understanding its internal statements.

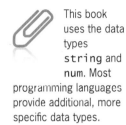 This book uses the data types **string** and **num**. Most programming languages provide additional, more specific data types.

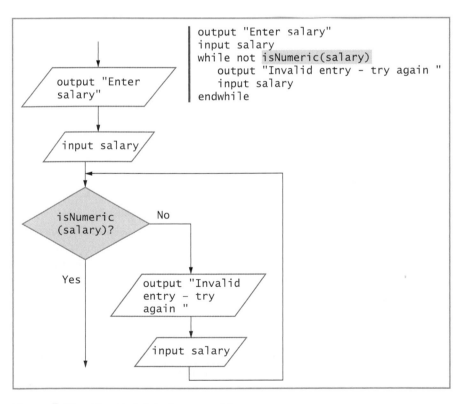

```
output "Enter salary"
input salary
while not isNumeric(salary)
    output "Invalid entry - try again "
    input salary
endwhile
```

Figure 5-21 Checking data for correct type

Besides allowing you to check whether a value is numeric, some languages contain methods such as `isChar()`, which checks whether a value is a character data type; `isWhitespace()`, which checks whether a value is a nonprinting character, such as a space or tab; and `isUpper()`, which checks whether a value is a capital letter.

In many languages, you accept all user data as a string of characters, and then use built-in methods to attempt to convert the characters to the correct data type for your application. When the conversion methods succeed, you have useful data; when the conversion methods fail because the user has entered the wrong data type, you can take appropriate action, such as issuing an error message, reprompting the user, or forcing the data to a default value.

Validating Reasonableness and Consistency of Data

Data items can be the correct type and within range, but still be incorrect. You have experienced this phenomenon yourself if anyone has ever misspelled your name or overbilled you. The data might have been the correct type—that is, alphabetic letters were used in your name—but the name itself was incorrect. Many data items cannot be checked for reasonableness; for example, the names Catherine, Katherine, and Kathryn are equally reasonable, but only one spelling is correct for a particular woman.

However, many data items can be checked for reasonableness. If you make a purchase on May 3, 2012, then the payment cannot possibly be due prior to that date. Perhaps within your organization, you cannot make more than $20.00 per hour if you work in Department 12. If your zip code is 90201, your state of residence cannot be New York. If your store's cash on hand was $3000 when it closed on Tuesday, it should not be a different value when it opens on Wednesday. If a customer's title is "Ms.", the customer's gender should be "F". Each of these examples involves comparing two data items for reasonableness or consistency. You should consider making as many such comparisons as possible when writing your own programs.

Good defensive programs try to foresee all possible inconsistencies and errors. The more accurate your data, the more useful information you will produce as output from your programs.

Frequently, testing for reasonableness and consistency involves using additional data files. For example, to check that a user has entered a valid county of residence for a state, you might use a file that contains every county name within every state in the United States, and check the user's county against those contained in the file.

When you become a professional programmer, you want your programs to work correctly as a source of professional pride. On a more basic level, you do not want to be called in to work at 3 a.m. when the overnight run of your program fails because of errors you created.

TWO TRUTHS & A LIE

Common Loop Applications

1. An accumulator is a variable that you use to gather or accumulate values.

2. An accumulator typically is initialized to 0.

3. An accumulator is typically reset to 0 after it is output.

The false statement is #3. There is typically no need to reset an accumulator after it is output.

Chapter Summary

- When you use a loop in a computer program, you can write one set of instructions that operates on multiple, separate sets of data.

- Three steps must occur in every loop: You must initialize a loop control variable, compare the variable to some value that controls whether the loop continues or stops, and alter the variable that controls the loop.

- When you must use loops within loops, you use nested loops. When nesting loops, you must maintain two individual loop control variables and alter each at the appropriate time.

- Common mistakes that programmers make when writing loops include neglecting to initialize the loop control variable, neglecting to alter the loop control variable, using the wrong comparison with the loop control variable, and including statements inside the loop that belong outside the loop.

- Most computer languages support a for statement or for loop that you can use with definite loops when you know how many times a loop will repeat. The for statement uses a loop control variable that it automatically initializes, evaluates, and increments.

- Loops are used in many applications—for example, to accumulate totals in business reports. Loops are also used to ensure that user data entries are valid by continuously reprompting the user.

Key Terms

A **loop control variable** is a variable that determines whether a loop will continue.

A **definite loop** is one for which the number of repetitions is a predetermined value.

A **counted loop** or **counter-controlled loop** is a loop whose repetitions are managed by a counter.

Incrementing a variable is adding a constant value to it, frequently 1.

Decrementing a variable is decreasing it by a constant value, frequently 1.

A **counter** is any numeric variable you use to count the number of times an event has occurred.

An **indefinite loop** is one for which you cannot predetermine the number of executions.

Nested loops occur when a loop structure exists within another loop structure.

An **outer loop** contains another when loops are nested.

An **inner loop** is contained within another when loops are nested.

A **stub** is a method without statements that is used as a placeholder.

A **for statement**, or **for loop**, can be used to code definite loops. The for statement contains a loop control variable that it automatically initializes, evaluates, and increments.

A **step value** is a number you use to increase a loop control variable on each pass through a loop.

A **summary report** lists only totals, without individual detail records.

An **accumulator** is a variable that you use to gather or accumulate values.

When you **validate data**, you make sure data items are meaningful and useful. For example, you ensure that values are the correct data type or that they fall within an acceptable range.

Defensive programming is a technique with which you try to prepare for all possible errors before they occur.

GIGO ("garbage in, garbage out") means that if your input is incorrect, your output is worthless.

Forcing a data item means you override incorrect data by setting it to a specific value.

Review Questions

1. The structure that allows you to write one set of instructions that operates on multiple, separate sets of data is the _____.

   a. sequence

   b. selection

   c. loop

   d. case

2. The loop that frequently appears in a program's mainline logic _____.

   a. always depends on whether a variable equals 0

   b. works correctly based on the same logic as other loops

   c. is an unstructured loop

   d. is an example of an infinite loop

3. Which of the following is *not* a step that must occur with every correctly working loop?

   a. Initialize a loop control variable before the loop starts.

   b. Set the loop control value equal to a sentinel during each iteration.

   c. Compare the loop control value to a sentinel during each iteration.

   d. Alter the loop control variable during each iteration.

4. The statements executed within a loop are known collectively as the _____.

   a. loop body

   b. loop controls

   c. sequences

   d. sentinels

5. A counter keeps track of _____.

   a. the number of times an event has occurred

   b. the number of machine cycles required by a segment of a program

   c. the number of loop structures within a program

   d. the number of times software has been revised

6. Adding 1 to a variable is also called _____ it.

   a. digesting

   b. resetting

   c. decrementing

   d. incrementing

7. Which of the following is a definite loop?

   a. a loop that executes as long as a user continues to enter valid data

   b. a loop that executes 1000 times

   c. both of the above

   d. none of the above

8. Which of the following is an indefinite loop?

   a. a loop that executes exactly 10 times

   b. a loop that follows a prompt asking a user how many repetitions to make and uses that value to control the loop

   c. both of the above

   d. none of the above

9. When you decrement a variable, you _____.

   a. set it to 0

   b. reduce it by one-tenth

   c. subtract 1 from it

   d. remove it from a program

10. When two loops are nested, the loop that is contained by the other is the _____ loop.

    a. captive

    b. unstructured

    c. inner

    d. outer

11. When loops are nested, _____.

    a. they typically share a loop control variable

    b. one must end before the other begins

    c. both must be the same type—definite or indefinite

    d. none of the above

12. Most programmers use a `for` loop _____.

    a. for every loop they write

    b. when a loop will not repeat

    c. when they do not know the exact number of times a loop will repeat

    d. when they know the exact number of times a loop will repeat

13. A report that lists only totals, with no details about individual records, is a(n) _____ report.

    a. accumulator

    b. final

    c. summary

    d. detailless

14. Typically, the value added to a counter variable is _____.

    a. 0

    b. 1

    c. 10

    d. 100

15. Typically, the value added to an accumulator variable is _____.

    a. 0

    b. 1

    c. the same for each iteration

    d. different in each iteration

16. After an accumulator or counter variable is displayed at the end of a program, it is best to _____.

    a. delete the variable from the program

    b. reset the variable to 0

    c. subtract 1 from the variable

    d. none of the above

17. When you _____, you make sure data items are the correct type and fall within the correct range.

    a. validate data

    b. employ offensive programming

    c. use object orientation

    d. count loop iterations

18. Overriding a user's entered value by setting it to a predetermined value is known as _____.

    a. forcing

    b. accumulating

    c. validating

    d. pushing

19. To ensure that a user's entry is the correct data type, frequently you _____.

    a. prompt the user, asking if the user is sure the type is correct

    b. use a method built into the programming language

    c. include a statement at the beginning of the program that lists the data types allowed

    d. all of the above

20. Variables might hold incorrect values even when they are _____ .

    a. the correct data type

    b. within a required range

    c. coded by the programmer rather than input by a user

    d. all of the above

Exercises

1. What is output by each of the pseudocode segments in Figure 5-22?

a.
```
a = 1
b = 2
c = 5
while a < c
    a = a + 1
    b = b + c
endwhile
output a, b, c
```

b.
```
d = 4
e = 6
f = 7
while d > f
    d = d + 1
    e = e - 1
endwhile
output d, e, f
```

c.
```
g = 4
h = 6
while g < h
    g = g + 1
endwhile
output g, h
```

d.
```
j = 2
k = 5
n = 9
while j < k
    m = 6
    while m < n
        output "Goodbye"
        m = m + 1
    endwhile
    j = j + 1
endwhile
```

e.
```
j = 2
k = 5
m = 6
n = 9
while j < k
    while m < n
        output "Hello"
        m = m + 1
    endwhile
    j = j + 1
endwhile
```

f.
```
p = 2
q = 4
while p < q
    output "Adios"
    r = 1
    while r < q
        output "Adios"
        r = r + 1
    endwhile
    p = p + 1
endwhile
```

Figure 5-22 Pseudocode segments for Exercise 1

2. Design the logic for a program that outputs every number from 1 through 10.

3. Design the logic for a program that outputs every number from 1 through 10 along with its square and cube.

4. Design the logic for a program that outputs every even number from 2 through 30.

5. Design the logic for a program that outputs numbers in reverse order from 10 down to 1.

6. a. The No Interest Credit Company provides zero-interest loans to customers. Design an application that gets customer account data, including an account number, customer name, and balance due. Output the account number and name, then output the customer's projected balance each month for the next 10 months. Assume that there is no finance charge on this account, that the customer makes no new purchases, and that the customer pays off the balance with equal monthly payments, which are 10 percent of the original bill.

   b. Modify the No Interest Credit Company application so it executes continuously for any number of customers until a sentinel value is supplied for the account number.

7. a. The Some Interest Credit Company provides loans to customers at 1.5 percent interest per month. Design an application that gets customer account data, including an account number, customer name, and balance due. Output the account number and name; then output the customer's projected balance each month for the next 10 months. Assume that when the balance reaches $10 or less, the customer can pay off the account. At the beginning of every month, 1.5 percent interest is added to the balance, and then the customer makes a payment equal to 5 percent of the current balance. Assume the customer makes no new purchases.

   b. Modify the Some Interest Credit Company application so it executes continuously for any number of customers until a sentinel value is supplied for the account number.

8. Secondhand Rose Resale Shop is having a seven-day sale during which the price of any unsold item drops 10 percent each day. For example, an item that costs $10.00 on the first day costs 10 percent less, or $9.00, on the second day. On the third day, the same item is 10 percent less than $9.00, or $8.10. Design an application that allows a user to input a price until an appropriate sentinel value is entered. Output is the price of each item on each day, one through seven.

9. The Howell Bank provides savings accounts that compound interest on a yearly basis. In other words, if you deposit $100 for two years at 4 percent interest, at the end of one year you will have $104. At the end of two years, you will have the $104 plus 4 percent of that, or $108.16. Design a program that accepts an account number, the account owner's first and last names, and a balance. The program operates continuously until an appropriate sentinel value is entered for the account number. Output the projected running total balance for each account for each of the next 20 years.

10. Mr. Roper owns 20 apartment buildings. Each building contains 15 units that he rents for $800 per month each. Design the application that would output 12 payment coupons for each of the 15 apartments in each of the 20 buildings. Each coupon should contain the building number (1 through 20), the apartment number (1 through 15), the month (1 through 12), and the amount of rent due.

11. a. Design a program for the Hollywood Movie Rating Guide, in which users continuously enter a value from 0 to 4 that indicates the number of stars they are awarding to the Guide's featured movie of the week. The program executes continuously until a user enters a negative number to quit. If a user enters a star value that does not fall in the correct range, reprompt the user continuously until a correct value is entered. At the end of the program, display the average star rating for the movie.

    b. Modify the movie-rating program so that a user gets three tries to enter a valid rating. After three incorrect entries, the program issues an appropriate message and continues with a new user.

    c. Modify the movie-rating program so that the user is prompted continuously for a movie title until "ZZZZZ" is entered. Then, for each movie, continuously accept star-rating values until a negative number is entered. Display the average rating for each movie.

12. The Café Noir Coffee Shop wants some market research on its customers. When a customer places an order, a clerk asks for the customer's zip code and age. The clerk enters that data as well as the number of items the customer orders. The program operates continuously until the clerk enters a 0 for zip code at the end of the day. When the clerk enters an invalid zip code (more than 5 digits) or an invalid age (defined as less than 10 or more than 110), the program reprompts the clerk continuously.

When the clerk enters fewer than 1 or more than 12 items, the program reprompts the clerk two more times. If the clerk enters a high value on the third attempt, the program accepts the high value, but if the clerk enters a negative value on the third attempt, an error message is displayed and the order is not counted. At the end of the program, display a count of the number of items ordered by customers from the same zip code as the coffee shop (54984), and a count from other zip codes. Also display the average customer age, as well as counts of the number of items ordered by customers under 30 and by customers 30 and older.

Find the Bugs

13. Your student disk contains files named DEBUG05-01.txt, DEBUG05-02.txt, and DEBUG05-03.txt. Each file starts with some comments that describe the problem. Comments are lines that begin with two slashes (//). Following the comments, each file contains pseudocode that has one or more bugs you must find and correct.

Game Zone

14. In Chapter 2, you learned that in many programming languages you can generate a random number between 1 and a limiting value named LIMIT by using a statement similar to randomNumber = random(LIMIT). In Chapter 4, you created the logic for a guessing game in which the application generates a random number and the player tries to guess it. Now, create the guessing game itself. After each guess, display a message indicating whether the player's guess was correct, too high, or too low. When the player eventually guesses the correct number, display a count of the number of guesses that were required.

15. Create the logic for a game that simulates rolling two dice by generating two numbers between 1 and 6 inclusive. The player chooses a number between 2 and 12 (the lowest and highest totals possible for two dice). The player then "rolls" two dice up to three times. If the number chosen by the user comes up, the user wins and the game ends. If the number does not come up within three rolls, the computer wins.

16. Create the logic for the dice game Pig, in which a player can compete with the computer. The object of the game is to be the first to score 100 points. The user and computer take turns "rolling" a pair of dice following these rules:

- On a turn, each player rolls two dice. If no 1 appears, the dice values are added to a running total for the turn, and the player can choose whether to roll again or pass the turn to the other player. When a player passes, the accumulated turn total is added to the player's game total.

- If a 1 appears on one of the dice, the player's turn total becomes 0; in other words, nothing more is added to the player's game total for that turn, and it becomes the other player's turn.

- If a 1 appears on both of the dice, not only is the player's turn over, but the player's entire accumulated total is reset to 0.

- When the computer does not roll a 1 and can choose whether to roll again, generate a random value from 1 to 2. The computer will then decide to continue when the value is 1 and decide to quit and pass the turn to the player when the value is not 1.

 Up for Discussion

17. Suppose you wrote a program that you suspect is in an infinite loop because it keeps running for several minutes with no output and without ending. What would you add to your program to help you discover the origin of the problem?

18. Suppose you know that every employee in your organization has a seven-digit ID number used for logging on to the computer system. A loop would be useful to guess every combination of seven digits in an ID. Are there any circumstances in which you should try to guess another employee's ID number?

19. If every employee in an organization had a seven-digit ID number, guessing all the possible combinations would be a relatively easy programming task. How could you alter the format of employee IDs to make them more difficult to guess?

Arrays

In this chapter, you will learn about:

◎ Arrays and how they occupy computer memory

◎ Manipulating an array to replace nested decisions

◎ Using constants with arrays

◎ Searching an array

◎ Using parallel arrays

◎ Searching an array for a range match

◎ Remaining within array bounds

◎ Using a `for` loop to process arrays

Understanding Arrays and How They Occupy Computer Memory

An **array** is a series or list of values in computer memory, all of which have the same name and data type but are differentiated with special numbers called subscripts. Usually, all the values in an array have something in common; for example, they might represent a list of employee ID numbers or a list of prices for items sold in a store. A **subscript**, also called an **index**, is a number that indicates the position of a particular item within an array.

Whenever you require multiple storage locations for physical objects, you are using a real-life counterpart of a programming array. For example, if you store important papers in a series of file folders and label each folder with a consecutive letter of the alphabet, then you are using the equivalent of an array.

When you look down the left side of a tax table to find your income level before looking to the right to find your income tax obligation, you are using an array. Similarly, if you look down the left side of a train schedule to find your station before looking to the right to find the train's arrival time, you are also using an array.

Each of these real-life arrays helps you organize real-life objects. You *could* store all your papers or mementos in one huge cardboard box, or find your tax rate or train's arrival time if both were printed randomly in one large book. However, using an organized storage and display system makes your life easier in each case. Using a programming array will accomplish the same results for your data.

 Some programmers refer to an array as a *table* or a *matrix*.

How Arrays Occupy Computer Memory

When you declare an array, you declare a structure that contains multiple data items. Each item within an array has the same name and the same data type; each separate item is one **element** of the array. Each array element occupies an area in memory next to, or contiguous to, the others. You can indicate the number of elements an array will hold—the **size of the array**—when you declare the array along with your other variables and constants. For example, you might declare an uninitialized three-element numeric array named someVals as follows:

```
num someVals[3]
```

All array elements have the same group name, but each individual element also has a unique subscript indicating how far away it is from the first element. Therefore, any array's subscripts are always

A common error by beginning programmers is to forget that array subscripts start with 0. If you assume that an array's first subscript is 1, you will always be "off by one" in your array manipulation.

Remember that a variable can hold only one value at a time. Each array element is a single variable.

In all languages, subscript values must be integers (whole numbers) and sequential. Some languages use 1 as the first array subscript, and some allow you to choose a starting subscript.

a sequence of integers such as 0 through 4 or 0 through 9. In most modern languages, such as Visual Basic, Java, C++, and C#, the first array element is accessed using subscript 0, and this book follows that convention.

Depending on the syntax rules of the programming language you use, you place the subscript within parentheses or square brackets following the group name. This book will use square brackets to hold array element subscripts so that you don't mistake array names for method names. Also, many newer programming languages such as C++, Java, and C# use the bracket notation.

Figure 6-1 shows an array named someVals that contains three elements, so the elements are someVals[0], someVals[1], and someVals[2]. This array's elements have been assigned values. The value stored in someVals[0] is 25; someVals[1] holds 36, and someVals[2] holds 47. The element someVals[0] is zero numbers away from the beginning of the array—in other words, it is located at the same memory address as the array. The element someVals[1] is one number away from the beginning of the array and someVals[2] is two numbers away.

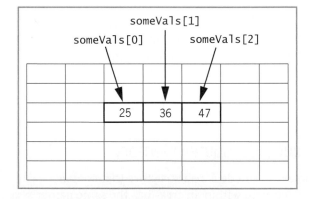

Figure 6-1 Appearance of a three-element array in computer memory

Providing array values sometimes is called **populating the array**.

After you declare an array, you can assign values to some or all of the elements individually, as shown in the following example:

```
num someVals[3]
someVals[0] = 25
someVals[1] = 36
someVals[2] = 47
```

Alternatively, you can initialize array elements when you declare the array. Most programming languages use a statement similar to the following to declare a three-element array and assign values to it:

```
num someVals[3] = 25, 36, 47
```

When you use a list of values to initialize an array, the first value you list is assigned to the first array element, and the subsequent values are assigned in order. In other words, `someVals[0]` is 25, `someVals[1]` is 36, and `someVals[2]` is 47. Many programming languages allow you to initialize an array with fewer values than there are array elements declared, but no language allows you to initialize an array using more values.

After an array has been declared and appropriate values have been assigned to specific elements, you can use the elements in the same way you would use any other data item of the same type. For example, you can input values to array elements and you can output them, and if the elements are numeric, you can perform arithmetic with them.

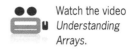

Watch the video *Understanding Arrays.*

The precise syntax used to declare an array varies. In some languages, the array size can be inferred from the size of a supplied list of initial values. For example, if you write the following, an array of four elements is created:

```
num someVals[] = 6, 8, 2, 4
```

In some languages, the brackets that indicate an array are placed following the data type, as in:

```
num[] someVals = 6, 8, 2, 4
```

Other languages require that you use terms to allocate memory or that you place the list of values between brackets. Even though the syntax used to declare arrays differs, the concepts are the same.

TWO TRUTHS & A LIE

Understanding Arrays and How They Occupy Computer Memory

1. In an array, each element has the same data type.

2. Each array element is accessed using a subscript, which can be a number or a string.

3. Array elements always occupy adjacent memory locations.

The false statement is #2. An array subscript must be a number. It can be a named constant, an unnamed constant, or a variable.

Manipulating an Array to Replace Nested Decisions

Consider an application requested by a Human Resources department to produce statistics on employees' claimed dependents. The department wants a report that lists the number of employees who have claimed 0, 1, 2, 3, 4, or 5 dependents. (Assume you know that no employees have more than five dependents.) For example, Figure 6-2 shows a typical report.

Without using an array, you could write the application that produces counts for the six categories of dependents (for each number of dependents, 0 through 5) by using a series of decisions. Figure 6-3 shows the pseudocode and flowchart for the decision-making part of such an application. Although this program works, its length and complexity are unnecessary once you understand how to use an array.

Dependents	Count
0	43
1	35
2	24
3	11
4	5
5	7

Figure 6-2   Typical Dependents report

In Figure 6-3, the variable dep is compared to 0. If it is 0, 1 is added to count0. If it is not 0, then dep is compared to 1. It is either added to count1 or compared to 2, and so on. Each time the application executes this decision-making process, 1 is added to one of the five variables that acts as a counter for one of the possible numbers of dependents. The dependent-counting application in Figure 6-3 works, but even with only six categories of dependents, the decision-making process is unwieldy. What if the number of dependents might be any value from 0 to 10, or 0 to 20? With either of these scenarios, the basic logic of the program would remain the same; however, you would need to declare many additional variables to hold the counts, and you would need many additional decisions.

The decision-making process in Figure 6-3 accomplishes its purpose, and the logic is correct, but the process is cumbersome and certainly not recommended. Follow the logic here so that you understand how the application works. In the next pages, you will see how to make the application more elegant.

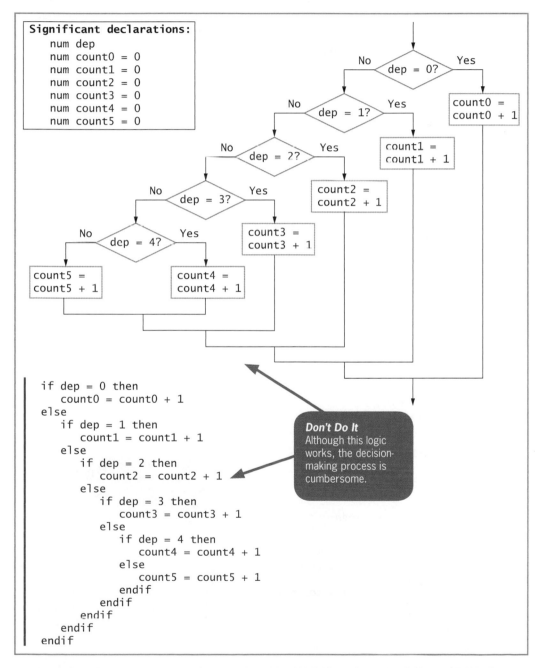

Figure 6-3 Flowchart and pseudocode of decision-making process using a series of decisions—the hard way

Using an array provides an alternate approach to this programming problem, which greatly reduces the number of statements you need. When you declare an array, you provide a group name for a number of associated variables in memory. For example, the six dependent count accumulators can be redefined as a single array named count. The individual elements become count[0], count[1], count[2], count[3], count[4], and count[5], as shown in the revised decision-making process in Figure 6-4.

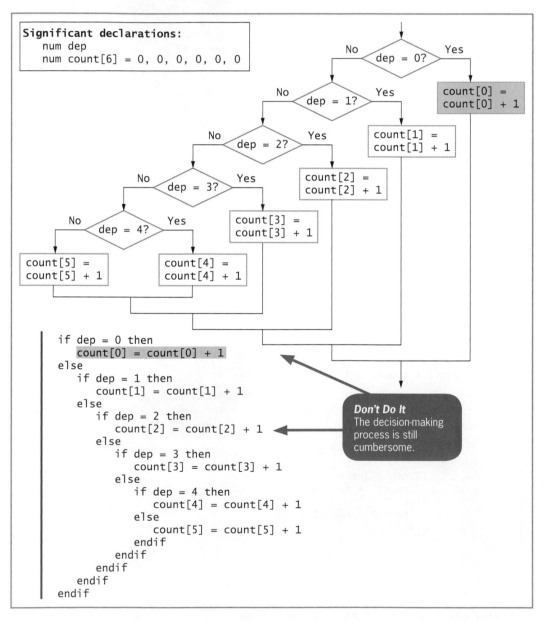

Figure 6-4 Flowchart and pseudocode of decision-making process—but still the hard way

The shaded statement in Figure 6-4 shows that when dep is 0, 1 is added to count[0]. You can see similar statements for the rest of the count elements; when dep is 1, 1 is added to count[1]; when dep is 2, 1 is added to count[2], and so on. When the dep value is 5, it means it was not 1, 2, 3, or 4, so 1 is added to count[5]. In other words, 1 is added to one of the elements of the count array instead of to an individual variable named count0, count1, count2, count3, count4, or count5. Is this version a big improvement over the original in Figure 6-3? Of course, it isn't. You still have not taken advantage of the benefits of using the array in this application.

The true benefit of using an array lies in your ability to use a variable as a subscript to the array, instead of using a literal constant such as 0 or 5. Notice in the logic in Figure 6-4 that within each decision, the value you are comparing to dep and the constant you are using as a subscript in the resulting "Yes" process are always identical. That is, when dep is 0, the subscript used to add 1 to the count array is 0; when dep is 1, the subscript used for the count array is 1, and so on. Therefore, you can just use dep as a subscript to the array. You can rewrite the decision-making process as shown in Figure 6-5.

236

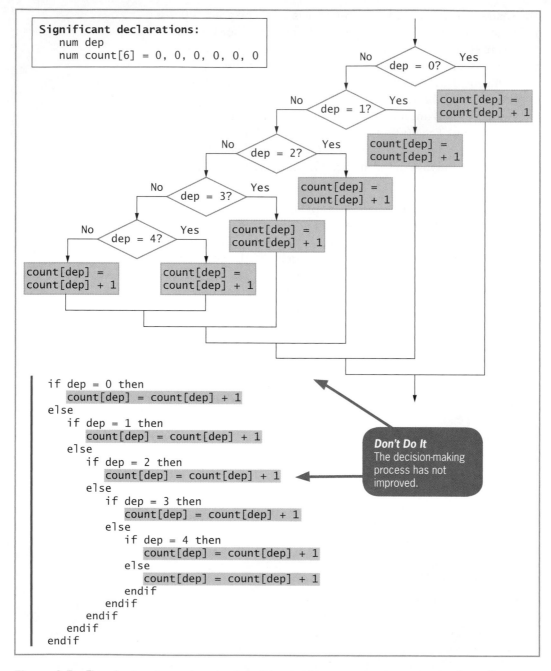

Significant declarations:
```
num dep
num count[6] = 0, 0, 0, 0, 0, 0
```

```
if dep = 0 then
    count[dep] = count[dep] + 1
else
    if dep = 1 then
        count[dep] = count[dep] + 1
    else
        if dep = 2 then
            count[dep] = count[dep] + 1
        else
            if dep = 3 then
                count[dep] = count[dep] + 1
            else
                if dep = 4 then
                    count[dep] = count[dep] + 1
                else
                    count[dep] = count[dep] + 1
                endif
            endif
        endif
    endif
endif
```

Don't Do It
The decision-making process has not improved.

Figure 6-5   Flowchart and pseudocode of decision-making process using an array—but still a hard way

The code segment in Figure 6-5 looks no more efficient than the one in Figure 6-4. However, notice the shaded statements in Figure 6-5— the process that occurs after each decision is exactly the same. In each case, no matter what the value of dep is, you always add 1 to count[dep]. If you will always take the same action no matter what the answer to a question is, why ask the question? Instead, you can rewrite the decision-making process, as shown in Figure 6-6.

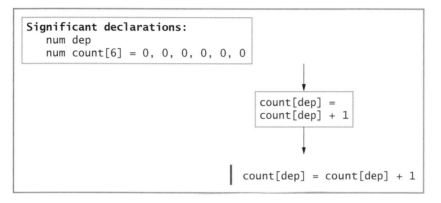

```
Significant declarations:
    num dep
    num count[6] = 0, 0, 0, 0, 0, 0
```

```
count[dep] =
count[dep] + 1
```

```
count[dep] = count[dep] + 1
```

Figure 6-6 Flowchart and pseudocode of efficient decision-making process using an array

The single statement in Figure 6-6 eliminates the *entire* decision-making process that was the original highlighted section in Figure 6-5! When dep is 2, 1 is added to count[2]; when dep is 4, 1 is added to count[4], and so on. *Now* you have a big improvement to the original process. What's more, this process does not change whether there are 20, 30, or any other number of possible categories. To use more than five accumulators, you would declare additional count elements in the array, but the categorizing logic would remain the same as it is in Figure 6-6.

Figure 6-7 shows an entire program that takes advantage of the array to produce the report that shows counts for dependent categories. Variables and constants are declared and, in the getReady() module, a first value for dep is entered into the program. In the countDependents() module, 1 is added to the appropriate element of the count array and the next value is input. The loop in the mainline logic in Figure 6-7 is an indefinite loop; it continues as long as the user does not enter the sentinel value. When data entry is complete, the finishUp() module displays the report. First, the heading is output, then dep is reset to 0, and each dep and count[dep] are output in a loop. The first output statement contains 0 (as the number of dependents) and the value stored in count[0]. Then, 1 is added to dep and the same set of instructions is used again to display the counts for each number of dependents. The loop in the finishUp() module is a definite loop; it executes precisely six times.

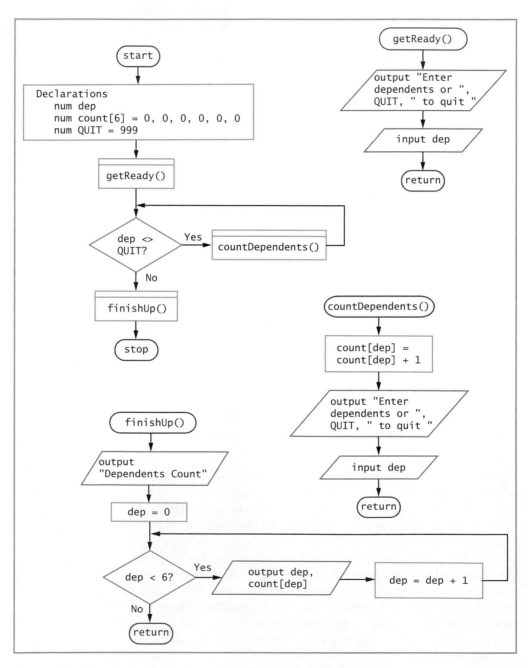

Figure 6-7   Flowchart and pseudocode for Dependents Report program

```
start
   Declarations
      num dep
      num count[6] = 0, 0, 0, 0, 0, 0
      num QUIT = 999
   getReady()
   while dep <> QUIT
      countDependents()
   endwhile
   finishUp()
stop

getReady()
   output "Enter dependents or ", QUIT, " to quit "
   input dep
return

countDependents()
   count[dep] = count[dep] + 1
   output "Enter dependents or ", QUIT, " to quit "
   input dep
return

finishUp()
   output "Dependents Count"
   dep = 0
   while dep < 6
      output dep, count[dep]
      dep = dep + 1
   endwhile
return
```

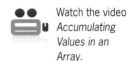

Watch the video *Accumulating Values in an Array.*

Figure 6-7 Flowchart and pseudocode for Dependents Report program (continued)

The dependent-counting program would have *worked* when it contained a long series of decisions and output statements, but the program is easier to write when you use an array and access its values using the number of dependents as a subscript. Additionally, the new program is more efficient, easier for other programmers to understand, and easier to maintain. Arrays are never mandatory, but often they can drastically cut down on your programming time and make your logic easier to understand.

Learning to use arrays correctly can make many programming tasks far more efficient and professional. When you understand how to use arrays, you will be able to provide elegant solutions to problems that otherwise would require tedious programming steps.

TWO TRUTHS & A LIE

Manipulating an Array to Replace Nested Decisions

1.   You can use an array to replace a long series of decisions.

2.   You realize a major benefit to using arrays when you use a numeric constant as a subscript as opposed to using a variable.

3.   The process of displaying every element in a 10-element array is basically no different from displaying every element in a 100-element array.

The false statement is #2. You realize a major benefit to using arrays when you use a variable as a subscript as opposed to using a constant.

Using Constants with Arrays

In Chapter 2, you learned that named constants hold values that do not change during a program's execution. When working with arrays, you can use constants in several ways:

- To hold the size of an array

- As the array values

- As a subscript

Using a Constant as the Size of an Array

The program in Figure 6-7 still contains one minor flaw. Throughout this book you have learned to avoid "magic numbers;" that is, unnamed constants. As the totals are output in the loop at the end of the program in Figure 6-7, the array subscript is compared to the constant 6. The program can be improved if you use a named constant instead. In most programming languages you can take one of two approaches:

- You can declare a named numeric constant such as num ARRAY_SIZE = 6. Then you can use this constant every time you access the array, always making sure any subscript you use remains less than the constant value.

- In many languages, when you declare an array, a constant that represents the array size is automatically provided for each array you create. For example, in Java, after you declare an array named `count`, its size is stored in a field named `count.length`. In both C# and Visual Basic, the array size is `count.Length`. (The difference is the uppercase "L" in `Length`.)

Besides making your code easier to modify, using a named constant makes the code easier to understand.

Using Constants as Array Element Values

Sometimes the values stored in arrays should be constants. For example, suppose you create an array that holds names for the months of the year. The first month is always "January"—the value should not change. You might create an array as follows:

Recall that the convention in this book is to use all upper-case letters in constant identifiers.

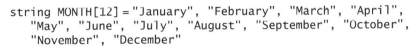

```
string MONTH[12] = "January", "February", "March", "April",
    "May", "June", "July", "August", "September", "October",
    "November", "December"
```

Using a Constant as an Array Subscript

Occasionally you will want to use a numeric constant as a subscript to an array. For example, to display the first value in an array named `salesArray`, you might write a statement that uses an unnamed, literal constant as follows:

```
output salesArray[0]
```

You might also have occasion to use a named constant as a subscript. For example, if `salesArray` holds sales values for each of 20 branches in your company, and Indiana is state 5, you could output the value for Indiana as follows:

```
output salesArray[5]
```

However, if you declare a named constant as `num INDIANA = 5`, then you can display the same value using this statement:

```
output salesArray[INDIANA]
```

An advantage to using a named constant in this case is that the statement becomes self-documenting—anyone who reads your statement more easily understands that your intention is to display the sales value for Indiana.

TWO TRUTHS & A LIE

Using Constants with Arrays

1. If you create a named constant equal to an array size, you can use it as a subscript to the array.

2. If you create a named constant equal to an array size, you can use it as a limit against which to compare subscript values.

3. In Java, C#, and Visual Basic, when you declare an array, a constant that represents the array size is automatically provided.

The false statement is #1. If the constant is equal to the array size, then it is larger than any valid array subscript.

Searching an Array

In the dependent-counting application in this chapter, the array's subscript variable conveniently held small whole numbers—the number of dependents allowed was 0 through 5—and the dep variable directly accessed the array. Unfortunately, real life doesn't always happen in small integers. Sometimes you don't have a variable that conveniently holds an array position; sometimes you have to search through an array to find a value you need.

Consider a mail-order business in which orders come in with a customer name, address, item number, and quantity ordered. Assume the item numbers from which a customer can choose are three-digit numbers, but perhaps they are not consecutively numbered 001 through 999. Instead, over the years, items have been deleted and new items have been added to the inventory. For example, there might no longer be an item with number 105 or 129. Sometimes there might be a hundred-number gap or more between items. For example, let's say that this season you are offering only six items: 106, 108, 307, 405, 457, and 688. In an office without a computer, if a customer orders item 307, a clerical worker can tell whether the order is valid by looking down the list and verifying that 307 is on it. In a similar fashion, a computer program can use a loop to test the ordered item number against each VALID_ITEM. When you search through a list from one end to the other, you are performing a **linear search**. See Figure 6-8.

In a similar fashion, a computer program can use a loop to test the ordered item number against each VALID_ITEM. In Figure 6-8, the six valid items are shown in the shaded array declaration VALID_ITEM. (The array is declared as constant because the item numbers will never change.) You could use a series of six decisions to compare each customer order's item number to each of the six allowed values. However, a superior approach is to create an array that holds the list of valid item numbers. Then you can search through the array for an exact match to the ordered item. If you search through the entire array without finding a match for the item the customer ordered, you can take action. For example, the program in Figure 6-8 displays an error message and adds 1 to a counter of bad items.

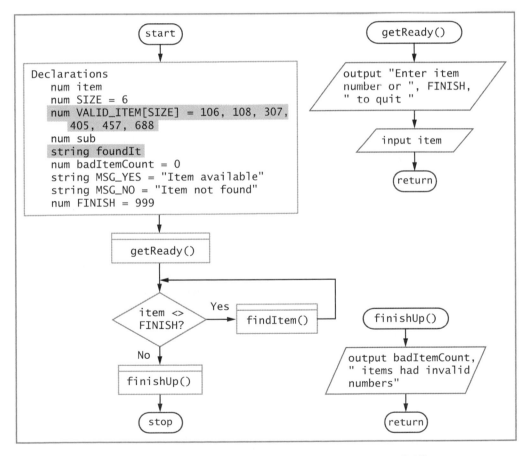

Figure 6-8 Flowchart and pseudocode for program that verifies item availability

244

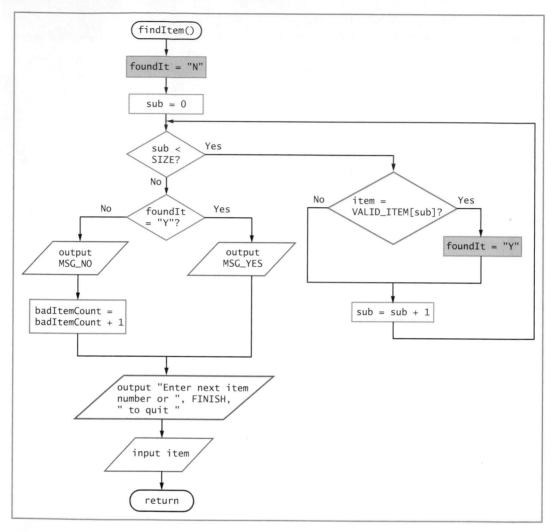

Figure 6-8 Flowchart and pseudocode for program that verifies item availability (continued)

```
start
   Declarations
      num item
      num SIZE = 6
      num VALID_ITEM[SIZE] = 106, 108, 307,
         405, 457, 688
      num sub
      string foundIt
      num badItemCount = 0
      string MSG_YES = "Item available"
      string MSG_NO = "Item not found"
      num FINISH = 999
   getReady()
   while item <> FINISH
      findItem()
   endwhile
   finishUp()
stop

getReady()
   output "Enter item number or ", FINISH, " to quit "
   input item
return

findItem()
   foundIt = "N"
   sub = 0
   while sub < SIZE
      if item = VALID_ITEM[sub] then
         foundIt = "Y"
      endif
      sub = sub + 1
   endwhile
   if foundIt = "Y" then
      output MSG_YES
   else
      output MSG_NO
      badItemCount = badItemCount + 1
   endif
   output "Enter next item number or ", FINISH, " to quit "
   input item
return

finishUp()
   output badItemCount, " items had invalid numbers"
return
```

Figure 6-8   Flowchart and pseudocode for program that verifies item availability (continued)

246

Instead of the string `foundIt` variable in the method in Figure 6-8, you might prefer to use a numeric variable that you set to 1 or 0. Most programming languages also support a Boolean data type that you can use for `foundIt`; when you declare a variable to be Boolean, you can set its value to true or false.

The technique for verifying that an item number exists involves setting a subscript to 0 and setting a flag variable to indicate that you have not yet determined whether the customer's order is valid. A **flag** is a variable that you set to indicate whether some event has occurred; frequently it holds a true or false value. For example, you can set a string variable named `foundIt` to "N", indicating "No". (See the first shaded statement in the `findItem()` method in Figure 6-8.) Then you compare the customer's ordered item number to the first item in the array. If the customer-ordered item matches the first item in the array, you can set the flag variable to "Y", or any other value that is not "N". (See the last shaded statement in the `findItem()` method in Figure 6-8.) If the items do not match, you increase the subscript and continue to look down the list of numbers stored in the array. If you check all six valid item numbers and the customer item matches none of them, then the flag variable `foundIt` still holds the value "N". If the flag variable is "N" after you have looked through the entire list, you can issue an error message indicating that no match was found.

TWO TRUTHS & A LIE

Searching an Array

1. Only whole numbers can be stored in arrays.

2. Only whole numbers can be used as array subscripts.

3. A flag is a variable that you set to indicate whether some event has occurred.

The false statement is #1. Whole numbers can be stored in arrays, but so can many other objects, including strings and numbers with decimal places.

Using Parallel Arrays

When you read a customer's order in a mail-order company program, you usually want to accomplish more than simply verifying the item's existence. For example, you might want to determine the price of the ordered item, multiply that price by the quantity ordered, and display the amount owed.

Suppose you have a list of item numbers and their associated prices. One array named VALID_ITEM contains six elements; each element is a valid item number. The other array also has six elements. The array is named VALID_PRICE; each element is a price of an item. Each price in the VALID_PRICE array is conveniently and purposely in the same position as the corresponding item number in the VALID_ITEM array. Two corresponding arrays such as these are **parallel arrays** because each element in one array is associated with the element in the same relative position in the other array. Figure 6-9 shows how the parallel arrays might look in computer memory.

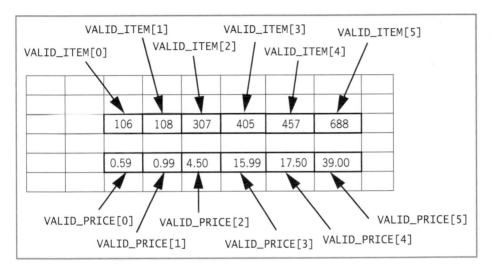

Figure 6-9   Parallel arrays in memory

When you use parallel arrays:

- Two or more arrays contain related data.

- A subscript relates the arrays. That is, elements at the same position in each array are logically related.

Figure 6-10 shows a program that declares parallel arrays. The VALID_PRICE array is shaded; each element in it corresponds to a valid item number.

 When you create parallel arrays, each array can be a different data type.

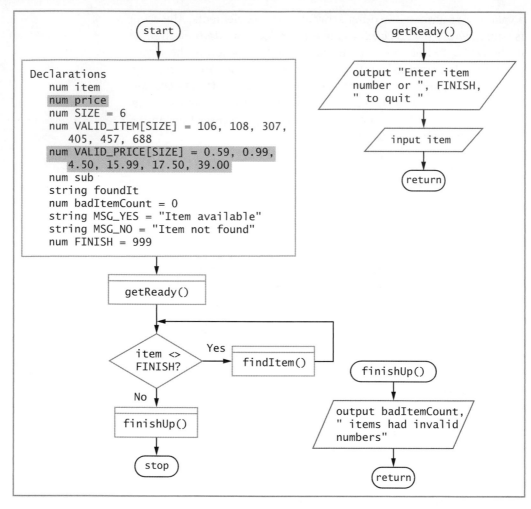

Figure 6-10 Flowchart and pseudocode of program that finds an item price using parallel arrays

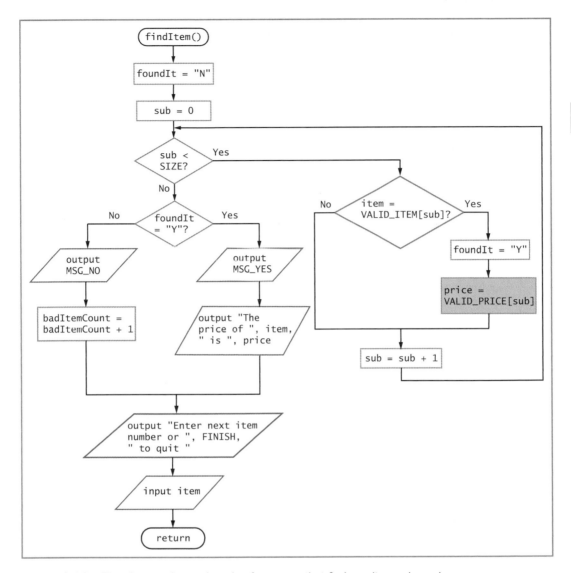

Figure 6-10   Flowchart and pseudocode of program that finds an item price using parallel arrays (continued)

```
start
    Declarations
        num item
        num price
        num SIZE = 6
        num VALID_ITEM[SIZE] = 106, 108, 307,
            405, 457, 688
        num VALID_PRICE[SIZE] = 0.59, 0.99,
            4.50, 15.99, 17.50, 39.00
        num sub
        string foundIt
        num badItemCount = 0
        string MSG_YES = "Item available"
        string MSG_NO = "Item not found"
        num FINISH = 999
    getReady()
    while item <> FINISH
        findItem()
    endwhile
    finishUp()
stop

getReady()
    output "Enter item number or ", FINISH, " to quit "
    input item
return

findItem()
    foundIt = "N"
    sub = 0
    while sub < SIZE
        if item = VALID_ITEM[sub] then
            foundIt = "Y"
            price = VALID_PRICE[sub]
        endif
        sub = sub + 1
    endwhile
    if foundIt = "Y" then
        output MSG_YES
        output "The price of ", item, " is ", price
    else
        output MSG_NO
        badItemCount = badItemCount + 1
    endif
    output "Enter next item number or ", FINISH, " to quit "
    input item
return

finishUp()
    output badItemCount, " items had invalid numbers"
return
```

Figure 6-10   Flowchart and pseudocode of program that finds an item price using parallel arrays (continued)

Some programmers object to using a cryptic variable name for a subscript, such as sub in Figure 6-10, because such names are not descriptive. These programmers would prefer a name like priceIndex. Others approve of short names when the variable is used only in a limited area of a program, as it is used here, to step through an array. Programmers disagree on many style issues like this one. As a programmer, it is your responsibility to find out what conventions are used among your peers in an organization.

As the program in Figure 6-10 receives a customer's order, it looks through each of the VALID_ITEM values separately by varying the subscript sub from 0 to the number of items available. When a match for the item number is found, the program pulls the corresponding parallel price out of the list of VALID_PRICE values and stores it in the price variable. (See shaded statements in Figure 6-10.)

The relationship between an item's number and its price is an **indirect relationship**. That means you don't access a price directly by knowing the item number. Instead, you determine the price by knowing an item number's position. Once you find a match for the ordered item number in the VALID_ITEM array, you know that the price of that item is in the same position in the other array, VALID_PRICE. When VALID_ITEM[sub] is the correct item, VALID_PRICE[sub] must be the correct price, so sub links the parallel arrays.

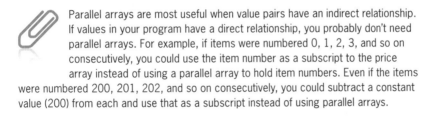

Parallel arrays are most useful when value pairs have an indirect relationship. If values in your program have a direct relationship, you probably don't need parallel arrays. For example, if items were numbered 0, 1, 2, 3, and so on consecutively, you could use the item number as a subscript to the price array instead of using a parallel array to hold item numbers. Even if the items were numbered 200, 201, 202, and so on consecutively, you could subtract a constant value (200) from each and use that as a subscript instead of using parallel arrays.

Suppose that a customer orders item 457. Walk through the logic yourself to see if you come up with the correct price per item, $17.50. Then, suppose that a customer orders item 458. Walk through the logic and see whether the appropriate "Item not found" message is displayed.

Improving Search Efficiency

The mail-order program in Figure 6-10 is still a little inefficient. If many customers order item 106 or 108, the prices are found on the first or second pass through the loop. However, the program continues searching through the item array until sub reaches the value SIZE. One way to stop the search when the item has been found and foundIt is set to "Y" is to change the loop-controlling question. Instead of simply continuing the loop while the number of comparisons does not exceed the array size, you should continue the loop while the searched item is not found *and* the number of comparisons has not exceeded the array size. Leaving a loop as soon as a match is found improves the program's efficiency. The larger the array, the more beneficial it becomes to exit the searching loop as soon as you find the desired value.

Figure 6-11 shows the improved version of the findItem() module with the altered loop-controlling question shaded.

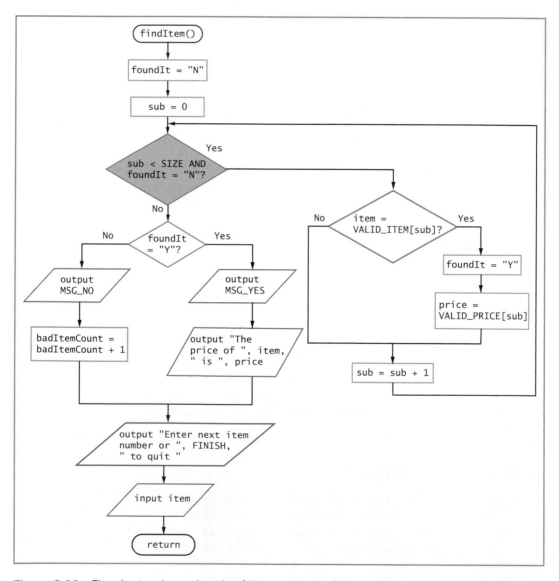

Figure 6-11   Flowchart and pseudocode of the module that finds an item price, exiting the loop as soon as it is found

Watch the video *Using Parallel Arrays*.

```
findItem()
   foundIt = "N"
   sub = 0
   while sub < SIZE AND foundIt = "N"
      if item = VALID_ITEM[sub] then
         foundIt = "Y"
         price = VALID_PRICE[sub]
      endif
      sub = sub + 1
   endwhile
   if foundIt = "Y" then
      output MSG_YES
      output "The price of ", item, " is ", price
   else
      output MSG_NO
      badItemCount = badItemCount + 1
   endif
   output "Enter next item number or ", FINISH, " to quit "
   input item
return
```

253

Figure 6-11 Flowchart and pseudocode of the module that finds an item price, exiting the loop as soon as it is found (continued)

Notice that the price-finding program is most efficient when the most frequently ordered items are stored at the beginning of the array. Only the seldom-ordered items require loops before finding a match. Often, you can improve sort efficiency by rearranging array elements.

As you study programming, you will learn search techniques other than a linear search. For example, a **binary search** starts looking in the middle of a sorted list, and then determines whether it should continue higher or lower.

TWO TRUTHS & A LIE

Using Parallel Arrays

1. Parallel arrays must be the same data type.

2. Parallel arrays usually contain the same number of elements.

3. You can improve the efficiency of searching through parallel arrays by using an early exit.

The false statement is #1. Parallel arrays do not need to be the same data type. For example, you might look up a name in a string array to find each person's age in a parallel numeric array.

Searching an Array for a Range Match

Customer order item numbers need to match available item numbers exactly to determine the correct price of an item. Sometimes, however, programmers want to work with ranges of values in arrays. In Chapter 4, you learned that a range of values is any series of values—for example, 1 through 5 or 20 through 30.

Suppose a company decides to offer quantity discounts when a customer orders multiple items, as shown in Figure 6-12.

Quantity	Discount %
0–8	0
9–12	10
13–25	15
26 or more	20

Figure 6-12   Discounts on orders by quantity

You want to be able to read in customer order data and determine a discount percentage based on the value in the quantity field. For example, if a customer has ordered 20 items, you want to be able to output "Your discount is 15 percent". One ill-advised approach might be to set up an array with as many elements as any customer might ever order, and store the appropriate discount for each possible number, as shown in Figure 6-13. This array is set up to contain the discount for 0 items, 1 item, 2 items, and so on. This approach has at least three drawbacks:

- It requires a very large array that uses a lot of memory.

- You must store the same value repeatedly. For example, each of the first nine elements receives the same value, 0, and each of the next four elements receives the same value, 10.

- How do you know you have enough array elements? Is a customer order quantity of 75 items enough? What if a customer orders 100 or 1000 items? No matter how many elements you place in the array, there's always a chance that a customer will order more.

```
numeric DISCOUNT[76]
 = 0, 0, 0, 0, 0, 0, 0, 0, 0,
   0.10, 0.10, 0.10, 0.10,
   0.15, 0.15, 0.15, 0.15, 0.15,
   0.15, 0.15, 0.15, 0.15, 0.15,
   0.15, 0.15, 0.15,
   0.20, 0.20, 0.20, 0.20, 0.20,
   0.20, 0.20, 0.20, 0.20, 0.20,
   0.20, 0.20, 0.20, 0.20, 0.20,
   0.20, 0.20, 0.20, 0.20, 0.20,
   0.20, 0.20, 0.20, 0.20, 0.20,
   0.20, 0.20, 0.20, 0.20, 0.20,
   0.20, 0.20, 0.20, 0.20, 0.20,
   0.20, 0.20, 0.20, 0.20, 0.20,
   0.20, 0.20, 0.20, 0.20, 0.20,
   0.20, 0.20, 0.20, 0.20, 0.20
```

Don't Do It
Although this array is usable, it is repetitious, prone to error, and difficult to use.

255

Figure 6-13 Usable—but inefficient—discount array

A better approach is to create two parallel arrays, each with four elements, as shown in Figure 6-14. Each

```
num DISCOUNT[4]   =   0, 0.10, 0.15, 0.20
num QUAN_LIMIT[4] = 0,    9,   13,   26
```

Figure 6-14 Parallel arrays to use for determining discount

discount rate is listed once in the DISCOUNT array, and the low end of each quantity range is listed in the QUAN_LIMIT array.

To find the correct discount for any customer's ordered quantity, you can start with the *last* quantity range limit (QUAN_LIMIT[3]). If the quantity ordered is at least that value, 26, the loop is never entered and the customer gets the highest discount rate (DISCOUNT[3], or 20 percent). If the quantity ordered is not at least QUAN_LIMIT[3]— that is, if it is less than 26—then you reduce the subscript and check to see if the quantity is at least QUAN_LIMIT[2], or 13. If so, the customer receives DISCOUNT[2], or 15 percent, and so on. Figure 6-15 shows a program that accepts a customer's quantity ordered and determines the appropriate discount rate.

256

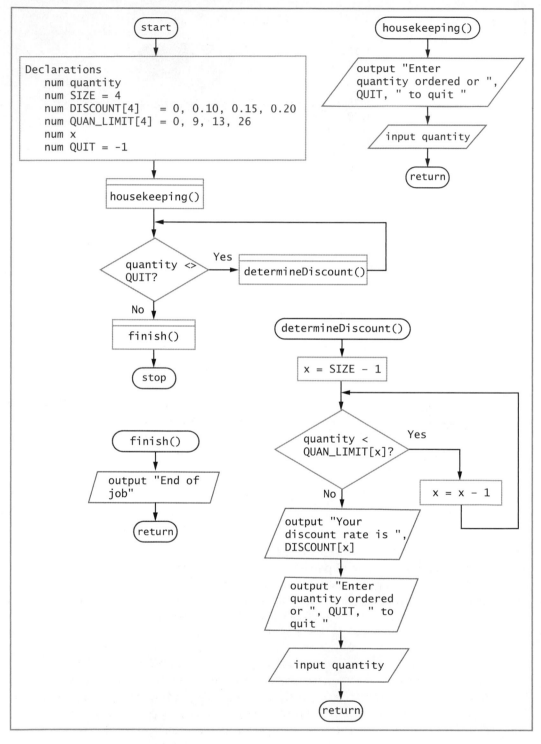

Figure 6-15   Program that determines discount rate

```
start
   Declarations
      num quantity
      num SIZE = 4
      num DISCOUNT[4] =   0, 0.10, 0.15, 0.20
      num QUAN_LIMIT[4] = 0,    9,   13,   26
      num x
      num QUIT = -1
   housekeeping()
   while quantity <> QUIT
     determineDiscount()
   endwhile
   finish()
stop

housekeeping()
   output "Enter quantity ordered or ", QUIT, " to quit "
   input quantity
return

determineDiscount()
   x = SIZE - 1
   while quantity < QUAN_LIMIT[x]
      x = x - 1
   endwhile
   output "Your discount rate is ", DISCOUNT[x]
   output "Enter quantity ordered or ", QUIT, " to quit "
   input quantity
return

finish()
   output "End of job"
return
```

Figure 6-15 Program that determines discount rate (continued)

When using an array to store range limits, you use a loop to make a series of comparisons that would otherwise require many separate decisions. The program that determines customer discount rates is written using fewer instructions than would be required if you did not use an array, and modifications to your method will be easier to make in the future.

An alternate approach to the one taken in Figure 6-15 is to store the high end of every range in an array. Then you start with the *lowest* element and check for values *less than or equal to* each array element value.

257

TWO TRUTHS & A LIE

Searching an Array for a Range Match

1. To help locate a range within which a value falls, you can store the highest value in each range in an array.

2. To help locate a range within which a value falls, you can store the lowest value in each range in an array.

3. When using an array to store range limits, you use a series of comparisons that would otherwise require many separate loop structures.

The false statement is #3. When using an array to store range limits, you use a loop to make a series of comparisons that would otherwise require many separate rate decisions.

Remaining within Array Bounds

Every array has a finite size. You can think of an array's size in one of two ways—either by the number of elements in the array or by the number of bytes in the array. Arrays are always composed of elements of the same data type, and elements of the same data type always occupy the same number of bytes of memory, so the number of bytes in an array is always a multiple of the number of elements in an array. For example, in Java, integers occupy 4 bytes of memory, so an array of 10 integers occupies exactly 40 bytes.

In every programming language, when you access data stored in an array, it is important to use a subscript containing a value that accesses memory occupied by the array. For example, examine the program in Figure 6-16. The method accepts a numeric value for monthNum and displays the name associated with that month.

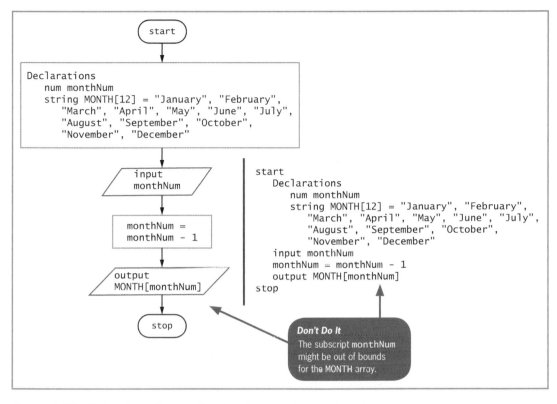

Figure 6-16 Determining the month string from user's numeric entry

 In the program in Figure 6-16, notice that 1 is subtracted from monthNum when it is used as a subscript. Although most people think of January as month 1, its name occupies the location in the array with the 0 subscript. With values that seem naturally to start with 1, like month numbers, some programmers would prefer to create a 13-element array and simply never use the zero-position element. That way, each "natural" month number would be the correct value to access its data without subtracting. Other programmers dislike wasting memory by creating an extra, unused element. Although workable programs can be created with or without the extra array element, professional programmers should follow the conventions and preferences of their colleagues and managers.

The logic in Figure 6-16 makes a questionable assumption: that every number entered by the user is a valid month number. If the user enters a number that is too small or too large, one of two things will happen depending on the programming language you use. When you use a subscript value that is negative or higher than the number of elements in an array:

- Some programming languages will stop execution of the program and issue an error message.

260

A user might enter an invalid number, or might not enter a number at all. In Chapter 5, you learned that many languages have a built-in method with a name like isNumeric() that can test for such mistakes.

- Other programming languages will not issue an error message but will access a value in a memory location that is outside the area occupied by the array. That area might contain garbage, or worse, it accidentally might contain the name of an incorrect month.

Either way, a logical error occurs. When you use a subscript that is not within the range of acceptable subscripts, your subscript is said to be **out of bounds**. Users enter incorrect data frequently; a good program should be able to handle the mistake and not allow the subscript to be out of bounds.

You can improve the program in Figure 6-16 by adding a test that ensures the subscript used to access the array is within the array bounds. After you test the input value to ensure it is between 1 and 12 inclusive, you might take one of the following approaches if it is not:

- Display an error message and end the program.

- Use a default value for the month. For example, when an entered month is invalid, you might want to use a default value of December.

- Continuously reprompt the user for a new value until it is valid.

Which technique you use depends on the requirements of your program.

TWO TRUTHS & A LIE

Remaining Within Array Bounds

1. Elements in an array frequently are different data types, so calculating the amount of memory the array occupies is difficult.

2. If you attempt to access an array with a subscript that is too small, some programming languages will stop execution of the program and issue an error message.

3. If you attempt to access an array with a subscript that is too large, some programming languages access an incorrect memory location outside the array bounds.

The false statement is #1. Array elements are always the same data type, and elements of the same data type always occupy the same number of bytes of memory, so the number of bytes in an array is always a multiple of the number of elements in an array.

Using a for Loop to Process Arrays

In Chapter 5, you learned about the for loop—a loop that, in a single statement, initializes a loop control variable, compares it to a limit, and alters it. The for loop is a particularly convenient tool when working with arrays because you frequently need to process every element of an array from beginning to end. As with a while loop, when you use a for loop, you must be careful to stay within array bounds, remembering that the highest usable array subscript is one less than the size of the array. Figure 6-17 shows a for loop that correctly displays all the department names in an array declared as DEPTS. Notice that dep is incremented through one less than the number of departments because with a five-item array, the subscripts you can use are 0 through 4.

```
start
   Declarations
      num dep
      num SIZE = 5
      string DEPTS[SIZE] = "Accounting", "Personnel",
         "Technical", "Customer Service", "Marketing"
   for dep = 0 to SIZE - 1 step 1
      output DEPTS[dep]
   endfor
stop
```

Figure 6-17 Pseudocode that uses a for loop to display an array of department names

The loop in Figure 6-17 is slightly inefficient because, as it executes five times, the subtraction operation that deducts 1 from SIZE occurs each time. Five subtraction operations do not consume much computer power or time, but in a loop that processes thousands or millions of array elements, the program's efficiency would be compromised. Figure 6-18 shows a superior solution. A new constant called ARRAY_LIMIT is calculated once, then used repeatedly in the comparison operation to determine when to stop cycling through the array.

```
start
   Declarations
      num dep
      num SIZE = 5
      num ARRAY_LIMIT = SIZE - 1
      string DEPTS[SIZE] = "Accounting", "Personnel",
         "Technical", "Customer Service", "Marketing"
   for dep = 0 to ARRAY_LIMIT step 1
      output DEPTS[dep]
   endfor
stop
```

Figure 6-18 Pseudocode that uses a more efficient for loop to output department names

TWO TRUTHS & A LIE

Using a for Loop to Process Arrays

1. The for loop is a particularly convenient tool when working with arrays.

2. You frequently need to process every element of an array from beginning to end.

3. An advantage to using a for loop to process array elements is that you don't need to be concerned about array bounds.

The false statement is #3. As with a while loop, when you use a for loop, you must be careful to stay within array bounds.

Chapter Summary

- An array is a series or list of values in computer memory, all of which have the same name and data type but are differentiated with special numbers called subscripts. Each array element occupies an area in memory next to, or contiguous to, the others.

- You often can use a variable as a subscript to an array, which allows you to replace multiple nested decisions with many fewer statements.

- Constants can be used to hold an array's size or to represent its values. Using a named constant for an array's size makes the code easier to understand and less likely to contain an error. Array values are declared as constant when they should not change during program execution.

- Searching through an array to find a value you need involves initializing a subscript, using a loop to test each array element, and setting a flag when a match is found.

- With parallel arrays, each element in one array is associated with the element in the same relative position in the other array.

- When you need to compare a value to a range of values in an array, you can store either the low- or high-end value of each range for comparison.

- When you access data stored in an array, it is important to use a subscript containing a value that accesses memory occupied by the array. When you use a subscript that is not within the defined range of acceptable subscripts, your subscript is said to be out of bounds.

- The for loop is a particularly convenient tool when working with arrays because you frequently need to process every element of an array from beginning to end.

Key Terms

An **array** is a series or list of values in computer memory, all of which have the same name but are differentiated with special numbers called subscripts.

A **subscript**, also called an **index**, is a number that indicates the position of a particular item within an array.

An **element** is a single data item in an array.

The **size of the array** is the number of elements it can hold.

Populating an array is the act of assigning values to the array elements.

A **linear search** is a search through a list from one end to the other.

A **flag** is a variable that you set to indicate whether some event has occurred.

In **parallel arrays**, each element in one array is associated with the element in the same relative position in the other array(s).

An **indirect relationship** describes the relationship between parallel arrays in which an element in the first array does not directly access its corresponding value in the second array.

A **binary search** is one that starts in the middle of a sorted list, and then determines whether it should continue higher or lower to find a target value.

Out of bounds describes an array subscript that is not within the range of acceptable subscripts for the array.

Review Questions

1. A subscript is a(n) _____.

   a. element in an array

   b. alternate name for an array

   c. number that represents the highest value stored within an array

   d. number that indicates the position of an array element

2. Each variable in an array must have the same _____ as the others.

   a. data type

   b. subscript

   c. value

   d. memory location

3. Each data item in an array is called a(n) _____.

   a. data type

   b. subscript

   c. component

   d. element

4. The subscripts of any array are always _____.

   a. integers

   b. fractions

   c. characters

   d. strings of characters

5. Suppose you have an array named `number`, and two of its elements are `number[1]` and `number[4]`. You know that _____.

   a. the two elements hold the same value

   b. the array holds exactly four elements

   c. there are exactly two elements between those two elements

   d. the two elements are at the same memory location

6. Suppose you want to write a program that inputs customer data and displays a summary of the number of customers who owe more than $1000 each, in each of 12 sales regions. Customer data variables include `name`, `zipCode`, `balanceDue`, and `regionNumber`. At some point during record processing, you would add 1 to an array element whose subscript would be represented by _____.

   a. `name`

   b. `zipCode`

   c. `balanceDue`

   d. `regionNumber`

7. The most useful type of subscript for manipulating arrays is a _____.

   a. numeric constant

   b. variable

   c. character

   d. filename

8. A program contains a seven-element array that holds the names of the days of the week. At the start of the program, you display the day names using a subscript named `dayNum`. You display the same array values again at the end of the program, where you _____ as a subscript to the array.

   a. must use `dayNum`

   b. can use `dayNum`, but can also use another variable

   c. must not use `dayNum`

   d. must use a numeric constant instead of a variable

9. Suppose you have declared an array as follows:
   `num values[4] = 0, 0, 0, 0`. Which of the following is an allowed operation?

   a. `values[2] = 17`

   b. `input values[0]`

   c. `values[3] = values[0] + 10`

   d. all of the above

10. Filling an array with values during a program's execution is known as _____ the array.

   a. executing

   b. colonizing

   c. populating

   d. declaring

11. Using an array can make a program _____.

   a. easier to understand

   b. illegal in some modern languages

   c. harder to maintain

   d. all of the above

12. A _____ is a variable that you set to indicate whether some event has occurred.

   a. subscript

   b. banner

   c. counter

   d. flag

13. What do you call two arrays in which each element in one array is associated with the element in the same relative position in the other array?

   a. cohesive arrays

   b. parallel arrays

   c. hidden arrays

   d. perpendicular arrays

14. In most modern programming languages, the highest subscript you should use with a 10-element array is _____.

   a. 8

   b. 9

   c. 10

   d. 11

15. Parallel arrays _____.

    a. frequently have an indirect relationship

    b. never have an indirect relationship

    c. must be the same data type

    d. must not be the same data type

16. Each element in a five-element array can hold _____ value(s).

    a. one

    b. five

    c. at least five

    d. an unlimited number of

17. After the annual dog show in which the Barkley Dog Training Academy awards points to each participant, the academy assigns a status to each dog based on the following criteria:

Points Earned	Level of Achievement
0–5	Good
6–7	Excellent
8–9	Superior
10	Unbelievable

    The academy needs a program that compares a dog's points earned with the grading scale, so that each dog can receive a certificate acknowledging the appropriate level of achievement. Of the following, which set of values would be most useful for the contents of an array used in the program?

    a. 0, 6, 9, 10

    b. 5, 7, 8, 10

    c. 5, 7, 9, 10

    d. any of these

18. When you use a subscript value that is negative or higher than the number of elements in an array, _____.

   a.   execution of the program stops and an error message is issued

   b.   a value in a memory location that is outside the area occupied by the array will be accessed

   c.   a value in a memory location that is outside the area occupied by the array will be accessed, but only if the value is the correct data type

   d.   the resulting action depends on the programming language used

19. In every array, a subscript is out of bounds when it is _____.

   a.   negative

   b.   0

   c.   1

   d.   999

20. You can access every element of an array using a _____.

   a.   `while` loop

   b.   `for` loop

   c.   both of the above

   d.   none of the above

Exercises

1. a.   Design the logic for a program that allows a user to enter 10 numbers, then displays them in the reverse order of their entry.

   b.   Modify the reverse-display program so that the user can enter up to 10 numbers until a sentinel value is entered.

2. a.   Design the logic for a program that allows a user to enter 10 numbers, then displays each number and its difference from the numeric average of the numbers entered.

   b.   Modify the program in Exercise 2a so that the user can enter up to 10 numbers until a sentinel value is entered.

3. a. The city of Cary is holding a special census. The city has collected data on cards that each hold the voting district and age of a citizen. The districts are numbered 1 through 22, and residents' ages range from 0 through 105. Design a program that allows a clerk to go through the cards, entering the district for each citizen until an appropriate sentinel value is entered. The output is a list of all 22 districts and the number of residents in each.

    b. Modify Exercise 3a so the clerk enters both the district and age on each card. Produce a count of the number of residents in each of the 22 districts and a count of residents in each of the following age groups: under 18, 18 through 30, 31 through 45, 46 through 64, and 65 and older.

4. a. The Midville Park District maintains five soccer teams, as shown in the table. Design a program that accepts a player's team number and displays the player's team name.

    b. Modify the Midville Park District program so that after the last player has been entered, the program displays a count of the number of players registered for each team.

Team Number	Team Name
1	Goal Getters
2	The Force
3	Top Guns
4	Shooting Stars
5	Midfield Monsters

5. a. Watson Elementary School contains 30 classrooms numbered 1 through 30. Each classroom can contain any number of students up to 35. Each student takes an achievement test at the end of the school year and receives a score from 0 through 100. Write a program that accepts data for each student in the school—student ID, classroom number, and score on the achievement test. Design a program that lists the total points scored for each of the 30 classrooms.

    b. Modify the Watson Elementary School program so that each classroom's average of the test scores is output, rather than each classroom's total.

6. The Billy Goat Fast-Food restaurant sells the following products:

Product	Price ($)
Cheeseburger	2.49
Pepsi	1.00
Chips	0.59

Design the logic for an application that allows a user to enter an ordered item continuously until a sentinel value is entered. After each item, display its price or the message "Sorry, we do not carry that" as output. After all items have been entered, display the total price for the order.

7. Design the application logic for a company that wants a report containing a breakdown of payroll by department. Input includes each employee's department number, hourly salary, and number of hours worked. The output is a list of the seven departments in the company

Department Number	Department Name
1	Personnel
2	Marketing
3	Manufacturing
4	Computer Services
5	Sales
6	Accounting
7	Shipping

and the total gross payroll (rate times hours) for each department. The department names are shown in the accompanying table.

8. Design a program that computes pay for employees. Allow a user to continuously input employees' names until an appropriate sentinel value is entered. Also input each employee's hourly wage and hours worked. Compute

Weekly Gross Pay ($)	Withholding Percent (%)
0.00–200.00	10
200.01–350.00	14
350.01–500.00	18
500.01 and up	22

each employee's gross pay (hours times rate), withholding tax percentage (based on the accompanying table), withholding tax amount, and net pay (gross pay minus withholding tax). Display all the results for each employee. After the last employee has been entered, display the sum of all the hours worked, the total gross payroll, the total withholding for all employees, and the total net payroll.

9. The Perfect Party Catering Company hosts events for clients. Create an application that accepts an event number, the event host's last name, and numeric month, day, and year values representing

Code	Entrée	Price per Person ($)
1	Roast beef	24.50
2	Salmon	19.00
3	Linguine	16.50
4	Chicken	18.00

the event date. The application should also accept the number of guests who will attend the event and a numeric meal code that represents the entrée the event hosts will serve. As each client's data is entered, verify that the month, day, year, and meal code are valid; if any of these is not valid, continue to prompt the user until it is. The valid meal codes are shown in the accompanying table.

Design the logic for an application that outputs each event number, host name, validated date, meal code, entrée name, number of guests, gross total price for the party, and price for the party after discount. The gross

Number of Guests	Discount ($)
1–25	0
26–50	75
51–100	125
101–250	200
251 and over	300

total price for the party is the meal price per guest times the number of guests. The final price includes a discount based on the accompanying table.

10. a. *Daily Life Magazine* wants an analysis of the demographic characteristics of its readers. The Marketing department has collected reader survey records containing the age, gender, marital status, and annual income of readers. Design an application that allows a user to enter reader data and, when data entry is complete, produces a count of readers by age groups as follows: under 20, 20–29, 30–39, 40–49, and 50 and older.

   b. Modify the *Daily Life Magazine* program so that it produces a count of readers by gender within age group— that is, under-20 females, under-20 males, and so on.

   c. Modify the *Daily Life Magazine* program so that it produces a count of readers by income groups as follows: under $30,000, $30,000–$49,999, $50,000–$69,999, and $70,000 and up.

11. Glen Ross Vacation Property Sales employs seven salespeople, as shown in the accompanying table.

When a salesperson makes a sale, a record is created, including the date, time, and dollar amount of the sale. The time is expressed in hours and minutes, based on a 24-hour clock. The sale amount is expressed in whole dollars. Salespeople earn a commission that differs for each sale, based on the rate schedule in the accompanying table.

ID Number	Salesperson Name
103	Darwin
104	Kratz
201	Shulstad
319	Fortune
367	Wickert
388	Miller
435	Vick

Sale Amount ($)	Commission Rate (%)
0–50,999	4
51,000–125,999	5
126,000–200,999	6
201,000 and up	7

Design an application that produces each of the following:

a. A list of each salesperson number, name, total sales, and total commissions

b. A list of each month of the year as both a number and a word (for example, "01 January"), and the total sales for the month for all salespeople

c. A list of total sales as well as total commissions earned by all salespeople for each of the following time frames, based on hour of the day: 00–05, 06–12, 13–18, and 19–23

Find the Bugs

12. Your student disk contains files named DEBUG06-01.txt, DEBUG06-02.txt, and DEBUG06-03.txt. Each file starts with some comments that describe the problem. Comments are lines that begin with two slashes (//). Following the comments, each file contains pseudocode that has one or more bugs you must find and correct.

Game Zone

13. Create the logic for a Magic 8 Ball© game in which the user enters a question such as "What does my future hold?". The computer randomly selects one of eight possible vague answers, such as "It remains to be seen".

14. Create the logic for an application that contains an array of 10 multiple-choice questions related to your favorite hobby. Each question contains three answer choices. Also create a parallel array that holds the correct answer to each question—A, B, or C. Display each question and verify that the user enters only A, B, or C as the answer—if not, keep prompting the user until a valid response is entered. If the user responds to a question correctly, display "Correct!"; otherwise, display "The correct answer is " and the letter of the correct answer. After the user answers all the questions, display the number of correct and incorrect answers.

15. a. Create the logic for a dice game. The application randomly "throws" five dice for the computer and five dice for the player. After each random throw, store the results in an array. The application displays all the values, which can be from 1 to 6 inclusive for each die. Decide the winner based on the following hierarchy of die values. Any higher combination beats a lower one; for example, five of a kind beats four of a kind.

   - Five of a kind

   - Four of a kind

   - Three of a kind

   - A pair

   For this game, the numeric dice values do not count. For example, if both players have three of a kind, it's a tie, no matter what the values of the three dice are.

Figure 6-19   Typical execution of the dice game

   Additionally, the game does not recognize a full house (three of a kind plus two of a kind). Figure 6-19 shows how the game might be played in a command-line environment.

b. Improve the dice game so that when both players have the same combination of dice values, the higher value wins. For example, two 6s beats two 5s.

16. Design the logic for the game Hangman, in which the user guesses letters in a hidden word. Store the letters of a word in an array of characters. Display a dash for each missing letter. Allow the user to continuously guess a letter until all the letters in the word are guessed correctly. As the user enters each guess, display the word again, filling in the guess if it was correct. For example, if the hidden word is "computer," first display "--------". After the user guesses "p", the display becomes "---p----". Make sure that when a user makes a correct guess, all the matching letters are filled in. For example, if the word is "banana" and the user guesses "a", all three "a" characters must be filled in.

17. Create two parallel arrays that represent a standard deck of 52 playing cards. One array is numeric and holds the values 1 through 13 (representing Ace, 2 through 10, Jack, Queen, and King). The other array is a string array and holds suits ("Clubs", "Diamonds", "Hearts", and "Spades"). Create the arrays so that all 52 cards are represented. Create a War card game that randomly selects two cards (one for the player and one for the computer) and declares a winner or a tie based on the numeric value of the two cards. The game should play for 26 rounds, dealing a full deck with no repeated cards. For this game, assume that the lowest card is the Ace. Display the values of the player's and computer's cards, compare their values, and determine the winner. When all the cards in the deck are exhausted, display a count of the number of times the player wins, the number of times the computer wins, and the number of ties.

Here are some hints:

• Start by creating an array of all 52 playing cards.

• Select a random number for the deck position of the player's first card and assign the card at that array position to the player.

• Move every higher-positioned card in the deck "down" one to fill in the gap. In other words, if the player's first random number is 49, select the card at position 49 (both the numeric value and the string), move the card that was in position 50 to position 49, and move the card that was in position 51 to position 50. Only 51 cards remain in the deck after the player's first card is dealt, so the available-card array is smaller by one.

- In the same way, randomly select a card for the computer and "remove" the card from the deck.

 Up for Discussion

18. A train schedule is an everyday, real-life example of an array. Think of at least four more.

19. Every element in an array always has the same data type. Why is this necessary?

CHAPTER 7

File Handling and Applications

In this chapter, you will learn about:

◎ Computer files

◎ The data hierarchy

◎ Performing file operations

◎ Sequential files and control break logic

◎ Merging sequential files

◎ Master and transaction file processing

◎ Random access files

Understanding Computer Files

In Chapter 1, you learned that computer memory, or random access memory (RAM), is temporary storage. When you write a program that stores a value in a variable, you are using temporary storage; the value you store is lost when the program ends or the computer loses power. This type of storage is volatile.

Permanent storage, on the other hand, is not lost when a computer loses power; it is nonvolatile. When you write a program and save it to a disk, you are using permanent storage.

 When discussing computer storage, *temporary* and *permanent* refer to volatility, not length of time. For example, a *temporary* variable might exist for several hours in a very large program or one that runs in an infinite loop, but a *permanent* piece of data might be saved and then deleted by a user within a few seconds. Because you can erase data from files, some programmers prefer the term *persistent storage* to permanent storage. In other words, you can remove data from a file stored on a device such as a disk drive, so it is not technically permanent. However, the data remains in the file even when the computer loses power, so, unlike in RAM, the data persists.

A **computer file** is a collection of data stored on a nonvolatile device in a computer system. Files exist on **permanent storage devices**, such as hard disks, DVDs, USB drives, and reels of magnetic tape. The two broad categories of files are:

- **Text files**, which contain data that can be read in a text editor because the data has been encoded using a scheme such as ASCII or Unicode. Text files might include facts and figures used by business programs, such as a payroll file that contains employee numbers, names, and salaries. The programs in this chapter will use text files.

- **Binary files**, which contain data that has not been encoded as text. Examples include images and music.

Although their contents vary, files have many common characteristics, as follows:

- Each has a name. The name often includes a dot and a file extension that describes the type of the file. For example, .txt is a plain text file, .dat is a data file, and .jpg is an image file in Joint Pictures Expert Group format.

- Each file has a specific time of creation and a time it was last modified.

 Watch the video *Understanding Files.*

- Each file occupies space on a section of a storage device; that is, each file has a size. Sizes are measured in bytes. A **byte** is a small

Appendix A contains more information on bytes and how file sizes are expressed.

unit of storage; for example, in a simple text file, a byte holds only one character. Because a byte is so small, file sizes usually are expressed in **kilobytes** (thousands of bytes), **megabytes** (millions of bytes), or **gigabytes** (billions of bytes).

Figure 7-1 shows how some files look when you view them in Microsoft Windows.

278

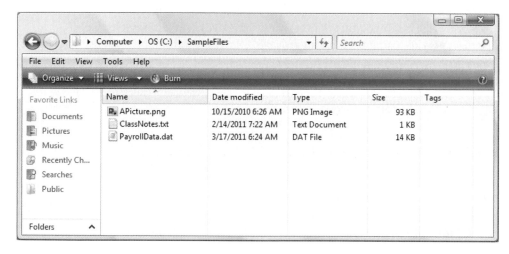

Figure 7-1 Three stored files showing their names, dates of modification, and sizes

Organizing Files

Computer files on a storage device are the electronic equivalent of paper files stored in file cabinets. With a physical file cabinet, the easiest way to store a document is to toss it into a drawer without a folder. However, for better organization, most office clerks place paper documents in folders and most computer users organize their files into folders or directories. **Directories** and **folders** are organization units on storage devices; each can contain multiple files as well as additional directories. The combination of the disk drive plus the complete hierarchy of directories in which a file resides is its **path**. For example, in the Windows operating system, the following line would be the complete path for a file named PayrollData.dat on the C drive in a folder named SampleFiles within a folder named Logic:

The terms *directory* and *folder* are used synonymously to mean an entity that organizes files. *Directory* is the more general term; the term *folder* came into use in graphical systems. For example, Microsoft began calling directories *folders* with the introduction of Windows 95.

`C:\Logic\SampleFiles\PayrollData.dat`

TWO TRUTHS & A LIE

Understanding Computer Files

1. Temporary storage is usually volatile.

2. Computer files exist on permanent storage devices, such as RAM.

3. A file's path is the hierarchy of folders in which it is stored.

The false statement is #2. Computer files exist on permanent storage devices, such as hard disks, floppy disks, USB drives, reels or cassettes of magnetic tape, and compact discs.

Understanding the Data Hierarchy

When businesses store data items on computer systems, they are often stored in a framework called the **data hierarchy** that describes the relationships between data components. The data hierarchy consists of the following:

Computers also recognize characters you cannot enter from a standard keyboard, such as foreign-alphabet characters like ϕ or Σ.

- **Characters** are letters, numbers, and special symbols, such as "A", "7", and "$". Anything you can type from the keyboard in one keystroke (including a space or a tab) is a character. Characters are made up of smaller elements called bits, but just as most human beings can use a pencil without caring whether atoms are flying around inside it, most computer users can store characters without caring about these bits.

- **Fields** are single useful data items that are composed of one or more characters. Fields include items such as lastName, middleInitial, streetAddress, or annualSalary.

- **Records** are groups of fields that go together for some logical reason. A random name, address, and salary aren't very useful, but if they're *your* name, *your* address, and *your* salary, then that's your record. An inventory record might contain fields for item number, color, size, and price; a student record might contain ID number, grade point average, and major.

- **Files** are groups of related records. The individual records of each student in your class might go together in a file called Students. dat. Similarly, records of each person at your company might be in a file called Personnel.dat. Some files can have just a few records. For example, a student file for a college seminar might have only 10 records. Others, such as the file of credit-card holders for a major department-store chain or policy holders of a large insurance company, can contain thousands or even millions of records.

A **database** holds groups of files, often called **tables**, that together serve the information needs of an organization. Database software establishes and maintains relationships between fields in these tables, so that users can pull related data items together in a format that allows businesspeople to make managerial decisions efficiently. Chapter 14 of the comprehensive version of this text covers database creation.

TWO TRUTHS & A LIE

Understanding the Data Hierarchy

1. In the data hierarchy, a field is a single data item, such as lastName, streetAddress, Or annualSalary.

2. In the data hierarchy, fields are grouped together to form a record; records are groups of fields that go together for some logical reason.

3. In the data hierarchy, related records are grouped together to form a field.

The false statement is #3. Related records form a file.

Performing File Operations

To use data files in your programs, you need to understand several file operations:

- Declaring a file
- Opening a file
- Reading from a file
- Writing to a file
- Closing a file

Declaring a File

The InputFile and OutputFile types are capitalized in this book because their equivalents are capitalized in most programming languages. This approach helps to distinguish these complex types from simple types such as num and string.

Most languages support several types of files, but the broadest types are files that can be used for input and files that can be used for output. Each type of file has a data type defined in the language you are using. You declare files in the same way you declare variables and constants—by giving each file a data type and an identifier. For example, you might declare two files as follows:

```
InputFile employeeData
OutputFile updatedData
```

The identifiers given to files, such as `employeeData` and `updatedData`, are internal to the program, just as variable names are. To make a program read a file's data from a storage device, you also need to associate the program's internal filename with the operating system's name for the file. Often, this association is accomplished when you open the file.

Opening a File

In most programming languages, before an application can use a data file, it must **open the file**. Opening a file locates it on a storage device and associates a variable name within your program with the file. For example, if the identifier `employeeData` has been declared as type `InputFile`, then you might make a statement similar to the following:

```
open employeeData "EmployeeData.dat"
```

This statement associates the file named "EmployeeData.dat" on the storage device with the program's internal name `employeeData`. Usually, you can also specify a more complete path when the data file is not in the same directory as the program, as in the following:

```
open employeeData "C:\CompanyFiles\CurrentYear\
    EmployeeData.dat"
```

Reading Data From a File

Before you can use stored data within a program, you must load the data into computer memory. You never use the data values that are stored on a storage device directly. Instead, you use a copy that is transferred into memory. When you copy data from a file on a storage device into RAM, you **read from the file**.

Especially when data items are stored on a hard disk, their location might not be clear to you—data just seems to be "in the computer." To a casual computer user, the lines between permanent storage and temporary memory are often blurred because many newer programs automatically save data for you periodically without asking your permission. However, at any moment in time, the version of a file in memory might differ from the version that was last saved to a storage device.

If data items have been stored in a file and a program needs them, you can write separate programming statements to input each field, as in the following example:

```
input name from employeeData
input address from employeeData
input payRate from employeeData
```

Most languages also allow you to write a single statement in the following format:

```
input name, address, payRate from employeeData
```

 Most programming languages provide a way for you to use a group name for record data, as in the following statement:

```
input EmployeeRecord from employeeData
```

When this format is used, you need to define the separate fields that compose an EmployeeRecord when you declare the variables for the program.

 The way the program knows how much data to input for each variable differs among programming languages. In many languages, a delimiter such as a comma is stored between data fields. In other languages, the amount of data retrieved depends on the data types of the variables in the input statement.

You usually do not want to input several items in a single statement when you read data from a keyboard, because you want to prompt the user for each item separately as you input it. However, when you retrieve data from a file, prompts are not needed. Instead, each item is retrieved in sequence and stored in memory at the appropriate named location.

Figure 7-2 shows how an input statement works. When the input statement executes, each field is copied and placed in the appropriate variable in computer memory. Nothing on the disk indicates a field name associated with any of the data; the variable names exist within the program only. For example, another program could use the same file as input and call the fields surname, street, and salary.

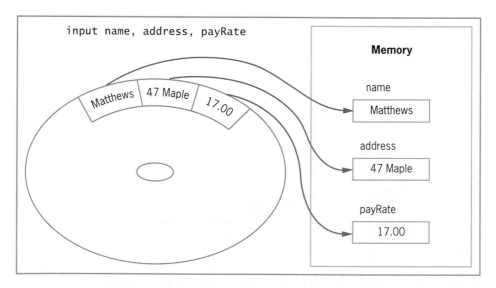

Figure 7-2   Reading three data items from a storage device into memory

When you read data from a file, you must read all the fields that are stored even though you might not want to use all of them. For example, suppose you want to read an employee data file that contains names, addresses, and pay rates for each employee, and you want to output a list of names. Even though you are not concerned with the address or pay rate fields, you must read them into your program for each employee before you can get to the name for the next employee.

Writing Data to a File

When you store data in a computer file on a persistent storage device, you **write to the file**. This means you copy data from RAM to the file. When you write data to a file, you write the contents of the fields using a statement such as the following:

```
output name, address, payRate to updatedData
```

When you write data to a file, you usually do not include explanations that make data easier for humans to interpret; you just write facts and figures. For example, you do not include column headings or write explanations such as "The pay rate is ", nor do you include commas, dollar signs, or percent signs in numeric values. Those embellishments are appropriate for output on a monitor or on paper, but not for storage.

Closing a File

When you finish using a file, the program should **close the file**—that is, the file is no longer available to your application. Failing to close an input file (a file from which you are reading data) usually does not present serious consequences; the data still exists in the file. However, if you fail to close an output file (a file to which you are writing data), the data might become inaccessible. You should always close every file you open, and you should close the file as soon as you no longer need it. When you leave a file open for no reason, you use computer resources, and your computer's performance suffers. Also, particularly within a network, another program might be waiting to use the file.

A Program that Performs File Operations

Figure 7-3 contains a program that opens two files, reads employee data from the input file, alters the employee's pay rate, writes the updated record to an output file, and closes the files. The statements that use the files are shaded.

 In most programming languages, if you read data from a keyboard or write it to the display monitor, you do not need to open the device. The keyboard and monitor are the **default input and output devices**, respectively.

284

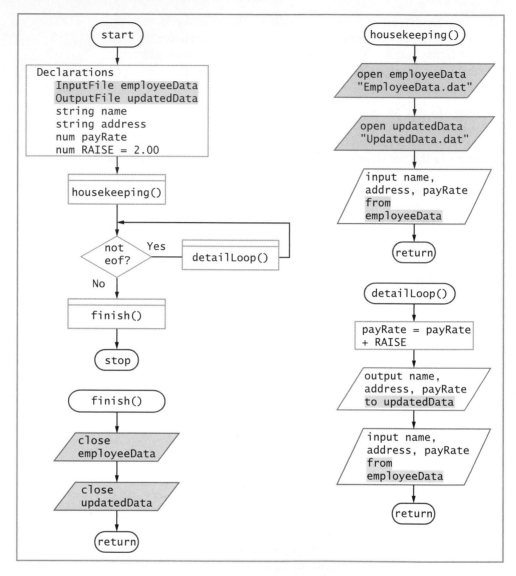

Figure 7-3   Flowchart and pseudocode for program that uses a file

```
start
    Declarations
        InputFile employeeData
        OutputFile updatedData
        string name
        string address
        num payRate
        num RAISE = 2.00
    housekeeping()
    while not eof
        detailLoop()
    endwhile
    finish()
stop

housekeeping()
    open employeeData "EmployeeData.dat"
    open updatedData "UpdatedData.dat"
    input name, address, payRate from employeeData
return

detailLoop()
    payRate = payRate + RAISE
    output name, address, payRate to updatedData
    input name, address, payRate from employeeData
return

finish()
    close employeeData
    close updatedData
return
```

Figure 7-3 Flowchart and pseudocode for program that uses a file (continued)

 The convention in this book is to place file open and close statements in parallelograms in flowcharts, because they are operations closely related to input and output.

In the program in Figure 7-3, each employee's data is read into memory. Then the `payRate` variable in memory is increased by $2.00. The value of the pay rate on the input storage device is not altered. After the employee's pay rate is increased, the name, address, and newly altered pay rate values are stored in the output file. When processing is complete, the input file retains the original data and the output file contains the revised data. Many organizations would keep the original file as a backup file. A **backup file** is a copy that is kept in case values need to be restored to their original state. The backup copy is called a **parent file** and the newly revised copy is a **child file**.

 Watch the video *File Operations*.

 Logically, the verbs "print," "write," and "display" mean the same thing—all produce output. However, in conversation, programmers usually reserve the word "print" for situations in which they mean "produce hard copy output." Programmers are more likely to use "write" when talking about sending records to a data file, and "display" when sending records to a monitor. In some programming languages, there is no difference in the verb you use for output, no matter what type of hardware you use; you simply assign different output devices (such as printers, monitors, and disk drives) as needed to programmer-named objects that represent them.

In many organizations, both data files and printed report files are sent to disk storage devices when they are created. Later, as time becomes available on an organization's busy printers (often after business hours), the report disk files are copied to paper.

Throughout this book you have been encouraged to think of input as basically the same process, whether it comes from a user typing interactively at a keyboard or from a stored file on a disk or other media. That concept remains a valid one as you read the rest of this chapter, which discusses applications that commonly use stored file data. Such applications could be executed by a data-entry operator from a keyboard, but it is more common for the data used in these applications to have been entered, validated, and sorted earlier in another application, and then processed as input from files to achieve the results discussed in this chapter.

TWO TRUTHS & A LIE

Performing File Operations

1. The identifiers given to files are internal to the program; you must associate them with the operating system's name for the file.

2. When you read from a file, you copy values from memory to a storage device.

3. If you fail to close an input file, usually no serious consequences will occur; the data still exists in the file.

The false statement is #2. When you read from a file, you copy values from a storage device into memory. When you write to a file, you copy values from memory to a storage device.

Understanding Sequential Files and Control Break Logic

A **sequential file** is a file in which records are stored one after another in some order. Frequently, records in a sequential file are organized based on the contents of one or more fields. Examples of sequential files include:

- A file of employees stored in order by ID number

- A file of parts for a manufacturing company stored in order by part number

- A file of customers for a business stored in alphabetical order by last name

 Files that are stored in order by some field have been sorted; they might have been sorted manually before they were saved, or a program might have sorted them. You can learn about sorting techniques in Chapter 8 of the comprehensive version of this book.

Understanding Control Break Logic

A **control break** is a temporary detour in the logic of a program. In particular, programmers use a **control break program** when a change in the value of a variable initiates special actions or causes special or unusual processing to occur. You usually write control break programs to organize output for programs that handle data records organized logically in groups based on the value in a field. As you read records, you examine the same field in each record, and when you encounter a record that contains a different value from the ones that preceded it, you perform a special action. For example, you might generate a report that lists all company clients in order by state of residence, with a count of clients after each state's client list. See Figure 7-4 for an example of a **control break report** that breaks after each change in state.

```
Company Clients by State of Residence

Name          City            State

Albertson     Birmingham      Alabama
Davis         Birmingham      Alabama
Lawrence      Montgomery      Alabama
                              Count for Alabama      3

Smith         Anchorage       Alaska
Young         Anchorage       Alaska
Davis         Fairbanks       Alaska
Mitchell      Juneau          Alaska
Zimmer        Juneau          Alaska
                              Count for Alaska       5

Edwards       Phoenix         Arizona
                              Count for Arizona      1
```

Figure 7-4   A control break report with totals after each state

Other examples of control break reports produced by control break programs could include:

- All employees listed in order by department number, with a new page started for each department

- All books for sale in a bookstore listed in order by category (such as reference or self-help), with a count following each category of book

- All items sold in order by date of sale, with a different ink color for each new month

Each of these reports shares two traits:

- The records used in each report are listed in order by a specific variable: state, department, category, or date.

- When that variable changes, the program takes special action: starts a new page, prints a count or total, or switches ink color.

 With some newer languages, such as SQL, the details of control breaks are handled automatically. Still, understanding how control break programs work improves your competence as a programmer.

To generate a control break report, your input records must be organized in sequential order based on the field that will cause the breaks. In other words, to write a program that produces a report of customers by state, like the one in Figure 7-4, the records must be grouped by state before you begin processing. Frequently, this grouping will mean placing the records in alphabetical order by state, although they could just as easily be ordered by population, governor's name, or any other factor, as long as all of one state's records are together.

Suppose you have an input file that contains client names, cities, and states, and you want to produce a report like the one in Figure 7-4. The basic logic of the program works like this:

- Each time you read a client's record from the input file, you determine whether the client resides in the same state as the previous client.

- If so, you simply output the client's data, add 1 to a counter, and read another record, without any special processing. If there are 20 clients in a state, these steps are repeated 20 times in a row—read a client's data, count it, and output it.

- Eventually you will read a record for a client who is not in the same state. At that point, before you output the data for the first client in the new state, you must output the count for the previous state. You must also reset the counter to 0 so it is ready to start counting customers in the next state. Then, you can proceed to handle client records for the new state, and you continue to do so until the next time you encounter a client from a different state. This type of program contains a **single-level control break**, a break in the logic of the program (in this case, pausing or detouring to output a count) that is based on the value of a single variable (in this case, the state).

The technique you must use to "remember" the old state so you can compare it with each new client's state is to create a special variable, called a **control break field**, to hold the previous state. As you read each new record, comparing the new and old state values determines when it is time to output the count for the previous state.

Figure 7-5 shows the mainline logic and getReady() module for a program that produces the report in Figure 7-4. In the mainline logic, the control break variable oldState is declared in the shaded statement. In the getReady() module, the report headings are output, the file is opened, and the first record is read into memory. Then, the state value in the first record is copied to the oldState variable. (See shading.) Note that it would be incorrect to initialize oldState when it is declared. When you declare the variables at the beginning of the main program, you have not yet read the first record; therefore, you don't know what the value of the first state will be. You might assume it is "Alabama" because that is the first state alphabetically, and you might be right, but perhaps the first state is "Alaska" or even "Wyoming". You are assured of storing the correct first state value if you copy it from the first input record.

290

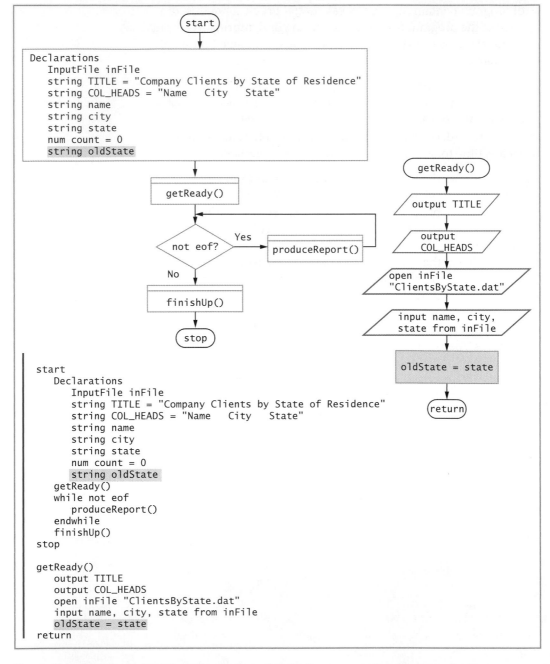

Figure 7-5 Mainline logic and `getReady()` module for the program that produces clients by state report

Within the produceReport() module in Figure 7-6, the first task is to check whether state holds the same value as oldState. For the first record, on the first pass through this method, the values are equal (because you set them to be equal right after getting the first input record in the getReady() module). Therefore, you proceed by outputting the first client's data, adding 1 to count, and inputting the next record.

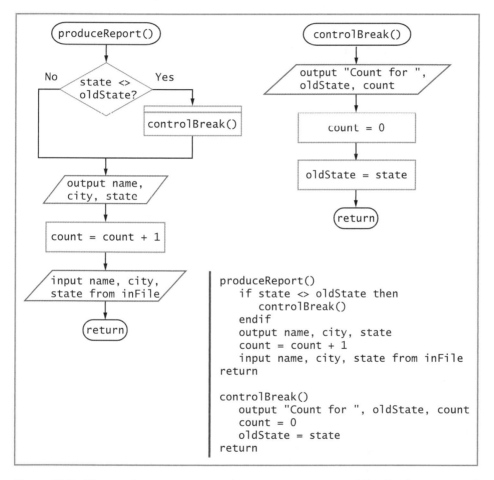

```
produceReport()
    if state <> oldState then
        controlBreak()
    endif
    output name, city, state
    count = count + 1
    input name, city, state from inFile
return

controlBreak()
    output "Count for ", oldState, count
    count = 0
    oldState = state
return
```

Figure 7-6 The produceReport() and controlBreak() modules for the program that produces clients by state

As long as each new record holds the same state value, you continue outputting, counting, and inputting, never pausing to output the count. Eventually, you will read in data for a client whose state is different from the previous one. That's when the control break occurs. Whenever a new state differs from the old one, three tasks must be performed:

- The count for the previous state must be output.

- The count must be reset to 0 so it can start counting records for the new state.

- The control break field must be updated.

When the produceReport() module receives a client record for which state is not the same as oldState, you cause a break in the normal flow of the program. The new client record must "wait" while the count for the just-finished state is output and count and the control break field oldState acquire new values.

Watch the video *Control Break Logic*.

The produceReport() module continues to output client names, cities, and states until the end of file is reached; then the finishUp() module executes. As shown in Figure 7-7, the module that executes after processing the last record in a control break program must complete any required processing for the last group that was handled. In this case, the finishUp() module must display the count for the last state that was processed. After the input file is closed, the logic can return to the main program, where the program ends.

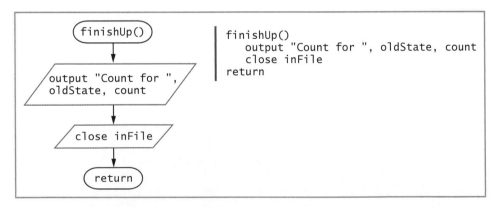

Figure 7-7　The finishUp() module for the program that produces clients by state report

> ## TWO TRUTHS & A LIE
>
> ### Understanding Sequential Files and Control Break Logic
>
> 1. In a control break program, a change in the value of a variable initiates special actions or causes special or unusual processing to occur.
>
> 2. When a control break variable changes, the program takes special action.
>
> 3. To generate a control break report, your input records must be organized in sequential order based on the first field in the record.
>
> The false statement is #3. Your input records must be organized in sequential order based on the field that will cause the breaks.

Merging Sequential Files

Businesses often need to merge two or more sequential files. **Merging files** involves combining two or more files while maintaining the sequential order. For example:

- Suppose you have a file of current employees in ID number order and a file of newly hired employees, also in ID number order. You need to merge these two files into one combined file before running this week's payroll program.

- Suppose you have a file of parts manufactured in the Northside factory in part-number order and a file of parts manufactured in the Southside factory, also in part-number order. You need to merge these two files into one combined file, creating a master list of available parts.

- Suppose you have a file that lists last year's customers in alphabetical order and another file that lists this year's customers in alphabetical order. You want to create a mailing list of all customers in order by last name.

Before you can easily merge files, two conditions must be met:

- Each file must contain the same record layout.

- Each file used in the merge must be sorted in the same order (ascending or descending) based on the same field.

For example, suppose your business has two locations, one on the East Coast and one on the West Coast, and each location maintains a customer file in alphabetical order by customer name. Each file contains fields for name and customer balance. You can call the fields in the East Coast file eastName and eastBalance, and the fields in the West Coast file westName and westBalance. You want to merge the two files, creating one combined file containing records for all customers. Figure 7-8 shows some sample data for the files; you want to create a merged file like the one shown in Figure 7-9.

East Coast File		West Coast File	
eastName	eastBalance	westName	westBalance
Able	100.00	Chen	200.00
Brown	50.00	Edgar	125.00
Dougherty	25.00	Fell	75.00
Hanson	300.00	Grand	100.00
Ingram	400.00		
Johnson	30.00		

Figure 7-8   Sample data contained in two customer files

mergedName	mergedBalance
Able	100.00
Brown	50.00
Chen	200.00
Dougherty	25.00
Edgar	125.00
Fell	75.00
Grand	100.00
Hanson	300.00
Ingram	400.00
Johnson	30.00

Figure 7-9   Merged customer file

The mainline logic for a program that merges two files is similar to the main logic you've used before in other programs: it contains preliminary, housekeeping tasks; a detail module that repeats until the end of the program; and some clean-up, end-of-job tasks. However, most programs you have studied processed records until an eof condition was met, either because an input data file reached its end or because a user entered a sentinel value in an interactive program. In a program that merges files, there are two input files, so checking for eof in one of them is insufficient. Instead, the program can check a flag variable with a name such as bothAtEnd. For example, you might initialize bothAtEnd to N, but change its value to Y after you have encountered eof in both input files.

Figure 7-10 shows the mainline logic for a program that merges the files shown in Figure 7-8. After the getReady() module executes, the shaded question that sends the logic to the finishUp() module tests the bothAtEnd variable. When it holds Y, the program ends.

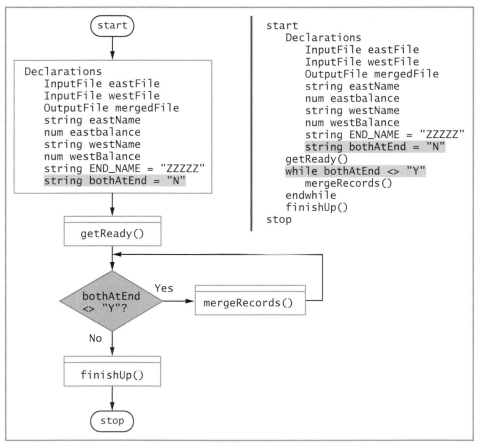

Figure 7-10 Mainline logic of a program that merges files

The getReady() module is shown in Figure 7-11. It opens three files—the input files for the east and west customers, and an output file in which to place the merged records. The program then reads one record from each input file. If either file has reached its end, the END_NAME constant is assigned to the variable that holds that file's customer name. The getReady() module then checks to see whether both files are finished (admittedly, a rare occurrence in the getReady() portion of the program's execution) and sets the bothAtEnd flag variable to Y if they are. Assuming there is at least one record available, the logic would then enter the mergeRecords() module.

296

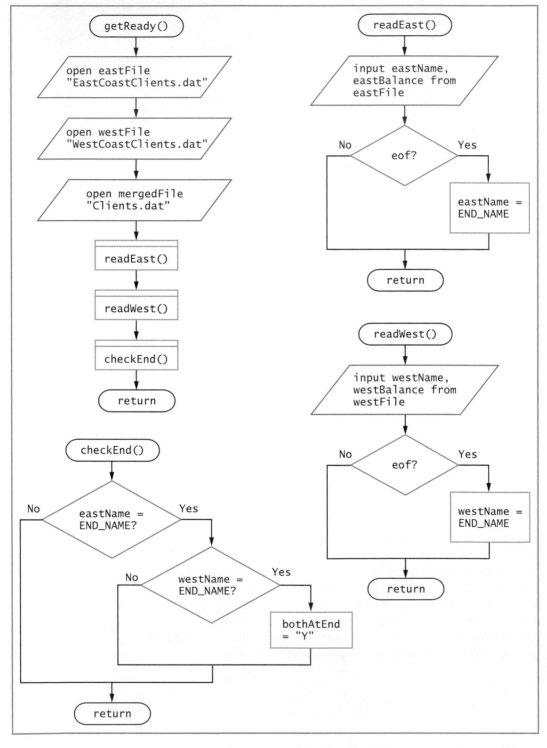

Figure 7-11 The getReady() method for a program that merges files, and the methods it calls

```
getReady()
    open eastFile "EastCoastClients.dat"
    open westFile "WestCoastClients.dat"
    open mergedFile "Clients.dat"
    readEast()
    readWest()
    checkEnd()
return

readEast()
    input eastName, eastBalance from eastFile
    if eof then
        eastName = END_NAME
    endif
return

readWest()
    input westName, westBalance from westFile
    if eof then
        westName = END_NAME
    endif
return

checkEnd()
    if eastName = END_NAME then
        if westName = END_NAME then
            bothAtEnd = "Y"
        endif
    endif
return
```

Figure 7-11 The getReady() method for a program that merges files, and the methods it calls (continued)

When you begin the mergeRecords() module in the program using the files shown in Figure 7-8, two records—one from eastFile and one from westFile—are sitting in the memory of the computer. One of these records needs to be written to the new output file first. Which one? Because the two input files contain records stored in alphabetical order, and you want the new file to store records in alphabetical order, you first output the input record that has the lower alphabetical value in the name field. Therefore, the process begins as shown in Figure 7-12.

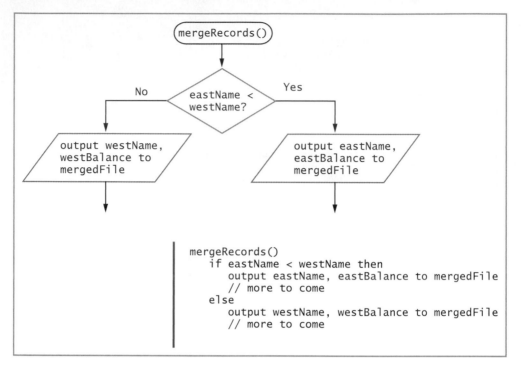

Figure 7-12   Start of merging process

Using the sample data from Figure 7-8, you can see that the "Able" record from the East Coast file should be written to the output file, while Chen's record from the West Coast file waits in memory. The eastName value "Able" is alphabetically lower than the westName value "Chen".

After you write Able's record, should Chen's record be written to the output file next? Not necessarily. It depends on the next eastName following Able's record in eastFile. When data records are read into memory from a file, a program typically does not "look ahead" to determine the values stored in the next record. Instead, a program usually reads the record into memory before making decisions about its contents. In this program, you need to read the next eastFile record into memory and compare it to "Chen". Because in this case the next record in eastFile contains the name "Brown", another eastFile record is written; no westFile records are written yet.

After the first two eastFile records, is it Chen's turn to be written now? You really don't know until you read another record from eastFile and compare its name value to "Chen". Because this record contains the name "Dougherty", it is indeed time to write

Chen's record. After Chen's record is written, should you now write Dougherty's record? Until you read the next record from westFile, you don't know whether that record should be placed before or after Dougherty's record.

Therefore, the merging method proceeds like this: Compare two records, write the record with the lower alphabetical name, and read another record from the *same* input file. See Figure 7-13.

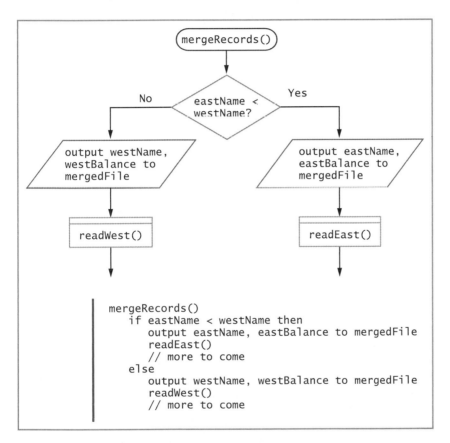

```
mergeRecords()
    if eastName < westName then
        output eastName, eastBalance to mergedFile
        readEast()
        // more to come
    else
        output westName, westBalance to mergedFile
        readWest()
        // more to come
```

Figure 7-13 Continuation of development of merging process

Recall the names from the two original files in Figure 7-8, and walk through the processing steps.

1. Compare "Able" and "Chen". Write Able's record. Read Brown's record from eastFile.

2. Compare "Brown" and "Chen". Write Brown's record. Read Dougherty's record from eastFile.

3. Compare "Dougherty" and "Chen". Write Chen's record. Read Edgar's record from westFile.

4. Compare "Dougherty" and "Edgar". Write Dougherty's record. Read Hanson's record from eastFile.

5. Compare "Hanson" and "Edgar". Write Edgar's record. Read Fell's record from westFile.

6. Compare "Hanson" and "Fell". Write Fell's record. Read Grand's record from westFile.

7. Compare "Hanson" and "Grand". Write Grand's record. Read from westFile, encountering eof. This causes westName to be set to END_NAME.

What happens when you reach the end of the West Coast file? Is the program over? It shouldn't be because records for Hanson, Ingram, and Johnson all need to be included in the new output file, and none of them is written yet. Because the westName field is set to END_NAME, and END_NAME has a very high alphabetic value ("ZZZZZ"), each subsequent eastName will be lower than the value of westName, and the rest of the eastName file will be processed. With a different set of data, the eastFile might have ended first. In that case, eastName would be set to END_NAME, and each subsequent westFile record would be processed.

Figure 7-14 shows the complete mergeRecords() module and the finishUp() module.

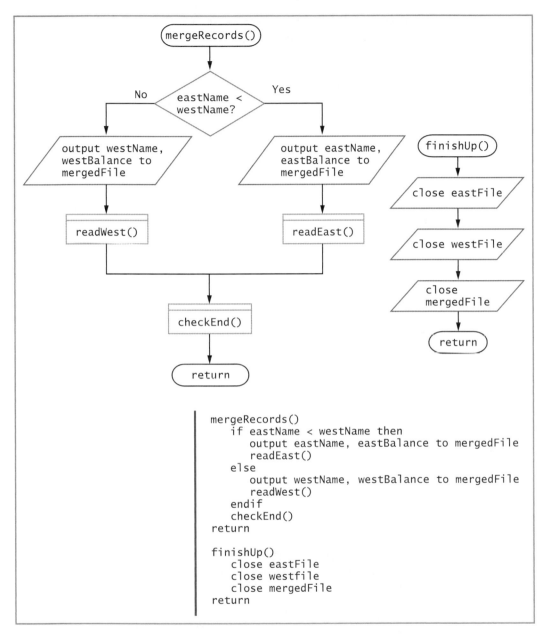

```
mergeRecords()
    if eastName < westName then
        output eastName, eastBalance to mergedFile
        readEast()
    else
        output westName, westBalance to mergedFile
        readWest()
    endif
    checkEnd()
return

finishUp()
    close eastFile
    close westfile
    close mergedFile
return
```

Figure 7-14 The mergeRecords() and finishUp() modules for the file-merging program

 As the value for END_NAME, you might choose to use 10 or 20 Zs instead of only five. Although it is unlikely that a person will have the last name ZZZZZ, you should make sure that the high value you choose is actually higher than any legitimate value.

After Grand's record is processed, `westFile` is read and `eof` is encountered, so `westName` gets set to `END_NAME`. Now, when you enter the loop again, `eastName` and `westName` are compared, and `eastName` is still "Hanson". The `eastName` value (Hanson) is lower than the `westName` value (ZZZZZ), so the data for `eastName`'s record writes to the output file, and another `eastFile` record (Ingram) is read.

The complete run of the file-merging program now executes the first six of the seven steps listed previously, and then proceeds, as shown in Figure 7-14 and as follows, starting with a modified Step 7:

7. Compare "Hanson" and "Grand". Write Grand's record. Read from `westFile`, encountering `eof` and setting `westName` to "ZZZZZ".

8. Compare "Hanson" and "ZZZZZ". Write Hanson's record. Read Ingram's record.

9. Compare "Ingram" and "ZZZZZ". Write Ingram's record. Read Johnson's record.

10. Compare "Johnson" and "ZZZZZ". Write Johnson's record. Read from `eastFile`, encountering `eof` and setting `eastName` to "ZZZZZ".

11. Now that both names are "ZZZZZ", set the flag `bothAtEnd` equal to Y.

 Watch the video *Merging Files*.

When the `bothAtEnd` flag variable equals Y, the loop is finished, the files are closed, and the program ends.

 If two names are equal during the merge process—for example, when there is a "Hanson" record in each file—then both Hansons will be included in the final file. When `eastName` and `westName` match, `eastName` is not lower than `westName`, so you write the `westFile` "Hanson" record. After you read the next `westFile` record, `eastName` will be lower than the next `westName`, and the `eastFile` "Hanson" record will be output. A more complicated merge program could check another field, such as first name, when last name values match.

 You can merge any number of files. To merge more than two files, the logic is only slightly more complicated; you must compare the key fields from all the files before deciding which file is the next candidate for output.

TWO TRUTHS & A LIE

Merging Sequential Files

1. A sequential file is a file in which records are stored one after another in some order. Most frequently, the records are stored based on the contents of one or more fields within each record.

2. Merging files involves combining two or more files while maintaining the sequential order.

3. Before you can easily merge files, each file must contain the same number of records.

The false statement is #3. Before you can easily merge files, each file must contain the same record layout and each file used in the merge must be sorted in the same order based on the same field.

Master and Transaction File Processing

In the last section, you learned how to merge related sequential files in which each record in each file contained the same fields. Some related sequential files, however, do not contain the same fields. Instead, some related files have a master-transaction relationship. A **master file** holds complete and relatively permanent data; a **transaction file** holds more temporary data. For example, a master customer file might hold customers' names, addresses, and phone numbers, and a customer transaction file might contain data that describes a customer's most recent purchase.

Commonly, you gather transactions for a period of time, store them in a file, and then use them one by one to update matching records in a master file. You **update the master file** by making appropriate changes to the values in its fields based on the recent transactions. For example, a file containing transaction purchase data for a customer might be used to update each balance due field in a customer record master file.

Here are a few other examples of files that have a master-transaction relationship:

- A library maintains a master file of all patrons and a transaction file with information about each book or other items checked out.

When a child file is updated, it becomes a parent, and its parent becomes a grandparent. Individual organizations create policies concerning the number of generations of backup files they will save before discarding them.

The terms "parent" and "child" refer to file backup generations, but they are used for a different purpose in object-oriented programming. When you base a class on another using inheritance, the original class is the parent and the derived class is the child. You can learn about these concepts in Chapters 10 and 11 of the comprehensive version of this book.

- A college maintains a master file of all students and a transaction file for each course registration.

- A telephone company maintains a master file for every telephone line (number) and a transaction file with information about every call.

When you update a master file, you can take two approaches:

- You can actually change the information in the master file. When you use this approach, the information that existed in the master file prior to the transaction processing is lost.

- You can create a copy of the master file, making the changes in the new version. Then, you can store the previous, parent version of the master file for a period of time, in case there are questions or discrepancies regarding the update process. The updated, child version of the file becomes the new master file used in subsequent processing. This approach is used in a program later in this chapter.

The logic you use to perform a match between master and transaction file records is similar to the logic you use to perform a merge. As with a merge, you must begin with both files sorted in the same order on the same field. Figure 7-15 shows the mainline logic for a program that matches files. The master file contains a customer number, name, and a field that holds the total dollar amount of all purchases the customer has made previously. The transaction file holds data for sales, including a transaction number, the number of the customer who made the transaction, and the amount of the transaction.

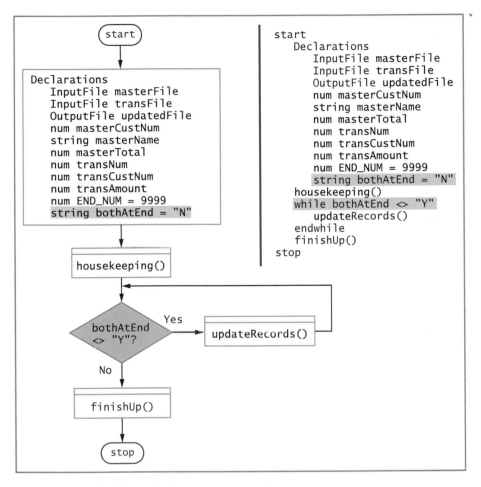

Figure 7-15 Mainline logic for master-transaction program

Figure 7-16 contains the housekeeping() module for the program, and the modules it calls. These modules are very similar to their counterparts in the file-merging program earlier in the chapter. When the program begins, one record is read from each file. When any file ends, the field used for matching is set to a high value, 9999, and when both files are at end, a flag variable is set so the mainline logic can test for the end of processing.

In the file-merging program presented earlier in this chapter, you placed "ZZZZZ" in the customer name field at the end of the file because string fields were being compared. In this example, because you are using numeric fields (customer numbers), you can store 9999 in them at the end of the file. The assumption is that 9999 is higher than any valid customer number.

306

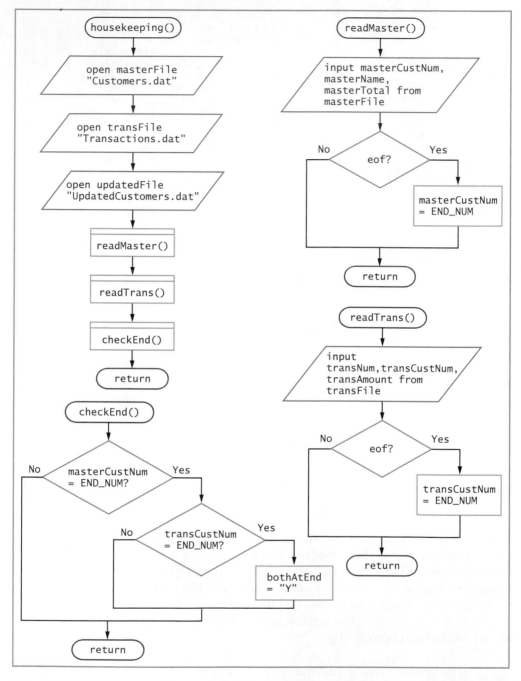

Figure 7-16 The housekeeping() module for master-transaction program, and the modules it calls

Imagine that you will update master file records by hand instead of using a computer program, and imagine that each master and transaction record is stored on a separate piece of paper. The easiest way to accomplish the update is to sort all the master records by customer number and place them in a stack, and then sort all the transactions by customer number (not transaction number) and place them in another stack. You then would examine the first transaction, and look through the master records until you found a match. Any master records without transactions would be placed in a "completed" stack without changes. When a transaction matched a master record, you would correct the master record using the new transaction amount, and then go on to the next transaction. Of course, if there is no matching master record for a transaction, then you would realize an error had occurred, and you would probably set the transaction aside before continuing. The `updateRecords()` module works exactly the same way.

In the file-merging program presented earlier in this chapter, your first action in the program's detail loop was to determine which file held the record with the lower value; then, you wrote that record. In a matching program, you are trying to determine not only whether one file's comparison field is larger than another's; it's also important to know if they are *equal*. In this example, you want to update the master file record's `masterTotal` field only if the transaction record `transCustNum` field contains an exact match for the customer number in the master file record. Therefore, you compare `masterCustNum` from the master file and `transCustNum` from the transaction file. Three possibilities exist:

- The `transCustNum` value equals `masterCustNum`. In this case, you add `transAmount` to `masterTotal`, and then write the updated master record to the output file. Then, you read in both a new master record and a new transaction record.

- The `transCustNum` value is higher than `masterCustNum`. This means a sale was not recorded for that customer. That's all right; not every customer makes a transaction every period, so you simply write the original customer record with exactly the same information it contained when input. Then, you get the next customer record to see if this customer made the transaction currently under examination.

- The `transCustNum` value is lower than `masterCustNum`. This means you are trying to apply a transaction for which no master record exists, so there must be an error, because a transaction should always have a master record. You can handle this error in a variety of ways; here, you will write an error message to an output device before reading the next transaction record. A human operator can then read the message and take appropriate action.

 The logic used here assumes there can be only one transaction per customer. In the exercises at the end of this chapter, you will develop the logic for a program in which the customer can have multiple transactions.

Whether `transCustNum` was higher than, lower than, or equal to `masterCustNum`, after reading the next transaction or master record (or both), you check whether both `masterCustNum` and `transCustNum` have been set to 9999. When both are 9999, you set the `bothAtEnd` flag to Y.

Figure 7-17 shows the `updateRecords()` module that carries out the logic of the file-matching process. Figure 7-18 shows some sample data you can use to walk through the logic for this program.

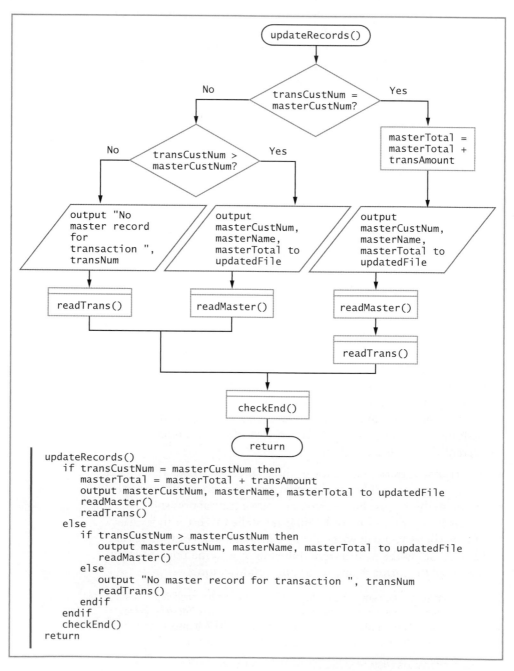

```
updateRecords()
   if transCustNum = masterCustNum then
      masterTotal = masterTotal + transAmount
      output masterCustNum, masterName, masterTotal to updatedFile
      readMaster()
      readTrans()
   else
      if transCustNum > masterCustNum then
         output masterCustNum, masterName, masterTotal to updatedFile
         readMaster()
      else
         output "No master record for transaction ", transNum
         readTrans()
      endif
   endif
   checkEnd()
return
```

Figure 7-17   The `updateRecords()` module for the master-transaction program

Master File		Transaction File	
masterCustNum	masterTotal	transCustNum	transAmount
100	1000.00	100	400.00
102	50.00	105	700.00
103	500.00	108	100.00
105	75.00	110	400.00
106	5000.00		
109	4000.00		
110	500.00		

Figure 7-18   Sample data for the file-matching program

The program proceeds as follows:

1. Read customer 100 from the master file and customer 100 from the transaction file. Customer numbers are equal, so 400.00 from the transaction file is added to 1000.00 in the master file, and a new master file record is written with a 1400.00 total sales figure. Then, read a new record from each input file.

2. The customer number in the master file is 102 and the customer number in the transaction file is 105, so there are no transactions today for customer 102. Write the master record exactly the way it came in, and read a new master record.

3. Now, the master customer number is 103 and the transaction customer number is still 105. This means customer 103 has no transactions, so you write the master record as is and read a new one.

4. Now, the master customer number is 105 and the transaction number is 105. Because customer 105 had a 75.00 balance and now has a 700.00 transaction, the new total sales figure for the master file is 775.00, and a new master record is written. Read one record from each file.

5. Now, the master number is 106 and the transaction number is 108. Write customer record 106 as is, and read another master.

6. Now, the master number is 109 and the transaction number is 108. An error has occurred. The transaction record indicates that you made a sale to customer 108, but there is no master record for customer number 108. Either the transaction is incorrect (there is an error in the transaction's customer number) or the transaction is correct but you have failed to create a master record. Either way, write an error message so that a

clerk is notified and can handle the problem. Then, get a new transaction record.

7. Now, the master number is 109 and the transaction number is 110. Write master record 109 with no changes and read a new one.

8. Now, the master number is 110 and the transaction number is 110. Add the 400.00 transaction to the previous 500.00 balance in the master file, and write a new master record with 900.00 in the masterTotal field. Read one record from each file.

9. Because both files are finished, end the job. The result is a new master file in which some records contain exactly the same data they contained going in, but others (for which a transaction has occurred) have been updated with a new total sales figure. The original master and transaction files that were used as input can be saved for a period of time as backups.

Figure 7-19 shows the finishUp() module for the program. After all the files are closed, the updated master customer file contains all the customer records it originally contained, and each holds a current total based on the recent group of transactions.

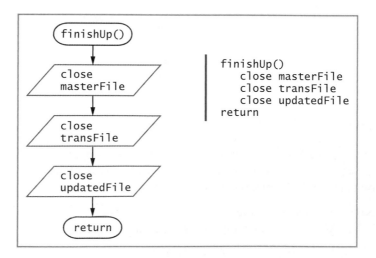

Figure 7-19   The finishUp() module for the master-transaction program

311

TWO TRUTHS & A LIE

Master and Transaction File Processing

1. You use a master file to hold temporary data related to transaction file records.

2. You use a transaction file to hold data that is used to update a master file.

3. The saved version of a master file is the parent file; the updated version is the child file.

The false statement is #1. You use a master file to hold relatively permanent data.

Random Access Files

The examples of files that have been written to and read from in this chapter are sequential access files, which means that you access the records in sequential order from beginning to end. For example, if you wrote an employee record with an ID number 234, and then you created a second record with an ID number 326, you would see when you retrieved the records that they remain in the original data-entry order. Businesses store data in sequential order when they use the records for **batch processing**, or processing that involves performing the same tasks with many records, one after the other. For example, when a company produces paychecks, the records for the pay period are gathered in a batch and the checks are calculated and printed in sequence. It really doesn't matter whose check is produced first because none are distributed to employees until all have been printed.

Besides indicating a system that works with many records, the term *batch processing* can also be used to mean a system in which you issue many operating-system commands as a group.

For many applications, sequential access is inefficient. These applications, known as **real-time** applications, require that a record be accessed immediately while a client is waiting. A program in which the user makes direct requests is an **interactive program**. For example, if a customer telephones a department store with a question about a monthly bill, the customer service representative does not need or want to access every customer account in sequence. With tens of thousands of account records to read, it would take too long to access the customer's record. Instead, customer service representatives require **random access files**, files in which records can be located in any order. Files in which records must be accessed

312

immediately are also called **instant access files**. Because they enable you to locate a particular record directly (without reading all of the preceding records), random access files are also called **direct access files**. You can declare a random access file with a statement similar to the following:

```
RandomFile customerFile
```

You associate this name with a stored file similarly to how you associate an identifier with sequential input and output files. You also can use read, write, and close operations with a random access file similarly to the way you use them with sequential files. However, with random access files you have the additional capability to find a record directly. For example, you might be able to use a statement similar to the following to find customer number 712 on a random access file:

```
seek record 712
```

This feature is particularly useful in random access processing. Consider a business with 20,000 customer accounts. When the customer who has the 14,607th record in the file acquires a new telephone number, it is convenient to directly access the 14,607th record and write the new telephone number to the file in the location in which the old number was previously stored.

TWO TRUTHS & A LIE

Random Access Files

1. A batch program usually uses instant access files.

2. In a real-time application, a record is accessed immediately while a client is waiting.

3. An interactive program usually uses random access files.

The false statement is #1. A batch program usually uses sequential files; interactive programs use random, instant access files.

Chapter Summary

- A computer file is a collection of data stored on a nonvolatile device in a computer system. Although the contents of files differ, each file occupies space on a section of a storage device, and each has a name and a specific time of creation or last modification. Computer files are organized in directories or folders. A file's complete list of directories is its path.

- Data items in a file usually are stored in a hierarchy. Characters are letters, numbers, and special symbols, such as "A", "7", and "$". Fields are single useful data items that are composed of one or more characters. Records are groups of fields that go together for some logical reason. Files are groups of related records.

- When you use a data file in a program, you must declare it and open it; opening a file associates an internal program identifier with the name of a physical file on a storage device. When you read from a file, the data is copied into memory. When you write to a file, the data is copied from memory to a storage device. When you are done with a file, you close it.

- A sequential file is a file in which records are stored one after another in some order. A control break program is one that reads a sequential file and performs special processing based on a change in one or more fields in each record in the file.

- Merging files involves combining two or more files while maintaining the sequential order.

- Some related sequential files are master files that hold relatively permanent data, and transaction files that hold more temporary data. Commonly, you gather transactions for a period of time, store them in a file, and then use them one by one to update matching records in a master file.

- Real-time, interactive applications require random access files in which records can be located in any order. Files in which records must be accessed immediately are also called instant access files and direct access files.

313

Key Terms

A **computer file** is a collection of data stored on a nonvolatile device in a computer system.

Permanent storage devices hold nonvolatile data; examples include hard disks, DVDs, USB drives, and reels of magnetic tape.

Text files contain data that can be read in a text editor.

Binary files contain data that has not been encoded as text.

A **byte** is a small unit of storage; for example, in a simple text file, a byte holds only one character.

A **kilobyte** is approximately 1000 bytes.

A **megabyte** is a million bytes.

A **gigabyte** is a billion bytes.

Directories are organization units on storage devices; each can contain multiple files as well as additional directories. In a graphic system, directories are often called *folders*.

Folders are organization units on storage devices; each can contain multiple files as well as additional folders. Folders are graphic directories.

A file's **path** is the combination of its disk drive and the complete hierarchy of directories in which the file resides.

The **data hierarchy** is a framework that describes the relationships between data components. The data hierarchy contains characters, fields, records, and files.

Characters are letters, numbers, and special symbols, such as "A", "7", and "$".

Fields are single useful data items that are composed of one or more characters.

Records are groups of fields that go together for some logical reason.

Files are groups of related records.

A **database** holds groups of files and provides methods for easy retrieval and organization.

Tables are files in a database.

Opening a file locates it on a storage device and associates a variable name within your program with the file.

Reading from a file copies data from a file on a storage device into RAM.

Writing to a file copies data from RAM to persistent storage.

Closing a file makes it no longer available to an application.

Default input and output devices are those that do not require opening. Usually they are the keyboard and monitor, respectively.

A **backup file** is a copy that is kept in case values need to be restored to their original state.

A **parent file** is a copy of a file before revision.

A **child file** is a copy of a file after revision.

A **sequential file** is a file in which records are stored one after another in some order.

A **control break** is a temporary detour in the logic of a program.

A **control break program** is one in which a change in the value of a variable initiates special actions or causes special or unusual processing to occur.

A **control break report** is a form of output that includes special processing after each group of records.

A **single-level control break** is a break in the logic of the program to perform special processing based on the value of a single variable.

A **control break field** holds a value that causes special processing in a control break program.

Merging files involves combining two or more files while maintaining the sequential order.

A **master file** holds complete and relatively permanent data.

A **transaction file** holds temporary data that you use to update a master file.

To **update a master file** involves making changes to the values in its fields based on transactions.

Batch processing involves performing the same tasks with many records, one after the other.

Real-time applications require that a record be accessed immediately while a client is waiting.

In an **interactive program**, the user makes direct requests, as opposed to one in which input comes from a file.

In **random access files**, records can be located in any order.

Instant access files are random access files in which records must be accessed immediately.

Direct access files are random access files.

Review Questions

1. Random access memory is _____.

    a. permanent

    b. volatile

    c. persistent

    d. continual

2. Which is true of text files?

    a. Text files contain data that can be read in a text editor.

    b. Text files commonly contain images and music.

    c. Both of the Above.

    d. None of the Above.

3. Every file on a storage device has a _____.

    a. name

    b. size

    c. both of the above

    d. none of the above

4. Which of the following is true regarding the data hierarchy?

    a. Files contain records.

    b. Characters contain fields.

    c. Fields contain files.

    d. Fields contain records.

5. The process of _____ a file locates it on a storage device and associates a variable name within your program with the file.

    a. opening

    b. closing

    c. declaring

    d. defining

6. When you write to a file, you _____.

   a. move data from a storage device to memory

   b. copy data from a storage device to memory

   c. move data from memory to a storage device

   d. copy data from memory to a storage device

7. Unlike when you print a report, when a program's output is a data file, you do not _____.

   a. include headings or other formatting

   b. open the files

   c. include all the fields represented as input

   d. all of the above

8. When you close a file, it _____.

   a. is no longer available to the program

   b. cannot be reopened

   c. becomes associated with an internal identifier

   d. ceases to exist

9. A file in which records are stored one after another in some order is a(n) _____ file.

   a. temporal

   b. sequential

   c. random

   d. alphabetical

10. When you combine two or more sorted files while maintaining their sequential order based on a field, you are _____ the files.

   a. tracking

   b. collating

   c. merging

   d. absorbing

11. A control break occurs when a program _____.

    a. takes one of two alternate courses of action for every record

    b. ends prematurely, before all records have been processed

    c. pauses to perform special processing based on the value of a field

    d. passes logical control to a module contained within another program

12. Which of the following is an example of a control break report?

    a. a list of all customers of a business in zip code order, with a count of the number of customers who reside in each zip code

    b. a list of all students in a school, arranged in alphabetical order, with a total count at the end of the report

    c. a list of all employees in a company, with a message "Retain" or "Dismiss" following each employee record

    d. a list of some of the patients of a medical clinic—those who have not seen a doctor for at least two years

13. A control break field _____.

    a. always is output prior to any group of records on a control break report

    b. always is output after any group of records on a control break report

    c. never is output on a report

    d. causes special processing to occur

14. Whenever a control break occurs during record processing in any control break program, you must _____.

    a. declare a control break field

    b. set the control break field to 0

    c. update the value in the control break field

    d. output the control break field

15. Assume you are writing a program to merge two files named FallStudents and SpringStudents. Each file contains a list of students enrolled in a programming logic course during the semester indicated, and each file is sorted in student ID number order. After the program compares two records and subsequently writes a Fall student to output, the next step is to _____.

    a. read a SpringStudents record

    b. read a FallStudents record

    c. write a SpringStudents record

    d. write another FallStudents record

16. When you merge records from two or more sequential files, the usual case is that the records in the files _____.

    a. contain the same data

    b. have the same format

    c. are identical in number

    d. are sorted on different fields

17. A file that holds more permanent data than a transaction file is a _____ file.

    a. master

    b. primary

    c. key

    d. mega-

18. A transaction file is often used to _____ another file.

    a. augment

    b. remove

    c. verify

    d. update

19. The saved version of a file that does not contain the most recently applied transactions is known as a _____ file.

    a. master

    b. child

    c. parent

    d. relative

20. Random access files are used most frequently in all of the following except _____.

    a. interactive programs

    b. batch processing

    c. real-time applications

    d. programs requiring direct access

Exercises

Your student disk contains one or more comma-delimited sample data files for each exercise in this section and the Game Zone section. You might want to use these files in any of several ways:

- You can look at the file contents to better understand the types of data each program uses.

- You can use the files' contents as sample data when you desk-check the logic of your flowcharts or pseudocode.

- You can use the files as input files if you implement the solutions in a programming language and write programs that accept file input.

- You can use the data as guides for entering appropriate values if you implement the solutions in a programming language and write interactive programs.

- When multiple files are included for an exercise, it reminds you that the problem requires different procedures when the number of data records varies.

1. The Vernon Hills Mail-Order Company often sends multiple packages per order. For each customer order, output enough mailing labels to use on each of the boxes that will be mailed. The mailing labels contain the customer's complete name and address, along with a box number in the form "Box 9 of 9". For example, an order that requires three boxes produces three labels: "Box 1 of 3", "Box 2 of 3", and "Box 3 of 3". Design an

application that reads records that contain a customer's title (for example, "Mrs."), first name, last name, street address, city, state, zip code, and number of boxes. The application must read the records until eof is encountered. Produce enough mailing labels for each order.

2. The Springwater Township School District has two high schools—Jefferson and Audubon. Each school maintains a student file with fields containing student ID, last name, first name, and address. Each file is in student ID number order. Design the logic for a program that merges the two files into one file containing a list of all students in the district, maintaining student ID number order.

3. The Redgranite Library keeps a file of all books borrowed every month. Each file is in Library of Congress number order and contains additional fields for author and title.

   a. Design the logic for a program that merges the files for January and February to create a list of all books borrowed in the two-month period.

   b. Modify the library program so that if a book number has more than one record, you output the book information only once.

   c. Modify the library program so that if a book number has more than one record, you not only output the book information only once, you output a count of the total number of times the book was borrowed.

4. Hearthside Realtors keeps a transaction file for each salesperson in the office. Each transaction record contains the salesperson's first name, date of the sale, and sale price. The records for the year are sorted in ascending sale price order. Two salespeople, Diane and Mark, have formed a partnership. Design the logic that produces a merged list of their transactions (including name of salesperson, date, and price) in descending order by price.

5. Dartmoor Medical Associates maintains two patient files—one for the Lakewood office and one for the Hanover office. Each record contains the name, address, city, state, and zip code of a patient, with the files maintained in zip code order. Design the logic that merges the two files to produce one combined name-and-address file, which the office staff can use for addressing mailings of the practice's monthly Healthy Lifestyles newsletter.

6. a. The Willmington Walking Club maintains a master file that contains a record for each of its members. Fields in the master file include the walker's ID number, first name, last name, and total miles walked to the nearest one-tenth of a mile. Every week, a transaction file is produced. It contains a walker's ID number and the number of miles the walker has logged that week. Each file is sorted in walker ID number order. Design the logic for a program that matches the master and transaction file records and updates the total miles walked for each club member by adding the current week's miles to the cumulative total. Not all walkers submit walking reports each week. The output is the updated master file and an error report that lists any transaction records for which no master record exists.

   b. Modify the walking club program to output a certificate of achievement each time a walker exceeds the 500-mile mark. The certificate, which contains the walker's name and an appropriate congratulatory message, is output during the execution of the update program when a walker's mile total surpasses 500.

7. a. The Timely Talent Temporary Help Agency maintains an employee master file that contains an employee ID number, last name, first name, address, and hourly rate for each temporary worker. The file has been sorted in employee ID number order. Each week, a transaction file is created with a job number, address, customer name, employee ID, and hours worked for every job filled by Timely Talent workers. The transaction file is also sorted in employee ID order. Design the logic for a program that matches the master and transaction file records, and outputs one line for each transaction, indicating job number, employee ID number, hours worked, hourly rate, and gross pay. Assume that each temporary worker works, at most, one job per week; output one line for each worker who has worked that week.

   b. Modify the help agency program so that any temporary worker can work any number of separate jobs in a week. Print one line for each job that week.

   c. Modify the help agency program so that it accumulates the worker's total pay for all jobs in a week and outputs one line per worker.

Find the Bugs

8. Your student disk contains files named DEBUG07-01.txt,
    DEBUG07-02.txt, and DEBUG07-03.txt. Each file starts with
    some comments that describe the problem. Comments are
    lines that begin with two slashes (//). Following the com-
    ments, each file contains pseudocode that has one or more
    bugs you must find and correct.

Game Zone

9. The International Rock Paper Scissors Society holds regional
    and national championships. Each region holds a semifinal
    competition in which contestants play 500 games of Rock
    Paper Scissors. The top 20 competitors in each region are
    invited to the national finals. Assume you are provided with
    files for the East, Midwest, and Western regions. Each file
    contains the following fields for the top 20 competitors: last
    name, first name, and number of games won. The records in
    each file are sorted in alphabetical order. Merge the three files
    to create a file of the top 60 competitors who will compete in
    the national championship.

10. In the Game Zone section of Chapter 5, you designed a
    guessing game in which the application generates a random
    number and the player tries to guess it. After each guess, you
    displayed a message indicating whether the player's guess
    was correct, too high, or too low. When the player eventu-
    ally guessed the correct number, you displayed a score that
    represented a count of the number of guesses that were
    required. Modify the game so that when it starts, the player
    enters his or her name. After a player plays the game exactly
    five times, save the best (lowest) score from the five games
    to a file. If the player's name already exists in the file, update
    the record with the new lowest score. If the player's name
    does not already exist in the file, create a new record for the
    player. After the file is updated, display all the best scores
    stored in the file.

Up for Discussion

324

11. Suppose you are hired by a police department to write a program that matches arrest records with court records detailing the ultimate outcome or verdict for each case. You have been given access to current files so that you can test the program. Your friend works in the personnel department of a large company and must perform background checks on potential employees. (The job applicants sign a form authorizing the check.) Police records are open to the public and your friend could look up police records at the courthouse, but it would take many hours per week. As a convenience, should you provide your friend with outcomes of any arrest records of job applicants?

12. Suppose you are hired by a clinic to match a file of patient office visits with patient master records to print various reports. While working with the confidential data, you notice the name of a friend's fiancé. Should you tell your friend that the fiancé is seeking medical treatment? Does the type of treatment affect your answer?

CHAPTER 8

Advanced Array Concepts, Indexed Files, and Linked Lists

In this chapter, you will learn about:

◎ The need for sorting data

◎ Swapping two values in computer memory

◎ The bubble sort

◎ Multidimensional arrays

◎ Indexed files and linked lists

The sorting process is usually reserved for a relatively small number of data items. If thousands of customer records are stored, and they frequently need to be accessed in order based on different fields (alphabetical order by customer name one day, zip code order the next), the records would probably not be sorted at all, but would be indexed or linked. You learn about indexing and linking later in this chapter.

The **median** value in a list is the value of the middle item when the values are listed in order. It is not the same as the arithmetic average, or **mean**. The median is used as a statistic in many cases because it represents a more typical case—half the values are below it and half are above it. Unlike the median, the mean is skewed by a few very high or low values.

As you learned in Chapter 7, when you create a control break report, the records must have been sorted in order by the control break field.

Understanding the Need for Sorting Records

When you store data records, they exist in some type of order; that is, one record is first, another second, and so on. When records are in **sequential order**, they are arranged one after another on the basis of the value in a particular field. Examples include employee records stored in numeric order by Social Security number or department number, or in alphabetic order by last name or department name. Even if the records are stored in a random order—for example, the order in which a clerk felt like entering them—they still are *in order*, although probably not the order desired for processing or viewing. Such data records need to be **sorted**, or placed in order, based on the contents of one or more fields. When you sort data, you can sort either in **ascending order**, arranging records from lowest to highest value within a field, or **descending order**, arranging records from highest to lowest value. Here are some examples of occasions when you would need to sort records:

- A college stores students' records in ascending order by student ID number, but the registrar wants to view the data in descending order by credit hours earned so he can contact students who are close to graduation.

- A department store maintains customer records in ascending order by customer number, but at the end of a billing period, the credit manager wants to contact customers whose balances are 90 or more days overdue. The manager wants to list these overdue customers in descending order by the amount owed, so the customers with the largest debt can be contacted first.

- A sales manager keeps records for her salespeople in alphabetical order by last name, but needs to list the annual sales figure for each salesperson so she can determine the median annual sale amount.

When computers sort data, they always use numeric values when making comparisons between values. This is clear when you sort records by fields such as a numeric customer ID or balance due. However, even alphabetic sorts are numeric, because computer data is stored as a number using a series of 0s and 1s. Ordinary computer users seldom think about the numeric codes behind the letters, numbers, and punctuation marks they enter from their keyboards or see on a monitor. However, they see the consequence of the values behind letters when they see data sorted in alphabetical order. In every popular computer coding scheme, "B" is numerically one greater than "A", and "y" is numerically one less than "z". Unfortunately, whether "A" is represented by a number that is greater or smaller than the number representing "a" depends on your system. Therefore, to obtain the most useful and accurate list of alphabetically sorted records, either the data-entry personnel should be consistent in the use of capitalization, or the programmer should convert all the data to consistent capitalization.

As a professional programmer, you might never have to write a program that sorts data, because organizations can purchase prewritten, or "canned," sorting programs. Additionally, many popular language compilers come with built-in methods that can sort data for you. However, it is beneficial to understand the sorting process so that you can write a special-purpose sort when needed. Understanding the sorting process also improves your array-manipulating skills.

 Because "A" is always less than "B", alphabetic sorts are ascending sorts. The most popular coding schemes include ASCII, Unicode, and EBCDIC. In each code, a number represents a specific computer character. Appendix A contains additional information about these codes.

327

TWO TRUTHS & A LIE

Understanding the Need for Sorting Records

1. When you sort data in ascending order, you arrange records from lowest to highest based on the value in a specific field.

2. Normal alphabetical order, in which A precedes B, is descending order.

3. When computers sort data, they use numeric values when making comparisons, even when string values are compared.

The false statement is #2. Normal alphabetical order is ascending.

Understanding How to Swap Two Values

Computer professionals have developed many sorting techniques, and swapping two values is a concept that is central to most of them. When you **swap values** stored in two variables, you exchange their values; you set the first variable equal to the value of the second, and the second variable equal to the value of the first. However, there is a trick to swapping any two values. Assume you have declared two variables as follows:

```
num score1 = 90
num score2 = 85
```

You want to swap the values so that score1 is 85 and score2 is 90. If you first assign score1 to score2 using a statement such as score2 = score1, both score1 and score2 hold 90 and the value 85 is lost. Similarly, if you first assign score2 to score1 using a statement such as `score1 = score2`, both variables hold 85 and the value 90 is lost.

 Watch the video *Swapping Values.*

To correctly swap two values, you create a temporary variable to hold one of the scores. Then you can accomplish the swap, as shown in Figure 8-1. First, the value in `score2`, 85, is assigned to a temporary holding variable, named `temp`. Then, the `score1` value, 90, is assigned to `score2`. At this point, both `score1` and `score2` hold 90. Then, the 85 in `temp` is assigned to `score1`. Therefore, after the swap process, `score1` holds 85 and `score2` holds 90.

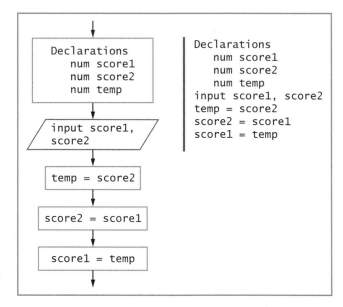

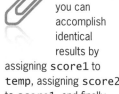 In Figure 8-1, you can accomplish identical results by assigning `score1` to `temp`, assigning `score2` to `score1`, and finally assigning `temp` to `score2`.

Figure 8-1 Program segment that swaps two values

TWO TRUTHS & A LIE

Understanding How to Swap Two Values

1. Swapping is a concept used in many types of sorts.

2. When you swap the values stored in two variables, you reverse their positions.

3. If you are careful, you can swap two values without creating any additional variables.

The false statement is #3. Swapping values requires a temporary variable so that you don't lose one of the values.

Using a Bubble Sort

One of the simplest sorting techniques to understand is a bubble sort. You can use a bubble sort to arrange records in either ascending or descending order. In a **bubble sort**, items in a list are compared with each other in pairs. When an item is out of order, it swaps values with the item below it. With an ascending bubble sort, after each adjacent pair of items in a list has been compared once, the largest item in the list will have "sunk" to the bottom. After many passes through the list, the smallest items rise to the top like bubbles in a carbonated drink.

 A bubble sort is sometimes called a **sinking sort**.

 When you learn a sort method, programmers say you are learning an algorithm. An **algorithm** is a list of instructions that accomplishes a task.

Assume that you want to sort five student test scores in ascending order. Figure 8-2 shows a program in which a constant is declared to hold an array's size, and then the array is declared to hold five scores. (The other variables and constants, which are shaded in the figure, will be discussed in the next paragraphs when they are used.) The program calls three main procedures—one to input the five scores, one to sort them, and the final one to display the sorted result.

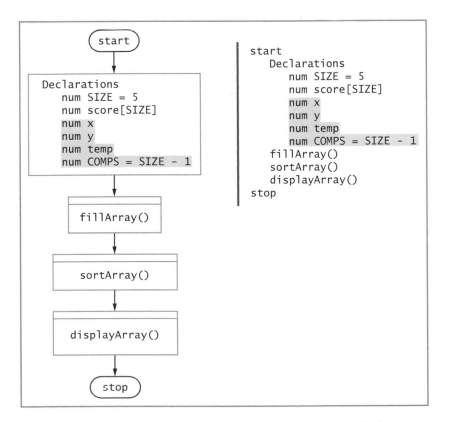

Figure 8-2 Mainline logic for program that accepts, sorts, and displays scores

Figure 8-3 shows the fillArray() method. Within the method, a subscript, x, is initialized to 0 and each array element is filled in turn. After a user enters five scores, control returns to the main program.

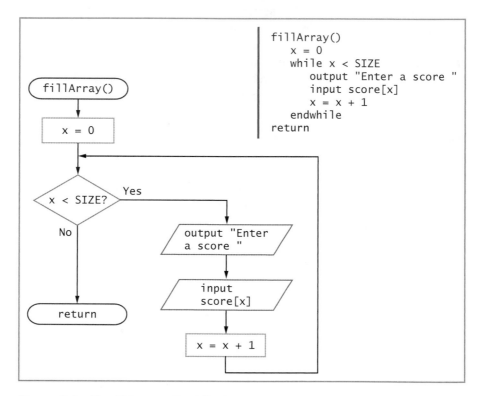

```
fillArray()
    x = 0
    while x < SIZE
        output "Enter a score "
        input score[x]
        x = x + 1
    endwhile
return
```

Figure 8-3   The fillArray() method

The sortArray() method in Figure 8-4 sorts the array elements by making a series of comparisons of adjacent element values and swapping them if they are out of order. To begin sorting this list of scores, you compare the first two scores, score[0] and score[1]. If they are out of order—that is, if score[0] is larger than score[1]—you want to reverse their positions, or swap their values.

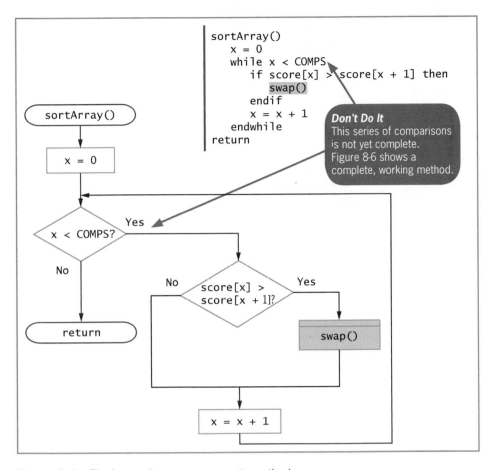

```
sortArray()
    x = 0
    while x < COMPS
        if score[x] > score[x + 1] then
            swap()
        endif
        x = x + 1
    endwhile
return
```

Don't Do It
This series of comparisons is not yet complete. Figure 8-6 shows a complete, working method.

Figure 8-4   The incomplete sortArray() method

For example, assume the five entered scores are:

```
score[0] = 90
score[1] = 85
score[2] = 65
score[3] = 95
score[4] = 75
```

In this list, score[0] is 90 and score[1] is 85, so you want to exchange the values of the two elements. You call the swap() method, which places the scores in slightly better order than they were originally. Figure 8-5 shows the swap() method. This module switches any two adjacent elements in the score array.

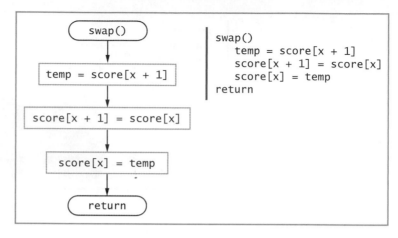

Figure 8-5   The swap() method

Notice the similarities between Figures 8-5 and 8-1.

In Figure 8-4, the number of comparisons made is based on the value of the constant named COMPS, which was initialized to the value of SIZE – 1. That is, for an array of size 5, the COMPS constant will be 4. The comparisons that are made, therefore, are as follows:

```
score[0] > score[1]?
score[1] > score[2]?
score[2] > score[3]?
score[3] > score[4]?
```

Each element in the array is compared to the one that follows it. When x becomes COMPS, the while loop ends. If it continued when x became equal to COMPS, then the next comparison would be score[4] > score[5]?. This would cause an error because the highest allowed subscript in a five-element array is 4. You must execute the decision score[x] > score[x + 1]? four times—when x is 0, 1, 2, and 3.

For a descending sort in which you want to end up with the highest value first, write the decision so that you perform the switch when score[x] is *less than* score[x + 1].

For an ascending sort, you need to perform the swap() method whenever any given element of the score array has a value greater than the next element. For any x, if the xth element is not greater than the element at position x + 1, the swap should not take place. For example, when score[x] is 90 and score[x + 1] is 85, a swap should occur. On the other hand, when score[x] is 65 and score[x + 1] is 95, then no swap should occur.

As a complete example of how this application works, suppose you have these original scores:

```
score[0] = 90
score[1] = 85
score[2] = 65
score[3] = 95
score[4] = 75
```

The logic of the sortArray() method proceeds like this:

1. Set x to 0.

2. The value of x is less than 4 (COMPS), so enter the loop.

3. Compare score[x], 90, to score[x + 1], 85. The two scores are out of order, so they are switched.

    The list is now:

    ```
    score[0] = 85
    score[1] = 90
    score[2] = 65
    score[3] = 95
    score[4] = 75
    ```

4. After the swap, add 1 to x, so x is 1.

5. Return to the top of the loop. The value of x is less than 4, so enter the loop a second time.

6. Compare score[x], 90, to score[x + 1], 65. These two values are out of order, so swap them.

    Now the result is:

    ```
    score[0] = 85
    score[1] = 65
    score[2] = 90
    score[3] = 95
    score[4] = 75
    ```

7. Add 1 to x, so x is now 2.

8. Return to the top of the loop. The value of x is less than 4, so enter the loop.

9. Compare score[x], 90, to score[x + 1], 95. These values are in order, so no switch is made.

10. Add 1 to x, making it 3.

11. Return to the top of the loop. The value of x is less than 4, so enter the loop.

12. Compare score[x], 95, to score[x + 1], 75. These two values are out of order, so switch them.

    Now the list is as follows:

    ```
    score[0] = 85
    score[1] = 65
    score[2] = 90
    score[3] = 75
    score[4] = 95
    ```

13. Add 1 to x, making it 4.

14. Return to the top of the loop. The value of x is 4, so do not enter the loop again.

When x reaches 4, every element in the list has been compared with the one adjacent to it. The highest score, 95, has "sunk" to the bottom of the list. However, the scores still are not in order. They are in slightly better ascending order than they were when the process began, because the largest value is at the bottom of the list, but they still out of order. You need to repeat the entire procedure so that 85 and 65 (the current score[0] and score[1] values) can switch places, and 90 and 75 (the current score[2] and score[3] values) can switch places. Then, the scores will be 65, 85, 75, 90, and 95. You will have to go through the list yet again to swap 85 and 75.

As a matter of fact, if the scores had started out in the worst possible order (95, 90, 85, 75, 65), the comparison process would have to take place four times. In other words, you would have to pass through the list of values four times, making appropriate swaps, before the numbers would appear in perfect ascending order. You need to place the loop in Figure 8-4 within another loop that executes four times.

Figure 8-6 shows the complete logic for the sortArray() module. The module uses a loop control variable named y to cycle through the list of scores four times. (The initialization, comparison, and alteration of this loop control variable are shaded in the figure.) With an array of five elements, it takes four comparisons to work through the array once, comparing each pair, and it takes four sets of those comparisons to ensure that every element in the entire array is in sorted order.

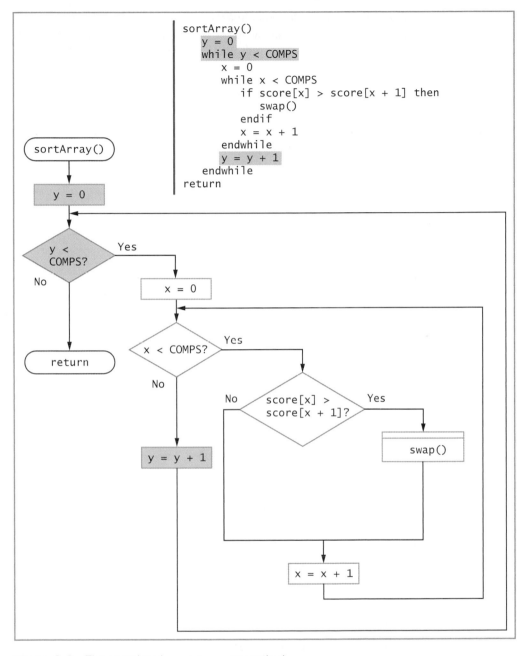

Figure 8-6 The completed sortArray() method

In the **sortArray()** method in Figure 8-6, it is important that **x** is reset to 0 for each new value of **y** so that the comparisons always start at the top of the list.

When you sort the elements in an array this way, you use nested loops—an inner loop that swaps out-of-order pairs, and an outer loop that goes through the list multiple times. The general rules are:

- The greatest number of pair comparisons you need to make during each loop is *one less* than the number of elements in the array. You use an inner loop to make the pair comparisons.

- The number of times you need to process the list of values is *one less* than the number of elements in the array. You use an outer loop to control the number of times you walk through the list.

 Watch the video *The Bubble Sort.*

As an example, if you want to sort a 10-element array, you make nine pair comparisons on each of nine rotations through the loop, executing a total of 81 score comparison statements.

The last method called by the score-sorting program in Figure 8-2 is the one that displays the sorted array contents. Figure 8-7 shows this method.

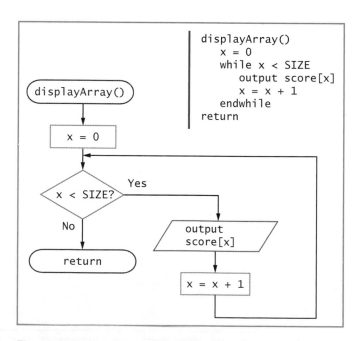

Figure 8-7   The `displayArray()` method

Sorting a List of Variable Size

In the score-sorting program in the previous section, a SIZE constant was initialized to the number of elements to be sorted at the start of the program. Sometimes, you don't want to create such a value because you might not know how many array elements will hold valid values. For example, sometimes when you run the program, you might want to sort only three or four scores, and sometimes you might want to sort 20. In other words, what if the size of the list to be sorted might vary? Rather than sorting a fixed number of array elements, you can count the input scores, and then sort just that many.

To keep track of the number of elements stored in an array, you can create the application shown in Figure 8-8. As in the original version of the program, you call the fillArray() method, and when you input each score, you increase x by 1 to place each new score into a successive element of the score array. After you input one score value and place it in the first element of the array, x is 1. After a second score is input and placed in score[1], x is 2, and so on. After you reach the end of input, x holds the number of scores that have been placed in the array, so you can store x in numberOfEls, and compute comparisons as numberOfEls - 1. With this approach, it doesn't matter if there are not enough score values to fill the array. The sortArray() and displayArray() methods use comparisons and numberOfEls instead of COMPS and SIZE to process the array. For example, if 35 scores are input, numberOfEls will be set to 35 in the fillArray() module, and when the program sorts, it will use 34 as a cutoff point for the number of pair comparisons to make. The sorting program will never make pair comparisons on array elements 36 through 100—those elements will just "sit there," never being involved in a comparison or swap.

338

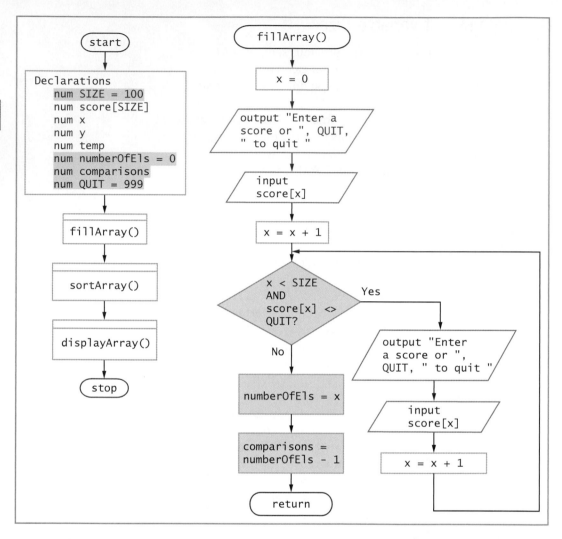

Figure 8-8   Score-sorting application in which number of elements to sort can vary

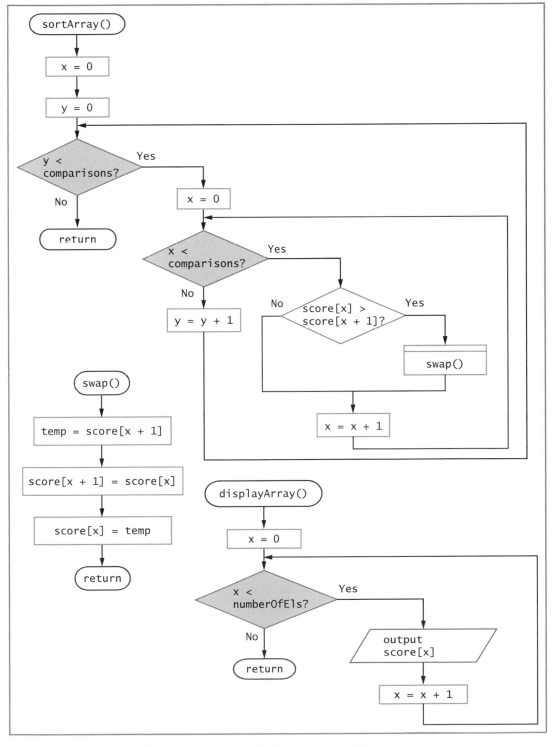

Figure 8-8 Score-sorting application in which number of elements to sort can vary (continued)

In the fillArray() method in Figure 8-8, notice that a priming read has been added to the method. If the user enters the QUIT value at the first input, then the number of elements to be sorted will be 0.

When you count the input values and use the numberOfEls variable, it does not matter if there are not enough scores to fill the array. However, an error occurs if you attempt to store more values than the array can hold. When you don't know how many elements will be stored in an array, you must overestimate the number of elements you declare.

```
start
    Declarations
        num SIZE = 100
        num score[SIZE]
        num x
        num y
        num temp
        num numberOfEls = 0
        num comparisons
        num QUIT = 999
    fillArray()
    sortArray()
    displayArray()
stop

fillArray()
    x = 0
    output "Enter a score or ", QUIT, " to quit "
    input score[x]
    x = x + 1
    while x < SIZE AND score[x] <> QUIT
        output "Enter a score or ", QUIT, " to quit "
        input score[x]
        x = x + 1
    endwhile
    numberOfEls = x
    comparisons = numberOfEls - 1
return

sortArray()
    x = 0
    y = 0
    while y < comparisons
        x = 0
        while x < comparisons
            if score[x] > score[x + 1] then
                swap()
            endif
            x = x + 1
        endwhile
        y = y + 1
    endwhile
return

swap()
    temp = score[x + 1]
    score[x + 1] = score[x]
    score[x] = temp
return

displayArray()
    x = 0
    while x < numberOfEls
        output score[x]
        x = x + 1
    endwhile
return
```

Figure 8-8   Score-sorting application in which number of elements to sort can vary (continued)

Refining the Bubble Sort to Reduce Unnecessary Comparisons

You can make additional improvements to the bubble sort created in the previous sections. As illustrated in Figure 8-8, when you perform the sorting module for a bubble sort, you pass through a list, making comparisons and swapping values if two adjacent values are out of order. If you are performing an ascending sort, then after you have made one pass through the list, the largest value is guaranteed to be in its correct final position at the bottom of the list. Similarly, the second-largest element is guaranteed to be in its correct second-to-last position after the second pass through the list, and so on. If you continue to compare every element pair in the list on every pass through the list, you are comparing elements that are already guaranteed to be in their final correct position. In other words, after the first pass through the list, you no longer need to check the bottom element; after the second pass, you don't need to check the two bottom elements.

On each pass through the array, you can afford to stop your pair comparisons one element sooner. You can avoid comparing the already-in-place values by creating a new variable, `pairsToCompare`, and setting it equal to the value of `numberOfEls` - 1. On the first pass through the list, every pair of elements is compared, so `pairsToCompare` *should* equal `numberOfEls` - 1. In other words, with five array elements to sort, four pairs are compared, and with 50 elements to sort, 49 pairs are compared. On each subsequent pass through the list, `pairsToCompare` should be reduced by 1. For example, after the first pass is completed, it is not necessary to check the bottom element. See Figure 8-9 to examine the use of the `pairsToCompare` variable.

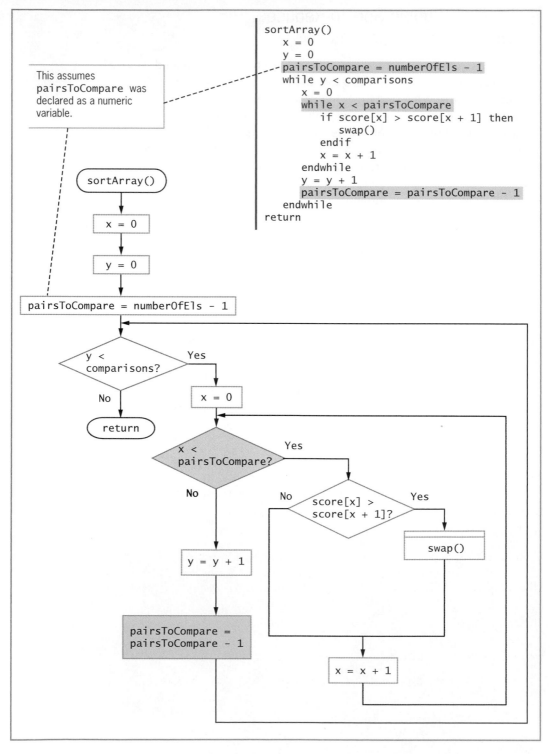

Figure 8-9   Flowchart and pseudocode for `sortArray()` method using `pairsToCompare` variable

Refining the Bubble Sort to Eliminate Unnecessary Passes

You could also improve the bubble sort module in Figure 8-9 by reducing the number of passes through the array. If array elements are badly out of order or in reverse order, many passes through the list are required to place it in order; it takes one fewer pass than the value in numberOfEls to complete all the comparisons and swaps needed to sort the list. However, when the array elements are in order or nearly in order to start, all the elements might be correctly arranged after only a few passes through the list. All subsequent passes result in no swaps. For example, assume the original scores are as follows:

```
score[0] = 65
score[1] = 75
score[2] = 85
score[3] = 90
score[4] = 95
```

The bubble sort module in Figure 8-9 would pass through the array list four times, making four sets of pair comparisons. It would always find that each score[x] is *not* greater than the corresponding score[x + 1], so no switches would ever be made. The scores would end up in the proper order, but they *were* in the proper order in the first place; therefore, a lot of time would be wasted.

A possible remedy is to add a flag variable set to a "continue" value on any pass through the list in which any pair of elements is swapped (even if just one pair), and which holds a different "finished" value when no swaps are made—that is, when all elements in the list are already in the correct order. For example, you can create a variable named didSwap and set it to "No" at the start of each pass through the list. You can change its value to "Yes" each time the swap() module is performed (that is, each time a switch is necessary).

If you ever make it through the entire list of pairs without making a switch, the didSwap flag will *not* have been set to "Yes", meaning that no swap has occurred and that the array elements must already be in the correct order. This might be on the first or second pass through the array list, or it might not be until a much later pass. If the array elements are already in the correct order at any point, you can stop making passes through the list.

Figure 8-10 illustrates a module that sorts scores and uses a didSwap flag. At the beginning of the sortArray() module, initialize didSwap to "Yes" before entering the comparison loop the first time. Then, immediately set didSwap to "No". When a switch occurs—that is, when the swap() module executes—set didSwap to "Yes".

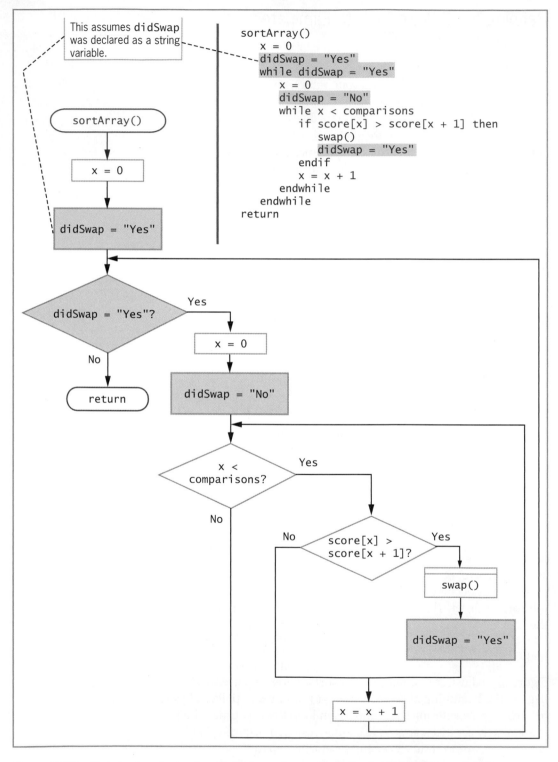

Figure 8-10 Flowchart and pseudocode for `sortArray()` method using `didSwap` variable

Other Sorts

The bubble sort works well and is relatively easy for novice array users to understand and manipulate, but even with all the improvements you added to the original bubble sort in previous sections, it is actually one of the least efficient sorting methods available. Some alternate algorithms—including the insertion sort, selection sort, cocktail sort, gnome sort, and quick sort—are more efficient because they usually require fewer comparisons. You can find algorithms for these sorts in many programming textbooks and on the Web.

With the addition of the flag variable in Figure 8-10, you no longer need the variable y, which was keeping track of the number of passes through the list. Instead, you just keep going through the list until you can make a complete pass without any switches.

345

Remember that you might never have to write your own sorting method. Many languages come with prewritten sorting methods that you use as black boxes. However, taking the time to understand some sorting procedures enhances your ability to work with arrays.

TWO TRUTHS & A LIE

Using a Bubble Sort

1. You can use a bubble sort to arrange records in ascending or descending order.

2. In a bubble sort, items in a list are compared with each other in pairs, and when an item is out of order, it swaps values with the item below it.

3. With any bubble sort, after each adjacent pair of items in a list has been compared once, the largest item in the list will have "sunk" to the bottom.

The false statement is #3. Statement #3 is true of an ascending bubble sort. However, with a descending bubble sort, the smallest item in the list will have "sunk" to the bottom after each adjacent pair of items in a list has been compared once.

Using Multidimensional Arrays

In Chapter 6, you learned that an array is a series or list of values in computer memory, all of which have the same name and data type but are differentiated with special numbers called subscripts. Usually, all the values in an array have something in common; for example, they might represent a list of employee ID numbers or a list of prices for items sold in a store. A subscript, also called an index, is a number that indicates the position of a particular item within an array.

An array whose elements you can access using a single subscript is a **one-dimensional array** or **single-dimensional array**. The array has only one dimension because its data can be stored in a table that has just one dimension—height. If you know the vertical position of a one-dimensional array's element, you can find its value.

Floor	Rent ($)
0	350
1	400
2	475
3	600
4	1000

Table 8-1   Rent schedule based on floor

For example, suppose you own an apartment building and charge five different rent amounts for apartments on different floors (including floor 0, the basement), as shown in Table 8-1.

You could declare the following array to hold the rent values:

```
num RENT_BY_FLOOR[5] = 350, 400, 475, 600, 1000
```

The location of any rent value in Table 8-1 depends on only a single variable—the floor of the building. So, when you create a single-dimensional array to hold rent values, you need just one subscript to identify the row.

Sometimes, however, locating a value in an array depends on more than one variable. If you must represent values in a table or grid that contains rows and columns instead of a single list, then you might want to use a **two-dimensional array**. A two-dimensional array contains two dimensions: height and width. That is, the location of any element depends on two factors. For example, if an apartment's rent depends on two variables—both the floor of the building and the number of bedrooms—then you want to create a two-dimensional array.

As an example of how useful two-dimensional arrays can be, assume that you own an apartment building with five floors, and that each of the floors has studio apartments (with no bedroom) and one- and two-bedroom apartments. Table 8-2 shows the rental amounts.

Floor	Studio apartment	1-bedroom apartment	2-bedroom apartment
0	350	390	435
1	400	440	480
2	475	530	575
3	600	650	700
4	1000	1075	1150

Table 8-2   Rent schedule based on floor and number of bedrooms

To determine a tenant's rent, you need to know two pieces of information: the floor on which the tenant rents an apartment and the number of bedrooms in the apartment. Each element in a two-dimensional array requires two subscripts to reference it—one subscript to determine the row and a second to determine the column. Thus, the 15 separate rent values for a two-dimensional array based on the rent table in Table 8-2 would be arranged in five rows and three columns and defined as follows:

```
num RENT_BY_FLOOR_AND_BDRMS[5][3]= {350, 390, 435},
                                    {400, 440, 480},
                                    {475, 530, 575},
                                    {600, 650, 700},
                                    {1000, 1075, 1150}
```

Figure 8-11 shows how the one- and two-dimensional rent arrays might appear in computer memory.

A Single-Dimensional Array

```
num RENT_BY_FLOOR[5] = 350,
400, 475, 600, 1000
```

350
400
475
600
1000

A Two-Dimensional Array

```
num RENT_BY_FLOOR_AND_BDRMS[5][3] =
              {350, 390, 435},
              {400, 440, 480},
              {475, 530, 575},
              {600, 650, 700},
              {1000, 1075, 1150}
```

350	390	435
400	440	480
475	530	575
600	650	700
1000	1075	1150

Figure 8-11   One- and two-dimensional arrays in memory

When you declare a one-dimensional array, you type a set of square brackets after the array type and name. To declare a two-dimensional array, many languages require you to type two sets of brackets after the array type and name. For each element in the array, the first square bracket holds the number of rows, and the second one holds the number of columns. In other words, the two dimensions represent the array's height and its width.

 Instead of two sets of brackets to indicate a position in a two-dimensional array, some languages use a single set of brackets but separate the subscripts with commas. Therefore, the elements in row 1, column 2 would be RENT_BY_FLOOR_AND_BDRMS[1, 2].

Watch the video *Two-Dimensional Arrays*.

In the RENT_BY_FLOOR_AND_BDRMS array declaration, the values that are assigned to each row are enclosed in braces to help you picture the placement of each number in the array. The first row of the array holds the three rent values 350, 390, and 435 for floor 0; the second row holds 400, 440, and 480 for floor 1; and so on.

You access a two-dimensional array value using two subscripts, in which the first subscript represents the row and the second one represents the column. For example, some of the values in the array are as follows:

- RENT_BY_FLOOR_AND_BDRMS[0][0] is 350

- RENT_BY_FLOOR_AND_BDRMS[0][1] is 390

When mathematicians use a two-dimensional array, they often call it a **matrix** or a **table**; you might have used a two-dimensional array called a spreadsheet.

- RENT_BY_FLOOR_AND_BDRMS[0][2] is 435

- RENT_BY_FLOOR_AND_BDRMS[4][0] is 1000

- RENT_BY_FLOOR_AND_BDRMS[4][1] is 1075

- RENT_BY_FLOOR_AND_BDRMS[4][2] is 1150

If you declare two variables to hold the floor number and bedroom count as num floor and num bedrooms, any tenant's rent is RENT_BY_FLOOR_AND_BDRMS[floor][bedrooms].

Figure 8-12 shows a program that continuously displays rents for apartments based on renter requests for bedrooms and floor. Notice that although significant setup is required to provide all the values for the rents, the basic program is extremely brief and easy to follow.

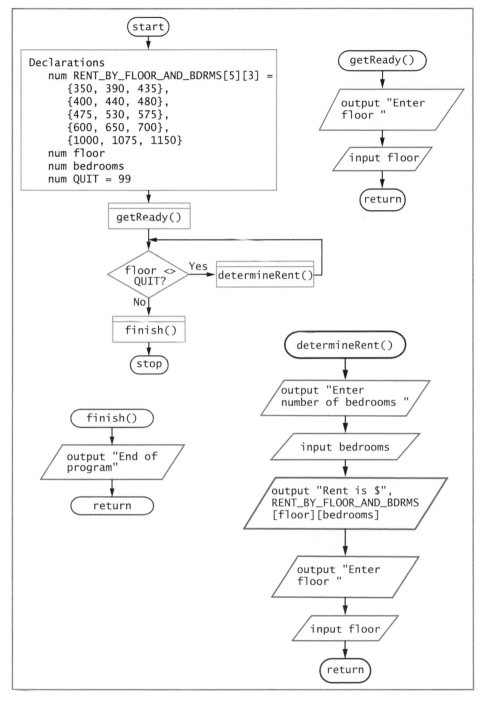

Figure 8-12 A program that determines rents

```
start
   Declarations
      num RENT_BY_FLOOR_AND_BDRMS[5][3] = {350, 390, 435},
                                          {400, 440, 480},
                                          {475, 530, 575},
                                          {600, 650, 700},
                                          {1000, 1075, 1150}
      num floor
      num bedrooms
      num QUIT = 99
   getReady()
   while floor <> QUIT
      determineRent()
   endwhile
   finish()
stop

getReady()
   output "Enter floor "
   input floor
return

determineRent()
   output "Enter number of bedrooms "
   input bedrooms
   output "Rent is $", RENT_BY_FLOOR_AND_BDRMS[floor][bedrooms]
   output "Enter floor "
   input floor
return

finish()
   output "End of program"
return
```

Figure 8-12   A program that determines rents (continued)

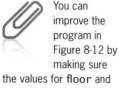

You can improve the program in Figure 8-12 by making sure the values for **floor** and **bedrooms** are within range before using them as array subscripts.

Two-dimensional arrays are never actually *required* in order to achieve a useful program. The same 15 categories of rent information could be stored in three separate single-dimensional arrays of five elements each. Of course, don't forget that even one-dimensional arrays are never required for you to be able to solve a problem. You could also declare 15 separate rent variables and make 15 separate decisions to determine the rent.

Besides one- and two-dimensional arrays, many programming languages also support **three-dimensional arrays**. For example, if you own an apartment building with a number of floors and different numbers of bedrooms available in apartments on each floor, you can use a two-dimensional array to store the rental fees, but if you own several apartment buildings, you might want to employ a third dimension to store the building number. For example, if a three-dimensional array is stored on paper, you might need to know an element's row, column, and page to access it, as shown in Figure 8-13.

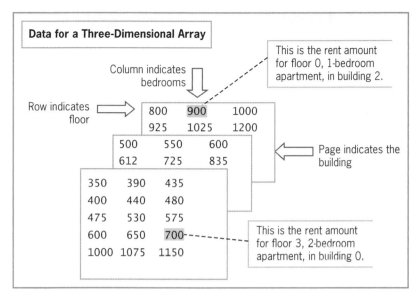

Data for a Three-Dimensional Array

Column indicates bedrooms

Row indicates floor

This is the rent amount for floor 0, 1-bedroom apartment, in building 2.

| 800 | 900 | 1000 |
| 925 | 1025 | 1200 |

| 500 | 550 | 600 |
| 612 | 725 | 835 |

Page indicates the building

350	390	435
400	440	480
475	530	575
600	650	700
1000	1075	1150

This is the rent amount for floor 3, 2-bedroom apartment, in building 0.

Figure 8-13 Picturing a three-dimensional array

If you declare a three-dimensional array named RENT_BY_3_FACTORS, then you can use an expression such as RENT_BY_3_FACTORS[floor] [bedrooms][building], which refers to a specific rent figure for an apartment whose floor and bedroom numbers are stored in the floor and bedrooms variables, and whose building number is stored in the building variable. Specifically, RENT_BY_3_FACTORS[0][1][2] refers to a one-bedroom apartment on floor 0 of building 2.

Both two- and three- dimensional arrays are examples of **multidimensional arrays**, which are arrays that have more than one dimension. Some languages allow many dimensions. For example, in C# and Visual Basic, an array can have 32 dimensions. However, it's usually hard for people to keep track of more than three dimensions.

TWO TRUTHS & A LIE

Using Multidimensional Arrays

1. In every multidimensional array, the location of any element depends on two factors.

2. For each element in a two-dimensional array, the first subscript represents the row number, and the second one represents the column.

3. Multidimensional arrays are never actually *required* in order to achieve a useful program.

The false statement is #1. In a two-dimensional array, the location of any element depends on two factors, but in a three-dimensional array, it depends on three factors, and so on.

Using Indexed Files and Linked Lists

Sorting a list of five or even 100 scores does not require significant computer resources. However, many data files contain thousands of records, and each record might contain dozens of data fields. Sorting large numbers of data records requires considerable time and computer memory. When a large data file needs to be processed in ascending or descending order based on a particular field, it is usually more efficient to store and access records based on their logical order than to sort and access them in their physical order. **Physical order** refers to a "real" order for storage; an example would be writing the names of 10 friends, each one on an index card. You can arrange the cards alphabetically by the friends' last names, chronologically by age of the friendship, or randomly by throwing the cards in the air and picking them up as you find them. Whichever way you do it, the records still follow each other in *some* order. In addition to their current physical order, you can think of the cards as having a **logical order**; that is, a virtual order, based on any criterion you choose— from the tallest friend to the shortest, from the one who lives farthest away to the closest, and so on. Sorting the cards in a new physical order can take a lot of time; using the cards in their logical order without physically rearranging them is often more efficient.

Using Indexed Files

A common method of accessing records in logical order is to use an index. Using an index involves identifying a key field for each record. A record's **key field** is the field whose contents make the record unique among all records in a file. For example, multiple employees can have the same last name, first name, salary, or street address, but each employee possesses a unique employee identification number, so an ID number field might make a good key field for a personnel file. Similarly, a product number makes a good key field in an inventory file.

As pages in a book have numbers, computer memory and storage locations have **addresses**. In Chapter 1, you learned that every variable has a numeric address in computer memory; likewise, every data record on a disk has a numeric address where it is stored. You can store records in any physical order on the disk, but when you **index** records, you store a list of key fields paired with the storage address for the corresponding data record. Then you can use the index to find the records in order based on their addresses.

When you use an index, you can store records on a **random-access storage device**, such as a disk, from which records can be accessed in any order. Each record can be placed in any physical location on the disk, and you can use the index as you would use the index in the back of a book. If you pick up a 600-page American history book because you need some facts about Betsy Ross, you do not want to start on page one and work your way through the book. Instead, you turn to the index, discover that Betsy Ross is mentioned on page 418, and go directly to that page.

Chapter 7 contains a discussion of random access files.

You do not need to determine a record's exact physical address in order to use it. A computer's operating system takes care of locating available storage for your records.

You can picture an index based on ID numbers by looking at the index in Figure 8-14. The index is stored on a portion of the disk. The address in the index refers to other scattered locations on the disk.

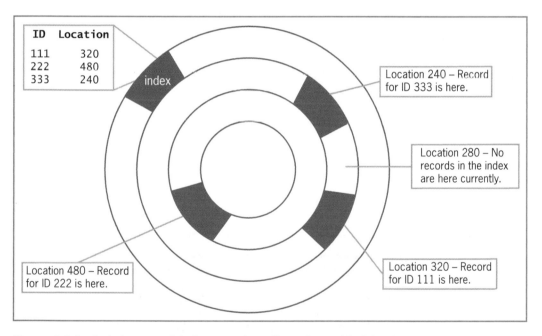

Figure 8-14 An index on a disk that associates ID numbers with disk addresses

When you want to access the data for employee 333, you tell your computer to look through the ID numbers in the index, find a match, and then proceed to the memory location specified. Similarly, when you want to process records in order based on ID number, you tell your system to retrieve records at the locations in the index in sequence. Thus, even though employee 111 may have been hired last and the record is stored at the highest physical address on the disk, if the employee record has the lowest ID number, it will be accessed first during any ordered processing.

Watch the video *Using an Indexed File.*

When a record is removed from an indexed file, it does not have to be physically removed. Its reference can simply be deleted from the index, and then it will not be part of any further processing.

Using Linked Lists

Another way to access records in a desired order, even though they might not be physically stored in that order, is to create a linked list. In its simplest form, creating a **linked list** involves creating one extra field in every record of stored data. This extra field holds the physical address of the next logical record. For example, a record that holds a customer's ID, name, and phone number might contain the following fields:

```
idNum
name
phoneNum
nextCustAddress
```

Every time you use a record, you access the next record based on the address held in the nextCustAddress field.

Every time you add a new record to a linked list, you search through the list for the correct logical location of the new record. For example, assume that customer records are stored at the addresses shown in Table 8-3 and that they are linked in customer ID order. Notice that the addresses of the records are not shown in sequential order. The records are shown in their logical order by idNum, with each one's nextCustAddress field holding the address of the record shown in the following line.

Address	idNum	name	phoneNum	nextCustAddress
0000	111	Baker	234-5676	7200
7200	222	Vincent	456-2345	4400
4400	333	Silvers	543-0912	6000
6000	444	Donovan	328-8744	eof

Table 8-3   Sample linked customer list

You can see from Table 8-3 that each customer's record contains a nextCustAddress field that stores the address of the next customer who follows in customer ID number order (and not necessarily in address order). For any individual customer, the next logical customer's address might be physically distant.

Examine the file shown in Table 8-3, and suppose a new customer with number 245 and the name Newberg is acquired. Also suppose that the computer operating system finds an available storage location for Newberg's data at address 8400. In this case, the procedure to add Newberg to the list is:

1. Create a variable named `currentAddress` to hold the address of the record in the list you are currently examining. Store the address of the first record in the list, 0000, in this variable.

2. Compare the new customer Newberg's ID, 245, with the current (first) record's ID, 111 (in other words, the ID at address 0000). The value 245 is higher than 111, so you save the first customer's address (the address you are currently examining), 0000, in a variable you can name `saveAddress`. The `saveAddress` variable always holds the address you just finished examining. The first customer's record contains a link to the address of the next logical customer—7200. Store the 7200 in the `currentAddress` variable.

3. Examine the second customer record, the one that physically exists at the address 7200, which is currently held in the `currentAddress` variable.

4. Compare Newberg's ID, 245, with the ID stored in the record at `currentAddress`, 222. The value 245 is higher, so save the current address, 7200, in `saveAddress` and store its `nextCustAddress` address field, 4400, in the `currentAddress` variable.

5. Compare Newberg's ID, 245, with 333, which is the ID at `currentAddress` (4400). Up to this point, 245 had been higher than each ID tested, but this time the value 245 is lower, so that means customer 245 should logically precede customer 333. Set the `nextCustAddress` field in Newberg's record (customer 245) to 4400, which is the address of customer 333 and the address currently stored in `currentAddress`. This means that in any future processing, Newberg's record will logically be followed by the record containing 333. Also set the `nextCustAddress` field of the record located at `saveAddress` (7200, Vincent, customer 222, the customer who logically preceded Newberg) to the new customer Newberg's address, 8400. The updated list appears in Table 8-4.

Address	idNum	name	phoneNum	nextCustAddress
0000	111	Baker	234-5676	7200
7200	222	Vincent	456-2345	8400
8400	245	Newberg	222-9876	4400
4400	333	Silvers	543-0912	6000
6000	444	Donovan	328-8744	eof

Table 8-4   Updated customer list

Watch the video *Using a Linked List.*

As with indexing, when removing records from a linked list, the records do not need to be physically deleted from the medium on which they are stored. If you need to remove customer 333 from the preceding list, all you need to do is change Newberg's `nextCustAddress` field to the value in Silvers' `nextCustAddress` field, which is Donovan's address: 6000. In other words, the value of 6000 is obtained not by knowing to which record Newberg should point, but by knowing to which record Silvers previously pointed. When Newberg's record points to Donovan, Silvers' record is then bypassed during any further processing that uses the links to travel from one record to the next.

More sophisticated linked lists store *two* additional fields with each record. One field stores the address of the next record, and the other field stores the address of the *previous* record so that the list can be accessed either forward or backward.

TWO TRUTHS & A LIE

Using Indexed Files and Linked Lists

1. When a large data file needs to be processed in order based on a particular field, it is usually most efficient to sort the records.

2. A record's key field is the field whose contents make the record unique among all records in a file.

3. Creating a linked list requires you to create one extra field for every record; this extra field holds the physical address of the next logical record.

The false statement is #1. It is usually most efficient to store and access records based on their logical order than to sort and access them in their physical order.

Chapter Summary

- Frequently, data records need to be sorted, or placed in order, based on the contents of one or more fields. When you sort data, you can sort either in ascending order, arranging records from lowest to highest value, or descending order, arranging records from highest to lowest value.

- Swapping two values is a concept that is central to most sorting techniques. When you swap the values stored in two variables, you reverse their positions using a temporary variable to hold one of the values during the swap process.

- In a bubble sort, items in a list are compared with each other in pairs. When an item is out of order, it swaps values with the item below it. With an ascending bubble sort, after each adjacent pair of items in a list has been compared once, the largest item in the list will have "sunk" to the bottom. After many passes through the list, the smallest items rise to the top like bubbles in a carbonated drink.

- Sometimes, the size of the list to be sorted might vary. Rather than initializing a constant to a fixed value, you can count the values to be sorted, and then give a variable the value of the number of array elements to use.

- You can improve a bubble sort by stopping pair comparisons one element sooner on each pass through the array being sorted.

- You can improve a bubble sort by adding a flag variable that you set to a "continue" value on any pass through the sort in which any pair of elements is swapped (even if just one pair), and that holds a different "finished" value when no swaps are made—that is, all elements in the list are already in the correct order.

- Two-dimensional arrays have both rows and columns of values. You must use two subscripts when you access an element in a two-dimensional array. Many languages support arrays with even more dimensions.

- You can use an index or linked list to access data records in a logical order that differs from their physical order. Using an index involves identifying a physical address and key field for each record. Creating a linked list involves creating an extra field within every record to hold the physical address of the next logical record.

Key Terms

Sequential order describes the arrangement of records when they are stored one after another on the basis of the value in a particular field.

Sorted records are in order based on the contents of one or more fields.

Ascending order describes the arrangement of records from lowest to highest, based on a value within a field.

Descending order describes the arrangement of records from highest to lowest, based on a value within a field.

The **median** value in a list is the value in the middle position when the values are sorted.

The **mean** value in a list is the arithmetic average.

To **swap values** is to exchange the values of two variables.

A **bubble sort** is a sort in which you arrange records in either ascending or descending order by comparing items in a list in pairs; when an item is out of order, it swaps values with the item below it.

A **sinking sort** is another name for a bubble sort.

An **algorithm** is a list of instructions that accomplishes a task.

A **one-dimensional array** or **single-dimensional array** is a list accessed using a single subscript.

Two-dimensional arrays have both rows and columns of values; you must use two subscripts when you access an element in a two-dimensional array.

Matrix and **table** are terms used by mathematicians to describe a two-dimensional array.

Three-dimensional arrays are arrays in which each element is accessed using three subscripts.

Multidimensional arrays are lists with more than one dimension.

A list's **physical order** is the order in which it is actually stored.

A list's **logical order** is the order in which you use it, even though it is not necessarily physically stored in that order.

A record's **key field** is the field whose contents make the record unique among all records in a file.

Addresses identify computer memory and storage locations.

When you **index** records, you store a list of key fields paired with the storage address for the corresponding data record.

A **random-access storage device**, such as a disk, is one from which records can be accessed in any order.

A **linked list** contains an extra field in every record of stored data; this extra field holds the physical address of the next logical record.

Review Questions

1. Employee records stored in order from highest-paid to lowest-paid have been sorted in _____ order.

   a. ascending

   b. descending

   c. staggered

   d. recursive

2. Student records stored in alphabetical order by last name have been sorted in _____ order.

   a. ascending

   b. descending

   c. staggered

   d. recursive

3. When computers sort data, they always _____.

   a. place items in ascending order

   b. use a bubble sort

   c. use numeric values when making comparisons

   d. begin the process by locating the position of the lowest value

4. Which of the following code segments correctly swaps the values of variables named x and y?

   a. ```
x = y
y = temp
x = temp
```
```

b. `temp = x`

`x = y`

`y = temp`

c. `x = y`

`temp = x`

`y = temp`

d. `temp = x`

`y = x`

`x = temp`

5. Which type of sort compares list items in pairs, swapping any two adjacent values that are out of order?

   a. bubble sort

   b. indexed sort

   c. insertion sort

   d. selection sort

6. To sort a list of eight values using a bubble sort, the greatest number of times you would have to pass through the list making comparisons is _____.

   a. six

   b. seven

   c. eight

   d. nine

7. To sort a list of eight values using a bubble sort, the greatest number of pair comparisons you would have to make before the sort is complete is _____.

   a. seven

   b. eight

   c. 49

   d. 64

8. When you do not know how many items need to be sorted in a program, you can create an array that has _____.

   a. variable-sized elements

   b. at least as many elements as the number you predict you will need

   c. at least one element less than the number you predict you will need

   d. You cannot sort items if you do not know how many there will be when you write the program.

9. In a bubble sort, on each pass through the list that must be sorted, you can stop making pair comparisons _____.

   a. one comparison sooner

   b. two comparisons sooner

   c. one comparison later

   d. two comparisons later

10. When performing a bubble sort on a list of 10 values, you can stop making passes through the list of values as soon as _____ on a single pass through the list.

    a. no swaps are made

    b. exactly one swap is made

    c. no more than nine swaps are made

    d. no more than 10 swaps are made

11. The bubble sort is _____.

    a. the most efficient sort

    b. a relatively fast sort compared to others

    c. a relatively easy sort to understand

    d. all of the above

12. Data stored in a table that can be accessed using row and column numbers is stored as a _____ array.

   a. single-dimensional

   b. two-dimensional

   c. three-dimensional

   d. nondimensional

13. A two-dimensional array declared as `num myArray[6][7]` has _____ columns.

   a. 5

   b. 6

   c. 7

   d. 8

14. In a two-dimensional array declared as `num myArray[6][7]`, the highest row number is _____.

   a. 5

   b. 6

   c. 7

   d. 8

15. If you access a two-dimensional array with the expression `output myArray[2][5]`, the output value will be _____.

   a. 0

   b. 2

   c. 5

   d. impossible to tell from the information given

16. Three-dimensional arrays _____.

   a. are supported in many modern programming languages

   b. always contain at least nine elements

   c. are used only in object-oriented languages

   d. all of the above

17. Student records are stored in ID number order, but accessed by grade point average for a report. Grade point average order is a(n) _____ order.

    a. imaginary

    b. physical

    c. logical

    d. illogical

18. When you store a list of key fields paired with the storage address for the corresponding data record, you are creating _____.

    a. a directory

    b. a three-dimensional array

    c. a linked list

    d. an index

19. When a record in an indexed file is not needed for further processing, _____.

    a. its first character must be replaced with a special character, indicating it is a deleted record

    b. its position must be retained, but its fields must be replaced with blanks

    c. it must be physically removed from the file

    d. the record can stay in place physically, but its reference is removed from the index

20. With a linked list, every record _____.

    a. is stored in sequential order

    b. contains a field that holds the address of another record

    c. contains a code that indicates the record's position in an imaginary list

    d. is stored in a physical location that corresponds to a key field

Exercises

1. Design an application that accepts 10 numbers and displays them in descending order.

2. Design an application that accepts eight friends' first names and displays them in alphabetical order.

3. a. Professor Zak allows students to drop the two lowest scores on the ten 100-point quizzes she gives during the semester. Design an application that accepts a student name and 10 quiz scores. Output the student's name and total points for the student's eight highest-scoring quizzes.

   b. Modify the application in Exercise 3a so that the student's mean and median scores on the eight best quizzes are displayed.

4. The village of Ringwood conducted a census and created records that contain household data, including income. Ringwood has exactly 75 households. Write a program into which a village statistician can enter each of the 75 household income values, and determine the mean and median household income.

5. The village of Marengo conducted a census and collected records that contain household data, including the number of occupants in each household. The exact number of household records has not yet been determined, but you know that Marengo has fewer than 300 households. Develop the logic for a program that allows a user to enter each household size and determine the mean and median household size in Marengo.

6. The Hinner College Foundation holds an annual fundraiser for which the foundation director maintains records. Write a program that accepts donor names and contribution amounts continuously. Assume that there are at least five donors, but never more than 300. Develop the logic for a program that sorts the donation amounts in descending order and then displays the five most generous donors and their donation amounts.

7. The Spread-a-Smile Greeting Card Store maintains customer records with data fields for first name, last name, address, and total purchases in dollars. At the end of each month, the store manager invites the five customers with the greatest value of purchases to an exclusive sales event. Develop the logic for a program that reads in 100 customer records and stores the first and last names and total purchases in three parallel arrays. Then sort the arrays so that records are in descending order by purchase amount for the month. The output lists the names of the top five customers.

8. The MidAmerica Bus Company charges fares to passengers based on the number of travel zones they cross. Additionally, discounts are provided for multiple passengers traveling together. Ticket fares are shown in the following table:

	Zones crossed			
Passengers	0	1	2	3
1	7.50	10.00	12.00	12.75
2	14.00	18.50	22.00	23.00
3	20.00	21.00	32.00	33.00
4	25.00	27.50	36.00	37.00

Develop the logic for a program that accepts the number of passengers and zones crossed as input. The output is the ticket charge.

9. In golf, par represents a standard number of strokes a player will need to complete a hole. Instead of using an absolute score, players can compare their scores on a hole to the par figure and determine whether they are above or below par. Families can play nine holes of miniature golf at the Family Fun Miniature Golf Park. So that family members can compete fairly, the course provides a different par for each hole based on the player's age. The par figures are shown in the following table:

	Holes								
Age	1	2	3	4	5	6	7	8	9
4 and under	8	8	9	7	5	7	8	5	8
5–7	7	7	8	6	5	6	7	5	6
8–11	6	5	6	5	4	5	5	4	5
12–15	5	4	4	4	3	4	3	3	4
16 and over	4	3	3	3	2	3	2	3	3

a. Develop the logic for a program that accepts a player's name, age, and nine-hole score as input. Display the player's name and score on each of the nine holes, with one of the phrases "Over par", "Par", or "Under par" next to each score.

b. Modify the program in Exercise 9a so that, at the end of the golfer's report, the total score is displayed. Include the player's total score in relation to par for the entire course.

10. Parker's Consulting Services pays its employees an hourly rate based on two criteria—number of years of service and last year's performance rating, which is a whole number, 0 through 5. Employee records contain ID number, last and first names, year hired, and performance score. The salary schedule is outlined in the following table:

Years of service	Performance score					
	0	1	2	3	4	5
0	8.50	9.00	9.75	10.30	12.00	13.00
1	9.50	10.25	10.95	11.30	13.50	15.25
2	10.50	11.00	12.00	13.00	15.00	17.60
3	11.50	12.25	14.00	14.25	15.70	18.90
4 or more	12.50	13.75	15.25	15.50	17.00	20.00

In addition to the pay rates shown, an employee with more than 10 years of service receives an extra 5 percent per hour for each year over 10. Develop the logic for a program that continuously accepts employee data and prints each employee's ID number, name, and correct hourly salary for the current year.

11. The Roadmaster Driving School allows students to sign up for any number of driving lessons. The school allows up to four attempts to pass the driver's license test; if all the attempts are unsuccessful, then the student's tuition is returned. The school maintains an archive containing student records for those who have successfully passed the licensing test over the last year. Each record contains a student ID number, name, number of driving lessons completed, and the number of the attempt on which the student passed the licensing test. Records are stored in alphabetical order by student name. The school administration is interested in

examining the correlation between the number of lessons taken and the number of attempts required to pass the test. Develop the logic for a program that would produce a table for the school. Each row represents the number of lessons taken: 0–9, 10–19, 20–29, and 30 or more. Each column represents the number of test attempts in order to pass—1 through 4.

12. The Stevens College Testing Center creates a record each time a student takes a placement test. Students are tested in any of 12 subject areas: Art, Biology, Chemistry, Computer Science, English, German, History, Math, Music, Psychology, Sociology, or Spanish. Each record contains the student's ID number, the test subject area, and a percent score on the test. Records are maintained in the order they are entered as the tests are taken. The college wants a report that lists each of the 12 tests along with a count of the number of students who have received scores in each of the following categories: at least 90 percent, 80 through 89 percent, 70 through 79 percent, and below 70 percent. Develop the logic that produces the report.

Find the Bugs

13. Your student disk contains files named DEBUG08-01.txt, DEBUG08-02.txt, and DEBUG08-03.txt. Each file starts with some comments that describe the problem. Comments are lines that begin with two slashes (//). Following the comments, each file contains pseudocode that has one or more bugs you must find and correct.

Game Zone

14. In the Game Zone section of Chapter 6, you designed the logic for a quiz that contains questions about a topic of your choice. (Each question was a multiple-choice question with three answer options.) Now, modify the program so it allows the user to retake the quiz up to four additional times or until the user achieves a perfect score, whichever comes first. At the end of all the quiz attempts, display a recap of the user's scores.

15. In the Game Zone section of Chapter 5, you designed a guessing game in which the application generates a random number and the player tries to guess it. After each guess, you displayed a message indicating whether the player's guess was correct, too high, or too low. When the player eventually guessed the correct number, you displayed a score that represented a count of the number of guesses that were required. Now, modify that program to allow a player to replay the game as many times as he likes, up to 20 times. When the player is done, display the scores from highest to lowest, and display the mean and median scores.

16. a. Create a TicTacToe game. In this game, two players alternate placing Xs and Os into a grid until one player has three matching symbols in a row, either horizontally, vertically, or diagonally. Create a game that displays a three-by-three grid containing the digits 1 through 9, similar to the first window shown in Figure 8-15. When the user chooses a position by typing a number, place an X in the appropriate spot. For example, after the user chooses 3, the screen looks like the second window in Figure 8-15. Generate a random number for the position where the computer will place an O. Do not allow the player or the computer to place a symbol where one has already been placed. When either the player or computer has three symbols in a row, declare a winner. If all positions have been used and no one has three symbols in a row, declare a tie.

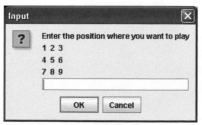 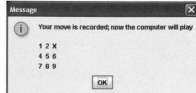

Figure 8-15   A TicTacToe game

b. In the TicTacToe game in Exercise 16a, the computer's selection is chosen randomly. Improve the game so that when the computer has two Os in any row, column, or diagonal, it selects the winning position for its next move rather than selecting a position randomly.

Up for Discussion

17. Now that you are becoming comfortable with arrays, you can see that programming is a complex subject. Should all literate people understand how to program? If so, how much programming should they understand?

18. What are language standards? At this point in your study of programming, what do they mean to you?

19. This chapter discusses sorting data. Suppose a large hospital hires you to write a program that displays lists of potential organ recipients. The hospital's doctors will consult this list if they have an organ that can be transplanted. The hospital administrators instruct you to sort potential recipients by last name and display them sequentially in alphabetical order. If more than 10 patients are waiting for a particular organ, the first 10 patients are displayed; a doctor can either select one of these or move on to view the next set of 10 patients. You worry that this system gives an unfair advantage to patients with last names that start with A, B, C, and D. Should you write and install the program? If you do not, many transplant opportunities will be missed while the hospital searches for another programmer to write the program. Are there different criteria you would want to use to sort the patients?

Advanced Modularization Techniques

In this chapter, you will learn about:

- ◎ Methods with no parameters
- ◎ Methods that require a single parameter
- ◎ Methods that require multiple parameters
- ◎ Methods that return a value
- ◎ Passing arrays to methods
- ◎ Overloading methods
- ◎ Avoiding ambiguous methods
- ◎ Using predefined methods
- ◎ Method design issues, including implementation hiding, cohesion, and coupling
- ◎ Recursion

Using Methods with No Parameters

In Chapter 2, you learned about many features of program modules, also called methods. You also learned much of the vocabulary associated with methods. For example:

- A **method** is a program module that contains a series of statements that carry out a task; you can invoke or call a method from another program or method.

- Any program can contain an unlimited number of methods, and each method can be called an unlimited number of times.

- The rules for naming methods are different in every programming language, but they are often similar to the language's rules for variable names. In this text, method names are followed by a set of parentheses.

- A method must include a **method header** (also called the declaration or definition) and a **method body**. The last statement in the body is a **return statement**.

- Variables and constants are **in scope** within, or **local** to, only the method in which they are declared.

Figure 9-1 shows a program that allows a user to enter a preferred language (English or Spanish) and then, using the chosen language, asks the user to enter his or her weight. The program then calculates the user's weight on the moon as 16.6 percent of the person's weight on Earth. The main program contains two variables and a constant, all of which are local to the main program. The program calls the displayInstructions() method, which contains its own local variable and constants that are invisible to the main program. The method prompts the user for a language indicator and displays a prompt in the selected language. Figure 9-2 shows a typical program execution in a command-line environment.

Especially in newer object-oriented programming languages, modules are most often called methods, so the term *methods* will be used in this chapter.

The opposite of local is global. When a data item is known to all of a program's modules, it is a **global data item**. In general, programmers prefer local data items because when data is contained within the method that uses it, the method is more portable and less prone to error. In Chapter 2, you learned that when a method is described as *portable*, it can easily be moved to another application and used there.

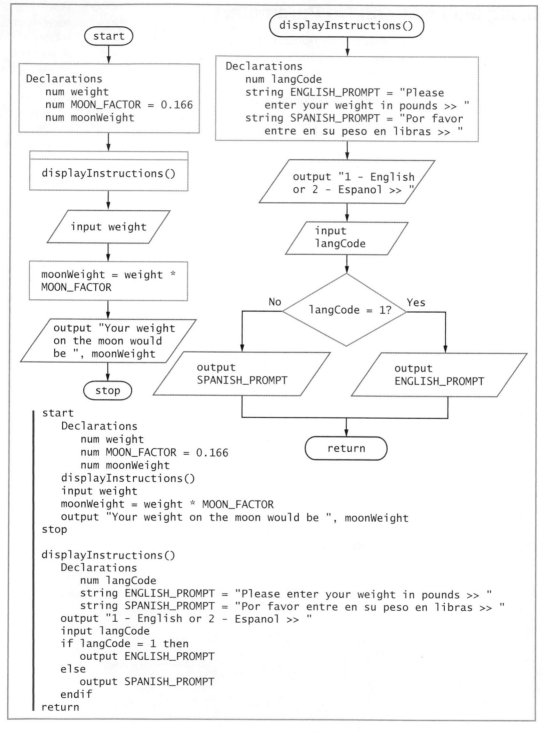

Figure 9-1   A program that calculates the user's weight on the moon

In Chapter 2, you learned that this book uses a rectangle with a horizontal stripe across the top to represent a method call statement in a flowchart. Some programmers prefer to use a rectangle with two vertical stripes at the sides; a popular flowcharting program called Visual Logic uses the same convention. As a way to remember that this symbol represents an external method call, picture the rectangle with the vertical stripes as a window with drapery on each side, then imagine that your program has to "look outside" to find the external method.

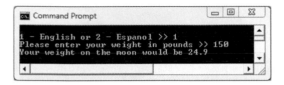

Figure 9-2 Output of moon weight calculator program in Figure 9-1

In the program in Figure 9-1, the main program and the called method each contain only what is needed at the local level. However, sometimes two or more parts of a program require access to the same data. When methods must share data, you can pass the data into and return the data out of methods. In this chapter, you will learn that when you call a method from a program or other method, you must know three things:

- The name of the called method

- What type of information to send to the method, if any

- What type of return data to expect from the method, if any

TWO TRUTHS & A LIE

Using Methods with No Parameters

1. Any program can contain an unlimited number of methods, but each method can be called once.

2. A method includes a header and a body.

3. Variables and constants are in scope within, or local to, only the method in which they are declared.

The false statement is #1. Each method can be called an unlimited number of times.

Parameter and *argument* are closely related terms. A calling method sends an argument to a called method. A called method accepts the value as its parameter.

Creating Methods that Require a Single Parameter

Some methods require information to be sent in from the outside. When you pass a data item into a method from a calling program, it is called an **argument to the method**, or more simply, an argument. When the method receives the data item, it is called a **parameter to the method**, or more simply, a parameter.

If a method could not receive parameters, you would have to write an infinite number of methods to cover every possible situation. As a real-life example, when you make a restaurant reservation, you do not need to employ a different method for every date of the year at every possible time of day. Rather, you can supply the date and time as information to the person who carries out the method. The method that records the reservation is carried out in the same manner, no matter what date and time are supplied. In a program, if you design a method to square numeric values, it makes sense to design a `square()` method that you can supply with a parameter that represents the value to be squared, rather than having to develop a `square1()` method that squares the value 1, a `square2()` method that squares the value 2, and so on. To call a `square()` method that accepts a parameter, you might write a statement like `square(17)` or `square(86)` and let the method use whatever argument you send.

Watch the video *Methods With a Parameter.*

When you write the declaration for a method that can receive a parameter, you must include the following items within the method declaration parentheses:

• The type of the parameter

• A local name for the parameter

For example, suppose you decide to improve the moon weight program in Figure 9-1 by making the final output more user-friendly and adding the explanatory text in the chosen language. It makes sense that if the user can request a prompt in a specific language, the user would want to see the output explanation in the same language. However, in Figure 9-1, the `langCode` variable is local to the `displayInstructions()` method and therefore cannot be used in the main program. You could rewrite the program by taking several approaches:

• You could rewrite the program without including any methods. That way, you could prompt the user for a language preference, and display the prompt and the result in the appropriate language.

In Chapter 2, you learned that this book uses a rectangle with a horizontal stripe across the top to represent a method call statement in a flowchart. Some programmers prefer to use a rectangle with two vertical stripes at the sides; a popular flowcharting program called Visual Logic uses the same convention. As a way to remember that this symbol represents an external method call, picture the rectangle with the vertical stripes as a window with drapery on each side, then imagine that your program has to "look outside" to find the external method.

```
Command Prompt                                    _ □ ⌘
1 - English or 2 - Espanol >> 1
Please enter your weight in pounds >> 150
Your weight on the moon would be 24.9
```

Figure 9-2 Output of moon weight calculator program in Figure 9-1

In the program in Figure 9-1, the main program and the called method each contain only what is needed at the local level. However, sometimes two or more parts of a program require access to the same data. When methods must share data, you can pass the data into and return the data out of methods. In this chapter, you will learn that when you call a method from a program or other method, you must know three things:

- The name of the called method

- What type of information to send to the method, if any

- What type of return data to expect from the method, if any

TWO TRUTHS & A LIE

Using Methods with No Parameters

1. Any program can contain an unlimited number of methods, but each method can be called once.

2. A method includes a header and a body.

3. Variables and constants are in scope within, or local to, only the method in which they are declared.

The false statement is #1. Each method can be called an unlimited number of times.

This approach would work, but you would not be taking advantage of the benefits provided by modularization. Those benefits include making the main program more streamlined and abstract, and making the displayInstructions() method a self-contained unit that can easily be transported to other programs—for example, applications that might determine a user's weight on Saturn or Mars.

- You could retain the displayInstructions() method, but make at least the langCode variable global by declaring it outside of any methods. If you took this approach, you would lose some of the portability of the displayInstructions() method because everything the method used would not be contained within the method.

- You could retain the displayInstructions() method as is with its own local declarations, but add a section to the main program that also asks the user for a preferred language for displaying the result. The disadvantage to this approach is that during one execution of the program, the user must answer a preferred language question twice.

- You could store the variable that holds the language code in the main program so that it could be used to determine the result language. You could also retain the displayInstructions() method, but pass the language code to it so the prompt would appear in the appropriate language. This is the best choice, and is illustrated in Figures 9-3 and 9-4.

376

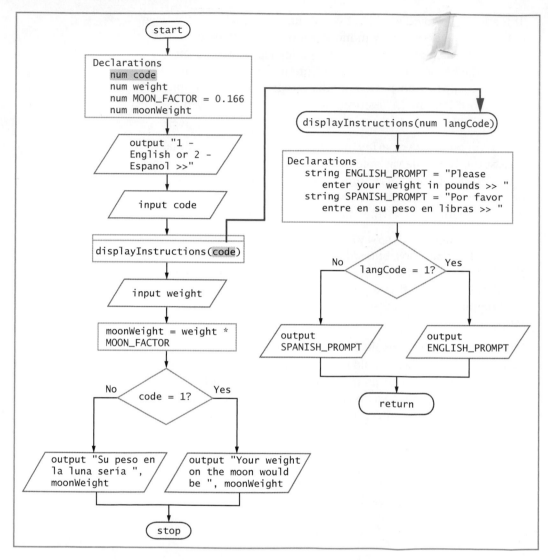

Figure 9-3   Moon weight program that passes an argument to a method

```
start
   Declarations
      num code
      num weight
      num MOON_FACTOR = 0.166
      num moonWeight
   output "1 - English or 2 - Espanol >>"
   input code
   displayInstructions(code)
   input weight
   moonWeight = weight * MOON_FACTOR
   if code = 1 then
      output "Your weight on the moon would be ", moonWeight
   else
      output "Su peso en la luna sería ", moonWeight
   endif
stop

displayInstructions(num langCode)
   Declarations
      string ENGLISH_PROMPT = "Please enter your weight in pounds >> "
      string SPANISH_PROMPT = "Por favor entre en su peso en libras >> "
   if langCode = 1 then
      output ENGLISH_PROMPT
   else
      output SPANISH_PROMPT
   endif
return
```

Figure 9-3 Moon weight program that passes an argument to a method (continued)

Figure 9-4 Typical execution of moon weight program in Figure 9-3

In the main program in Figure 9-3, a numeric variable named code is declared and the user is prompted for a value. The value then is passed to the displayInstructions() method. The value of the language code is stored in two places in memory:

- The main method stores the code in the variable code and passes it to displayInstructions() as an argument.

- The displayInstructions() method accepts the parameter as langCode. Within the method, langCode takes on the value that code had in the main program.

You can think of the parentheses in a method declaration as a funnel into the method—parameters listed there hold values that are "dropped in" to the method.

A variable passed into a method is **passed by value**; that is, a copy of its value is sent to the method and stored in a new memory location accessible to the method. The displayInstructions() method could be called using any numeric value as an argument, whether it is a variable, a named constant, or a literal constant. If the value used as an argument in the call to a method is a variable, it might possess the same identifier as the parameter declared in the method header, or a different one. Within a method, the passed variable is simply a temporary placeholder; it makes no difference what name the variable "goes by" in the calling program.

Each time a method executes, any parameter variables listed in the method header are redeclared—that is, a new memory location is reserved and named. When the method ends at the return statement, the locally declared parameter variable ceases to exist. For example, Figure 9-5 shows a program that declares a variable, assigns a value to it, displays it, and sends it to a method. Within the method, the parameter is displayed, altered, and displayed again. When control returns to the main program, the original variable is displayed one last time. As the execution in Figure 9-6 shows, even though the variable in the method was altered, the original variable in the main program retains its starting value because it never was altered; it occupies a different memory address from the variable in the method.

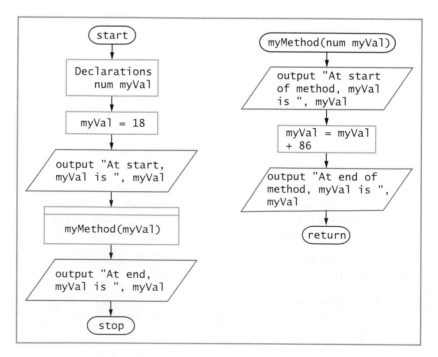

Figure 9-5   A program that calls a method in which the argument and parameter have the same identifier

```
Command Prompt
At start, myVal is 18
At start of method, myVal is 18
At end of method, myVal is 104
At end, myVal is 18
```

Figure 9-6   Execution of the program in Figure 9-5

TWO TRUTHS & A LIE

Creating Methods that Require a Single Parameter

1. A value sent to a method from a calling program is a parameter.

2. When you write the declaration for a method that can receive a parameter, you must include the type and local name in the method declaration parentheses.

3. When a variable is used as an argument in a method call, it can have the same identifier as the parameter in the method header.

The false statement is #1. A calling method sends an argument; when the method receives the value, it is a parameter.

Creating Methods that Require Multiple Parameters

A method can require more than one parameter. You create and use a method with multiple parameters by doing the following:

- You list the arguments within the method call, separated by commas.

- You list a data type and local identifier for each parameter within the method header's parentheses, separating each declaration with a comma.

For example, suppose you want to create a `computeTax()` method that calculates a tax on any value passed into it. You can create a method to which you pass two values—the amount to be taxed as well as a percentage figure by which to tax it. Figure 9-7 shows a method that accepts two such parameters.

The arguments sent to a method in a method call are its **actual parameters**. The variables in the method declaration that accept the values from the actual parameters are **formal parameters**.

380

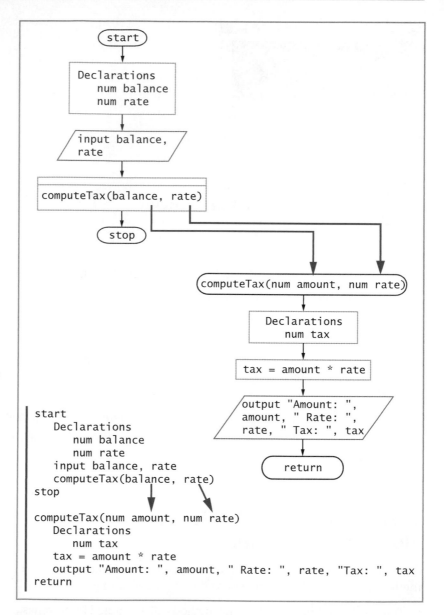

```
start
    Declarations
        num balance
        num rate
    input balance, rate
    computeTax(balance, rate)
stop

computeTax(num amount, num rate)
    Declarations
        num tax
    tax = amount * rate
    output "Amount: ", amount, " Rate: ", rate, "Tax: ", tax
return
```

Figure 9-7　A program that calls a `computeTax()` method that requires two parameters

 A declaration for a method that receives two or more arguments must list the type for each parameter separately, even if the parameters have the same type.

 In Figure 9-7, notice that one of the arguments to the method has the same name as the corresponding method parameter, and the other has a different name from its corresponding parameter. Each could have the same identifier as its counterpart, or all could be different. Each identifier is local to its own method.

In Figure 9-7, two parameters (`num amount` and `num rate`) appear within the parentheses in the method header. A comma separates each parameter, and each requires its own declared type (in this case, both are numeric) as well as its own identifier. When multiple values are passed to a method, they are accepted by the parameters in the order in which they are passed. Arguments must be passed in

Watch the video *Methods With Multiple Parameters*.

the correct order. A call of `computeTax(rate, balance)` instead of `computeTax(balance, rate)` would result in incorrect values being displayed in the output statement. You can write a method so that it takes any number of parameters in any order. However, when you call a method, the arguments you send to the method must match in order—both in number and in type—the parameters listed in the method declaration.

When multiple parameters appear in a method header, they comprise a **parameter list**. If method arguments are the same type—for example, two numeric arguments—passing them to a method in the wrong order results in a logical error; the program will compile and execute, but produce incorrect results. If a method expects arguments of diverse types—for example, a number and a string—then passing arguments in the wrong order is a syntax error, and the program will not compile.

A method's name and parameter list constitute the method's **signature**.

TWO TRUTHS & A LIE

Creating Methods that Require Multiple Parameters

1. You indicate that a method requires multiple parameters by listing their data types and local identifiers within the method header's parentheses and separating them by commas.

2. You pass multiple arguments to a method by listing the arguments within the method call and separating them with commas.

3. When you call a method, you must include at least one more argument than the number of parameters listed in the method declaration.

The false statement is #3. When you call a method, the arguments you send must match in order—both in number and in type—the arguments listed in the method declaration.

Creating Methods that Return a Value

A variable declared within a method ceases to exist when the method ends—it goes out of scope. When you want to retain a value that exists when a method ends, you can return the value from the method back to the calling method. When a method returns a value, the method must have a return type that matches the data type of the value that is returned. The **return type** for a method indicates the data type of the value that the method will send back to the location where

Along with an identifier and parameter list, a return type is part of a method's declaration. Some programmers claim a method's return type is part of its signature, but this is not the case. Only the method name and parameter list constitute the signature.

Up to this point, this book has not included return types for methods because all the methods have been void methods. From this point forward, a return type is included with every method.

the method call was made. It can be any type, which includes numeric and string, as well as other more specific types in the programming language you are using. Of course, a method can also return nothing, in which case the return type is void, and the method is a **void method**. (The term *void* means "nothing" or "empty".) A method's return type is known more succinctly as a **method's type**. A method's type is listed in front of the method name when the method is defined.

For example, a method that returns the number of hours an employee has worked might have the following header:

```
num getHoursWorked()
```

This method returns a numeric value, so its type is num.

When a method returns a value, you usually want to use the returned value in the calling method, although this is not required. For example, Figure 9-8 shows how a program might use the value returned by the getHoursWorked() method. A variable named hours is declared in the main program. The getHoursWorked() method call is part of an assignment statement. When the method is called, the logic transfers to the getHoursWorked() method, which contains a variable named workHours. A value is obtained for this variable, and is returned to the main program where it is assigned to hours. After the logic returns to the main program from the getHoursWorked() method, the method's local variable workHours no longer exists. However, its value has been stored in the main program where, as hours, it can be displayed and used in a calculation.

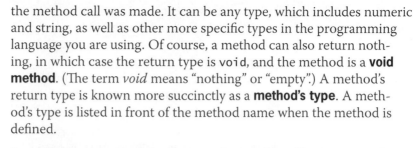

As an example of when you might call a method but not use its returned value, consider a method that gets a character from the keyboard and returns its value to the calling program. If you wanted to tell the user to "Press any key," you could call the method to accept the character from the keyboard, but you would not care which key was pressed or which key value was returned.

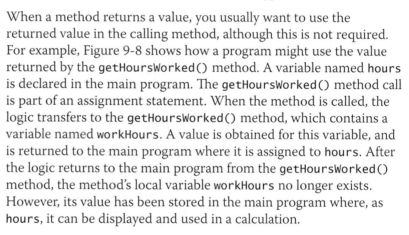

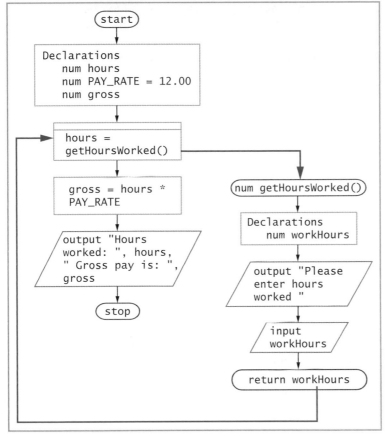

Figure 9-8 A payroll program that calls a method that returns a value

In Figure 9-8, notice the return type num that precedes the method name in the getHoursWorked() method header. A method's declared return type must match the type of the value used in the return statement; if it does not, the program will not compile. A numeric value is correctly included in the return statement that is the last statement within the getHoursWorked() method. When you place a value in a return statement, the value is sent from the called method back to the calling method.

You are not required to assign a method's return value to a variable in order to use the value. Instead, you can use a method's returned value directly, without storing it. You use a method's value in the same way you would use any variable of the same type. For example, you can output a return value in a statement such as the following:

```
output "Hours worked is ", getHoursWorked()
```

 A method's **return** statement can return one value at most. The value can be a simple data type or it can be a more complex type—for example, a structure or an object. You will learn to create objects in Chapter 10.

 The value returned from a method is not required to be a variable. Instead, you might return a constant, as in **return 0**.

Because getHoursWorked() returns a numeric value, you can use the method call getHoursWorked() in the same way that you would use any simple numeric value. Figure 9-9 shows an example of a program that uses a method's return value directly without storing it. The value of the shaded workHours variable returned from the method is used directly in the calculation of gross in the main program.

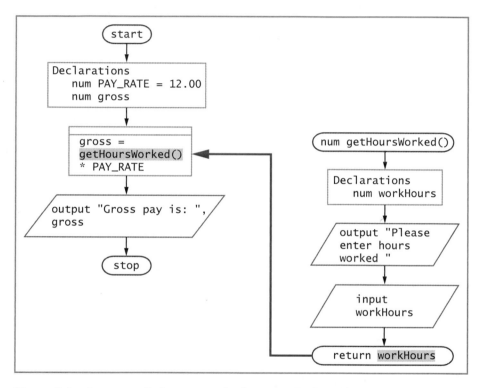

Figure 9-9   A program that uses a method's returned value without storing it

When a program needs to use a method's returned value in more than one place, it makes sense to store the returned value in a variable instead of calling the method multiple times. A program statement that calls a method requires more computer time and resources than a statement that does not call any outside methods. Programmers use the term **overhead** to describe any extra time and resources required by an operation.

In most programming languages, you technically are allowed to include multiple return statements in a method, although this practice is not recommended. For example, consider the findLargest() method in Figure 9-10. The method accepts three parameters and returns the largest of the values. Although this method works correctly (and you might see this technique used in programs written by others), you should not place more than one `return` statement in a method. In Chapter 3, you learned that structured logic requires each structure to contain one entry point and one exit point. The `return` statements in Figure 9-10 violate this convention by leaving decision structures before they are complete. Figure 9-11 shows the superior and recommended way to handle the problem. In Figure 9-11, the largest value is stored in a variable. Then, when the nested decision structure is complete, the stored value is returned.

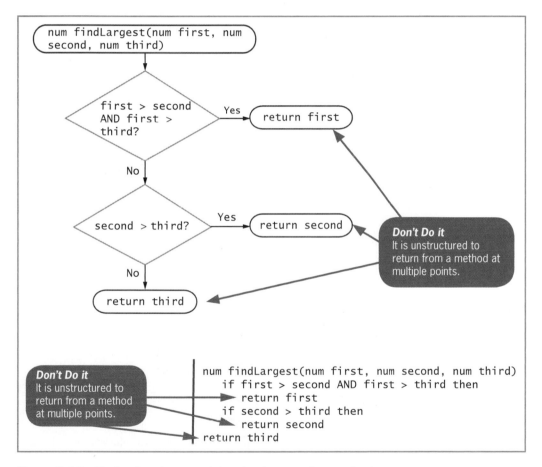

Figure 9-10   Unstructured approach to returning one of several values

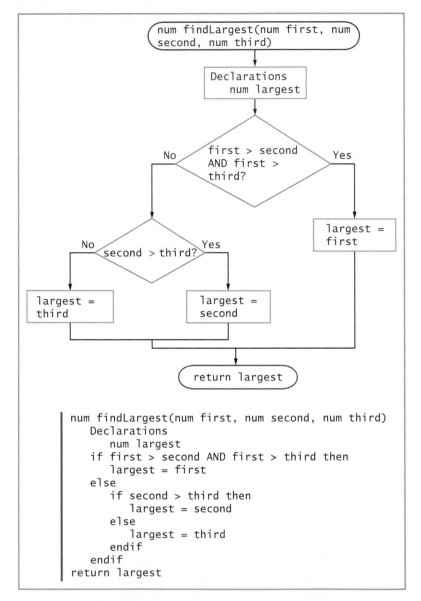

```
num findLargest(num first, num second, num third)
    Declarations
        num largest
    if first > second AND first > third then
        largest = first
    else
        if second > third then
            largest = second
        else
            largest = third
        endif
    endif
return largest
```

Figure 9-11 Recommended, structured approach to returning one of several values

When you want to use a method, you should know four things:

- What the method does in general, but not necessarily how it carries out tasks internally

- The method's name

- The method's required parameters, if any

Using an IPO Chart

When designing methods to use within larger programs, some programmers find it helpful to use an **IPO chart**, a tool that identifies and categorizes each item needed within the method as pertaining to input, processing, or output. For example, consider a method that finds the smallest of three numeric values. When you think about designing this method, you can start by placing each of its components in one of the three processing categories, as shown in Figure 9-12.

Input	Processing	Output
First value Second value Third value	If the first value is smaller than each of the other two, save it as the smallest value; otherwise, if the second value is smaller than the third, save it as the smallest value; otherwise, save the third value as the smallest value	Smallest value

Figure 9-12   IPO chart for the method that finds the smallest of three numeric values

The IPO chart in Figure 9-12 provides an overview of the processing steps involved in the method. Like a flowchart or pseudocode, an IPO chart is just another tool to help you plan the logic of your programs. Many programmers create an IPO chart only for specific methods in their programs and as an alternative to flowcharting or writing pseudocode. IPO charts provide an overview of input to the method, the processing steps that must occur, and the result.

This book emphasizes creating flow-charts and pseudocode. You can find many more examples of IPO charts on the Web.

TWO TRUTHS & A LIE

Creating Methods that Return a Value

1. The return type for a method can be any type, which includes numeric, character, and string, as well as other more specific types that exist in the programming language you are using.

2. A method's return type must be the same type as one of the method's parameters.

3. You are not required to use a method's returned value.

The false statement is #2. The return type of a method can be any type. The return type must match the type of value in the method's return statement. A method's return type is not required to match any of the method's parameters.

Passing an Array to a Method

In Chapter 6, you learned that you can declare an array to create a list of elements, and that you can use any individual array element in the same manner you would use any single variable of the same type. For example, suppose you declare a numeric array as follows:

```
num someNums[12]
```

You can subsequently output someNums[0] or perform arithmetic with someNums[11], just as you would for any simple variable that is not part of an array. Similarly, you can pass a single array element to a method in exactly the same manner you would pass a variable or constant.

Consider the program shown in Figure 9-13. This program creates an array of four numeric values and then outputs them. Next, the program calls a method named tripleTheValue() four times, passing each of the array elements in turn. The method outputs the passed value, multiplies it by 3, and outputs it again. Finally, back in the calling program, the four numbers are output again. Figure 9-14 shows an execution of this program in a command-line environment.

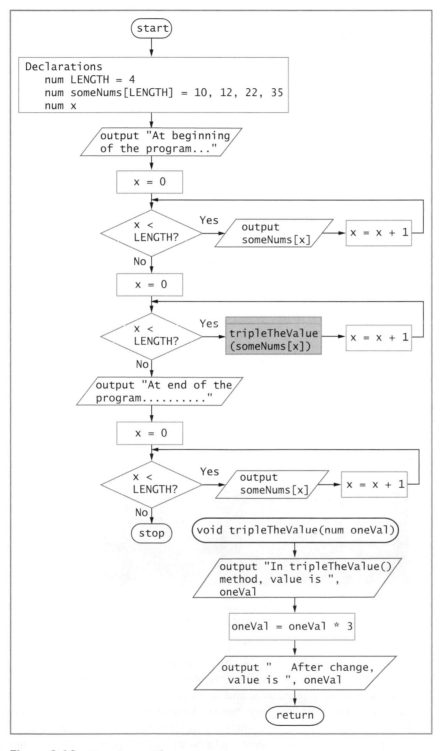

Figure 9-13 PassArrayElement program

```
start
    Declarations
        num LENGTH = 4
        num someNums[LENGTH] = 10, 12, 22, 35
        num x
    output "At beginning of the program..."
    x = 0
    while x < LENGTH
        output someNums[x]
        x = x + 1
    endwhile
    x = 0
    while x < LENGTH
        tripleTheValue(someNums[x])
        x = x + 1
    endwhile
    output "At end of the program.........."
    x = 0
    while x < LENGTH
        output someNums[x]
        x = x + 1
    endwhile
stop

void tripleTheValue(numeric oneVal)
    output "In tripleTheValue() method, value is ", oneVal
    oneVal = oneVal * 3
    output "      After change, value is ", oneVal
return
```

Figure 9-13   PassArrayElement program (continued)

Figure 9-14   Output of PassArrayElement program

As you can see in Figure 9-14, the program displays the four original values, then passes each to the tripleTheValue() method, where it is displayed, multiplied by 3, and displayed again. After the method executes four times, the logic returns to the main program where the four values are displayed again, showing that they are unchanged by the new assignments within tripleTheValue(). The oneVal variable is local to the tripleTheValue() method; therefore, any changes to it are not permanent and are not reflected in the array declared in the main program. Each `oneVal` variable in the `tripleTheValue()` method holds only a copy of the array element passed into the method, and the `oneVal` variable that holds each newly assigned, larger value exists only while the `tripleTheValue()` method is executing. In all respects, a single array element acts just like any single variable of the same type would.

Instead of passing a single array element to a method, you can pass an entire array as an argument. You can indicate that a method parameter must be an array by placing square brackets after the data type in the method's parameter list. When you pass an array to a method, changes you make to array elements within the method are permanent; that is, they are reflected in the original array that was sent to the method. Arrays, unlike simple built-in types, are **passed by reference**; the method receives the actual memory address of the array and has access to the actual values in the array elements.

The program shown in Figure 9-15 creates an array of four numeric values. After the numbers are output, the entire array is passed to a method named `quadrupleTheValues()`. Within the method header, the parameter is declared as an array by using square brackets after the parameter type. Within the method, the numbers are output, which shows that they retain their values from the main program upon entering the method. Then the array values are multiplied by 4. Even though `quadrupleTheValues()` returns nothing to the calling program, when the program displays the array for the last time within the mainline logic, all of the values have been changed to their new quadrupled values. Figure 9-16 shows an execution of the program. Because arrays are passed by reference, the `quadrupleTheValues()` method "knows" the address of the array declared in the calling program and makes its changes directly to the original array that was declared in the calling program.

The name of an array represents a memory address, and the subscript used with an array name represents an offset from that address.

Simple nonarray variables usually are passed to methods by value. Many programming languages provide the means to pass variables by reference as well as by value. The syntax to accomplish this differs among the languages that allow it; you will learn this technique when you study a specific language.

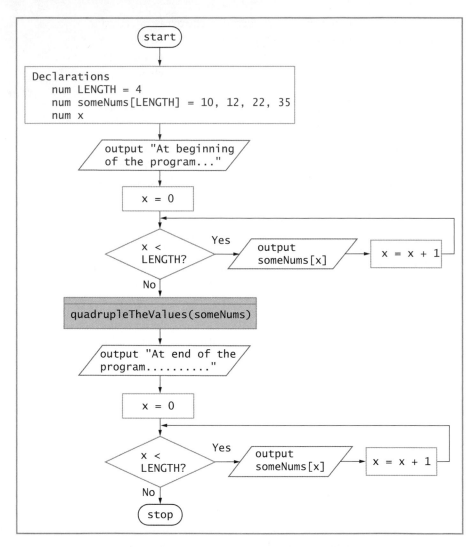

Figure 9-15   PassEntireArray program

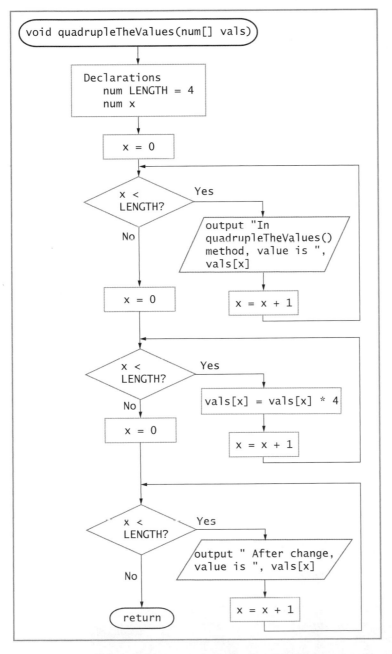

Figure 9-15 PassEntireArray program (continued)

```
start
   Declarations
      num LENGTH = 4
      num someNums[LENGTH] = 10, 12, 22, 35
      num x
   output "At beginning of the program..."
   x = 0
   while x < LENGTH
      output someNums[x]
      x = x + 1
   endwhile
   quadrupleTheValues(someNums)
   output "At end of the program.........."
   x = 0
   while x < LENGTH
      output someNums[x]
      x = x + 1
   endwhile
stop

void quadrupleTheValues(num[] vals)
   Declarations
      num LENGTH = 4
      num x
   x = 0
   while x < LENGTH
      output "In quadrupleTheValues() method, value is ", vals[x]
      x = x + 1
   endwhile
   x = 0
   while x < LENGTH
      vals[x] = vals[x] * 4
      x = x + 1
   endwhile
   x = 0
   while x < LENGTH
      output "        After change, value is ", vals[x]
      x = x + 1
   endwhile
return
```

Figure 9-15   PassEntireArray program (continued)

Figure 9-16   Output of the PassEntireArray program

When an array is a method parameter, the square brackets in the method header remain empty and do not hold a size. The array name that is passed is a memory address that indicates the start of the array. Depending on the language in which you are working, you can control the values you use for a subscript to the array in different ways. In some languages, you might also want to pass a constant that indicates the array size to the method. In other languages, you can access the automatically created length field for the array. Either way, the array size itself is never implied when you use the array name. The array name only indicates the starting point from which subscripts will be used.

TWO TRUTHS & A LIE

Passing an Array to a Method

1. You can pass an entire array as a method's argument.

2. You can indicate that a method parameter must be an array by placing square brackets after the data type in the method's parameter list.

3. Arrays, unlike simple built-in types, are passed by value; the method receives a copy of the original array.

The false statement is #3. Arrays, unlike simple built-in types, are passed by reference; the method receives the actual memory address of the array and has access to the actual values in the array elements.

Overloading Methods

In programming, **overloading** involves supplying diverse meanings for a single identifier. When you use the English language, you frequently overload words. When you say "break a window," "break bread," "break the bank," and "take a break," you describe four very different actions that use different methods and produce different results. However, anyone who speaks English comprehends your meaning because "break" is understood in the context of the discussion.

When you **overload a method**, you write multiple methods with a shared name but different parameter lists. When you call an overloaded method, the language translator understands which version of the method to use based on the arguments used. For example, suppose you create a method to print a message and the amount due on a customer bill, as shown in Figure 9-17. The method receives a numeric parameter that represents the customer's balance and prints two lines of output. Assume you also need a method that is similar to printBill(), except the new method applies a

 In most programming languages, some operators are overloaded. For example, a + between two values indicates addition, but a single + to the left of a value means the value is positive. The + sign has different meanings based on the arguments used with it.

Overloading a method is an example of **polymorphism**—the ability of a method to act appropriately depending on the context. Literally, *polymorphism* means "many forms."

discount to the customer bill. One solution to this problem would be to write a new method with a different name—for example, `printBillWithDiscount()`. A downside to this approach is that a programmer who uses your methods must remember the different names you gave to each slightly different version. It is more natural for your methods' clients to use a single well-designed method name for the task of printing bills, but to be able to provide different arguments as appropriate. In this case, you can overload the `printBill()` method so that, in addition to the version that takes a single numeric argument, you can create a version that takes two numeric arguments—one that represents the balance and one that represents the discount rate. Figure 9-17 shows the two versions of the `printBill()` method.

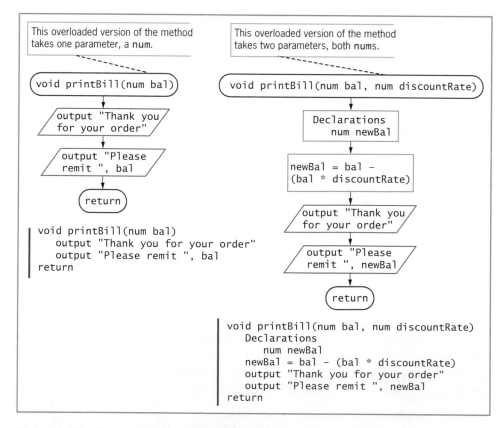

Figure 9-17   Two overloaded versions of the `printBill()` method

If both versions of `printBill()` are included in a program and you call the method using a single numeric argument, as in `printBill(custBalance)`, the first version of the method in Figure 9-17 executes. If you use two numeric arguments in the call, as in `printBill(custBalance, rate)`, the second version of the method executes.

If it suited your needs, you could provide more versions of the printBill() method, as shown in Figure 9-18. The first version accepts a numeric parameter that holds the customer's balance, and a string parameter that holds an additional message that can be customized for the bill recipient and displayed on the bill. For example, if a program makes a method call such as the following, this version of printBill() will execute:

```
printBill(custBal, "Due in 10 days")
```

The second version of the method in Figure 9-18 accepts three parameters, providing a balance, discount rate, and customized message. For example, the following method call would use this version of the method:

```
printBill(balanceDue, discountRate, specialMessage)
```

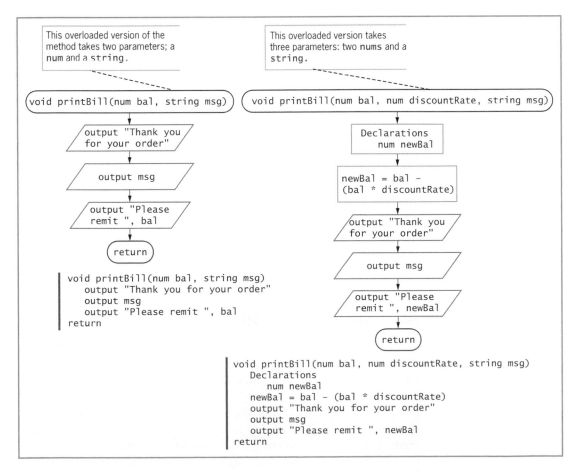

Figure 9-18 Two additional overloaded versions of the printBill() method

398

 In many programming languages, the `output` statement is actually an overloaded method that you call. It is convenient that you use a single name, such as `output`, whether you want to output a number, a `string`, or any combination of the two.

Overloading methods is never required in a program. Instead, you could create multiple methods with unique identifiers such as `printBill()` and `printBillWithDiscountAndMessage()`. Overloading methods does not reduce your work when creating a program; you need to write each method individually. The advantage is provided to your method's clients; those who use your methods need to remember just one appropriate name for all related tasks.

 Even if you write two or more overloaded versions of a method, many program clients will use just one version. For example, suppose you develop a bill-creating program that contains all four versions of the `printBill()` method just discussed, and then sell it to different companies. An organization that adopts your program and its methods might only want to use one or two versions of the method. You probably own many devices for which only some of the features are meaningful to you; for example, some people who own microwave ovens only use the Popcorn button or never use Defrost.

TWO TRUTHS & A LIE

Overloading Methods

1. In programming, overloading involves supplying diverse meanings for a single identifier.

2. When you overload a method, you write multiple methods with different names but identical parameter lists.

3. A method can be overloaded as many times as you want.

The false statement is #2. When you overload a method, you write methods with a shared name but different parameter lists.

Avoiding Ambiguous Methods

When you overload a method, you run the risk of creating **ambiguous methods**—a situation in which the compiler cannot determine which method to use. Every time you call a method, the compiler decides whether a suitable method exists; if so, the method executes, and if not, you receive an error message. For example, suppose you write two versions of a `printBill()` method, as shown in the program in Figure 9-19. One version of the method is intended to accept a customer balance and a discount rate, and the other is intended to accept a customer balance and a discount amount expressed in dollars.

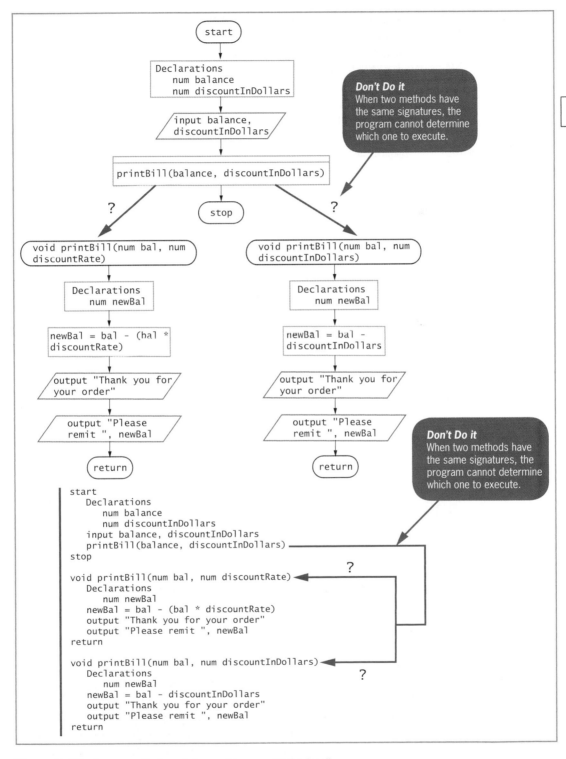

Figure 9-19 Program that contains ambiguous method call

An overloaded method is not ambiguous on its own—it becomes ambiguous only if you make a method call that matches multiple method signatures. A program with potentially ambiguous methods will run without problems if you don't make any method calls that match more than one method.

Watch the video *Overloading Methods.*

Each of the two versions of printBill() in Figure 9-19 is a valid method on its own. However, when the two versions exist in the same program, a problem arises. When the main program calls printBill() using two numeric arguments, the compiler cannot determine which version to call. You might think that the version of the method with a parameter named discountInDollars would execute, because the method call uses the identifier discountInDollars. However, the compiler determines which version of a method to call based on argument data types only, not their identifiers. Because both versions of the printBill() method could accept two numeric parameters, the compiler cannot determine which version to execute, so an error occurs and program execution stops.

Methods can be overloaded correctly by providing different parameter lists for methods with the same name. Methods with identical names that have identical parameter lists but different return types are not overloaded—they are ambiguous. For example, the following two method headers create ambiguity.

```
string aMethod(num x)
num aMethod(num y)
```

The compiler determines which of several versions of a method to call based on parameter lists, not return types. When the method call aMethod(17) is made, the compiler will not know which of the two methods to execute because both possibilities take a numeric argument.

All the popular object-oriented programming languages support multiple numeric data types. For example, Java, C#, C++, and Visual Basic all support integer (whole number) data types that are different from floating-point (decimal place) data types. Many languages have even more specialized numeric types, such as signed and unsigned. Methods that accept different specific types are correctly overloaded.

Using Predefined Methods

All modern programming languages contain many methods that have already been written for programmers. Predefined methods might originate from several sources:

• Some prewritten methods are built into a language. For example, methods that perform input and output are usually predefined.

• When you work on a program in a team, each programmer might be assigned specific methods to create, and your methods will interact with methods written by others.

• If you work for a company, many standard methods may already have been written and you will be required to use them. For example, the company might have a standard method that displays its logo.

Predefined methods save you time and effort. For example, in most languages, printing a message on the screen involves using a built-in method. When you want to display "Hello" on the command prompt screen in C#, you write the following:

```
Console.WriteLine("Hello");
```

In Java, you write:

```
System.out.println("Hello");
```

In these statements, you can recognize `WriteLine()` and `println()` as method names because they are followed by parentheses; the

In C#, the convention is to begin method names with an uppercase letter. In Java, method names conventionally begin with a lowercase letter. The WriteLine() and println() methods follow their respective language's convention.

parentheses hold an argument that represents the message to display. If these methods were not written for you, you would have to know the low-level details of how to manipulate pixels on a display screen to get the characters to print. Instead, by using the prewritten methods, you can concentrate on the higher-level task of displaying a useful and appropriate message.

The WriteLine() and println() methods are both overloaded in their respective languages. For example, if you pass a string to either method, the version of the method that accepts a string parameter executes, but if you pass a number, another version that accepts a numeric parameter executes.

Most programming languages also contain a variety of mathematical methods, such as those that compute a square root or the absolute value of a number. Other methods retrieve the current date and time from the operating system or select a random number to use in a game application. These methods were written as a convenience for you—computing a square root and generating random numbers are complicated tasks, so it is convenient to have methods already written, tested, and available to you when you need them. The names of the methods that perform these functions differ among programming languages, so you need to research the language's documentation to use them. For example, many of a language's methods are described in introductory programming language textbooks, and you can also find language documentation online.

When you want to use a predefined method, you should know the same four details that you should understand about any method you use:

- What the method does in general—for example, compute a square root.

- The method's name—for example, it might be sqrt().

- The method's required parameters—for example, a square root method might require a single numeric parameter. There might be multiple overloaded versions of the method from which you can choose.

- The method's return type—for example, a square root method most likely returns a numeric value that is the square root of the argument passed to the method.

You do not need to know how the method is implemented—that is, how the instruction statements are written within it. Like all methods, you can use built-in methods without worrying about their low-level implementation details.

TWO TRUTHS & A LIE

Using Predefined Methods

1. The name of a method that performs a specific function (such as generating a random number) is likely to be the same in various programming languages.

2. When you want to use a predefined method, you should know what the method does in general, its name, required parameters, and return type.

3. When you want to use a predefined method, you do not need to know how the method works internally to be able to use the method effectively.

The false statement is #1. Methods that perform standard functions are likely to have different names in various languages.

Method Design Issues: Implementation Hiding, Cohesion, and Coupling

To design high-quality methods, you should consider several program qualities:

- You should employ implementation hiding; that is, a method's client should not need to understand a method's internal mechanisms.

- You should strive to increase cohesion.

- You should strive to reduce coupling.

Understanding Implementation Hiding

An important principle of modularization is the notion of **implementation hiding**, the encapsulation of method details. That is, when a program makes a request to a method, it doesn't know the details of how the method is executed. For example, when you make a real-life restaurant reservation, you do not need to know how the reservation is actually recorded at the restaurant—perhaps it is written in a book, marked on a large chalkboard, or entered into a computerized database. The implementation details don't concern you as a patron, and if the restaurant changes its methods from one year to the next, the change does not affect your use of the reservation method—you still call and provide your name, a date, and a time.

With well-written methods, using implementation hiding means that a method that calls another must know only the following:

- The name of the called method

- What type of information to send to the method

- What type of return data to expect from the method

In other words, the calling method needs to understand only the **interface to the method** that is called. The interface is the only part of a method with which the method's **client** (or method's caller) inter-acts. The program does *not* need to know how the method works internally. Additionally, if you substitute a new, improved method implementation, as long as the interface to the method does not change, you won't need to make changes in any methods that call the altered method.

Programmers refer to hidden implementation details as existing in a **black box**—you can examine what goes in and what comes out, but not the details of how it works inside.

Another example of style to consider when writing a method is to hide the implementation details that have no meaning for the user. For example, unless you are writing a method for demonstration or educational purposes, or to help debug the method, you usually do not want to expose variable and constant identifiers to the outside world. Suppose you have declared a variable named additionResult. The output statement "The result of the addition is 102" is more meaningful to users than "The value of additionResult is 102".

Increasing Cohesion

When you begin to design computer programs, it is difficult to decide how much to put into a method. For example, a process that requires 40 instructions can be contained in a single method, two 20-instruction methods, 20 two-instruction methods, or many other combinations. In most programming languages, any of these combinations is allowed; you can write a program that executes and produces correct results no matter how you divide the individual steps into methods. However, placing too many or too few instructions in a single method makes a program harder to follow and reduces flexibility.

To help determine the appropriate division of tasks among methods, you want to analyze each method's **cohesion**, which refers to how the internal statements of a method serve to accomplish the method's purpose. In highly cohesive methods, all the operations are related, or "go together." Such methods are **functionally cohesive**—all their operations contribute to the performance of a single task. Functionally cohesive methods usually are more reliable than those that have low cohesion; they are considered stronger, and they make programs easier to write, read, and maintain.

For example, consider a method that calculates gross pay. The method receives parameters that define a worker's pay rate and number of hours worked. The method computes gross pay and displays it. The cohesion of this method is high because each of its instructions contributes to one task—computing gross pay. If you can write a sentence describing what a method does using only two words—for example, "Compute gross," "Cube value," or "Display record"—the method is probably functionally cohesive.

You might work in a programming environment that has a rule such as "No method will be longer than can be printed on one page" or "No method will have more than 30 lines of code." The rule maker is trying to achieve more cohesion, but such rules are arbitrary. A two-line method could have low cohesion and—although less likely—a 40-line method might have high cohesion. Because good, functionally cohesive methods perform only one task, they tend to be short. However, the issue is not size. If it takes 20 statements to perform one task within a method, the method is still cohesive.

Most programmers do not consciously make decisions about cohesiveness for each method they write. Rather, they develop a "feel" for what types of tasks belong together, and for which subsets of tasks should be diverted to their own methods.

Reducing Coupling

Coupling is a measure of the strength of the connection between two program methods; it expresses the extent to which information is exchanged by methods. Coupling is either tight or loose, depending on how much one method depends on information from another. **Tight coupling**, which occurs when methods excessively depend on each other, makes programs more prone to errors. With tight coupling, you have many data paths to keep track of, many chances for bad data to pass from one method to another, and many chances for one method to alter information needed by another method. **Loose coupling** occurs when methods do not depend on others. In general, you want to reduce coupling as much as possible because connections between methods make them more difficult to write, maintain, and reuse.

Imagine four cooks wandering in and out of a kitchen while preparing a stew. If each is allowed to add seasonings at will without the knowledge of the other cooks, you could end up with a culinary disaster. Similarly, if four payroll program methods can alter your gross pay without the "knowledge" of the other methods, you could end up with a financial disaster. A program in which several methods have access to your gross pay figure has methods that are tightly

406

coupled. A superior program would control access to the payroll figure by limiting its passage to methods that need it.

You can evaluate whether coupling between methods is loose or tight by looking at how methods share data.

- Tight coupling occurs when methods have access to the same globally defined variables. When one method changes the value stored in a variable, other methods are affected. Because you should avoid tight coupling, all the examples in this book avoid using global variables. However, be aware that you might see them used in programs written by others.

- Loose coupling occurs when a copy of data that must be shared is passed from one method to another. That way, the sharing of data is always purposeful—variables must be explicitly passed to and from methods that use them. The loosest (best) methods pass single arguments rather than many variables or entire records, if possible.

Additionally, there is a time and a place for shortcuts. If you need a result from spreadsheet data in a hurry, you can type two values and take a sum rather than creating a formula with proper cell references. If a memo must go out in five minutes, you don't have to change fonts or add clip art with your word processor. Similarly, if you need a quick programming result, you might very well use cryptic variable names, tight coupling, and minimal cohesion. When you create a professional application, however, you should keep professional guidelines in mind.

TWO TRUTHS & A LIE

Method Design Issues: Implementation Hiding, Cohesion, and Coupling

1. A calling method must know the interface to any method it calls.

2. You should try to avoid loose coupling, which occurs when methods do not depend on others.

3. Functional cohesion occurs when all operations in a method contribute to the performance of only one task.

The false statement is #2. You should aim for loose coupling so that methods are independent.

Understanding Recursion

Recursion occurs when a method is defined in terms of itself. A method that calls itself is a **recursive method**. Some programming languages do not allow a method to call itself, but those that do can be used to create recursive methods that produce interesting effects.

Figure 9-20 shows a simple example of recursion. The program calls an infinity() method, which displays "Help! " and calls itself again (see the shaded statement). The second call to infinity() displays "Help!" and generates a third call. The result is a large number of repetitions of the infinity() method. The output is shown in Figure 9-21.

```
start
    infinity()
stop

infinity()
    output "Help! "
    infinity()
return
```

Figure 9-20   A program that calls a recursive method

Figure 9-21   Output of program in Figure 9-20

Every time you call a method, the address to which the program should return at the completion of the method is stored in a memory location called the **stack**. When a method ends, the address is retrieved from the stack and the program returns to the location from which the method call was made. For example, suppose a program calls methodA() and that methodA() calls methodB(). When the program calls methodA(), a return address is stored in the stack, and then methodA() begins execution. When methodA() calls methodB(),

Using recursion successfully requires a thorough understanding of looping. You learned about loops in Chapter 5.

An everyday example of recursion is printed on shampoo bottles: "Lather, rinse, repeat."

a return address in `methodA()` is stored in the stack and `methodB()` begins execution. When `methodB()` ends, the last entered address is retrieved from the stack and program control returns to complete `methodA()`. When `methodA()` ends, the remaining address is retrieved from the stack and program control returns to the main program method to complete it.

Like all computer memory, the stack has a finite size. When the program in Figure 9-20 calls the `infinity()` method, the stack receives so many return addresses that it eventually overflows. The recursive calls will end after an excessive number of repetitions and the program issues error messages.

Of course, there is no practical use for an infinitely recursive program. Just as you must be careful not to create endless loops, when you write useful recursive methods you must provide a way for the recursion to stop eventually.

Figure 9-22 shows an application that uses recursion productively. The program calls a recursive method that computes the sum of every integer from 1 up to and including the method's argument value. For example, the sum of every integer up to and including 3 is 1 + 2 + 3, or 6, and the sum of every integer up to and including 4 is 1 + 2 + 3 + 4, or 10.

```
start
   Declarations
      num LIMIT = 10
      num number
   number = 1
   while number <= LIMIT
      output "When number is ", number,
         " then cumulativeSum(number) is ",
         cumulativeSum(number)
      number = number + 1
   endwhile
return

num cumulativeSum(num number)
   Declarations
      num returnVal
   if number = 1 then
      returnVal = number
   else
      returnVal = number + cumulativeSum(number - 1)
   endif
return returnVal
```

Figure 9-22   Program that uses a recursive `cumulativeSum()` method

When thinking about cumulative summing relationships, remember that the sum of all the integers up to and including any number is that number plus the sum of the integers for the next lowest number. In other words, consider the following:

- The sum of the digits from 1, up to and including 1, is simply 1.

- The sum of the digits from 1 through 2 is the previous sum, plus 2.

- The sum of the digits from 1 through 3 is the previous sum, plus 3.

- The sum of the digits 1 through 4 is the previous sum, plus 4.

- And so on.

The recursive cumulativeSum() method in Figure 9-22 uses this knowledge. For each number, its cumulative sum consists of itself plus the cumulative sum of all the previous lesser numbers.

The program in Figure 9-22 calls the cumulativeSum() method 10 times in a loop to show the cumulative sum of every integer from 1 through 10. Figure 9-23 shows the output.

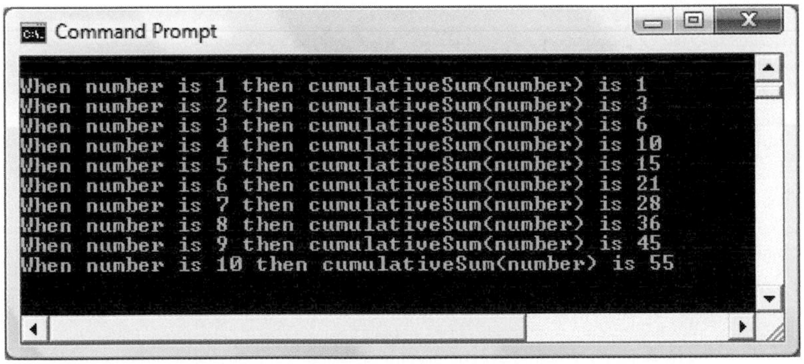

Figure 9-23 Output of program in Figure 9-22

If you examine Figures 9-22 and 9-23 together, you can see the following:

- When 1 is passed to the cumulativeSum() method, the if statement within the method determines that the argument is equal to 1, returnVal becomes 1, and 1 is returned for output.

- On the next pass through the loop, 2 is passed to the cumulativeSum() method. When the method receives 2 as an argument, the if statement within the method is false, and returnVal is set to 2 plus the value of cumulativeSum(1). This second call to cumulativeSum() using 1 as an argument returns a 1, so when the method ends, it returns 2 + 1, or 3.

- On the third pass through the loop within the calling program, 3 is passed to the `cumulativeSum()` method. When the method receives 3 as an argument, the `if` statement within the method is false and the method returns 3 plus the value of `cumulativeSum(2)`. The value of this call is 2 plus `cumulativeSum(1)`. The value of `cumulativeSum(1)` is 1. Ultimately, `cumulativeSum(3)` is 3 + 2 + 1.

 Watch the video *Recursion.*

Following the logic of a recursive method is difficult, and programs that use recursion are error-prone and hard to debug. For these reasons, some business organizations forbid their programmers from using recursive logic in company programs. Additionally, many of the problems solved by recursive methods can be solved in a more straightforward way. For example, examine the program in Figure 9-24. This program produces the same result as the previous recursive program, but in a more straightforward fashion.

```
start
    Declarations
        num number
        num total
        num LIMIT = 10
    total = 0;
    number = 1
    while number <= LIMIT
        total = total + number
        output "When number is ", number,
            " then the cumulative sum of 1 through",
            number, " is ", total
        number = number + 1
    endwhile
stop
```

Figure 9-24   Nonrecursive program that computes cumulative sums

A humorous illustration of recursion is found in this sentence: "In order to understand recursion, you must first understand recursion." A humorous dictionary entry is "Recursion: See Recursion." These examples contain an element of truth, but useful recursion algorithms always have a point at which the infinite loop is exited. In other words, the base case, or exit case, is always reached at some point.

TWO TRUTHS & A LIE

Understanding Recursion

1. A method that calls itself is a recursive method.

2. Every time you call a method, the address to which the program should return at the completion of the method is stored in a memory location called the stack.

3. Following the logic of a recursive method is usually much easier than following the logic of an ordinary program, so recursion makes debugging easier.

The false statement is #3. Following the logic of a recursive method is difficult, and programs that use recursion are error-prone and hard to debug.

Chapter Summary

- A method is a program module that contains a series of statements that carry out a task. Any program can contain an unlimited number of methods, and each method can be called an unlimited number of times. A method must include a header, a body, and a `return` statement that marks the end of the method. Variables and constants are in scope within, or local to, only the method within which they are declared.

- When you pass a data item into a method from a calling program, it is called an argument to the method. When the method receives the data item, it is called a parameter to the method. When you write the declaration for a method that can receive a parameter, you must include the data type and a local name for the parameter within the method declaration parentheses.

- You indicate that a method requires multiple arguments by listing their data types and local identifiers within the method header's parentheses. You can pass multiple arguments to a called method by listing the arguments within the method call and separating them with commas. When you call a method, the arguments you send to the method must match in order—both in number and in type—the parameters listed in the method declaration.

- When a method returns a value, the method must have a return type. A method's return type indicates the data type of the value that the method will send back to the location where the method call was made; it is also known as a method's type, and is indicated in front of the method name when the method is defined. When a method returns a value, you usually want to use the returned value in the calling method, although this is not required.

- You can pass a single array element to a method in exactly the same manner you would pass a variable or constant. Additionally, you can pass an entire array to a method. You can indicate that a method parameter must be an array by placing square brackets after the data type in the method's parameter list. When you pass an array to a method, it is passed by reference; that is, the method receives the actual memory address of the array and has access to the actual values in the array elements.

- When you overload a method, you write multiple methods with a shared name but different parameter lists. The compiler understands your meaning based on the arguments you use when you call the method.

- Overloading a method introduces the risk of creating ambiguous methods—a situation in which the compiler cannot determine which method to use. Every time you call a method, the compiler decides whether a suitable method exists; if so, the method executes, and if not, you receive an error message. Methods can be overloaded correctly by providing different parameter lists for methods with the same name.

- All modern programming languages contain many prewritten methods that are built into a language to save you time and effort.

- With well-written methods, the implementation is hidden. To use a method, you need only know the name of the called method, what type of information to send to the method, and what type of return data to expect from the method. When writing methods, you should strive to achieve high cohesion and loose coupling.

- Recursion occurs when a method is defined in terms of itself. Following the logic of a recursive method is difficult, and programs that use recursion are error-prone and hard to debug.

Key Terms

A **method** is a program module that contains a series of statements that carry out a task.

A **method header** precedes a method; the header includes the method identifier and possibly other necessary identifying information.

A **method body** contains all the statements in the method.

A method's **`return` statement** marks the end of the method and identifies the point at which control returns to the calling method.

In scope describes the status of active variables and constants declared within a method.

Local variables are declared within each method that uses them.

A **global data item** is known to all the methods in a program.

An **argument to a method** is a value passed to a method in the call to the method.

A **parameter to a method** is a data item passed into the method from the outside.

A variable passed into a method is **passed by value**; that is, a copy of its value is sent to the method and stored in a new memory location accessible to the method.

Actual parameters are the arguments in a method call.

Formal parameters are the variables in the method declaration that accept the values from the actual parameters.

A **parameter list** is all the data types and parameter names that appear in a method header.

A method's **signature** includes its name and argument list.

A method's **return type** indicates the data type of the value that the method will send back to the location where the method call was made.

A **void method** returns no value.

A **method's type** is the type of its return value.

Overhead refers to all the resources and time required by an operation.

An **IPO chart** identifies and categorizes each item needed within the method as pertaining to input, processing, or output.

When an item is **passed by reference** to a method, the method receives the actual memory address item. Arrays are passed by reference.

Overloading involves supplying diverse meanings for a single identifier.

Polymorphism is the ability of a method to act appropriately depending on the context.

When you **overload a method**, you create multiple versions with the same name but different parameter lists.

Ambiguous methods are those that the compiler cannot distinguish because they have the same name and parameter types.

Implementation hiding is a programming principle that describes the encapsulation of method details.

The **interface to a method** includes the method's return type, name, and arguments. It is the part that a client sees and uses.

A method's **client** is a program or other method that uses the method.

A **black box** is the analogy programmers use to refer to hidden method implementation details.

Cohesion is a measure of how the internal statements of a method serve to accomplish the method's purpose.

Functional cohesion occurs when all operations in a method contribute to the performance of only one task. Functional cohesion is the highest level of cohesion; you should strive for it in all methods you write.

Coupling is a measure of the strength of the connection between two program methods.

Tight coupling occurs when methods excessively depend on each other; it makes programs more prone to errors.

Loose coupling occurs when methods do not depend on others.

Recursion occurs when a method is defined in terms of itself.

A **recursive method** is a method that calls itself.

The **stack** is a memory location that holds addresses to which methods should return.

Review Questions

1. Which of the following is true?

    a. A program can call one method at most.

    b. A program can contain a method that calls another method.

    c. A method can contain one or more other methods.

    d. All of these are true.

2. Which of the following must every method have?

    a. a header

    b. a parameter list

    c. a return value

    d. all of these

3. Which of the following is most closely related to the concept of *local*?

    a. abstract

    b. object-oriented

    c. in scope

    d. program level

4. Although the terms *parameter* and *argument* are closely related, the difference is that *argument* refers to _____.

    a. a passed constant

    b. a value in a method call

    c. a formal parameter

    d. a variable that is local to a method

5. A method's interface is its _____.

    a. signature

    b. return type

    c. identifier

    d. parameter list

6. When you write the declaration for a method that can receive a parameter, which of the following must be included in the method declaration?

    a. the name of the argument that will be used to call the method

    b. a local name for the parameter

    c. the return value for the method

    d. two of these

7. When you use a variable name in a method call, it _____ as the variable in the method header.

    a. can have the same name

    b. cannot have the same name

    c. must have the same name

    d. cannot have the same data type

8. Assume you have written a method with the header `void myMethod(num a, string b)`. Which of the following is a correct method call?

    a. `myMethod(12)`

    b. `myMethod(12, "Hello")`

    c. `myMethod("Goodbye")`

    d. It is impossible to tell.

9. Assume you have written a method with the header `num yourMethod(string name, num code)`. The method's type is _____.

    a. `num`

    b. `string`

    c. `num` and `string`

    d. `void`

10. Assume you have written a method with the header
    `string myMethod(num score, string grade)`. Also assume
    you have declared a numeric variable named `test`. Which of
    the following is a correct method call?

    a. `myMethod()`

    b. `myMethod(test)`

    c. `myMethod(test, test)`

    d. `myMethod(test, "A")`

11. The value used in a method's `return` statement
    must _____.

    a. be numeric

    b. be a variable

    c. match the data type used before the method name in the
       header

    d. two of the above

12. When a method receives a copy of the value stored in an
    argument used in the method call, it means the variable
    was _____.

    a. unnamed

    b. passed by value

    c. passed by reference

    d. assigned its original value when it was declared

13. A void method _____.

    a. contains no statements

    b. requires no parameters

    c. returns nothing

    d. has no name

14. When an array is passed to a method, it is _____.

    a. passed by reference

    b. passed by value

    c. unnamed in the method

    d. unalterable in the method

15. When you overload a method, you write multiple methods with the same _____.

  a. name

  b. parameter list

  c. number of parameters

  d. return type

16. A program contains a method with the header
num calculateTaxes(num amount, string name). Which of the following methods can coexist in the same program with no possible ambiguity?

  a. num calculateTaxes(string name, num amount)

  b. string calculateTaxes(num money, string taxpayer)

  c. num calculateTaxes(num annualPay, string taxpayerId)

  d. All of these can coexist without ambiguity.

17. Methods in the same program with identical names and identical parameter lists are _____.

  a. overloaded

  b. overworked

  c. overwhelmed

  d. ambiguous

18. Methods in different programs with identical names and identical parameter lists are _____.

  a. overloaded

  b. illegal

  c. both of these

  d. none of these

19. The notion of _____ most closely describes the way a calling method is not aware of the statements within a called method.

  a. abstraction

  b. object-oriented

  c. implementation hiding

  d. encapsulation

20. Programmers should strive to _____.

    a. increase coupling

    b. increase cohesion

    c. both of the above

    d. neither a nor b

Exercises

1. Create an IPO chart for each of the following methods:

    a. The method that produces your paycheck

    b. The method that calculates your semester tuition bill

    c. The method that calculates your monthly car payment

2. Create the logic for a program that continuously prompts the user for a number of dollars until the user enters 0. Pass each entered amount to a conversion method that displays a breakdown of the passed amount into the fewest bills; in other words, the method calculates the number of 20s, 10s, 5s, and 1s needed.

3. Create the logic for a program that calculates and displays the amount of money you would have if you invested $1000 at 5 percent interest for one year. Create a separate method to do the calculation and return the result to be displayed.

4. a. Create the logic for a program that calculates the due date for a bill. Prompt the user for the month, day, and year a bill is received. Calculate the day the bill is due to be paid as one month later. Print each date in turn by passing its month, day, and year to a method that displays slashes between the parts of the date—for example, 6/24/2012.

    b. Modify the method in Exercise 4a so it displays each date using a string for the month—for example, June 24, 2012.

5. a. Create the logic for a program that performs arithmetic functions. Design the program to contain two numeric variables, and prompt the user for values for the variables. Pass both variables to methods named sum() and difference(). Create the logic for the methods sum() and difference(); they compute the sum of and difference between the values of two arguments, respectively. Each method should perform the appropriate computation and display the results.

   b. Add a method named product() to the program in Exercise 5a. The product() method should compute the result when multiplying two numbers, but not display the answer. Instead, it should return the answer to the calling program, which displays the answer.

6. Create the logic for a program that continuously prompts a user for a numeric value until the user enters 0. The application passes the value in turn to a method that squares the number and to a method that cubes the number. The program displays the results before reprompting the user. Create the two methods that square and cube a number passed to them, and then return the calculated value.

7. Create the logic for a program that calls a method that computes the final price for a sales transaction. The program contains variables that hold the price of an item, the salesperson's commission expressed as a percentage, and the customer discount expressed as a percentage. Create a calculatePrice() method that determines the final price and returns the value to the calling method. The calculatePrice() method requires three arguments: product price, salesperson commission rate, and customer discount rate. A product's final price is the original price plus the commission amount minus the discount amount. The customer discount is taken as a percentage of the total price after the salesperson commission has been added to the original price.

8. Create the logic for a program that continuously prompts the user for two numeric values that represent the sides of a rectangle. Include two overloaded methods that compute a rectangle's area. One method takes two numeric parameters and calculates the area by multiplying the parameters. The other takes a single numeric parameter, which is squared to

calculate area. Each method displays its calculated result. Accept input and respond as follows:

- When the user enters a negative number for the first value, end the program.

- If the user enters a negative number for the second value, continue to reprompt the user until the second value is not negative.

- If both numbers entered are greater than 0, call the method version that accepts two parameters and pass it both values.

- If one of the values entered is 0 but the other is not, call the version of the method that accepts just one parameter and pass it the nonzero value.

- If both the entered values are 0, display an error message.

9. a. Plan the logic for an insurance company program to determine policy premiums. The program continuously prompts the user for an insurance policy number. When the user enters an appropriate sentinel value, end the program. Call a method that prompts each user for the type of policy needed—health or auto. While the user's response does not indicate health or auto, continue to prompt the user. When the value is valid, return it from the method. Pass the user's response to a new method where the premium is set and returned—$250 for a health policy or $175 for an auto policy. Display the results for each policy.

    b. Modify Exercise 9a so that the premium setting method calls one of two additional methods—one that determines the health premium or one that determines the auto premium. The health insurance method asks users whether they smoke; the premium is $250 for smokers and $190 for nonsmokers. The auto insurance method asks users to enter the number of traffic tickets they have received in the last three years. The premium is $175 for drivers with three or more tickets, $140 for those with one or two tickets, and $95 for those with no tickets. Each of these two methods returns the premium amount to the calling method, which returns the amount to be displayed.

10. Plan the logic for a program that continuously prompts a user for a customer number until an appropriate sentinel value is entered. Also prompt each user for the stock number of an item being ordered and the quantity ordered. If the customer number is not between 1000 and 7999 inclusive, and is not the sentinel, continue to prompt until a valid customer number is entered. If the stock number of the item is not between 201 and 850 inclusive, continue to prompt for the stock number. Pass the stock number to a method that a colleague at your organization has written; the method's signature is `num getPrice(num stockNumber)`. The `getPrice()` method accepts a stock number and returns the price of the item. Multiply the price by the quantity ordered, giving the total due. Pass the customer number and the calculated price to a prewritten method whose signature is `void displayBill(num custNum, num price)`. This method determines the customer's name and address by using the customer ID number, and calculates the final bill, including tax, using the price. Organize your program using as many methods as you think are appropriate. You do not need to write the `getPrice()` and `displayBill()` methods—assume they have already been written.

11. Create the logic for a program that computes weekly salary. Include two overloaded methods named `computeWeeklySalary()`. One version accepts an annual salary as a number and calculates weekly salary as 1/52 of the annual amount. The other accepts a number of hours worked per week and an hourly pay rate, and calculates weekly salary as a product of the two. Each method returns the weekly salary to the calling program. The main program prompts the user for the type of calculation to perform; then, based on the user's response, the program prompts for appropriate data, calls the correct method, and displays the result.

12. Create the logic for a program that prompts a user for three numbers and stores them in an array. Pass the array to a method that reverses the order of the numbers. Display the reversed numbers in the main program.

13. Create the logic for a program that prompts a user for 10 numbers and stores them in an array. Pass the array to a method that calculates the arithmetic average of the numbers and returns the value to the calling program. Display each number and how far it is from the arithmetic average. Continue to prompt the user for additional sets of 10 numbers until the user wants to quit.

14. The Information Services Department at the Springfield Library has created methods with the following signatures:

Signature	Description
num getNumber(num high, num low)	Prompts the user for a number. Continues to prompt until the number falls between designated high and low limits. Returns a valid number.
string getCharacter()	Prompts the user for a character string and returns the entered string.
num lookUpISBN(string title)	Accepts the title of a book and returns the ISBN. Returns a 0 if the book cannot be found.
string lookUpTitle(num isbn)	Accepts the ISBN of a book and returns a title. Returns a space character if the book cannot be found.
string isBookAvailable(num isbn)	Accepts an ISBN, searches the library database, and returns a "Y" or "N" indicating whether the book is currently available.

a. Design an interactive program that does the following, using the prewritten methods whenever they are appropriate.

- Prompt the user for and read a library card number, which must be between 1000 and 9999.

- Prompt the user for and read a search option—1 to search for a book by ISBN, 2 to search for a book by title, and 3 to quit. If the entry is invalid, repeat the request.

- While the user does not enter 3, prompt for an ISBN or title based on the user's previous selection. If the user enters an ISBN, get and display the book's title and ask the user to enter a "Y" or "N" to confirm whether the title is correct.

- If the user has entered a valid ISBN or a title that matches a valid ISBN, check whether the book is available, and display an appropriate message for the user.

- The user can continue to search for books until he or she enters 3 as the search option.

b. Develop the logic that implements each of the methods in Exercise 14a.

15. Each of the programs in Figure 9-25 uses a recursive method. Try to determine the output in each case.

a.
```
start
    output recursiveA(0)
stop
num recursiveA(num x)
    num result
    if x = 0 then
        result = x
    else
        result = x *
            (recursiveA(x - 1))
    endif
return result
```

b.
```
start
    output recursiveB(2)
stop
num recursiveB(num x)
    num result
    if x = 0 then
        result = x
    else
        result = x *
            (recursiveB(x - 1))
    endif
return result
```

c.
```
start
    output recursiveC(2)
stop
num recursiveC(num x)
    num result
    if x = 1 then
        result = x
    else
        result = x *
            (recursiveC(x - 1))
    endif
return result
```

Figure 9-25   Problems for Exercise 15

 Find the Bugs

16. Your student disk contains files named DEBUG09-01.txt, DEBUG09-02.txt, and DEBUG09-03.txt. Each file starts with some comments that describe the problem. Comments are lines that begin with two slashes (//). Following the comments, each file contains pseudocode that has one or more bugs you must find and correct.

 Game Zone

17. In the Game Zone sections of Chapters 6 and 8, you designed the logic for a quiz that contains questions about a topic of your choice. Now, modify the program so it contains an array of five multiple-choice quiz questions related to the topic of your choice. Each question contains four answer choices. Also create a parallel array that holds the correct answer to each question—A, B, C, or D. In turn, pass each question to a method that displays the question and accepts the player's answer. If the player does not enter a valid answer choice, force the player to reenter the choice. Return the user's valid (but not necessarily correct) answer to the main program. After the user's answer is returned to the main program, pass it and the correct answer to a method that determines whether the values are equal and displays an appropriate

message. After the user answers all five questions, display the number of correct and incorrect answers that the user chose.

18. In the Game Zone section of Chapter 6, you designed the logic for the game Hangman, in which the user guesses letters in a hidden word. Improve the game to store an array of 10 words. One at a time, pass each word to a method that allows the user to continuously guess letters until the game is solved. The method returns the number of guesses it took to complete the word. Store the number in an array before returning to the method for the next word. After all 10 words have been guessed, display a summary of the number of guesses required for each word as well as the average number of guesses per word.

 ## Up for Discussion

19. One advantage to writing a program that is subdivided into methods is that such a structure allows different programmers to write separate methods, thus dividing the work. Would you prefer to write a large program by yourself, or to work on a team in which each programmer produces one or more methods? Why?

20. In this chapter, you learned that hidden implementations are often said to exist in a black box. What are the advantages and disadvantages to this approach in both programming and real life?

Object-Oriented Programming

In this chapter, you will learn about:

- ◎ The basic principles of object-oriented programming
- ◎ Classes
- ◎ Public and private access
- ◎ Different ways to organize classes
- ◎ Instance methods
- ◎ Static methods
- ◎ Using objects

Principles of Object-Oriented Programming

Object-oriented programming (**OOP**) is a style of programming that focuses on an application's data and the methods you need to manipulate that data. OOP uses all of the concepts you are familiar with from modular procedural programming, such as variables, methods, and passing values to methods. Methods in object-oriented programs continue to use sequence, selection, and looping structures and make use of arrays. However, object-oriented programming adds several new concepts to programming and involves a different way of thinking. A considerable amount of new vocabulary is involved as well. First, you will read about object-oriented programming concepts in general, and then you will learn the specific terminology.

 Throughout this book, the terms *module* and *method* have been used interchangeably. In Chapter 9, you learned that object-oriented programmers prefer the term *method*, so it will be used in this chapter.

Five important features of object-oriented languages are:

- Classes

- Objects

- Polymorphism

- Inheritance

- Encapsulation

Classes and Objects

In object-oriented terminology, a **class** is a term that describes a group or collection of objects with common attributes. An **object** is one **instance** of a class. For example, your redChevroletAutomobile WithTheDent is an instance of the class that is made up of all automobiles, and your GoldenRetrieverDogNamedGinger is an instance of the class that is made up of all dogs. A class is like a blueprint from which many houses might be constructed, or like a recipe from which many meals can be prepared. One house and one meal are each an instance of their class.

Objects both in the real world and in object-oriented programming are made up of attributes and methods. **Attributes** are the characteristics that define an object as part of a class. For example, some of your automobile's attributes are its make, model, year, and purchase price. Other attributes include whether the automobile is currently running, its gear, its speed, and whether it is dirty. All automobiles possess the same attributes, but not, of course, the same values for those attributes. Similarly, your dog has the attributes of its breed, name, age, and whether its shots are current. Methods are the actions that alter, use, or retrieve the attributes. For example, an automobile has methods for changing and discovering its speed, and a dog has methods for setting and finding out its shot status.

Thinking of items as instances of a class allows you to apply your general knowledge of the class to its individual members. A particular instance of an object takes its attributes from the general category. If your friend purchases an `Automobile`, you know it has a model name, and if your friend gets a `Dog`, you know the dog has a breed. You might not know the current state of your friend's `Automobile`, such as its current speed, or the status of her `Dog`'s shots, but you do know what attributes exist for the `Automobile` and `Dog` classes, which allows you to imagine these objects reasonably well before you see them. You know enough to ask the `Automobile`'s model, and not its breed; you know enough to ask the `Dog`'s name and not its engine size. As another example, when you use a new application on your computer, you expect each component to have specific, consistent attributes, such as a button being clickable or a window being closeable, because each component gains these attributes as a member of the general class of GUI (graphical user interface) components.

428

Most programmers who use more modern languages employ the format in which class names begin with an uppercase letter and multiple-word identifiers are run together, such as `SavingsAccount` or `TemporaryWorker`. Each new word within the identifier starts with an uppercase letter. In Chapter 2, you learned that this format is known as *Pascal casing*.

Much of your understanding of the world comes from your ability to categorize objects and events into classes. As a young child, you learned the concept of "animal" long before you knew the word. Your first encounter with an animal might have been with the family dog, a neighbor's cat, or a goat at a petting zoo. As you developed speech, you might have used the same term for all of these creatures, gleefully shouting "Doggie!" as your parents pointed out cows, horses, and sheep in picture books or along the roadside on drives in the country. As you grew more sophisticated, you learned to distinguish dogs from cows; still later, you learned to distinguish breeds. Your understanding of the class "animal" helps you see the similarities between dogs and cows, and your understanding of the class "dog" helps you see the similarities between a Great Dane and a Chihuahua. Understanding classes gives you a framework for categorizing new experiences. You might not know the term "okapi," but when you learn it's an animal, you begin to develop a concept of what an okapi might be like.

When you think in an object-oriented manner, everything is an object, and every object is a member of a class. You can think of any inanimate physical item as an object—your desk, your computer, and your house are all called "objects" in everyday conversation. You can think of living things as objects, too—your houseplant, your pet fish, and your sister are objects. Events are also objects—the stock purchase you made, the mortgage closing you attended, and your graduation party are all objects.

Everything is an object, and every object is a member of a more general class. Your desk is a member of the class that includes all desks, and your pet fish is a member of the class that contains all fish. An object-oriented programmer would say that the desk in your office is an instance, or one tangible example, of the Desk class and your fish is an instance of the Fish class. These statements represent **is-a relationships** because you can say, "My oak desk with the scratch on top *is a* Desk and my goldfish named Moby *is a* Fish." Your goldfish, my guppy, and the zoo's shark each constitute one instance of the Fish class.

The concept of a class is useful because of its reusability. For example, if you invite me to a graduation party, I automatically know many things about the object (the party). I assume there will be attributes such as a starting time, a number of guests, some quantity of food, and some nature of gifts. I understand parties because of my previous knowledge of the Party class, of which all parties are members. I don't know the number of guests or the date or time of this particular party, but I understand that because all parties have a date and time, then this one must as well. Similarly, even though every stock purchase is unique, each must have a dollar amount and a number of shares. All objects have predictable attributes because they are members of certain classes.

The data components of a class that belong to every instantiated object are the class's **instance variables**. Also, object attributes are often called **fields** to help distinguish them from other variables you might use. The set of all the values or contents of a class object's instance variables is known as its **state**. For example, the current state of a particular party might be 8 p.m. and Friday; the state of a particular stock purchase might be $10 and five shares.

In addition to their attributes, class objects have methods associated with them, and every object that is an instance of a class possesses the same methods. For example, at some point you might want to issue invitations for a party. You might name the method issueInvitations(), and it might display some text as well as the values of the party's date and time fields. Your graduation party, then, might possess the identifier myGraduationParty. As a member of the Party class, it might have data members for the date and time, like all parties, and it might have a method to issue invitations. When you use the method, you might want to be able to send an argument to issueInvitations() that indicates how many copies to print. When you think of an object and its methods, it's as though you can send a message to the object to direct it to accomplish a particular task—you can tell the party object named myGraduationParty to print the number of invitations you request. Even though yourAnniversaryParty is also a member of the Party

Object-oriented programmers also use the term *is-a* when describing inheritance. You will learn about inheritance later in this chapter and in Chapter 11.

Object-oriented programmers sometimes say an object is one **instantiation** of a class; this is just another form of *instance*.

In grammar, a noun is equivalent to an object and the values of a class's attributes are adjectives—they describe the characteristics of the objects. An object can also have methods, which are equivalent to verbs.

class, and even though it also has an `issueInvitations()` method, you will send a different argument value to `yourAnniversaryParty`'s `issueInvitations()` method than I send to `myGraduationParty`'s corresponding method. Within any object-oriented program, you continuously make requests to objects' methods, often including arguments as part of those requests.

When you program in object-oriented languages, you frequently create classes from which objects will be instantiated. You also write applications to use the objects, along with their data and methods. Often, you will write programs that use classes created by others; other times, you might create a class that other programmers will use to instantiate objects within their own programs. A program or class that instantiates objects of another prewritten class is a **class client** or **class user**. For example, your organization might already have written a class named `Customer` that contains attributes such as `name`, `address`, and `phoneNumber`, and you might create clients that include arrays of thousands of `Customer`s. Similarly, in a GUI operating environment, you might write applications that include prewritten components that are members of classes with names like `Window` and `Button`. You expect each component on a GUI screen to have specific, consistent attributes because each component gains these attributes as a member of its general class.

Polymorphism

The real world is full of objects. Consider a door. A door needs to be opened and closed. You open a door with an easy-to-use interface known as a doorknob. Object-oriented programmers would say you are "passing a message" to the door when you "tell" it to open by turning its knob. The same message (turning a knob) has a different result when applied to your radio than when applied to a door. The procedure you use to open something—call it the "open" procedure— works differently on a door to a room than it does on a desk drawer, a bank account, a computer file, or your eyes. However, even though these procedures operate differently using the different objects, you can call each of these procedures "open." In object-oriented programming, procedures are called methods.

With object-oriented programming, you focus on the objects that will be manipulated by the program—for example, a customer invoice, a loan application, or a menu from which the user will select an option. You define the characteristics of those objects and the methods each of the objects will use; you also define the information that must be passed to those methods.

You can create multiple methods with the same name, which will act differently and appropriately when used with different types of objects. In Chapter 9, you learned that this concept is called *polymorphism*, and you learned to overload methods. For example, you might use a method named `print()` to print a customer invoice, loan application, or envelope. Because you use the same method name, `print()`, to describe the different actions needed to print these diverse objects, you can write statements in object-oriented programming languages that are more like English; you can use the same method name to describe the same type of action, no matter what type of object is being acted upon. Using the method name `print()` is easier than remembering `printInvoice()`, `printLoanApplication()`, and so on. In English, you understand the difference between "running a race," "running a business," and "running a computer program." Object-oriented languages understand verbs in context, just as people do.

As another example of the advantages to using one name for a variety of objects, consider a screen you might design for a user to enter data into an application you are writing. Suppose the screen contains a variety of objects—some forms, buttons, scroll bars, dialog boxes, and so on. Suppose also that you decide to make all the objects blue. Instead of having to memorize the method names that these objects use to change color—perhaps `changeFormColor()`, `changeButtonColor()`, and so on—your job would be easier if the creators of all those objects had developed a `setColor()` method that works appropriately with each type of object.

Purists find a subtle difference between overloading and polymorphism. Some reserve the term *polymorphism* (or **pure polymorphism**) for situations in which one method body is used with a variety of arguments. For example, a single method that can be used with any type of object is polymorphic. The term *overloading* is applied to situations in which you define multiple functions with a single name—for example, three functions, all named `display()`, that display a number, an employee, and a student, respectively. Certainly, the two terms are related; both refer to the ability to use a single name to communicate multiple meanings. For now, think of overloading as a primitive type of polymorphism.

Inheritance

Another important concept in object-oriented programming is **inheritance**, which is the process of acquiring the traits of one's predecessors. In the real world, a new door with a stained glass window inherits most of its traits from a standard door. It has the same purpose, it opens and closes in the same way, and it has the

Watch the video *An Introduction to Object-Oriented Programming*.

same knob and hinges. The door with the stained glass window simply has one additional trait—its window. Even if you have never seen a door with a stained glass window, when you encounter one you know what it is and how to use it because you understand the characteristics of all doors. With object-oriented programming, once you create an object, you can develop new objects that possess all the traits of the original object plus any new traits you desire. If you develop a `CustomerBill` class of objects, there is no need to develop an `OverdueCustomerBill` class from scratch. You can create the new class to contain all the characteristics of the already developed one, and simply add necessary new characteristics. This not only reduces the work involved in creating new objects, it makes them easier to understand because they possess most of the characteristics of already developed objects.

Encapsulation

Real-world objects often employ encapsulation and information hiding. **Encapsulation** is the process of combining all of an object's attributes and methods into a single package. **Information hiding** is the concept that other classes should not alter an object's attributes— only the methods of an object's own class should have that privilege. Outside classes should only be allowed to make a request that an attribute be altered; then it is up to the class's methods to determine whether the request is appropriate. When using a door, you usually are unconcerned with the latch or hinge construction features, and you don't have access to the interior workings of the knob or know what color of paint might have been used on the inside of the door panel. You care only about the functionality and the interface, the user-friendly boundary between the user and internal mechanisms of the device. Similarly, the detailed workings of objects you create within object-oriented programs can be hidden from outside programs and modules if you want them to be. When the details are hidden, programmers can focus on the functionality and the interface, as people do with real-life objects.

Outside classes make requests to alter an attribute by using a set method. You will learn more about set methods later in this chapter.

Information hiding is also called **data hiding**.

In summary, understanding object-oriented programming means that you must consider five of its integral components: classes, objects, polymorphism, inheritance, and encapsulation.

> ## TWO TRUTHS & A LIE
>
> ### Principles of Object-Oriented Programming
>
> 1. Learning about object-oriented programming is difficult because it does not use the concepts you already know, such as declaring variables and using modules.
>
> 2. In object-oriented terminology, a class is a term that describes a group or collection of objects with common attributes; an instance of a class is an existing object of a class.
>
> 3. A program or class that instantiates objects of another prewritten class is a class client or class user.
>
> The false statement is #1. Object-oriented programming makes use of many of the features of procedural programming, including declaring variables and using modules.

Defining Classes and Creating Class Diagrams

A class is a category of things; an object is a specific instance of a class. A **class definition** is a set of program statements that tell you the characteristics of the class's objects and the methods that can be applied to its objects.

A class definition can contain three parts:

- Every class has a name.

- Most classes contain data, although this is not required.

- Most classes contain methods, although this is not required.

For example, you can create a class named Employee. Each Employee object will represent one employee who works for an organization. Data members, or attributes of the Employee class, include fields such as lastName, hourlyWage, and weeklyPay.

The methods of a class include all actions you want to perform with the class. Appropriate methods for an Employee class might include setHourlyWage(), getHourlyWage(), and calculateWeeklyPay(). The job of setHourlyWage() is to provide values for an Employee's wage data field, the purpose of getHourlyWage() is to retrieve the wage value, and the purpose of calculateWeeklyPay() is to multiply the Employee's hourlyWage by the number of hours in a workweek to calculate a weekly salary. With object-oriented languages, you think of the class name, data, and methods as a single encapsulated unit.

Declaring a class does not create any actual objects. A class is just an abstract description of what an object will be like if any objects are ever actually instantiated. Just as you might understand all the characteristics of an item you intend to manufacture long before the first item rolls off the assembly line, you can create a class with fields and methods long before you instantiate any objects that are members of that class. After an object has been instantiated, its methods can be accessed using the object's identifier, a dot, and a method call. When you declare a simple variable that is a built-in data type, you write a statement such as one of the following:

```
num money
string name
```

When you write a program that declares an object that is a class data type, you write a statement such as the following:

```
Employee myAssistant
```

In some object-oriented programming languages, you need to add more to the declaration statement to actually create an Employee object. For example, in Java, you would write:

```
Employee myAssistant = new Employee();
```

You will understand more about the format of this statement when you learn about constructors in Chapter 11.

When you declare the myAssistant object, it contains all the data fields and has access to all the methods contained within the class. In other words, a larger section of memory is set aside than when you declare a simple variable, because an Employee contains several fields. You can use any of an Employee's methods with the myAssistant object. The usual syntax is to provide an object name, a dot (period), and a method name. For example, you can write a program that contains statements such as the ones shown in the pseudocode in Figure 10-1.

Of course, the program segment in Figure 10-1 is very short. In a more useful real-life program, you might read employee data from a data file before assigning it to the object's fields, each Employee might contain dozens of fields, and your application might create hundreds or thousands of objects.

```
start
    Declarations
        Employee myAssistant
    myAssistant.setLastName("Reynolds")
    myAssistant.setHourlyWage(16.75)
    output "My assistant makes ",
        myAssistant.getHourlyWage(), " per hour"
stop
```

Figure 10-1   Application that declares and uses an Employee object

When you write a statement such as `myAssistant.setHourlyWage` `(16.75)`, you are making a call to a method that is contained within the `Employee` class. Because `myAssistant` is an `Employee` object, it is allowed to use the `setHourlyWage()` method that is part of its class.

When you write the application in Figure 10-1, you do not need to know what statements are written within the `Employee` class methods, although you could make an educated guess based on the methods' names. Before you could execute the application in Figure 10-1, someone would have to write appropriate statements within the `Employee` class methods. If you wrote the methods, of course you would know their contents, but if another programmer has already written the methods, you could use the application without knowing the details contained in the methods. In Chapter 9, you learned that the ability to use methods without knowing the details of their contents (called a "black box") is a feature of encapsulation. The real world is full of many black box devices. For example, you can use your television and microwave oven without knowing how they work internally—all you need to understand is the interface. Similarly, with well-written methods that belong to classes you use, you need not understand how they work internally to be able to use them; you need only understand the ultimate result when you use them.

In the client program segment in Figure 10-1, the focus is on the object—the `Employee` named `myAssistant`—and the methods you can use with that object. This is the essence of object-oriented programming.

In older object-oriented programming languages, simple numbers and characters are said to be **primitive data types**; this distinguishes them from objects that are class types. In the newest programming languages, every item you name, even one that is a numeric or string type, is an object that is a member of a class that contains both data and methods.

Creating Class Diagrams

Programmers often use a class diagram to illustrate class features or to help plan them. A **class diagram** consists of a rectangle divided into three sections, as shown in Figure 10-2. The top section contains the name of the class, the middle section contains the names and data types of the attributes, and the bottom section contains the methods. This generic class diagram shows two attributes and three methods, but a given class might have any number of either, including none. Figure 10-3 shows the class diagram for the `Employee` class.

Besides referring to `Employee` as a class, many programmers would refer to it as a **user-defined type**; a more accurate term is **programmer-defined type**. Object-oriented programmers typically refer to a class like `Employee` as an **abstract data type** (**ADT**); this term implies that the type's data can be accessed only through methods.

435

Some programmers write only client programs, never creating nonclient classes themselves, but using only classes that others have created.

When you instantiate objects, the data fields of each are stored at separate memory locations. However, all members of the same class share one copy of the class's methods. You will learn more about this concept later in this chapter.

Class diagrams are a type of Unified Modeling Language (UML) diagram. Chapter 13 covers the UML.

Class name
Attribute 1 : data type Attribute 2 : data type
Method 1() : data type Method 2() : data type Method 3() : data type

Figure 10-2   Generic class diagram

Employee
lastName: string hourlyWage: num weeklyPay: num
setLastName(name : string) : void setHourlyWage(wage : num) : void getLastName() : string getHourlyWage() : num getWeeklyPay() : num calculateWeeklyPay() : void

Figure 10-3   Employee class diagram

By convention, a class diagram lists the names of the data items first. Each name is followed by a colon and the data type. Similarly, method names are followed by their data types. Listing the names first emphasizes the purposes of the fields and methods more than their types.

Class diagrams are useful for communicating about a class's contents with nonprogrammers.

Figures 10-2 and 10-3 both show that a class diagram is intended to be only an overview of class attributes and methods. A class diagram shows *what* data items and methods the class will use, not the details of the methods nor *when* they will be used. It is a design tool that helps you see the big picture in terms of class requirements. Figure 10-3 shows the Employee class that contains three data fields that represent an employee's name, hourly pay rate, and weekly pay amount. Every Employee object created in any program that uses this class will contain these three data fields. In other words, when you declare an Employee object, you declare three fields with one statement and reserve enough memory to hold all three fields.

Figure 10-3 also shows that the Employee class contains six methods. For example, the first method is defined as follows:

```
setLastName(name : string) : void
```

This notation means that the method name is setLastName(), that it takes a single string parameter named name, and that it returns nothing.

Various books, Web sites, and organizations will use class diagrams that list the method name only, as in the following:

```
setLastName()
```

Some developers choose to list the method name and return type only, as in:

```
setLastName() : void
```

Some developers list the method name and return type as well as the parameter type, as in the following:

```
setLastName(string) : void
```

Still other developers list an appropriate identifier for the parameter, but not its type, as in the following:

```
setLastName(name) : void
```

This book will take the approach of being as complete as possible, so the class diagrams you see here will contain each method's identifier, parameter list with types, and return type. You should use the format your instructor prefers. When you are on the job, use the format your supervisor and coworkers understand.

The Employee class diagram shows that two of the six methods take parameters (setLastName() and setHourlyWage()). The diagram also shows the return type for each method—three void methods, two numeric methods, and one string method. The class diagram does not tell you what takes place inside the method (although you might be able to make an educated guess). Later, when you write the code that actually creates the Employee class, you include method implementation details. For example, Figure 10-4 shows some pseudocode you can use to show the details for the methods contained within the Employee class.

```
class Employee
    Declarations
        string lastName
        num hourlyWage
        num weeklyPay

    void setLastName(string name)
        lastName = name
    return

    void setHourlyWage(num wage)
        hourlyWage = wage
        calculateWeeklyPay()
    return

    string getLastName()
    return lastName

    num getHourlyWage()
    return hourlyWage

    num getWeeklyPay()
    return weeklyPay

    void calculateWeeklyPay()
        Declarations
            num WORK_WEEK_HOURS = 40
        weeklyPay = hourlyWage * WORK_WEEK_HOURS
    return
endClass
```

Figure 10-4 Pseudocode for Employee class described in the class diagram in Figure 10-3

In Figure 10-4, the `Employee` class attributes or fields are identified with a data type and a field name. In addition to listing the data fields required, Figure 10-4 shows the complete methods for the `Employee` class. The purposes of the methods can be divided into three categories:

- Two of the methods accept values from the outside world; these methods, by convention, start with the prefix *set*. These methods are used to set the data fields in the class.

- Three of the methods send data to the outside world; these methods, by convention, start with the prefix *get*. These methods return field values to a client program.

- One method performs work within the class; this method is named `calculateWeeklyPay()`. This method does not communicate with the outside; its purpose is to multiply `hourlyWage` by the number of hours in a week.

The Set Methods

In Figure 10-4, two of the methods begin with the word *set*; they are `setLastName()` and `setHourlyWage()`. They are known as **set methods** because their purpose is to set the values of data fields within the class. Each accepts data from the outside and assigns it to a field within the class. There is no requirement that such methods start with the prefix *set*; the prefix is merely conventional and clarifies the intention of the methods. The method `setLastName()` is implemented as follows:

```
void setLastName(string name)
   lastName = name
return
```

In this method, a string `name` is passed in as a parameter and assigned to the field `lastName`. Because `lastName` is contained in the same class as this method, the method has access to the field and can alter it.

Similarly, the method `setHourlyWage()` accepts a numeric parameter and assigns it to the class field `hourlyWage`. This method also calls the `calculateWeeklyPay()` method, which sets `weeklyPay` based on `hourlyWage`. By writing the `setHourlyWage()` method to call the `calculateWeeklyPay()` method automatically, you guarantee that the `weeklyPay` field is updated any time `hourlyWage` changes.

 Methods that set values are called **mutator methods**.

When you create an `Employee` object with a statement such as `Employee mySecretary`, you can use statements such as the following:

```
mySecretary.setLastName("Johnson")
mySecretary.setHourlyWage(15.00)
```

Similarly, you could pass variables or named constants to the methods as long as they were the correct data type. For example, if you write a program in which you make the following declaration, then the assignment in the next statement is valid.

```
num PAY_RATE_TO_START = 8.00
mySecretary.setHourlyWage(PAY_RATE_TO_START)
```

 In some languages—for example, Visual Basic and C#—you can create a **property** instead of creating a set method. Using a property provides a way to set a field value using a simpler syntax. By convention, if a class field is hourlyWage, its property would be HourlyWage, and in a program you could make a statement similar to mySecretary.HourlyWage = PAY_RATE_TO_START. The implementation of the property HourlyWage (with an uppercase initial letter) would be written in a format very similar to that of the setHourlyWage() method.

Just like any other methods, the methods that manipulate fields within a class can contain any statements you need. For example, a more complicated setHourlyWage() method might be written as in Figure 10-5. In this version, the wage passed to the method is tested against minimum and maximum values, and is assigned to the class field hourlyWage only if it falls within the prescribed limits. If the wage is too low, the MINWAGE value is substituted, and if the wage is too high, the MAXWAGE value is substituted.

```
void setHourlyWage(num wage)
   Declarations
      num MINWAGE = 6.00
      num MAXWAGE = 70.00
   if wage < MINWAGE then
      hourlyWage = MINWAGE
   else
      if wage > MAXWAGE then
         hourlyWage = MAXWAGE
      else
         hourlyWage = wage
      endif
   endif
   calculateWeeklyPay()
return
```

Figure 10-5   More complex setHourlyWage() method

Similarly, if the set methods in a class required them, the methods could contain output statements, loops, array declarations, or any other legal programming statements. However, if the main purpose of a method is not to set a field value, then the method should not be named with the set prefix.

The Get Methods

In the `Employee` class in Figure 10-4, three of the methods begin with the prefix *get*: `getLastName()`, `getHourlyWage()`, and `getWeeklyPay()`. The purpose of a **get method** is to return a value to the world outside the class. The methods are implemented as follows:

```
string getLastName()
return lastName

num getHourlyWage()
return hourlyWage

num getWeeklyPay()
return weeklyPay
```

Each of these methods simply returns the value in the field implied by the method name. Like set methods, any of these get methods could also contain more complicated statements as needed. For example, in a more complicated class, you might want to return the hourly wage of an employee only if the user had also passed an appropriate access code to the method, or you might want to return the weekly pay value as a string with a dollar sign attached instead of as a numeric value.

Methods that get values from class fields are known as **accessor methods**.

When you declare an `Employee` object such as `Employee mySecretary`, you can then make statements in a program similar to the following:

```
Declarations
    string employeeName
employeeName = mySecretary.getLastName()
output "Wage is ", mySecretary.getHourlyWage()
output "Pay for half a week is ", mySecretary.
    getWeeklyPay() * 0.5
```

In other words, the value returned from a get method can be used as any other variable of its type would be used. You can assign the value to another variable, display it, perform arithmetic with it, or make any other statement that works correctly with the returned data type.

In some languages—for example, Visual Basic and C#—instead of creating a get method, you can add statements to the property to return a value using simpler syntax. For example, if you create an `HourlyWage` property, you could write a program that contains the statement `output mySecretary.HourlyWage`.

Work Methods

The `Employee` class in Figure 10-4 contains one method that is neither a get nor a set method. This method, `calculateWeeklyPay()`, is a **work method** within the class. It contains a locally named constant that represents the hours in a standard workweek, and it computes the weeklyPay field value by multiplying hourlyWage by the named constant. The method is written as follows:

```
void calculateWeeklyPay()
   Declarations
      num WORK_WEEK_HOURS = 40
   weeklyPay = hourlyWage * WORK_WEEK_HOURS
return
```

Some programmers call work methods **help methods** or **facilitators**.

441

No values need to be passed into this method, and no value is returned from it because this method does not communicate with the outside world. Instead, this method is called only from within another method in the same class (the setHourlyWage() method), and that method is called from the outside world. Any time a program uses the setHourlyWage() method to alter an Employee's hourlyWage field, calculateWeeklyPay() is called to recalculate the weeklyPay field.

Programmers who are new to class creation often are tempted to pass the hourlyWage value into the setWeeklyPay() method so it can use the value in its calculation. Although this technique would work, it is not required. The setWeeklyPay() method has direct access to the hourlyWage field by virtue of being a member of the same class.

No setWeeklyPay() method is included in this Employee class because the intention is that weeklyPay is set only each time the setHourlyWage() method is used. If you wanted programs to be able to set the weeklyPay field directly, you would have to write a method to allow it.

For example, Figure 10-6 shows a program that declares an Employee object and sets the hourly wage value. The program displays the weeklyPay value. Then a new value is assigned to hourlyWage and weeklyPay is displayed again. As you can see from the output in Figure 10-7, the weeklyPay value has been recalculated even though it was never set directly by the client program.

```
start
   Declarations
      num LOW = 9.00
      num HIGH = 14.65
      Employee myGardener
   myGardener.setLastName("Greene")
   myGardener.setHourlyWage(LOW)
   output "My gardener makes ",
      myGardener.getWeeklyPay(), " per week"
   myGardener.setHourlyWage(HIGH)
   output "My gardener makes ",
      myGardener.getWeeklyPay(), " per week"
stop
```

Figure 10-6   Program that sets and displays Employee data two times

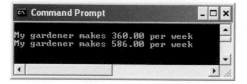

Figure 10-7 Execution of program in Figure 10-6

TWO TRUTHS & A LIE

Defining Classes and Creating Class Diagrams

1. Every class has a name, data, and methods.

2. After an object has been instantiated, its methods can be accessed using the object's identifier, a dot, and a method call.

3. A class diagram consists of a rectangle divided into three sections; the top section contains the name of the class, the middle section contains the names and data types of the attributes, and the bottom section contains the methods.

The false statement is #1. Most classes contain data and methods, although neither is required.

Understanding Public and Private Access

When you buy a product with a warranty, one of the common conditions of the warranty is that the manufacturer must perform all repair work. For example, if your computer has a warranty and something goes wrong with its operation, you cannot open the system unit yourself, remove and replace parts, and then expect to get your money back for a device that does not work properly. Instead, when something goes wrong with your computer, you must take the device to a technician approved by the manufacturer. The manufacturer guarantees that your machine will work properly only if the manufacturer can control how the internal mechanisms of the machine are modified.

Similarly, in object-oriented design, usually you do not want any outside programs or methods to alter your class's data fields unless you have control over the process. For example, you might design a class that performs a complicated statistical analysis on some data and stores the result. You would not want others to be able to alter your carefully crafted result. As another example, you might design a class from which others can create an innovative and useful GUI screen object. In this case you would not want others altering the dimensions of your artistic design. To prevent outsiders from changing your data fields in ways you do not endorse, you force other programs and methods to use a method that is part of the class, such as setLastName() and setHourlyWage(), to alter data. (Earlier in this chapter, you learned that the principle of keeping data private and inaccessible to outside classes is known as information hiding or data hiding.) Object-oriented programmers usually specify that their data fields will have **private access**—that is, the data cannot be accessed by any method that is not part of the class. The methods themselves, like setHourlyWage(), support **public access**—other programs and methods may use the methods that control access to the private data. Figure 10-8 shows a complete Employee class to which access specifiers have been added to describe each attribute and method. An **access specifier** (or **access modifier**) is the adjective defining the type of access (public or private) that outside classes will have to the attribute or method. In the figure, each access specifier is shaded.

```
class Employee
   Declarations
      private string lastName
      private num hourlyWage
      private num weeklyPay

   public void setLastName(string name)
      lastName = name
   return

   public void setHourlyWage(num wage)
      hourlyWage = wage
      calculateWeeklyPay()
   return

   public string getLastName()
   return lastName

   public num getHourlyWage()
   return hourlyWage

   public num getWeeklyPay()
   return weeklyPay

   private void calculateWeeklyPay()
      Declarations
         num WORK_WEEK_HOURS = 40
      weeklyPay = hourlyWage * WORK_WEEK_HOURS
   return
endClass
```

Figure 10-8　Employee class including public and private access specifiers

In many object-oriented programming languages, if you do not declare an access specifier for a data field or method, then it is private by default. This book will follow the convention of explicitly specifying access for every class member.

Watch the video *Creating a Class.*

In some object-oriented programming languages, such as C++, you can label a set of data fields or methods as public or private using the access specifier name just once, then following it with a list of the items in that category. In other languages, such as Java, you use the specifier public or private with each field or method. For clarity, this book will label each field and method as public or private.

In Figure 10-8, each of the data fields is private; that means each field is inaccessible to an object declared in a program. In other words, if a program declares an `Employee` object, such as `Employee myAssistant`, then the following statement is illegal:

`myAssistant.hourlyWage = 15.00`

Don't Do It
You cannot assign a value to a private variable using a statement in another class.

Instead, `hourlyWage` can be assigned only through a public method as follows:

`myAssistant.setHourlyWage(15.00)`

If you made `hourlyWage` public instead of private, then a direct assignment statement would work, but you would violate an important principle of OOP—that of data hiding using encapsulation. Data fields should usually be private and a client application should be able to access them only through the public interfaces; that is, through the class's public methods. That way, if you have restrictions on the value of `hourlyWage`, those restrictions will be enforced by the public method that acts as an interface to the private data field. Similarly, a public get method might control how a private value is retrieved. Perhaps you do not want clients to have access to an `Employee`'s `hourlyWage` if it is more than a specific value, or perhaps you always want to return it to the client as a string with a dollar sign attached. Even when a field has no data value requirements or restrictions, making data private and providing public set and get methods establishes a framework that makes such modifications easier in the future.

In the `Employee` class in Figure 10-8, only one method is not public; the `calculateWeeklyPay()` method is private. That means if you write a program and declare an `Employee` object such as `Employee myAssistant`, then the following statement is not permitted:

`myAssistant.calculateWeeklyPay()`

Don't Do It
The `calculateWeeklyPay()` method is not accessible outside the class.

Because it is private, the only way to call the `calculateWeeklyPay()` method is from within another method that already belongs to the class. In this example, it is called from the `setHourlyWage()` method. This prevents any client program from setting `hourlyWage` to one value while setting `weeklyPay` to some incompatible value. By making the `calculateWeeklyPay()` method private, you ensure that the class retains full control over when and how it is used. Classes most often contain private data and public methods, but as you have just seen, they can contain private methods. Classes can contain public data items as well. For example, an `Employee` class might contain a public constant data field named MINIMUM_WAGE; outside programs then would be able to access that value without using a method. Public data fields are not required to be named constants, but they frequently are.

Many programmers like to specify in their class diagrams whether each component in a class is public or private. Figure 10-9 shows the conventions that are typically used. A minus sign (–) precedes the items that are private; a plus sign (+) precedes those that are public.

When you learn more about inheritance in Chapter 11, you will learn about an additional access specifier—the protected access specifier. You use an octothorpe, also called a pound sign or number sign (#), to indicate protected access.

445

Employee
-lastName : string -hourlyWage : num -weeklyPay : num
+setLastName(name : string) : void +setHourlyWage(wage : num) : void +getLastName() : string +getHourlyWage() : num +getWeeklyPay() : num -calculateWeeklyPay() : void

Figure 10-9 Employee class diagram with public and private access specifiers

In object-oriented programming languages, the main program is most often written as a method named main() or Main(), and that method is virtually always defined as public.

TWO TRUTHS & A LIE

Understanding Public and Private Access

1. Object-oriented programmers usually specify that their data fields will have private access.

2. Object-oriented programmers usually specify that their methods will have private access.

3. In a class diagram, a minus sign (–) precedes the items that are private; a plus sign (+) precedes those that are public.

The false statement is #2. Object-oriented programmers usually specify that their methods will have public access.

Organizing Classes

The Employee class in Figure 10-9 contains just three data fields and six methods; most classes you create for professional applications will have many more. For example, in addition to requiring a last name and pay information, real employees require an employee number, a first name, address, phone number, hire date, and so on, as well as methods to set and get those fields. As classes grow in complexity, deciding how to organize them becomes increasingly important.

A unique identifier is one that should have no duplicates within an application. For example, an organization might have many employees with the last name Johnson or an hourly wage of $10.00, but only one employee will have employee number 12438.

Although there is no requirement to do so, most programmers place data fields in some logical order at the beginning of a class. For example, an ID number is most likely used as a unique identifier for each employee (what database users often call a **primary key**), so it makes sense to list the employee ID number first in the class. An employee's last name and first name "go together," so it makes sense to store these two Employee components adjacently. Despite these common-sense rules, you have a lot of flexibility in how you position your data fields within any class. For example, depending on the class, you might choose to store the data fields alphabetically, or you might choose to group together all the fields that are the same data type. Alternatively, you might choose to store all public data items first, followed by private ones, or vice versa.

In some languages you can organize a class's data fields and methods in any order within a class. For example, you could place all the methods first, followed by all the data fields, or you could organize the class so that several data fields are followed by methods that use them, and then several more data fields might be followed by the methods that use them. This book will follow the convention of placing all data fields first so that you can see their names and data types before reading the methods that use them. This format also echoes the way data and methods appear in standard class diagrams.

For ease in locating a class's methods, many programmers store them in alphabetical order. Other programmers arrange them in pairs of get and set methods, in the same order as the data fields are defined. Another option is to list all accessor (get) methods together and all mutator (set) methods together. Depending on the class, there might be other orders that result in logically functional groupings. Of course, if your company distributes guidelines for organizing class components, you must follow those rules.

Understanding Instance Methods

Class objects have data and methods associated with them, and every object that is an instance of a class is assumed to possess the same data and have access to the same methods. For example, Figure 10-10 shows a class diagram for a simple Student class containing just one private data field that holds a student's grade point average. The class also contains get and set methods for the field. Figure 10-11 shows the pseudocode for the Student class. This class becomes the model for a new data type named Student; when Student objects eventually are created, each will have its own gradePointAverage field and have access to methods to get and set it.

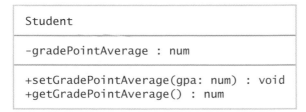

Figure 10-10 Class diagram for Student class

```
class Student
    Declarations
        private num gradePointAverage

    public void setGradePointAverage(num gpa)
        gradePointAverage = gpa
    return

    public num getGradePointAverage()
    return gradePointAverage
endClass
```

Figure 10-11 Pseudocode for the Student class

In the Student class in Figure 10-11, the method setGradePointAverage() takes one argument—a value for the Student's grade point average. The identifier gpa is local to the setGradePointAverage() method, and holds a value that will come into the method from the outside. Within the method, the value in gpa is assigned to gradePointAverage, which is a field within the class. The setGradePointAverage() method assigns a value to the gradePointAverage field for each separate Student object you create. Therefore, a method such as setGradePointAverage() is called an **instance method** because it operates correctly yet differently (using different values) for each separate instance of the Student class. In other words, if you create 100 Students and assign grade point averages to each of them, you need 100 storage locations in computer memory to store each unique grade point average.

Figure 10-12 shows a program that creates three Student objects and assigns values to their gradePointAverage fields. It also shows how the Student objects look in memory after the values have been assigned.

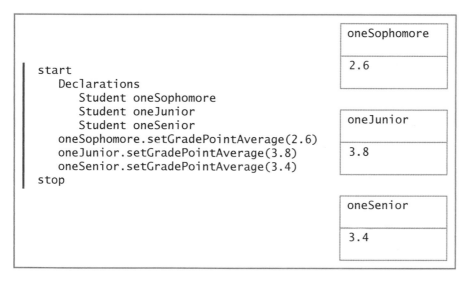

Figure 10-12 `StudentDemo` program and how `Student` objects look in memory

It makes sense for each `Student` object in Figure 10-12 to have its own `gradePointAverage` field, but it does not make sense for each `Student` to have its own copy of the methods that get and set `gradePointAverage`. Any method might have dozens of instructions in it, and to make 100 copies of identical methods would be inefficient. Instead, even though every `Student` has its own `gradePointAverage` field, only one copy of each of the methods `getGradePointAverage()` and `setGradePointAverage()` is stored in memory, but any instantiated object of the class can use the single copy.

Because only one copy of each instance method is stored, the computer needs a way to determine whose `gradePointAverage` is being set or retrieved when one of the methods is called. The mechanism that handles this problem is illustrated in Figure 10-13. When a method call such as `oneSophomore.setGradePointAverage(2.6)` is made, the true method call, which is invisible and automatically constructed, includes the memory address of the `oneSophomore` object. (These method calls are represented by the three narrow boxes in the center of Figure 10-13.)

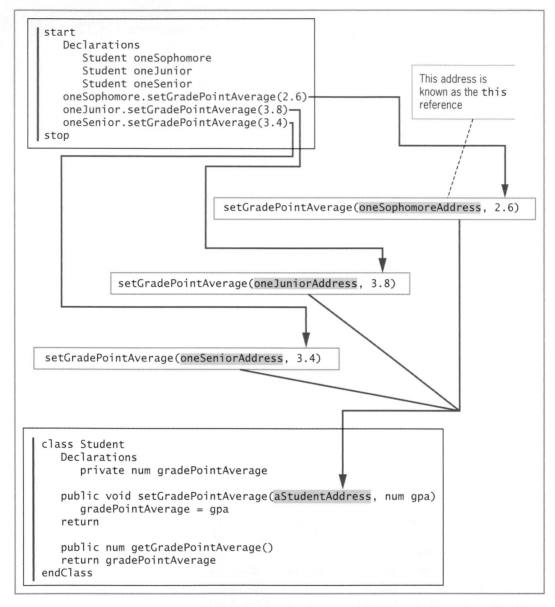

Figure 10-13 How Student addresses are passed from an application to an instance method of the Student class

Within the setGradePointAverage() method in the Student class, an invisible and automatically created parameter is added to the list. (For illustration purposes, this parameter is named aStudentAddress and is shaded in the Student class definition in Figure 10-13. In fact, no parameter is created with that name.) This parameter accepts the address of a Student object because the instance method belongs to the `Student` class; if this method belonged to another class—`Employee`, for example—then the method would accept an address for that type of object. The shaded addresses in Figure 10-13 are not written as code in any program—they are "secretly" sent and received behind the scenes. The address variable in Figure 10-13 is a `this` reference. A **`this` reference** is an automatically created variable that holds the address of an object and passes it to an instance method whenever the method is called. It is called a `this` reference because it refers to "this particular object" that is using the method at the moment. In the application in Figure 10-13, when `oneSophomore` uses the `setGradePointAverage()` method, the address of the `oneSophomore` object is contained in the `this` reference. Later in the program, when the `oneJunior` object uses the `setGradePointAverage()` method, the `this` reference will hold the address of that `Student` object.

Watch the video *The `this` Reference.*

Figure 10-13 shows each place the `this` reference is used in the `Student` class. It is implicitly passed as a parameter to each instance method. You never explicitly refer to the `this` reference when you write the method header for an instance method; Figure 10-13 just shows where it implicitly exists. Within each instance method, the `this` reference is implied any time you refer to one of the class data fields. For example, when you call `setGradePointAverage()` using a `oneSophomore` object, the `gradePointAverage` that is assigned within the method is the "*this* `gradePointAverage`", or the one that belongs to the `oneSophomore` object. The phrase "this `gradePointAverage`" usually is written as `this`, followed by a dot, followed by the field name—`this.gradePointAverage`.

The `this` reference exists throughout any instance method. You can explicitly use the `this` reference with data fields, as shown in the methods in the `Student` class in Figure 10-14, but you are not required to do so. Figure 10-14 shows where the `this` reference can be used implicitly, but where you can (but do not have to) use it explicitly. When you write an instance method in a class, the following two identifiers within the method always mean exactly the same thing:

- any field name

- `this`, followed by a dot, followed by the same field name

For example, within the `setGradePointAverage()` method, `gradePointAverage` and `this.gradePointAverage` refer to exactly the same memory location.

```
class Student
    Declarations
        private num gradePointAverage

    public void setGradePointAverage(num gpa)
        this.gradePointAverage = gpa
    return

    public num getGradePointAverage()
    return this.gradePointAverage
endClass
```

You can write **this** as a reference in these locations

Figure 10-14   Explicitly using **this** in the **Student** class

In a class method, the **this** reference can be used only with identifiers that are field names. For example, in Figure 10-14 you could not refer to **this.gpa** because **gpa** is not a class field—it is only a local variable.

Your organization might prefer that you explicitly use the **this** reference for clarity even though it is not required to create a workable program. It is the programmer's responsibility to follow the conventions established at work or by clients.

The syntax for using **this** differs among programming languages. For example, within a class in C++, you can refer to the **Student** class **gradePointAverage** value as **this->gradePointAverage** or **(*this).gradePointAverage**, but in Java you refer to it as **this.gradePointAverage**. In Visual Basic, the **this** reference is named **Me**, so the variable would be **Me.gradePointAverage**.

Usually you neither want nor need to use the **this** reference explicitly within the methods you write, but the **this** reference is always there, working behind the scenes, so that the data field for the correct object can be accessed.

As an example of an occasion when you might use the **this** reference explicitly, consider the following **setGradePointAverage()** method and compare it to the version in the **Student** class in Figure 10-14.

```
public void setGradePointAverage(num gradePointAverage)
    this.gradePointAverage = gradePointAverage
return
```

In this version of the method, the programmer has chosen to use the variable name **gradePointAverage** as the parameter to the method as well as the instance field within the class. This means that **gradePointAverage** is the name of a local variable within the method whose value is received by passing; it is also the name of a class field. To differentiate the two, you explicitly use the **this** reference with the copy of **gradePointAverage** that is a member of the class. Omitting the **this** reference in this case would result in the local parameter **gradePointAverage** being assigned to itself. The class's instance variable would not be set.

Any time a local variable in a method has the same identifier as a class field, the class field is hidden. This applies whether the local variable is a passed parameter or simply one that is declared within the method. In these cases, you must use a **this** reference to refer to the class field.

453

Understanding Static Methods

Some methods do not require a `this` reference; that is, the `this` reference makes no sense for them either implicitly or explicitly. For example, the `displayStudentMotto()` method in the `Student` class in Figure 10-15 does not use any data fields from the class, so it does not matter which `Student` object calls it. If you write a program in which you declare 100 `Student` objects, the `displayStudentMotto()` method executes in exactly the same way for each of them; it does not need to know whose motto is displayed and it does not need to access any specific object addresses. As a matter of fact, you might want to display the `Student` motto without instantiating any `Student` objects. Therefore, the `displayStudentMotto()` method can be written as a **class method** instead of an instance method.

```
public static void displayStudentMotto()
    output "Every student is an individual"
    output "in the pursuit of knowledge."
    output "Every student strives to be"
    output "a literate, responsible citizen."
return
```

Figure 10-15 Student class `displayStudentMotto()` method

454

In everyday language, the word *static* means "stationary"; it is the opposite of *dynamic*, which means "changing." In other words, static methods are always the same for the class, whereas nonstatic methods act differently depending on the object used to call them.

All the methods you have worked with in earlier chapters of this book, such as those that performed a calculation or produced some output, were static methods. That is, you did not create objects to call them.

When you write a class, you can indicate two types of methods:

- **Static methods** are those for which no object needs to exist, like the displayStudentMotto() method in Figure 10-15. Static methods do not receive a this reference as an implicit parameter. Typically, static methods include the word static in the method header, as shown shaded in Figure 10-15.

- **Nonstatic methods** are methods that exist to be used with an object created from a class. These instance methods receive a this reference to a specific object. In most programming languages, you use the word static when you want to declare a static class member and do not use any special word when you want a class member to be nonstatic. In other words, methods in a class are nonstatic instance methods by default.

In most programming languages, you use a static method with the class name, as in the following:

Student.displayStudentMotto()

In other words, no object is necessary with a static method.

In some languages, notably C++, besides using a static method with the class name, you are also allowed to use a static method with any object of the class, as in oneSophomore.displayStudentMotto().

TWO TRUTHS & A LIE

Understanding Static Methods

1. Class methods do not receive a this reference.

2. Static methods do not receive a this reference.

3. Nonstatic methods do not receive a this reference.

The false statement is #3. Nonstatic methods receive a this reference automatically.

Using Objects

After you create a class from which you want to instantiate objects, you can use the objects like you would use any other simpler data type. For example, consider the `InventoryItem` class in Figure 10-16. The class represents items a company manufactures and holds in inventory. Each item has a number, description, and price. The class contains a get and set method for each of the three fields.

```
class InventoryItem
   Declarations
      private string inventoryNumber
      private string description
      private num price

   public void setInventoryNumber(string number)
      inventoryNumber = number
   return

   public void setDescription(string description)
      this.description = description
   return

   public void setPrice(num price)
      if(price < 0)
         this.price = 0
      else
         this.price = price
   return

   public string getInventoryNumber()
   return inventoryNumber

   public string getDescription()
   return description

   public num getPrice()
   return price

endClass
```

Notice the uses of the `this` reference to differentiate between the method parameter and the class field.

Figure 10-16 `InventoryItem` class

Once you declare an `InventoryItem` object, you can use it in many of the ways you would use a simple numeric or string variable. For example, you could pass an `InventoryItem` object to a method or return one from a method. Figure 10-17 shows a program that declares an `InventoryItem` object and passes it to a method for display. The `InventoryItem` is declared in the main program and assigned values. Then the completed item is passed to a method where it is displayed. Figure 10-18 shows the execution of the program.

```
start
    Declarations
        InventoryItem oneItem
    oneItem.setInventoryNumber("1276")
    oneItem.setDescription("Mahogany chest")
    oneItem.setPrice(450.00)
    displayItem(oneItem)
stop

public static void displayItem(InventoryItem item)
    Declarations
        num TAX_RATE = 0.06
        num tax
        num pr
        num total
    output "Item #", item.getInventoryNumber()
    output item.getDescription()
    pr = item.getPrice()
    tax = pr * TAX_RATE
    total = pr + tax
    output "Price is $", pr, " plus $", tax, " tax"
    output "Total is $", total
return
```

Figure 10-17   Application that declares and uses an `InventoryItem` object

Figure 10-18   Execution of application in Figure 10-17

The `InventoryItem` declared in the main program in Figure 10-17 is passed to the `displayItem()` method in much the same way a numeric or string variable would be. The method receives a copy of the `InventoryItem` that is known locally by the identifier item. Within the method, the field values of the local item can be retrieved, displayed, and used in arithmetic statements in the same way they could have been in the main program where the `InventoryItem` was originally declared.

Figure 10-19 shows a more realistic application that uses `InventoryItem` objects. In the main program, an `InventoryItem` is declared and the user is prompted for a number. As long as the user does not enter the QUIT value, a loop is executed in which the entered inventory item number is passed to the `getItemValues()` method. Within that method, a local `InventoryItem` object is declared. This local object is used to gather and hold the user's input values. The user is prompted for a description and price; then the passed item number, as well as the newly obtained description and price, are assigned to the local InventoryItem object via its set methods. The completed object is returned to the program where it is assigned to the InventoryItem object. That item is then passed to the displayItem() method. As in the previous example, the method calculates tax and displays results. Figure 10-20 shows a typical execution.

```
start
   Declarations
      InventoryItem oneItem
      string itemNum
      string QUIT = "0"
   output "Enter item number or ", QUIT, " to quit… "
   input itemNum
   while itemNum <> "0"
      oneItem = getItemValues(itemNum)
      displayItem(oneItem)
      output "Enter next item number or ", QUIT, " to quit… "
      input itemNum
   endwhile
stop

public static InventoryItem getItemValues(string number)
   Declarations
      InventoryItem inItem
      string desc
      num price
   output "Enter description… "
   input desc
   output "Enter price… "
   input price
   inItem.setInventoryNumber(number)
   inItem.setDescription(desc)
   inItem.setPrice(price)
return inItem

public static void displayItem(InventoryItem item)
   Declarations
      num TAX_RATE = 0.06
      num tax
      num pr
      num total
   output "Item #", item.getInventoryNumber()
   output item.getDescription()
   pr = item.getPrice()
   tax = pr * TAX_RATE
   total = pr + tax
   output "Price is $", pr, " plus $", tax, " tax"
   output "Total is $", total
return
```

Figure 10-19   Application that uses InventoryItem objects

In Figure 10-19, notice that the return type for the getItemValues()
method is InventoryItem. A method can return only a single value.
Therefore, it is convenient that the getItemValues() method can encapsulate two strings and a number in a single InventoryItem object that it
returns to the main program.

Figure 10-20 Typical execution of program in Figure 10-19

TWO TRUTHS & A LIE

Using Objects

1. You can pass an object to a method.

2. Because only one value can be returned from a method, you cannot return an object that holds more than one field.

3. You can declare an object locally within a method.

The false statement is #2. An object can be returned from a method.

Chapter Summary

- Classes are the basic building blocks of object-oriented programming. When you think in an object-oriented manner, everything is an object, and every object is an instance of a class. A class's fields, or instance variables, hold its data, and every object that is an instance of a class possesses the same methods. A program or class that instantiates objects of another prewritten class is a class client or class user. In addition to classes and objects, three important features of object-oriented languages are polymorphism, inheritance, and encapsulation.

- A class definition is a set of program statements that tell you the characteristics of the class's objects and the methods that can be applied to its objects. A class definition can contain a name, data, and methods. Programmers often use a class diagram to illustrate class features. The purposes of many methods contained in a class can be divided into three categories: set methods, get methods, and work methods.

- Object-oriented programmers usually specify that their data fields will have private access—that is, the data cannot be accessed by any method that is not part of the class. The methods frequently support public access, which means that other programs and methods may use the methods that control access to the private data. In a class diagram, a minus sign (–) precedes the items that are private; a plus sign (+) precedes those that are public.

- As classes grow in complexity, deciding how to organize them becomes increasingly important. Depending on the class, you might choose to store the data fields by listing a key field first, listing fields alphabetically, or by data type or accessibility. Methods might be stored in alphabetical order or in pairs of get and set methods.

- An instance method operates correctly yet differently for every object instantiated from a class. When an instance method is called, a `this` reference that holds the object's memory address is automatically passed to the method.

- Some methods do not require a `this` reference. When you write a class, you can indicate two types of methods: static methods, which are also known as class methods and do not receive a `this` reference as an implicit parameter; and nonstatic methods, which are instance methods and do receive a `this` reference.

- After you create a class from which you want to instantiate objects, you can use the objects as you would use any other simpler data type.

459

Key Terms

Object-oriented programming (**OOP**) is a style of programming that focuses on an application's data and the methods you need to manipulate that data.

A **class** describes a group or collection of objects with common attributes.

An **object** is one tangible example of a class; it is an instance of a class.

An **instance** is one tangible example of a class; it is an object.

Attributes are the characteristics that define an object as part of a class.

An **is-a relationship** exists between an object and its class.

An **instantiation** of a class is an instance.

A class's **instance variables** are the data components that belong to every instantiated object.

Fields are object attributes or data.

The **state** of an object is the set of all the values or contents of its instance variables.

A **class client** or **class user** is a program or class that instantiates objects of another prewritten class.

Pure polymorphism describes situations in which one method body is used with a variety of arguments.

Inheritance is the process of acquiring the traits of one's predecessors.

Encapsulation is the process of combining all of an object's attributes and methods into a single package.

Information hiding (or **data hiding**) is the concept that other classes should not alter an object's attributes—only the methods of an object's own class should have that privilege.

A **class definition** is a set of program statements that tell you the characteristics of the class's objects and the methods that can be applied to its objects.

A **user-defined type**, or **programmer-defined type**, is a type that is not built into a language, but is created by the programmer.

An **abstract data type** (**ADT**) is a programmer-defined type such as a class.

Primitive data types are simple numbers and characters that are not class types.

A **class diagram** consists of a rectangle divided into three sections that show the name, data, and methods of a class.

A **set method** sets the values of a data field within a class.

Mutator methods are ones that set values in a class.

A **property** provides methods that allow you to get and set a class field value using a simple syntax.

A **get method** returns a value from a class.

Accessor methods get values from class fields.

Work methods perform tasks within a class.

Help methods and **facilitators** are other names for work methods.

Private access, as applied to a class's data or methods, specifies that the data or method cannot be used by any method that is not part of the same class.

Public access, as applied to a class's data or methods, specifies that other programs and methods may use the specified data or methods.

An **access specifier** (or **access modifier**) is the adjective that defines the type of access outside classes will have to the attribute or method.

A **primary key** is a unique identifier for each object in a database.

An **instance method** operates correctly yet differently for each class object. An instance method is nonstatic and receives a `this` reference.

A **this reference** is an automatically created variable that holds the address of an object and passes it to an instance method whenever the method is called.

A **class method** is a static method. Class methods are not instance methods and do not receive a `this` reference.

Static methods are those for which no object needs to exist. Static methods are not instance methods and do not receive a `this` reference.

Nonstatic methods are methods that exist to be used with an object created from a class; they are instance methods and receive a `this` reference.

Review Questions

1. Which of the following means the same as *object*?

    a. class

    b. field

    c. instance

    d. category

2. Which of the following means the same as *instance variable*?

    a. field

    b. instance

    c. category

    d. class

3. A program that instantiates objects of another prewritten class is a(n) _____.

    a. object

    b. client

    c. instance

    d. GUI

4. The relationship between an instance and a class is a(n) _____ relationship.

    a. has-a

    b. is-a

    c. polymorphic

    d. hostile

5. Which of these does not belong with the others?

    a. instance variable

    b. attribute

    c. object

    d. field

6. The process of acquiring the traits of one's predecessors
   is _____.

   a. inheritance

   b. encapsulation

   c. polymorphism

   d. orientation

7. When discussing classes and objects, *encapsulation* means
   that _____.

   a. all the fields belong to the same object

   b. all the fields are private

   c. all the fields and methods are grouped together

   d. all the methods are public

8. Every class definition must contain _____.

   a. a name

   b. data

   c. methods

   d. all of the above

9. Assume a working program contains the following statement:

   `myDog.setName("Bowser")`

   Which of the following do you know?

   a. `setName()` is a public method

   b. `setName()` accepts a string parameter

   c. both of these

   d. none of these

10. Assume a working program contains the following statement:

    `name = myDog.getName()`

    Which of the following do you know?

    a. `getName()` returns a string

    b. `getName()` returns a value that is the same data type as `name`

    c. both of these

    d. none of these

11. A class diagram _____.

   a.   provides an overview of a class's data and methods

   b.   provides method implementation details

   c.   is never used by nonprogrammers because it is too
        technical

   d.   all of the above

12. Which of the following is the most likely scenario for a
     specific class?

   a.   Its data is private and its methods are public.

   b.   Its data is public and its methods are private.

   c.   Its data and methods are both public.

   d.   Its data and methods are both private.

13. An instance method _____.

   a.   is static

   b.   receives a `this` reference

   c.   both of these

   d.   none of these

14. Assume you have created a class named `Dog` that contains
     a data field named `weight` and an instance method named
     `setWeight()`. Further assume the `setWeight()` method
     accepts a numeric parameter named `weight`. Which of the
     following statements correctly sets a `Dog`'s weight within the
     `setWeight()` method?

   a.   `weight = weight`

   b.   `this.weight = this.weight`

   c.   `weight = this.weight`

   d.   `this.weight = weight`

15. A static method is also known as a(n) _____
     method.

   a.   instance

   b.   public

   c.   private

   d.   class

16. By default, methods contained in a class are _____ methods.

    a. static

    b. nonstatic

    c. class

    d. public

17. Assume you have created a class named MyClass, and that a working program contains the following statement:

    output MyClass.number

    Which of the following do you know?

    a. number is a numeric field

    b. number is a static field

    c. number is an instance variable

    d. all of the above

18. Assume you have created an object named myObject and that a working program contains the following statement:

    output myObject.getSize()

    Which of the following do you know?

    a. size is a private numeric field

    b. size is a static field

    c. size is a public instance variable

    d. all of the above

19. Assume you have created a class named MyClass and that it contains a private field named myField and a nonstatic public method named myMethod(). Which of the following is true?

    a. myMethod() has access to and can use myField

    b. myMethod() does not have access to and cannot use myField

    c. myMethod() can use myField but cannot pass it to other methods

    d. myMethod() can use myField only if myField is passed to myMethod() as a parameter

20. An object can be _____.

    a. stored in an array

    b. passed to a method

    c. returned from a method

    d. all of the above

Exercises

1. Identify three objects that might belong to each of the following classes:

    a. `Automobile`

    b. `NovelAuthor`

    c. `CollegeCourse`

2. Identify three different classes that might contain each of these objects:

    a. Wolfgang Amadeus Mozart

    b. My pet cat named Socks

    c. Apartment 14 at 101 Main Street

3. Design a class named `CustomerRecord` that holds a customer number, name, and address. Include methods to set the values for each data field and display the values for each data field. Create the class diagram and write the pseudocode that defines the class.

4. Design a class named `House` that holds the street address, price, number of bedrooms, and number of baths in a house. Include methods to set the values for each data field, and include a method that displays all the values for a `House`. Create the class diagram and write the pseudocode that defines the class.

5. Design a class named `Loan` that holds an account number, name of account holder, amount borrowed, term, and interest rate. Include methods to set values for each data field and a method that displays all the loan information. Create the class diagram and write the pseudocode that defines the class.

6. Complete the following tasks:

   a. Design a class named Book that holds a stock number, author, title, price, and number of pages for a book. Include methods to set and get the values for each data field. Create the class diagram and write the pseudocode that defines the class.

   b. Design an application that declares two Book objects and sets and displays their values.

   c. Design an application that declares an array of 10 Books. Prompt the user for data for each of the Books, then display all the values.

7. Complete the following tasks:

   a. Design a class named Pizza. Data fields include a string field for toppings (such as pepperoni), numeric fields for diameter in inches (such as 12), and price (such as 13.99). Include methods to get and set values for each of these fields. Create the class diagram and write the pseudocode that defines the class.

   b. Design an application that declares two Pizza objects and sets and displays their values.

   c. Design an application that declares an array of 10 Pizzas. Prompt the user for data for each of the Pizzas, then display all the values.

8. Complete the following tasks:

   a. Design a class named HousePlant. A HousePlant has fields for a name (for example, "Philodendron"), a price (for example, 29.99), and a field that indicates whether the plant has been fed in the last month (for example, "Yes"). Create the class diagram and write the pseudocode that defines the class.

   b. Design an application that declares two HousePlant objects and sets and displays their values.

   c. Design an application that declares an array of 10 HousePlants. Prompt the user for data for each of the HousePlants, then display all the values.

Find the Bugs

9. Your student disk contains files named DEBUG10-01.txt, DEBUG10-02.txt, and DEBUG10-03.txt. Each file starts with some comments that describe the problem. Comments are lines that begin with two slashes (//). Following the comments, each file contains pseudocode that has one or more bugs you must find and correct.

Game Zone

10. a. Playing cards are used in many computer games, including versions of such classics as Solitaire, Hearts, and Poker. Design a Card class that contains a string data field to hold a suit (spades, hearts, diamonds, or clubs) and a numeric data field for a value from 1 to 13. Include get and set methods for each field. Write an application that randomly selects two playing cards and displays their values.

    b. Using two Card objects, design an application that plays a simple version of the card game War. Deal two Cards— one for the computer and one for the player. Determine the higher card, then display a message indicating whether the cards are equal, the computer won, or the player won. (Playing cards are considered equal when they have the same value, no matter what their suit is.) For this game, assume the Ace (value 1) is low. Make sure that the two Cards dealt are not the same Card. For example, a deck cannot contain more than one Queen of Spades.

Up for Discussion

11. In this chapter, you learned that instance data and methods belong to objects (which are class members), but that static data and methods belong to a class as a whole. Consider the real-life class named StateInTheUnitedStates. Name some real-life attributes of this class that are static attributes and instance attributes. Create another example of a real-life class and discuss what its static and instance members might be.

12. Some programmers use a system called Hungarian notation when naming their variables and class fields. What is Hungarian notation and why do many object-oriented programmers feel it is not a valuable style to use?

More Object-Oriented Programming Concepts

In this chapter, you will learn about:

- ◎ Constructors
- ◎ Destructors
- ◎ Composition
- ◎ Inheritance
- ◎ GUI objects
- ◎ Exception handling
- ◎ The advantages of object-oriented programming

An Introduction to Constructors

In object-oriented terminology, "default constructor" means one with no parameters. The constructor that is automatically supplied for a class is a default constructor because it has no parameters, but not all default constructors are supplied automatically.

In Chapter 10 you learned that you can create classes to encapsulate data and methods, and that you can instantiate objects from the classes you define. For example, you can create an `Employee` class that contains fields such as `lastName`, `hourlyWage`, and `weeklyPay`, and methods that set and return values for those fields. When you use a class such as `Employee` to instantiate an object with a statement such as `Employee chauffeur`, you are actually calling a method named `Employee()` that is provided by default by the compiler of the object-oriented (OO) language in which you are working. A constructor method, or more simply, a **constructor**, is a method that establishes an object. A **default constructor** is one that requires no arguments. In OO languages, a default constructor is created automatically by the compiler for every class you write.

When you create a class without writing a constructor, you get access to an automatically supplied one. However, if you write a constructor for any class, whether you write a default (parameterless) constructor or one that requires parameters, you lose the automatically created constructor.

When the prewritten, default constructor for the `Employee` class is called (the constructor is the method named `Employee()`), it establishes one `Employee` object with the identifier provided. Depending on the programming language, a default constructor might provide initial values for the object's data fields; for example, a language might set all numeric fields to zero by default. If you do not want an object's fields to hold these default values, or if you want to perform additional tasks when you create an instance of a class, you can write your own constructor. Any constructor you write must have the same name as the class it constructs, and constructor methods cannot have a return type. Normally, you declare constructors to be public so that other classes can instantiate objects that belong to the class.

For example, if you want every `Employee` object to have a starting hourly wage of $10.00 as well as the correct weekly pay for that wage, then you could write the constructor for the `Employee` class that appears in Figure 11-1. Any `Employee` object instantiated will have an `hourlyWage` field value equal to 10.00, a `weeklyPay` field equal to $400.00, and a `lastName` field equal to the default value for strings in the programming language in which this class is implemented.

```
class Employee
    Declarations
        private string lastName
        private num hourlyWage
        private num weeklyPay

    public Employee()
        hourlyWage = 10.00
        calculateWeeklyPay()
    return

    public void setLastName(string name)
        lastName = name
    return

    public void setHourlyWage(num wage)
        hourlyWage = wage
        calculateWeeklyPay()
    return

    public string getLastName()
    return lastName

    public num getHourlyWage()
    return hourlyWage

    public num getWeeklyPay()
    return weeklyPay

    private void calculateWeeklyPay()
        Declarations
            num WORK_WEEK_HOURS = 40
        weeklyPay = hourlyWage * WORK_WEEK_HOURS
    return
endClass
```

Figure 11-1   Employee class with a default constructor that sets hourlyWage and weeklyPay

The Employee constructor in Figure 11-1 calls the calculateWeeklyPay() method. You can write any statement you want in a constructor; it is just a method. Although you usually have no reason to do so, you could output a message from a constructor, declare local variables, or perform any other task. You can place the constructor anywhere inside the class, outside of any other method. Often, programmers list the constructor first among the methods, because it is the first method used when an object is created.

Figure 11-2 shows a program in which two Employee objects are declared and their hourlyWage values are displayed. In the output in Figure 11-3, you can see that even though the setHourlyWage() method is never used in the program, the Employees possess valid hourly wages as set by their constructors.

```
start
    Declarations
        Employee myPersonalTrainer
        Employee myInteriorDecorator
    output "Trainer's wage: ",
        myPersonalTrainer.getHourlyWage()
    output "Decorator's wage: ",
        myInteriorDecorator.getHourlyWage()
stop
```

Figure 11-2 Program that declares `Employee` objects using class in Figure 11-1

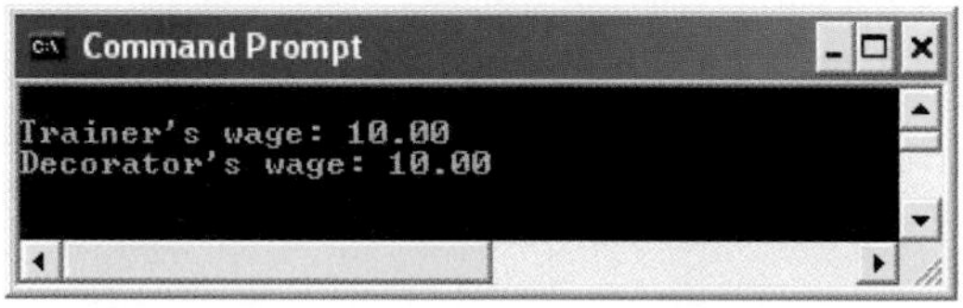

Figure 11-3 Output of program in Figure 11-2

If the `Employee` class contained it, you could use its `setHourlyWage()` method to assign values to individual objects after construction. A constructor assigns its values at the time an object is created.

A potentially superior way to write the `Employee` class constructor that initializes every `Employee`'s `hourlyWage` field to 10.00 is shown in Figure 11-4. In this version of the constructor, a named constant with the value 10.00 is passed to `setHourlyWage()`. Using this technique provides several advantages:

- The statement to call `calculateWeeklyPay()` is no longer required in the constructor because the constructor calls `setHourlyWage()`, which calls `calculateWeeklyPay()`.

- In the future, if restrictions should be imposed on `hourlyWage`, the code will need to be altered in only one location. For example, if `setHourlyWage()` is modified to disallow rates that are too high and too low, the code will change only in the `setHourlyWage()` method and will not have to be modified in the constructor. This reduces the amount of work required and reduces the possibility for error.

```
public Employee()
    Declarations
        num DEFAULT_WAGE = 10.00
    setHourlyWage(DEFAULT_WAGE)
return
```

Figure 11-4 Alternate and efficient version of the `Employee` class constructor

Of course, if different `hourlyWage` requirements are needed at initialization than are required when the value is set after construction, then different code statements will be written in the constructor than those written in the `setHourlyWage()` method.

Constructors with Parameters

Instead of forcing every `Employee` to be constructed with the same initial values, you might choose to create `Employee` objects with values that differ for each employee. For example, to initialize each `Employee` with a unique `hourlyWage`, you can pass a numeric value to the constructor; in other words, you can write constructors that receive arguments. Figure 11-5 shows an `Employee` class constructor that receives an argument. With this constructor, an argument is passed using a statement similar to one of the following:

```
Employee partTimeWorker(8.81)
Employee partTimeWorker(valueEnteredByUser)
```

When the constructor executes, the numeric value within the constructor call is passed to `Employee()`, where the parameter `rate` takes on the value of the argument. The value is assigned to `hourlyWage` within the constructor.

```
public Employee(num rate)
   hourlyWage = rate
   calculateWeeklyPay()
return
```

Figure 11-5   `Employee` constructor that accepts a parameter

When you create an `Employee` class with a constructor such as the one shown in Figure 11-5, then every `Employee` object you create must use a numeric argument. In other words, with this new version of the class, the declaration statement `Employee partTimeWorker` no longer works. Once you write a constructor for a class, you no longer receive the automatically written default constructor. If a class's only constructor requires an argument, you must provide an argument for every object of that class you create.

Overloading Class Methods and Constructors

In Chapter 9, you learned that you can overload methods by writing multiple versions of a method with the same name but different argument lists. In the same way, you can overload instance methods and constructors. For example, Figure 11-6 shows a version of the

Employee class that contains two constructors. One version requires no argument and the other requires a numeric argument.

```
class Employee
    Declarations
        private string lastName
        private num hourlyWage
        private num weeklyPay

    public Employee()
        hourlyWage = 10.00
        calculateWeeklyPay()
    return

    public Employee(num rate)
        hourlyWage = rate
        calculateWeeklyPay()
    return

    public void setLastName(string name)
        lastName = name
    return

    public void setHourlyWage(num wage)
        hourlyWage = wage
        calculateWeeklyPay()
    return

    public string getLastName()
    return lastName

    public num getHourlyWage()
    return hourlyWage

    public num getWeeklyPay()
    return weeklyPay

    private void calculateWeeklyPay()
        Declarations
            num WORK_WEEK_HOURS = 40
        weeklyPay = hourlyWage * WORK_WEEK_HOURS
    return
endClass
```

Recall from Chapter 9 that a method's name and parameter list together are its signature.

Figure 11-6 Employee class with overloaded constructors

When you use Figure 11-6's version of the class, then you can make statements like both of the following:

```
Employee deliveryPerson
Employee myButler(25.85)
```

When you declare an `Employee` using the first statement, an `hourlyWage` of 10.00 is automatically set because the statement uses the parameterless version of the constructor. When you declare an `Employee` using the second statement, `hourlyWage` is set to the passed value. Any method or constructor in a class can be overloaded, and you can provide as many versions as you want. For example, you could add a third constructor to the `Employee` class, as shown in Figure 11-7. This version can coexist with the other two because the parameter list is different from either existing version. With the constructor in Figure 11-7, you can specify the hourly rate for the `Employee` as well as a name. If an application makes a statement similar to the following, then this two-parameter version would execute:

Watch the video *Constructors*.

475

```
Employee myMaid(22.50, "Parker")
```

```
public Employee(num rate, string name)
    lastName = name
    hourlyWage = rate
    calculateWeeklyPay()
return
```

Figure 11-7 A third possible `Employee` class constructor

You might create an `Employee` class with several constructor versions to provide flexibility for client programs. A particular client program might use only one version, and a different client might use another.

TWO TRUTHS & A LIE

An Introduction to Constructors

1. A constructor is a method that establishes an object.

2. A default constructor is defined as one that is created automatically.

3. Depending on the programming language, a default constructor might provide initial values for the object's data fields.

The false statement is #2. A default constructor is one that takes no arguments. Although the automatically created constructor for a class is a default constructor, not all default constructors are created automatically.

Understanding Destructors

The rules for creating and naming destructors vary among programming languages. For example, in Visual Basic classes, the destructor is called `Finalize`.

A **destructor** contains the actions you require when an instance of a class is destroyed. Most often, an instance of a class is destroyed when the object goes out of scope. As with constructors, if you do not explicitly create a destructor for a class, one is provided automatically.

The most common way to declare a destructor explicitly is to use an identifier that consists of a tilde (˜) followed by the class name. You cannot provide any parameters to a destructor; it must have an empty parameter list. As a consequence, destructors cannot be overloaded; a class can have one destructor at most. Like a constructor, a destructor has no return type.

Figure 11-8 shows an `Employee` class that contains only one field (`idNumber`), a constructor, and a shaded destructor. Although it is unusual for a constructor or destructor to output anything, these display messages so that you can see when the objects are created and destroyed. When you execute the program in Figure 11-9, you instantiate two `Employee` objects, each with its own `idNumber` value. When the program ends, the two `Employee` objects go out of scope, and the destructor for each object is called automatically. Figure 11-10 shows the output.

```
class Employee
    Declarations
        private string idNumber
    public Employee(string empID)
        idNumber = empId
        output "Employee ", idNumber, " is created"
    return
    public ~Employee()
        output "Employee ", idNumber, " is destroyed"
    return
endClass
```

Figure 11-8   `Employee` class with destructor

```
start
    Declarations
        Employee aWorker("101")
        Employee anotherWorker("202")
stop
```

Figure 11-9   Program that declares two `Employee` objects

Figure 11-10   Output of program in Figure 11-9

The program in Figure 11-9 never explicitly calls the `Employee` class destructor, yet you can see from the output that the destructor executes twice. Destructors are invoked automatically; you usually do not explicitly call one, although in some languages you can. Interestingly, you can see from the output in Figure 11-10 that the last object created is the first object destroyed; the same relationship would hold true no matter how many objects the program instantiated if the objects went out of scope at the same time.

For now, you have little reason to create a destructor except to demonstrate how it is called automatically. Later, when you write more sophisticated programs that work with files, databases, or large quantities of computer memory, you might want to perform specific clean-up or close-down tasks when an object goes out of scope. Then you will place appropriate instructions within a destructor.

An instance of a class becomes eligible for destruction when it is no longer possible for any code to use it—that is, when it goes out of scope. In many languages, the actual execution of an object's destructor might occur at any time after the object becomes eligible for destruction.

477

TWO TRUTHS & A LIE

Understanding Destructors

1. Unlike with constructors, you must explicitly create a destructor if you want one for a class.

2. You cannot provide any parameters to a destructor; it must have an empty argument list.

3. Destructors cannot be overloaded; a class can have one destructor at most.

The false statement is #1. As with constructors, if you do not explicitly create a destructor for a class, one is provided automatically.

Understanding Composition

A class can contain objects of another class as data members. For example, you might create a class named Date that contains a month, day, and year, and add two Date fields to an Employee class to hold the Employee's birth date and hire date. Then you might create a class named Department that represents every department in a company, and create each Department class member to contain an array of 50 Employee objects. Placing a class object within another class object is known as **composition**. The relationship created is also called a **has-a relationship** because one class "has an" instance of another.

When your classes contain objects that are members of other classes, your programming task becomes increasingly complex. For example, you sometimes must refer to a method by a very long name. Suppose you create a Department class that contains an array of Employee objects (those who work in that department), and a method named getHighestPaidEmployee() that returns a single Employee object. Suppose the Employee class contains a method named getHireDate() that returns a Date object that is an Employee's hire date. Further suppose that the Date class contains a method that returns the year portion of the Date. Then an application might contain a statement such as the following:

```
display salesDepartment.getHighestPaidEmployee().
    getHireDate().getYear()
```

Additionally, when classes contain objects that are members of other classes, all the corresponding constructors and destructors execute in a specific order. As you work with object-oriented programming languages, you will learn to manage these complex issues.

TWO TRUTHS & A LIE

Understanding Composition

1. A class can contain objects of another class as data members.

2. Composition occurs when you use a class object within another class object.

3. Composition is called an is-a relationship because one class "is an" instance of another.

The false statement is #3. Composition is called a has-a relationship because one class "has an" instance of another.

Understanding Inheritance

Understanding classes helps you organize objects in real life. Understanding inheritance helps you organize them more precisely. Inheritance is the principle that you can apply your knowledge of a general category to more specific objects. You are familiar with the concept of inheritance from all sorts of situations. When you use the term *inheritance*, you might think of genetic inheritance. You know from biology that your blood type and eye color are the products of inherited genes.

You might choose to own plants and animals based on their inherited attributes. You plant impatiens next to your house because they thrive in the shade; you adopt a poodle because you know poodles don't shed. Every plant and pet has slightly different character-istics, but within a species, you can count on many consistent inherited attributes and behaviors. In other words, you can reuse the knowledge you gain about general categories and apply it to more specific categories. Similarly, the classes you create in object-oriented programming languages can inherit data and methods from existing classes. When you create a class by making it inherit from another class, you are provided with data fields and methods automatically; you can reuse fields and methods that are already written and tested.

You already know how to create classes and how to instantiate objects that are members of those classes. For example, consider the Employee class in Figure 11-11. The class contains two data fields, empNum and weeklySalary, as well as methods that get and set each field.

```
class Employee
    Declarations
        private string empNum
        private num weeklySalary

    public void setEmpNum(string number)
        empNum = number
    return

    public string getEmpNum()
    return empNum

    public void setWeeklySalary(num salary)
        weeklySalary = salary
    return

    public num getWeeklySalary()
    return weeklySalary
endClass
```

Figure 11-11   An Employee class

Suppose you hire a new type of Employee who earns a commission as well as a weekly salary. You can create a class with a name such as CommissionEmployee, and provide this class with three fields (empNum, weeklySalary, and commissionRate) and six methods (to get and set each of the three fields). However, this work would duplicate much of the work that you have already done for the Employee class. The wise and efficient alternative is to create the class CommissionEmployee so it inherits all the attributes and methods of Employee. Then, you can add just the single field and two methods (the get and set methods for the new field) that are additions within the new class. Figure 11-12 depicts these relationships. The complete CommissionEmployee class is shown in Figure 11-13.

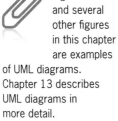

Recall that a plus sign in a class diagram indicates public access and a minus sign indicates private access.

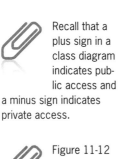

Figure 11-12 and several other figures in this chapter are examples of UML diagrams. Chapter 13 describes UML diagrams in more detail.

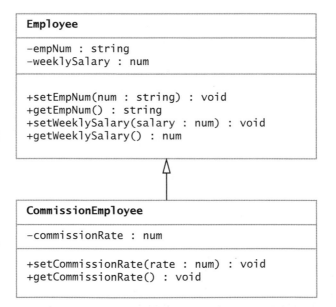

Employee
–empNum : string –weeklySalary : num
+setEmpNum(num : string) : void +getEmpNum() : string +setWeeklySalary(salary : num) : void +getWeeklySalary() : num

CommissionEmployee
–commissionRate : num
+setCommissionRate(rate : num) : void +getCommissionRate() : void

Figure 11-12   CommissionEmployee inherits from Employee

```
class CommissionEmployee inheritsFrom Employee
    Declarations
        private num commissionRate

    public void setCommissionRate(num rate)
        commissionRate = rate
    return

    public num getCommissionRate()
    return commissionRate
endClass
```

Figure 11-13   CommissionEmployee class

The class in Figure 11-13 uses the phrase "inheritsFrom Employee" (see shading) to indicate inheritance. Each programming language uses its own syntax. For example, using Java you would write "extends", in Visual Basic you would write "inherits", and in C++ and C# you would use a colon between the new class name and the one from which it inherits.

When you use inheritance to create the CommissionEmployee class, you acquire the following benefits:

- You save time, because you need not re-create the Employee fields and methods.

- You reduce the chance of errors, because the Employee methods have already been used and tested.

- You make it easier for anyone who has used the Employee class to understand the CommissionEmployee class, because such users can concentrate on the new features only.

- You reduce the chance for errors and inconsistencies in shared fields. For example, if your company decides to change employee ID numbers from four digits to five, and you have code in the Employee class constructor that ensures valid ID numbers, then when you change the code in the Employee class, its descendents automatically acquire the change. Without inheritance, not only would you make the change in many separate places, but the likelihood would increase that you would forget to make the change in one of the classes.

In part, the concept of class inheritance is useful because it makes class code reusable. However, you do not use inheritance simply to save work. When properly used, inheritance always involves a general-to-specific relationship.

The ability to use inheritance makes programs easier to write, easier to understand, and less prone to errors. Imagine that besides CommissionEmployee, you want to create several other more specific Employee classes (perhaps PartTimeEmployee, including a field for hours worked, or DismissedEmployee, including a reason for dismissal). By using inheritance, you can develop each new class correctly and more quickly.

Understanding Inheritance Terminology

A class that is used as a basis for inheritance, like Employee, is called a **base class**. When you create a class that inherits from a base class (such as CommissionEmployee), it is a **derived class** or **extended class**. When presented with two classes that have a base-derived relationship, you can tell which class is the base class and which is the derived class by using the two classes in a sentence with the phrase "is a." A derived class always "is a" case or instance of the more general base class. For example, a Tree class may be a base class to an Evergreen class. Every Evergreen "is a" Tree; however, it is not true that every Tree is an Evergreen. Thus, Tree is the base class and Evergreen is the derived class. Similarly, a CommissionEmployee "is an" Employee—not always the other way around—so Employee is the base class and CommissionEmployee is derived.

It is also convenient to think of a derived class as building upon its base class by providing the "adjectives" or additional descriptive terms for the "noun." Frequently, the names of derived classes are formed in this way, as in CommissionEmployee or EvergreenTree.

Do not think of a subclass as a "subset" of another class—in other words, possessing only parts of its base class. In fact, a derived class usually contains more than its parent.

You can use the terms **superclass** and **subclass** as synonyms for base class and derived class. Thus, Evergreen can be called a subclass of the Tree superclass. You can also use the terms **parent class** and **child class**. A CommissionEmployee is a child to the Employee parent.

As an alternative way to discover which of two classes is the base class and which is the derived class, you can try saying the two class names together (although this technique might not work with every base-subclass pair). When people say their names together in the English language, they state the more specific name before the all-encompassing family name, such as "Mary Johnson." Similarly, with classes, the order that "makes more sense" is the child-parent order. Thus, because "Evergreen Tree" makes more sense than "Tree Evergreen," you can deduce that Evergreen is the child class.

Finally, you usually can distinguish base classes from their derived classes by size. Although it is not required, a derived class is generally larger than its base class, in the sense that it usually has additional fields and methods. A subclass description may look small, but any subclass contains all of its base class's fields and methods as well as its own more specific fields and methods.

A derived class can be further extended. In other words, a subclass can have a child of its own. For example, after you create a Tree class and derive Evergreen, you might derive a Spruce class from Evergreen. Similarly, a Poodle class might derive from Dog, Dog from DomesticPet, and DomesticPet from Animal. The entire list of parent classes from which a child class is derived constitutes the **ancestors** of the subclass.

After you create the Spruce class, you might be ready to create Spruce objects. For example, you might create theTreeInMyBackYard, or you might create an array of 1000 Spruce objects for a tree farm.

A child inherits all the members of all its ancestors. In other words, when you declare a Spruce object, it contains all the attributes and methods of both an Evergreen and a Tree, and a CommissionEmployee contains all the attributes and methods of an Employee. In other words, the members of Employee and CommissionEmployee are as follows:

- Employee contains two fields and four methods, as shown in Figure 11-11.

- CommissionEmployee contains three fields and six methods, even though you do not see all of them in Figure 11-13.

Although a child class contains all the data fields and methods of its parent, a parent class does not gain any child class members. Therefore, when `Employee` and `CommissionEmployee` classes are defined as in Figures 11-11 and 11-13, the statements in Figure 11-14 are all valid in an application. The `salesperson` object can use all the methods of its parent, and it can use its own `setCommissionRate()` and `getCommissionRate()` methods. Figure 11-15 shows the output of the program as it would appear in a command-line environment.

```
start
   Declarations
      Employee manager
      CommissionEmployee salesperson
   manager.setEmpNum("111")
   manager.setWeeklySalary(700.00)
   salesperson.setEmpNum("222")
   salesperson.setWeeklySalary(300.00)
   salesperson.setCommissionRate(0.12)
   output "Manager ", manager.getEmpNum(), manager.getWeeklySalary()
   output "Salesperson ", salesperson.getEmpNum(),
      salesperson.getWeeklySalary(), salesperson.getCommissionRate()
stop
```

Figure 11-14   EmployeeDemo application that declares two Employee objects

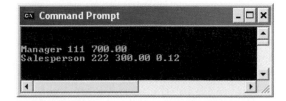

Figure 11-15   Output of the program in Figure 11-14

The following statements would not be allowed in the `EmployeeDemo` application in Figure 11-14 because `manager`, as an `Employee` object, does not have access to the methods of the `CommissionEmployee` child class:

Don't Do It
These base class objects cannot use methods that belong to their class's child.

```
manager.setCommissionRate(0.08)
output manager.getCommissionRate()
```

When you create your own inheritance chains, you want to place fields and methods at their most general level. In other words, a method named `grow()` rightfully belongs in a `Tree` class, whereas `leavesTurnColor()` does not, because the method applies to only some of the `Tree` child classes. Similarly, a `leavesTurnColor()` method would be better located in a `DeciduousTree` class than separately within the `Oak` or `Maple` child classes.

As with subclasses of doctors, it is convenient to think of derived classes as *specialists*. That is, their fields and methods are more specialized than those of the parent class.

In some programming languages, such as C#, Visual Basic, and Java, every class you create is a child of one ultimate base class, often called the `Object` class. The `Object` class usually provides you with some basic functionality that all the classes you create inherit—for example, the ability to show its memory location and name.

It makes sense that a parent class object does not have access to its child's data and methods. When you create the parent class, you do not know how many future child classes might be created, or what their data or methods might look like. In addition, derived classes are more specific. A `Cardiologist` class and an `Obstetrician` class are children of a `Doctor` class. You do not expect all members of the general parent class `Doctor` to have the `Cardiologist`'s `repairHeartValve()` method or the `Obstetrician`'s `performCaesarianSection()` method. However, `Cardiologist` and `Obstetrician` objects have access to the more general `Doctor` methods `takeBloodPressure()` and `billPatients()`.

Accessing Private Members of a Parent Class

In Chapter 10 you learned that when you create classes, the most common scenario is for methods to be public but for data to be private. Making data private is an important object-oriented programming concept. By making data fields private, and allowing access to them only through a class's methods, you protect the ways in which data can be altered and used.

When a data field within a class is private, no outside class can use it—including a child class. The principle of data hiding would be lost if all you had to do to access a class's private data was to create a child class. However, it can be inconvenient when the methods of a child class cannot directly access its own inherited data.

For example, suppose you hire some employees who do not earn a weekly salary as defined in the `Employee` class, but who are paid by the hour. You might create an `HourlyEmployee` class that descends from `Employee`, as shown in Figure 11-16. The class contains two new fields, `hoursWorked` and `hourlyRate`, and a get and set method for each.

```
Employee

-empNum : string
-weeklySalary : num

+setEmpNum(number: string) : void
+getEmpNum() : string
+setWeeklySalary(salary : num) : void
+getWeeklySalary() : num
```

```
HourlyEmployee

-hoursWorked : num
-hourlyRate : num

+setHoursWorked(hours : num) : void
+getHoursWorked() : num
+setHourlyRate(rate : num) : void
+getHourlyRate() : num
```

Figure 11-16 Class diagram for `HourlyEmployee` class

You can implement the new class as shown in Figure 11-17. Whenever you set either `hoursWorked` or `hourlyRate`, you want to modify `weeklySalary` based on the product of the hours and rate. The logic makes sense, but the code does not compile. The two shaded statements show that the `HourlyEmployee` class is attempting to modify the `weeklySalary` field. Although every `HourlyEmployee` *has* a `weeklySalary` field by virtue of being a child of `Employee`, the `HourlyEmployee` class methods do not have access to the `weeklySalary` field, because `weeklySalary` is private within the `Employee` class. In this case, the `weeklySalary` field is **inaccessible** to any class other than the one in which it is defined.

 Watch the video
Inheritance.

486

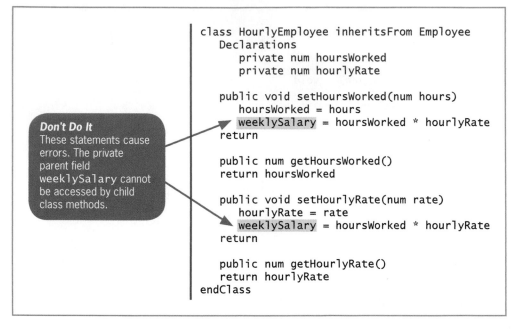

```
                          class HourlyEmployee inheritsFrom Employee
                             Declarations
                                 private num hoursWorked
                                 private num hourlyRate

                             public void setHoursWorked(num hours)
                                 hoursWorked = hours
                                 weeklySalary = hoursWorked * hourlyRate
                             return

                             public num getHoursWorked()
                             return hoursWorked

                             public void setHourlyRate(num rate)
                                 hourlyRate = rate
                                 weeklySalary = hoursWorked * hourlyRate
                             return

                             public num getHourlyRate()
                             return hourlyRate
                          endClass
```

Don't Do It
These statements cause errors. The private parent field weeklySalary cannot be accessed by child class methods.

Figure 11-17   Implementation of HourlyEmployee class that attempts to access weeklySalary

One solution to this dilemma would be to make weeklySalary public in the parent Employee class. Then the child class could use it. However, that action would violate the important object-oriented principle of data hiding. Good object-oriented style dictates that your data should be altered only by the properties and methods you choose and only in ways that you can control. If outside classes could alter an Employee's private fields, then the fields could be assigned values that the Employee class could not control. In such a case, the principle of data hiding would be destroyed, causing the behavior of the object to be unpredictable.

Therefore, OO programming languages allow a medium-security access specifier that is more restrictive than public but less restrictive than private. The **protected access modifier** is used when you want no outside classes to be able to use a data field, except classes that are children of the original class. Figure 11-18 shows a rewritten Employee class that uses the protected access modifier on one of its data fields (see shading). When this modified class is used as a base class for another class such as HourlyEmployee, the child class's methods will be able to access any protected items (fields or methods) originally defined in the parent class. When the Employee class is defined with a protected weeklySalary field, as shown in Figure 11-18, the code in the HourlyEmployee class in Figure 11-17 works correctly.

```
class Employee
    Declarations
        private string empNum
        protected num weeklySalary

    public void setEmpNum(string number)
        empNum = number
    return

    public string getEmpNum()
    return empNum

    public void setWeeklySalary(num salary)
        weeklySalary = salary
    return

    public num getWeeklySalary()
    return weeklySalary
endClass
```

Figure 11-18 Employee class with a protected field

Figure 11-19 contains the class diagram for the version of the Employee class shown in Figure 11-18. Notice the weeklySalary field is preceded with an octothorpe (#)—the character that conventionally is used in class diagrams to indicate protected class members.

Employee
-empNum : string #weeklySalary : num
+setEmpNum(number: string) : void +getEmpNum() : string +setWeeklySalary(salary : num) : void +getWeeklySalary() : num

Figure 11-19 Employee class with protected member

If weeklySalary is defined as protected instead of private in the Employee class, it means either that the creator of the Employee class knew that a child class would want to access the field, or the Employee class was revised after it became known the child class would need access to the field.

If the Employee class's creator did not foresee that a field would need to be accessible, or if it is not preferable to revise the class, then weeklySalary will remain private. It is still possible to correctly set an HourlyEmployee's weekly pay—the HourlyEmployee is just required to use the same means as any other class would. That is, the HourlyEmployee class can use the public method setWeeklySalary()

that already exists in the parent class. Any class, including a child, can use a public member of the base class. So, assuming weeklySalary remains private in Employee, Figure 11-20 shows how HourlyEmployee could be written to correctly set weeklySalary().

```
class HourlyEmployee inheritsFrom Employee
    Declarations
        private num hoursWorked
        private num hourlyRate

    public void setHoursWorked(num hours)
        hoursWorked = hours
        setWeeklySalary(hoursWorked * hourlyRate)
    return

    public num getHoursWorked()
    return hoursWorked

    public void setHourlyRate(num rate)
        hourlyRate = rate
        setWeeklySalary(hoursWorked * hourlyRate)
    return

    public num getHourlyRate()
    return hourlyRate
endClass
```

Figure 11-20   The HourlyEmployee class when weeklySalary remains private

In the version of HourlyEmployee in Figure 11-20, the shaded statements within setHoursWorked() and setHourlyRate() assign a value to the corresponding child class field (hoursWorked or hourlyRate, respectively). Each method then calls the public parent class method setWeeklySalary(). In this example, no **protected** access modifiers are needed for any fields in the parent class, and the creators of the parent class did not have to foresee that a child class would eventually need to access any of its fields. Instead, any child classes of Employee simply follow the same access rules as any other outside class would. As an added benefit, if the parent class method setWeeklySalary() contained additional code (for example, to require a minimum base weekly pay for all employees), then that code would be enforced even for HourlyEmployees.

So, in summary, when a child class must access a private field of its parent's class, you can take one of several approaches:

- You can modify the parent class to make the field public. Usually, this is not advised, because it violates the principle of data hiding.

- You can modify the parent class to make the field protected so that child classes have access to it, but other outside classes do not. This is necessary if no public methods to modify the field are desired within the parent class. You should be aware that some programmers oppose making any data fields nonprivate. They feel that public methods should always control data access, even by a class's children.

- The child class can use a public method within the parent class that modifies the field, just as any other outside class would. This is frequently, but not always, the best option.

Using the protected access modifier for a field can be convenient, and it also improves program performance a little by using a field directly instead of "going through" another method. Also, using the protected access modifier is occasionally necessary when no existing public method accesses a field in a way required by the specifications for the child class. However, protected data members should be used sparingly. Whenever possible, the principle of data hiding should be observed, and even child classes should have to go through methods to "get to" their parent's private data.

The likelihood of future errors increases when child classes are allowed direct access to a parent's fields. For example, if the company decides to add a bonus to every Employee's weekly salary, you might make a change in the setWeeklySalary() method. If a child class is allowed direct access to the Employee field weeklySalary without using the setWeeklySalary() method, then any child class objects will not receive the bonus.

Some OO languages, such as C++, allow a subclass to inherit from more than one parent class. For example, you might create an InsuredItem class that contains data fields pertaining to each possession for which you have insurance (for example, value and purchase date), and an Automobile class that contains data fields pertaining to an automobile (for example, vehicle identification number, make, model, and year). When you create an InsuredAutomobile class for a car rental agency, you might want to include InsuredItem information and methods as well as Automobile information and methods, so you might want to inherit from both. The capability to inherit from more than one class is called **multiple inheritance**.

Classes that depend on field names from parent classes are said to be **fragile** because they are prone to errors—that is, they are easy to "break."

Sometimes, a parent class is so general that you never intend to create any specific instances of the class. For example, you might never create an object that is "just" an Employee; each Employee is more specifically a SalariedEmployee, HourlyEmployee, or ContractEmployee. A class such as Employee that you create only to extend from, but not to instantiate objects from, is an abstract class. An **abstract class** is one from which you cannot create any concrete objects, but from which you can inherit.

Using Inheritance to Achieve Good Software Design

When an automobile company designs a new car model, it does not build every component of the new car from scratch. The company might design a new feature completely from scratch; for example, at some point someone designed the first air bag. However, many of a new car's features are simply modifications of existing features. The manufacturer might create a larger gas tank or more comfortable seats, but even these new features still possess many properties of their predecessors in the older models. Most features of new car models are not even modified; instead, existing components, such as air filters and windshield wipers, are included on the new model without any changes.

Similarly, you can create powerful computer programs more easily if many of their components are used either "as is" or with slight modifications. Inheritance makes your job easier because you don't have to create every part of a new class from scratch. Professional programmers constantly create new class libraries for use with OO languages. Having these classes available to use and extend makes programming large systems more manageable. When you create a useful, extendable superclass, you and other future programmers gain several advantages:

- Subclass creators save development time because much of the code needed for the class has already been written.

- Subclass creators save testing time because the superclass code has already been tested and probably used in a variety of situations. In other words, the superclass code is **reliable**.

- Programmers who create or use new subclasses already understand how the superclass works, so the time it takes to learn the new class features is reduced.

- When you create a new subclass, neither the superclass source code nor the translated superclass code is changed. The superclass maintains its integrity.

When you consider classes, you must think about the commonalities between them, and then you can create superclasses from which to inherit. You might be rewarded professionally when you see your own superclasses extended by others in the future.

TWO TRUTHS & A LIE

Understanding Inheritance

1. When you create a class by making it inherit from another class, you save time, because you need not re-create the base class fields and methods.

2. A class that is used as a basis for inheritance is called a base class, derived class, or extended class.

3. When a data field within a class is private, no outside class can use it—including a child class.

The false statement is #2. A class that is used as a basis for inheritance is called a base class, superclass, or parent class. A derived class is a subclass, extended class, or child class.

One Example of Using Predefined Classes: Creating GUI Objects

When you purchase or download an object-oriented programming language compiler, it comes packaged with many predefined, built-in classes. The classes are stored in **libraries**—collections of classes that serve related purposes. Some of the most useful are the classes you can use to create graphical user interface (GUI) objects such as frames, buttons, labels, and text boxes. You place these GUI components within interactive programs so that users can manipulate them using input devices, most frequently a keyboard and a mouse. For example, if you want to place a clickable button on the screen using a language that supports GUI applications, you instantiate an object that belongs to the already created class named `Button`. In many object-oriented languages, a class with a name similar to `Button` is already created. It contains private data fields such as `text` and `height` and public methods such as `setText()` and `setHeight()` that allow you to place instructions on your `Button` object and to change its vertical size, respectively.

 In some languages, such as Java, libraries are also called **packages**.

If no predefined GUI object classes existed, you could create your own. However, this would present several disadvantages:

- It would be a lot of work. Creating graphical objects requires a substantial amount of code and at least a modicum of artistic talent.

492

- It would be repetitious work. Almost all GUI programs require standard components such as buttons and labels. If each programmer created the classes that represent these components from scratch, much of this work would be repeated unnecessarily.

- The components would look different in various applications. If each programmer created his or her own component classes, objects like buttons would look and operate slightly differently in different applications. Users prefer standardization in their components—title bars on windows that are a uniform height, buttons that appear to be pressed when clicked, frames and windows that contain maximize and minimize buttons in predictable locations, and so on. By using standard component classes, programmers are assured that the GUI components in their programs have the same look and feel as those in other programs.

In programming languages that supply existing GUI classes, you are often provided with a **visual development environment** in which you can create programs by dragging components such as buttons and labels onto a screen and arranging them visually. Then you write programming statements to control the actions that take place when a user manipulates the controls by clicking them using a mouse, for example. Many programmers never create any classes of their own from which they will instantiate objects, but only write classes that are applications that use built-in GUI component classes. Some languages—for example, Visual Basic and C#—lend themselves very well to this type of programming.

 In several languages, the visual development environment is known by the acronym **IDE**, which stands for Integrated Development Environment.

In Chapter 12, you will learn more about creating programs that use GUI objects.

TWO TRUTHS & A LIE

One Example of Using Predefined Classes: Creating GUI Objects

1. Collections of classes that serve related purposes are called annals.

2. GUI components are placed within interactive programs so that users can manipulate them using input devices.

3. By using standard component classes, programmers are assured that the GUI components in their programs have the same look and feel as those in other programs.

The false statement is #1. Libraries are collections of classes that serve related purposes.

Understanding Exception Handling

A great deal of the effort that goes into writing programs involves checking data items to make sure they are valid and reasonable. Professional data-entry operators who create the files used in business computer applications (for example, typing data from phone or mail orders) spend their entire working day entering facts and figures that your applications use; operators can and do make typing errors. When programs depend on data entered by average users who are not trained typists, the likelihood of errors is even greater.

In procedural programs, programmers handled errors in various ways that were effective, but the techniques had some drawbacks. The introduction of object-oriented programming has led to a new model called exception handling.

 Programmers use the phrase *GIGO* to describe what happens when worthless or invalid input causes inaccurate or unrealistic results. GIGO is an acronym for "garbage in, garbage out."

493

Drawbacks to Traditional Error-Handling Techniques

In traditional programming, probably the most often used error-handling outcome was to terminate the program, or at least the method in which the offending statement occurred. For example, suppose a program prompts a user to enter an insurance premium type from the keyboard, and that the entered value should be "A" or "H" for *Auto* or *Health*. Figure 11-21 shows a segment of pseudocode that causes the determinePremium() method to end if policyType is invalid; in the shaded if statement, the method ends abruptly when policyType is not "A" or "H". This method of handling an error is not only unforgiving, it isn't even structured. Recall that a structured method should have one entry and one exit point. The method in Figure 11-21 contains two exit points at the two return statements.

```
public void determinePremium()
    Declarations
        string policyType
        string AUTO = "A"
        string HEALTH = "H"
    output "Please enter policy type "
    input policyType
    if policyType <> AUTO AND policyType not <> HEALTH then
        return
    else
        // Calculations for auto and health premiums go here
    endif
return
```

Don't Do It
A structured method should not have multiple return statements.

Figure 11-21 A method that handles an error in an unstructured manner

In the example in Figure 11-21, if `policyType` is an invalid value, the method in which the code appears is terminated. The client program might continue with an invalid value or it might stop working. If the program that contains this method is part of a business program or a game, the user may be annoyed. However, an early termination in a program that monitors a hospital patient's vital signs or navigates an airplane might cause results that are far more serious.

Rather than ending a method prematurely just because it encounters a piece of invalid data, a more elegant solution involves looping until the data item becomes valid, as shown in the highlighted portion of Figure 11-22. As long as the value of `policyType` is invalid, the user is continuously prompted to enter a new value. Only when `policyType` is "A" or "H" does the method continue.

```
public void determinePremium()
    Declarations
        string policyType
        string AUTO = "A"
        string HEALTH = "H"
    output "Please enter policy type "
    input policyType
    while policyType <> AUTO AND policyType <> HEALTH
        output "You must enter ", AUTO, " or ", HEALTH
        input policyType
    endwhile
    // Calculations for auto and health premiums go here
return
```

Figure 11-22   Method that handles an error using a loop

The error-handling logic shown in Figure 11-22 has at least two shortcomings:

• The method is not as reusable as it could be.

• The method is not as flexible as it might be.

One of the principles of modular and object-oriented programming is reusability. The method in Figure 11-22 is only reusable under limited conditions. The `determinePremium()` method allows the user to reenter policy data any number of times, but other programs in the insurance system may need to limit the number of chances the user gets to enter correct data, or may allow no second chance at all. A more flexible `determinePremium()` method would simply calculate the premium amount without deciding what to do about data errors.

The determinePremium() method will be most flexible if it can detect an error and then notify the calling program or method that an error has occurred. Each client who uses the determinePremium() method then can handle the mistake appropriately for the current application.

The other drawback to forcing the user to reenter data is that the technique works only with interactive programs. A more flexible program accepts any kind of input, including data stored on a disk. Program errors can occur as a result of many factors—for example, a disk drive might not be ready, a file might not exist on the disk, or stored data items might be invalid. You cannot continue to reprompt a disk file for valid data the way you can reprompt a user in an interactive program; if stored data is invalid, it remains invalid.

In the next section you will learn object-oriented exception-handling techniques that overcome the limitations of traditional error handling.

The Object-Oriented Exception Handling Model

Object-oriented programs employ a more specific group of techniques for handling errors called **exception handling**. The techniques check for and manage errors. The generic name used for errors in object-oriented languages is **exceptions** because, presumably, errors are not usual occurrences; they are the "exceptions" to the rule.

In object-oriented terminology, an exception is an object that represents an error. You **try** some code that might **throw an exception**. If an exception is thrown, it is passed to a block of code that can **catch the exception**, which means to receive it in a block that can handle the problem. In some languages, the exception object that is thrown can be any data type—a number, a string, or a programmer-created object. Even when programmers use a language in which any data type can be thrown, most programmers throw an object of the built-in class Exception, or they derive a class from the built-in Exception class. For example, Figure 11-23 shows a determinePremium() method that throws an exception only if policyType is neither "H" nor "A". If policyType is invalid, an object of type Exception named mistake is instantiated and thrown from the method by a throw statement. A **throw statement** is one that sends an Exception object out of the current code block or method so it can be handled elsewhere. If policyType is "H" or "A", the method continues, the premium is calculated, and the method ends naturally.

```
public void determinePremium()
   Declarations
      string policyType
      string AUTO = "A"
      string HEALTH = "H"
   output "Please enter policy type "
   input policyType
   if policyType <> AUTO AND policyType <> HEALTH then
      Declarations
         Exception mistake
      throw mistake
   else
      // Calculations for auto and health premiums go here
   endif
return
```

Figure 11-23 A method that creates and throws an `Exception` object

When you create a segment of code in which something might go wrong, you place the code in a **try block**, which is a block of code you attempt to execute while acknowledging that an exception might occur. A `try` block consists of the keyword `try`, followed by any number of statements, including some that might cause an exception to be thrown. If a statement in the block causes an exception, the remaining statements in the `try` block do not execute and the `try` block is abandoned. For pseudocode purposes, you can end a `try` block with a sentinel such as `endtry`.

You almost always code at least one `catch` block immediately following a `try` block. A **catch block** is a segment of code that can handle an exception that might be thrown by the `try` block that precedes it. Each `catch` block "catches" one type of exception—in many languages the caught object must be of type `Exception` or one of its child classes. You create a `catch` block by typing the following elements:

- The keyword `catch`, followed by parentheses that contain an `Exception` type and an identifier

- Statements that take the action you want to use to handle the error condition

- An `endcatch` statement to indicate the end of the `catch` block in the pseudocode

Figure 11-24 shows a client program that calls the `determinePremium()` method. Because `determinePremium()` has the potential to throw an exception, the call to the method is contained in a `try` block. If `determinePremium()` throws an exception, the `catch` block in the program executes; if all goes well and `determinePremium()` does not throw an exception, the `catch` block is bypassed.

```
start
    try
        perform determinePremium()
    endtry
    catch(Exception mistake)
        output "A mistake occurred"
    endcatch
        // Other statements that would execute whether
        // or not the exception was thrown could go here
    stop
```

A catch block looks a lot like a method named catch() that takes an argument that is some type of Exception. However, it is not a method; it has no return type, and you can't call it directly.

Figure 11-24 A program that contains a try...catch pair

In the program in Figure 11-24, a message is displayed when the exception is thrown. Another application might take different actions. For example, you might write an application in which the catch block forces the policyType to "H" or to "A", or reprompts the user for a valid value. Various programs can use the determinePremium() method and handle any error in the way that is most appropriate for the application.

Some programmers refer to a catch block as a catch clause.

In the method in Figure 11-24, the variable mistake in the catch block is an object of type Exception. The object is not used within the catch block, but it could be. For example, depending on the language, the Exception class might contain a method named getMessage() that returns a string that explains the cause of the error. In that case, you could place a statement such as output mistake.getMessage() in the catch block.

Even when a program uses a method that throws an exception, the exceptions are created and thrown only occasionally, when something goes wrong. Programmers sometimes refer to a situation in which nothing goes wrong as the **sunny day case**.

In the application in Figure 11-24, the try and catch operations reside in the same method. Actually, this is not much different from including an if...else pair to handle the mistake. In reality, trys and their corresponding catches frequently reside in separate methods. This technique increases the client's flexibility in error handling.

The general principle of exception handling in object-oriented programming is that a method that uses data should be able to detect errors, but not be required to handle them. The handling should be left to the application that uses the object, so that each application can use each method appropriately.

Watch the video *Exception Handling.*

Using Built-in Exceptions and Creating Your Own Exceptions

Many (but not all) OO languages provide many built-in `Exception` types. For example, Java, Visual Basic, and C# each provide dozens of categories of `Exceptions` that you can use in your programs. Every object-oriented language has an automatically created exception with a name similar to `ArrayOutOfBoundsException` that is thrown when you attempt to use an invalid subscript with an array. Similarly, an exception with a name like `DivideByZeroException` might be generated automatically if your program attempts the invalid arithmetic action of dividing a number by zero.

Although some actions, such as dividing by zero, are errors in every programming situation, the built-in `Exceptions` in a programming language cannot cover *every* condition that might be an `Exception` in your applications. For example, you might want to declare an `Exception` when your bank balance is negative or when an outside party attempts to access your e-mail account. Most organizations have specific rules for exceptional data; for example, an employee number must not exceed three digits, or an hourly salary must not be less than the legal minimum wage. Of course, you can handle these potential error situations with `if` statements, but you can also create your own `Exceptions`.

Depending on the language you are using, you might be able to extend from other throwable classes as well as `Exception`.

To create your own throwable `Exception`, you usually extend a built-in `Exception` class. For example, you might create a class named `NegativeBankBalanceException` or `EmployeeNumberTooLargeException`. Each would be a subclass of the more general, built-in `Exception` class. By inheriting from the `Exception` class, you gain access to methods contained in the parent class, such as those that display a default message describing the `Exception`.

When you create an `Exception`, it's conventional to end its name with `Exception`, as in `NegativeBankBalanceException`.

In most object-oriented programming languages, a method can throw any number of exceptions. A `catch` block must be available for each type of exception that might be thrown.

TWO TRUTHS & A LIE

Understanding Exception Handling

1. In object-oriented terminology, you try some code that might throw an exception. The exception can then be caught and handled.

2. A catch block is a segment of code that can handle an exception that might be thrown by the try block preceding it.

3. The general principle of exception handling in object-oriented programming is that a method that uses data should be able to detect and handle most common errors.

The false statement is #3. The general principle of exception handling in object-oriented programming is that a method that uses data should be able to detect errors, but not be required to handle them.

Reviewing the Advantages of Object-Oriented Programming

In Chapter 10 and in this chapter, you have been exposed to many concepts related to OO programming. Using the features of object-oriented programming languages provides many benefits as you develop programs. Whether you instantiate objects from classes you have created or from those created by others, you save development time because each object automatically includes appropriate, reliable methods and attributes. When using inheritance, you can develop new classes more quickly by extending classes that already exist and work; you need to concentrate only on new features added by the new class. When using existing objects, you need to concentrate only on the interface to those objects, not on the internal instructions that make them work. By using polymorphism, you can use reasonable, easy-to-remember names for methods and concentrate on their purpose rather than on memorizing different method names.

> **TWO TRUTHS & A LIE**
>
> Reviewing the Advantages of Object-Oriented Programming
>
> 1. When you instantiate objects in programs, you save development time because each object automatically includes appropriate, reliable methods and attributes.
>
> 2. When using inheritance, you can develop new classes more quickly by extending existing classes that already work.
>
> 3. By using polymorphism, you can avoid the strict rules of procedural programming and take advantage of more flexible object-oriented methods.
>
> The false statement is #3. By using polymorphism, you can use reasonable, easy-to-remember names for methods and concentrate on their purpose rather than on memorizing different method names.

Chapter Summary

- A constructor is a method that establishes an object. A default constructor is one that requires no arguments; in OO languages, a default constructor is created automatically by the compiler for every class you write. If you want to perform specific tasks when you create an instance of a class, then you can write your own constructor. Any constructor you write must have the same name as the class it constructs, and constructor methods cannot have a return type. Once you write a constructor for a class, you no longer receive the automatically written default constructor. If a class's only constructor requires an argument, then you must provide an argument for every object of the class that you create.

- A destructor contains the actions you require when an instance of a class is destroyed. Most often, an instance of a class is destroyed when the object goes out of scope. As with constructors, if you do not explicitly create a destructor for a class, one is automatically provided. The most common way to declare a destructor explicitly is to use an identifier that consists of a tilde (˜) followed by the class name. You cannot provide any parameters to a destructor; it must have an empty argument list. As a consequence, destructors cannot be overloaded; a class can have one destructor at most. Like a constructor, a destructor has no return type.

- A class can contain objects of another class as data members. Using a class object within another class object is known as composition.

- Inheritance is the principle that you can apply knowledge of a general category to more specific objects. The classes you create in object-oriented programming languages can inherit data and methods from existing classes. When you create a class by making it inherit from another class, you are provided with data fields and methods automatically; you can reuse fields and methods that are already written and tested. Using inheritance helps you save time, reduces the chance of errors and inconsistencies, and makes it easier for readers to understand your classes. A class that is used as a basis for inheritance is called a base class. A class that inherits from a base class is a derived class or extended class. The terms *superclass* and *parent class* are synonyms for *base class*. The terms *subclass* and *child class* are synonyms for *derived class.*

- Some of the most useful classes packaged in language libraries are those used to create graphical user interface (GUI) objects such as frames, buttons, labels, and text boxes. In programming languages that supply existing GUI classes, a visual development environment is often provided in which you can create programs by dragging components such as buttons and labels onto a screen and arranging them visually.

- Exception-handling techniques are used to handle errors in object-oriented programs. When you try a block of code, you attempt to use it while acknowledging that an exception might occur. If an exception does occur, it is thrown. A catch block of the correct type can receive the exception and handle it. The general principle of exception handling in object-oriented programming is that a method that uses data should be able to detect errors, but not be required to handle them. The handling should be left to the application that uses the object, so that each application can use each method appropriately. Many OO languages provide built-in Exception types. You can also create your own by extending the Exception class.

- When you instantiate objects in programs, you save development time because each object automatically includes appropriate, reliable methods and attributes. You can develop new classes more quickly by extending existing classes that already work, and you can use reasonable, easy-to-remember names for methods.

Key Terms

A **constructor** is an automatically called method that establishes an object.

A **default constructor** is one that requires no arguments.

A **destructor** is an automatically called method that contains the actions you require when an instance of a class is destroyed.

Composition is the technique of placing a class object within another class object.

A **has-a relationship** is the type that exists when using composition.

A **base class** is one that is used as a basis for inheritance.

A **derived class** or **extended class** is one that is extended from a base class.

Superclass and **parent class** are synonyms for *base class*.

Subclass and **child class** are synonyms for *derived class*.

The **ancestors** of a derived class are the entire list of parent classes from which the class is derived.

Inaccessible describes any field or method that cannot be reached because of a logical error.

The **protected access modifier** is used when you want no outside classes to be able to use a data field, except classes that are children of the original class.

Fragile describes classes that depend on field names from parent classes. They are prone to errors—that is, they are easy to "break."

Multiple inheritance is the capability to inherit from more than one class.

An **abstract class** is one from which you cannot create any concrete objects, but from which you can inherit.

Reliable describes code that has already been tested and used in a variety of situations.

Libraries are stored collections of classes that serve related purposes.

Packages are another name for libraries in some languages.

A **visual development environment** is one in which you can create programs by dragging components such as buttons and labels onto a screen and arranging them visually.

IDE is the acronym for Integrated Development Environment, which is the visual development environment in some programming languages.

Exception handling is a set of techniques for handling errors in object-oriented programs.

Exception is the generic term used for an error in object-oriented languages. Presumably, errors are not usual occurrences; they are the "exceptions" to the rule.

In object-oriented terminology, you **try** a method that might throw an exception.

To **throw an exception** is to pass it out of a block where it occurs, usually to a block that can handle it.

To **catch an exception** is to receive it from a throw so it can be handled.

A **throw statement** is one that sends an Exception object out of a method so it can be handled elsewhere.

A **try block** is a block of code you attempt to execute while acknowledging that an exception might occur. A try block consists of the keyword try, followed by any number of statements, including some that might cause an exception to be thrown.

A **catch block** is a segment of code that can handle an exception that might be thrown by the try block that precedes it.

A **sunny day case** is a case in which nothing goes wrong.

Review Questions

1. When you instantiate an object, the automatically created method that is called is a(n) _____.

    a. creator

    b. initiator

    c. constructor

    d. architect

2. Every class has _____.

    a. exactly one constructor

    b. at least one constructor

    c. at least two constructors

    d. a default constructor and a programmer-written constructor

3. Which of the following can be overloaded?

    a.   constructors

    b.   instance methods

    c.   both of these

    d.   none of these

4. A default constructor is _____.

    a.   another name that is used only for a class's automatically created constructor

    b.   a constructor that requires no arguments

    c.   a constructor that sets a value for every field in a class

    d.   the only constructor that is explicitly written in a class

5. When you write a constructor that receives a parameter, _____.

    a.   the parameter must be numeric

    b.   the parameter must be used to set a data field

    c.   the automatically created default constructor no longer exists

    d.   the constructor body must be empty

6. When you write a constructor that receives no parameters, _____.

    a.   the automatically created constructor no longer exists

    b.   it becomes known as the default constructor

    c.   both of the above

    d.   none of the above

7. Most often, a destructor is called when _____.

    a.   an object is created

    b.   an object goes out of scope

    c.   you make an explicit call to it

    d.   a value is returned from a class method

8. Which of the following is not a similarity between constructors and destructors?

    a. Both can be automatically called.

    b. Both have the same name as the class.

    c. Both have no return type.

    d. Both can be overloaded.

9. Advantages of creating a class that inherits from another include all of the following except:

    a. You save time because subclasses are created automatically from those that come built-in as part of a programming language.

    b. You save time because you need not re-create the fields and methods in the original class.

    c. You reduce the chance of errors because the original class's methods have already been used and tested.

    d. You make it easier for anyone who has used the original class to understand the new class.

10. Employing inheritance reduces errors because _____.

    a. the new classes have access to fewer data fields

    b. the new classes have access to fewer methods

    c. you can copy and paste methods that you already created

    d. many of the methods you need have already been used and tested

11. A class that is used as a basis for inheritance is called a _____.

    a. derived class

    b. subclass

    c. child class

    d. base class

12. Which of the following is another name for a derived class?

    a. base class

    b. child class

    c. superclass

    d. parent class

13. Which of the following is *not* another name for a derived class?

    a. extended class

    b. superclass

    c. child class

    d. subclass

14. Which of the following is true?

    a. A base class usually has more fields than its descendent.

    b. A child class can also be a parent class.

    c. A class's ancestors consist of its entire list of children.

    d. To be considered object oriented, a class must have a child.

15. Which of the following is true?

    a. A derived class inherits all the members of its ancestors.

    b. A derived class inherits only the public members of its ancestors.

    c. A derived class inherits only the private members of its ancestors.

    d. A derived class inherits none of the members of its ancestors.

16. Which of the following is true?

    a. A class's data members are usually public.

    b. A class's methods are usually public.

    c. both of the above

    d. none of the above

17. A _____ is a collection of predefined built-in classes that you can use when writing programs.

    a. vault

    b. black box

    c. library

    d. store

18. An environment in which you can develop GUI programs by dragging components to their desired positions is a(n) _____.

    a. visual development environment

    b. integrated compiler

    c. text-based editor

    d. GUI formatter

19. In object-oriented programs, errors are known as _____.

    a. faults

    b. gaffes

    c. exceptions

    d. omissions

20. The general principle of exception handling in object-oriented programming is that a method that uses data should _____.

    a. be able to detect errors, but not be required to handle them

    b. be able to handle errors, but not detect them

    c. be able to handle and detect errors

    d. not be able to detect or handle errors

Exercises

1. Complete the following tasks:

    a. Design a class named Circle with fields named radius, area, and diameter. Include a constructor that sets the radius to 1. Include get methods for each field, but include a set method only for the radius. When the radius is set, do not allow it to be zero or a negative number. When the radius is set, calculate the diameter (twice the radius) and the area (the radius squared times pi, which is approximately 3.14). Create the class diagram and write the pseudocode that defines the class.

    b. Design an application that declares two Circles. Set the radius of one manually, but allow the other to use the default value supplied by the constructor. Then, display each Circle's values.

2. Complete the following tasks:

    a. Design a class named Square with fields that hold the length of a side, the length of the perimeter, and the area. Include a constructor that sets the length of a side to 1. Include get methods for each field, but include a set method only for the length of a side, and do not allow a side to be zero or negative. When the side is set, calculate the perimeter length (four times the side length) and the area (a side squared). Create the class diagram and write the pseudocode that defines the class.

    b. Design an application that declares two Squares. Set the side length of one manually, but allow the other to use the default value supplied by the constructor. Then, display each Square's values.

    c. Create a child class named Cube. Cube contains an additional data field named depth, and a computeSurfaceArea() method that overrides the parent method appropriately for a cube.

    d. Create the logic for an application that instantiates a Square object and a Cube object and displays the surface areas of both objects.

3. Complete the following tasks:

    a. Design a class named GirlScout with fields that hold a name, troop number, and dues owed. Include get and set methods for each field. Include a static method that displays the Girl Scout motto ("To obey the Girl Scout law"). Include three overloaded constructors as follows:

- A default constructor that sets the name to "XXX" and the numeric fields to 0

- A constructor that allows you to pass values for all three fields

- A constructor that allows you to pass a name and troop number but sets dues owed to 0

Create the class diagram and write the pseudocode that defines the class.

b. Design an application that declares three GirlScout objects using a different constructor version with each object. Display each GirlScout's values. Then display the motto.

4. Complete the following tasks:

a. Create a class named Commission that includes two numeric variables: a sales figure and a commission rate. Also create two overloaded methods named computeCommission(). The first method takes two numeric arguments representing sales and rate, multiplies them, and then displays the results. The second method takes a single argument representing sales. When this method is called, the commission rate is assumed to be 7.5 percent and the results are displayed.

b. Create an application that demonstrates how both method versions can be called.

5. Complete the following tasks:

a. Create a class named Pay that includes five numeric variables: hours worked, hourly pay rate, withholding rate, gross pay, and net pay. Also create three overloaded computeNetPay() methods. When computeNetPay() receives values for hours, pay rate, and withholding rate, it computes the gross pay and reduces it by the appropriate withholding amount to produce the net pay. (Gross pay is computed as hours worked multiplied by hourly pay rate.) When computeNetPay() receives two arguments, they represent the hours and pay rate, and the withholding rate is assumed to be 15 percent. When computeNetPay() receives one argument, it represents the number of hours worked, the withholding rate is assumed to be 15 percent, and the hourly rate is assumed to be 6.50.

b. Create an application that demonstrates all the methods.

6. Complete the following tasks:

   a. Design a class named Book that holds a stock number, author, title, price, and number of pages for a book. Include methods to set and get the values for each data field. Also include a displayInfo() method that displays each of the Book's data fields with explanations.

   b. Design a class named TextBook that is a child class of Book. Include a new data field for the grade level of the book. Override the Book class displayInfo() method so that you accommodate the new grade-level field.

   c. Design an application that instantiates an object of each type and demonstrates all the methods.

7. Complete the following tasks:

   a. Design a class named Player that holds a player number and name for a sports team participant. Include methods to set the values for each data field and output the values for each data field.

   b. Design two classes named BaseballPlayer and BasketballPlayer that are child classes of Player. Include a new data field in each class for the player's position. Include an additional field in the BaseballPlayer class for batting average. Include a new field in the BasketballPlayer class for free-throw percentage. Override the Player class methods that set and output the data so that you accommodate the new fields.

   c. Design an application that instantiates an object of each type and demonstrates all the methods.

8. Complete the following tasks:

   a. Create a class named Tape that includes fields for length and width in inches, and create get and set methods for each field.

   b. Derive two subclasses—VideoCassetteTape and AdhesiveTape. The VideoCassetteTape class includes a numeric field to hold playing time in minutes and get and set methods for the field. The AdhesiveTape class includes a numeric field that holds a stickiness factor—a value from 1 to 10—and get and set methods for the field.

   c. Design a program that instantiates one object of each of the three classes, and demonstrate using all the methods defined for each class.

9. Complete the following tasks:

   a. Create a class named Order that performs order processing of a single item. The class has four fields: customer
   name, customer number, quantity ordered, and unit
   price. Include set and get methods for each field. The set
   methods prompt the user for values for each field. This
   class also needs a computePrice() method to compute
   the total price (quantity multiplied by unit price) and a
   method to display the field values.

   b. Create a subclass named ShippedOrder that overrides
   computePrice() by adding a shipping and handling
   charge of $4.00.

   c. Create the logic for an application that instantiates an
   object of each of these two classes. Prompt the user for
   data for the Order object and display the results; then
   prompt the user for data for the ShippedOrder object and
   display the results.

   d. Create the logic for an application that continuously
   prompts a user for order information until the user
   enters "ZZZ" for the customer name or 10 orders have
   been taken, whichever comes first. Ask the user whether
   each order will be shipped, and create an Order or a
   ShippedOrder appropriately. Store each order in an array.
   When the user is done entering data, display all the order
   information taken as well as the total price that was
   computed for each order.

10. Complete the following tasks:

   a. Design a method that calculates the cost of a painting job
   for College Student Painters. Variables include whether
   the job is location "I" for interior, which costs $100, or "E"
   for exterior, which costs $200. The method should throw
   an exception if the location code is invalid.

   b. Write a method that calls the method designed in
   Exercise 10a. If the method throws an exception, force
   the price of the job to 0.

   c. Write a method that calls the method designed in
   Exercise 10a. If the method throws an exception, require
   the user to reenter the location code.

   d. Write a method that calls the method designed in
   Exercise 10a. If the method throws an exception, force
   the location code to "E" and the price to $200.

11. Complete the following tasks:

a. Design a method that calculates the cost of a semester's tuition for a college student at Mid-State University. Variables include whether the student is an in-state resident ("I" for in-state or "O" for out-of-state) and the number of credit hours for which the student is enrolling. The method should throw an exception if the residency code is invalid. Tuition is $75 per credit hour for in-state students and $125 per credit hour for out-of-state students. If a student enrolls in six hours or fewer, there is an additional $100 surcharge. Any student enrolled in 19 hours or more pays only the rate for 18 credit hours.

b. Write a method that calls the method designed in Exercise 11a. If the method throws an exception, force the tuition to 0.

Find the Bugs

12. Your student disk contains files named DEBUG11-01.txt, DEBUG11-02.txt, and DEBUG11-03.txt. Each file starts with some comments that describe the problem. Comments are lines that begin with two slashes (//). Following the comments, each file contains pseudocode that has one or more bugs you must find and correct.

Game Zone

13. a. Computer games often contain different characters or creatures. For example, you might design a game in which alien beings possess specific characteristics such as color, number of eyes, or number of lives. Create an Alien class. Include at least three data members of your choice. Include a constructor that requires a value for each data field and a method named toString() that returns a string that contains a complete description of the Alien.

b. Create two classes—Martian and Jupiterian—that descend from Alien. Supply each with a constructor that sets the Alien data fields with values you choose. For example, you can decide that a Martian has four eyes but a Jupiterian has only two.

c. Create an application that instantiates one Martian and one Jupiterian. Call the toString() method with each object and display the results.

14. In Chapter 2, you learned that in many programming languages you can generate a random number between 1 and a limiting value named `LIMIT` by using a statement similar to `randomNumber = random(LIMIT)`. In Chapters 4 and 5, you created and fine-tuned the logic for a guessing game in which the application generates a random number and the player tries to guess it. As written, the game should work as long as the player enters numeric guesses. However, if the player enters a letter or other non-numeric character, the game throws an automatically generated exception. Improve the game by handling any exception so that the user is informed of the error and allowed to attempt correct data entry again.

15. a. In Chapter 10, you developed a `Card` class that contains a string data field to hold a suit and a numeric data field for a value from 1 to 13. Now extend the class to create a class called `BlackjackCard`. In the game of Blackjack, each card has a point value as well as a face value. These two values match for cards with values of 2 through 10, and the point value is 10 for Jacks, Queens, and Kings (face values 11 through 13). For a simplified version of the game, assume that the value of the Ace is 11. (In the official version of Blackjack, the player chooses whether each Ace is worth 1 or 11 points.)

    b. Randomly assign values to 10 `BlackjackCard` objects, then design an application that plays a modified version of Blackjack. In this version, the objective is to accumulate cards whose total value equals 21, or whose value is closer to 21 than the opponent's total value without exceeding 21. Deal five `BlackjackCards` each to the player and the computer. Make sure that each `BlackjackCard` is unique. For example, a deck cannot contain more than one Queen of Spades.

        Determine the winner as follows:

        • If the player's first two, first three, first four, or all five cards have a total value of exactly 21, the player wins, even if the computer also achieves a total of 21.

        • If the player's first two cards do not total exactly 21, sum as many as needed to achieve the highest possible total that does not exceed 21. For example, suppose the player's five cards are valued as follows: 10, 4, 5, 9, 2. In that case, the player's total for the first three cards is 19; counting any more cards would cause the total to exceed 21.

514

- After you have determined the player's total, sum the computer's cards in sequence. For example, suppose the computer's cards are 10, 10, 5, 6, 7. The first two cards total 20; you would not use the third card because it would cause the total to exceed 21.

- The winner has the highest total among the cards used. For example, if the player's total using the first three cards is 19 and the computer's total using the first two cards is 20, the computer wins.

Display a message that indicates whether the game ended in a tie, the computer won, or the player won.

Up for Discussion

16. Many programmers think object-oriented programming is a superior approach to procedural programming. Others think it adds a level of complexity that is not needed in many scenarios. Find and summarize arguments on both sides. With which side do you agree?

17. Many object-oriented programmers are opposed to using multiple inheritance. Find out why and decide whether you agree with this stance.

18. If you are completing all the programming exercises in this book, you can see how much work goes into planning a full-blown professional program. How would you feel if someone copied your work without compensating you? Investigate the magnitude of software piracy in our society. What are the penalties for illegally copying software? Are there circumstances under which it is acceptable to copy a program? If a friend asked you to make a copy of a program for him, would you? What do you suggest we do about this problem, if anything?

Event-Driven GUI Programming, Multithreading, and Animation

In this chapter, you will learn about:

◎ The principles of event-driven programming

◎ The actions that GUI components can initiate

◎ Designing graphical user interfaces

◎ The steps to developing an event-driven application

◎ Multithreading

◎ Creating animation

Understanding Event-Driven Programming

From the 1950s, when businesses began to use computers to help them perform many jobs, through the 1970s, almost all interactive dialogues between people and computers took place at the command prompt (or on the command line). In Chapter 1 you learned that the command line is the location on your computer screen at which you type entries to communicate with the computer's **operating system**—the software that you use to run a computer and manage its resources. In the early days of computing, interacting with a computer operating system was difficult because the user had to know the exact syntax to use when typing commands, and had to spell and type those commands accurately. (Syntax is the correct sequence of words and symbols that form the operating system's command set.) Figure 12-1 shows a command in the Windows operating system.

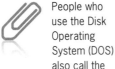

People who use the Disk Operating System (DOS) also call the command line the **DOS prompt**.

Figure 12-1   Command prompt screen

If you use the Windows operating system on a PC, you can locate the command prompt by clicking Start, and pointing to the command prompt window shortcut on the Start menu. Alternatively, you can point to All Programs in Vista or Windows XP (or Programs in some earlier operating systems), then Accessories, and then click Command Prompt.

Although you frequently use the command line to communicate with the operating system, you also sometimes communicate with software through the command line. For example, when you issue a command to execute some applications, you can include data values that the program uses.

Fortunately for today's computer users, operating system software allows them to use a mouse or other pointing device to select pictures, or **icons**, on the screen. As you learned in Chapter 1, this type of environment is a graphical user interface, or GUI. Computer users can expect to see a standard interface in the GUI programs they use. Rather than memorizing difficult commands that must be typed at a command line, GUI users can select options from menus and click buttons to make their preferences known to a program. Users can select objects that look like their real-world counterparts and get the expected results. For example, users may select an icon that looks like a pencil when they want to write a memo, or they may drag an icon shaped like a folder to another icon that resembles a recycling bin when they want to delete a file. Figure 12-2 shows a Windows program named Paint in which icons representing pencils, paint cans, and so on appear on clickable buttons. Performing an operation on an icon (for example, clicking or dragging it) causes an **event**—an occurrence that generates a message sent to an object.

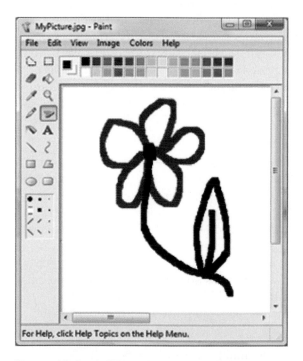

Figure 12-2   A GUI application that contains buttons and icons

GUI programs are frequently called **event-driven** or **event-based** because actions occur in response to user-initiated events such as clicking a mouse button. When you program with event-driven languages, the emphasis is on the objects that the user can manipulate, such as text boxes, buttons, and menus, and on the events that the user can initiate with those objects, such as typing, pointing, clicking, or double-clicking. The programmer writes instructions within modules that execute each type of event.

For the programmer, event-driven programs require unique considerations. The program logic you have developed within many of the methods of this book is procedural; each step occurs in the order the programmer determines. In a procedural application, if you write statements that display a prompt and accept a user's response, the processing goes no further until the input is completed. When you write a procedural program and call moduleA() before calling moduleB(), you have complete control over the order in which all the statements will execute. In contrast, with most event-driven programs, the user might initiate any number of events in any order. For example, when you use an event-driven word-processing program, you have dozens of choices at your disposal at any moment. You can type words, select text with the mouse, click a button to change text to bold or italics, choose a menu item such as Save or Print, and so on. With each word-processing document you create, you choose options in any order that seems appropriate at the time. The word-processing program must be ready to respond to any event you initiate. The programmers who created the word-processing program are not guaranteed that you will always select Bold before you select Italics, or that you will always select Save before you select Quit, so they must write programs that are more flexible than their procedural counterparts.

You first learned the term *procedural programming* in Chapter 1.

When an object should listen for events, you must write two types of statements. You write the statement or statements that define the object as a listener, and you write the statements that constitute the event.

Within an event-driven program, a component from which an event is generated is the **source of the event**. A button that a user can click to cause some action is an example of a source; a text box that one can use to enter typed characters is another source. An object that is "interested in" an event to which you want it to respond is a **listener**. It "listens for" events so it knows when to respond. Not all objects can receive all events—you probably have used programs in which clicking many areas of the screen has no effect at all. In the programs you write, if you want an object such as a button to be a listener for an event such as a mouse click, you must write the appropriate program statements.

In object-oriented languages, the procedural modules that depend on user-initiated events are often called *scripts*.

Although event-driven programming is relatively new, the instructions that programmers write to respond to events are still simply sequences, selections, and loops. Event-driven programs still have methods that declare variables, use arrays, and contain all the attributes of their procedural-program ancestors. The user's screen in an event-driven program might contain buttons or check boxes with labels like "Sort Records," "Merge Files," or "Total Transactions," but each of these processes uses the same kind of programming logic you have learned throughout this book for programs that did not have a graphical interface. Writing event-driven programs involves thinking of possible events as the modules that constitute the programs and writing the statements that link user selections to those modules.

TWO TRUTHS & A LIE

Understanding Event-Driven Programming

1. GUI programs are called event-driven or event-based because actions occur in response to user-initiated events such as clicking a mouse button.

2. With event-driven programs, the user might initiate any number of events in any order.

3. Within an event-driven program, a component from which an event is generated, such as a button, is a listener, and an object that is "interested in" an event is the source of the event.

The false statement is # 3. Within an event-driven program, a component from which an event is generated is the source of the event, and an object that is "interested in" an event to which you want it to respond is a listener.

User-Initiated Actions and GUI Components

To understand GUI programming, you need to have a clear picture of the possible events a user can initiate. These include the events listed in Table 12-1.

Event	Description of User's Action
Key press	Pressing a key on the keyboard
Mouse point or mouse over	Placing the mouse pointer over an area on the screen
Mouse click or left mouse click	Pressing the left mouse button
Right mouse click	Pressing the right mouse button
Mouse double-click	Pressing the left mouse button two times in rapid sequence
Mouse drag	Holding down the left mouse button while moving the mouse over the desk surface

Table 12-1　Common user-initiated events

 Most languages allow you to distinguish between many additional events. For example, you might be able to initiate different events when a keyboard key or a mouse key is pressed, while it is held down, and when it is released.

You also need to be able to picture common GUI components. Table 12-2 describes some common GUI components, and Figure 12-3 shows how they look on a screen.

Component	Description
Label	A rectangular area that displays text
Text box	A rectangular area into which the user can type text
Check box	A label placed beside a small square; you can click the square to display or remove a check mark; this component allows the user to select or deselect an option
Option buttons	A group of options that are similar to check boxes, but that are mutually exclusive. When the options are square, they are often called a check box group. When they are round, they are often called radio buttons.
List box	When the user clicks a list box, a menu of items appears. Depending on the options the programmer sets, you might be able to make only one selection, or you might be able to make multiple selections.
Button	A rectangular object you can click; when you do, its appearance usually changes to look pressed.

Table 12-2 Common GUI components

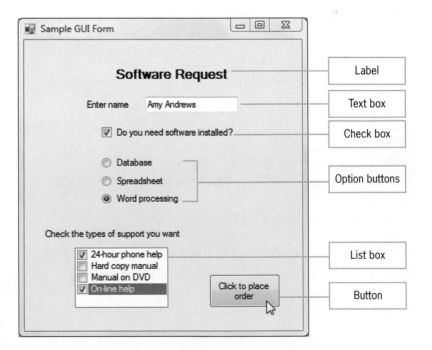

Figure 12-3 Common GUI components

When you program in a language that supports event-driven logic, you do not create the GUI components you need from scratch. Instead, you call prewritten methods that draw the GUI components on the screen for you. The components themselves are constructed using existing classes complete with names, attributes, and methods. In some programming languages, you can work in a text environment and write statements that instantiate GUI objects. In other languages, you can work in a graphical environment, drag GUI objects onto your screen from a toolbox, and arrange them appropriately for your application. Some languages offer both options. Either way, you do not think about the details of constructing the components. Instead, you concentrate on the actions that you want to take place when a user initiates an event from one of the components. Thus, GUI components are excellent examples of the best principles of object-oriented programming (OOP)—they represent objects with attributes and methods that operate like black boxes, making them easy for you to use.

When you use already created GUI components, you are instantiating objects, each of which belongs to a prewritten class. For example, you might use a `Button` object when you want the user to be able to click a button to make a selection. Depending on the programming language you use, the `Button` class might contain attributes or properties such as the text written on the `Button` and the position of the `Button` on the screen. The class might also contain methods such as `setText()` and `setPosition()`. For example, Figure 12-4 shows how a built-in `Button` class might have been written.

Although in many languages you can place square option buttons in a group and force them to be mutually exclusive, users conventionally expect a group of mutually exclusive buttons to appear as round radio buttons.

521

GUI components are often referred to as *widgets*, which some sources claim is a combination of the terms *window* and *gadgets*. Originally, "widget" comes from the 1924 play "Beggar on Horseback," by George Kaufman and Marc Connelly. In the play, a young composer gets engaged to the daughter of a rich businessman, and foresees spending his life doing pointless work in a bureaucratic big business that manufactures widgets, items whose purpose is never explained.

Watch the video *GUI Components*.

```
class Button
    Declarations
        private string text
        private num x_position
        private num y_position

    public void setText(string messageOnButton)
        text = messageOnButton
    return

    public void setPosition(num x, num y)
        x_position = x
        y_position = y
    return
endClass
```

Figure 12-4   `Button` class

The x_position and y_position of the Button object defined in Figure 12-4 refer to horizontal and vertical coordinates where the Button appears on an object, such as a window that appears on the screen during program execution. A **pixel** is one of the tiny dots of light that form a grid on your screen. The term *pixel* derives from combining the first syllables of *picture* and *element*. You will use x- and y-positions again when you learn about animation later in this chapter.

An important advantage of using GUI data-entry objects is that you can often control much of what a user enters by limiting the user's options. When you provide a user with a finite set of buttons to click, or a limited number of menu items from which to choose, the user cannot make unexpected, illegal, or bizarre choices. For example, if you provide only two buttons so the user must click "Yes" or "No", you can eliminate writing code for invalid entries.

The Button class shown in Figure 12-4 is an abbreviated version so you can easily see its similarity to a class such as Employee, which you read about in Chapter 11. The figure shows three fields and two set methods. A working Button class in most programming languages would contain many more fields and methods. For example, a full-blown class might also contain get methods for the text and position, and other fields and methods to manipulate a Button's font, color, size, and so on.

To create a Button object in a client program, you would write a statement similar to the following:

```
Button myProgramButton
```

In this statement, Button is the type and myProgramButton is the name of the object you create. To use a Button's methods, you would write statements such as the following:

```
myProgramButton.setText("Click here")
myProgramButton.setPosition(10, 30)
```

Different GUI classes support different attributes and methods. For example, a CheckBox class might contain a method named getCheckedStatus() that returns true or false, indicating whether the CheckBox object has been checked. A Button, however, would have no need for such a method.

TWO TRUTHS & A LIE

User-Initiated Actions and GUI Components

1. In a GUI program, a key press is a common user-initiated event and a check box is a typical GUI component.

2. When you program in a language that supports event-driven logic, you call prewritten methods that draw the GUI components on the screen for you.

3. An advantage of using GUI objects is that each class you use to create the objects supports identical methods and attributes.

The false statement is # 3. Different GUI classes support different attributes and methods.

Designing Graphical User Interfaces

You should consider several general design principles when creating a program that will use a GUI:

- The interface should be natural and predictable.

- The interface should be attractive, easy to read, and nondistracting.

- To some extent, it's helpful if the user can customize your applications.

- The program should be forgiving.

- The GUI is only a means to an end.

The Interface Should Be Natural and Predictable

The GUI program interface should represent objects like their real-world counterparts. In other words, it makes sense to use an icon that looks like a recycling bin when you want to allow a user to drag files or other components to the bin to delete them. Using a recycling bin icon is a "natural" concept in that people use one in real life when they want to discard actual items; dragging files to the bin is a "natural" event because that's what people do with real-life items they discard. Using a recycling bin for discarded items is also predictable, because users are already familiar with the icon in other programs. Some icons may be natural in terms of meaning, but if they are not predictable as well, then they are not as effective. An icon that depicts a recycling truck is just as "natural" as far as corresponding to real-world recycling, but because other programs do not use a truck icon for this purpose, it is not as predictable.

GUIs should also be predictable in their layout. For example, when a user must enter personal information in text boxes, the street address is expected to come before the city and state. Also, when you use a menu bar, it is at the top of the screen in most GUI programs, and the first menu item is almost always *File*. If you design a program interface in which the menu runs vertically down the right side of the screen, or in which *File* is the last menu option instead of the first, you will confuse users. Either they will make mistakes when using your program, or they may give up using it entirely. It doesn't matter if you can prove that your layout plan is more efficient than the standard one—if you do not use a predictable layout, your program will meet rejection from users in the marketplace.

Many studies have proven that the Dvorak keyboard layout is more efficient for typists than the QWERTY keyboard layout that most of us use. The QWERTY keyboard layout gets its name from the first six letter keys in the top row. With the Dvorak layout, which gets its name from its inventor, the most frequently used keys are in the home row, allowing typists to complete many more keystrokes per minute. However, the Dvorak keyboard has not caught on with the computer-buying public because it is not predictable to users who have already learned the QWERTY keyboard.

Stovetops in kitchens often have an unnatural interface, making unfamiliar stoves more difficult for you to use. Most stovetops have four burners arranged in two rows, but the knobs that control the burners frequently sit in a single horizontal row. Because there is not a natural correlation between the placement of a burner and its control, you are more likely to select the wrong knob when adjusting the burner's flame or heating element.

An excellent way to learn about good GUI design is to pay attention to the design features used in popular applications and in Web sites you visit. Notice that the designs you like to use feel more "natural."

Dimming a component is also called *graying* the component. Dimming a component provides another example of predictability—users with computer experience do not expect to be able to use a dimmed component.

GUI programmers sometimes refer to screen space as *real estate*. Just as a plot of real estate becomes unattractive when it supports no open space, your screen becomes unattractive when you fill the limited space with too many components.

The Interface Should Be Attractive, Easy to Read, and Nondistracting

If your interface is attractive, people are more likely to use it. If it is easy to read, they are less likely to make mistakes, more likely to want to use it, and more likely to consider it attractive. When it comes to GUI design, fancy fonts and weird color combinations are the signs of amateur designers. In addition, you should make sure that unavailable screen options are either sufficiently dimmed or removed, so the user does not waste time clicking components that aren't functional.

Screen designs should not be distracting. When a screen has too many components, users can't find what they're looking for. When a component is no longer needed, it should be removed from the interface. You also want to avoid distracting users with overly creative design elements. When users click a button to open a file, they might be amused the first time a filename dances across the screen or the speakers play a tune. But after one or two experiences with your creative additions, users find that intruding design elements hamper the actual work of the program.

To Some Extent, It's Helpful If the User Can Customize Your Applications

Every user works in his or her own way. If you are designing an application that will use numerous menus and toolbars, it's helpful if users can position the components in the order with which it's easiest for them to work. Users often appreciate being able to change features like color schemes. Allowing a user to change the background color in your application may seem frivolous to you, but to users who are color-blind or visually impaired, it might make the difference in whether they use your application at all. The screen design issues that make programs easier to use for people with physical limitations are known as **accessibility** issues.

The Program Should Be Forgiving

Perhaps you have had the inconvenience of accessing a voice mail system in which you selected several sequential options, only to find yourself at a dead end with no recourse but to hang up and redial the number. Good program design avoids similar problems. You should always provide an escape route to accommodate users who make bad choices or change their minds. By providing a Back button or functional Escape key, you provide more functionality to your users.

The GUI Is Only a Means to an End

The most important principle of GUI design is to remember always that any GUI is only an interface. Using a mouse to click items and drag them around is not the point of any business program except those that train people how to use a mouse. Instead, the point of a graphical interface is to help people be more productive. To that end, the design should help the user see what options are available, allow the use of components in the ordinary way, and not force the user to concentrate on how to interact with your application. The real work of any GUI program is done after the user clicks a button or makes a list box selection. Then, actual program tasks take place.

Many programs are used internationally. If you can allow the user to work in a choice of languages, you might be able to market your program more successfully in other countries.

It can be helpful if you provide an option for the user to revert to the default settings after making changes. Some users might be afraid to alter an application's features if they are not sure they can easily return to the original settings.

TWO TRUTHS & A LIE

Designing Graphical User Interfaces

1. In order to keep the user's attention, a well-designed GUI interface should contain unique and creative controls.

2. In order to be most useful to users, a GUI interface should be attractive, easy to read, and nondistracting.

3. To avoid frustrating users, a well-designed program should be forgiving.

The false statement is #1. A GUI interface should be natural and predictable.

The Steps to Developing an Event-Driven Application

In Chapter 1, you first learned the steps to developing a computer program. They are:

1. Understanding the problem.

2. Planning the logic.

3. Coding the program.

4. Translating the program into machine language.

5. Testing the program.

6. Putting the program into production.

7. Maintaining the program.

When you develop an event-driven application, you expand on Step 2, planning the logic, and include three new substeps as follows:

2a. Creating storyboards.

2b. Defining the objects.

2c. Defining the connections between the screens the user will see.

For example, suppose you want to create a simple, interactive program that determines premiums for prospective insurance customers. They should be able to use a graphical interface to select a policy type—health or auto. Next, users answer pertinent questions about their age, driving record, and whether they smoke. Although most insurance premium amounts would be based on more characteristics than these, assume that policy rates are determined using the factors shown in Table 12-3. The final output of the program is a second screen that shows the semiannual premium amount for the chosen policy.

Health Policy Premiums	Auto Policy Premiums
Base rate: $500	Base rate: $750
Add $100 if over age 50	Add $400 if more than 2 tickets
Add $250 if smoker	Subtract $200 if over age 50

Table 12-3   Insurance premiums based on customer characteristics

Creating Storyboards

A **storyboard** represents a picture or sketch of a screen the user will see when running a program. Filmmakers have long used storyboards to illustrate key moments in the plots they are developing; similarly, GUI storyboards represent "snapshot" views of the screens the user will encounter during the run of a program. If the user could view up to four screens during the insurance premium program, then you would draw four storyboard cells, or frames.

Figure 12-5 shows two storyboard sketches for the insurance program. They represent the introductory screen at which the user selects a premium type and answers questions, and the final screen that displays the semiannual premium.

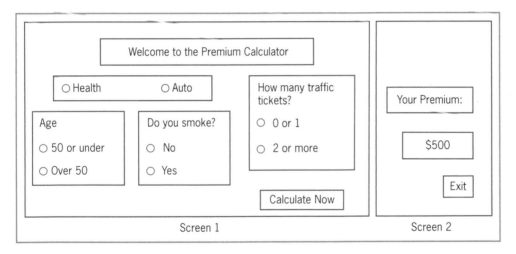

Figure 12-5   Storyboard for insurance program

Defining the Storyboard's Objects in an Object Dictionary

An event-driven program may contain dozens or even hundreds of objects. To keep track of them, programmers often use an object dictionary. An **object dictionary** is a list of the objects used in a program, including which screens they are used on and whether any code, or script, is associated with them.

Figure 12-6 shows an object dictionary for the insurance premium program. The type and name of each object to be placed on a screen is listed in the two left columns. The third column shows the screen number on which the object appears. The next column names any variables that are affected by an action on the object. The right column indicates whether any code or script is associated with the object. For example, the label named welcomeLabel appears on the first screen. It has no associated actions—it does not call any methods or change any variables; it is just a label. The calcButton, however, does cause execution of a method named calcRoutine(). This method calculates the semiannual premium amount and stores it in the premiumAmount variable. Depending on the programming language you use, you might need to name calcRoutine() something similar to calcButton.click(). In languages that use this format, a standard method named click() holds the statements that execute when the user clicks the calcButton.

528

Some organizations also include the disk location where an object is stored as part of the object dictionary.

Object Type	Name	Screen Number	Variables Affected	Script?
Label	welcomeLabel	1	none	none
RadioButton	healthRadioButton	1	premiumAmount	none
RadioButton	autoRadioButton	1	premiumAmount	none
Label	ageLabel	1	none	none
RadioButton	lowAgeRadioButton	1	premiumAmount	none
RadioButton	highAgeRadioButton	1	premiumAmount	none
Label	smokeLabel	1	none	none
RadioButton	smokeNoRadioButton	1	premiumAmount	none
RadioButton	smokeYesRadioButton	1	premiumAmount	none
Label	ticketsLabel	1	none	none
RadioButton	lowTicketsRadioButton	1	premiumAmount	none
RadioButton	highTicketsRadioButton	1	premiumAmount	none
Button	calcButton	1	premiumAmount	calcRoutine()
Label	premiumLabel	2	none	none
Label	premAmtLabel	2	none	none
Button	exitButton	2	none	exitRoutine()

Figure 12-6   Object dictionary for insurance premium program

Defining Connections Between the User Screens

The insurance premium program is small, but with larger programs you may need to draw the connections between the screens to show how they interact. Figure 12-7 shows an interactivity diagram for the screens used in the insurance premium program. An **interactivity diagram** shows the relationship between screens in an interactive GUI program. Figure 12-7 shows that the first screen calls the second screen, and the program ends.

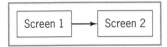

Figure 12-7 Diagram of interaction for insurance premium program

Figure 12-8 shows how a diagram might look for a more complicated program in which the user has several options available at Screens 1, 2, and 3. Notice how each of these three screens may lead to different screens, depending on the options the user selects at any one screen.

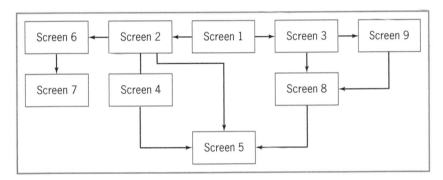

Figure 12-8 Interactivity diagram for a complicated program

Planning the Logic

In an event-driven program, you design the screens, define the objects, and define how the screens will connect. Then you can start to plan the insurance program class. For example, following the storyboard plan for the insurance program (see Figure 12-5), you need to create the first screen, which contains a label, four sets of radio buttons, and a button. Figure 12-9 shows the pseudocode that creates these components.

```
Declarations
    Label welcomeLabel
    RadioButton healthRadioButton
    RadioButton autoRadioButton
    Label ageLabel
    RadioButton lowAgeRadioButton
    RadioButton highAgeRadioButton
    Label smokeLabel
    RadioButton smokeNoRadioButton
    RadioButton smokeYesRadioButton
    Label ticketsLabel
    RadioButton lowTicketsRadioButton
    RadioButton highTicketsRadioButton
    Button calcButton

welcomeLabel.setText("Welcome to the Premium Calculator")
welcomeLabel.setPosition(30, 10)

healthRadioButton.setText("Health")
healthRadioButton.setPosition(15, 40)

autoRadioButton.setText("Auto")
autoRadioButton.setPosition(50, 40)

ageLabel.setText("Age")
ageLabel.setPosition(5, 60)

lowAgeRadioButton.setText("50 or under")
lowAgeRadioButton.setPosition(5, 70)

highAgeRadioButton.setText("Over 50")
highAgeRadioButton.setPosition(5, 80)

smokeLabel.setText("Do you smoke?")
smokeLabel.setPosition(40, 60)

smokeNoRadioButton.setText("No")
smokeNoRadioButton.setPosition(40, 70)

smokeYesRadioButton.setText("Yes")
smokeYesRadioButton.setPosition(40, 80)

ticketsLabel.setText("How many traffic tickets?")
ticketsLabel.setPosition(60, 50)

lowTicketsRadioButton.setText("0 or 1")
lowTicketsRadioButton.setPosition(60, 70)

highTicketsRadioButton.setText("2 or more")
highTicketsRadioButton.setPosition(60, 90)

calcButton.setText("Calculate Now")
calcButton.setPosition(60, 100)
calcButton.registerListener(calcRoutine())
```

Figure 12-9   Component definitions for first screen of insurance program

In Figure 12-9, the statement `calcButton.registerListener (calcRoutine())` specifies that `calcRoutine()` executes when a user clicks the `calcButton`. The syntax of this statement varies among programming languages.

In reality, you might generate more code than that shown in Figure 12-9 when you create the insurance program components. For example, each component might require a color and font. You might also want to initialize some components with default values to indicate they are selected. For example, you might want one radio button in a group to be selected already, which allows the user to click a different option only if he does not want the default value.

When you use an integrated development environment to create applications, you can drag components like those in Figure 12-9 onto a screen without explicitly writing all the statements shown in the pseudocode. In that case, the coding statements will be generated for you. It's beneficial to understand these statements so that you can more easily modify and debug your programs.

You also need to create the component onto which all the GUI elements in Figure 12-9 are placed. Depending on the language you are using, you might use a class with a name such as `Screen`, `Form`, or `Window`. Each of these generically is a **container**, or a class of objects whose main purpose is to hold other elements. The container class contains methods that allow you to set physical properties such as height and width, as well as methods that allow you to add the appropriate components to a container. Figure 12-10 shows how you would define a `Screen` class, set its size, and add the necessary components.

```
Declarations
    Screen screen1
screen1.setSize(150, 150)
screen1.add(welcomeLabel)
screen1.add(healthRadioButton)
screen1.add(autoRadioButton)
screen1.add(ageLabel)
screen1.add(lowAgeRadioButton)
screen1.add(highAgeRadioButton)
screen1.add(smokeLabel)
screen1.add(smokeNoRadioButton)
screen1.add(smokeYesRadioButton)
screen1.add(ticketsLabel)
screen1.add(lowTicketsRadioButton)
screen1.add(highTicketsRadioButton)
screen1.add(calcButton)
```

Figure 12-10   Statements that create `screen1`

Similarly, Figure 12-11 shows how you can create and define the components for the second screen in the insurance program and how to add the components to the container. Notice the label that holds the user's insurance premium is not filled with text, because the amount is not known until the user makes all the selections on the first screen.

```
Declarations
    Screen screen2
    Label premiumLabel
    Label premAmtLabel
    Button exitButton

screen2.setSize(100, 100)

premiumLabel.setText("Your Premium")
premiumLabel.setPosition(5, 30)

premAmtLabel.setPosition(20, 50)

exitButton.setText("Exit")
exitButton.setPosition(60, 80)
exitButton.registerListener(exitRoutine())

screen2.add(premiumLabel)
screen2.add(premAmtLabel)
screen2.add(exitButton)
```

Figure 12-11   Statements that define and create `screen2` and its components

After the GUI components are designed and arranged, you can plan the logic for each of the modules (or methods or scripts) that the program will use. For example, given the program requirements shown at the beginning of this section in Table 12-3, you can write the pseudocode for the `calcRoutine()` method of the insurance premium program, as shown in Figure 12-12. The `calcRoutine()` method does not execute until the user clicks the `calcButton`. At that point, the user's choices are sent to the method and used to calculate the premium amount.

```
public void calcRoutine()
   Declarations
      num HEALTH_AMT = 500
      num HIGH_AGE = 100
      num SMOKER = 250
      num AUTO_AMT = 750
      num HIGH_TICKETS = 400
      num HIGH_AGE_DRIVER_DISCOUNT = 200
      num premiumAmount
   if healthRadioButton.getChecked() then
      premiumAmount = HEALTH_AMT
      if highAgeRadioButton.getChecked() then
         premiumAmount = premiumAmount + HIGH_AGE
      endif
      if smokeYesRadioButton.getChecked() then
         premiumAmount = premiumAmount + SMOKER
      endif
   else
      premiumAmount = AUTO_AMT
      if highTicketsRadioButton.getChecked() then
         premiumAmount = premiumAmount + HIGH_TICKETS
      endif
      if highAgeRadioButton.getChecked() then
         premiumAmount = premiumAmount - HIGH_AGE_DRIVER_DISCOUNT
      endif
   endif
   premAmtLabel.setText(premiumAmount)
   screen1.remove()
   screen2.display()
return
```

Figure 12-12   Pseudocode for calcRoutine() method for insurance premium program

The pseudocode in Figure 12-12 should look very familiar to you—it declares numeric constants and a variable and uses decision-making logic you have used since the early chapters of this book. After the premium is calculated based on the user's choices, it is placed in the label that appears on the second screen. The basic structures of sequence, selection, and looping will continue to serve you well, whether you are programming in a procedural or event-driven environment.

The last two statements in the calcRoutine() method indicate that after the insurance premium is calculated and placed in its label, the first screen is removed and the second screen is displayed. Screen removal and display are accomplished differently in different languages; this example assumes that the appropriate methods are named remove() and display().

Two more program segments are needed to complete the insurance premium program. These include the main program that executes when the program starts and the last method that executes when the program ends. In many GUI languages, the process is slightly more complicated, but the general logic appears in Figure 12-13. The final method in the program is the one that is associated with the `exitButton` object on `screen2`. In Figure 12-13, this method is called `exitRoutine()`. In this program, the main program sets up the first screen and the last method removes the last screen.

```
start
    screen1.display()
stop

public void exitRoutine()
    screen2.remove()
return
```

Figure 12-13 The main program and `exitRoutine()` method for the insurance program

With most OOP languages, you must **register components**, or sign them up so that they can react to events initiated by other components. The details vary among languages, but the basic process is to write a statement that links the appropriate method (such as the `calcRoutine()` or `exitRoutine()` method) with an event such as a user's button click. In many development environments, the statement that registers a component to react to a user-initiated event is written for you automatically when you click components while designing your screen.

TWO TRUTHS & A LIE

The Steps to Developing an Event-Driven Application

1. A storyboard represents a diagram of the logic used in an interactive program.

2. An object dictionary is a list of the objects used in a program, including on which screens they are used and whether any code, or script, is associated with them.

3. An interactivity diagram shows the relationship between screens in an interactive GUI program.

The false statement is #1. A storyboard represents a picture or sketch of a screen the user will see when running a program.

Understanding Multithreading

A **thread** is the flow of execution of one set of program statements. When you execute a program statement by statement, from beginning to end, you are following a thread. Many applications follow a single thread; this means that at any one time the application executes only a single program statement. Every program you have studied so far in this book has contained a single thread.

Single-thread programs contain statements that execute in very rapid sequence, but a computer's central processing unit (CPU) can execute only one statement at a time, regardless of its processor speed. When you use a computer with multiple CPUs, the computer can execute multiple instructions simultaneously. All major OOP languages allow you to launch, or start, multiple threads, no matter which type of processing system you use. Using multiple threads of execution is known as **multithreading**. Figure 12-14 illustrates how multithreading executes in a multiprocessor system.

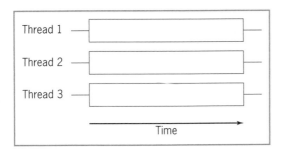

Figure 12-14   Executing multiple threads in a multiprocessor system

If a computer uses a single processor (as most desktop and laptop computers do), the multiple threads share the CPU's time, as shown in Figure 12-15. The CPU devotes a small amount of time to one task, then devotes a small amount of time to another task. The CPU never actually performs two tasks at the same instant. Instead, it performs a piece of one task and then a piece of another task. The CPU performs so quickly that each task seems to execute without interruption.

 With a single CPU, multiple threads execute *concurrently*, meaning they execute during the same time frame. They do not execute *simultaneously*, which would mean multiple threads were executing at the same instant.

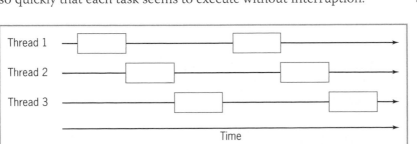

Figure 12-15   Executing multiple threads in a single-processor system

Watch the video
Multithreading.

Perhaps you have seen an expert chess player participate in chess games with several opponents at once. The chess player makes a move on the first playing board, and then moves to the second board against a second opponent while the first opponent analyzes the next move. The master player can go to the third board, make a move, and return to the first board before the first opponent is even ready to respond. To the first opponent, it might seem that the expert is devoting all of his time to the first game. Because he is so fast, the expert can play other opponents in the first opponent's "downtime." Executing multiple threads on a single CPU is a similar process. The CPU transfers its attention from thread to thread so quickly that the tasks don't even "miss" the CPU's attention.

Programmers sometimes use the terms *thread of execution* or *execution context* to describe a thread. They also describe a thread as a *lightweight process* because it is not a full-blown program. Rather, a thread must run within the context of a full, heavyweight program.

You use multithreading to improve the performance of your programs. Multithreaded programs often run faster, but more importantly, they are more user-friendly. With a multithreaded program, a user can continue to click buttons while your program is reading a data file. With multithreading, an animated figure can appear on one part of the screen while the user makes menu selections on another part of the screen. When you use the Internet, the benefits of multithreading increase. For example, you can begin to read a long text file, watch a video, or listen to an audio file while the rest of the file is still downloading. Web users are likely to abandon a site if downloading a file takes too long. When you use multithreading to perform concurrent tasks, you are more likely to retain visitors to your Web site—this is particularly important if your site sells a product or service.

Object-oriented languages often contain a built-in `Thread` class that contains methods to help handle multiple threads. For example, a `sleep()` method is frequently used to pause program execution for a specified amount of time. Computer instruction processing speed is so rapid that sometimes you have to slow processing down for human consumption. An application that frequently requires `sleep()` method calls is computer animation.

Creating Animation

Animation is the rapid sequence of still images, each slightly different from the previous one, that produces the illusion of movement. Many object-oriented languages offer built-in classes that contain methods you can use to draw geometric figures on the screen. The methods typically have names like drawLine(), drawCircle(), drawRectangle(), and so on. You place figures on the screen based on a graphing coordinate system. Typically, any component you place on the screen has a horizontal, or **x-axis**, position as well as a vertical, or **y-axis**, position. The upper-left corner of any display is position 0, 0. The first, or **x-coordinate**, value increases as you travel from left to right across the window. The second, or **y-coordinate**, value increases as you travel from top to bottom. Figure 12-16 shows four screen coordinate positions. The more to the right a spot is, the higher its x-coordinate value, and the lower a spot is, the higher its y-coordinate value.

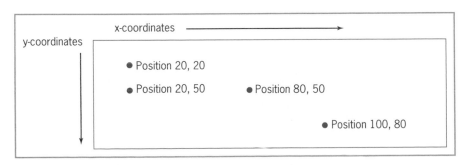

Figure 12-16 Selected screen coordinate positions

Cartoonists create animated films by drawing a sequence of frames or cells. These individual drawings are shown to the audience in rapid succession to give the illusion of natural movement. You create computer animation using the same techniques. If you display computer images as fast as your CPU can process them, you might not be able to see anything. Most computer animation employs a `Thread` class `sleep()` method to pause for short periods of time between animation cells, so the human brain has time to absorb each image's content.

Artists often spend a great deal of time creating the exact images they want to use in an animation sequence. As a simple example, Figure 12-17 shows pseudocode for a `MovingCircle` class. As its name implies, the class moves a circle across the screen. The class contains data fields to hold x- and y-coordinates that identify the location at which a circle appears. The constants `SIZE` and `INCREASE` respectively define the size of the first circle drawn and the relative increase in size and position of each subsequent circle. The `MovingCircle` class assumes you are working with a language that provides a `drawCircle()` method, which takes care of the details of creating a circle when it is given parameters for horizontal and vertical positions and radius. Assuming you are working with a language that provides a `sleep()` method to accept a pause time in milliseconds, the `SLEEP_TIME` constant provides a 100-millisecond gap before the production of each new circle.

```
public class MovingCircle
   Declarations
      private num x = 20
      private num y = 20
      private num LIMIT = 300
      private num SIZE = 40
      private num INCREASE = SIZE / 10
      private num SLEEP_TIME = 100

   public void main()
      while true
         repaintScreen()
      endwhile
   return

   public void repaintScreen()
      drawCircle(x, y, SIZE)
      x = x + INCREASE
      y = y + INCREASE
      Thread.sleep(SLEEP_TIME)
   return
endClass
```

Figure 12-17   The `MovingCircle` class

In most object-oriented languages, a method named `main()` executes automatically when a class object is created. The `main()` method in the `MovingCircle` class executes a continuous loop. A similar technique is used in many languages that support GUI interfaces. Program execution will cease only when the user quits the application by clicking a window's Close button on the screen, for example. In the `repaintScreen()` method of the `MovingCircle` class, a circle is drawn at the x, y position, then x and y are both increased. The application sleeps for one-tenth of a second (the `SLEEP_TIME` value), and then the `repaintScreen()` method draws a new circle more to the right, further down, and a little larger. The effect is a moving circle that leaves a trail of smaller circles behind as it moves diagonally across the screen. Figure 12-18 shows the output as a Java version of the application executes.

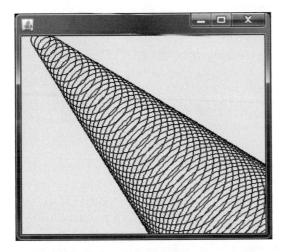

Figure 12-18   Output of the `MovingCircle` application

Although an object-oriented language might make it easy for you to draw geometric shapes, you can also substitute a variety of more sophisticated, predrawn animated images to achieve the graphic effects you want within your programs. An image is loaded in a separate thread of execution; this allows program execution to continue while the image loads. This is a significant advantage because loading a large image can be time consuming.

Many animated images are available on the Web for you to use freely. Use your search engine and keywords such as *gif files*, *jpeg files*, and *animation* to find sources for shareware and freeware files.

TWO TRUTHS & A LIE

Creating Animation

1. Typically, any component you place on a screen has a horizontal, or x-axis, position as well as a vertical, or y-axis, position.

2. The x-coordinate value increases as you travel from left to right across a window.

3. You almost always want to display animation cells as fast as your processor can handle them.

The false statement is #3. If you display computer images as fast as your CPU can process them, you might not be able to see anything, so most computer animation employs a method to pause for short periods of time between animation cells.

Chapter Summary

- Interacting with a computer operating system from the command line is difficult; it is easier to use an event-driven graphical user interface (GUI), in which users manipulate objects such as buttons and menus. Within an event-driven program, a component from which an event is generated is the source of the event. A listener is an object that is "interested in" an event to which you want it to respond.

- The possible events a user can initiate include a key press, mouse point, click, right-click, double-click, and drag. Common GUI components include labels, text boxes, buttons, check boxes, check box groups, option buttons, and list boxes. GUI components are excellent examples of the best principles of object-oriented programming; they represent objects with attributes and methods that operate like black boxes.

- When you create a program that will use a GUI, the interface should be natural, predictable, attractive, easy to read, and non-distracting. It's helpful if the user can customize your applications. The program should be forgiving, and you should not forget that the GUI is only a means to an end.

- Developing an event-driven application requires more steps than developing other programs, including creating storyboards, defining objects, and defining the connections between the screens the user will see.

- A thread is the flow of execution of one set of program statements. Many applications follow a single thread; using multiple threads of execution is known as multithreading.

- Animation is the rapid sequence of still images, each slightly different from the previous one, that produces the illusion of movement. Many object-oriented languages offer built-in classes that contain methods you can use to draw geometric figures on the screen. Typically, any component you place on the screen has a horizontal, or x-axis, position as well as a vertical, or y-axis, position.

Key Terms

An **operating system** is the software that you use to run a computer and manage its resources.

The **DOS prompt** is the command line in the DOS operating system.

Icons are small pictures on the screen that the user can select with a mouse.

An **event** is an occurrence that generates a message sent to an object.

In **event-driven** or **event-based** programs, actions occur in response to user-initiated events such as clicking a mouse button.

The **source of an event** is the component from which the event is generated.

A **listener** is an object that is "interested in" an event to which you want it to respond.

A **pixel** is a picture element, or one of the tiny dots of light that form a grid on your screen.

Accessibility issues are the screen design concerns that make programs easier to use for people with physical limitations.

A **storyboard** represents a picture or sketch of a screen the user will see when running a program.

An **object dictionary** is a list of the objects used in a program, including which screens they are used on and whether any code, or script, is associated with them.

An **interactivity diagram** shows the relationship between screens in an interactive GUI program.

A **container** is a class of objects whose main purpose is to hold other elements—for example, a window.

Registering components is the act of signing them up so they can react to events initiated by other components.

A **thread** is the flow of execution of one set of program statements.

Multithreading is using multiple threads of execution.

Animation is the rapid sequence of still images, each slightly different from the previous one, that together produce the illusion of movement.

The **x-axis** represents horizontal positions in a screen window.

The **y-axis** represents vertical positions in a screen window.

The **x-coordinate** value increases as you travel from left to right across a window.

The **y-coordinate** value increases as you travel from top to bottom across a window.

Review Questions

1. Compared to using a command line, an advantage to using an operating system that employs a GUI is _____.

    a. you can interact directly with the operating system

    b. you do not have to deal with confusing icons

    c. you do not have to memorize complicated commands

    d. all of the above

2. When users can initiate actions by clicking the mouse on an icon, the program is _____-driven.

    a. event

    b. prompt

    c. command

    d. incident

3. A component from which an event is generated is the _____ of the event.

    a. base

    b. icon

    c. listener

    d. source

4. An object that responds to an event is a _____.

    a. source

    b. listener

    c. transponder

    d. snooper

5. All of the following are user-initiated events except a _____.

    a. key press

    b. key drag

    c. right mouse click

    d. mouse drag

6. All of the following are typical GUI components except a _____.

    a. label

    b. text box

    c. list box

    d. button box

7. GUI components operate like _____.

    a. black boxes

    b. procedural functions

    c. looping structures

    d. command lines

8. Which of the following is *not* a principle of good GUI design?

   a. The interface should be predictable.

   b. The fancier the screen design, the better.

   c. The program should be forgiving.

   d. The user should be able to customize your applications.

9. Which of the following aspects of a GUI layout is most predictable and natural for the user?

   a. A menu bar runs down the right side of the screen.

   b. *Help* is the first option on a menu.

   c. A dollar sign icon represents saving a file.

   d. Pressing *Esc* allows the user to cancel a selection.

10. In most GUI programming environments, the programmer can change all of the following attributes of most components except their _____.

    a. color

    b. screen location

    c. size

    d. You can change all of these attributes.

11. Depending on the programming language used, you might _____ to change a screen component's attributes.

    a. use an assignment statement

    b. call a module

    c. enter a value into a list of properties

    d. all of the above

12. When you create an event-driven application, which of the following must be done before defining the objects you will use?

    a. Translate the program.

    b. Create storyboards.

    c. Test the program.

    d. Code the program.

13. A _____ is a sketch of a screen the user will see when running a program.

    a. flowchart

    b. hierarchy chart

    c. storyboard

    d. tale timber

14. A list of objects used in a program is an object _____.

    a. thesaurus

    b. glossary

    c. index

    d. dictionary

15. A(n) _____ diagram shows the connections between the various screens a user might see during a program's execution.

    a. interactivity

    b. help

    c. cooperation

    d. communication

16. The flow of execution of one set of program statements is a _____.

    a. thread

    b. string

    c. path

    d. route

17. When a computer contains a single CPU, it can execute _____ computer instruction(s) at a time.

    a. one

    b. several

    c. an unlimited number of

    d. from several to thousands (depending on the processor speed)

18. Multithreaded programs usually _____ than their procedural counterparts.

    a. run faster

    b. are harder to use

    c. are older

    d. all of the above

19. An object's horizontal position on the computer screen is its _____.

    a. a-coordinate

    b. h-coordinate

    c. x-coordinate

    d. y-coordinate

20. You create computer animation by _____.

    a. drawing an image and setting its animation property to true

    b. drawing a single image and executing it on a multiprocessor system

    c. drawing a sequence of frames that are shown in rapid succession

    d. Animation is not used in computer applications.

Exercises

1. Take a critical look at three GUI applications with which you are familiar—for example, a spreadsheet, a word-processing program, and a game. Describe how well each conforms to the GUI design guidelines listed in this chapter.

2. Select one element of poor GUI design in a program with which you are familiar. Describe how you would improve the design.

3. Select a GUI program that you have never used before. Describe how well it conforms to the GUI design guidelines listed in this chapter.

4. Design the storyboards, interactivity diagram, object dictionary, and any necessary scripts for an interactive program for customers of Sunflower Floral Designs.

    Allow customers the option of choosing a floral arrangement ($25 base price), cut flowers ($15 base price), or a corsage ($10 base price). Let the customer choose roses, daisies, chrysanthemums, or irises as the dominant flower. If the customer chooses roses, add $5 to the base price. After the customer clicks an Order Now button, display the price of the order.

5. Design the storyboards, interactivity diagram, object dictionary, and any necessary scripts for an interactive program for customers of Toby's Travels.

    Allow customers the option of at least five trip destinations and four means of transportation, each with a unique price. After the customer clicks the Plan Trip Now button, display the price of the trip.

6. Design the storyboards, interactivity diagram, object dictionary, and any necessary scripts for an interactive program for customers of The Mane Event Hair Salon.

    Allow customers the option of choosing a haircut ($15), coloring ($25), or perm ($45). After the customer clicks a Select button, display the price of the service.

 ## Find the Bugs

7. Your student disk contains files named DEBUG12-01.txt, DEBUG12-02.txt, and DEBUG12-03.txt. Each file starts with some comments that describe the problem. Comments are lines that begin with two slashes (//). Following the comments, each file contains pseudocode that has one or more bugs you must find and correct.

Game Zone

8. Design the storyboards, interactivity diagram, object dictionary, and any necessary scripts for an interactive program that allows a user to play a card game named Lucky Seven. In real life, the game can be played with seven cards, each containing a number from 1 through 7, that are shuffled and dealt number-side down. To start the game, a player turns over any card. The exposed number on the card determines the position (reading from left to right) of the next card that must be turned over. For example, if the player turns over the first card and its number is 7, the next card turned must be the seventh card (counting from left to right). If the player turns over a card whose number denotes a position that was already turned, the player loses the game. If the player succeeds in turning over all seven cards, the player wins.

   Instead of cards, you will use seven buttons labeled 1 through 7 from left to right. Randomly associate one of the seven values 1 through 7 with each button. (In other words, the associated value might or might not be equivalent to the button's labeled value.) When the player clicks a button, reveal the associated hidden value. If the value represents the position of a button already clicked, the player loses. If the revealed number represents an available button, force the user to click it—that is, do not take any action until the user clicks the correct button. After a player clicks a button, remove the button from play.

   For example, a player might click Button 7, revealing a 4. Then the player clicks Button 4, revealing a 2. Then the player clicks Button 2, revealing a 7. The player loses because Button 7 is already "used."

9. In the Game Zone sections of Chapters 6 and 9, you designed and fine-tuned the logic for the game Hangman, in which the user guesses letters in a series of hidden words. Design the storyboards, interactivity diagram, object dictionary, and any necessary scripts for a version of the game in which the user clicks lettered buttons to fill in the secret words. Draw a "hanged" person piece by piece with each missed letter. For example, when the user chooses a correct letter, place it in the appropriate position or positions in the word, but the first time the user chooses a letter that is not in the target word, draw a head for the "hanged" man. The second time the user makes

an incorrect guess, add a torso. Continue with arms and legs. If the complete body is drawn before the user has guessed all the letters in the word, display a message indicating that the player has lost the game. If the user completes the word before all the body parts are drawn, display a message that the player has won. Assume you can use built-in methods named drawCircle() and drawLine(). The drawCircle() method requires three parameters—the x- and y-coordinates of the center, and a radius size. The drawLine() method requires four parameters—the x- and y-coordinates of the start of the line, and the x- and y-coordinates of the end of the line.

 Up for Discussion

10. Making exciting, entertaining, professional-looking GUI applications becomes easier once you learn to include graphics images. You can copy graphics images from many locations on the Web. Should there be any restrictions on what graphics you use? Does it make a difference if you are writing programs for your own enjoyment as opposed to putting them on the Web where others can see them? Is using photographs different from using drawings? Does it matter if the photographs contain recognizable people? Would you impose any restrictions on images posted to your organization's Web site?

11. Playing computer games has been shown to increase the level of dopamine in the human brain. High levels of this substance are associated with addiction to drugs. Suppose you work for a company that manufactures games and it decides to research how its games can produce more dopamine in the brains of players. Would you support the company's decision?

12. When people use interactive programs on the Web, when do you feel it is appropriate to track which buttons they select or to record the data they enter? When is it not appropriate? Does it matter how long the data is stored? Does it matter if a profit is made from using the data?

13. Should there be limits on what is shown on the Web? Consider sites that might display pornography, child abuse, suicide, or assassination of a political leader. Does it make a difference if the offensive images are animated as opposed to being photos or footage of such activities?

System Modeling with the UML

In this chapter, you will learn about:

- ◎ The need for system modeling
- ◎ The UML
- ◎ Use case diagrams
- ◎ Class and object diagrams
- ◎ Sequence and communication diagrams
- ◎ State machine diagrams
- ◎ Activity diagrams
- ◎ Component, deployment, and profile diagrams
- ◎ Diagramming exception handling
- ◎ Deciding when to use the UML and which UML diagrams to use

Understanding the Need for System Modeling

Computer programs often stand alone to solve a user's specific problem. For example, a program might exist only to print paychecks for the current week. Most computer programs, however, are part of a larger system. Your company's payroll system might consist of dozens of programs, including programs that produce employee paychecks, apply raises to employee records, alter employee deduction options, and print federal and state tax forms at the end of the year. Each program you write as part of a system might be related to several others. Some programs depend on input from other programs in the system or produce output to be fed into other programs. Similarly, an organization's accounting, inventory, and customer ordering systems all consist of many interrelated programs. Producing a set of programs that operate together correctly requires careful planning. **System design** is the detailed specification of how all the parts of a system will be implemented and coordinated.

 Usually, system design refers to computer system design, but even a noncomputerized, manual system can benefit from good design techniques.

Many textbooks cover the theories and techniques of system design. If you continue to study in a Computer Information Systems program at a college or university, you probably will be required to take a semester-long course in system design. Explaining all the techniques of system design is beyond the scope of this book. However, some basic principles parallel those you have used throughout this book in designing individual programs:

- Large systems are easier to understand when you break them down into subsystems.

- Good modeling techniques are increasingly important as the size and complexity of systems increase.

- Good models promote communication among technical and nontechnical workers while ensuring good business solutions.

In other words, developing a model for a single program or an entire business system requires organization and planning. In this chapter, you learn the basics of one popular design tool, the **Unified Modeling Language (UML)**, which is based on these principles. The UML allows you to envision systems with an object-oriented perspective, breaking a system into subsystems, focusing on the big picture, and hiding the implementation details. In addition, the UML provides a means for programmers and businesspeople to communicate about system design. It also provides a way to plan to divide responsibilities for large systems. Understanding the UML's principles helps you design a variety of system types and talk about systems with the people who will use them.

 In addition to modeling a system before creating it, system analysts sometimes model an existing system to get a better picture of its operation. Creating a model for an existing system is called **reverse engineering**.

What is the UML?

You can purchase compilers for most programming languages from a variety of manufacturers, and you can purchase several different flowcharting programs. Similarly, you can purchase a variety of tools to help you create UML diagrams, but the UML itself is vendor-independent.

The UML is a standard way to specify, construct, and document systems that use object-oriented methods. The UML is a modeling language, not a programming language. The systems you develop using the UML probably will be implemented later in object-oriented programming languages such as Java, C++, C#, or Visual Basic. As with flowcharts, pseudocode, hierarchy charts, and class diagrams, the UML has its own notation that consists of a set of specialized shapes and conventions. You can use the UML's shapes to construct different kinds of software diagrams and model different kinds of systems. Just as you can use a flowchart or hierarchy chart to diagram real-life activities, organizational relationships, or computer programs, you can also use the UML for many purposes, including modeling business activities, organizational processes, or software systems.

The UML was created at Rational Software by Grady Booch, Ivar Jacobson, and Jim Rumbaugh. The Object Management Group (OMG) adopted the UML as a standard for software modeling in 1997. The OMG includes more than 800 software vendors, developers, and users who seek a common architectural framework for object-oriented programming. The UML is in its second major version; the current version is UML 2.2. You can view or download the entire UML specification and usage guidelines from the OMG at *www.uml.org*.

When you draw a flowchart or write pseudocode, your purpose is to illustrate the individual steps in a process. When you draw a hierarchy chart, you use more of a "big picture" approach. As with a hierarchy chart, you use the UML to create top-view diagrams of business processes that let you hide details and focus on functionality. This approach lets you start with a generic view of an application and introduce details and complexity later. UML diagrams are useful as you begin designing business systems, when customers who are not technically oriented must accurately communicate with the technical staff members who will create the actual systems. The UML was intentionally designed to be nontechnical so that developers, customers, and implementers (programmers) could all "speak the same language." If business and technical people can agree on what a system should do, the chances improve that the final product will be useful.

The UML is very large; its documentation is more than 800 pages, and new diagram types are added frequently. Currently, the UML provides 14 diagram types that you can use to model systems. Each of the diagram types lets you see a business process from a different angle, and appeals to a different type of user. Just as an architect, interior designer, electrician, and plumber use different diagram types to describe the same building, different computer users appreciate different perspectives. For example, a business user most values a system's use case diagrams because they illustrate who is doing what. On the other hand, programmers find class and object diagrams more useful because they help explain details of how to build classes and objects into applications.

The UML superstructure groups the diagram types into three categories—structure diagrams, behavior diagrams, and interaction diagrams.

- **Structure diagrams** emphasize the "things" in a system. These include:
  - Class diagrams
  - Object diagrams
  - Component diagrams
  - Composite structure diagrams
  - Package diagrams
  - Deployment diagrams
  - Profile diagrams
- **Behavior diagrams** emphasize what happens in a system. These include:
  - Use case diagrams
  - Activity diagrams
  - State machine diagrams

Interaction diagrams are considered to be a subset of behavior diagrams.

- **Interaction diagrams** emphasize the flow of control and data among the things in the system being modeled. These include:

  - Sequence diagrams

  - Communication diagrams

  - Timing diagrams

  - Interaction overview diagrams

554

Watch the video *The UML.*

You can categorize UML diagrams as those that illustrate the dynamic, or changing, aspects of a system and those that illustrate the static, or steady, aspects of a system. Dynamic diagrams include use case, sequence, communication, state machine, and activity diagrams. Static diagrams include class, object, component, deployment, and profile diagrams.

The UML Web site at *www.uml.org* provides links to several UML tutorials.

Each of the UML diagram types supports multiple variations, and explaining them all would require an entire textbook. This chapter presents an overview and simple examples of several diagram types, which provides a good foundation for further study of the UML.

TWO TRUTHS & A LIE

What is the UML?

1. The UML is a standard way to specify, construct, and document systems that use object-oriented methods; it is a modeling language.

2. The UML provides an easy-to-learn alternative to complicated programming languages such as Java, C++, C#, or Visual Basic.

3. The UML documentation is more than 800 pages.

The false statement is #2. The systems you develop using the UML probably will be implemented later in object-oriented programming languages such as Java, C++, C#, or Visual Basic.

Using Use Case Diagrams

The **use case diagram** shows how a business works from the perspective of those who actually use the business. This category includes many types of users—for example, employees, customers, and suppliers. Although users can also be governments, private organizations, machines, or other systems, it is easiest to think of them as people, so users are called actors and are represented by stick figures in use case diagrams. The actual use cases are represented by ovals.

Use cases do not necessarily represent all the functions of a system; they are the system functions or services that are visible to the system's actors. In other words, they represent the cases by which an actor uses and presumably benefits from the system. Determining all the cases for which users interact with systems helps you divide a system logically into functional parts.

Establishing use cases usually follows from analyzing the main events in a system. For example, from a librarian's point of view, two main events are `acquireNewBook()` and `checkOutBook()`. Figure 13-1 shows a use case diagram for these two events.

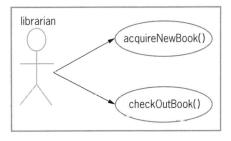

Figure 13-1   Use case diagram for librarian

In many systems, there are variations in use cases. The three possible types of variations are:

- Extend

- Include

- Generalization

An **extend variation** is a use case variation that shows functions beyond those found in a base case. In other words, an extend variation is usually an optional activity. For example, checking out a book for a new library patron who doesn't have a library card is slightly more complicated than checking out a book for an existing patron. Each variation in the sequence of actions required in a use case is a **scenario**. Each use case has at least one main scenario, but might have several more that are extensions or variations of the main one. Figure 13-2 shows how you would diagram the relationship between the use case `checkOutBook()` and the more specific scenario `checkOutBookForNewPatron()`. Extended use cases are shown in an oval with a dashed arrow pointing to the more general base case.

Many system developers would use the standard English form to describe activities in their UML diagrams—for example, `check out book` instead of `checkOutBook()`, which looks like a programming method call. Because you are used to seeing method names in camel casing and with trailing parentheses throughout this book, this discussion of the UML continues with the same format.

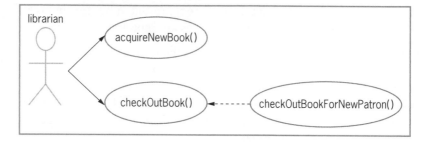

Figure 13-2   Use case diagram for librarian with scenario extension

For clarity, you can add "<<extend>>" near the line that shows a relationship extension. Such a feature, which adds to the UML vocabulary of shapes to make them more meaningful for the reader, is called a **stereotype**. Figure 13-3 includes a stereotype.

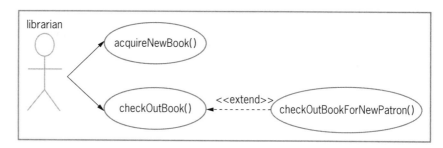

Figure 13-3   Use case diagram for librarian using stereotype

In addition to extend relationships, use case diagrams can also show include relationships. You use an **include variation** when a case can be part of multiple use cases. This concept is very much like that of a subroutine or submodule. You show an include use case in an oval with a dashed arrow pointing to the subroutine use case. For example, `issueLibraryCard()` might be a function of `checkOutBook()`, which is used when the patron checking out a book is new, but it might also be a function of `registerNewPatron()`, which occurs when a patron registers at the library but does not want to check out books yet. See Figure 13-4.

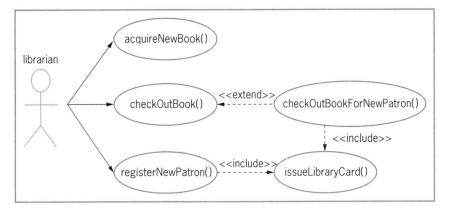

Figure 13-4   Use case diagram for librarian using include relationship

You use a **generalization variation** when a use case is less specific than others, and you want to be able to substitute the more specific case for a general one. For example, a library has certain procedures for acquiring new materials, whether they are videos, tapes, CDs, hardcover books, or paperbacks. However, the procedures might become more specific during a particular acquisition—perhaps the librarian must procure plastic cases for circulating videos or assign locked storage locations for CDs. Figure 13-5 shows the generalization `acquireNewItem()` with two more specific situations: acquiring videos and acquiring CDs. The more specific scenarios are attached to the general scenario with open-headed dashed arrows.

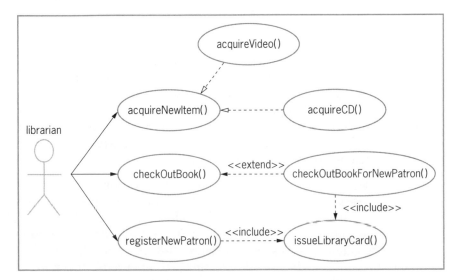

Figure 13-5   Use case diagram for librarian with generalizations

Many use case diagrams show multiple actors. For example, Figure 13-6 shows that a library clerk cannot perform as many functions as a librarian; the clerk can check out books and register new patrons but cannot acquire new materials.

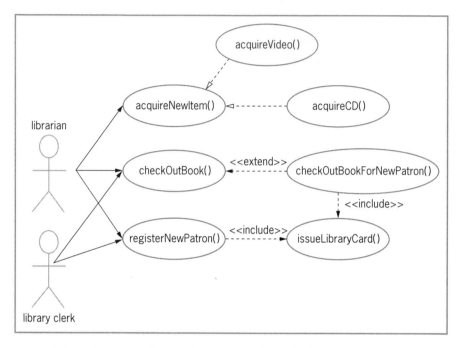

Figure 13-6 Use case diagram for librarian with multiple actors

While designing an actual library system, you could add many more use cases and actors to the use case diagram. The purpose of such a diagram is to encourage discussion between the system developer and the library staff. Library staff members do not need to know any of the technical details of the system that the analysts will eventually create, and they certainly do not need to understand computers or programming. However, by viewing the use cases, the library staff can visualize activities they perform while doing their jobs and correct the system developer if inaccuracies exist. The final software products developed for such a system are far more likely to satisfy users than those developed without this design step.

A use case diagram is only a tool to aid communication. No single "correct" use case diagram exists; you might correctly represent a system in several ways. For example, you might choose to emphasize the actors in the library system, as shown in Figure 13-7, or to emphasize system requirements, as shown in Figure 13-8. Diagrams that are too crowded are neither visually pleasing nor very useful. Therefore, the use case diagram in Figure 13-7 shows all the specific actors and their relationships, but purposely omits more specific system functions, whereas Figure 13-8 shows many actions that are often hidden from users but purposely omits more specific actors. For example, the activities carried out to `manageNetworkOutage()`, if done properly, should be invisible to library patrons checking out books.

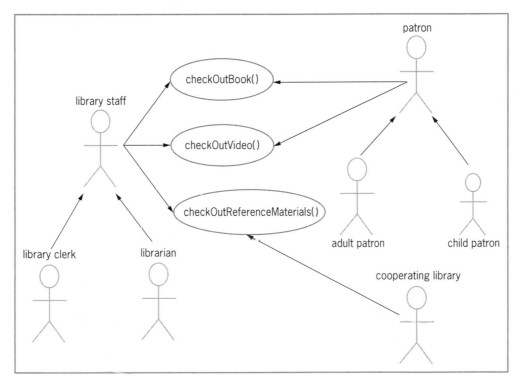

Figure 13-7   Use case diagram emphasizing actors

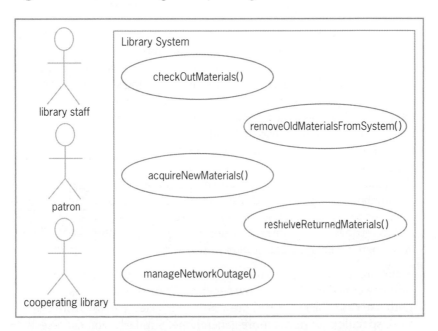

Figure 13-8   Use case diagram emphasizing system requirements

In Figure 13-8, the relationship lines between the actors and use cases have been removed because the emphasis is on the system requirements, and too many lines would make the diagram confusing. When system developers omit parts of diagrams for clarity, they refer to the missing parts as **elided**. For the sake of clarity, eliding extraneous information is perfectly acceptable. The main purpose of UML diagrams is to facilitate clear communication.

TWO TRUTHS & A LIE

Using Use Case Diagrams

1. A use case diagram shows how a business works from the perspective of those who approach it from the outside, or those who actually use the business.

2. Users are called actors and are represented by stick figures in use case diagrams. The actual use cases are represented by ovals.

3. Use cases are important because they describe all the functions of a system.

The false statement is #3. Use cases do not necessarily represent all the functions of a system; they are the system functions or services that are visible to the system's actors.

Using Class and Object Diagrams

You use a class diagram to illustrate the names, attributes, and methods of a class or set of classes. Class diagrams are more useful to a system's programmers than to its users because they closely resemble code the programmers will write. A class diagram illustrating a single class contains a rectangle divided into three sections: the top section contains the name of the class, the middle section contains the names of the attributes, and the bottom section contains the names of the methods. Figure 13-9 shows the class diagram for a Book class. Each Book object contains an idNum, title, and author. Each Book object also contains methods to create a Book when it is acquired, and to retrieve or get title and author information when the Book object's idNum is supplied.

Book
idNum title author
create() getInfo(idNum)

Figure 13-9   Book class diagram

 You first used class diagrams in Chapter 10.

In the preceding section, you learned how to use generalizations with use case diagrams to show general and more specific use cases. With use case diagrams, you drew an open-headed arrow from the more specific case to the more general one. Similarly, you can use generalizations with class diagrams to show more general (or parent) classes and more specific (or child) classes that inherit attributes from parents. For example, Figure 13-10 shows Book and Video classes that are more specific than the general LibraryItem class. All LibraryItem objects contain an idNum and title, but each Book

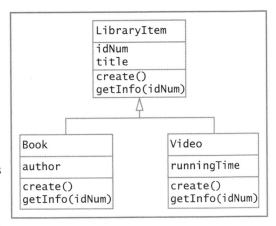

Figure 13-10 LibraryItem class diagram showing generalization

You learned about inheritance and parent and child classes in Chapter 11.

561

item also contains an author, and each Video item also contains a runningTime. Child classes contain all the attributes of their parents and usually contain additional attributes not found in the parent.

Class diagrams can include symbols that show the relationships between objects. You can show two types of relationships:

- An association relationship

- A whole-part relationship

An **association relationship** describes the connection or link between objects. You represent an association relationship between classes with a straight line. Frequently, you include information about the arithmetical relationship or ratio (called **cardinality** or **multiplicity**) of the objects. For example, Figure 13-11 shows the association relationship between a Library and the LibraryItems it lends. Exactly one Library object exists, and it can be associated with any number of LibraryItems from 0 to infinity, which is represented by an asterisk. Figure 13-12 adds the Patron class to the diagram and shows how you indicate that any number of Patrons can be associated with the Library, but that each Patron can borrow only up to five LibraryItems at a time, or currently might not be borrowing any. In addition, each LibraryItem can be associated with at most one Patron, but at any given time might not be on loan.

When a child class contains a method with the same signature as one in the parent class, the child class version **overrides** the version in the parent class. That is, by default, the child class version is used with any child class object. The create() and getInfo() methods in the Book and Video classes override the versions in the LibraryItem class.

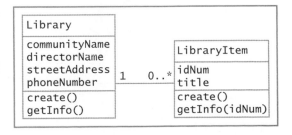

Figure 13-11 Class diagram with association relationship

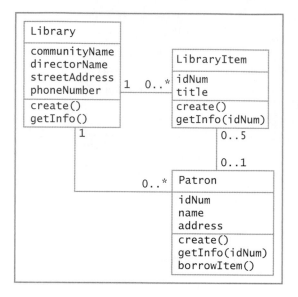

Figure 13-12   Class diagram with several association relationships

A **whole-part relationship** describes an association in which one or more classes make up the parts of a larger whole class. For example, 50 states "make up" the United States, and 10 departments might "make up" a company. This type of relationship is also called an **aggregation** and is represented by an open diamond at the "whole part" end of the line that indicates the relationship. You can also call a whole-part relationship a **has-a relationship** because the phrase describes the association between the whole and one of its parts; for example, "The library has a Circulation Department." Figure 13-13 shows a whole-part relationship for a Library.

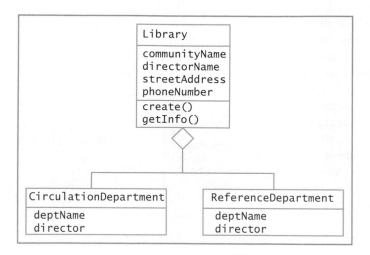

Figure 13-13   Class diagram with whole-part relationship

Object diagrams are similar to class diagrams, but they model specific instances of classes. You use an object diagram to show a snapshot of an object at one point in time, so you can more easily understand its relationship to other objects. Imagine looking at the travelers in a major airport. If you try to watch them all at once, you see a flurry of activity, but it is hard to understand all the tasks (buying a ticket, checking luggage, and so on) a traveler must accomplish to take a trip. However, if you concentrate on one traveler and follow his or her actions through the airport from arrival to takeoff, you get a clearer picture of the required activities. An object diagram serves the same purpose; you concentrate on a specific instance of a class to better understand how a class works.

Figure 13-14 contains an object diagram showing the relationship between one Library, LibraryItem, and Patron. Notice the similarities between Figures 13-12 and 13-14. If you need to describe the relationship between three classes, you can use either model—a class diagram or an object diagram—interchangeably. You simply use the model that seems clearer to you and your intended audience.

Watch the video *Class and Object Diagrams.*

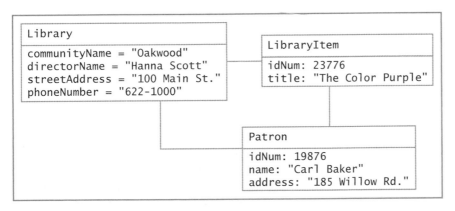

Figure 13-14 Object diagram for Library

564

Using Sequence and Communication Diagrams

You use a **sequence diagram** to show the timing of events in a single use case. A sequence diagram makes it easier to see the order in which activities occur. The horizontal axis (x-axis) of a sequence diagram represents objects, and the vertical axis (y-axis) represents time. You create a sequence diagram by placing objects that are part of an activity across the top of the diagram along the x-axis, starting at the left with the object or actor that begins the action. Beneath each object on the x-axis, you place a vertical dashed line that represents the period of time the object exists. Then, you use horizontal arrows to show how the objects communicate with each other over time.

For example, Figure 13-15 shows a sequence diagram for a scenario that a librarian can use to create a book check-out record. The librarian begins a `create()` method with `Patron idNum` and `Book idNum` information. The `BookCheckOutRecord` object requests additional `Patron` information (such as `name` and `address`) from the `Patron` object with the correct `Patron idNum`, and additional Book information (such as `title` and `author`) from the `Book` object with the correct `Book idNum`. When `BookCheckOutRecord` contains all the data it needs, a completed record is returned to the librarian.

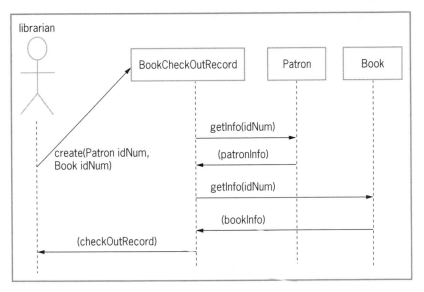

In Figures 13-15 and 13-16, `patronInfo` and **bookInfo** represent group items that contain all of a `Patron`'s and `Book`'s data. For example, `patronInfo` might contain `idNum`, `lastName`, `firstName`, `address`, and `phoneNumber`, all of which have been defined as attributes of that class.

Figure 13-15   Sequence diagram for checking out a `Book` for a `Patron`

A **communication diagram** emphasizes the organization of objects that participate in a system. It is similar to a sequence diagram, except that it contains sequence numbers to represent the precise order in which activities occur. Communication diagrams focus on object roles instead of the times that messages are sent. Figure 13-16 shows the same sequence of events as Figure 13-15, but the steps to creating a `BookCheckOutRecord` are clearly numbered. Decimal numbered steps (1.1, 1.2, and so on) represent substeps of the main steps. Checking out a library book is a fairly straightforward event, so a sequence diagram sufficiently illustrates the process. Communication diagrams become more useful with more complicated systems.

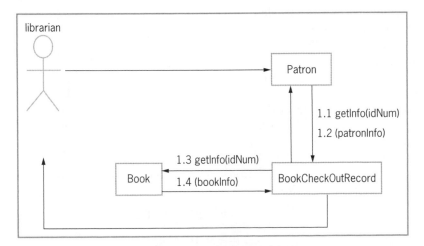

Figure 13-16   Communication diagram for checking out a `Book` for a `Patron`

TWO TRUTHS & A LIE

Using Sequence and Communication Diagrams

1. You use a sequence diagram to show the timing of events in a single use case.

2. A communication diagram emphasizes the timing of events in multiple use cases.

3. Communication diagrams focus on object roles instead of the times that messages are sent.

The false statement is #2. A communication diagram emphasizes the organization of objects that participate in a system.

Using State Machine Diagrams

A **state machine diagram** shows the different statuses of a class or object at different points in time. You use a state machine diagram to illustrate aspects of a system that show interesting changes in behavior as time passes. Conventionally, you use rounded rectangles to represent each state and labeled arrows to show the sequence in which events affect the states. A solid dot indicates the start and stop states for the class or object. Figure 13-17 contains a state machine diagram you can use to describe the states of a Book.

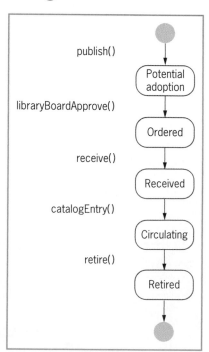

Figure 13-17 State machine diagram for states of a Book

To make sure that your diagrams are clear, you should use the correct symbol in each UML diagram you create, just as you should use the correct symbol in each program flowchart. However, if you create a flowchart and use a rectangle for an input or output statement where a parallelogram is conventional, others will still understand your meaning. Similarly, with UML diagrams, the exact shape you use is not nearly as important as the sequence of events and relationships between objects.

TWO TRUTHS & A LIE

Using State Machine Diagrams

1. A state machine diagram shows the permanent status of fixed data in a class.

2. You use a state machine diagram to illustrate aspects of a system that show interesting changes in behavior as time passes.

3. Conventionally, you use rounded rectangles to represent each state and labeled arrows to show the sequence in which events affect the states.

The false statement is #1. A state machine diagram shows the different statuses of a class or object at different points in time.

Using Activity Diagrams

The UML diagram that most closely resembles a conventional flowchart is an activity diagram. In an **activity diagram**, you show the flow of actions of a system, including branches that occur when decisions affect the outcome. Conventionally, activity diagrams use flowchart start and stop symbols (called lozenges) to describe actions and solid dots to represent start and stop states. Like flowcharts, activity diagrams use diamonds to describe decisions. Unlike the diamonds in flowcharts, the diamonds in UML activity diagrams usually are empty; the possible outcomes are documented along the branches emerging from the decision symbol. As an example, Figure 13-18 shows a simple activity diagram with a single branch.

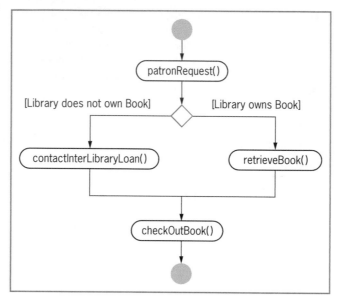

Figure 13-18 Activity diagram showing branch

In the first major version of the UML (UML 1.0), each lozenge was an activity. Starting with the second major version (UML 2.0), each lozenge is an action and a group of actions is an activity.

Many real-life systems contain actions that are meant to occur simultaneously. For example, when you apply for a home mortgage with a bank, a bank officer might perform a credit or background check, while an appraiser determines the value of the house you are buying. When both actions are complete, the loan process continues. UML activity diagrams use forks and joins to show simultaneous activities. A **fork** is similar to a decision, but whereas the flow of control follows only one path after a decision, a fork defines a branch in which all paths are followed simultaneously. A **join**, as its name implies, reunites the flow of control after a fork. You indicate forks and joins with thick straight lines. Figure 13-19 shows how you might model the way an interlibrary loan system processes book requests. When a request is received, simultaneous searches begin at three local libraries that are part of the library system.

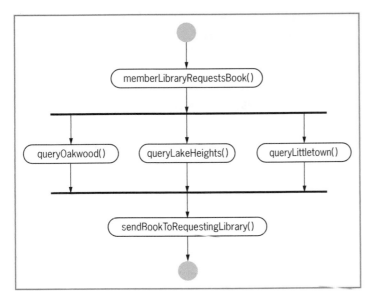

Figure 13-19 Activity diagram showing fork and join

A fork does not have to indicate strictly simultaneous activity. The actions in the branches for a fork might only be concurrent or interleaved.

An activity diagram can contain a time signal. A **time signal** indicates that a specific amount of time should pass before an action starts. The time signal looks like two stacked triangles (resembling the shape of an hourglass). Figure 13-20 shows a time signal indicating that if a patron requests a book, and the book is checked out to another patron, then only if the book's due date has passed should a request to return the book be issued. In activity diagrams for other systems, you might see explanations at time signals, such as "10 hours have passed" or "at least January 1". If an action is time-dependent, whether by a fraction of a second or by years, using a time signal is appropriate.

The time signal was a new feature starting in UML 2.0.

The connector is a fairly recent addition to the UML. It is a small circle used to connect diagrams that continue on a new page.

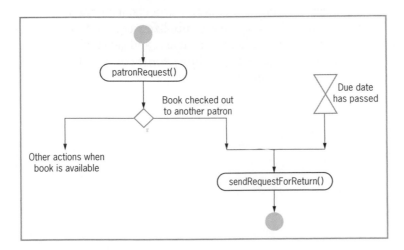

Figure 13-20 A time signal starting an action

TWO TRUTHS & A LIE

Using Activity Diagrams

1. The activity diagram is the UML diagram that most closely resembles a hierarchy chart.

2. Like flowcharts, activity diagrams use diamonds to describe decisions, but unlike the diamonds in flowcharts, the diamonds in UML activity diagrams are usually empty.

3. In an activity diagram, a fork is similar to a decision; a join, as its name implies, reunites the flow of control after a fork.

The false statement is #1. The activity diagram is the UML diagram that most closely resembles a conventional flowchart.

Using Component, Deployment, and Profile Diagrams

Component and deployment diagrams model the physical aspects of systems. You use a **component diagram** when you want to emphasize the files, database tables, documents, and other components that a system's software uses. You use a **deployment diagram** when you want to focus on a system's hardware. You can use a variety of icons in each type of diagram, but each icon must convey meaning to the reader. Figures 13-21 and 13-22 show component and deployment diagrams, respectively, that illustrate aspects of a library system. Figure 13-21 contains icons that symbolize paper and Internet requests for library items, the library database, and two tables that constitute the database. Figure 13-22 shows some commonly used icons that represent hardware components.

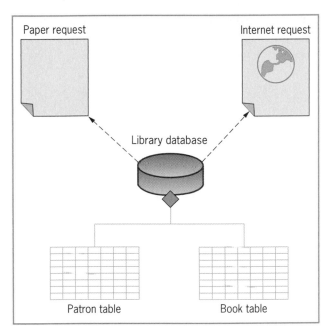

Figure 13-21   Component diagram

In Figure 13-21, notice the filled diamond connecting the two tables to the database. Just as it does in a class diagram, the diamond aggregation symbol shows the whole-part relationship of the tables to the database. You use an open diamond when a part might belong to several wholes (for example, **Door** and **Wall** objects belong to many **House** objects), but you use a filled diamond when a part can belong to only one whole at a time (the **Patron** table can belong only to the **Library** database). You can use most UML symbols in multiple types of diagrams.

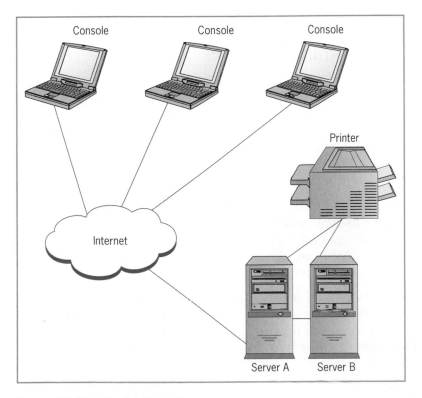

Figure 13-22   Deployment diagram

The **profile diagram** is the newest UML diagram type. It is used to extend a UML model for a particular domain (such as financial or healthcare applications) or a particular platform (such as .NET or Java).

TWO TRUTHS & A LIE

Using Component, Deployment, and Profile Diagrams

1. You use a component diagram when you want to emphasize the files, database tables, documents, and other components that a system's software uses.

2. You use a deployment diagram when you want to focus on a system's software components.

3. You can use a variety of icons in each type of UML diagram, but each icon must convey meaning to the reader.

The false statement is #2. You use a deployment diagram when you want to focus on a system's hardware.

Diagramming Exception Handling

You learned the object-oriented technique of exception handling in Chapter 11.

Exception handling is a set of the object-oriented techniques used to handle program errors. When a segment of code might cause an error, you can place that code in a `try` block. If the error occurs, an object called an exception is thrown, or sent, to a `catch` block where appropriate action can be taken. For example, depending on the application, a `catch` block might display a message, assign a default value to a field, or prompt the user for direction.

In the UML, a `try` block is called a **protected node** and a `catch` block is a **handler body node**. In a UML diagram, a protected node is enclosed in a rounded rectangle and any exceptions that might be thrown are listed next to arrows shaped like lightning bolts, which extend to the appropriate handler body node.

Figure 13-23 shows an example of an activity that uses exception handling. When a library patron tries to check out a book, the patron's card is scanned and the book is scanned. These actions might cause three errors—the patron owes fines, and so cannot check out new books; the patron's card has expired, requiring a new card application; or the book might be on hold for another patron. If no exceptions occur, the activity proceeds to the `checkOutBook()` process.

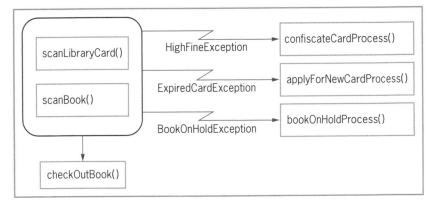

Figure 13-23   Exceptions in the Book check-out activity

TWO TRUTHS & A LIE

Diagramming Exception Handling

1. In the UML, a `try` block is called a protected node.

2. In the UML, a `catch` block is a handler body node.

3. In a UML diagram, both protected nodes and handler body nodes are enclosed in rounded rectangles.

The false statement is #3. In a UML diagram, a protected node is enclosed in a rounded rectangle and any exceptions that might be thrown are listed next to arrows shaped like lightning bolts, which extend to the appropriate handler body node.

Deciding When to Use the UML and Which UML Diagrams to Use

The UML is widely recognized as a modeling standard, but it is also frequently criticized. The criticisms include:

*   *Size*—The UML is often criticized as being too large and complex. Many of the diagrams are infrequently used, and some critics claim several are redundant.

*   *Imprecision*—The UML is a combination of rules and English. In particular, problems occur when the diagrams are applied to tasks other than those implemented in object-oriented programming languages.

- *Complexity*—Because of its size and imprecision, the UML is relatively difficult to learn.

Still, under the right circumstances, the UML can increase communication between developers and users of a system. Each of the UML diagram types provides a different view of a system. Just as a portrait artist, psychologist, and neurosurgeon each prefer a different conceptual view of your head, the users, managers, designers, and technicians of computer and business systems each prefer specific system views. Very few systems require diagrams of all UML types; you can illustrate the objects and activities of many systems by using a single diagram, or perhaps one that is a hybrid of two or more basic types. No view is superior to the others; you can achieve the most complete picture of any system by using several views. The most important reason you use any UML diagram is to communicate clearly and efficiently with the people for whom you are designing a system.

TWO TRUTHS & A LIE

Deciding When to Use the UML and Which UML Diagrams to Use

1. The UML has been hailed as a practically perfect design tool because it is concise and easy to learn.

2. Very few systems require diagrams of all UML types; you can illustrate the objects and activities of many systems by using a single diagram, or perhaps one that is a hybrid of two or more basic types.

3. The most important reason you use any UML diagram is to communicate clearly and efficiently with the people for whom you are designing a system.

The false statement is #1. The UML is often criticized as being too large and complex. Many of the diagrams are infrequently used, and some critics claim several are redundant. Because of its size and imprecision, the UML is relatively difficult to learn.

Chapter Summary

- System design is the detailed specification of how all the parts of a system will be implemented and coordinated. Good designs make systems easier to understand. The UML (Unified Modeling Language) provides a means for programmers and businesspeople to communicate about system design.

- The UML is a standard way to specify, construct, and document systems that use object-oriented methods. The UML has its own notation, with which you can construct software diagrams that model different kinds of systems. The UML provides 14 diagram types that you use at the beginning of the design process.

- A use case diagram shows how a business works from the perspective of those who approach it from the outside, or those who actually use the business. The diagram often includes actors, represented by stick figures, and use cases, represented by ovals. Use cases can include variations such as extend relationships, include relationships, and generalizations.

- You use a class diagram to illustrate the names, attributes, and methods of a class or set of classes. A class diagram of a single class contains a rectangle divided into three sections: the name of the class, the names of the attributes, and the names of the methods. Class diagrams can show generalizations and the relationships between objects. Object diagrams are similar to class diagrams, but they model specific instances of classes at one point in time.

- You use a sequence diagram to show the timing of events in a single use case. The horizontal axis (x-axis) of a sequence diagram represents objects, and the vertical axis (y-axis) represents time. A communication diagram emphasizes the organization of objects that participate in a system. It is similar to a sequence diagram, except that it contains sequence numbers to represent the precise order in which activities occur.

- A state machine diagram shows the different statuses of a class or object at different points in time.

- In an activity diagram, you show the flow of actions of a system, including branches that occur when decisions affect the outcome. UML activity diagrams use forks and joins to show simultaneous activities.

575

576

- You use a component diagram when you want to emphasize the files, database tables, documents, and other components that a system's software uses. You use a deployment diagram when you want to focus on a system's hardware. A profile diagram is used to extend a UML model for a particular domain or platform.

- Exception handling is diagrammed in the UML using a rounded rectangle to represent a `try` block protected node. Any exceptions that might be thrown are listed next to arrows shaped like lightning bolts, which extend to the appropriate handler body node.

- Each of the UML diagram types provides a different view of a system. Very few systems require diagrams of all UML types; the most important reason to use any UML diagram is to communicate clearly and efficiently with the people for whom you are designing a system.

Key Terms

System design is the detailed specification of how all the parts of a system will be implemented and coordinated.

The **Unified Modeling Language (UML)** is a standard way to specify, construct, and document systems that use object-oriented methods.

Reverse engineering is the process of creating a model of an existing system.

Structure diagrams emphasize the "things" in a system.

Behavior diagrams emphasize what happens in a system.

Interaction diagrams emphasize the flow of control and data among the things in the system being modeled.

The **use case diagram** is a UML diagram that shows how a business works from the perspective of those who approach it from the outside, or those who actually use the business.

An **extend variation** is a use case variation that shows functions beyond those found in a base case.

A **scenario** is a variation in the sequence of actions required in a use case.

A **stereotype** is a feature that adds to the UML vocabulary of shapes to make them more meaningful for the reader.

An **include variation** is a use case variation that you use when a case can be part of multiple use cases in a UML diagram.

A **generalization variation** is used in a UML diagram when a use case is less specific than others, and you want to be able to substitute the more specific case for a general one.

Elided describes the omitted parts when UML diagrams are edited for clarity.

When a method **overrides** another, it is used by default in place of one with the same signature.

An **association relationship** describes the connection or link between objects in a UML diagram.

Cardinality and **multiplicity** refer to the arithmetic relationships between objects.

A **whole-part relationship** describes an association in which one or more classes make up the parts of a larger whole class.

An **aggregation** is a whole-part relationship.

A **has-a relationship** is a whole-part relationship; the phrase describes the association between the whole and one of its parts.

Object diagrams are UML diagrams that are similar to class diagrams, but they model specific instances of classes.

A **sequence diagram** is a UML diagram that shows the timing of events in a single use case.

A **communication diagram** is a UML diagram that emphasizes the organization of objects that participate in a system.

A **state machine diagram** is a UML diagram that shows the different statuses of a class or object at different points in time.

An **activity diagram** is a UML diagram that shows the flow of actions of a system, including branches that occur when decisions affect the outcome.

A **fork** is a feature of a UML activity diagram; it is similar to a decision, but whereas the flow of control follows only one path after a decision, a fork defines a branch in which all paths are followed simultaneously.

A **join** is a feature of a UML activity diagram; it reunites the flow of control after a fork.

A **time signal** is a UML diagram symbol that indicates that a specific amount of time has passed before an action is started.

A **component diagram** is a UML diagram that emphasizes the files, database tables, documents, and other components that a system's software uses.

A **deployment diagram** is a UML diagram that focuses on a system's hardware.

A **profile diagram** is used to extend a UML model for a particular domain or platform.

A **protected node** is the UML diagram name for an exception-throwing try block.

A **handler body node** is the UML diagram name for an exception-handling catch block.

Review Questions

1. The detailed specification of how all the parts of a system will be implemented and coordinated is called _____.

   a. programming

   b. paraphrasing

   c. system design

   d. structuring

2. The primary purpose of good modeling techniques is to _____.

   a. promote communication

   b. increase functional cohesion

   c. reduce the need for structure

   d. reduce dependency between modules

3. The Unified Modeling Language provides standard ways to do all of the following to business systems except _____ them.

   a. construct

   b. document

   c. describe

   d. destroy

4. The UML is commonly used to model all of the following except _____.

   a. computer programs

   b. business activities

   c. organizational processes

   d. software systems

5. The UML was intentionally designed to be _____.

   a. low-level, detail-oriented

   b. used with Visual Basic

   c. nontechnical

   d. inexpensive

6. The UML diagrams that show how a business works from the perspective of those who actually use the business, such as employees or customers, are _____ diagrams.

   a. communication

   b. use case

   c. state machine

   d. class

7. Which of the following is an example of a relationship that would be portrayed as an extend relationship in a use case diagram for a hospital?

   a. the relationship between the head nurse and the floor nurses

   b. admitting a patient who has never been admitted before

   c. serving a meal

   d. scheduling the monitoring of patients' vital signs

8. The people shown in use case diagrams are called _____.

   a. workers

   b. clowns

   c. actors

   d. relatives

9. One aspect of use case diagrams that makes them difficult to learn is that _____.

    a. they require programming experience to understand

    b. they use a technical vocabulary

    c. there is no single right answer for any case

    d. all of the above

10. The arithmetic association relationship between a college student and college courses would be expressed as _____.

    a. 1   0

    b. 1   1

    c. 1   0..*

    d. 0..* 0..*

11. In the UML, object diagrams are most similar to _____ diagrams.

    a. use case

    b. activity

    c. class

    d. sequence

12. In any given situation, you should choose the type of UML diagram that is _____.

    a. shorter than others

    b. clearer than others

    c. more detailed than others

    d. closest to the programming language you will use to implement the system

13. A whole-part relationship can be described as a(n) _____ relationship.

    a. parent-child

    b. has-a

    c. is-a

    d. creates-a

14. The timing of events is best portrayed in a(n) _____ diagram.

    a. sequence

    b. use case

    c. communication

    d. association

15. A communication diagram is closest to a(n) _____ diagram.

    a. activity

    b. use case

    c. deployment

    d. sequence

16. A(n) _____ diagram shows the different statuses of a class or object at different points in time.

    a. activity

    b. state machine

    c. sequence

    d. deployment

17. The UML diagram that most closely resembles a conventional flowchart is a(n) _____ diagram.

    a. activity

    b. state machine

    c. sequence

    d. deployment

18. You use a _____ diagram when you want to emphasize the files, database tables, documents, and other components that a system's software uses.

    a. state machine

    b. component

    c. deployment

    d. use case

19. The UML diagram that focuses on a system's hardware is a(n) _____ diagram.

    a. deployment

    b. sequence

    c. activity

    d. use case

20. When using the UML to describe a single system, most designers would use _____.

    a. a single type of diagram

    b. at least three types of diagrams

    c. most of the available types of diagrams

    d. all the types of diagrams

Exercises

1. Complete the following tasks:

   a. Develop a use case diagram for a convenience food store. Include an actor representing the store manager and use cases for orderItem(), stockItem(), and sellItem().

   b. Add more use cases to the diagram you created in Exercise 1a. Include two generalizations for stockItem() called stockPerishable() and stockNonPerishable(). Also include an extension to sellItem() called checkCredit() for when a customer purchases items using a credit card.

   c. Add a customer actor to the use case diagram you created in Exercise 1b. Show that the customer participates in sellItem(), but not in orderItem() or stockItem().

2. Develop a use case diagram for a department store credit card system. Include at least two actors and four use cases.

3. Develop a use case diagram for a college registration system. Include at least three actors and five use cases.

4. Develop a class diagram for a Video class that describes objects a video store customer can rent. Include at least four attributes and three methods.

5. Develop a class diagram for a Shape class. Include generalizations for child classes Rectangle, Circle, and Triangle.

6. Develop a class diagram for a BankLoan class. Include generalizations for child classes Mortgage, CarLoan, and EducationLoan.

7. Develop a class diagram for a college registration system. Include at least three classes that cooperate to achieve student registration.

8. Develop a sequence diagram that shows how a clerk at a mail-order company places a customer Order. The Order accesses Inventory to check availability. Then, the Order accesses Invoice to produce a customer invoice that returns to the clerk.

9. Develop a state machine diagram that shows the states of a CollegeStudent from PotentialApplicant to Graduate.

10. Develop a state machine diagram that shows the states of a Book from Concept to Publication.

11. Develop an activity diagram that illustrates how to build a house.

12. Develop an activity diagram that illustrates how to prepare dinner.

13. Develop the UML diagram of your choice that illustrates some aspect of your life.

14. Complete the following tasks:

a. Develop the UML diagram of your choice that best illustrates some aspect of a place you have worked.

b. Develop a different UML diagram type that illustrates the same functions as the diagram you created in Exercise 14a.

Find the Bugs

15. Your student disk contains files named DEBUG13-01.doc, DEBUG13-02.doc, and DEBUG13-03.doc. Each file contains some comments that describe a problem and a UML diagram that has one or more bugs you must find and correct.

 Game Zone

16. Develop a use case diagram for a baseball game. Include actors representing a player and an umpire. Create use cases for `hitBall()`, `runBases()`, and `makeCallAtBase()`. Include two generalizations for `makeCallAtBase()` called `callSafe()` and `callOut()`.

17. Develop a class diagram for a `CardGame` class. Include generalizations for child classes `SolitaireCardGame` and `OpponentCardGame`.

18. Choose a child's game such as Hide and Seek or Duck, Duck, Goose and describe it using UML diagrams of your choice.

 Up for Discussion

19. Which do you think you would enjoy doing more on the job—designing large systems that contain many programs, or writing the programs themselves? Why?

20. In earlier chapters, you considered ethical dilemmas in writing programs that select candidates for organ transplants. Are the ethical responsibilities of a system designer different from those of a programmer? If so, how?

Using Relational Databases

In this chapter you will learn about:

- ◎ Relational database fundamentals
- ◎ Creating databases and table descriptions
- ◎ Primary keys
- ◎ Database structure notation
- ◎ Adding, deleting, updating, and sorting records within a table
- ◎ Creating queries
- ◎ Relationships between tables
- ◎ Poor table design
- ◎ Anomalies, normal forms, and normalization
- ◎ Database performance and security issues

Understanding Relational Database Fundamentals

In Chapter 7, you learned that when you store data items for use within computer systems, they are often stored in a data hierarchy that is organized as follows:

- **Characters** are the smallest usable units of data—for example, a letter, digit, or punctuation mark is a character. When characters are stored in a computer, they are created from smaller pieces called bits, which represent computer circuitry, but human users seldom care about bits; characters have meaning to users.

- **Fields** are formed from groups of characters and represent a piece of information, such as `firstName`, `lastName`, or `socialSecurityNumber`.

- **Records** are formed from groups of related fields. The fields go together because they represent attributes of some entity, such as an employee, a customer, an inventory item, or a bank account.

- **Files** are composed of associated records; for example, a file might contain a record for each employee in a company or each account at a bank.

In Chapter 6, you learned that arrays are also sometimes called tables. Arrays (stored in memory) and tables (stored in databases) are similar in that both contain rows and columns. When an array has multiple columns, all must have the same data type. The same is not true for tables stored in databases.

Most organizations store many files that contain the data they need to operate their businesses; for example, businesses often need to maintain files containing data about employees, customers, inventory items, and orders. Many organizations use a database to organize the information in these files. A **database** holds a group of files that an organization needs to support its applications. In a database, the files often are called **tables** because you can arrange their contents in rows and columns. Real-life examples of these tables abound. For example, consider the listings in a telephone book. Each listing might contain four columns, as shown in Figure 14-1—last name, first name, street address, and phone number. Although your local phone directory might not store its data in this format, it could. You can see that each column represents a field and that each row represents one record. You can picture a table within a database in the same way.

Sometimes, one record or row is also called an **entity**; however, many definitions of *entity* exist in database texts. One column (field) can also be called an **attribute**.

Last name	First name	Address	Phone
Abbott	William	123 Oak Lane	490-8920
Ackerman	Kimberly	467 Elm Drive	787-2781
Adams	Stanley	8120 Pine Street	787-0129
Adams	Violet	347 Oak Lane	490-8912
Adams	William	12 Second Street	490-3667

Figure 14-1 A telephone book table

Figure 14-1 includes five records, each representing a unique person. It is relatively easy to scan this short list of names to find a person's phone number; of course, telephone books contain many more records. Some users, such as telemarketers or even the phone company, might prefer to have records organized in telephone-number order. Others might prefer to have records organized in street-address order. Most people, however, prefer a telephone book in which the records are organized as shown, in alphabetical order by last name. It is most convenient for different users when a computerized database is used to store data because the data can easily be sorted and displayed to fit each user's needs.

Unless you are using a telephone book for a very small town, a last name alone often is not sufficient to identify a person. In the example in Figure 14-1, three people have the last name of Adams. For these records, you need to examine the first name before you can determine the correct phone number. In a large city, many people might have the same first and last names; in that case, you might also need to examine the street address to identify a person. As with the telephone book, most computerized database tables need to have a way to identify each record uniquely, even if it means using multiple columns. A value that uniquely identifies a record is called a **primary key**, or a **key** for short. Key fields are often defined as a single table column, but as with the telephone book, keys can be constructed from multiple columns; such a key is a **compound key**, or **composite key**.

You learn more about key fields and compound keys later in this chapter.

Telephone books are republished periodically because changes have occurred—people have left or moved into the city, canceled service, or changed phone numbers. With computerized database tables, you also need to add, delete, and modify records, although usually with more frequency than phone books are published.

Computerized database tables frequently contain thousands of records, or rows, and each row might contain entries in dozens of columns. Handling and organizing all the data in an organization's tables requires sophisticated software. **Database management software** is a set of programs that allows users to:

- Create table descriptions.
- Identify keys.
- Add, delete, and update records within a table.
- Arrange records within a table so they are sorted by different fields.
- Write questions that select specific records from a table for viewing.

- Write questions that combine information from multiple tables. This is possible because the database management software establishes and maintains relationships between the columns in the tables. A group of database tables from which you can make these connections is a **relational database**.

- Create reports that allow users to easily interpret your data, and create forms that allow users to view and enter data using an easy-to-manage interactive screen.

- Keep data secure by employing sophisticated security measures.

Each database management software package operates differently; however, with each, you perform the same types of tasks.

TWO TRUTHS & A LIE

Understanding Relational Database Fundamentals

1. Files are composed of associated records, and records are composed of fields.

2. In a database, files are often called tables because you can arrange their contents in rows and columns.

3. Key fields are always defined as a single table column.

The false statement is #3. Key fields are often defined as a single table column, but keys can be constructed from multiple columns; such a key is a compound key.

Creating Databases and Table Descriptions

Creating a useful database requires planning and analysis. You must decide what data will be stored, how that data will be divided between tables, and how the tables will interrelate. Before you create any tables, you must create the database itself. With most database software packages, creating the database that will hold the tables requires nothing more than naming it and indicating the physical location, perhaps a hard disk drive, where the database will be stored. When you save a table, it is conventional to provide a name that begins with the prefix "tbl"—for example, tblCustomers. Your databases often become filled with a variety of objects—tables, forms for data entry, reports that organize the data for viewing, queries that select subsets of data for viewing, and so on. Using naming conventions, such as beginning each table name with a prefix that identifies it as a table, helps you keep track of the objects in your system.

Before you can enter any data into a database table, you must design the table. At minimum, this involves two tasks:

- You must decide what columns your table needs, and provide names for them.

- You must provide a data type for each column.

For example, assume you are designing a customer database table. Figure 14-2 shows some column names and data types you might use.

When you save a table description, many database management programs suggest a default, generic table description name such as Table1. Usually, a more descriptive name is more useful as you create objects.

Column	Data type
customerID	text
lastName	text
firstName	text
streetAddress	text
balanceOwed	numeric

Figure 14-2 Customer table description

A table description closely resembles the list of variables that you have used with every program throughout this book.

It is important to think carefully about the original design of a database. After the database has been created and data has been entered, it could be difficult and time consuming to make changes.

The table description in Figure 14-2 uses just two data types—text and numeric. Text columns can hold any type of characters—letters or digits. Numeric columns can hold numbers only. Depending on the database management software you use, you might have many more sophisticated data types at your disposal. For example, some database software divides the numeric data type into several subcategories such as integer (whole number only) values and double-precision numbers (numbers that contain decimals). Other options might include special categories for currency numbers (representing dollars and cents), dates, and Boolean columns (representing true or false). At the least, all database software recognizes the distinction between text and numeric data.

Throughout this book, you have been aware of the distinction that computers make between text and numeric data. Because of the way computers handle data, every type of software observes this distinction. Throughout this book, the term "string" has been used to describe text fields. The term "text" is used in this chapter only because popular database packages use this term.

590

Unassigned variables within computer programs might be empty (containing a null value), or might contain unknown or garbage values. Similarly, columns in database tables might also contain null or unknown values. When a field in a database contains a null value, it does not mean that the field holds a 0 or a space; it means that no data has been entered for the field at all. Although *null* and *empty* are used synonymously by many database developers, the terms have slightly different meanings to some professionals, such as Visual Basic programmers.

The table description in Figure 14-2 uses one-word column names and camel casing, in the same way that variable names have been defined throughout this book. Many database software packages allow multiple-word column names with embedded spaces, but many database table designers prefer single-word names because they resemble variable names in programs. In addition, when you write programs that access a database table, the single-word field names can be used "as is," without special syntax to indicate the names that represent a single field. Also, when you use a single word to label each database column, it is easier to understand whether just one column is being referenced, or several.

Watch the video *Creating Databases*.

The `customerID` column in Figure 14-2 is defined as text. If `customerID` numbers are composed entirely of digits, this column could also be defined as numeric. However, many database designers feel that columns should be defined as numeric only if necessary—that is, only if they might be used in arithmetic calculations. The description in Figure 14-2 follows this convention by declaring `customerID` as text.

Many database management software packages allow you to add a narrative description of each data column to a table. These comments become part of the table, but do not affect the way it operates; they simply serve as documentation for those who are reading a table description. For example, you might want to make a note that `customerID` should consist of five digits, or that `balanceOwed` should not exceed a given limit. Some software allows you to specify that values for a certain column are required—the user cannot create a record without providing data for these columns. In addition, you might be able to indicate range limits for a column—high and low values between which the column contents must fall.

In some database programs, the comments fields are called *memos*.

TWO TRUTHS & A LIE

Creating Databases and Table Descriptions

1. When you save a table, it is conventional to provide a name that begins with the prefix "table".

2. Designing a table involves deciding what columns your table needs, providing names for them, and providing a data type for each column.

3. Many database table designers prefer single-word column names because they resemble variable names in programs, they can be easily used in programs, and they make it easier to understand whether just one column is being referenced, or several.

The false statement is # 1. When you save a table, it is conventional to provide a name that begins with the prefix "tbl".

Identifying Primary Keys

In most tables you create for a database, you want to identify a column, or possibly a combination of columns, as the table's key column or field, also called the primary key. The primary key in a table is the column that makes each record different from all others. For example, in the customer table in Figure 14-2, the logical choice for a primary key is the `customerID` column—each customer record entered into the customer table has a unique value in this column. Many customers might have the same first name or last name (or both), and multiple customers might have the same street address or balance due. However, each customer possesses a unique ID number.

Other typical examples of primary keys include:

*   A student ID number in a table that contains college student information

*   A part number in a table that contains inventory items

*   A state abbreviation in a table that contains sales information for each state in the United States

In each of these examples, the primary key uniquely identifies the row. For example, each student has a unique ID number assigned by the college. Other columns in a student table would not be adequate keys—many students have the same last name, first name, hometown, or major.

Often, keys are numbers. Usually, assigning a number to each row in a table is the simplest and most efficient method of obtaining a useful key. However, a table's key can be a text field, as in the state abbreviation example.

Sometimes, several columns could serve as the key. For example, if an employee record contains both a company-assigned employee ID and a Social Security number, then both columns are **candidate keys**. After you choose a primary key from among candidate keys, the remaining candidate keys become **alternate keys**. (Many database developers would object to using a Social Security number as a primary key because of privacy issues.)

The primary key is important for several reasons:

- You can configure your database software to prevent multiple records from containing the same value in this column, thus avoiding data-entry errors.

- You can sort your records in this order before displaying or printing them.

In some database software packages, such as Microsoft Access, you indicate a primary key simply by selecting a column name and clicking a button that is labeled with a key icon.

- You use the primary key column when setting up relationships between this table and others that will become part of the same database.

- You need to understand the concept of the primary key when you normalize a database—a concept you will learn more about later in this chapter.

In some tables, when no identifying number has been assigned to the rows, a primary key must be constructed from multiple columns. A multicolumn key is a compound key. For example, consider Figure 14-3, which might be used by a residence hall administrator to store data about students living on a university campus. Each room in a building has a number and two students, each assigned to either bed A or bed B.

hall	room	bed	lastName	firstName	major
Adams	101	A	Fredricks	Madison	Chemistry
Adams	101	B	Garza	Lupe	Psychology
Adams	102	A	Liu	Jennifer	CIS
Adams	102	B	Smith	Crystal	CIS
Browning	101	A	Patel	Sarita	CIS
Browning	101	B	Smith	Margaret	Biology
Browning	102	A	Jefferson	Martha	Psychology
Browning	102	B	Bartlett	Donna	Spanish
Churchill	101	A	Wong	Cheryl	CIS
Churchill	101	B	Smith	Madison	Chemistry
Churchill	102	A	Patel	Jennifer	Psychology
Churchill	102	B	Jones	Elizabeth	CIS

Figure 14-3   Table containing residence hall student records

In Figure 14-3, no single column can serve as a primary key. Many students live in the same residence hall, and the same room numbers exist in the different residence halls. In addition, some students have the same last name, first name, or major. It is even possible that two students with the same first name, last name, or major are assigned to the same room. In this case, the best primary key is a multicolumn key that combines residence hall, room number, and bed number (hall, room, and bed). "Adams 101 A" identifies a single room and student, as does "Churchill 102 B".

A primary key should be **immutable**, meaning that a value does not change during normal operation. In other words, in Figure 14-3, "Adams 102 A" will always pertain to a fixed location, even though the resident or her major might change. Of course, the school might choose to change the name of a residence hall—for example, to honor a benefactor—but that action would fall outside the range of "normal operation."

Even if only one student was named Smith, for example, or only one Psychology major was listed in Figure 14-3, those fields still would not be good primary key candidates because of the potential for future Smiths and Psychology majors within the database. Analyzing existing data is not a fool-proof way to select a good key; you must also consider likely future data.

As an alternative to selecting three columns to create the compound key for the table in Figure 14-3, many database designers would prefer that the college uniquely number every bed on campus and add a new column to the database that contains the ID number. Many database designers feel that a primary key should be short to minimize the amount of storage required for it in all the tables that refer to it.

Usually, after you have identified the necessary fields, data types, and the primary key, you are ready to save your table description and begin to enter data.

594

Understanding Database Structure Notation

 Some database designers insert an asterisk after the key instead of underlining it.

 The key does not have to be the first attribute listed in a table reference, but frequently it is.

A shorthand way to describe a table is to use the table name followed by parentheses containing all the field names, with the primary key underlined. Thus, when a table is named tblStudents and contains columns named idNumber, lastName, firstName, and gradePointAverage, and idNumber is the key, you can reference the table using the following notation:

tblStudents(<u>idNumber</u>, lastName, firstName, gradePointAverage)

Although this shorthand notation does not provide information about data types or range limits on values, it does provide a quick overview of the table's structure.

TWO TRUTHS & A LIE

Understanding Database Structure Notation

1. A shorthand way to describe a table is to use the table name followed by parentheses containing all the field names.

2. Typically, when you describe a table using database structure notation, the primary key is underlined.

3. Database structure notation provides information about column names, their data types, and their range limits.

The false statement is #3. Although this shorthand notation does not provide information about data types or range limits on values, it does provide a quick overview of the table's structure.

Adding, Deleting, Updating, and Sorting Records within Tables

Entering data into an existing table is not difficult, but it requires a good deal of time and accurate typing. Depending on the application, the contents of the tables might be entered over the course of months or years by many data-entry personnel. Entering data of the wrong type is not allowed by most database applications. In addition, you might have set up your table to prevent duplicate data in specific fields, or to prevent data entry outside of specified bounds in certain fields. With some database software, you type data into rows representing each record, and columns representing each field in each record, much as you would enter data into a spreadsheet. With other software, you can create on-screen forms to make data entry more user-friendly. Some software does not allow you to enter a partial record; that is, you might not be allowed to leave any fields blank.

 In Chapter 12, you learned that computer professionals use the acronym GIGO, which stands for "garbage in, garbage out." It means that if you enter invalid input data into an application, the output results will be worthless.

Deleting and modifying records in a database table are also relatively easy tasks. In most organizations, most of the important data is in a constant state of change. Keeping the data records up to date is a vital part of any database management system.

 In many database systems, some "deleted" records are not physically removed. Instead, they are just marked as deleted so they will not be used to process active records. For example, a company might want to retain data about former employees, but not process them with current personnel reports. On the other hand, an employee record that was entered by mistake would be permanently removed from the database.

When sorting records on multiple fields, the software first uses a primary sort—for example, by last name. After all records with the same primary sort key are grouped, the software sorts by the secondary key—for example, first name.

Sorting the Records in a Table

Database management software generally allows you to sort a table based on any column, letting you view the data in the way that is most useful to you. For example, you might want to view inventory items in alphabetical order, or from the most to least expensive. You can also sort by multiple columns—for example, you might sort employees by first name within last name (so that Aaron Black is listed before Andrea Black), or by department within first name within last name (so that Aaron Black in Department 1 is listed before another Aaron Black in Department 6).

After rows are sorted, they usually can be grouped. For example, you might want to sort customers by their zip code, or employees by the department in which they work; in addition, you might want counts or subtotals at the end of each group. Database software allows you to create displays in the formats that suit your needs.

TWO TRUTHS & A LIE

Adding, Deleting, Updating, and Sorting Records within Tables

1. Depending on the application, the contents of the tables in a database system might be entered over the course of months or years by many data-entry personnel.

2. In most organizations, most of the important data is permanent.

3. Database management software generally allows you to sort and group data, letting you view the data in the way that is most useful to you.

The false statement is #2. In most organizations, most of the important data is in a constant state of change. Keeping the data records up to date is a vital part of any database management system.

Creating Queries

Data tables often contain hundreds or thousands of rows; making sense out of that much information is a daunting task. Frequently, you want to view subsets of data from a table you have created. For example, you might want to examine only those customers with an address in a specific state, only those inventory items whose quantity in stock

TWO TRUTHS & A LIE

Understanding Database Structure Notation

1. A shorthand way to describe a table is to use the table name followed by parentheses containing all the field names.

2. Typically, when you describe a table using database structure notation, the primary key is underlined.

3. Database structure notation provides information about column names, their data types, and their range limits.

The false statement is #3. Although this shorthand notation does not provide information about data types or range limits on values, it does provide a quick overview of the table's structure.

Adding, Deleting, Updating, and Sorting Records within Tables

Entering data into an existing table is not difficult, but it requires a good deal of time and accurate typing. Depending on the application, the contents of the tables might be entered over the course of months or years by many data-entry personnel. Entering data of the wrong type is not allowed by most database applications. In addition, you might have set up your table to prevent duplicate data in specific fields, or to prevent data entry outside of specified bounds in certain fields. With some database software, you type data into rows representing each record, and columns representing each field in each record, much as you would enter data into a spreadsheet. With other software, you can create on-screen forms to make data entry more user-friendly. Some software does not allow you to enter a partial record; that is, you might not be allowed to leave any fields blank.

In Chapter 12, you learned that computer professionals use the acronym GIGO, which stands for "garbage in, garbage out." It means that if you enter invalid input data into an application, the output results will be worthless.

Deleting and modifying records in a database table are also relatively easy tasks. In most organizations, most of the important data is in a constant state of change. Keeping the data records up to date is a vital part of any database management system.

In many database systems, some "deleted" records are not physically removed. Instead, they are just marked as deleted so they will not be used to process active records. For example, a company might want to retain data about former employees, but not process them with current personnel reports. On the other hand, an employee record that was entered by mistake would be permanently removed from the database.

To select all fields for each record in a table, you can use the asterisk as a wildcard; a **wildcard** is a symbol that means "any" or "all." For example, the following statement would select all columns for every customer whose state is "WI", not just specifically named columns:

```
SELECT * from tblCustomer WHERE state = "WI"
```

To select all customers from a table, you can omit the WHERE clause in a SELECT-FROM-WHERE statement. In other words, the following statement selects all columns for all customers:

```
SELECT * FROM tblCustomer
```

You learned about making selections in computer programs much earlier in this book, and you have probably noticed that SELECT-FROM-WHERE statements serve the same purpose as programming decisions. As with decision statements in programs, SQL allows you to create compound conditions using AND or OR operators. In addition, you can precede any condition with a NOT operator to achieve a negative result. In summary, Figure 14-4 shows a database table named **tblInventory** with the following structure:

```
tblInventory(itemNumber, description, quantityInStock, price)
```

The table contains five records. Figure 14-5 lists several typical SQL SELECT statements you might use with **tblInventory**, and explains each.

itemNumber	description	quantityInStock	price
144	Pkg 12 party plates	250	$14.99
231	Helium balloons	180	$2.50
267	Paper streamers	68	$1.89
312	Disposable tablecloth	20	$6.99
383	Pkg 20 napkins	315	$2.39

Figure 14-4 The tblInventory table

has fallen below the normal reorder point, or only those employees who participate in an insurance plan. Besides limiting records, you might also want to limit the columns that you view. For example, student records might contain dozens of fields, but a school administrator might only be interested in looking at names and grade point averages. The questions you use to extract the appropriate records from a table and specify the fields to be viewed are called queries; a **query** is a question using the syntax that the database software can understand.

Depending on the software you use, you might create a query by filling in blanks (a process called **query by example**) or by writing statements similar to those in many programming languages. The most common language that database administrators use to access data in their tables is **Structured Query Language**, or **SQL**. The basic form of the SQL statement that retrieves selected records from a table is **SELECT-FROM-WHERE**. This statement:

- *Selects* the columns you want to view

- *From* a specific table

- *Where* one or more conditions are met

SQL is frequently pronounced *sequel*; however, several SQL product Web sites insist that the official pronunciation is *S-Q-L*. Similarly, some people pronounce GUI as *gooey* and others insist that it should be *G-U-I*. In general, a preferred pronunciation evolves in an organization. The TLA, or three-letter abbreviation, is the most popular type of abbreviation in technical terminology.

Conventionally, SQL keywords such as **SELECT** appear in all uppercase; this book follows that convention.

For example, suppose a customer table named `tblCustomer` contains data about your business customers and that the structure of the table is as follows:

`tblCustomer(custId, lastName, state)`

Then, a statement such as the following would display a new table containing two columns—`custId` and `lastName`—and only as many rows as needed to hold those customers whose `state` column contains "WI":

`SELECT custId, lastName FROM tblCustomer WHERE state = "WI"`

Besides using = to mean "equal to," you can use the comparison operators > (greater than), < (less than), >= (greater than or equal to), and <= (less than or equal to). As you have already learned from working with programming variables throughout this book, text field values are contained within quotes, but numeric values are not.

In database management systems, a particular way of looking at a database is sometimes called a **view**. Typically, a view arranges records in some order and makes only certain fields visible. The different views provided by database software are virtual; that is, they do not affect the physical organization of the database.

SQL statement	Explanation
SELECT itemNumber, price FROM tblInventory	Shows only the item number and price for all five records.
SELECT * FROM tblInventory WHERE price > 5.00	Shows all fields from only those records where price is over $5.00— items 144 and 312.
SELECT itemNumber FROM tblInventory WHERE quantityInStock > 200 AND price > 10.00	Shows item number 144—the only record that has a quantity greater than 200 as well as a price greater than $10.00.
SELECT description, price FROM tblInventory WHERE description = "Pkg 20 napkins" OR itemNumber < 200	Shows the description and price fields for the package of 12 party plates and the package of 20 napkins. Each selected record must satisfy only one of the two criteria.
SELECT itemNumber FROM tblInventory WHERE NOT price < 14.00	Shows the item number for the only record where the price is not less than $14.00—item 144.

Figure 14-5   Sample SQL statements and explanations

TWO TRUTHS & A LIE

Creating Queries

1. A query is a question you use to extract appropriate fields and records from a table.

2. The most common language that database administrators use to access data in their tables is Structured Query Language, or SQL.

3. The basic form of the SQL command that retrieves selected records from a table is RETRIEVE-FROM-SELECTION.

The false statement is # 3. The basic form of the SQL command that retrieves selected records from a table is SELECT-FROM-WHERE.

Understanding Relationships Between Tables

Most database applications require many tables, and require that the tables be related. The connection between two tables is a **relationship**, and the database containing the relationships is called a relational database. Connecting two tables based on the values in a common column is called a **join operation**, or more simply, a **join**; the column on which they are connected is the **join column**. The table that is displayed as the result of the query is a virtual table—it uses some of its data from each joined table without disrupting the contents of the originals. For example, in Figure 14-6, the `customerNumber` column is the join column that could produce a virtual image when a user makes a query. When a user asks to see the name of a customer associated with a specific order number, or a list of the customers who have ordered a specific item, a joined table is produced. Three types of relationships can exist between tables:

- One-to-many
- Many-to-many
- One-to-one

tblCustomers

customerNumber	customerName
214	Kowalski
215	Jackson
216	Lopez
217	Thompson
218	Vitale

tblOrders

orderNumber	customerNumber	orderQuantity	orderItem	orderDate
10467	215	2	HP203	10/15/2009
10468	218	1	JK109	10/15/2009
10469	215	4	HP203	10/16/2009
10470	216	12	ML318	10/16/2009
10471	214	4	JK109	10/16/2009
10472	215	1	HP203	10/16/2009
10473	217	10	JK109	10/17/2009

Figure 14-6   Sample customers and orders

Understanding One-to-Many Relationships

In a **one-to-many relationship**, one row in a table can be related to many rows in another table. It is the most common type of relationship between tables. Consider the following tables:

```
tblCustomers(customerNumber, customerName)
tblOrders(orderNumber, customerNumber, orderQuantity,
    orderItem, orderDate)
```

The `tblCustomers` table contains one row for each customer, and `customerNumber` is the primary key. The `tblOrders` table contains one row for each order, and each order is assigned an orderNumber, which is the primary key in this table.

In most businesses, a single customer can place many orders. In the sample data in Figure 14-6, customer 215 has placed three orders. One row in the tblCustomers table can correspond to, and be related to, many rows in the tblOrders table. This means there is a one-to-many relationship between the two tables tblCustomers and tblOrders. The "one" table (tblCustomers) is the **base table** in this relationship, and the "many" table (tblOrders) is the **related table**.

When two tables have a one-to-many relationship, it is based on the values in one or more columns in the tables. In this example, the column, or attribute, that links the two tables together is the customerNumber attribute. In the tblCustomers table, customerNumber is the primary key, but in the tblOrders table, customerNumber is not a key—it is a **nonkey attribute**. When a column that is not a key in a table contains an attribute that is a key in a related table, the column is called a **foreign key**. When a base table is linked to a related table in a one-to-many relationship, the primary key of the base table is always related to the foreign key in the related table. In the example in Figure 14-6, customerNumber in the tblOrders table is a foreign key.

A key in a base table and the foreign key in the related table do not need to have the same name; they only need to contain the same type of data. Some database management software programs automatically create a relationship if the columns in two tables you select have the same name and data type. However, if this is not the case (for example, if the column is named customerNumber in one table and custID in another), you can explicitly instruct the software to create the relationship.

Understanding Many-to-Many Relationships

Another example of a one-to-many relationship is depicted with the following tables:

```
tblItems(itemNumber, itemName, itemPurchaseDate,
    itemPurchasePrice, itemCategoryId)
tblCategories(categoryId, categoryName,
    categoryInsuredAmount)
```

Assume you are creating these tables to keep track of all the items in your household for insurance purposes. You want to store data about your sofa, stereo, refrigerator, and so on. The tblItems table contains the item number, name, purchase date, and purchase price of each item. In addition, this table contains the ID number of the category (Appliance, Jewelry, Antique, and so on) to which the item belongs. You need these categories because your insurance policy has specific coverage limits for different types of property. For example, with many insurance policies, antiques might have a different coverage limit than appliances, or jewelry might have a different limit than furniture. Sample data for these tables is shown in Figure 14-7.

tblItems

itemNumber	itemName	itemPurchaseDate	itemPurchasePrice	itemCategoryId
1	Sofa	1/13/2003	$6,500	5
2	Stereo	2/10/2005	$1,200	6
3	Refrigerator	5/12/2005	$750	1
4	Diamond ring	2/12/2006	$42,000	2
5	TV	7/11/2006	$285	6
6	Rectangular pine coffee table	4/21/2007	$300	5
7	Round pine end table	4/21/2007	$200	5

tblCategories

categoryId	categoryName	categoryInsuredAmount
1	Appliance	$30,000
2	Jewelry	$15,000
3	Antique	$10,000
4	Clothing	$25,000
5	Furniture	$5,000
6	Electronics	$2,500
7	Miscellaneous	$5,000

Figure 14-7 Sample items and categories: a one-to-many relationship

The primary key of the tblItems table is itemNumber, a unique identifying number that you have assigned to each item you own. (You might even prepare labels with these numbers and stick a label on each item in an inconspicuous place.) The tblCategories table contains the category names and the maximum insured amounts for the specific categories. For example, one row in this table has a categoryName of "Jewelry" and a categoryInsuredAmount of $15,000. The primary key for the tblCategories table is categoryId, a uniquely assigned value for each property category.

The two tables in Figure 14-7 have a one-to-many relationship. Which is the "one" table and which is the "many" table? Or, asked in another way, which is the base table and which is the related table? You have probably determined that the tblCategories table is the base table (the "one" table) because one category can describe many items that you own. Therefore, the tblItems table is the related table (the "many" table); that is, many items fall into each category. The two tables are linked with the category ID attribute, which is the primary key in the base table (tblCategories) and a foreign key in the related table (tblItems).

In Figure 14-7, one row in the tblCategories table relates to multiple items you own. The opposite is not true—one item in the tblItems table cannot relate to multiple categories in the tblCategories table. The row in the tblItems table that describes the "rectangular pine coffee table" relates to one specific category in the tblCategories table—the Furniture category. However, what if you own a sofa that has a built-in DVD player, or a diamond ring that is an antique?

The structure of the tables shown in Figure 14-7 and the relationship between those tables are designed to keep track of possessions for insurance purposes. If you needed help categorizing your sofa with a built-in DVD player, you might call your insurance agent. If the agent says that the item is considered a piece of furniture for insurance purposes, then the existing table structures and relationships are adequate. If the agent says the sofa is considered a special type of hybrid item that has a specific maximum insured amount, you could create a new row in the tblCategories table to describe this special hybrid category—perhaps Electronic Furniture. This new category would acquire a category number, and you could associate the DVD-sofa with the new category using the foreign key in the tblItems table.

However, if your insurance agent didn't know whether to categorize the sofa as furniture or electronics, the item would present a problem to your database. You may want to categorize your new sofa as both a furniture item *and* an electronic item. The existing table structures, with their one-to-many relationship, would not support this because the current design limits any specific item to only one category. When you insert a row into the tblItems table to describe the new DVD-sofa, you can assign the Furniture code to the foreign key itemCategoryId, or you can assign the Electronics code, but not both.

If you want to assign the new DVD-sofa to both categories (Furniture and Electronics), you have to change the design of the table structures and relationships, because there is no longer a one-to-many relationship between the two tables. Now, there is a **many-to-many relationship**—one in which multiple rows in each table can correspond to multiple rows in the other. In this example, one row in the tblCategories table (for example, Furniture) can relate to many rows in the tblItems table (for example, sofa and coffee table), *and* one row in the tblItems table (for example, the sofa with the built-in DVD player) can relate to multiple rows in the tblCategories table.

The tblItems table contains a foreign key named itemCategoryId. If you want to change the application so that one specific row in the tblItems table can link to many rows (and, therefore, many

604

categoryIds) in the tblCategories table, you cannot continue to maintain the foreign key itemCategoryId in the tblItems table, because one item may be assigned to many categories. You could change the structure of the tblItems table so that you can assign multiple itemCategoryIds to one specific row in that table, but as you will learn later in this chapter, that approach leads to many problems using the data. Therefore, it is not an option.

The simplest way to support a many-to-many relationship between the tblItems and tblCategories tables is to remove the itemCategoryId attribute (what was once the foreign key) from the tblItems table, producing:

tblItems(<u>itemNumber</u>, itemName, itemPurchaseDate, itemPurchasePrice)

The tblCategories table structure remains the same:

tblCategories(<u>categoryId</u>, categoryName, categoryInsuredAmount)

With just the preceding two tables, there is no way to know that any specific rows in the tblItems table link to any specific rows in the tblCategories table, so you create a new table called tblItemsCategories that contains the primary keys from the two tables you want to link in a many-to-many relationship. This table is depicted as:

tblItemsCategories(<u>itemNumber</u>, <u>categoryId</u>)

Notice that this new table contains a compound primary key—both itemNumber and categoryId are underlined. The itemNumber value of 1 might be associated with many categoryIds. Therefore, itemNumber alone cannot be the primary key because the same value may occur in many rows. Similarly, a categoryId might relate to many different itemNumbers; this would disallow using just the categoryId as the primary key. However, combining the two attributes itemNumber and categoryId results in a unique primary key value for each row of the tblItemsCategories table.

The purpose of all this is to create a many-to-many relationship between the tblItems and tblCategories tables. The tblItemsCategories table contains two attributes; together, these attributes are the primary key. In addition, each of these attributes separately is a foreign key to one of the two original tables. The itemNumber attribute in the tblItemsCategories table is a foreign key that links to the primary key of the tblItems table. The categoryId attribute in the tblItemsCategories table links to the primary key of the tblCategories table. Now, there is a one-to-many relationship between the tblItems table (the "one," or base table) and the tblItemsCategories table (the "many," or related table); there is also a one-to-many relationship between the tblCategories table (the "one," or base table) and the tblItemsCategories table (the "many," or related table). This, in effect, implies a many-to-many relationship between the two base tables (tblItems and tblCategories).

Figure 14-8 shows the new tables holding a few items. The sofa (itemNumber 1) in the tblItems table is associated with the Furniture category (categoryId 5) in the tblCategories table because the first row of the tblItemsCategories table contains a 1 and a 5. Similarly, the stereo (itemNumber 2) in the tblItems table is associated with the Electronics category (categoryId 6) in the tblCategories table because the tblItemsCategories table has a row containing the values 2, 6.

tblItems

itemNumber	itemName	itemPurchaseDate	itemPurchasePrice
1	Sofa	1/13/2003	$6,500
2	Stereo	2/10/2005	$1,200
3	Sofa with DVD player	5/24/2010	$8,500
4	Coffee table with built-in refrigerator	6/24/2007	$12,000
5	Grandpa's pocket watch	4/7/1925	$100

tblItemsCategories

itemNumber	categoryId
1	5
2	6
3	5
3	6
4	1
4	5
5	2
5	3

tblCategories

categoryId	categoryName	categoryInsuredAmount
1	Appliance	$30,000
2	Jewelry	$15,000
3	Antique	$10,000
4	Clothing	$25,000
5	Furniture	$5,000
6	Electronics	$2,500
7	Miscellaneous	$5,000

Figure 14-8 Sample items, categories, and item categories: a many-to-many relationship

The fancy sofa with the built-in DVD player (itemNumber 3 in the tblItems table) occurs in two rows in the tblItemsCategories table: once with a categoryId of 5 (Furniture) and once with a categoryId of 6 (Electronics). Similarly, the coffee table with the built-in refrigerator (a piece of furniture that is an appliance) and Grandpa's pocket watch (an antique piece of jewelry) both belong to multiple categories. The tblItemsCategories table, then, allows the establishment of a many-to-many relationship between the two base tables, tblItems and tblCategories.

Understanding One-to-One Relationships

Another reason to create tables with one-to-one relation-ships is to avoid lots of empty columns, or **nulls**, if a subset of columns is applicable only to specific types of rows in the main table.

You learn more about security issues later in this chapter.

In a **one-to-one relationship**, a row in one table corresponds to exactly one row in another table. This type of relationship is easy to understand, but is the least frequently encountered. When one row in a table corresponds to a row in another table, the columns could be combined into a single table. A common reason you create a one-to-one relationship is security. For example, Figure 14-9 shows two tables, tblEmployees and tblSalaries. Each employee in the tblEmployees table has exactly one salary in the tblSalaries table. The salaries could have been added to the tblEmployees table as an additional column; the salaries are separate because you want some clerks to be allowed to view only names, addresses, and other nonsensitive data, so you give them permission to access only the tblEmployees table. Others who work in payroll or administration can create queries and view joined tables that include the salary information.

tblEmployees					tblSalaries	
empId	empLast	empFirst	empDept	empHireDate	empId	empSalary
101	Parker	Laura	3	4/07/2000	101	$42,500
102	Walters	David	4	1/19/2001	102	$28,800
103	Shannon	Ewa	3	2/28/2005	103	$36,000

Figure 14-9   Employees and salaries tables: a one-to-one relationship

TWO TRUTHS & A LIE

Understanding Relationships Between Tables

1. In a one-to-many relationship, one row in a table can be related to many rows in another table; this is the most common type of relationship between tables.

2. In a many-to-many relationship, multiple rows in a table each correspond to a single row in many different tables.

3. In a one-to-one relationship, a row in one table corresponds to exactly one row in another table; this type of relationship is easy to understand, but is the least frequently encountered.

The false statement is #2. A many-to-many relationship is one in which multiple rows in each table can correspond to multiple rows in the other.

Recognizing Poor Table Design

As you create database tables to hold the data used by an organization, you will often find the table design, or structure, inadequate to support the needs of the application. In other words, even if a table contains all the attributes required by a specific application, the structural design of the table may make the application cumbersome to use and prone to data errors.

607

For example, assume that you have been hired by an Internet-based college to design a database to keep track of its students. After meeting with the college administrators, you determine that you need to know the following information:

- Students' names

- Students' addresses

- Students' cities

- Students' states

- Students' zip codes

- ID numbers for classes in which students are enrolled

- Titles for classes in which students are enrolled

 In a real-life example, you could think of many other data requirements for the college. The number of attributes is small in this example for simplicity.

Figure 14-10 contains the `Students` table. Assume that because the Internet-based college is new, only three students have already enrolled. Besides the columns you identified as being necessary, notice the addition of the `studentId` attribute. Given the earlier discussions, you probably recognize that this is the best choice for a primary key, because many students can have the same names and even the same addresses. Although the table in Figure 14-10 contains a column for each data requirement from the preceding list, the table is poorly designed and will create many problems.

studentId	name	address	city	state	zip	class	classTitle
1	Rodriguez	123 Oak	Schaumburg	IL	60193	CIS101 PHI150 BIO200	Computer Literacy Ethics Genetics
2	Jones	234 Elm	Wild Rose	WI	54984	CHM100 MTH200	Chemistry Calculus
3	Mason	456 Pine	Dubuque	IA	52004	HIS202	World History

Figure 14-10 `Students` table before normalization

What if a college administrator wanted to view a list of courses offered by the Internet-based college? You can see six courses listed for the three students, so you can assume that at least six courses are offered. But, could there also be a Psychology course, or a class whose code is CIS102? You can't tell from the table because no students have enrolled in those classes. It would be good to know all the classes offered by your institution, regardless of whether any students have enrolled in them.

Consider another potential problem: What if student Mason withdraws from the school, and his row is deleted from the table? You would lose some valuable information that has nothing to do with student Mason, but is important for running the college. For instance, if Mason's row is deleted, you no longer know from the remaining data in the table whether the college offers any History classes, because Mason was the only student enrolled in a class with the HIS prefix (the HIS202 class).

Why is it so important to discuss the deficiencies of the existing table structure? You have probably heard the saying, "Pay me now or pay me later." This is especially true for table design. If you do not take the time to ensure well-designed table structures during the initial database design, users will spend plenty of time later fixing data errors, typing the same information multiple times, and being frustrated by the inability to cull important subsets of information from the database. If you had created this table structure as a solution to the college's needs, you probably would not be hired for future database projects.

TWO TRUTHS & A LIE

Recognizing Poor Table Design

1. The structural design of a table is excellent when the table contains all the attributes required by a specific application.

2. In a poorly designed database, you might risk losing important data when specific records are deleted.

3. If you do not take the time to ensure well-designed table structures during the initial database design, users will spend plenty of time later fixing data errors, typing the same information multiple times, and being frustrated by the inability to cull important subsets of information from the database.

The false statement is #1. Even if a table contains all the attributes required by a specific application, the structural design of the table may make the application cumbersome to use and prone to data errors.

Understanding Anomalies, Normal Forms, and Normalization

Database management programs can maintain all the relationships you need. As you add, delete, and modify records within your database tables, the software keeps track of all the relationships you have established, so that you can view any needed joins any time you want. The software, however, can only maintain useful relationships if you have planned ahead to create a set of database tables that satisfies the users' needs, supports all the applications you will need, and avoids potential problems. This process is called **normalization**.

The normalization process helps you reduce data redundancies and anomalies. **Data redundancy** is the unnecessary repetition of data. An **anomaly** is an irregularity in a database's design that causes problems and inconveniences. Three common types of anomalies are:

- Update anomalies

- Delete anomalies

- Insert anomalies

If you look ahead to the college database table in Figure 14-11, you will see an example of an **update anomaly**, or a problem that occurs when the data in a table needs to be altered. Because the table contains redundant data, if student Rodriguez moves to a new residence, you have to change the address, city, state, and zip values in more than one location. Of course, this table example is small; imagine if additional data were stored about Rodriguez, such as birth date, e-mail address, major field of study, and previous schools attended.

The database table in Figure 14-10 contains a **delete anomaly**, or a problem that occurs when a row is deleted. If student Jones withdraws from the college and his entries are deleted from the table, important data regarding the classes CHM100 and MTH200 are lost.

With an **insert anomaly**, problems occur when new rows are added to a table. In the table in Figure 14-10, if a new student named Ramone has enrolled in the college, but has not yet registered for any specific classes, then you can't insert a complete row for student Ramone; the only way to do so would be to "invent" at least one phony class for him. It would be valuable to the college to be able to maintain data on all enrolled students, regardless of whether they have registered for specific classes—for example, the college might want to send catalogs and registration information to these students.

 With some database software, you can enter an incomplete row.

When you normalize a database table, you walk through a series of steps that allows you to remove redundancies and anomalies.

609

Normalization involves altering a table so that it satisfies one or more of three **normal forms**, or sets of rules for constructing a well-designed database. The three normal forms are:

In a 1970 paper titled "A Relational Model of Data for Large Shared Data Banks," Dr. E. F. Codd listed seven normal forms. For business applications, 3NF is usually sufficient, and so only 1NF through 3NF are discussed in this chapter.

- **First normal form**, also known as **1NF**, in which you eliminate repeating groups

- **Second normal form**, or **2NF**, in which you eliminate partial key dependencies

- **Third normal form**, or **3NF**, in which you eliminate transitive dependencies

Each normal form is structurally better than the one preceding it. In any well-designed database, you almost always want to convert all tables to 3NF.

First Normal Form

A table that contains repeating groups is **unnormalized**. A **repeating group** is a subset of rows in a database table that all depend on the same key. A table in 1NF contains no repeating groups of data.

The table in Figure 14-10 violates this 1NF rule. The `class` and `classTitle` attributes repeat multiple times for some of the students. For example, student Rodriguez is taking three classes; her `class` attribute contains a repeating group. To remedy this situation, and to transform the table to 1NF, you simply repeat the rows for each repeating group of data. Figure 14-11 contains the revised table.

studentId	name	address	city	state	zip	class	classTitle
1	Rodriguez	123 Oak	Schaumburg	IL	60193	CIS101	Computer Literacy
1	Rodriguez	123 Oak	Schaumburg	IL	60193	PHI150	Ethics
1	Rodriguez	123 Oak	Schaumburg	IL	60193	BIO200	Genetics
2	Jones	234 Elm	Wild Rose	WI	54984	CHM100	Chemistry
2	Jones	234 Elm	Wild Rose	WI	54984	MTH200	Calculus
3	Mason	456 Pine	Dubuque	IA	52004	HIS202	World History

Figure 14-11   Students table in 1NF

The repeating groups have been eliminated from the table in Figure 14-11. However, there is still a problem—the primary key, `studentId`, is no longer unique for each row in the table. For example, the table now contains three rows in which `studentId` equals 1. You can fix this problem and create a primary key simply by adding the `class` attribute to the primary key, creating a compound key. (Other problems still exist, as you will see later in this chapter.) The table's key then becomes a combination of **studentId** and **class**. By knowing the **studentId** *and* **class**, you can identify one, and only one, row in the table—for example, a combination of **studentId** 1 and **class** BIO200 identifies a single row. Using the notation discussed earlier in this chapter, the table in Figure 14-11 can be described as:

```
tblStudents(studentId, name, address, city, state, zip,
    class, classTitle)
```

Both the **studentId** and **class** attributes are underlined, showing that they are both part of the key.

When you combine two columns to create a compound key, you are **concatenating the columns**.

The table in Figure 14-11 is now in 1NF because there are no repeating groups and the primary key attributes are defined. Satisfying the "no repeating groups" condition is also called making the columns **atomic attributes**; that is, making them as small as possible, containing an undividable piece of data. In 1NF, all values for an intersection of a row and column must be atomic. Recall the table in Figure 14-10, in which the **class** attribute for **studentId** 1 (Rodriguez) contained three entries: CIS101, PH1150, and BIO200. This violated the 1NF atomicity rule because these three classes represented a set of values rather than one specific value. The table in Figure 14-11 does not repeat this problem because, for each row in the table, the **class** attribute contains one and only one value. The same is true for the other attributes that were part of the repeating group.

Database developers also refer to operations or transactions as **atomic transactions** when they appear to execute completely or not at all.

Think back to the earlier discussion about why we normalize tables in the first place. Does Figure 14-11 still have redundancies? Are there still anomalies? Yes to both questions. Recall that you want to have your tables in 3NF before actually defining them to the database. Currently, the table in Figure 14-11 is only in 1NF.

In Figure 14-11, notice that Student 1, Rodriguez, is taking three classes. If you were responsible for typing data into this table, would you want to type this student's name, address, city, state, and zip code for each of the three classes? For one of her classes, you might mistype her name as "Rodrigues" instead of "Rodriguez". Or, you might misspell the city of "Schaumburg" as "Schamburg" for one of Rodriguez's classes. A college administrator might look at the table and not know whether Rodriguez's correct city of residence is Schaumburg or Schamburg. If you queried the database to select or count the number of classes being taken by students residing in "Schaumburg," one of Rodriguez's classes would be missed.

Misspelling "Rodriguez" is an example of a data integrity error. You learn more about this type of error later in this chapter.

Consider the student Jones, who is taking two classes. If Jones changes his residence, how many times will you need to retype his new address, state, city, and zip code? What if Jones is taking six classes?

Second Normal Form

To improve the design of the table in Figure 14-11 and bring the table to 2NF, you need to eliminate all **partial key dependencies**; that is, no column should depend on only part of the key. For a table to be in 2NF, it must be in 1NF and all nonkey attributes must be dependent on the entire primary key.

In the table in Figure 14-11, the key is a combination of `studentId` and `class`. Consider the `name` attribute. Does the `name` "Rodriguez" depend on the entire primary key? In other words, do you need to know that the `studentId` is 1 *and* that the `class` is CIS101 to determine that the `name` is "Rodriguez"? No, it is sufficient to know that the `studentId` is 1 to know that the `name` is "Rodriguez". Therefore, the `name` attribute is only partially dependent on the primary key, and so the table violates 2NF. The same is true for the other attributes of `address`, `city`, `state`, and `zip`. If you know, for example, that `studentId` is 3, then you also know that the student's `city` is "Dubuque"; you do not need to know any `class` codes.

Similarly, examine the `classTitle` attribute in the first row of the table in Figure 14-11. This attribute has a value of "Computer Literacy". In this case, you do not need to know both the `studentId` and the `class` to predict the `classTitle` "Computer Literacy". Rather, just the `class` attribute, which is only part of the compound key, is required. Also, class "PHI150" will always have the associated `classTitle` "Ethics", regardless of the particular students who are taking that class. So, `classTitle` represents a partial key dependency.

You bring a table into 2NF by eliminating the partial key dependencies. To accomplish this, you create multiple tables so that each non-key attribute of each table is dependent on the *entire* primary key for the specific table within which the attribute occurs. If the resulting tables are still in 1NF and there are no partial key dependencies, then those tables will also be in 2NF.

Figure 14-12 contains three tables: `tblStudents`, `tblClasses`, and `tblStudentClasses`. To create the `tblStudents` table, you simply take the attributes from the original table that depend on the `studentId` attribute and group them into a new table—`name`, `address`, `city`, `state`, and `zip` all can be determined by the `studentId` alone. The primary key to the `tblStudents` table is `studentId`. Similarly, you can create the `tblClasses` table simply by grouping the attributes from the 1NF table that depend on the `class` attribute. In this application, only one attribute from the original table, the `classTitle` attribute, depends on the `class` attribute. The first two tables in Figure 14-12 can be notated as:

```
tblStudents(studentId, name, address, city, state, zip)
tblClasses(class, classTitle)
```

tblStudents

studentId	name	address	city	state	zip
1	Rodriguez	123 Oak	Schaumburg	IL	60193
2	Jones	234 Elm	Wild Rose	WI	54984
3	Mason	456 Pine	Dubuque	IA	52004

tblClasses

class	classTitle
CIS101	Computer Literacy
PHI150	Ethics
BIO200	Genetics
CHM100	Chemistry
MTH200	Calculus
HIS202	World History

tblStudentClasses

studentId	class
1	CIS101
1	PHI150
1	BIO200
2	CHM100
2	MTH200
3	HIS202

Figure 14-12 Students table in 2NF

The tblStudents and tblClasses tables contain all the attributes from the original table. Remember the prior redundancies and anomalies. Several improvements have occurred:

- You have eliminated the update anomalies. The name "Rodriguez" occurs just once in the tblStudents table. The same is true for Rodriguez's address, city, state, and zip code. The original table contained three rows for student Rodriguez. By eliminating the redundancies, you have fewer anomalies. If Rodriguez changes her residence, you only need to update one row in the tblStudents table.

- You have eliminated the insert anomalies. With the new configuration, you can insert a complete row into the tblStudents table even if the student has not yet enrolled in any classes. Similarly, you can add a complete row to the tblClasses table for a new class offering even though no students are currently taking the class.

- You have eliminated the delete anomalies. Recall from the original table that Mason was the only student taking HIS202. This caused a delete anomaly because the HIS202 class would disappear if Mason was removed. Now, if you delete Mason from the tblStudents table in Figure 14-12, the HIS202 class remains in the tblClasses list.

If you create the first two tables shown in Figure 14-12, you have eliminated many of the problems associated with the original version. However, if you have those two tables alone, you have lost some important information that you originally had while at 1NF—specifically, which students are taking which classes or which classes are being taken by which students. When breaking up a table into multiple tables, you need to consider the type of relationship among the resulting tables—you are designing a *relational* database, after all.

You know that the Internet-based college application requires that you keep track of which students are taking which classes. This implies a relationship between the tblStudents and tblClasses tables. Your job is to determine what type of relationship exists between the two tables. Recall from earlier in the chapter that the two most common types of relationships are one-to-many and many-to-many. This specific application requires that one specific student can enroll in many different classes, and that one specific class can be taken by many different students. Therefore, a many-to-many relationship exists between the tables tblStudents and tblClasses.

As you learned in the earlier example of categorizing insured items, you create a many-to-many relationship between two tables by creating a third table that contains the primary keys from the two tables that you want to relate. In this case, you create the tblStudentClasses table in Figure 14-12 as:

tblStudentClasses(studentId, class)

If you examine the rows in the tblStudentClasses table, you can see that the student with studentId 1, Rodriguez, is enrolled in three classes; studentId 2, Jones, is taking two classes; and studentId 3, Mason, is enrolled in only one class. Finally, the table requirements for the Internet-based college have been fulfilled.

Or have they? Earlier, you saw the many redundancies and anomalies that were eliminated by structuring the tables into 2NF, and the 2NF table structures certainly result in a much "better" database than the 1NF structures. But look again at the tblStudents table in Figure 14-12. As the college expands, what if you need to add 50 new students to this table, and all of the new students reside in Schaumburg, IL? If you were the data-entry person, would you want to type the city of "Schaumburg", the state of "IL", and the zip code of "60193" 50 times? This data is redundant, and you can improve the design of the tables to eliminate this redundancy.

Third Normal Form

3NF requires that a table be in 2NF and that it has no transitive dependencies. A **transitive dependency** occurs when the value of a nonkey attribute determines, or predicts, the value of another nonkey attribute. Clearly, the `studentId` attribute of the `tblStudents` table in Figure 14-12 is a determinant—if you know a particular `studentId` value, you can also know that student's `name`, `address`, `city`, `state`, and `zip`. But this is not considered a transitive dependency because the `studentId` attribute is the primary key for the `tblStudents` table, and, after all, the primary key's job is to determine the values of the other attributes in the row.

A problem arises, however, if a nonkey attribute determines another nonkey attribute. The `tblStudents` table in Figure 14-12 has five nonkey attributes: `name`, `address`, `city`, `state`, and `zip`.

The name is a nonkey attribute. If you know the value of `name` is "Rodriguez", do you also know the one specific address where Rodriguez resides? In other words, is this a transitive dependency? No, it isn't. Even though only one student is named "Rodriguez" now, there may be more in the future. So, though it may be tempting to consider that the `name` attribute is a determinant of `address`, it isn't. If your boss said, "Look at the `tblStudents` table and tell me Jones's address," you couldn't if you had 10 students named "Jones".

The `address` attribute is a nonkey attribute. Does it predict anything? If you know the value of `address` is "20 N. Main Street", can you determine which student is associated with that address? No, because in the future, many students might live at "20 N. Main Street", but they might live in different cities, or two students might live at the same address in the same city. Therefore, `address` does not cause a transitive dependency.

Similarly, the `city` and `state` attributes are not keys, but they are also not determinants because knowing their values alone is not sufficient to predict another nonkey attribute value. You might argue that if you know a city's name, you know the state, but many states contain cities named Union or Springfield, for example.

What about the nonkey attribute `zip`? If you know that the zip code is 60193, can you determine the value of any other nonkey attributes? Yes, a zip code of 60193 indicates that the `city` is Schaumburg and the `state` is IL. This is the "culprit" that is causing the redundancies in the `city` and `state` attributes. The attribute `zip` is a determinant because it determines `city` and `state`; therefore, the `tblStudents` table contains a transitive dependency and is not in 3NF.

To convert the tblStudents table to 3NF, simply remove the attributes that are determined by, or are **functionally dependent** on, the zip attribute. For example, if attribute zip determines attribute city, then attribute city is considered to be functionally dependent on attribute zip. So, as Figure 14-13 shows, the new tblStudents table is defined as:

tblStudents(studentId, name, address, zip)

tblStudents

studentId	name	address	zip
1	Rodriguez	123 Oak	60193
2	Jones	234 Elm	54984
3	Mason	456 Pine	52004

tblZips

zip	city	state
60193	Schaumburg	IL
54984	Wild Rose	WI
52004	Dubuque	IA

tblClasses

class	classTitle
CIS101	Computer Literacy
PHI150	Ethics
BIO200	Genetics
CHM100	Chemistry
MTH200	Calculus
HIS202	World History

tblStudentClasses

studentId	class
1	CIS101
1	PHI150
1	BIO200
2	CHM100
2	MTH200
3	HIS202

A functionally dependent relationship is sometimes written using an arrow that extends from the depended-upon attribute to the dependent attribute—for example, zip→city.

Figure 14-13 The complete Students database

Figure 14-13 also shows the tblZips table, which is defined as:

tblZips(zip, city, state)

The new tblZips table is related to the tblStudents table by the zip attribute. Using the two tables together, you can determine, for example, that studentId 3, Mason, in the tblStudents table resides in the city of Dubuque and the state of IA, attributes stored in the tblZips table. When you encounter a table with a functional dependence, you almost always can reduce data redundancy by creating two tables, as in Figure 14-13. With the new configuration, a data-entry operator must still type a zip code for each student, but you have eliminated redundancy and the possibility of introducing data-entry errors in city and state names.

Is the student-to-zip-code relationship a one-to-many, many-to-many, or one-to-one relationship? You know that one row in the tblZips table can relate to many rows in the tblStudents table—that is, many students can reside in zip code 60193. However, the opposite is not true—one row in the `tblStudents` table (a particular student) cannot relate to many rows in the `tblZips` table, because a particular student can only reside in one zip code. Therefore, there is a one-to-many relationship between the base table, `tblZips`, and the related table `tblStudents`. The link to the relationship is the `zip` attribute, which is a primary key in the `tblZips` table and a foreign key in the `tblStudents` table.

This was a lot of work, but it was worth it. The tables are in 3NF, and the redundancies and anomalies that would have contributed to an unwieldy, error-prone, inefficient database design have been eliminated.

Recall that the definition of 3NF is 2NF plus no transitive dependencies. What if you were considering changing the structure of the `tblStudents` table by adding an attribute to hold the students' Social Security numbers (`ssn`)? If you know a specific `ssn` value, you also know a particular student `name`, `address`, and so on; in other words, a specific value for `ssn` determines one and only one row in the `tblStudents` table. No two students have the same Social Security number (ruling out identity theft, of course). However, `studentId` is the primary key, `ssn` is a nonkey determinant, which, by definition, seems to violate the requirements of 3NF. However, if you add `ssn` to the `tblStudents` table, the table is still in 3NF because a determinant is allowed in 3NF if the determinant is also a candidate key. Recall that a candidate key is an attribute that could qualify as the primary key but has not been used as the primary key. In the example concerning the `zip` attribute of the `tblStudents` table (Figure 14-11), `zip` was a determinant of the `city` and `state` attributes. Therefore, the `tblStudents` table was not in 3NF because many rows in the `tblStudents` table could have the same value for `zip`, meaning `zip` was not a candidate key. The situation with the `ssn` column is different because `ssn` could be used as a primary key for the `tblStudents` table.

In summary:

- A table is in first normal form (1NF) when there are no repeating groups.

- A table is in second normal form (2NF) if it is in first normal form and no nonkey column depends on just part of the primary key.

- A table is in third normal form (3NF) if it is in second normal form and the only determinants are candidate keys.

Watch the video *Normalization.*

617

In general, you try to create a database in the highest normal form. However, when data items are stored in multiple tables, it takes longer to access related information than when it is all stored in a single table. So, for performance, you sometimes might **denormalize** a table, or reduce it to a lower normal form, by placing some repeated information back into the table. Deciding on the best form in which to store a body of data is a sophisticated art.

Not every table starts out denormalized. For example, a table might already be in third normal form when you first encounter it. On the other hand, a table might not be normalized, but after you put it in 1NF, you may find that it also satisfies the requirements for 2NF and 3NF.

TWO TRUTHS & A LIE

Understanding Anomalies, Normal Forms, and Normalization

1. Normalization helps you reduce data redundancies and anomalies.

2. Data redundancy is the unnecessary repetition of data.

3. First normal form is structurally better than third normal form.

The false statement is #3. Third normal form is structurally better than first and second normal form. In any well-designed database, you almost always want to convert all tables to 3NF.

Database Performance and Security Issues

Frequently, a company's database is its most valuable resource. If buildings, equipment, or inventory items are damaged or destroyed, they can be rebuilt or re-created. However, the information contained in a database is often irreplaceable. A company that has spent years building valuable customer profiles cannot re-create them at the drop of a hat; a company that loses billing or shipment information might not simply lose the current orders—the affected customers might defect to competitors who can serve them better. Keeping data secure is often a company's most economically crucial responsibility.

You can study entire books to learn all the details involved in data security. The major issues include:

- Providing data integrity

- Recovering lost data

- Avoiding concurrent update problems

- Providing authentication and permissions

- Providing encryption

Providing Data Integrity

Database software provides the means to ensure that data integrity is enforced; a database has **data integrity** when it follows a set of rules that makes the data accurate and consistent. For example, you might indicate that a quantity in an inventory record can never be negative, or that a price can never be higher than a predetermined value. In addition, you can enforce integrity between tables; for example, you might prohibit entering an insurance plan code for an employee if the code is not one of the types offered by the organization.

Recovering Lost Data

An organization's data can be destroyed in many ways—legitimate users can make mistakes, hackers or other malicious users can enter invalid data, and hardware problems can wipe out records or entire databases. **Recovery** is the process of returning the database to a correct form that existed before an error occurred.

Periodically making a backup copy of a database and keeping a record of every transaction are two of the simplest approaches to recovery. When an error occurs, you can replace the database with an error-free version that was saved at the last backup. Usually, changes to the database, called transactions, have occurred since the last backup; if so, you must then reapply those transactions.

Many organizations keep a copy of their data off-site (sometimes hundreds or thousands of miles away) so that if a disaster such as a fire or flood destroys data, the remotely stored copy can serve as a backup.

Avoiding Concurrent Update Problems

Large databases are accessible by many users at a time. The database is stored on a central computer, and users work at terminals in diverse locations. For example, several order clerks might be able to update customer and inventory tables concurrently. A **concurrent update problem** occurs when two database users need to modify the same record at the same time. Suppose two order clerks take a phone order for item number 101 in an inventory file. Each sees the quantity in stock—for example, 25—on her terminal. Each accepts the customer's order and subtracts 1 from inventory. Now, in each local terminal, the quantity is 24. One order gets written to the central database, then the other, and the final inventory is 24, not 23 as it should be.

Several approaches can be used to avoid this problem. With one approach, a lock can be placed on one record the moment it is accessed. A **lock** is a mechanism that prevents changes to a database for a period of time. While one order clerk makes a change, the other cannot access the record. Potentially, a customer on the phone with the second order clerk could be inconvenienced while the first clerk maintains the lock, but the data in the inventory table would remain accurate.

A **persistent lock** is a long-term database lock required when users want to maintain a consistent view of their data while making modifications over a long transaction.

Another approach to the concurrent update problem is to not allow users to update the original database at all, but to have them store transactions, which later can be applied to the database all at once, or in a **batch**—perhaps once or twice a day or after business hours. The problem with this approach is that the database will be out of date as soon as the first transaction occurs and until the batch processing takes place. For example, if several clerks place orders for the same item, the item might actually be out of stock. However, none of the clerks will realize this because the database will not reflect the orders until it is updated with the current batch of transactions.

Providing Authentication and Permissions

Most database software can authenticate that people who try to access an organization's data are legitimate users. **Authentication techniques** include storing and verifying passwords or even using physical characteristics, such as fingerprints or voice recognition, before users can view data. After being authenticated, the user typically receives authorization to all or part of the database. The **permissions** assigned to a user indicate which parts of the database the user can view, modify, or delete. For example, an order clerk might not be allowed to view or update personnel data, whereas a clerk in the personnel office might not be allowed to alter inventory data.

Providing Encryption

Database software can be used to encrypt data. **Encryption** is the process of coding data into a format that human beings cannot read. If unauthorized users gain access to database files, the data will be in a coded format that is useless to them. Only authorized users see the data in a readable format.

TWO TRUTHS & A LIE

Database Performance and Security Issues

1. A database has data integrity when it follows a set of rules that makes the data accurate and consistent.

2. Encryption is the process of returning the database to a correct form that existed before an error occurred.

3. A concurrent update problem occurs when two database users need to modify the same record at the same time.

The false statement is #2. Encryption is the process of coding data into a format that human beings cannot read. Recovery is the process of returning the database to a correct form that existed before an error occurred.

Chapter Summary

- A database holds a group of files that an organization needs to support its applications. In a database, the files are often called tables because you can arrange their contents in rows and columns. A value that uniquely identifies a record is called a primary key, a key field, or a key for short. Database management software is a set of programs that allows users to create and manage data.

- Creating a useful database requires planning and analysis. You must decide what data will be stored, how that data will be divided between tables, and how the tables will interrelate.

- In most tables you create for a database, you want to identify a column, or possibly a combination of columns, as the table's key column or field, also called the primary key. The primary key is important because you can configure your software to prevent multiple records from containing the same value in this column, thus avoiding data-entry errors. In addition, you can sort your records in primary key order before displaying or printing them, and you need to use this column when setting up relationships between the table and others that will become part of the same database.

- A shorthand way to describe a table is to use the table name followed by parentheses containing all the field names, with the primary key underlined.

- Entering data into an existing table requires a good deal of time and accurate typing. Depending on the application, the contents of the tables might be entered over the course of months or years by many data-entry personnel. Deleting and modifying records within a database table are relatively easy tasks. In most organizations, most of the important data is in a constant state of change.

- Database management software generally allows you to sort a table based on any column, letting you view the data in the way that is most useful to you. After rows are sorted, they usually can be grouped.

- Frequently, you want to cull subsets of data from a table you have created. The questions you use to extract the appropriate records from a table and specify the fields to be viewed are called queries. Depending on the software you use, you might create a query by filling in blanks (a process called query by example) or by writing statements similar to those in many programming languages. The most common language that database administrators use to access data in their tables is Structured Query Language, or SQL.

- Most database applications require many tables, and require that the tables be related. The three types of relationships are one-to-many, many-to-many, and one-to-one.

- As you create database tables to hold the data an organization needs, you will often find the table design, or structure, inadequate to support the needs of the application.

- Normalization is the process of designing and creating a set of database tables that satisfies the users' needs and avoids potential problems. Normalization helps you reduce data redundancies, update anomalies, delete anomalies, and insert anomalies. Normalization involves altering a table so that it satisfies one or more of three normal forms, or rules, for constructing a well-designed database. The three normal forms are first normal form, also known as 1NF, in which you eliminate repeating groups; second normal form, also known as 2NF, in which you eliminate partial key dependencies; and third normal form, also known as 3NF, in which you eliminate transitive dependencies.

- Frequently, a company's database is its most valuable resource. Major security issues include providing data integrity, recovering lost data, avoiding concurrent update problems, providing authentication and permissions, and providing encryption.

Key Terms

Characters are the smallest usable units of data—for example, a letter, digit, or punctuation mark.

Fields are formed from groups of characters and represent a piece of information, such as firstName, lastName, or socialSecurityNumber.

Records are formed from groups of related fields. The fields go together because they represent attributes of an entity, such as an employee, a customer, an inventory item, or a bank account.

Files are composed of associated records; for example, a file might contain a record for each employee in a company or each account at a bank.

A **database** holds a group of files, or tables, that an organization needs to support its applications.

A database **table** contains data in rows and columns.

An **entity** is one record or row in a database table.

An **attribute** is one field or column in a database table.

A **primary key**, or **key** for short, is a field or column that uniquely identifies a record.

A **compound key**, also known as a **composite key**, is a key constructed from multiple columns.

Database management software is a set of programs that allows users to create and manage data.

A **relational database** contains a group of tables from which you can make connections to produce virtual tables.

Candidate keys are columns or attributes that could serve as a primary key in a table.

Alternate keys are the remaining candidate keys after you choose a primary key.

Immutable means not changing during normal operation.

A **query** is a question using syntax that the database software can understand. Its purpose is often to display a subset of data.

Query by example is the process of creating a query by filling in blanks.

Structured Query Language, or **SQL**, is a commonly used language for accessing data in database tables.

The **SELECT-FROM-WHERE** SQL statement is the command that selects the fields you want to view from a specific table where one or more conditions are met.

A **view** is a particular way of looking at a database.

A **wildcard** is a symbol that means "any" or "all."

A **relationship** is a connection between two tables.

A **join operation**, or a **join**, connects two tables based on the values in a common column.

A **join column** is the column on which two tables are connected.

A **one-to-many relationship** is one in which one row in a table can be related to many rows in another table. It is the most common type of relationship among tables.

The **base table** in a one-to-many relationship is the "one" table.

The **related table** in a one-to-many relationship is the "many" table.

A **nonkey attribute** is any column in a table that is not a key.

A **foreign key** is a column that is not a key in a table, but contains an attribute that is a key in a related table.

A **many-to-many relationship** is one in which multiple rows in each of two tables can correspond to multiple rows in the other.

In a **one-to-one relationship**, a row in one table corresponds to exactly one row in another table.

In a database, empty columns are **nulls**.

Normalization is the process of designing and creating a set of database tables that satisfies the users' needs and avoids redundancies and anomalies.

Data redundancy is the unnecessary repetition of data.

An **anomaly** is an irregularity in the design of a database that causes problems and inconveniences.

An **update anomaly** is a problem that occurs when the data in a table needs to be altered; the result is repeated data.

A **delete anomaly** is a problem that occurs when a row in a table is deleted; the result is loss of related data.

An **insert anomaly** is a problem that occurs when new rows are added to a table; the result is incomplete rows.

Normal forms are rules for constructing a well-designed database.

First normal form, also known as **1NF**, is the normalization form in which you eliminate repeating groups.

Second normal form, or **2NF**, is the normalization form in which you eliminate partial key dependencies.

Third normal form, or **3NF**, is the normalization form in which you eliminate transitive dependencies.

An **unnormalized** table contains repeating groups.

A **repeating group** is a subset of rows in a database table that all depend on the same key.

To **concatenate columns** is to combine columns to produce a compound key.

Atomic attributes or columns are as small as possible so as to contain an undividable piece of data.

Atomic transactions appear to execute completely or not at all.

A **partial key dependency** occurs when a column in a table depends on only part of the table's key.

A **transitive dependency** occurs when the value of a nonkey attribute determines, or predicts, the value of another nonkey attribute.

Functionally dependent describes an attribute's relationship to another if it can be determined by the other attribute.

To **denormalize** a table is to place it in a lower normal form by placing some repeated information back into it.

A database has **data integrity** when it follows a set of rules that makes the data accurate and consistent.

Recovery is the process of returning the database to a correct form that existed before an error occurred.

A **concurrent update problem** occurs when two database users need to modify the same record at the same time.

A **lock** is a mechanism that prevents changes to a database for a period of time.

A **persistent lock** is a long-term database lock required when users want to maintain a consistent view of their data while making modifications over a long transaction.

A **batch** is a group of transactions applied all at once.

Authentication techniques include storing and verifying passwords or even using physical characteristics, such as fingerprints or voice recognition, before users can view data.

The **permissions** assigned to a user indicate which parts of the database the user can view, modify, and delete.

Encryption is the process of coding data into a format that human beings cannot read.

Review Questions

1. A field or column that uniquely identifies a row in a database table is a(n) _____.

   a. variable

   b. identifier

   c. principal

   d. key

2. Which of the following is *not* a feature of most database management software?

    a. sorting records in a table

    b. creating reports

    c. preventing poorly designed tables

    d. relating tables

3. Before you can enter any data into a database table, you must do all of the following except _____.

    a. determine the attributes the table will hold

    b. provide names for each attribute

    c. provide data types for each attribute

    d. determine maximum and minimum values for each attribute

4. Which of the following is the best key for a table containing a landlord's rental properties?

    a. `numberOfBedrooms`

    b. `amountOfMonthlyRent`

    c. `streetAddress`

    d. `tenantLastName`

5. A table's notation is: `tblClients(socialSecNum, lastName, firstName, `<u>`clientNumber`</u>`, balanceDue)`. You know that _____.

    a. the primary key is `socialSecNum`

    b. the primary key is `clientNumber`

    c. there are four candidate keys

    d. there is at least one numeric attribute

6. You can extract subsets of data from database tables using a(n) _____.

    a. query

    b. sort

    c. investigation

    d. subroutine

7. A database table has the structure tblPhoneOrders(orderNum, custName, custPhoneNum, itemOrdered, quantity). Which SQL statement could be used to extract all attributes for orders for item AB3333?

    a. SELECT * FROM tblPhoneOrders WHERE itemOrdered = "AB3333"

    b. SELECT tblPhoneOrders WHERE itemOrdered = "AB3333"

    c. SELECT itemOrdered FROM tblPhoneOrders WHERE = "AB3333"

    d. Two of these are correct.

8. Connecting two database tables based on the value of a column (producing a virtual view of a new table) is a _____ operation.

    a. merge

    b. concatenate

    c. join

    d. met

9. Heartland Medical Clinic maintains a database to keep track of patients. One table can be described as: tblPatients(patientId, name, address, primaryPhysicianCode). Another table contains physician codes along with other physician data; it is described as tblPhysicians(physicianCode, name, officeNumber, phoneNumber, daysOfWeekInOffice). In this example, the relationship is _____.

    a. one-to-one

    b. one-to-many

    c. many-to-many

    d. impossible to determine

10. Edgerton Insurance Agency sells life, home, health, and auto insurance policies. The agency maintains a database containing a table that holds policy data—each record contains the policy number, the customer's name and address, and type of policy purchased. For example, customer Michael Robertson is referenced in two records because he holds life and auto policies. Another table contains information on each type of policy the agency sells—coverage limits, term, and so on. In this example, the relationship is _____.

   a. one-to-one

   b. one-to-many

   c. many-to-many

   d. impossible to determine

11. Kratz Computer Repair maintains a database that contains a table that holds information about each repair job the company agrees to perform. The jobs table is described as: `tblJobs(jobId, dateStarted, customerId, technicianId, feeCharged)`. Each job has a unique ID number that serves as a key to this table. The `customerId` and `technicianId` columns in the table each link to other tables of customer information, such as name, address, and phone number, and technician information, such as name, office extension, and hourly rate. When the `tblJobs` and `tblCustomers` tables are joined, which is the base table?

   a. `tblJobs`

   b. `tblCustomers`

   c. `tblTechnicians`

   d. a combination of two tables

12. When a column that is not a key in a table contains an attribute that is a key in a related table, the column is called a(n) _____.

   a. foreign key

   b. merge column

   c. internal key

   d. primary column

13. The most common reason to construct a one-to-one relationship between two tables is _____.

   a. to save money

   b. to save time

   c. for security purposes

   d. so that neither table is considered "inferior"

14. The process of designing and creating a set of database tables that satisfies the users' needs and avoids potential problems is _____ __.

   a. purification

   b. normalization

   c. standardization

   d. structuring

15. The unnecessary repetition of data is called data _____.

   a. amplification

   b. echoing

   c. redundancy

   d. mining

16. Problems with database design are caused by irregularities known as _____.

   a. glitches

   b. anomalies

   c. bugs

   d. abnormalities

17. When you place a table into first normal form, you have eliminated _____.

   a. transitive dependencies

   b. partial key dependencies

   c. repeating groups

   d. all of the above

18. When you place a table into third normal form, you have eliminated _____.

   a. transitive dependencies

   b. partial key dependencies

   c. repeating groups

   d. all of the above

19. If a table contains no repeating groups, but a column depends on part of the table's key, the table is in _____ normal form.

   a. first

   b. second

   c. third

   d. fourth

20. Which of the following is not a database security issue?

   a. providing data integrity

   b. recovering lost data

   c. providing normalization

   d. providing encryption

Exercises

1. The Lucky Dog Grooming Parlor maintains data about each of its clients in a table named `tblClients`. Attributes include each dog's name, breed, and owner's name, all of which are text attributes. The only numeric attributes are an ID number assigned to each dog and the balance due on services. The table structure is `tblClients(dogId, name, breed, owner, balanceDue)`. Write the SQL statement that would select each of the following:

   a. names and owners of all Great Danes

   b. owners of all dogs with balance due over $100

   c. all attributes of dogs named "Fluffy"

   d. all attributes of poodles whose balance is no greater than $50

2. Consider the following table with the structure
   tblRecipes(recipeName, timeToPrepare, ingredients). If
   necessary, redesign the table so it satisfies 1NF, 2NF, and 3NF.

recipeName	timeToPrepare	ingredients
Baked lasagna	1 hour	1 pound lasagna noodles
		½ pound ground beef
		16 ounces tomato sauce
		½ pound ricotta cheese
		½ pound parmesan cheese
		1 onion
Fruit salad	10 minutes	1 apple
		1 banana
		1 bunch grapes
		1 pint blueberries
Marinara sauce	30 minutes	16 ounces tomato sauce
		¼ pound parmesan cheese
		1 onion

3. Consider the following table with the structure
   tblFriends(lastName, firstName, address, birthday,
   phoneNumbers, emailAddresses). If necessary, redesign the
   table so it satisfies 1NF, 2NF, and 3NF.

lastName	firstName	address	birthday	phoneNumbers	emailAddresses
Gordon	Alicia	34 Second St.	3/16	222-4343	agordon@mail.com
				349-0012	
Washington	Edward	12 Main St.	12/12	222-7121	ewash@mail.com
					coolguy@earth.com
Davis	Olivia	55 Birch Ave.	10/3	222-9012	olivia@abc.com
				333-8788	
				834-0112	

4. You have created the following table to keep track of your
   DVD collection. The structure is tblDVDs(movie, year,
   stars). If necessary, redesign the table so it satisfies 1NF,
   2NF, and 3NF.

movie	year	stars
The Departed	2006	Leonardo DiCaprio
		Matt Damon
Hairspray	2007	John Travolta
		Michelle Pfeiffer
		Christopher Walken
Catch Me If You Can	2002	Leonardo DiCaprio
		Tom Hanks
		Christopher Walken

5. The Midtown Ladies Auxiliary is sponsoring a scholarship for local high school students. They have constructed a table with the structure tblScholarshipApplicants(appId, lastName, hsAttended, hsAddress, gpa, honors, clubsActivities). The hsAttended and hsAddress attributes represent high school attended and its street address, respectively. The gpa attribute is a grade point average. The honors attribute holds awards received, and the clubsActivities attribute holds the names of clubs and activities in which the student participated. If necessary, redesign the table so it satisfies 1NF, 2NF, and 3NF.

appId	lastName	hsAttended	hsAddress	gpa	honors	clubsActivities
1	Wong	Central	1500 Main	3.8	Citizenship award	Future teachers
						Class officer
						Model airplane
						Soccer MVP
						Newspaper
2	Jefferson	Central	1500 Main	4.0	Valedictorian	Pep
					Citizenship award	Yearbook
						Homecoming court
						Football MVP
3	Mitchell	Highland	200 Airport	3.6	Class officer	Pep
						Homecoming court
						Future teachers
4	O'Malley	St. Joseph	300 Fourth	4.0	Valedictorian	Pep
						Chess
5	Abel	Central	1500 Main	3.7	Citizenship award	Yearbook
						Class officer

6. Assume you want to create a database to store information about your music collection. You want to be able to query the database for each of the following attributes:

- A particular title (for example, Tapestry or Beethoven's Fifth Symphony)

- Artist (for example, Carole King or the Chicago Symphony Orchestra)

- Format of the recording (for example, CD or tape)

- Style of music (for example, rock or classical)

- Year recorded

- Year acquired as part of your collection

- Recording company

- Address of the recording company

Design the tables you would need so they are all in third normal form. Create at least five sample data records for each table you create.

7. Design a group of database tables for the St. Charles Riding Academy. The academy teaches students to ride by starting them on horses that have been ranked according to their manageability, using a numeric score from 1 to 4. The data you need to store includes the following attributes:

- Student's last name

- Student's first name

- Student's address

- Student's age

- Student's emergency contact information—name and phone number

- Student's riding level—1, 2, 3, or 4

- Horse's name

- Horse's age

- Horse's color

- Horse's manageability level—1, 2, 3, or 4

- Horse's veterinarian's name

- Horse's veterinarian's phone number

Design the tables you would need so they are all in third normal form. Create at least five sample data records for each table you create.

Find the Bugs

8. Your student disk contains files named DEBUG14-01.doc, DEBUG14-02.doc, and DEBUG14-03.doc. Each file starts with some comments that describe the problem. Following the comments, each file contains a table that is not in 3NF. Create tables as needed to put the data in 3NF.

Game Zone

9. Massively Multiplayer Online Role-Playing Games (MMORPGs) are online computer role-playing games in which a large number of players interact with one another in a virtual world. Players assume the role of a fictional character and control that character's actions. MMORPGs are distinguished from smaller RPGs by the number of players and by the game's persistent world, usually hosted by the game's publisher, which continues to exist and evolve while the player is away from the game. Design the database you would use to host an MMORPG, including at least three tables.

Up for Discussion

10. In this chapter, a phone book was mentioned as an example of a database you use frequently. Name some other examples.

11. Suppose you have authority to browse your company's database. The company keeps information on each employee's past jobs, health insurance claims, and any criminal record. Also suppose that there is an employee at the company whom you want to ask out on a date. Should you use the database to obtain information about the person? If so, are there any limits on the data you should use? If not, should you be allowed to pay a private detective to discover similar data?

12. The FBI's National Crime Information Center (NCIC) is a computerized database of criminal justice information, including data on criminal histories, fugitives, stolen property, and missing persons. It is almost inevitable that such large systems will contain inaccuracies. Various studies have indicated that perhaps less than half the records in this database are complete, accurate, and unambiguous. Do you approve of this system or object to it? Would you change your mind if there were no inaccuracies? Is there a level of inaccuracy you would find acceptable to realize the benefits of such a system?

13. What type of data might be useful to a community in the wake of a natural disaster? Who should pay for the expense of gathering, storing, and maintaining this data?

Understanding Numbering Systems and Computer Codes

The numbering system with which you are most familiar is the decimal system—the system based on 10 digits, 0 through 9. When you use the decimal system, no other symbols are available; if you want to express a value larger than 9, you must resort to using multiple digits from the same pool of 10, placing them in columns.

When you use the decimal system, you analyze a multicolumn number by mentally assigning place values to each column. The value of the rightmost column is 1, the value of the next column to the left is 10, the next column is 100, and so on, multiplying the column value by 10 as you move to the left. There is no limit to the number of columns you can use; you simply keep adding columns to the left as you need to express higher values. For example, Figure A-1 shows how the value 305 is rep-

```
        Column value
     100    10    1
      3      0    5

      3 * 100 = 300
      0 * 10  =   0
      5 * 1   =   5
                 ---
                 305
```

Figure A-1 Representing 305 in the decimal system

resented in the decimal system. You simply sum the value of the digit in each column after it has been multiplied by the value of its column.

The binary numbering system works in the same way as the decimal numbering system, except that it uses only two digits, 0 and 1. When you use the binary system, if you want to express a value greater than 1, you must resort to using multiple columns, because no single symbol is available that represents any value other than 0 or 1. However, instead of each new column to the left being 10 times greater than

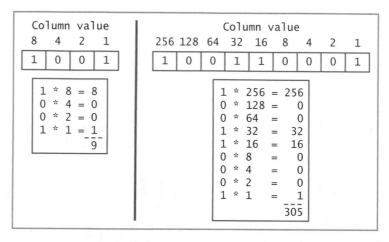

Figure A-2   Representing decimal values 9 and 305 in the binary system

the previous column, when you use the binary system, each new column is only two times the value of the previous column. For example, Figure A-2 shows how the numbers 9 and 305 are represented in the binary system. Notice that in both binary numbers, as well as in the decimal system, it is perfectly acceptable—and often necessary—to create numbers with 0 in one or more columns. As with the decimal system, the binary system has no limit to the number of columns—you can use as many as it takes to express a value.

A computer stores every piece of data it ever uses as a set of 0s and 1s. Each 0 or 1 is known as a bit, which is short for binary digit. Every computer uses 0s and 1s because all values in a computer are stored as electronic signals that are either on or off. This two-state system is most easily represented using just two digits.

Computers use a set of binary digits to represent stored characters. If computers used only one binary digit to represent characters, then only two different characters could be represented, because the single bit could be only 0 or 1. If computers used only two digits, then only four characters could be represented—the four codes 00, 01, 10, and 11, which in decimal values are 0, 1, 2, and 3, respectively. Many computers use sets of eight binary digits to represent each character they store, because using eight binary digits provides 256 different combinations. One combination can represent an "A", another a "B", still others "a" and "b", and so on. Two hundred fifty-six combinations are enough so that each capital letter, small letter, digit, and punctuation mark used in English has its own code; even a space has a code. For example, in some computers 01000001 represents the character "A". The binary number 01000001 has a decimal value of 65, but this numeric value is not important to ordinary computer users; it is simply a code that

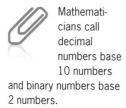

Mathematicians call decimal numbers base 10 numbers and binary numbers base 2 numbers.

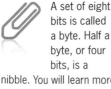

A set of eight bits is called a byte. Half a byte, or four bits, is a nibble. You will learn more about bytes later in this appendix.

stands for "A". The code that uses 01000001 to mean "A" is the American Standard Code for Information Interchange, or ASCII.

The ASCII code is not the only computer code; it is typical, and is the one used in most personal computers. The Extended Binary Coded Decimal Interchange Code, or EBCDIC, is an eight-bit code that is used in IBM mainframe computers. In these computers, the principle is the same—every character is stored as a series of binary digits. However, the actual values used are different. For example, in EBCDIC, an "A" is 11000001, or 193. Another code used by languages such as Java and C# is Unicode; with this code, 16 bits are used to represent each character. The character "A" in Unicode has the same decimal value as the ASCII "A", 65, but it is stored as 0000000001000001. Using 16 bits provides many more possible combinations than using only eight bits— 65,536 to be exact. With Unicode, not only are there enough available codes for all English letters and digits, but also for characters from many international alphabets.

Ordinary computer users seldom think about the numeric codes behind the letters, numbers, and punctuation marks they enter from their keyboards or see displayed on a monitor. However, they see the consequence of the values behind letters when they see data sorted in alphabetical order. When you sort a list of names, "Andrea" comes before "Brian", and "Caroline" comes after "Brian" because the numeric code for "A" is lower than the code for "B", and the numeric code for "C" is higher than the code for "B", no matter whether you are using ASCII, EBCDIC, or Unicode.

Table A-1 shows the decimal and binary values behind the most commonly used characters in the ASCII character set—the letters, numbers, and punctuation marks you can enter from your keyboard using a single key press.

Most of the values not included in Table A-1 have a purpose. For example, the decimal value 7 represents a bell—a dinging sound your computer can make, often used to notify you of an error or some other unusual condition.

Each binary number in Table A-1 is shown containing two sets of four digits; this convention makes the long eight-digit numbers easier to read.

Decimal number	Binary number	ASCII character	
32	0010 0000		Space
33	0010 0001	!	Exclamation point
34	0010 0010	"	Quotation mark, or double quote
35	0010 0011	#	Number sign, also called an octothorpe or a pound sign
36	0010 0100	$	Dollar sign
37	0010 0101	%	Percent
38	0010 0110	&	Ampersand
39	0010 0111	'	Apostrophe, single quote
40	0010 1000	(	Left parenthesis
41	0010 1001	)	Right parenthesis
42	0010 1010	*	Asterisk
43	0010 1011	+	Plus sign
44	0010 1100	,	Comma
45	0010 1101	-	Hyphen or minus sign
46	0010 1110	.	Period or decimal point
47	0010 1111	/	Slash or front slash
48	0011 0000	0	
49	0011 0001	1	
50	0011 0010	2	
51	0011 0011	3	
52	0011 0100	4	
53	0011 0101	5	
54	0011 0110	6	
55	0011 0111	7	
56	0011 1000	8	
57	0011 1001	9	
58	0011 1010	:	Colon
59	0011 1011	;	Semicolon
60	0011 1100	<	Less-than sign
61	0011 1101	=	Equal sign
62	0011 1110	>	Greater-than sign
63	0011 1111	?	Question mark
64	0100 0000	@	At sign
65	0100 0001	A	

Table A-1 Decimal and binary values for common ASCII characters

Decimal number	Binary number	ASCII character	
66	0100 0010	B	
67	0100 0011	C	
68	0100 0100	D	
69	0100 0101	E	
70	0100 0110	F	
71	0100 0111	G	
72	0100 1000	H	
73	0100 1001	I	
74	0100 1010	J	
75	0100 1011	K	
76	0100 1100	L	
77	0100 1101	M	
78	0100 1110	N	
79	0100 1111	O	
80	0101 0000	P	
81	0101 0001	Q	
82	0101 0010	R	
83	0101 0011	S	
84	0101 0100	T	
85	0101 0101	U	
86	0101 0110	V	
87	0101 0111	W	
88	0101 1000	X	
89	0101 1001	Y	
90	0101 1010	Z	
91	0101 1011	[	Opening or left bracket
92	0101 1100	\	Backslash
93	0101 1101	]	Closing or right bracket
94	0101 1110	^	Caret
95	0101 1111	_	Underline or underscore
96	0110 0000	`	Grave accent
97	0110 0001	a	
98	0110 0010	b	
99	0110 0011	c	
100	0110 0100	d	

Table A-1   Decimal and binary values for common ASCII characters (continued)

Decimal number	Binary number	ASCII character	
101	0110 0101	e	
102	0110 0110	f	
103	0110 0111	g	
104	0110 1000	h	
105	0110 1001	i	
106	0110 1010	j	
107	0110 1011	k	
108	0110 1100	l	
109	0110 1101	m	
110	0110 1110	n	
111	0110 1111	o	
112	0111 0000	p	
113	0111 0001	q	
114	0111 0010	r	
115	0111 0011	s	
116	0111 0100	t	
117	0111 0101	u	
118	0111 0110	v	
119	0111 0111	w	
120	0111 1000	x	
121	0111 1001	y	
122	0111 1010	z	
123	0111 1011	{	Opening or left brace
124	0111 1100	|	Vertical line or pipe
125	0111 1101	}	Closing or right brace
126	0111 1110	~	Tilde

Table A-1   Decimal and binary values for common ASCII characters (continued)

The Hexadecimal System

The hexadecimal numbering system is called the base 16 system because it uses 16 digits. As shown in Table A-2, the digits are 0 through 9 and A through F. Computer professionals often use the hexadecimal system to express addresses and instructions as they are stored in computer memory because hexadecimal provides convenient shorthand expressions for groups of binary values. In Table A-2, each hexadecimal value represents one of the 16 possible combinations of four-digit binary values.

Decimal value	Hexadecimal value	Binary value (shown using four digits)
0	0	0000
1	1	0001
2	2	0010
3	3	0011
4	4	0100
5	5	0101
6	6	0110
7	7	0111
8	8	1000
9	9	1001
10	A	1010
11	B	1011
12	C	1100
13	D	1101
14	E	1110
15	F	1111

Table A-2 Values in the decimal and hexadecimal systems

Therefore, instead of referencing memory contents as a 16-digit binary value, for example, programmers can use a 4-digit hexadecimal value.

In the hexadecimal system, each column is 16 times the value of the column to its right. Therefore, column values from right to left are 1, 16, 256, 4096, and so on. Figure A-3 shows how 171 and 305 are expressed in hexadecimal.

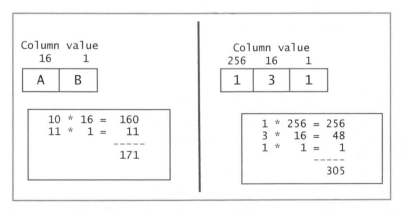

Figure A-3 Representing decimal values 171 and 305 in the hexadecimal system

Measuring Storage

In computer systems, both internal memory and external storage are measured in bits and bytes. Eight bits make a byte, and a byte frequently holds a single character (in ASCII or EBCDIC) or half a character (in Unicode). Because a byte is such a small unit of storage, the size of memory and files is often expressed in thousands or billions of bytes. Table A-3 describes some commonly used terms for storage measurement.

In the metric system, "kilo" means 1000. However, in Table A-3, notice that a kilobyte is 1024 bytes. The discrepancy occurs because everything stored in a computer is based on the binary system, so multiples of two are used in most measurements. If you multiply 2 by itself 10 times, the result is 1024, which is a little over 1000. Similarly, a gigabyte is 1,073,741,624 bytes, which is more than a billion.

Confusion arises because many hard-drive manufacturers use the decimal system instead of the binary system to describe storage. For example, if you buy a hard drive that holds 10 gigabytes, it actually holds exactly 10 billion bytes. However, in the binary system, 10 GB is 10,737,418,240 bytes, so when you check your hard drive's capacity, your computer will report that you don't quite have 10 GB, but only 9.31 GB.

Term	Abbreviation	Number of bytes using binary system	Number of bytes using decimal system	Example
Kilobyte	KB or kB	1024	one thousand	This appendix occupies about 85 kB on a hard disk.
Megabyte	MB	1,048,576 (1024 × 1024 kilobytes)	one million	One megabyte can hold an average book in text format. A 3½ inch diskette you might have used a few years ago held 1.44 megabytes.
Gigabyte	GB	1,073,741,824 (1,024 megabytes)	one billion	The hard drive or a fairly new laptop computer might be 160 gigabytes. An hour of HDTV video is about 4 gigabytes.
Terabyte	TB	1024 gigabytes	one trillion	The entire Library of Congress can be stored in 10 terabytes.
Petabyte	PB	1024 terabytes	one quadrillion	Popular Web sites such as YouTube and Google have 20 to 30 petabytes of activity per month.
Exabyte	EB	1024 petabytes	one quintillion	A popular expression claims that all words ever spoken by humans could be stored in text form in 5 exabytes.
Zettabyte	ZB	1024 exabytes	one sextillion	A popular expression claims that all words ever spoken by humans could be stored in audio form in 42 zettabytes.
Yottabyte	YB	1024 zettabytes	one septillion (a 1 followed by 24 zeros)	All data accessible on the Internet and in corporate networks is estimated to be 1 yottabyte.

Table A-3 Commonly used terms for computer storage

Flowchart Symbols

This appendix contains the flowchart symbols used in this book.

Terminal	(rounded rectangle)
Flowline	→
Input/Output	(parallelogram)
Process	(rectangle)
Decision	(diamond)
Internal module call	(rectangle with side bars at top)
External module call	(rectangle with vertical bars on sides)

Structures

This appendix contains diagrams of the structures allowed in structured programming. Although all logical problems can be solved using the three fundamental structures, the additional structures provide convenience in some situations. Each structure has one entry point and one exit point. At these points, structures can be stacked and nested.

Three Fundamental Structures

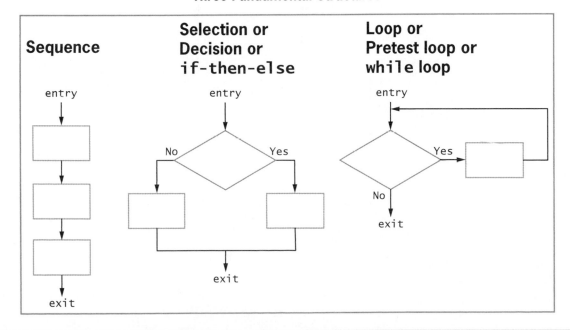

Additional Selection Structures

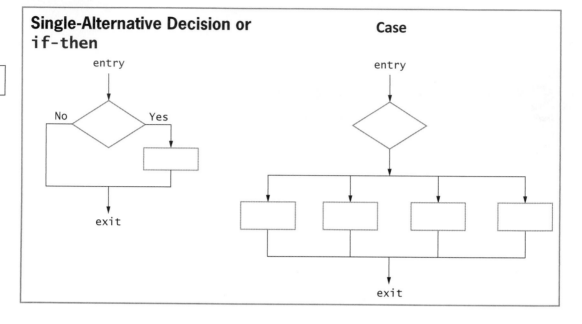

For more information on the case structure and posttest loops, see Appendix F.

Additional Loop Structure

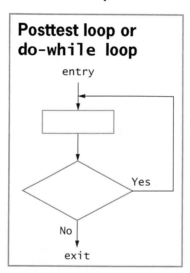

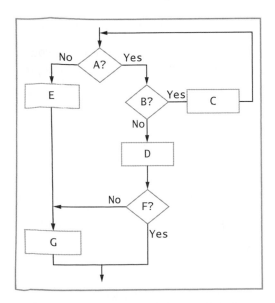

Solving Difficult Structuring Problems

In Chapter 3, you learned that you can solve any logical problem using only the three standard structures—sequence, selection, and loop. Modifying an unstructured program to make it adhere to structured rules often is a simple matter. Sometimes, however, structuring a more complicated program can be challenging. Still, no matter how complicated, large, or poorly structured a problem is, the same tasks can *always* be accomplished in a structured manner.

Consider the flowchart segment in Figure D-1. Is it structured?

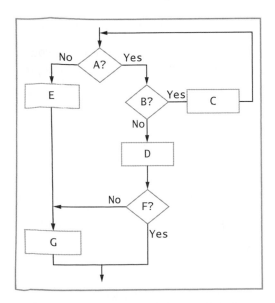

Figure D-1   Unstructured flowchart segment

No, it is not structured. To straighten out the flowchart segment, making it structured, you can use the "spaghetti" method. Using this method, you untangle each path of the flowchart as if you were attempting to untangle strands of spaghetti in a bowl. The objective is to create a new flowchart segment that performs exactly the same tasks as the first, but using only the three structures—sequence, selection, and loop.

To begin to untangle the unstructured flowchart segment, you start at the beginning with the decision labeled A, shown in Figure D-2. This step must represent the beginning of either a selection or a loop, because a sequence would not contain a decision.

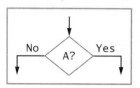

Figure D-2 Structuring, Step 1

If you follow the logic on the No, or left, side of the question in the original flowchart, you can pull up on the left branch of the decision. You encounter process E, followed by G, followed by the end, as shown in Figure D-3. Compare the "No" actions after Decision A in the first flowchart (Figure D-1) with the actions after Decision A in Figure D-3; they are identical.

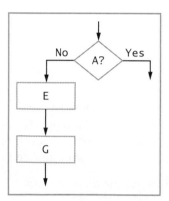

Figure D-3 Structuring, Step 2

Now continue on the right, or Yes, side of Decision A in Figure D-1. When you follow the flowline, you encounter a decision symbol, labeled B. Pull on B's left side, and a process, D, comes up next. See Figure D-4.

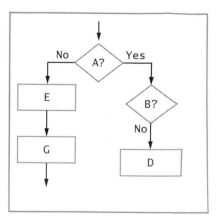

Figure D-4 Structuring, Step 3

After Step D in the original diagram, a decision labeled F comes up. Pull on its left, or No, side and you get a process, G, and then the end. When you pull on F's right, or Yes, side in the original flowchart, you simply reach the end, as shown in Figure D-5. Notice in Figure D-5 that the G process now appears in two locations. When you improve unstructured flowcharts so that they become structured, you often must repeat steps. This eliminates crossed lines and difficult-to-follow spaghetti logic.

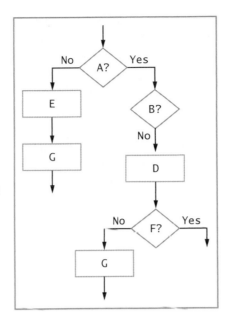

Figure D-5   Structuring, Step 4

The biggest problem in structuring the original flowchart segment from Figure D-1 follows the right, or Yes, side of the B decision. When the answer to B is Yes, you encounter process C, as shown in both Figures D-1 and D-6. The structure that begins with Decision C looks like a loop because it doubles back, up to Decision A. However, the rules of a structured loop say that it must have the appearance shown in Figure D-7: a question, followed by a structure, returning

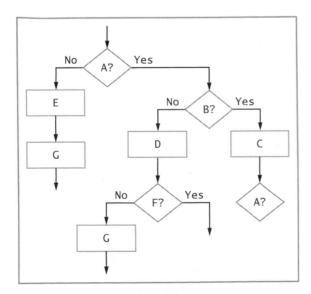

Figure D-6   Structuring, Step 5

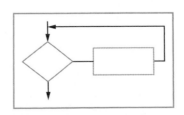

Figure D-7   A structured loop

right back to the question. In Figure D-1, if the path coming out of C returned right to B, there would be no problem; it would be a simple, structured loop. However, as it is, Question A must be repeated. The spaghetti technique says if things are tangled up, start repeating them. So repeat an A decision after C, as Figure D-6 shows.

In the original flowchart segment in Figure D-1, when A is Yes, Question B always follows. So, in Figure D-8, after A is Yes and B is Yes, Step C executes, and A is asked again; when A is Yes, B repeats. In the original, when B is Yes, C executes, so in Figure D-8, on the right side of B, C repeats. After C, A occurs. On the right side of A, B occurs. On the right side of B, C occurs. After C, A should occur again, and so on. Soon you should realize that, to follow the steps in the same order as in the original flowchart segment, you will repeat these same steps forever.

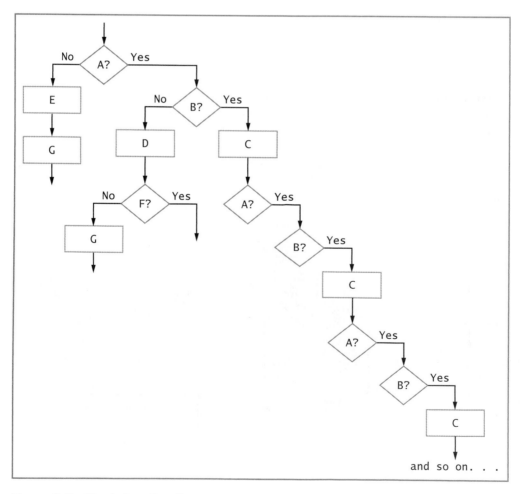

Figure D-8 Structuring, Step 6

If you continue with Figure D-8, you will never be able to end; every C is always followed by another A, B, and C. Sometimes, to make a program segment structured, you have to add an extra flag variable to get out of an infinite mess. A flag is a variable that you set to indicate a true or false state. Typically, a variable is called a flag when its only purpose is to tell you whether some event has occurred. You can create a flag variable named shouldRepeat and set its value to "Yes" or "No", depending on whether it is appropriate to repeat Decision A. When A is No, the shouldRepeat flag should be set

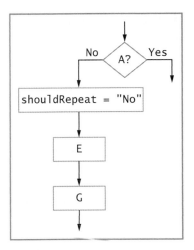

Figure D-9 Adding a flag to the flowchart

to "No" because, in this situation, you never want to repeat Question A again. See Figure D-9.

Similarly, after A is Yes, but when B is No, you never want to repeat Question A again, either. Figure D-10 shows that you set shouldRepeat to "No" when the answer to B is No. Then you continue with D and the F decision that executes G when F is No.

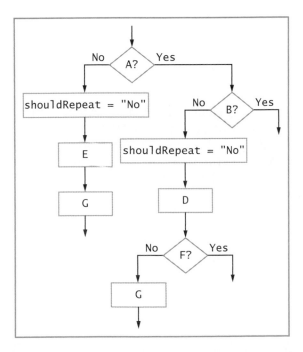

Figure D-10 Adding a flag to a second path in the flowchart

However, in the original flowchart segment in Figure D-1, when the B decision result is Yes, you *do* want to repeat A. So when B is Yes, perform the process for C and set the shouldRepeat flag equal to "Yes", as shown in Figure D-11.

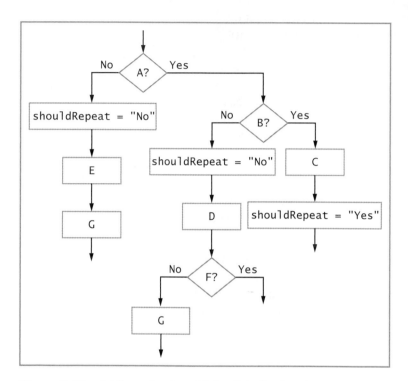

Figure D-11   Adding a flag to a third path in the flowchart

Now all paths of the flowchart can join together at the bottom with one final question: Is shouldRepeat equal to "Yes"? If it isn't, exit; but if it is, extend the flowline to go back to repeat Question A. See Figure D-12. Take a moment to verify that the steps that would execute following Figure D-12 are the same steps that would execute following Figure D-1.

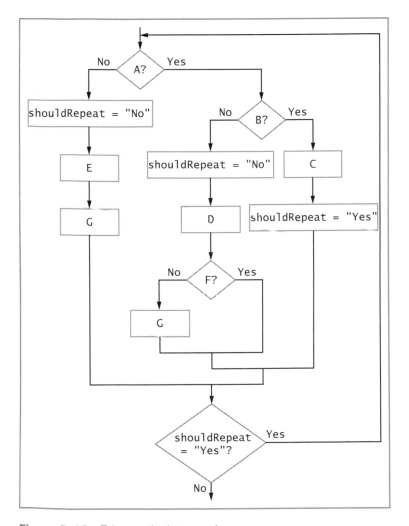

Figure D-12 Tying up the loose ends

- When **A** is No, **E** and **G** always execute.
- When **A** is Yes and **B** is No, **D** and decision **F** always execute.
- When **A** is Yes and **B** is Yes, **C** always executes and **A** repeats.

Figure D-12 contains three nested selection structures. Notice how the F decision begins a complete selection structure whose Yes and No paths join together when the structure ends. This F selection structure is within one path of the B decision structure; the B decision begins a complete selection structure, the Yes and No paths of which join together at the bottom. Likewise, the B selection structure resides entirely within one path of the A selection structure.

The flowchart segment in Figure D-12 performs identically to the original spaghetti version in Figure D-1. However, is this new flowchart segment structured? There are so many steps in the diagram, it is hard to tell. You may be able to see the structure more clearly if you create a module named aThroughG(). If you create the module shown in Figure D-13, then the original flowchart segment can be drawn as in Figure D-14.

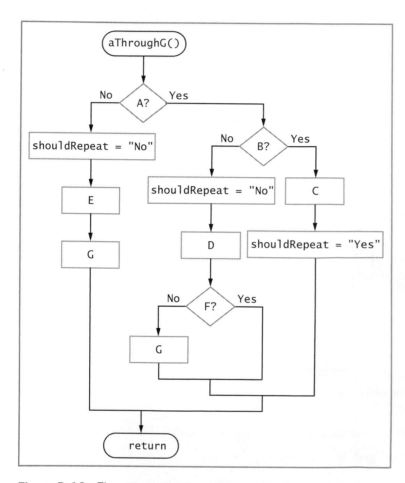

Figure D-13   The aThroughG() module

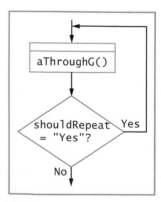

Figure D-14   Logic in Figure D-12, substituting a module for Steps A through G

Creating Print Charts

A printed report is a very common type of output. You can design a printed report on a printer spacing chart, which is also called a print chart or a print layout. Many modern-day programmers use various software tools to design their output, but you can also create a print chart by hand. This appendix provides some of the details for creating a traditional handwritten print chart. Even if you never design output on your own, you might see print charts in the documentation of existing programs.

Figure E-1 shows a printer spacing chart, which basically looks like graph paper. The chart has many boxes, and in each box the designer

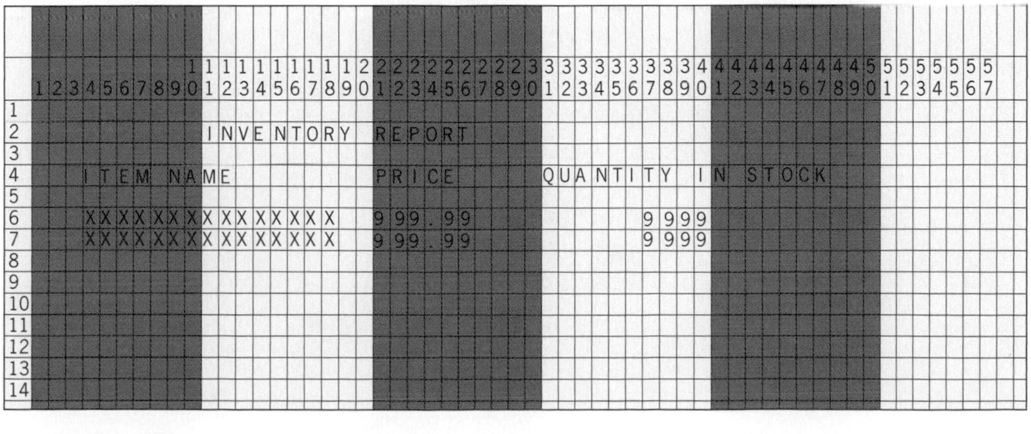

Figure E-1   A printer spacing chart

Now you can see that the completed flowchart segment in Figure D-14 is a do-until loop. If you prefer to use a while loop, you can redraw Figure D-14 to perform a sequence followed by a while loop, as shown in Figure D-15.

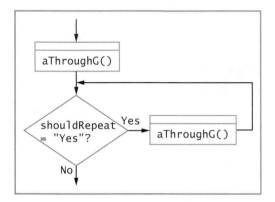

Figure D-15 Logic in Figure D-14, substituting a sequence and while loop for the do-until loop

It has taken some effort, but any logical problem can be made to conform to structured rules. It may take extra steps, including repeating specific steps and using some flag variables, but every logical problem can be solved using the three structures: sequence, selection, and loop.

The flowchart segment in Figure D-12 performs identically to the original spaghetti version in Figure D-1. However, is this new flowchart segment structured? There are so many steps in the diagram, it is hard to tell. You may be able to see the structure more clearly if you create a module named aThroughG(). If you create the module shown in Figure D-13, then the original flowchart segment can be drawn as in Figure D-14.

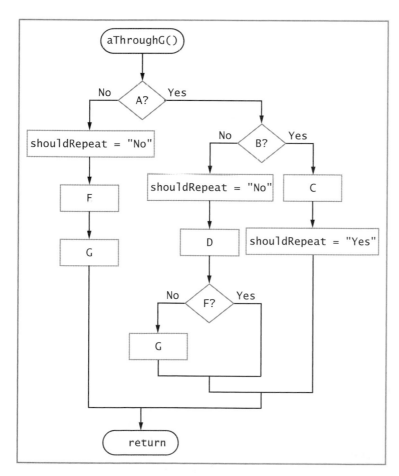

Figure D-13 The aThroughG() module

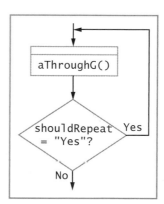

Figure D-14 Logic in Figure D-12, substituting a module for Steps A through G

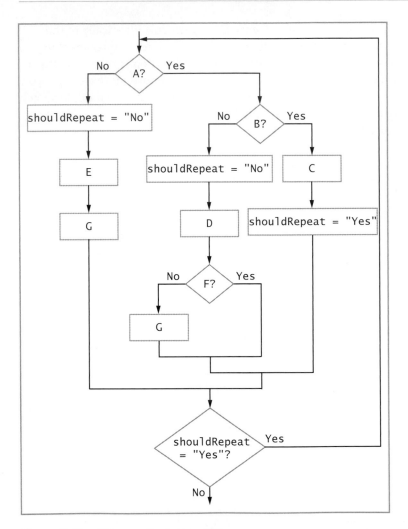

Figure D-12 Tying up the loose ends

- When **A** is No, **E** and **G** always execute.
- When **A** is Yes and **B** is No, **D** and decision **F** always execute.
- When **A** is Yes and **B** is Yes, **C** always executes and **A** repeats.

Figure D-12 contains three nested selection structures. Notice how the F decision begins a complete selection structure whose Yes and No paths join together when the structure ends. This F selection structure is within one path of the B decision structure; the B decision begins a complete selection structure, the Yes and No paths of which join together at the bottom. Likewise, the B selection structure resides entirely within one path of the A selection structure.

places one character that will be printed. The rows and columns in the chart usually are numbered for reference.

For example, suppose you want to create a printed report with the following features:

- A printed title, INVENTORY REPORT, that begins 11 spaces from the left edge of the page and one line down

- Column headings for ITEM NAME, PRICE, and QUANTITY IN STOCK, two lines below the title and placed over the actual data items that are displayed

- Variable data appearing below each of the column headings

The exact spacing and the use of uppercase or lowercase characters in the print chart make a difference. Notice that the constant data in the output—the items that remain the same in every execution of the report—do not need to follow the same rules as variable names in the program. Within a report, constants like INVENTORY REPORT and ITEM NAME can contain spaces. These headings exist to help readers understand the information presented in the report, not for a computer to interpret; there is no need to run the names together, as you do when choosing identifiers for variables.

A print layout typically shows how the variable data will appear on the report. Of course, the data will probably be different every time the program is executed. Thus, instead of writing in actual item names and prices, the users and programmers usually use Xs to represent generic variable characters, and 9s to represent generic variable numeric data. (Some programmers use Xs for both character and numeric data.) Each line containing Xs and 9s is a detail line, or a line that displays the data details. Detail lines typically appear many times per page, as opposed to heading lines, which contain the title and any column headings, and usually appear only once per page.

Even though an actual inventory report might eventually go on for hundreds or thousands of detail lines, writing two or three rows of Xs and 9s is sufficient to show how the data will appear. For example, if a report contains employee names and salaries, those data items will occupy the same print positions on output for line after line, whether the output eventually contains 10 employees or 10,000. A few rows of identically positioned Xs and 9s are sufficient to establish the pattern.

Two Variations on the Basic Structures— case and do-while

You can solve any logic problem you might encounter using only the three structures: sequence, selection, and loop. However, many programming languages allow two more structures: the case structure and the do-while loop. These structures are never *needed* to solve any problem—you can always use a series of selections instead of the case structure, and you can always use a sequence plus a while loop in place of the do-while loop. However, sometimes these additional structures are convenient. Programmers consider them all to be acceptable, legal structures.

The case Structure

You can use the case structure when there are several distinct possible values for a single variable you are testing and each value requires a different course of action. Suppose you work at a school at which tuition varies per credit hour, depending on whether a student is a freshman, sophomore, junior, or senior. The structured flowchart and pseudocode in Figure F-1 show a series of decisions that assigns different tuition values depending on the value of year.

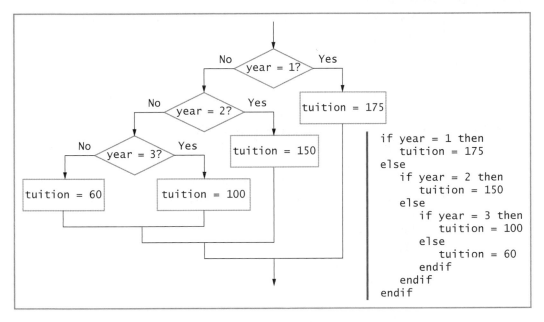

```
if year = 1 then
    tuition = 175
else
    if year = 2 then
        tuition = 150
    else
        if year = 3 then
            tuition = 100
        else
            tuition = 60
        endif
    endif
endif
```

Figure F-1 Flowchart and pseudocode of tuition decisions

The logic shown in Figure F-1 is absolutely correct and completely structured. The **year** = 3? selection structure is contained within the **year** = 2? structure, which is contained within the **year** = 1? structure. (In this example, if **year** is not 1, 2, or 3, it is assumed that the student receives the senior tuition rate.)

Even though the program segments in Figure F-1 are correct and structured, many programming languages permit using a **case** structure, as shown in Figure F-2. When using the **case** structure, you test a variable against a series of values, taking appropriate action based on the variable's value. Many people feel such programs are easier to read, and the **case** structure is allowed because the same results *could*

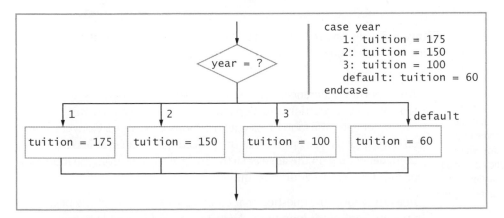

```
case year
    1: tuition = 175
    2: tuition = 150
    3: tuition = 100
    default: tuition = 60
endcase
```

Figure F-2 Flowchart and pseudocode of **case** structure that determines tuition

The term *default* used in Figure F-2 means "if none of the other cases is true." Various programming languages you learn may use different syntaxes for the default case.

You use the case structure only when a series of decisions is based on different values stored in a single variable. If multiple variables are tested, then you must use a series of decisions.

be achieved with a series of structured selections (thus making the program structured). That is, if the first program is structured and the second one reflects the first one point by point, then the second one must be structured also.

Even though a programming language permits you to use the case structure, you should understand that the case structure is just a convenience that might make a flowchart, pseudocode, or actual program code easier to understand at first glance. When you write a series of decisions using the case structure, the computer still makes a series of individual decisions, just as though you had used many if-then-else combinations. In other words, you might prefer looking at the diagram in Figure F-2 to understand the tuition fees charged by a school, but a computer actually makes the decisions as shown in Figure F-1—one at a time. When you write your own programs, it is always acceptable to express a complicated decision-making process as a series of individual selections.

The do-while Loop

Recall that a structured loop (often called a while loop) looks like Figure F-3. A special-case loop called a do-while loop looks like Figure F-4.

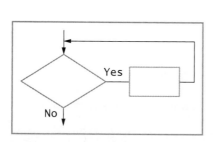

Figure F-3 The while loop, which is a pretest loop

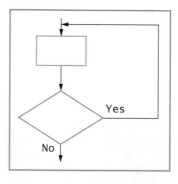

Figure F-4 Structure of a do-while loop, which is a posttest loop

Notice that the word "do" begins the name of the do-while loop. This should remind you that the action you "do" precedes testing the condition.

An important difference exists between these two structures. In a while loop, you ask a question and, depending on the answer, you might or might not enter the loop to execute the loop's procedure. Conversely, in do-while loops, you ensure that the procedure executes at least once; then, depending on the answer to the controlling question, the loop may or may not execute additional times.

In a while loop, the question that controls a loop comes at the beginning, or "top," of the loop body. A while loop is a pretest loop because a condition is tested before entering the loop even once. In a do-while loop, the question that controls the loop comes at the end, or "bottom," of the loop body. Do-while loops are posttest loops because a condition is tested after the loop body has executed.

You encounter examples of do-while looping every day. For example:

do
    pay a bill
while more bills remain to be paid

As another example:

do
    wash a dish
while more dishes remain to be washed

In these examples, the activity (paying bills or washing dishes) must occur at least one time. With a do-while loop, you ask the question that determines whether you continue only after the activity has been executed at least once.

You never are required to use a posttest loop. You can duplicate the same series of actions generated by any posttest loop by creating a sequence followed by a standard, pretest while loop. Consider the flowcharts and pseudocode in Figure F-5.

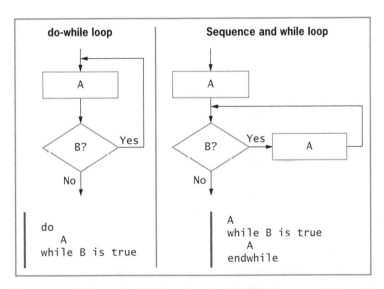

Figure F-5 Flowchart and pseudocode for do-while loop and while loop that do the same thing

On the left side of Figure F-5, A executes, and then B is asked. If B is yes, then A executes and B is asked again. On the right side of the figure, A executes, and then B is asked. If B is yes, then A executes and B is asked again. In other words, both sets of flowchart and pseudocode segments do exactly the same thing.

Because programmers understand that any posttest loop (`do-while`) can be expressed with a sequence followed by a `while` loop, most languages allow at least one of the versions of the posttest loop for convenience. Again, you are never required to use a posttest loop; you can always accomplish the same tasks with a sequence followed by a pretest `while` loop.

Recognizing the Characteristics Shared by All Structured Loops

As you examine Figures F-3 and F-4, notice that with the `while` loop, the loop-controlling question is placed at the beginning of the steps that repeat. With the `do-while` loop, the loop-controlling question is placed at the end of the sequence of the steps that repeat.

All structured loops, both pretest and posttest, share these two characteristics:

- The loop-controlling question must provide either entry to or exit from the repeating structure.

- The loop-controlling question provides the *only* entry to or exit from the repeating structure.

In other words, there is exactly one loop-controlling value, and it provides either the only entrance to or the only exit from the loop.

Some languages support a **do-until** loop, which is a posttest loop that iterates until the loop-controlling question is false. The **do-until** loop follows structured loop rules.

Recognizing Unstructured Loops

Figure F-6 shows an unstructured loop. It is not a `while` loop, which begins with a decision and, after an action, returns to the decision. It is also not a `do-while` loop, which begins with an action and ends with a decision that might repeat the action. Instead, it begins like a posttest loop (a `do-while` loop), with a process followed by a decision, but one branch of the decision does not repeat the initial process. Instead, it performs an additional new action before repeating the initial process.

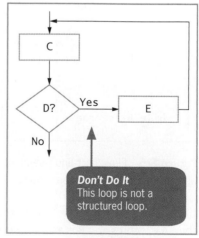

Figure F-6 Unstructured loop

If you need to use the logic shown in Figure F-6—performing a task, asking a question, and perhaps performing an additional task before looping back to the first process—then the way to make the logic structured is to repeat the initial process within the loop, at the end of the loop. Figure F-7 shows the same logic as Figure F-6, but now it is structured logic, with a sequence of two actions occurring within the loop.

Especially when you are first mastering structured logic, you might prefer to use only the three basic structures—sequence, selection, and `while` loop. Every logical problem can be solved using only these three structures, and you can understand all of the examples in this book using only these structures.

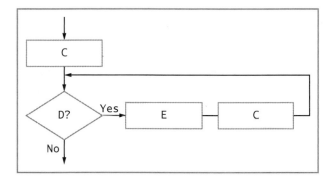

Figure F-7 Sequence and structured loop that accomplish the same tasks as Figure F-6

Glossary

A

abstract class A class from which you cannot create any concrete objects, but from which you can inherit.

abstract data type (ADT) A programmer-defined type, such as a class.

abstraction The process of paying attention to important properties while ignoring nonessential details.

access specifier (or access modifier) The adjective that defines the type of access outside classes will have to an attribute or method.

accessibility Describes screen design issues that make programs easier to use for people with physical limitations.

accessor methods Methods that get values from class fields.

accumulator A variable that you use to gather or accumulate values.

activity diagram A UML diagram that shows the flow of actions of a system, including branches that occur when decisions affect the outcome.

actual parameters The arguments in a method call.

addresses Computer memory and storage locations.

aggregation A whole-part relationship.

algorithm A list of instructions that accomplish a task; the sequence of steps necessary to solve any problem.

alphanumeric values The set of values that includes alphabetic characters, numbers, and punctuation.

alternate keys The remaining candidate keys after you choose a primary key in a database.

ambiguous methods Methods between which the compiler cannot distinguish because they have the same name and parameter types.

ancestors The entire list of parent classes from which a class is derived.

AND decision A decision in which two conditions must both be true for an action to take place.

animation The rapid sequence of still images, each slightly different from the previous one, that together produce the illusion of movement.

annotation symbol A flowcharting symbol that contains information that expands on what appears in another flowchart symbol; it is most often represented by a three-sided box that is connected to the step it references by a dashed line.

anomaly An irregularity in a database's design that causes problems and inconveniences.

application software Programs that carry out a task for the user.

argument to a method A value passed to a method in a call to the method.

array A series or list of variables in computer memory, all of which have the same name but are differentiated with subscripts.

ascending order Describes the arrangement of records from lowest to highest, based on a value within a field.

assignment operator The equal sign; it always requires the name of a memory location on its left side.

assignment statement A statement that stores the result of any calculation performed on its right side to the named location on its left side.

association relationship Describes the connection or link between objects in a UML diagram.

atomic attributes In a database, describes columns that are as small as possible so as to contain undividable pieces of data.

atomic transactions Transactions that appear to execute completely or not at all.

attribute One field or column in a database table; a characteristic that defines an object as part of a class.

authentication techniques Security techniques that include storing and verifying passwords and using physical characteristics, such as fingerprints or voice recognition, before users can view data.

B

backup file A copy that is kept in case values need to be restored to their original state.

base class A class that is used as a basis for inheritance.

base table The "one" table in a one-to-many relationship.

batch A group of transactions applied all at once.

batch processing Processing that performs the same tasks with many records in sequence.

behavior diagrams UML diagrams that emphasize what happens in a system.

binary decision A yes-or-no decision; so called because there are two possible outcomes.

binary files Files that contain data that has not been encoded as text.

binary language Computer language represented using a series of 0s and 1s.

binary operator An operator that requires two operands—one on each side.

binary search A search that starts in the middle of a sorted list, and then determines whether it should continue higher or lower to find a target value.

black box The analogy that programmers use to refer to hidden method implementation details.

block A group of statements that executes as a single unit.

Boolean expression An expression that represents only one of two states, usually expressed as true or false.

bubble sort A sort in which you arrange records in either ascending or descending order by comparing items in a list in pairs; when an item is out of order, it swaps values with the item below it.

byte A unit of computer storage. It can contain any of 256 combinations of 0s and 1s that often represent a character.

C

camel casing The format for naming variables in which the initial letter is lowercase, multiple-word variable names are run together, and each new word within the variable name begins with an uppercase letter.

candidate keys Columns or attributes that could serve as a primary key in a table.

cardinality Describes an arithmetic relationship between objects.

cascading if statement A series of nested if statements.

catch an exception To receive an exception from a throw so it can be handled.

catch block A segment of code that can handle an exception that might be thrown by the try block that precedes it.

central processing unit (CPU) The piece of hardware that processes data.

character A letter, number, or special symbol such as "A", "7", or "$"; the smallest usable unit of data.

child class A derived class.

child file A copy of a file after revision.

class A group or collection of objects with common attributes.

class client or **class user** A program or class that instantiates objects of another prewritten class.

class definition A set of program statements that define the characteristics of a class's objects and the methods that can be applied to its objects.

class diagram A tool for describing a class that consists of a rectangle divided into three sections that show the name, data, and methods of a class.

class method A static method. Class methods are not instance methods and do not receive a this reference.

client A program or other method that uses a method.

closing a file An action that makes a file no longer available to an application.

coding the program The act of writing the statements of a program in a programming language.

cohesion A measure of how the internal statements of a method serve to accomplish the method's purpose.

command line The location on your computer screen at which you enter text to communicate with the computer's operating system.

communication diagram A UML diagram that emphasizes the organization of objects that participate in a system.

compiler Software that translates a high-level language into machine language and tells you if you have used a programming language incorrectly. A compiler is similar to an interpreter; however, a compiler translates all the statements in a program prior to executing them.

component diagram A UML diagram that emphasizes the files, database tables, documents, and other components that a system's software uses.

composition The technique of placing a class object within another class object.

compound condition A condition constructed when you need to ask multiple questions before determining an outcome.

compound key, or **composite key** A key constructed from multiple columns.

computer file A collection of data stored on a nonvolatile device in a computer system.

computer memory The temporary, internal storage within a computer.

computer system A combination of all the components required to process and store data using a computer.

concatenate columns To combine database table columns to produce a compound key.

concurrent update problem A problem that can occur when two database users need to modify the same record at the same time.

conditional AND operator A symbol that you use to combine decisions so that two (or more) conditions must be true for an action to occur. Also called an AND operator.

conditional OR operator A symbol that you use to combine decisions when any one condition can be true for an action to occur. Also called an OR operator.

constructor An automatically called method that establishes an object.

container A class of objects whose main purpose is to hold other elements—for example, a window.

control break A temporary detour in the logic of a program.

control break field A variable that holds the value that signals a break in a program.

control break program A program in which a change in the value of a variable initiates special actions or causes special or unusual processing to occur.

control break report A report that lists items in groups. Frequently, each group is followed by a subtotal.

conversion The entire set of actions an organization must take to switch over to using a new program or set of programs.

counter Any numeric variable you use to count the number of times an event has occurred.

coupling A measure of the strength of the connection between two program methods.

D

data dictionary A list of every variable name used in a program, along with its type, size, and description.

data hierarchy Represents the relationship of databases, files, records, fields, and characters.

data integrity Describes a database when it follows a set of rules that makes the data accurate and consistent.

data redundancy The unnecessary repetition of data.

data type The characteristic of a variable that describes the kind of values the variable can hold and the types of operations that can be performed with it.

database A logical container that holds a group of files, often called tables, that together serve the information needs of an organization; a collection that holds a group of files, or tables, that an organization needs to support its applications.

database management software A set of programs that allows users to create and manage data.

dead path A logical path that can never be traveled.

debugging The process of finding and correcting program errors.

decision structure A program structure in which you ask a question, and, depending on the answer, you take one of two courses of action. Then, no matter which path you follow, you continue with the next task.

decision symbol A symbol that represents a decision in a flowchart, and is shaped like a diamond.

declaration A statement that names a variable and its data type.

declaring variables The process of naming program variables and assigning a type to them.

decrementing The act of changing a variable by decreasing it by a constant value, frequently 1.

default constructor A constructor that requires no arguments.

default input and output devices Hardware devices that do not require opening. Usually they are the keyboard and monitor, respectively.

defensive programming A technique with which you try to prepare for all possible errors before they occur.

definite loop A loop for which the number of repetitions is a predetermined value.

delete anomaly A problem that occurs when a row in a database table is deleted; the result is loss of related data.

denormalize To place a database table in a lower normal form by placing some repeated information back into it.

deployment diagram A UML diagram that focuses on a system's hardware.

derived class An extended class.

descending order Describes the arrangement of records from highest to lowest, based on a value within a field.

desk-checking The process of walking through a program solution on paper.

destructor An automatically called method that contains the actions you require when an instance of a class is destroyed.

detail loop tasks The steps that are repeated for each set of input data.

direct access files Random access files.

directories Organization units on storage devices; each can contain multiple files as well as additional directories. In a graphic system, directories are often called *folders*.

documentation All of the supporting material that goes with a program.

DOS prompt The command line in the DOS operating system.

dual-alternative if or **dual-alternative selection** A selection structure that defines one action to be taken when the tested condition is true, and another action to be taken when it is false.

dummy value A preselected value that stops the execution of a program.

E

echoing input The act of repeating input back to a user either in a subsequent prompt or in output.

element An array variable.

elided Describes the omitted parts when UML diagrams are edited for clarity.

else clause A part of a decision that holds the action or actions that execute only when the Boolean expression in the decision is false.

encapsulation The act of containing a task's instructions and data in the same method; the process of combining all of an object's attributes and methods into a single package.

encryption The process of coding data into a format that human beings cannot read.

end-of-job task A step you take at the end of the program to finish the application.

end-structure statements Statements that designate the ends of pseudocode structures.

entity One record or row in a database table.

eof An end-of-data file marker, short for "end of file."

event An occurrence that generates a message sent to an object.

event-driven or **event-based** Describes programs and actions that occur in response to user-initiated events such as clicking a mouse button.

exception The generic term used for an error in object-oriented languages. Presumably, errors are not usual occurrences; they are the "exceptions" to the rule.

exception-handling techniques The techniques for handling errors in object-oriented programs.

executing Having a computer use a written and compiled program. See also *running*.

extend variation A use case UML diagram variation that shows functions beyond those found in a base case.

extended class A derived class.

external documentation All the external material that programmers develop to support a program. Contrast with program comments, which are internal program documentation.

F

field A single data item, such as `lastName`, `streetAddress`, or `annualSalary`; a group of characters that represent a piece of information.

file A group of records that go together for some logical reason.

first normal form, or **1NF** The normalization form in which repeating groups in a database are eliminated.

flag A variable that you set to indicate whether some event has occurred.

floating-point value A fractional, numeric variable that contains a decimal point.

flowchart A pictorial representation of the logical steps it takes to solve a problem.

flowline An arrow that connects the steps in a flowchart.

folders Organization units on storage devices; each can contain multiple files as well as additional folders. Folders are graphic directories.

for statement A statement that can be used to code definite loops. It contains a loop control variable that it automatically initializes, evaluates, and increments. Also called a `for` loop.

foreign key A column that is not a key in a table, but contains an attribute that is a key in a related table.

fork A feature of a UML activity diagram; it is similar to a decision, but whereas the flow of control follows only one path after a decision, a fork defines a branch in which all paths are followed simultaneously.

formal parameters The variables in a method declaration that accept the values from the actual parameters.

fragile Describes classes that depend on field names from parent classes. Fragile classes are prone to errors; that is, they are easy to "break."

functional cohesion The type of cohesion that occurs when all operations in a method contribute to the performance of only one task.

functionally dependent Describes a relationship in which an attribute can be determined by another.

G

garbage Describes the unknown value stored in an unassigned variable.

generalization variation A variation used in a UML diagram when a use case is less specific than others, and you want to be able to substitute the more specific case for a general one.

get method A method that returns a value from a class.

gigabyte A billion bytes.

GIGO Acronym for "garbage in, garbage out"; it means that if your input is incorrect, your output is worthless.

global Describes variables that are known to an entire program.

global data item An item that is known to all the methods in a program.

goto-less programming A name to describe structured programming, because structured programmers do not use a "go to" statement.

graphical user interface (GUI) A program interface that uses screens to display program output and allows users to interact with a program in a graphical environment.

H

hardware The equipment of a computer system.

has-a relationship A whole-part relationship; the phrase describes the association between the whole and one of its parts. The type of relationship that exists when using composition.

help methods and **facilitators** Work methods.

hierarchy chart A diagram that illustrates modules' relationships to each other.

high-level programming language A programming language that is like English, as opposed to a low-level programming language.

housekeeping tasks Tasks that include steps you must perform at the beginning of a program to get ready for the rest of the program.

Hungarian notation A variable-naming convention in which a variable's data type or other information is stored as part of its name.

I

I/O symbol An input/output symbol.

icons Small pictures on the screen that the user can select with a mouse.

IDE The acronym for Integrated Development Environment, which is the visual development environment in some programming languages.

identifier A variable name.

if-then A structure similar to an if-then-else, but no alternative or "else" action is necessary.

if-then-else Another name for a selection structure.

immutable Not changing during normal operation.

implementation hiding A programming principle that describes the encapsulation of method details.

in scope The characteristic in which variables and constants apply only within the method in which they are declared.

inaccessible Describes any field or method that cannot be reached because of a logical error.

include variation A UML diagram variation that you use when a case can be part of multiple use cases.

incrementing Changing a variable by adding a constant value to it, frequently 1.

indefinite loop A loop for which you cannot predetermine the number of executions.

index The process of storing a list of key fields paired with the storage address for the corresponding data record.

indirect relationship Describes the relationship between parallel arrays in which an element in the first array does not directly access its corresponding value in the second array.

infinite loop A repeating flow of logic without an ending.

information hiding (or data hiding) The concept that other classes should not alter an object's attributes—only the methods of an object's own class should have that privilege.

inheritance The process of acquiring the traits of one's predecessors.

initializing a variable The act of assigning the first value to a variable, often at the same time the variable is created.

inner loop When loops are nested, the loop that is contained within the other loop.

input Describes the entry of data items into computer memory using hardware devices such as keyboards and mice.

input symbol A symbol that indicates an input operation, and is represented as parallelograms in flowcharts.

input/output symbol A parallelogram in flowcharts.

insert anomaly A problem that occurs in a database when new rows are added to a table; the result is incomplete rows.

instance A tangible example of a class; an object.

instance method A method that operates correctly yet differently for each class object. An instance method is nonstatic and receives a `this` reference.

instance variables The data components that belong to every instantiated object.

instant access files Random access files in which records must be accessed immediately.

instantiation An instance of a class.

integer A whole number.

integrated development environment (IDE) A software package that provides an editor, compiler, and other programming tools.

interaction diagrams UML diagrams that emphasize the flow of control and data among the things in the system being modeled.

interactive program A program in which a user makes direct requests, as opposed to one in which input comes from a file.

interactivity diagram A tool that shows the relationship between screens in an interactive GUI program.

interface to a method A method's return type, name, and arguments; the part of a method that a client sees and uses.

internal documentation Documentation within a program. See also *program comments*.

IPO chart A program development tool that delineates input, processing, and output tasks in a method.

is-a relationship A relationship that exists between an object and its class.

iteration Another name for a loop structure.

J

join A feature of a UML activity diagram; it reunites the flow of control after a fork.

join column The column on which two tables in a database are connected.

join operation A database operation that connects two tables based on the values in a common column.

K

key A field or column that uniquely identifies a record.

key field The field whose contents make a record unique among all records in a file.

keywords The limited word set that is reserved in a language.

kilobyte Approximately 1000 bytes.

L

left-to-right associativity Describes operators that evaluate the expression to the left first.

libraries Stored collections of classes that serve related purposes.

linear search A search through a list from one end to the other.

linked list A list that contains an extra field in every record of stored data; this extra field holds the physical address of the next logical record.

listener An object that is "interested in" an event to which you want it to respond.

local Describes variables that are declared within the method that uses them.

lock A mechanism that prevents changes to a database for a period of time.

logic Instructions given to the computer in a specific sequence, without leaving any instructions out or adding extraneous instructions.

logical error An error that occurs when incorrect instructions are performed, or when instructions are performed in the wrong order.

logical NOT operator A symbol that reverses the meaning of a Boolean expression.

logical order The order in which you use a list, even though it is not necessarily physically stored in that order.

loop A structure that repeats actions while a condition continues.

loop body The set of actions that occurs within a loop.

loop control variable A variable that determines whether a loop will continue.

loop structure A structure that repeats actions based on the answer to a question.

loose coupling Occurs when methods do not depend on others.

low-level language A programming language not far removed from machine language, as opposed to a high-level programming language.

lvalue The memory address identifier to the left of an assignment operator.

M

machine language A computer's on/off circuitry language; the low-level language made up of 1s and 0s that the computer understands.

magic number An unnamed numeric constant.

main program A program that runs from start to stop and calls other modules. Also called a main program method.

mainline logic The overall logic of a main program from beginning to end.

maintenance All the improvements and corrections made to a program after it is in production.

making a decision The act of testing a value.

making declarations The process of naming program variables and assigning a type to them.

many-to-many relationship A relationship in which multiple rows in each of two tables can correspond to multiple rows in the other.

master file A file that holds complete and relatively permanent data.

matrix A term sometimes used by mathematicians to describe a two-dimensional array.

mean An arithmetic average.

median The value in a list that is in the middle position when the values are sorted.

megabyte A million bytes.

merging files The act of combining two or more files while maintaining the sequential order.

method A program module that contains a series of statements that carries out a task.

method body A program component that contains all the statements in a method.

method header A program component that precedes a method; the header includes the method identifier and possibly other necessary identifying information.

method's type The type of a method's return value.

Microsoft Visual Studio IDE A software package that contains useful tools for creating programs in Visual Basic, C++, and C#.

mnemonic A memory device; variable identifiers act as mnemonics for hard-to-remember memory addresses.

modularization The process of breaking down a program into modules.

module A small program unit that you can use with other modules to make a program. Programmers also refer to modules as subroutines, procedures, functions, and methods.

module's body Part of a module that contains all the statements in the module.

module's header Part of a module that includes the module identifier and possibly other necessary identifying information.

module's return statement Part of a module that marks the end of the module and identifies the point at which control returns to the program or module that called the module.

multidimensional arrays Lists with more than one dimension.

multiple inheritance The act of inheriting from more than one class.

multiplicity Describes arithmetic relationships between objects.

multithreading Using multiple threads of execution.

mutator methods Methods that set values in a class.

N

named constant A named memory location, similar to a variable, except its value never changes during the execution of a program. Conventionally, constants are named using all capital letters.

nested decision A decision "inside of" another decision. Also called a nested if.

nested loop A loop structure within another loop structure; nesting loops are loops within loops.

nesting structures Placing a structure within another structure.

nonkey attribute Any column in a table that is not a key.

nonstatic methods Methods that exist to be used with an object created from a class; they are instance methods and receive a this reference.

nonvolatile Describes storage whose contents are retained when power is lost.

normal forms Rules for constructing a well-designed database.

normalization The process of designing and creating a set of database tables that satisfies the users' needs and avoids redundancies and anomalies.

null case The branch of a decision in which no action is taken.

nulls Empty columns in a database.

numeric constant A specific numeric value.

numeric variable A variable that holds numeric values.

O

object A tangible example of a class; it is an instance of a class.

object code Code that has been translated to machine language.

object diagrams UML diagrams that are similar to class diagrams, but that model specific instances of classes.

object dictionary A list of the objects used in a program, including which screens they are used on and whether any code, or script, is associated with them.

object-oriented programming (OOP) A style of programming that focuses on an application's data and the methods you need to manipulate that data. In other words, OOP focuses on objects, or "things," and describes their features, or attributes, and their behaviors.

one-dimensional or **single-dimensional array** A list accessed using a single subscript.

one-to-many relationship A relationship in which one row in a table can be related to many rows in another table. It is the most common type of relationship among tables.

one-to-one relationship A relationship in which a row in one table corresponds to exactly one row in another table.

opening a file The process of locating a file on a storage device, physically preparing it for reading, and associating it with an identifier inside a program.

operating system The software that you use to run a computer and manage its resources.

OR decision A decision that contains two (or more) decisions; if at least one condition is met, the resulting action takes place.

order of operations Describes the rules of precedence.

out of bounds Describes an array subscript that is not within the range of acceptable subscripts.

outer loop The loop that contains a nested loop.

output Describes the operation of retrieving information from memory and sending it to a device, such as a monitor or printer, so people can view, interpret, and work with the results.

output symbol A symbol that indicates an output operation, and is represented as parallelograms in flowcharts.

overhead All the resources and time required by an operation.

overload a method The act of creating multiple method versions with the same name but different parameter lists.

overloading Supplying diverse meanings for a single identifier.

override The action of using one method over another when the first is used by default in place of the second with the same signature.

P

packages Another name for libraries in some languages.

parallel arrays Two or more arrays in which each element in one array is associated with the element in the same relative position in the other array or arrays.

parameter list All the data types and parameter names that appear in a method header.

parameter to a method A data item passed into the method from the outside.

parent class A base class.

parent file A copy of a file before revision.

partial key dependency A condition that occurs when a column in a database table depends on only part of the table's key.

Pascal casing The format for naming variables in which the initial letter is uppercase, multiple-word variable names are run together, and each new word within the variable name begins with an uppercase letter.

passed by reference Describes a method parameter that represents the item's memory address.

passed by value Describes a variable for which a copy of its value is sent to a method and stored in a new memory location accessible to the method.

path The combination of the disk drive and the complete hierarchy of directories in which a file resides.

permanent storage devices Hardware devices that hold nonvolatile data; examples include hard disks, DVDs, USB drives, and reels of magnetic tape.

permissions Attributes assigned to a user to indicate which parts of a database the user can view, change, or delete.

persistent lock A long-term database lock required when users want to maintain a consistent view of their data while making modifications over a long transaction.

physical order The order in which a list is actually stored even though you might access it in a different logical order.

pixel A picture element; one of the tiny dots of light that forms a grid on your screen.

polymorphism The ability of a method to act appropriately depending on the context.

populating an array The act of assigning values to array elements.

portable Describes a module that can more easily be reused in multiple programs.

primary key A field or column that uniquely identifies a record; a unique identifier for each object in a database.

priming input or **priming read** The statement that reads the first input data record prior to starting a structured loop.

primitive data types Simple numbers and characters that are not class types.

private access Specifies privileges of class members; private access specifies that the data or method cannot be used by any method that is not part of the same class.

procedural programming A programming technique that focuses on the procedures that programmers create.

processing The acts of organizing data items, checking them for accuracy, and performing mathematical operations on them.

processing symbol Represented as a rectangle in flowcharts.

program A set of instructions for a computer.

program code The set of instructions a programmer writes in a programming language.

program comments Nonexecuting statements that programmers place within their code to explain program statements in English. See also *internal documentation*.

program development cycle The steps that occur during a program's lifetime.

program level The level at which global variables are declared.

programming The act of developing and writing programs.

programming language A language such as Visual Basic, C#, C++, Java, or COBOL, used to write programs.

prompt A message that is displayed on a monitor, asking the user for a response.

property A programming construct that provides methods that allow you to get and set a class field value using a simple syntax.

protected access modifier A modifier used when you want no outside classes to be able to use a data field, except classes that are children of the original class.

protected node The UML diagram name for an exception-throwing `try` block.

pseudocode An English-like representation of the logical steps it takes to solve a problem.

public access Specifies privileges of class members; public access specifies that other programs and methods may use the specified data or methods.

pure polymorphism A situation in which one method body is used with a variety of arguments.

Q

query A question asked using syntax that database software can understand. Its purpose is often to display a subset of data.

query by example The process of creating a query by filling in blanks.

R

random access files Files that contain records that can be located in any order.

random access memory (RAM) Temporary, internal computer storage.

random-access storage device A storage device, such as a disk, from which records can be accessed in any order.

range check Comparing a variable to a series of values that mark the limiting ends of ranges.

reading from a file The act of copying data from a file on a storage device into RAM.

real numbers Floating-point numbers.

real-time Describes applications that require a record to be accessed immediately while a client is waiting.

record A group of fields that go together for some logical reason—for example, because they represent attributes of some entity.

recovery The process of returning a database to a correct form that existed before an error occurred.

recursion A programming event that occurs when a method is defined in terms of itself.

recursive method A method that calls itself.

registering components The act of signing up components so they can react to events initiated by other components.

related table The "many" table in a one-to-many relationship.

relational comparison operator A symbol that expresses Boolean comparisons. Examples include =, >, <, >=, <=, and <>. These operators are also called relational operators or comparison operators.

relational database A group of tables from which you can make connections to produce virtual tables.

relationship A connection between two tables.

reliability The feature of modular programs that assures you a module has been tested and proven to function correctly.

repeating group A subset of rows in a database table that all depend on the same key.

repetition Another name for a loop structure.

return statement A statement that marks the end of the method and identifies the point at which control returns to the calling method.

return type The data type of the value that a method will send back to the location where the method call was made.

reusability The feature of modular programs that allows individual modules to be used in a variety of applications.

reverse engineering The process of creating a model of an existing system.

right-associativity and **right-to-left associativity** Describes operators that evaluate the expression to the right first.

rules of precedence Rules that dictate the order in which operations in the same statement are carried out.

running Having a computer use a written and compiled program. See also *executing*.

S

scenario A variation in the sequence of actions required in a use case UML diagram.

scripting language A language such as Python, Lua, Perl, or PHP used to write programs that are typed directly from a keyboard and stored as text rather than as binary executable files. Also called scripting programming languages or script languages.

second normal form, or **2NF** The normalization form in which partial key dependencies in a database are eliminated.

SELECT-FROM-WHERE An SQL statement that selects the fields you want to view from a specific table where one or more conditions are met.

selection structure A program structure in which you ask a question, and, depending on the answer, you take one of two courses of action. Then, no matter which path you follow, you continue with the next task.

self-documenting The term used for a program that contains meaningful data and module names that describe the program's purpose.

semantic error An error that occurs when a correct word is used in an incorrect context.

sentinel value A value that represents an entry or exit point.

sequence diagram A UML diagram that shows the timing of events in a single use case.

sequence structure A program structure in which you perform an action or task, and then you perform the next action, in order. A sequence can contain any number of tasks, but there is no chance to branch off and skip any of the tasks.

sequential file A file in which records are stored one after another in some order.

sequential order Describes the arrangement of records when they are stored one after another on the basis of the value in a particular field.

set method A method that sets the values of a data field within a class.

short-circuit evaluation A logical feature in which expressions in each part of a larger expression are evaluated only as far as necessary to determine the final outcome.

signature The name and parameter list of a method.

single-alternative if or **single-alternative selection** A selection structure in which action is required for only one branch of the decision. You call this form of the selection structure an **if-then**, because no "else" action is necessary.

677

single-level control break A break in the logic of a program based on the value of a single variable.

sinking sort Another name for a bubble sort.

size of the array The number of elements the array can hold.

software Programs that tell a computer what to do.

sorted Describes records that are in order based on the contents of one or more fields.

source code The readable statements of a program, written in a programming language.

source of an event The component from which an event is generated.

spaghetti code Snarled, unstructured program logic.

stack A memory location in which the computer keeps track of the correct memory address to which it should return after executing a module.

stacking structures Attaching program structures end to end.

state The set of all the values or contents of a class's instance variables.

state machine diagram A UML diagram that shows the different statuses of a class or object at different points in time.

static methods Methods for which no object needs to exist. Static methods are not instance methods and do not receive a `this` reference.

step value A number you use to increase a loop control variable on each pass through a loop.

stereotype A feature that adds to the UML vocabulary of shapes to make them more meaningful for the reader.

storage device Hardware that holds information for later retrieval.

storyboard A picture or sketch of a screen the user will see when running a program.

string constant (or **literal string constant**) A specific group of characters enclosed within quotation marks.

string variable A variable that can hold text that includes letters, digits, and special characters such as punctuation marks.

structure A basic unit of programming logic; each structure is a sequence, selection, or loop.

structure diagrams UML diagrams that emphasize the "things" in a system.

structured programs Programs that follow the rules of structured logic.

Structured Query Language (SQL) A commonly used language for accessing data in database tables.

stub A method without statements that is used as a placeholder.

subclass A derived class.

subscript A number that indicates the position of a particular item within an array.

summary report A report that lists only totals, without individual detail records.

sunny day case A case in program execution in which nothing goes wrong.

superclass A base class.

swap values To exchange the values of two variables.

syntax The rules of a language.

syntax error An error in language or grammar.

system design The detailed specification of how all the parts of a system will be implemented and coordinated.

system software The programs that you use to manage your computer.

T

table A database file that contains data in rows and columns; also, a term sometimes used by mathematicians to describe a two-dimensional array.

temporary variable A working variable that you use to hold intermediate results during a program's execution.

terminal symbol A symbol used at each end of a flowchart. Its shape is a lozenge. Also called a start/stop symbol.

text editor A program that you use to create simple text files; it is similar to a word processor, but without as many features.

text files Files that contain data that can be read in a text editor.

then clause Part of a decision that holds the action that results when the Boolean expression in the decision is true.

third normal form, or **3NF** The normalization form in which transitive dependencies in a database are eliminated.

this reference An automatically created variable that holds the address of an object and passes it to an instance method whenever the method is called.

thread The flow of execution of one set of program statements.

three-dimensional arrays Arrays in which each element is accessed using three subscripts.

throw an exception To pass an exception out of a block where it occurs, usually to a block that can handle it.

throw statement A programming statement that sends an `Exception` object out of a method or code block so it can be handled elsewhere.

tight coupling Occurs when methods excessively depend on each other; it makes programs more prone to errors.

time signal A UML diagram symbol that indicates a specific amount of time has passed before an action is started.

TOE chart A program development tool that lists tasks, objects, and events.

transaction file A file that holds temporary data that you use to update a master file.

transitive dependency A condition that occurs when the value of a nonkey attribute determines, or predicts, the value of another nonkey attribute.

trivial expression An expression that always evaluates to the same value.

truth table A diagram used in mathematics and logic to help describe the truth of an entire expression based on the truth of its parts.

try To execute code that might throw an exception.

try block A block of code you attempt to execute while acknowledging that an exception might occur. A `try` block consists of the keyword `try`, followed by any number of statements, including some that might cause an exception to be thrown.

two-dimensional arrays Arrays that have both rows and columns of values; you must use two subscripts when you access an element in a two-dimensional array.

U

UML A standard way to specify, construct, and document systems that use object-oriented methods. UML is an acronym for Unified Modeling Language.

unnamed constant A literal numeric or string value.

unnormalized Describes a database table that contains repeating groups.

unstructured programs Programs that do not follow the rules of structured logic.

update a master file To change the values in a file's fields based on transactions.

update anomaly A problem that occurs when the data in a table needs to be altered; the result is repeated data.

use case diagrams UML diagrams that show how a business works from the perspective of those who approach it from the outside, or those who actually use the business.

user-defined type, or **programmer-defined type** A type that is not built into a language, but that is created by the programmer.

users (or **end users)** People who employ and benefit from computer programs.

V

validating data Making sure data falls within an acceptable range.

variable A named memory location of a specific data type, whose contents can vary or differ over time.

view A particular way of looking at a database.

visible A characteristic of data items in which they "can be seen" only within the method in which they are declared.

visual development environment A programming environment in which you can create programs by dragging components such as buttons and labels onto a screen and arranging them visually.

void method A method that returns no value.

volatile A characteristic of internal memory, which loses its contents every time the computer loses power.

W

while loop or **while . . . do loop** A loop in which a process continues while some condition continues to be true.

whole-part relationship An association in which one or more classes make up the parts of a larger whole class.

wildcard A symbol that means "any" or "all."

work methods Methods that perform tasks within a class.

writing to a file The act of copying data from RAM to persistent storage.

X

x-axis An imaginary line that represents horizontal positions in a screen window.

x-coordinate A value that indicates screen position and increases as you travel from left to right across a window.

Y

y-axis An imaginary line that represents vertical positions in a screen window.

y-coordinate A value that indicates screen position and increases as you travel from top to bottom across a window.

Index